PHILIP'S

STR… LAS

W… ire

CW01582533

rst published in 2003 by

ilip's, a division of
ctopus Publishing Group Ltd
4 Heron Quays, London E14 4JP

rst edition 2003
ird impression 2005

BN-10 0-540-08337-2 (pocket)
BN-13 978-0-540-08337-4 (pocket)

rinted and bound in Spain
y Cayfosa-Quebecor

Contents

III **Key to map symbols**

IV **Key to map pages**

VI **Route planning**

VIII **Administrative and Postcode boundaries**

1 **Street maps** at 2½ inches to 1 mile

198 **Town maps** of Ludlow and Stratford-upon-Avon

199 **Index** of towns and villages

202 **Index** of streets, hospitals, industrial estates, railway stations, schools, shopping centres, universities and places of interest

Digital Data

The exceptionally high-quality mapping found in this atlas is available as digital data in TIFF format, which is easily convertible to other bitmapped (raster) image formats.

The index is also available in digital form as a standard database table. It contains all the details found in the printed index together with the National Grid reference for the map square in which each entry is named.

For further information and to discuss your requirements, please contact Philip's on 020 7644 6932 or james.mann@philips-maps.co.uk

Key to map symbols

22a	**Motorway** with junction number
	Primary route – dual/single carriageway
	A road – dual/single carriageway
	B road – dual/single carriageway
	Minor road – dual/single carriageway
	Other minor road – dual/single carriageway
	Road under construction
	Tunnel, covered road
	Rural track, private road or narrow road in urban area
	Gate or obstruction to traffic (restrictions may not apply at all times or to all vehicles)
	Path, bridleway, byway open to all traffic, road used as a public path
	Pedestrianised area
DY7	**Postcode boundaries**
	County and unitary authority boundaries
	Railway, tunnel, railway under construction
	Tramway, tramway under construction
	Miniature railway
Walsall	**Railway station**
	Private railway station
South Shields	**Metro station**
	Tram stop, tram stop under construction
	Bus, coach station

	Ambulance station
	Coastguard station
	Fire station
	Police station
	Accident and Emergency entrance to hospital
H	**Hospital**
	Place of worship
i	**Information Centre** (open all year)
P	**Parking**
P&R	**Park and Ride**
PO	**Post Office**
	Camping site
	Caravan site
	Golf course
	Picnic site
Prim Sch	**Important buildings, schools, colleges, universities and hospitals**
River Ouse	**Tidal water, water name**
	Non-tidal water – lake, river, canal or stream
	Lock, weir, tunnel
	Woods
	Built up area
Church	**Non-Roman antiquity**
ROMAN FORT	**Roman antiquity**
87 58	**Adjoining page indicators**

Acad	**Academy**	Inst	**Institute**	Recn Gd	**Recreation Ground**
Allot Gdns	**Allotments**	Ct	**Law Court**	Resr	**Reservoir**
Cemy	**Cemetery**	L Ctr	**Leisure Centre**	Ret Pk	**Retail Park**
C Ctr	**Civic Centre**	LC	**Level Crossing**	Sch	**School**
CH	**Club House**	Liby	**Library**	Sh Ctr	**Shopping Centre**
Coll	**College**	Mkt	**Market**	TH	**Town Hall/House**
Crem	**Crematorium**	Meml	**Memorial**	Trad Est	**Trading Estate**
Ent	**Enterprise**	Mon	**Monument**	Univ	**University**
Ex H	**Exhibition Hall**	Mus	**Museum**	Wks	**Works**
Ind Est	**Industrial Estate**	Obsy	**Observatory**	YH	**Youth Hostel**
IRB Sta	**Inshore Rescue Boat Station**	Pal	**Royal Palace**		
		PH	**Public House**		

■ The small numbers around the edges of the maps identify the 1 kilometre National Grid lines ■ The dark grey border on the inside edge of some pages indicates that the mapping does not continue onto the adjacent page

The scale of the maps on the pages numbered in blue is 3.92 cm to 1 km • 2½ inches to 1 mile • 1: 25344

0 ¼ ½ ¾ 1 mile

0 250 m 500 m 750 m 1 kilometre

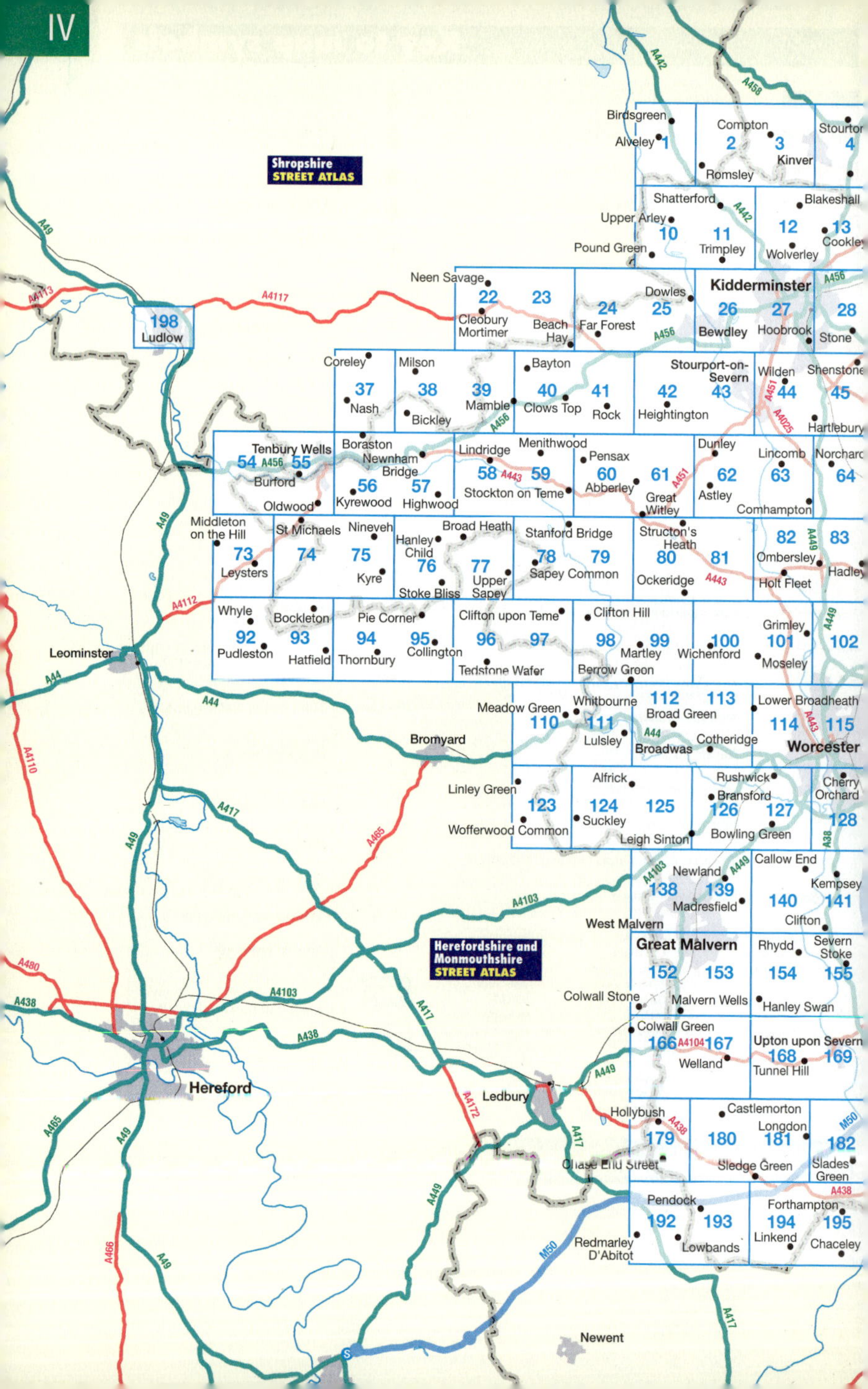
Shropshire STREET ATLAS
Herefordshire and Monmouthshire STREET ATLAS
198 Ludlow
Kidderminster
Worcester
Great Malvern
Hereford
Leominster
Bromyard
Ledbury
Newent
Tenbury Wells
Stourport-on-Severn
Bewdley
West Malvern
Birdsgreen
Alveley
Compton
Kinver
Romsley
Stourton
Shatterford
Upper Arley
Pound Green
Trimpley
Blakeshall
Wolverley
Cookley
Neen Savage
Cleobury Mortimer
Beach Hay
Far Forest
Dowles
Hoobrook
Stone
Coreley
Nash
Milson
Bickley
Mamble
Bayton
Clows Top
Rock
Heightington
Wilden
Shenstone
Hartlebury
Boraston
Newnham Bridge
Burford
Oldwood
Kyrewood
Highwood
Lindridge
Menithwood
Stockton on Teme
Pensax
Abberley
Great Witley
Dunley
Astley
Lincomb
Comhampton
Norchard
Middleton on the Hill
Leysters
St Michaels
Nineveh
Kyre
Hanley Child
Broad Heath
Stoke Bliss
Upper Sapey
Stanford Bridge
Sapey Common
Structon's Heath
Ockeridge
Ombersley
Holt Fleet
Hadley
Whyle
Pudleston
Bockleton
Hatfield
Pie Corner
Thornbury
Collington
Clifton upon Teme
Tedstone Wafer
Clifton Hill
Martley
Berrow Green
Wichenford
Grimley
Moseley
Meadow Green
Whitbourne
Lulsley
Broad Green
Broadwas
Cotheridge
Lower Broadheath
Linley Green
Wofferwood Common
Alfrick
Suckley
Leigh Sinton
Rushwick
Bransford
Bowling Green
Cherry Orchard
Newland
Madresfield
Callow End
Kempsey
Clifton
Rhydd
Severn Stoke
Colwall Stone
Malvern Wells
Hanley Swan
Colwall Green
Welland
Upton upon Severn
Tunnel Hill
Hollybush
Castlemorton
Longdon
Sledge Green
Slades Green
Chase End Street
Pendock
Lowbands
Forthampton
Linkend
Chaceley
Redmarley D'Abitot
1 2 3 4 10 11 12 13 22 23 24 25 26 27 28 37 38 39 40 41 42 43 44 45 54 55 56 57 58 59 60 61 62 63 64 73 74 75 76 77 78 79 80 81 82 83 92 93 94 95 96 97 98 99 100 101 102 110 111 112 113 114 115 123 124 125 126 127 128 138 139 140 141 152 153 154 155 166 167 168 169 179 180 181 182 192 193 194 195
A442
A458
A49
A4113
A4117
A456
A451
A4025
A443
A449
A44
A4112
A4110
A417
A465
A4103
A480
A438
A4104
A4172
A466
M50
A38

Key to map pages

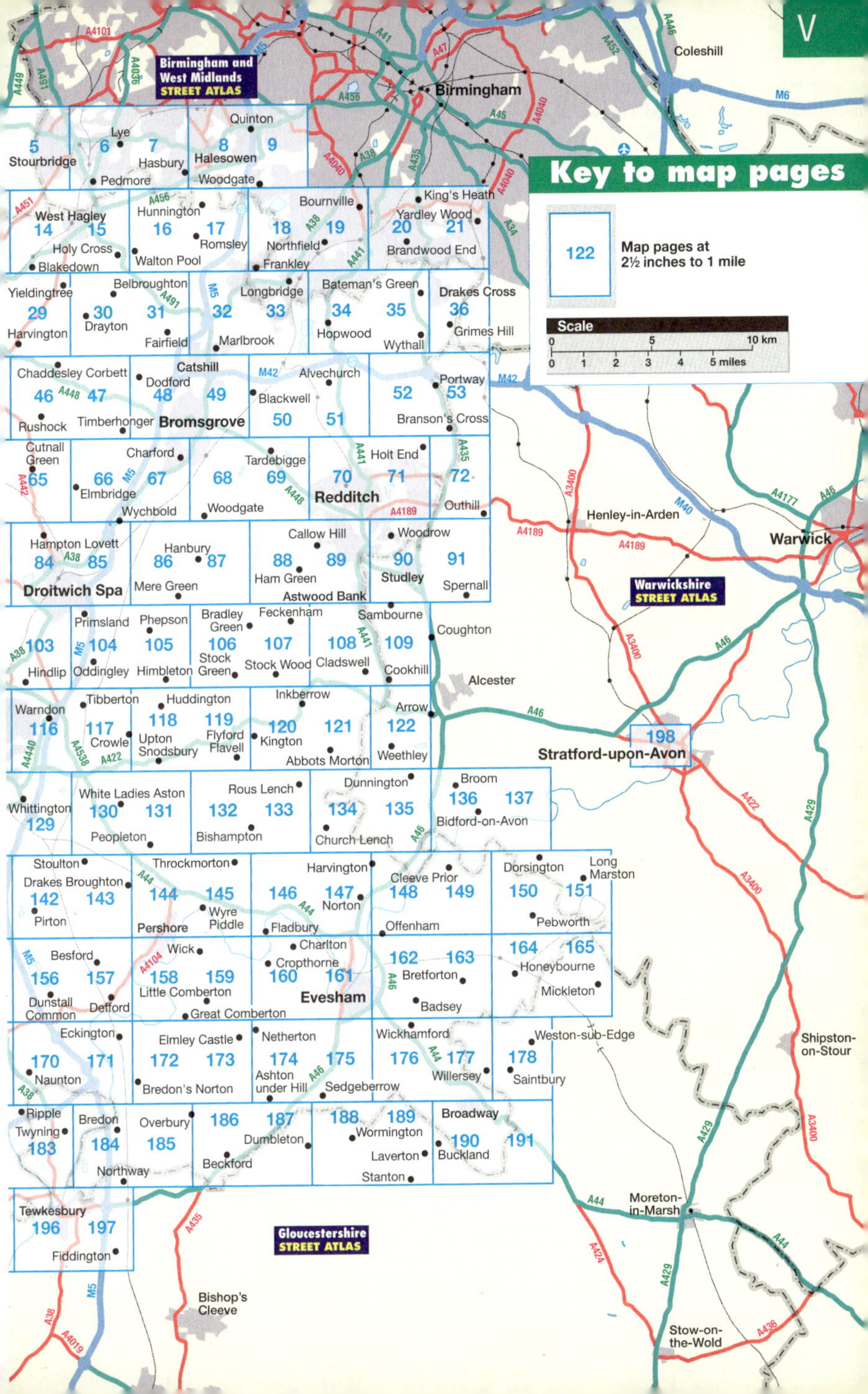

Route planning

West Midlands
Warwick
shire
BIRMINGHAM
COVENTRY
Solihull
Stourbridge
HALESOWEN
SMETHWICK
Rowley Regis
Brierley Hill
Bromsgrove
Redditch
Droitwich
Kenilworth
Warwick
Stratford-upon-Avon
Alcester
Studley
Henley-in-Arden
Evesham
Pershore
Broadway
Shipston-on-Stour
Moreton-in-Marsh
Stow-on-the-Wold
Bishop's Cleeve
Cheltenham
Chipping Campden
Shirley
Olton
Harborne
Edgbaston
Selly Oak
Bournville
Northfield
King's Norton
Longbridge
Rubery
Catshill
Marlbrook
Hollywood
Earlswood
Dorridge
Knowle
Balsall Common
Meriden
Hampton in Arden
Lapworth
Tanworth-in-Arden
Wootton Wawen
Snitterfield
Wellesbourne
Bidford-on-Avon
Welford-on-Avon
Long Marston
Mickleton
Ebrington
Blockley
Bourton on the Hill
Winchcombe
Southam
Prestbury
Hagley
Romsley
Frankley
Hopwood
Alvechurch
Tardebigge
Feckenham
Inkberrow
Abbots Morton
Harvington
Offenham
Bengeworth
Badsey
Wickhamford
Aston Somerville
Ashchurch
Teddington
Alderton
Toddington
Stanway
Snowshill
Temple Guiting
Condicote
Donnington
Kineton
Upper Swell
Lower Swell
Longborough
Sezincote
Evenlode
Adlestrop
Daylesford
Oddington
Kingham
Bledington
Barcheston
Tidmington
Burmington
Todenham
Aston Magna
Batsford
Ilmington
Admington
Armscote
Halford
Ettington
Alderminster
Atherstone on Stour
Clifford Chambers
Preston on Stour
Binton
Temple Grafton
Shottery
Bishopton
Wilmcote
Aston Cantlow
Great Alne
Little Alne
Coughton
Sambourne
Astwood Bank
Cookhill
Arrow
Exhall
Wixford
Broom
Dunnington
Salford Priors
Abbots Salford
Church Lench
Ab Lench
Atch Lench
Rous Lench
Flyford Flavell
Upton Snodsbury
Peopleton
Pinvin
Wyre Piddle
Fladbury
Cropthorne
Charlton
Little Comberton
Great Comberton
Elmley Castle
Bricklehampton
Kemerton
Beckford
Dumbleton
Wormington
Laverton
Stanton
Buckland
Childswickham
Saintbury
Weston Sub-Edge
Aston Subedge
Willersey
Hidcote Boyce
Charingworth
Paxford
Stretton-on-Fosse
Draycott
Lower Lemington
Little Wolford
Great Wolford
Barton on the Heath
Long Compton
Little Compton
Chastleton
Salford
Over Norton
Cornwell
Broadwell
Maugersbury
Naunton
Upper Slaughter
Guiting Power
Charlton Abbots
Hawling
Farmcote
Ford
Cutsdean
Didbrook
Hailes
Greet
Gretton
Gotherington
Oxenton
Dixton
Alstone
Fiddington
Stoke Orchard
Elmstone Hardwicke
Swindon
Woodmancote
Cleeve Hill
Battledown
Charlton Kings
M5
M42
M40
M6
A38
A44
A46
A422
A435
A441
A448
A429
A3400
A452
A45
A34
A41
A456
A491
A4189
A4177
A4023
A3400
B4035
B4632
B4077
B4084
B4088
B4089
B4090
B4091
B4092
B4093
B4101
B4102
B4104
B4086
B4087
B4439
B4078
B4079
B4080
B4081
B4082
B4450
B4068
B4455
B4632
Avon
Stour
Cannock
Bredon Hill
Meon Hill
Langley Hill
Alderton Hill
FRANKLEY SERVICES
HOPWOOD PARK SERVICES
STRENSHAM SERVICES (Northbound Only)
STRENSHAM SERVICES (Southbound Only)
BIRMINGHAM INTERNATIONAL

Administrative and Postcode boundaries

2

A
B
C
D
E
F
A442 Bridgnorth
Shropshire STREET ATLAS
8
7
85
6
5
84
4
3
83
2
1
82
75
76
77
Butter Cross
Lake House
Coton Springs
Waterfall
Cotori Dingle
A442
Blunder Bridge
Allum Bridge
PH
The Ridings
Turleygreen Farm
Turleygreen
Birdsgreen
PH
New Barns Farm
COOKS CROSS
BIRCH GROVE
CEDAR CL
MAPLE CR
COOKS CROSS
LIME CL
Arnside
The Hadleys
Howards End
Alveley Prim Sch
PH
Recreation Ground
HAZELGROVE
Woodlands
HONEYBOURNE RD
THE LEA
ROMSLEY VW
DADDLEBROOK ROAD
The Woodlands
Churchhouse Farm
HOLMES
ORCHARD
BRIDGE ROAD
MALLARDS CL
PH
GREENWAY AVENUE
Alveley
Bowhills
Hadleys Coppice
VICARAGE BANK
PO
ARDEN WY
Dumbolds Farm
Bow Hill Farm
Industrial Estate
CHURCH ROAD
CHAPEL RD
1 GREEN LEYS CR
2 MEADOWBROOK CL
3 WHITTALL CL
4 ARDEN WY
5 SEABRIGHT WY
6 GOLDEN ACRES
P
Visitor Centre
Townsend Farm
Severn Valley Country Park
WV15
A442
Hall Close Farm
Moat
Pool Hall Farm
Pool Hall
The Spinney
Little London Farm
Woodthorne
Fenn Green
Ladypitt Farm
Little London Coppice
High House Farm
SHAM LANE
Stanley
Severnside
Fenn Green Farm
Cabin Coppice
May House Farm
Butts Farm
Shropshire Farm
River Severn
LOWE LANE
Lowe Farm
LOWE LANE
Severn Valley Railway
Severn Way
Hooks Coppice
PH
A442
LOWE LANE
WV16
Hexton Farm
Far Things
Baynhams Farm
DY12
Coombys Farm
Kitlands Coppice

10

2

1

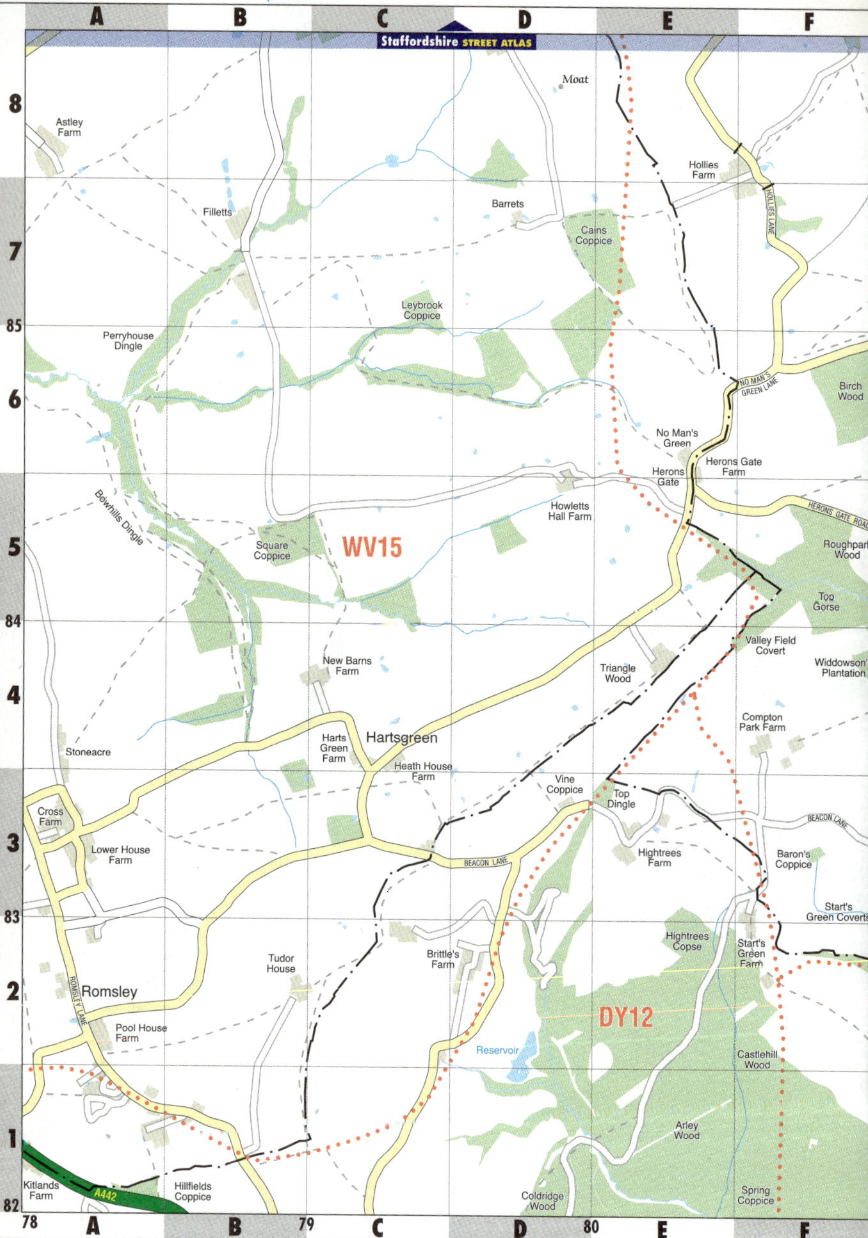
A
B
C
D
E
F
Staffordshire STREET ATLAS
8
7
85
6
5
84
4
3
83
2
1
82
78
79
80
Moat
Astley Farm
Hollies Farm
HOLLIES LANE
Filletts
Barrets
Cains Coppice
Leybrook Coppice
Perryhouse Dingle
NO MAN'S GREEN LANE
Birch Wood
No Man's Green
Herons Gate Farm
Herons Gate
Howletts Hall Farm
HERONS GATE ROAD
Bowhills Dingle
Square Coppice
WV15
Roughpark Wood
Top Gorse
Valley Field Covert
Widdowson's Plantation
New Barns Farm
Triangle Wood
Compton Park Farm
Stoneacre
Harts Green Farm
Hartsgreen
Heath House Farm
Vine Coppice
Top Dingle
Cross Farm
BEACON LANE
Lower House Farm
Hightrees Farm
Baron's Coppice
Start's Green Coverts
Hightrees Copse
Start's Green Farm
Tudor House
Brittle's Farm
Romsley
ROMSLEY LANE
DY12
Pool House Farm
Reservoir
Castlehill Wood
Arley Wood
Kitlands Farm
A442
Hillfields Coppice
Coldridge Wood
Spring Coppice

1
11

4

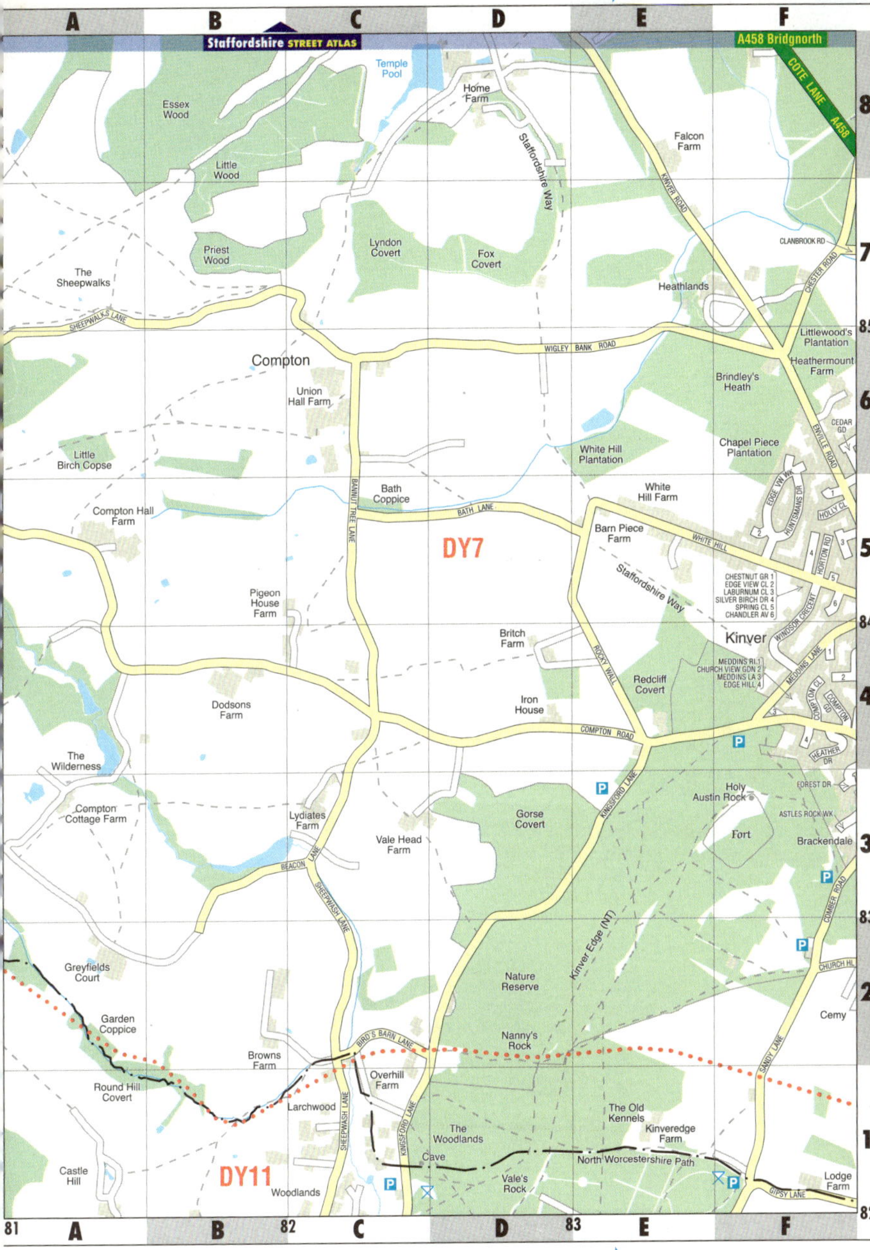

Staffordshire STREET ATLAS
A458 Bridgnorth
COTE LANE
A458
Temple Pool
Home Farm
Essex Wood
Little Wood
Staffordshire Way
Falcon Farm
KINVER ROAD
CLANBROOK RD
CHESTER ROAD
Priest Wood
Lyndon Covert
Fox Covert
The Sheepwalks
Heathlands
SHEEPWALKS LANE
Littlewood's Plantation
Compton
WIGLEY BANK ROAD
Heathermount Farm
Union Hall Farm
Brindley's Heath
CEDAR GD
ENVILLE ROAD
Little Birch Copse
White Hill Plantation
Chapel Piece Plantation
Bath Coppice
BANNUT TREE LANE
White Hill Farm
EDGE VW WK
HUNTSMANS DR
HOLLY CL
Compton Hall Farm
BATH LANE
DY7
Barn Piece Farm
WHITE HILL
HORTON RD
CHESTNUT GR 1
EDGE VIEW CL 2
LABURNUM CL 3
SILVER BIRCH DR 4
SPRING CL 5
CHANDLER AV 6
Pigeon House Farm
WINDSOR CRESCENT
Britch Farm
Kinver
ROCKY WALL
MEDDINS RI 1
CHURCH VIEW GDN 2
MEDDINS LA 3
EDGE HILL 4
MEDDINS LANE
Redcliff Covert
COMPTON CL
COMPTON GD
Dodsons Farm
Iron House
COMPTON ROAD
The Wilderness
HEATHER DR
KINGSFORD LANE
Holy Austin Rock
FOREST DR
Compton Cottage Farm
Lydiates Farm
Gorse Covert
ASTLES ROCK WK
Fort
Vale Head Farm
Brackendale
BEACON LANE
SHEEPWASH LANE
COMBER ROAD
Kinver Edge (NT)
Greyfields Court
Nature Reserve
CHURCH HL
Garden Coppice
Cemy
Nanny's Rock
BIRD'S BARN LANE
SANDY LANE
Browns Farm
Round Hill Covert
Overhill Farm
Larchwood
The Old Kennels
Kinveredge Farm
The Woodlands
Cave
North Worcestershire Path
Castle Hill
DY11
Woodlands
Vale's Rock
Lodge Farm
GIPSY LANE

12

4

3

A
B
C
D
E
F
Staffordshire STREET ATLAS
A449 Wolverhampton
8
7
85
6
5
84
4
3
83
2
1
82
84
85
86
Jesson's Plantation
Broom Hill
Clanbrook Covert
COTE LANE
A458
Clanbrook
The Fox Covert
PH
Kings Lodge Plantation
CLANBROOK ROAD
Littlewoods Common
Littlewood's Plantation
BRIDGNORTH ROAD
Prestwood Pumping Station
Top Barn
Stourton Farm
Holly Wood
GREENSFORGE LANE
Devil's Den
Weir
Monarch's Way
Prestwood Plantation
PRESTWOOD DRIVE
Halfcot Farm
WOLVERHAMPTON ROAD
A449
Stourton Bridge
PRESTWOOD RD
BEECHLAWN DRIVE
STOURTON CRESCENT
Stourton
A458 BRIDGNORTH ROAD
Stewponey Bridge
PH
HYDE LANE
CEDAR GARDENS
Gallowstree Elm
HILLBORO RISE
MAPLE CL
1 HYDE CL
2 WHITE HL
3 MEDDINS LA
Woodlands
Staffordshire & Worcester Canal
Dunsley Hall
GIBBET LANE
Potter's Cross
PO
Brindley Heath Jun Sch
Leisure Centre
Edgecliff High Sch
ENVILLE ROAD
CASTLE ST
FOLEY STREET
STERRYMERE GD
HAMPTON GROVE
BRINDLEY BRAE
DUNSLEY ROAD
BEECH CLOSE
DUNSLEY DRIVE
Dunsley
School Plantation
Gibbet Wood
JAMES ST
FOSTER STREET
FOSTER CRES
A4
1 MEDDINS CL
2 CHURCH VW GDNS
3 FOSTER CRES
4 FOREST DR
ORCHARD GR
DUNSLEY ROAD
GIBRALTAR
Woodside
The Coppice
DY7
COMPTON ROAD
STONE LANE
Kinver
LOCKSIDE DRIVE
FAIRFIELD DR
COMBER GR
River Stour
Foley Inf Sch
Liby
VICARAGE DR
COMBER ROAD
PO
HIGH STREET
MILL LANE
MILL FIELDS
BROCKLEY'S WK
PINE CL
LARCH CL
OAK CL
REDWOOD ROAD
HAWTHORNE WAY
LIME GR
ELM GROVE
WILLOW RD
1 THE COPELANDS
2 ASTLES ROCK WK
3 VICARAGE CT
THE COMPA
THE BURGESSES
Comber Copse
CHURCH HILL
DARK LANE
THE GRAZINGS
Snelgrove
CHURCH HILL
Woodside
CHURCH HILL
Cemy
Whittington Common
HORSE BRIDGE LANE
PH
Penhole Coppice
Whittington
WHITTINGTON HALL LANE
Hare Covert
COOKLEY LANE
WINDSOR HOLLOWAY
Whittington Bridge
Lower Whittington Farm
Highgrove Farm
Mill Coppice
A449
GIPSY LANE
DY11
Far Coppice

3
13

6
E8 3 LONGBOAT LA
F8 8 CORBETT HO

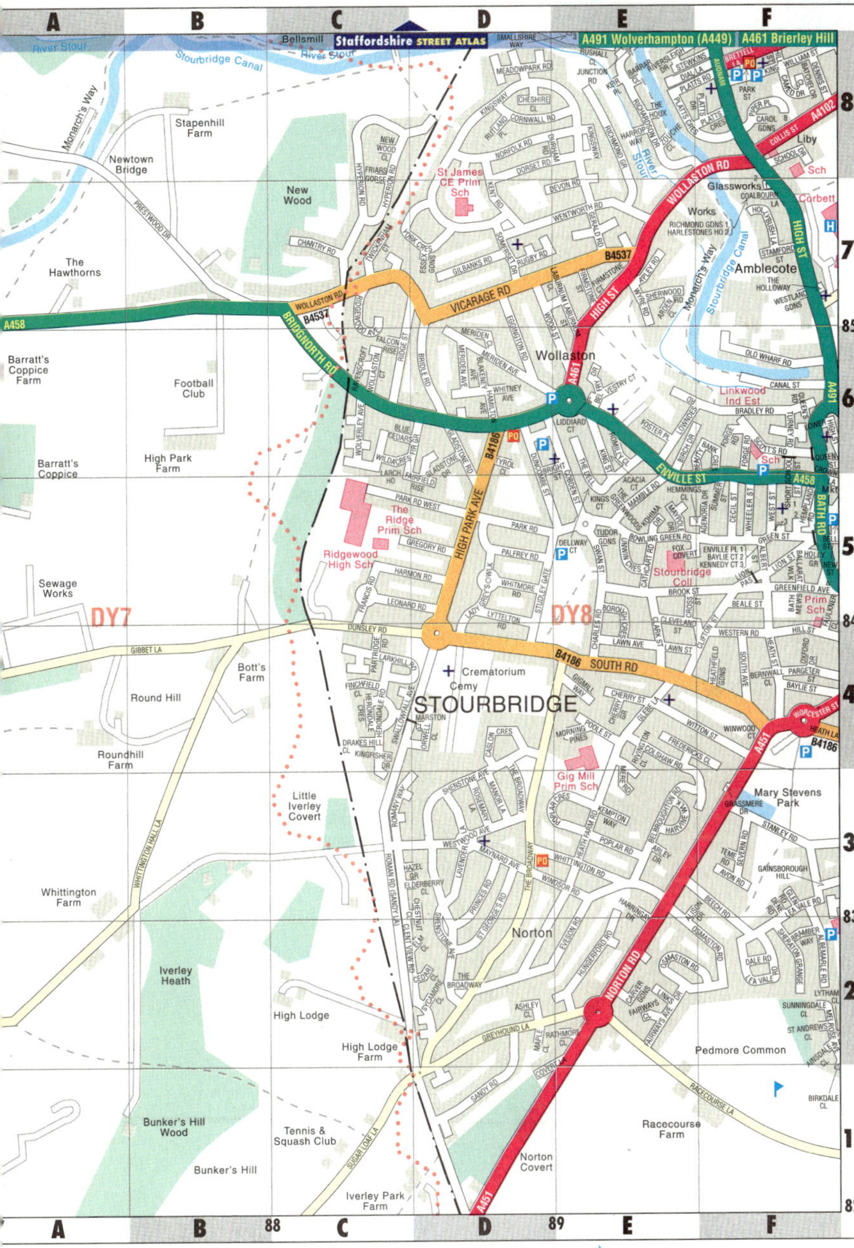

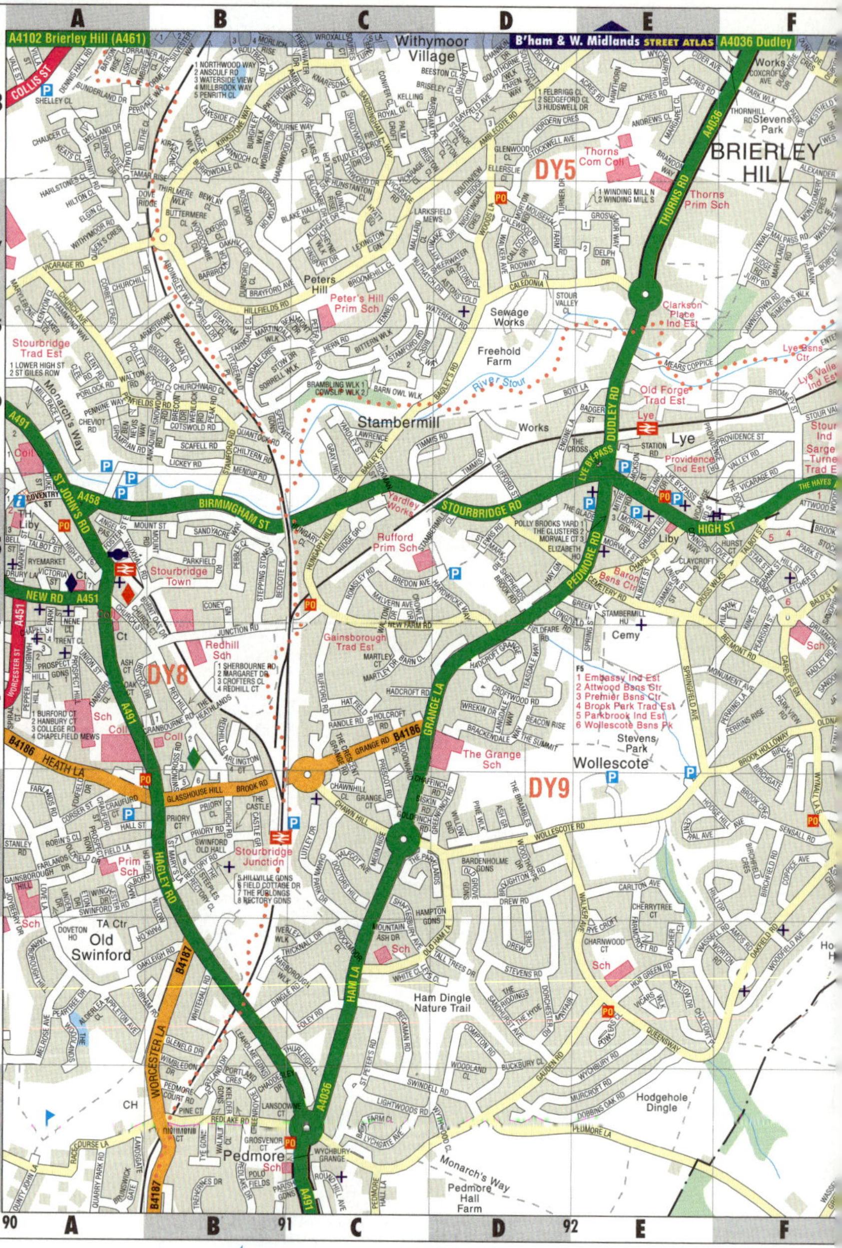
A4102 Brierley Hill (A461)
B'ham & W. Midlands STREET ATLAS
A4036 Dudley
Withymoor Village
BRIERLEY HILL
Stevens Park
Thorns Com Coll
Thorns Prim Sch
DY5
Peters Hill
Peter's Hill Prim Sch
Sewage Works
Freehold Farm
River Stour
Clarkson Place Ind Est
Lye Bsns Ctr
Lye Valley Ind Est
Old Forge Trad Est
Stourbridge Trad Est
1 LOWER HIGH ST
2 ST GILES ROW
Monarch's Way
Stambermill
Works
Lye
Providence Ind Est
BIRMINGHAM ST
STOURBRIDGE RD
HIGH ST
Yardley Works
Rufford Prim Sch
Stourbridge Town
Redhill Sch
DY8
Gainsborough Trad Est
Baron Bsns Ctr
Cemy
F5
1 Embassy Ind Est
2 Attwood Bsns Ctr
3 Premier Bsns Ctr
4 Brook Park Trad Est
5 Parkbrook Ind Est
6 Wollescote Bsns Pk
Stevens Park
Wollescote
The Grange Sch
DY9
Stourbridge Junction
Old Swinford
TA Ctr
Ham Dingle Nature Trail
Hodgehole Dingle
Pedmore
Pedmore Hall Farm
HAGLEY RD
HAM LA
GRANGE LA
PEDMORE RD
DUDLEY RD
THORNS RD
WORCESTER LA
QUEENSWAY
WOLLESCOTE RD
A491
A4036
B4186
B4187
A451
A458
90
91
92
A
B
C
D
E
F
1
2
3
4
5
6
7
8
82
83
84
85

8

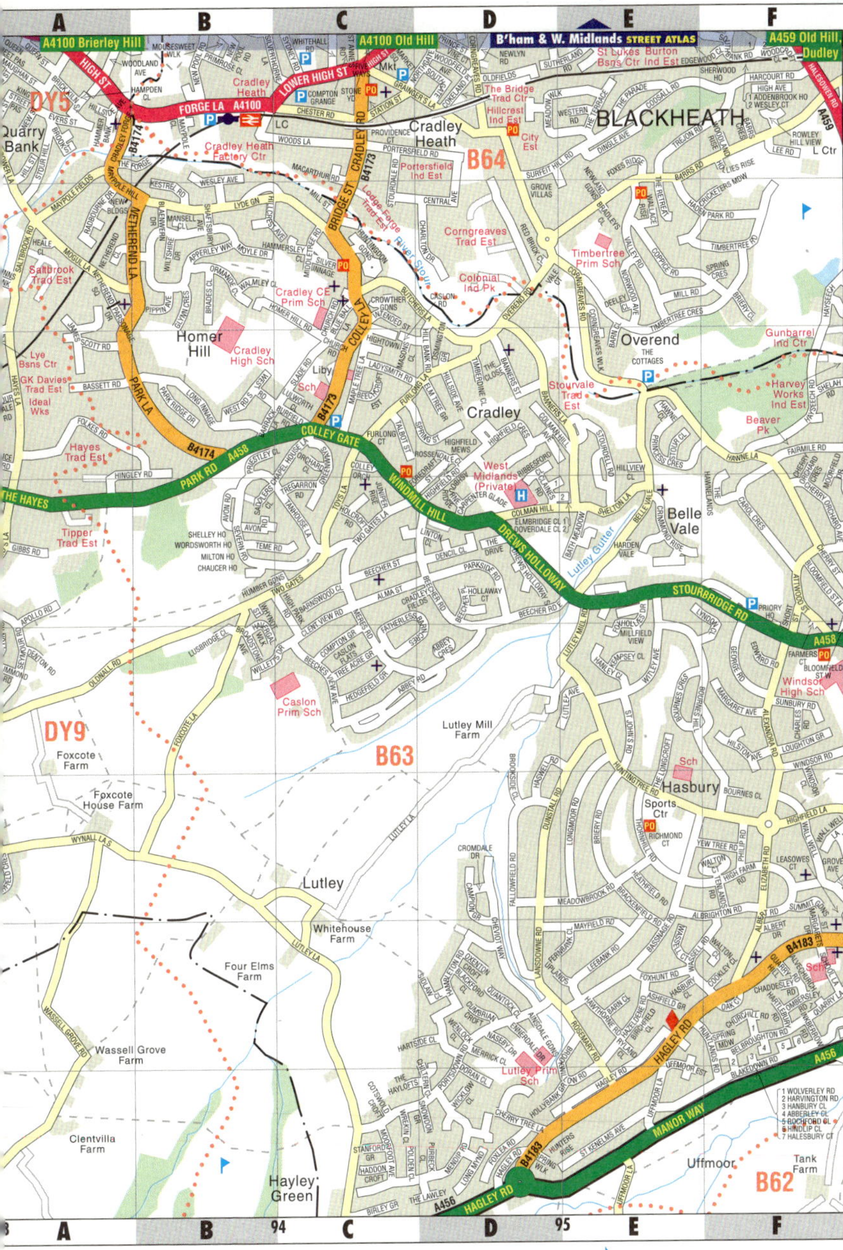
A4100 Brierley Hill
A4100 Old Hill
B'ham & W. Midlands STREET ATLAS
A459 Old Hill, Dudley
DY5
Quarry Bank
Cradley Heath
Cradley Heath Factory Ctr
Cradley Heath
BLACKHEATH
B64
Portersfield Ind Est
Lodge Forge Trad Est
Corngreaves Trad Est
Timbertree Prim Sch
Colonial Ind Pk
Saltbrook Trad Est
Cradley CE Prim Sch
Homer Hill
Cradley High Sch
Lye Bsns Ctr
GK Davies Trad Est
Ideal Wks
Liby
Sch
Overend
Gunbarrel Ind Ctr
Harvey Works Ind Est
Beaver Pk
Stourvale Trad Est
Cradley
Hayes Trad Est
West Midlands (Private)
Belle Vale
Tipper Trad Est
THE HAYES
PARK RD A458
COLLEY GATE
WINDMILL HILL
DREWS HOLLOWAY
STOURBRIDGE RD
A458
Lutley Gutter
Windsor High Sch
Caslon Prim Sch
DY9
Foxcote Farm
Foxcote House Farm
Lutley Mill Farm
B63
Hasbury
Sports Ctr
Sch
Lutley
Whitehouse Farm
Four Elms Farm
Wassell Grove Farm
Clentvilla Farm
Hayley Green
Lutley Prim Sch
HAGLEY RD
B4183
MANOR WAY
A456
Uffmoor
Tank Farm
B62
River Stour
City Est
Hillcrest Ind Est
The Bridge Trad Ctr
St Lukes Burton Bsns Ctr Ind Est
Mkt
1 ADDENBROOK HO
2 WESLEY CT
1 WOLVERLEY RD
2 HARVINGTON RD
3 HANBURY CL
4 ABBERLEY CL
5 ROCHFORD CL
6 HINDLIP CL
7 HALESBURY CT
A B C D E F
8 7 85 6 5 84 4 3 83 2 1 82
94 95

16

8

7

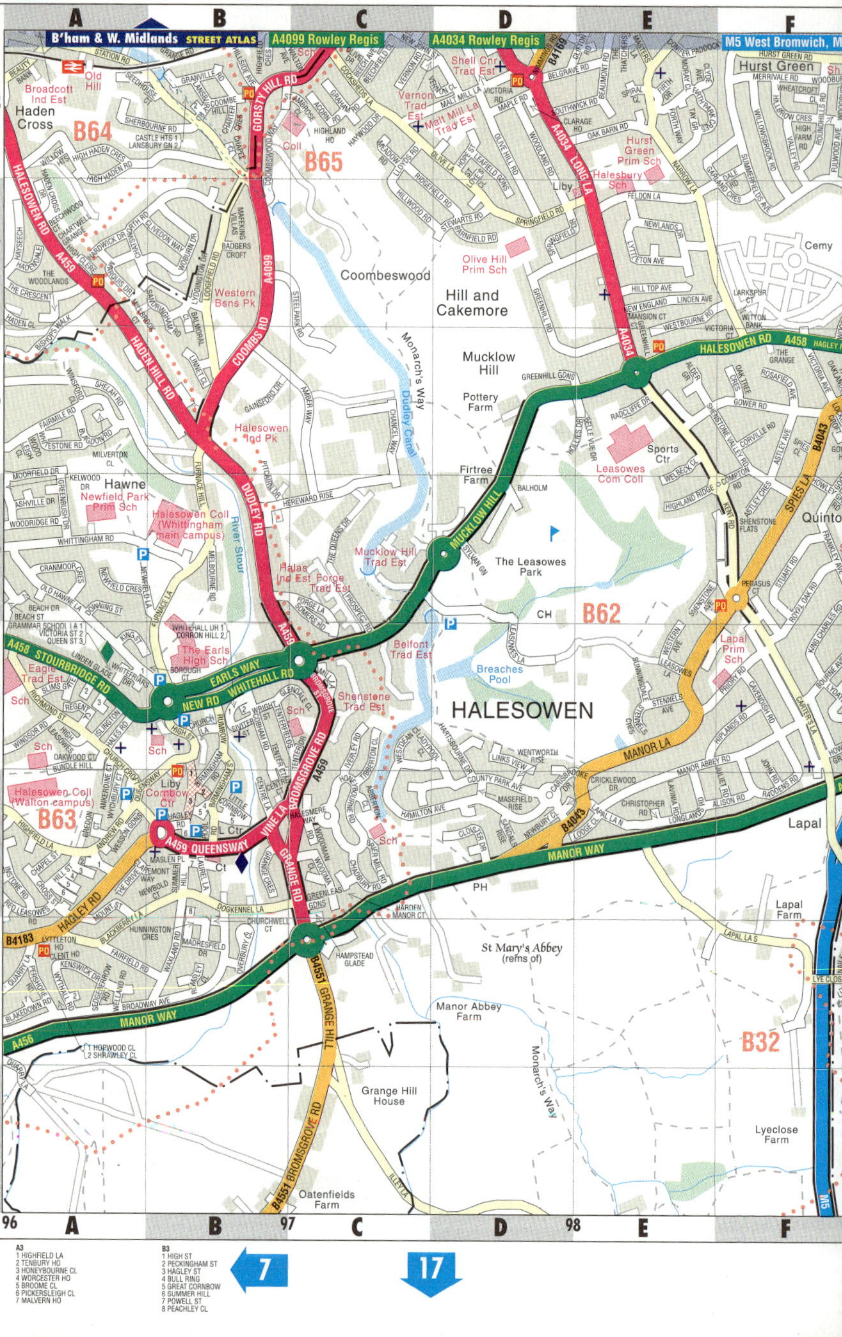

A3
1 HIGHFIELD LA
2 TENBURY HO
3 HONEYBOURNE CL
4 WORCESTER HO
5 BROOME CL
6 PICKERSLEIGH CL
7 MALVERN HO

B3
1 HIGH ST
2 PECKINGHAM ST
3 HAGLEY ST
4 BULL RING
5 GREAT CORNBOW
6 SUMMER HILL
7 POWELL ST
8 PEACHLEY CL

7
17

VERLEY CT
CKMANS CL
MBARDY CROFT
E GREEN

A7
1 ALBANY CT
2 WILLES CT
3 MILVERTON CT
4 REGENT CT
5 MANOR CT
6 VICTORIA CT

B7
1 BRINDLEY CT
2 VERNON CT
3 HINCKLEY CT
4 ASTBURY CT
5 DOWNING CT
6 AVERY CT

B8
1 ARROW HO
2 STOUR HO
3 AVON HO
4 SEVERN HO
5 RUSKIN CT
6 LAWRENCE CT

7 HENDERSON CT
8 REYNOLDS CT
9 OLD CRESCENT CT

18

1

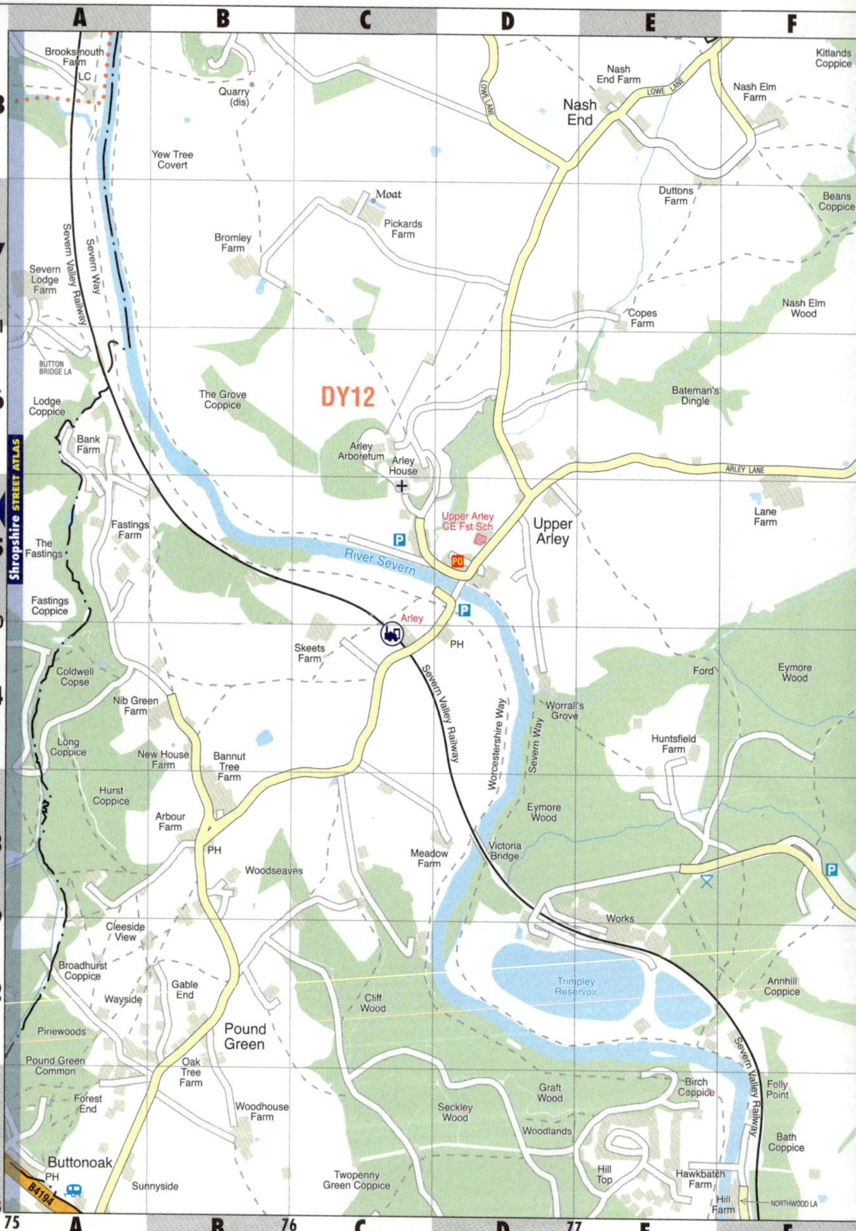

A
B
C
D
E
F
8
7
81
6
5
80
4
3
79
2
1
78
75
76
77
Brooksmouth Farm
LC
Quarry (dis)
Yew Tree Covert
Nash End Farm
LOWE LANE
Nash End
Nash Elm Farm
Kitlands Coppice
Moat
Pickards Farm
Bromley Farm
Duttons Farm
Beans Coppice
Severn Valley Railway
Severn Way
Severn Lodge Farm
Copes Farm
Nash Elm Wood
BUTTON BRIDGE LA
Lodge Coppice
The Grove Coppice
DY12
Bateman's Dingle
Bank Farm
Arley Arboretum
Arley House
ARLEY LANE
Upper Arley CE Fst Sch
Upper Arley
Lane Farm
Fastings Farm
The Fastings
River Severn
PO
P
Fastings Coppice
Arley
PH
Skeets Farm
Coldwell Copse
Ford
Eymore Wood
Nib Green Farm
Worrall's Grove
Huntsfield Farm
Long Coppice
New House Farm
Bannut Tree Farm
Worcestershire Way
Hurst Coppice
Arbour Farm
Eymore Wood
Meadow Farm
Victoria Bridge
Woodseaves
Works
Cleeside View
Broadhurst Coppice
Gable End
Wayside
Cliff Wood
Trimpley Reservoir
Annhill Coppice
Pinewoods
Pound Green
Pound Green Common
Oak Tree Farm
Graft Wood
Birch Coppice
Folly Point
Forest End
Seckley Wood
Woodhouse Farm
Woodlands
Bath Coppice
Buttonoak
B4194
Sunnyside
Twopenny Green Coppice
Hill Top
Hawkbatch Farm
Hill Farm
NORTHWOOD LA
Shropshire STREET ATLAS

25

2
12

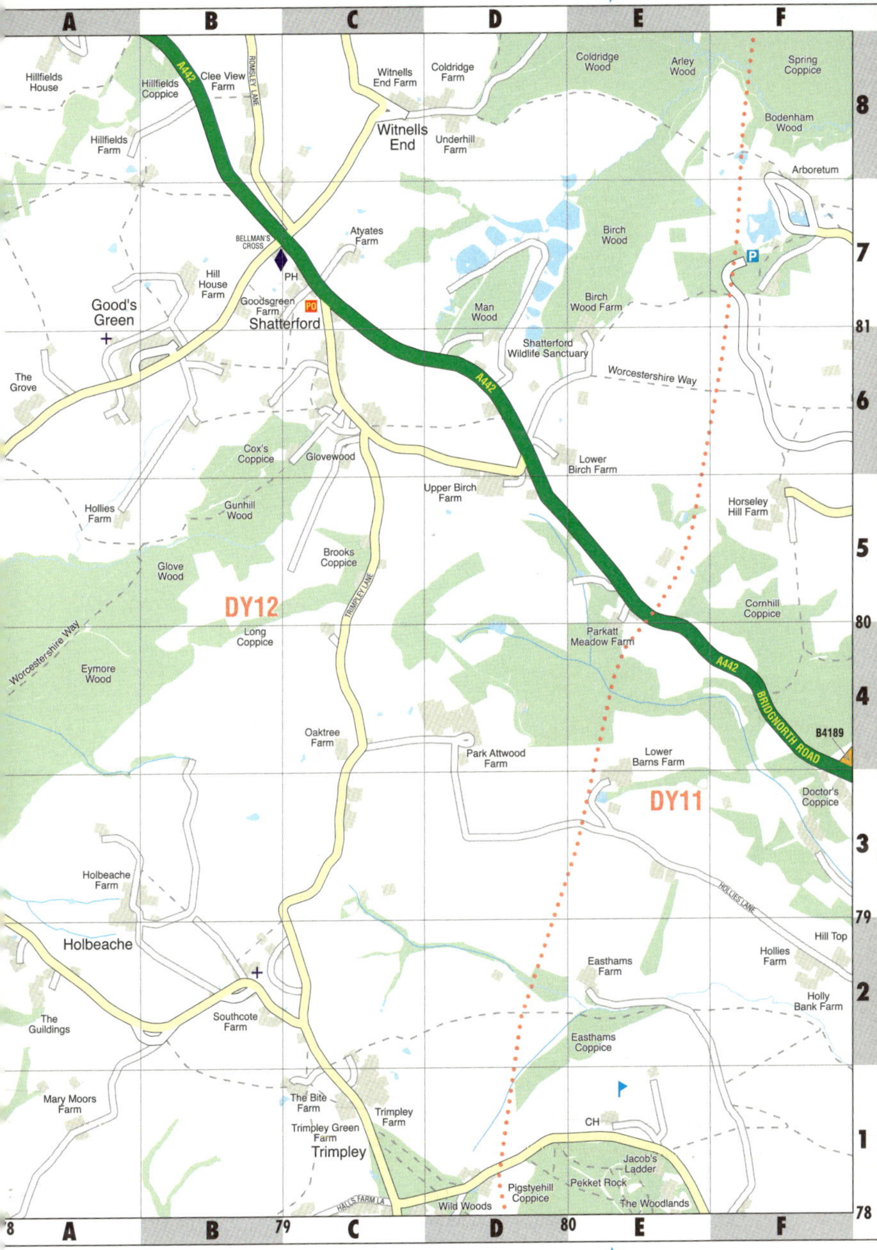
A
B
C
D
E
F
8
7
81
6
5
80
4
3
79
2
1
78
79
80
Hillfields House
Hillfields Coppice
Clee View Farm
ROMSLEY LANE
A442
Witnells End Farm
Coldridge Farm
Coldridge Wood
Arley Wood
Spring Coppice
Bodenham Wood
Hillfields Farm
Witnells End
Underhill Farm
Arboretum
BELLMAN'S CROSS
PH
Atyates Farm
Birch Wood
Hill House Farm
Good's Green
Goodsgreen Farm
PO
Shatterford
Man Wood
Birch Wood Farm
P
The Grove
Shatterford Wildlife Sanctuary
Worcestershire Way
Cox's Coppice
Glovewood
Lower Birch Farm
Upper Birch Farm
Horseley Hill Farm
Hollies Farm
Gunhill Wood
Brooks Coppice
Glove Wood
DY12
TRIMPLEY LANE
Cornhill Coppice
Long Coppice
Parkatt Meadow Farm
Worcestershire Way
Eymore Wood
BRIDGNORTH ROAD
B4189
Oaktree Farm
Park Attwood Farm
Lower Barns Farm
DY11
Doctor's Coppice
Holbeache Farm
HOLLIES LANE
Hill Top
Hollies Farm
Holbeache
Easthams Farm
Holly Bank Farm
The Guildings
Southcote Farm
Easthams Coppice
Mary Moors Farm
The Bite Farm
Trimpley Farm
CH
Trimpley Green Farm
Trimpley
Jacob's Ladder
Pekket Rock
Pigstyehill Coppice
HALLS FARM LA
Wild Woods
The Woodlands

26
12

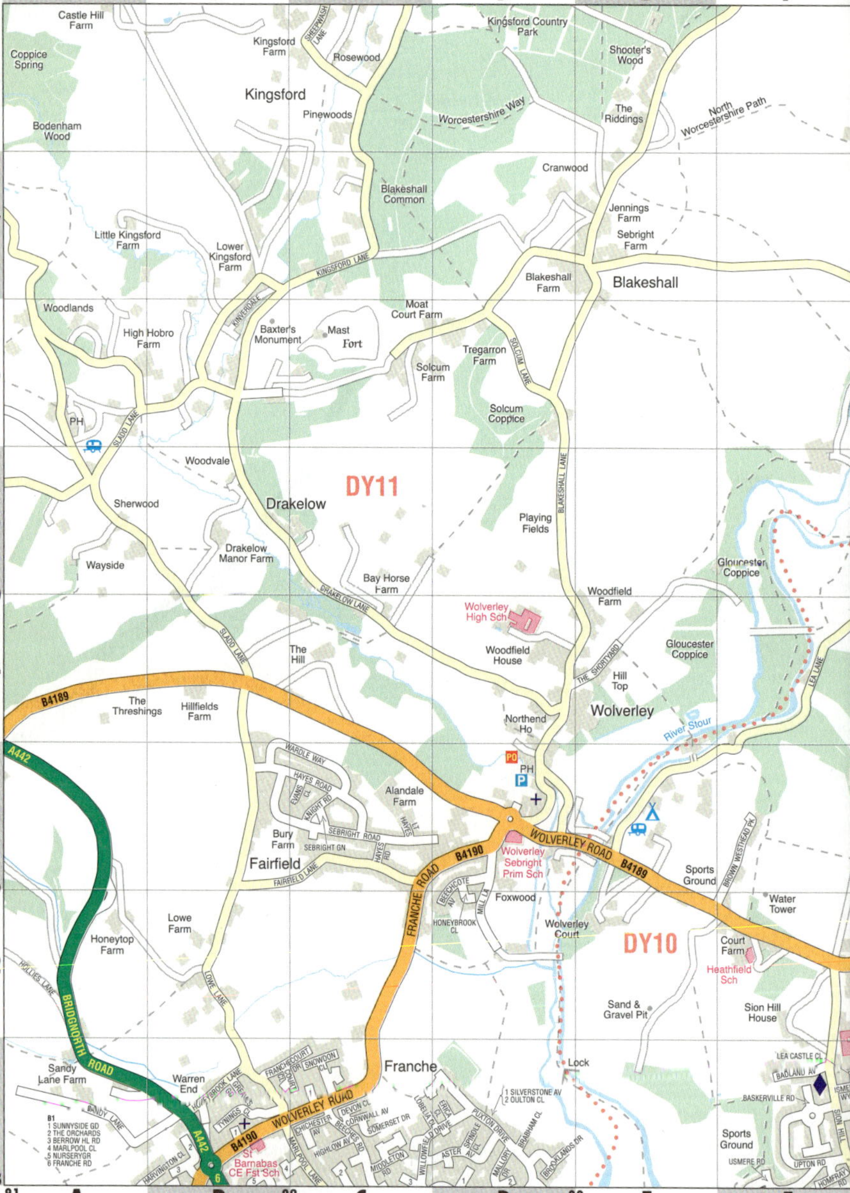
A
B
C
D
E
F
8
7
81
6
5
80
4
3
79
2
1
78
81
82
83
Castle Hill Farm
Coppice Spring
Kingsford Farm
Rosewood
Kingsford Country Park
Shooter's Wood
Kingsford
Pinewoods
Worcestershire Way
North Worcestershire Path
The Riddings
Bodenham Wood
Cranwood
Blakeshall Common
Jennings Farm
Sebright Farm
Little Kingsford Farm
Lower Kingsford Farm
KINGSFORD LANE
Blakeshall Farm
Blakeshall
Woodlands
Baxter's Monument
Mast
Fort
Moat Court Farm
High Hobro Farm
Tregarron Farm
SOLCUM LANE
Solcum Farm
PH
SLADD LANE
Solcum Coppice
Woodvale
DY11
BLAKESHALL LANE
Sherwood
Drakelow
Playing Fields
Wayside
Drakelow Manor Farm
Bay Horse Farm
Gloucester Coppice
DRAKELOW LANE
Woodfield Farm
Wolverley High Sch
The Hill
Woodfield House
THE SHORTYARD
Gloucester Coppice
Hill Top
B4189
The Threshings
Hillfields Farm
Wolverley
Northend Ho
River Stour
LEA LANE
A442
WARDLE WAY
HAYES ROAD
EVANS CL
KNIGHT RD
PO
PH
Alandale Farm
HAYES LT
SEBRIGHT ROAD
Bury Farm
SEBRIGHT GN
HAYES RD
Fairfield
FAIRFIELD LANE
B4190
FRANCHE ROAD
WOLVERLEY ROAD
B4189
Wolverley Sebright Prim Sch
BEECHCOTE AV
MILL LA
Foxwood
Sports Ground
BROWN WESTHEAD PK
Water Tower
Lowe Farm
HONEYBROOK CL
Wolverley Court
DY10
Court Farm
Heathfield Sch
Honeytop Farm
HOLLIES LANE
BRIDGNORTH ROAD
LOWE LANE
Sand & Gravel Pit
Sion Hill House
Sandy Lane Farm
Warren End
HONEYBROOK LANE
FRANCHECOURT DR
SNOWDON CL
Franche
Lock
LEA CASTLE CL
BADLAND AV
1 SILVERSTONE AV
2 OULTON CL
WOLVERLEY ROAD
DEVON CL
CORNWALL AV
SOMERSET DR
LOBELIA CL
ERICA CL
PUXTON DRIVE
BASKERVILLE RD
USMERE WY
SANDY LANE
TYNINGS CL
CHICHESTER AV
BEECHES RD
GOLDFIELD DRIVE
BRABHAM CL
SION HILL
B1
1 SUNNYSIDE GD
2 THE ORCHARDS
3 BERROW HL RD
4 MARLPOOL CL
5 NURSERYGR
6 FRANCHE RD
B4190
St Barnabas CE Fst Sch
HIGHLOW AV
MIDDLETON RD
WILLOWFIELD DRIVE
ASTER AV
SPINDLE CL
MALLORY DR
BROOKLANDS DR
Sports Ground
USMERE RD
UPTON RD
HOMFRAY RD
HARVINGTON CL
MARLPOOL LANE
A442

4
14

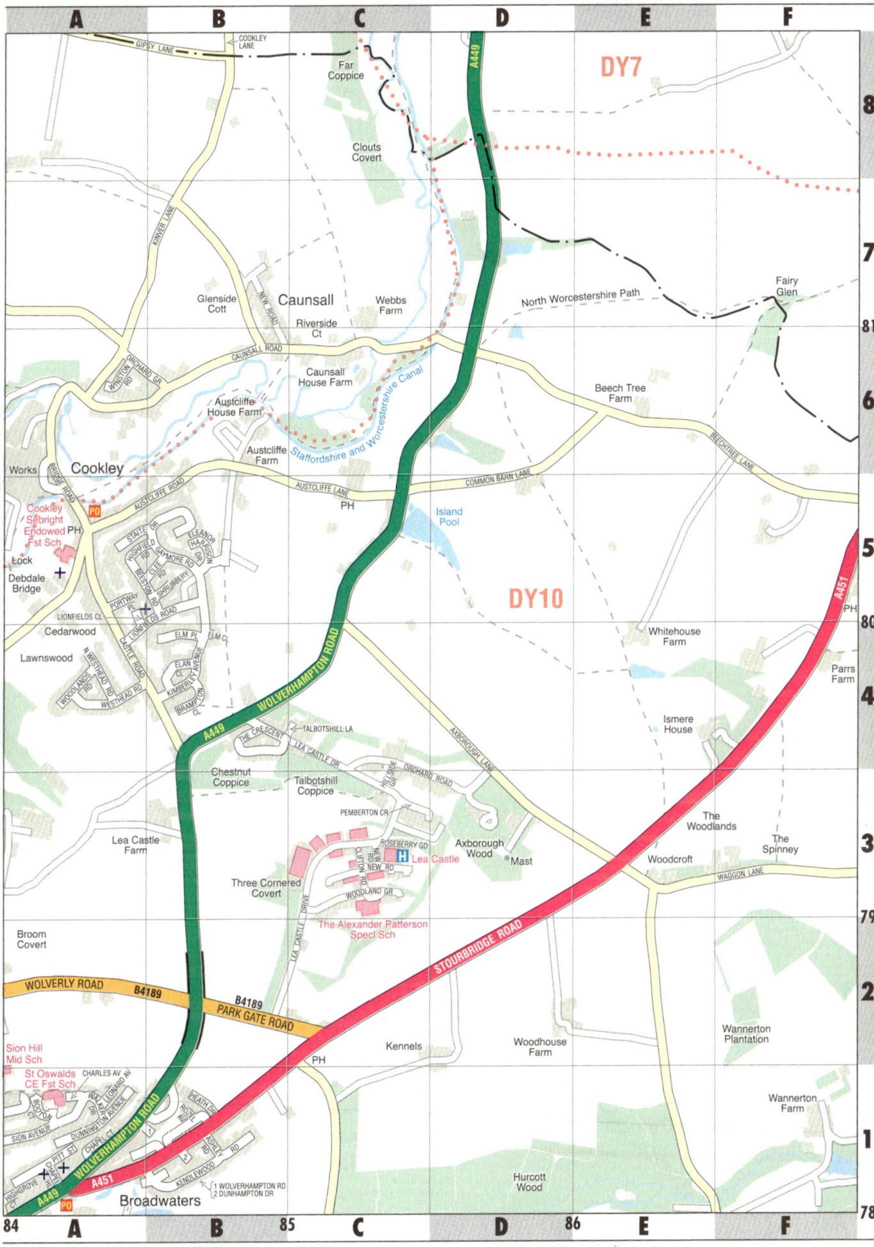
A
B
C
D
E
F
8
7
81
6
5
80
4
3
79
2
1
78
84
85
86
DY7
DY10
GIPSY LANE
COOKLEY LANE
Far Coppice
A449
Clouts Covert
KINVER LANE
Glenside Cott
NEW ROAD
Caunsall
Webbs Farm
Riverside Ct
North Worcestershire Path
Fairy Glen
CAUNSALL ROAD
WINSTON RD
ORCHARD GR
Caunsall House Farm
Austcliffe House Farm
Staffordshire and Worcestershire Canal
Beech Tree Farm
BEECHTREE LANE
Austcliffe Farm
Works
Cookley
BRIDGE ROAD
AUSTCLIFFE ROAD
AUSTCLIFFE LANE
COMMON BARN LANE
PH
PO
Cookley Sebright Endowed Fst Sch
Island Pool
STATE DR
ELEANOR HARRISON DR
HIGHFIELD RD
GAYMORE RD
Lock
Debdale Bridge
CLEE RD
BEESTON RD
SHRUBBERY
PORTWAY PL
LIONFIELDS RD
LIONFIELDS CL
Cedarwood
ELM PL
ELM CL
Whitehouse Farm
Parrs Farm
A451
Lawnswood
N WESTHEAD RD
WOODLANDS RD
WESTHEAD RD
CASTLE ROAD
ELAN CL
KIMBERLEY AVENUE
BRAMPTON CL
WOLVERHAMPTON ROAD
THE CRESCENT
TALBOTSHILL LA
LEA CASTLE DR
AXBOROUGH LANE
Ismere House
Chestnut Coppice
Talbotshill Coppice
HILLSIDE GR
ORCHARD ROAD
PEMBERTON CR
Lea Castle Farm
ROSEBERRY GD
Axborough Wood
Lea Castle
Mast
The Woodlands
The Spinney
Woodcroft
WAGGON LANE
CLIFTON RD
NEW RD
Three Cornered Covert
WOODLAND GR
LEA CASTLE DRIVE
The Alexander Patterson Specl Sch
Broom Covert
STOURBRIDGE ROAD
WOLVERLY ROAD
B4189
PARK GATE ROAD
Sion Hill Mid Sch
Kennels
Woodhouse Farm
Wannerton Plantation
St Oswalds CE Fst Sch
CHARLES AV
LEONARD AV
WALKER AVENUE
DUNNINGTON AVENUE
BOLTON CT
SION AVENUE
HEATH DR
ROZEL AV
ASHLEY RD
Wannerton Farm
PITT ST
CHAPEL CT
CHAPEL HL
HIGHGROVE CT
KENDLEWOOD RD
1 WOLVERHAMPTON RD
2 DUNHAMPTON DR
Broadwaters
Hurcott Wood

28
14

13
5

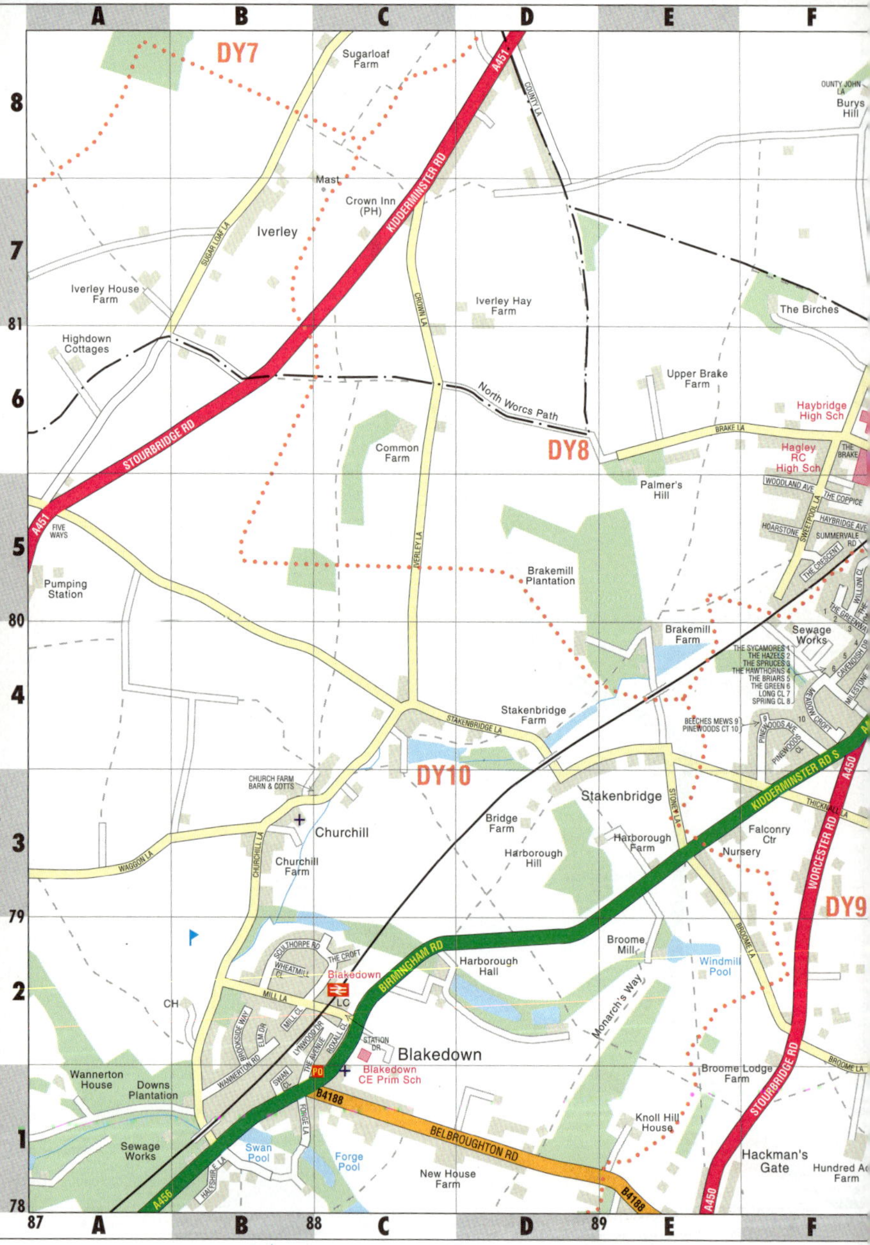
A
B
C
D
E
F
8
7
81
6
5
80
4
3
79
2
1
78
87
88
89
DY7
DY8
DY10
DY9
Sugarloaf Farm
A451
COUNTY LA
Burys Hill
Mast
Crown Inn (PH)
KIDDERMINSTER RD
Iverley
SUGAR LOAF LA
Iverley House Farm
CROWN LA
Iverley Hay Farm
The Birches
Highdown Cottages
Upper Brake Farm
North Worcs Path
Haybridge High Sch
STOURBRIDGE RD
Common Farm
BRAKE LA
Hagley RC High Sch
THE BRAKE
WOODLAND AVE
THE COPPICE
Palmer's Hill
HAYBRIDGE AVE
HOARSTONE
SWEETPOOL LA
SUMMERVALE RD
FIVE WAYS
IVERLEY LA
THE CRESCENT
Brakemill Plantation
Pumping Station
WILLOW CL
THE GREENWAY
Brakemill Farm
Sewage Works
THE SYCAMORES 1
THE HAZELS 2
THE SPRUCES 3
THE HAWTHORNS 4
THE BRIARS 5
THE GREEN 6
LONG CL 7
SPRING CL 8
CAVENDISH DR
MILESTONE
MEADOW CROFT
BEECHES MEWS 9
PINEWOODS CT 10
Stakenbridge Farm
STAKENBRIDGE LA
PINEWOODS AVE
PINEWOODS CL
A450
KIDDERMINSTER RD S
CHURCH FARM BARN & COTTS
Stakenbridge
THICKNALL LA
Churchill
Bridge Farm
STONE LA
Harborough Farm
Falconry Ctr
WORCESTER RD
CHURCHILL LA
Churchill Farm
Harborough Hill
Nursery
WAGGON LA
SCULTHORPE RD
THE CROFT
Broome Mill
WHEATMILL CL
Blakedown
BIRMINGHAM RD
Harborough Hall
Windmill Pool
BROOME LA
MILL LA
CH
LC
Monarch's Way
BROOKSIDE WAY
ELM DR
MILL CL
LYNWOOD DR
ROYALL CL
STATION DR
Blakedown
WANNERTON RD
THE AVENUE
PO
Blakedown CE Prim Sch
Wannerton House
Downs Plantation
SWAN CL
B4188
Broome Lodge Farm
FORGE LA
STOURBRIDGE RD
Knoll Hill House
Sewage Works
BELBROUGHTON RD
Swan Pool
Forge Pool
Hackman's Gate
HALFSHIRE LA
New House Farm
Hundred Ac Farm
A456

13
29

6
16

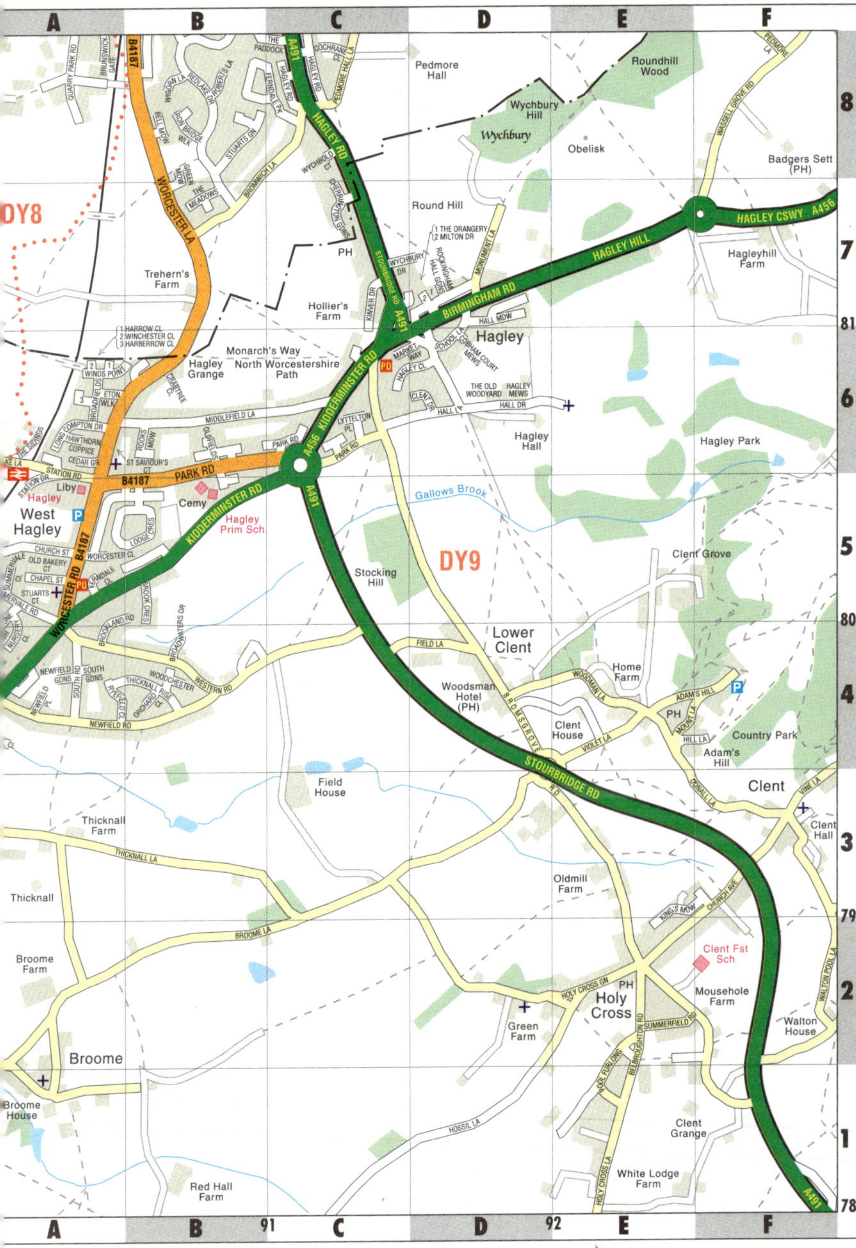
A
B
C
D
E
F
8
7
81
6
5
80
4
3
79
2
1
78
91
92
DY8
DY9
Pedmore Hall
Roundhill Wood
Wychbury Hill
Wychbury
Obelisk
Badgers Sett (PH)
Round Hill
HAGLEY CSWY A456
HAGLEY HILL
Hagleyhill Farm
BIRMINGHAM RD
Hagley
Trehern's Farm
Hollier's Farm
PH
Monarch's Way
North Worcestershire Path
Hagley Grange
WORCESTER LA
B4187
A491
A456
HAGLEY RD
STOURBRIDGE RD
KIDDERMINSTER RD
PARK RD
MIDDLEFIELD LA
Hagley Hall
Hagley Park
Gallows Brook
PO
Liby
Hagley
West Hagley
Cemy
Hagley Prim Sch
Stocking Hill
Clent Grove
Lower Clent
Home Farm
Woodsman Hotel (PH)
BROMSGROVE RD
Clent House
ADAM'S HILL
Country Park
Adam's Hill
Clent
Clent Hall
FIELD LA
WESTERN RD
NEWFIELD RD
Field House
Thicknall Farm
THICKNALL LA
Thicknall
Oldmill Farm
BROOME LA
Broome Farm
Broome
Broome House
Clent Fst Sch
Mousehole Farm
Walton House
HOLY CROSS GN
Holy Cross
Green Farm
SUMMERFIELD RD
Clent Grange
HOSSIL LA
White Lodge Farm
HOLY CROSS LA
Red Hall Farm
VIOLET LA
WOODMAN LA
CHURCH AVE
KING'S MDW
WALTON POOL LA
VINE LA
HILL LA
MOUNT LA
ODNALL LA
BELBROUGHTON RD
POOL FURLONG
1 HARROW CL
2 WINCHESTER CL
3 HARBERROW CL
1 THE ORANGERY
2 MILTON DR
HALL MDW
HALL DR
HALL LA
SCHOOL LA
COBHAM COURT MEWS
THE OLD WOODYARD
HAGLEY MEWS
MARKET WAY
HAGLEY CL
CLENT DR
LYTTELTON PL
WYCHBURY DR
ROCKINGHAM HALL GDNS
MONUMENT LA
KINVER DR
WYCHBOLD CT
BROMWICH LA
THE MEADOWS
STUARTS GN
IRON BRIDGE WLK
BELL MDW
REDLAKE DR
ROBERTS LA
FERNDALE PK
COCHRANE CL
PEDMORE HALL LA
THE PADDOCK
QUARRY PARK RD
BRUNSWICK GATE
PEDMORE LA
WASSELL GROVE RD
STATION RD
STATION DR
CEDAR GR
ST SAVIOUR'S CT
CHURCH ST
OLD BAKERY CT
CHAPEL ST
STUARTS CT
WORCESTER CL
LODGE CRES
BROOK CRES
BROOKLAND RD
BROADWATERS DR
NEWFIELD GDNS
SOUTH GDNS
SOUTH RD
NEWFIELD PL
WOODCHESTER
THICKNALL RISE
RYEFIELD CL
ORCHARD CL
WINDS POINT
ETON WLK
BROADFIELDS
HAWTHORN COPPICE
COMPTON DR
OLDFIELDS
ROCKS MDW
CRABTREE CL
THE SIDINGS

30
16

15
7

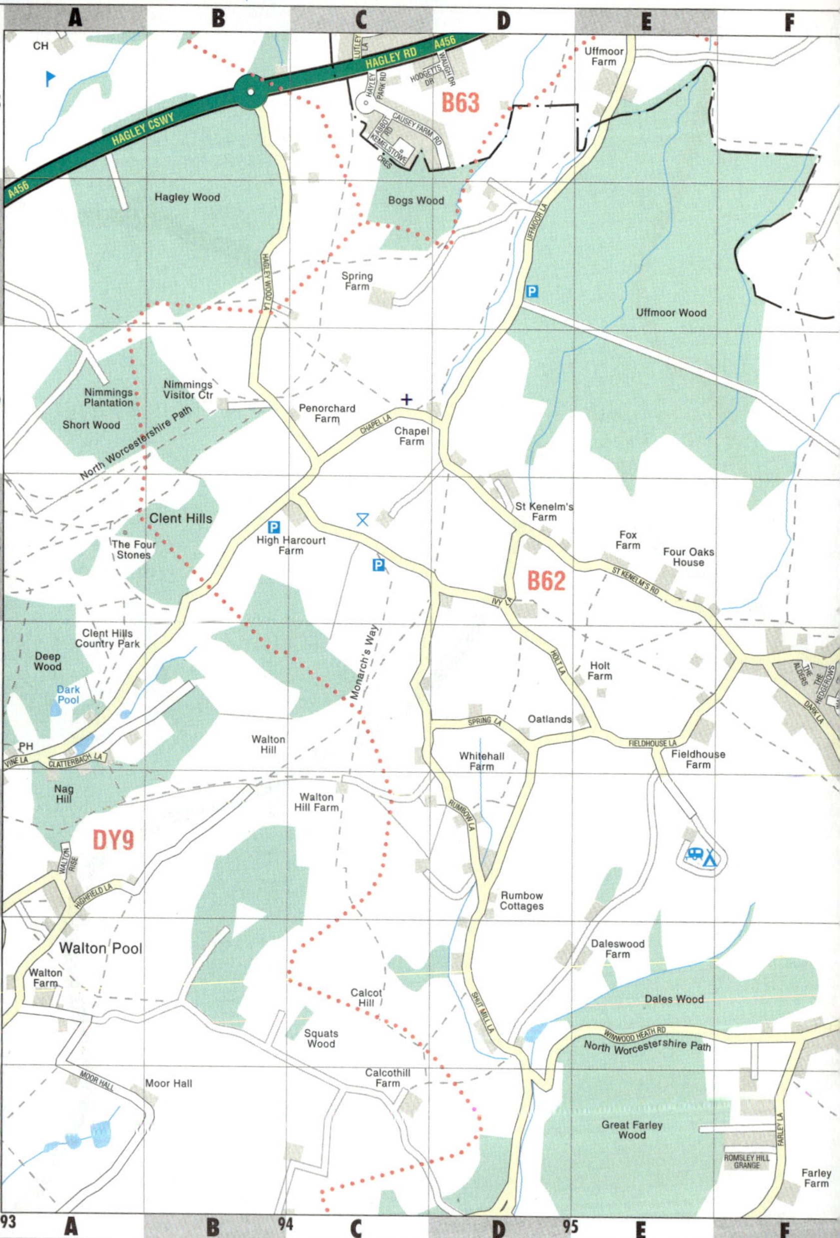
A
B
C
D
E
F
CH
A456
HAGLEY RD
HAGLEY CSWY
LUTLEY LA
HAYLEY PARK RD
HODGETTS DR
WAUGH DR
CAUSEY FARM RD
ABBOT RD
KEMELSTOWE CRES
B63
Uffmoor Farm
Hagley Wood
Bogs Wood
UFFMOOR LA
HAGLEY WOOD LA
Spring Farm
Uffmoor Wood
Nimmings Plantation
Nimmings Visitor Ctr
Short Wood
North Worcestershire Path
Penorchard Farm
CHAPEL LA
Chapel Farm
Clent Hills
The Four Stones
High Harcourt Farm
St Kenelm's Farm
Fox Farm
Four Oaks House
B62
ST KENELM'S RD
IVY LA
Clent Hills Country Park
Deep Wood
Dark Pool
Monarch's Way
HOLT LA
Holt Farm
THE ALDERS
THE HEDGEROWS
DARK LA
SPRING LA
Oatlands
Walton Hill
PH
VINE LA
CLATTERBACH LA
Whitehall Farm
FIELDHOUSE LA
Fieldhouse Farm
Nag Hill
Walton Hill Farm
RUMBOW LA
DY9
WALTON RISE
HIGHFIELD LA
Rumbow Cottages
Walton Pool
Daleswood Farm
Walton Farm
Calcot Hill
Dales Wood
SHUT MILL LA
Squats Wood
WINWOOD HEATH RD
North Worcestershire Path
MOOR HALL
Moor Hall
Calcothill Farm
Great Farley Wood
FARLEY LA
ROMSLEY HILL GRANGE
Farley Farm
8
7
81
6
5
80
4
3
79
2
1
78
93
94
95

15
31

8
18
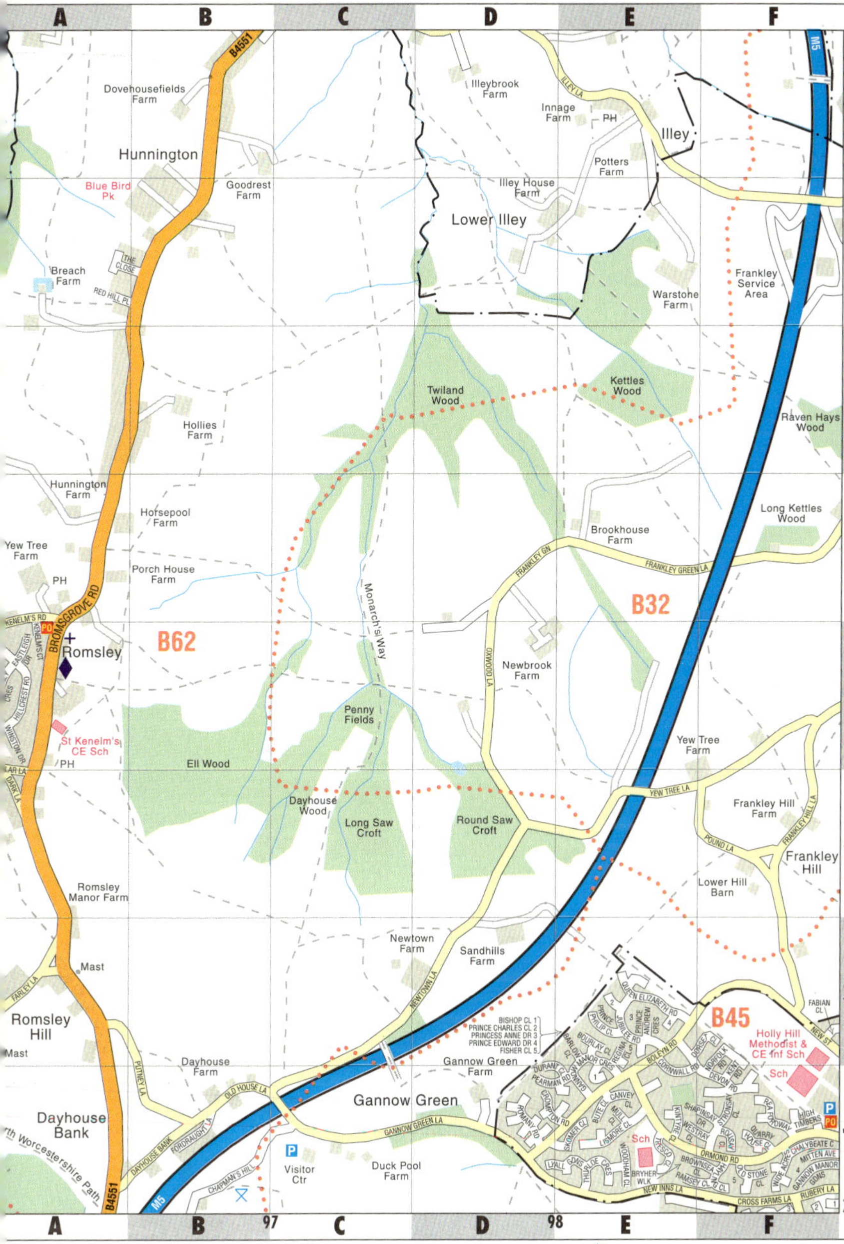

32
18

F1
1 BROOKDALE CL
2 CHADDERSLEY CL
3 RUBERY LA S
4 HOLLY HILL
5 CALDY WLK

17
9

A
B
C
D
E
F
8
7
81
6
5
80
4
3
79
2
1
78
99
00
01
Woodcock Hill
Bartley Green
Newman Coll
King Edward VI Five Ways Sch
Kitwell Prim Sch
Kitwell
Bartley Reservoir
Shenley Fields
Shenley Court Sch
Bromwich Wood
Westminster Farm
Raven Hays Wood
Scotland Farm
B32
Frankley
Frankley Green
Frankley Resr
Works
Ley Hill Prim Sch
Merritt's Brook
Bellfield Jun & Inf Sch
Frankley Beeches
Northfield Children's Farm
Frankley Lodge Farm
Egg Hill
Egghill Dingle
Egghill Farm
B31
B45
Frankley Schs
The Meadows Prim Sch
Frankley Ind Pk
Balaam's Wood
River Rea
Bedlam Wood
Birmingham Great Pk
CROMWELL LA
FRANKLEY LA
CHURCH HILL
FRANKLEY BEECHES RD
TESSALL LA
BRISTOL RD S
SHENLEY LA
A38
B4121

17
33

B7
1 HAMPSHIRE CT
2 DORSET CT
3 DEVON CT
4 BATH CT
5 CHESTER CT
6 CHELSEA CT

C7
1 WARWICK CT
2 RUTLAND CT
3 DANBIGH CT
4 RICHMOND CT
5 ESSEX CT
6 NORFOLK CT
7 SUSSEX CT
8 OXFORD CT
9 LINCOLN CT
10 WILTSHIRE CT
11 ASCOT CT
12 GUILDFORD CT
13 ARUNDEL CT
14 KENDAL CT
15 BRISTOL CT
16 EPSOM CT
17 KINGSTON CT
18 SANDOWN CT
19 DOVEDALE CT

20

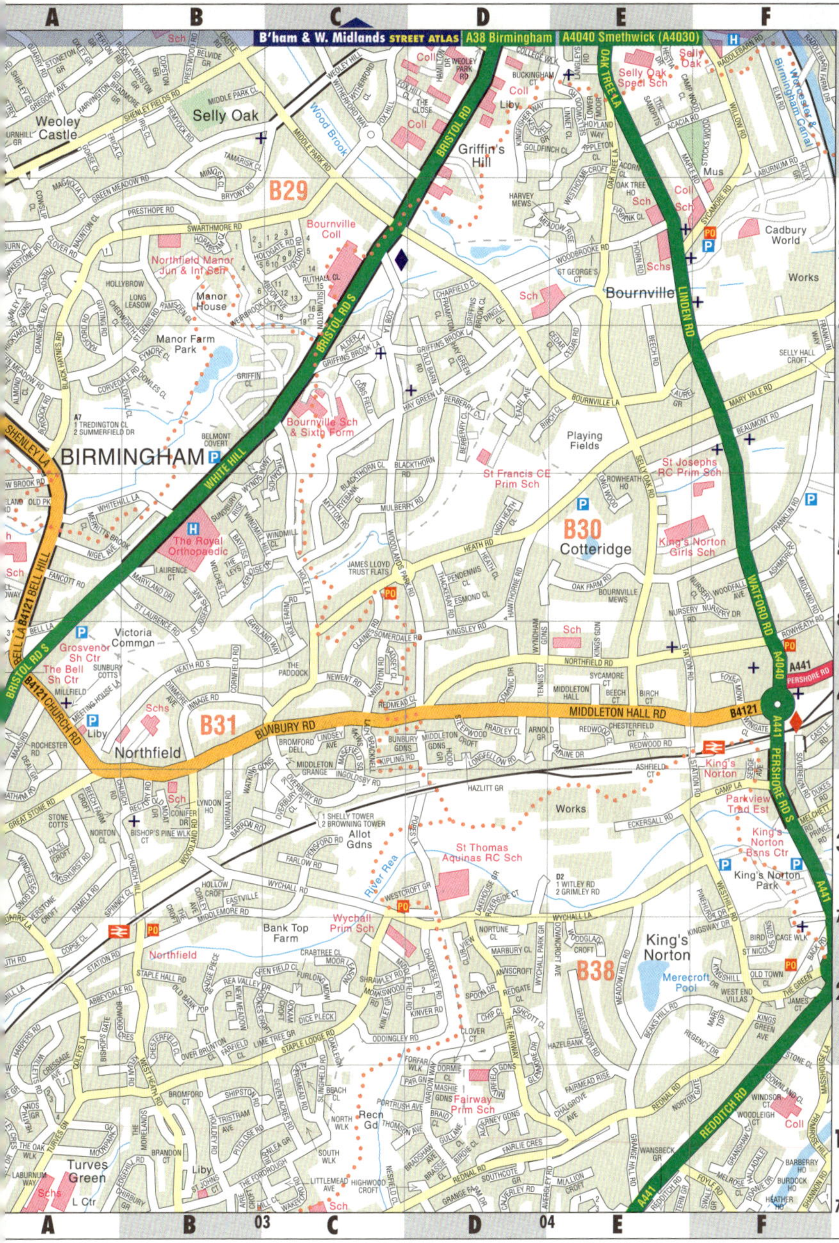

34

20

E1
1 BURFORD PARK RD
2 GROVEWOOD DR
3 WHITEBEAM CROFT
F1
1 WARRENS END

CENTENARY CL
ENBY TOWER
SANDOWN TOWER
WELLINGTON TOWER

CUTLERS ROUGH CL
SAXON WOOD CL
BELL HILL
VINEYARD RD

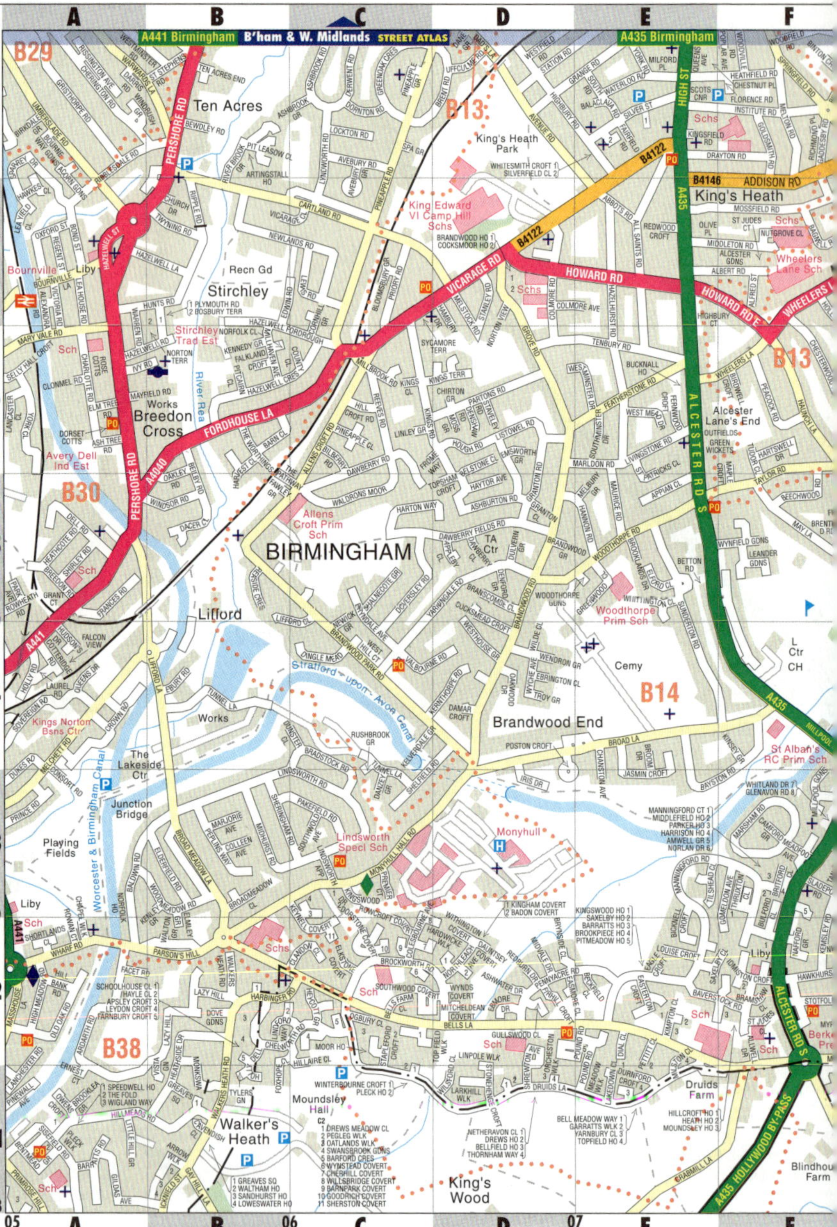
A441 Birmingham
B'ham & W. Midlands STREET ATLAS
A435 Birmingham
A B C D E F
8 7 81 6 5 80 4 3 79 2 1 78
05 06 07
B29
B13
B30
B14
B38
Ten Acres
Stirchley
Recn Gd
Stirchley Trad Est
Breedon Cross
Works
River Rea
Bournville
Liby
Sch
Avery Dell Ind Est
King's Heath Park
King Edward VI Camp Hill Schs
King's Heath
Schs
Wheelers Lane Sch
Alcester Lane's End
BIRMINGHAM
Allens Croft Prim Sch
TA Ctr
Woodthorpe Prim Sch
Cemy
Lifford
Stratford - upon - Avon Canal
Works
Kings Norton Bsns Ctr
The Lakeside Ctr
Junction Bridge
Playing Fields
Worcester & Birmingham Canal
Brandwood End
St Alban's RC Prim Sch
Monyhull
Lindsworth Specl Sch
Schs
Walker's Heath
Moundsley Hall
King's Wood
Druids Farm
Blindhouse Farm
PERSHORE RD
A4040
FORDHOUSE LA
VICARAGE RD
HOWARD RD
HOWARD RD E
B4122
B4146
ADDISON RD
HIGH ST
A435
ALCESTER RD S
A441
A435 HOLLYWOOD BY-PASS
BROAD LA
BELLS LA
PARSON'S HILL
WHARF RD
Liby
Sch
L Ctr
CH

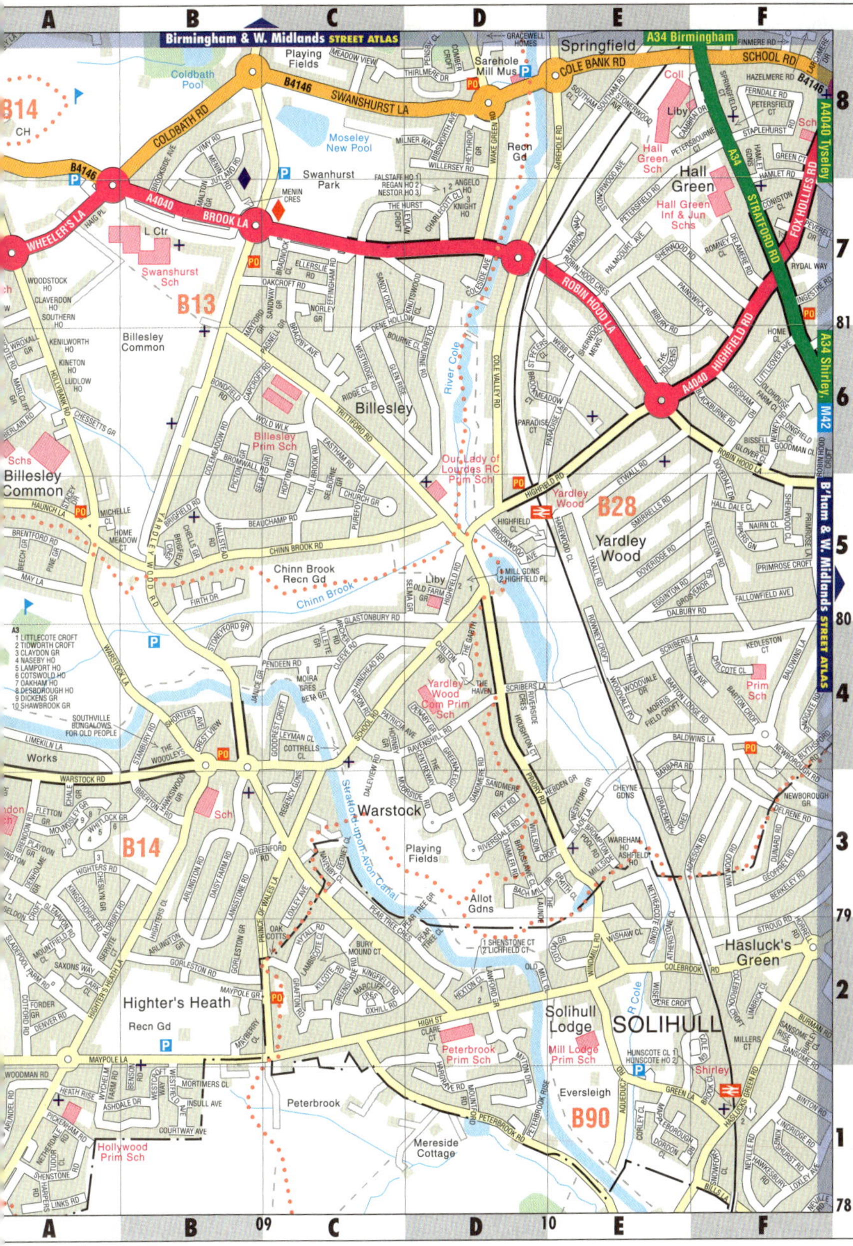
Birmingham & W. Midlands STREET ATLAS
A34 Birmingham
A40 40 Tyseley
A34 Shirley, M42
B'ham & W. Midlands STREET ATLAS
A
B
C
D
E
F
09
10
8
7
81
6
5
80
4
3
79
2
1
78
B14
B13
B28
B90
Springfield
Playing Fields
Coldbath Pool
Sarehole Mill Mus
Moseley New Pool
Swanhurst Park
Recn Gd
Hall Green
Hall Green Sch
Hall Green Inf & Jun Schs
Coll
Liby
L Ctr
Swanhurst Sch
Billesley Common
Billesley
Billesley Prim Sch
River Cole
Our Lady of Lourdes RC Prim Sch
Yardley Wood
Chinn Brook Recn Gd
Chinn Brook
Liby
Works
Yardley Wood Com Prim Sch
Prim Sch
Warstock
Stratford-upon-Avon Canal
Playing Fields
Allot Gdns
Hasluck's Green
Highter's Heath
Recn Gd
Solihull Lodge
SOLIHULL
Mill Lodge Prim Sch
Peterbrook Prim Sch
Peterbrook
Eversleigh
Shirley
Mereside Cottage
Hollywood Prim Sch
Sch
Schs
COLDBATH RD
SWANSHURST LA
B4146
A4040
BROOK LA
WHEELER'S LA
COLE BANK RD
SCHOOL RD
STRATFORD RD
ROBIN HOOD LA
HIGHFIELD RD
FOX HOLLIES RD
CHINN BROOK RD
WARSTOCK LA
WARSTOCK RD
YARDLEY WOOD RD
MAYPOLE LA
HIGH ST
COLEBROOK RD
PETERBROOK RD
HIGHTER'S HEATH LA

36

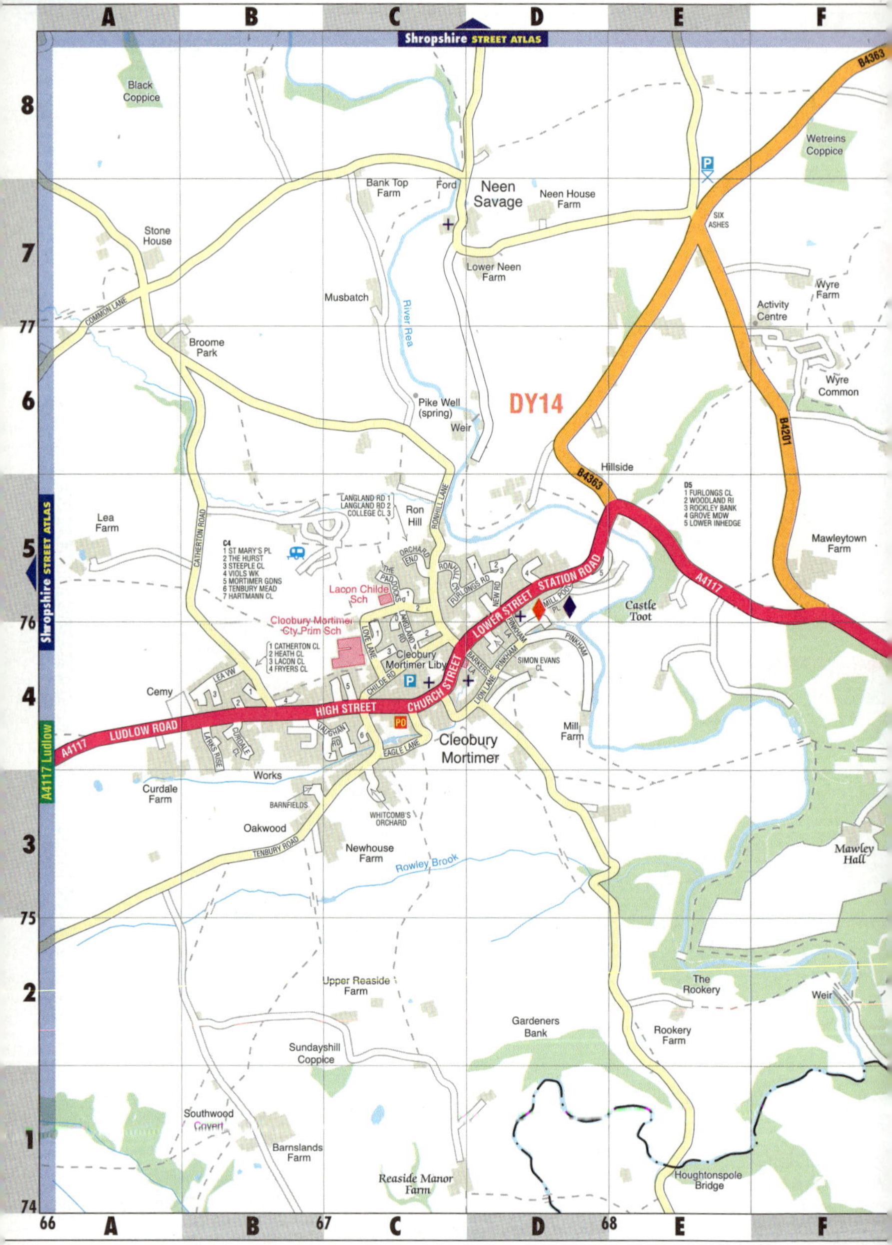
A
B
C
D
E
F
Shropshire STREET ATLAS
8
7
77
6
5
76
4
3
75
2
1
74
66
67
68
Black Coppice
Wetreins Coppice
B4363
Bank Top Farm
Ford
Neen Savage
Neen House Farm
SIX ASHES
Stone House
Lower Neen Farm
Musbatch
River Rea
Wyre Farm
Activity Centre
COMMON LANE
Broome Park
Wyre Common
Pike Well (spring)
Weir
DY14
B4201
Hillside
LANGLAND RD 1
LANGLAND RD 2
COLLEGE CL 3
Ron Hill
RONHILL LANE
D5
1 FURLONGS CL
2 WOODLAND RI
3 ROCKLEY BANK
4 GROVE MDW
5 LOWER INHEDGE
Lea Farm
CATHERTON ROAD
C4
1 ST MARY'S PL
2 THE HURST
3 STEEPLE CL
4 VIOLS WK
5 MORTIMER GDNS
6 TENBURY MEAD
7 HARTMANN CL
Mawleytown Farm
ORCHARD END
THE PADDOCKS
FURLONGS RD
NEW RD
STATION ROAD
A4117
Lacon Childe Sch
LOWER STREET
MILL POOL PL
Castle Toot
Cloobury Mortimer Cty Prim Sch
LANGLAND RD
PINKHAM
LOVE LANE
Cleobury Mortimer Liby
BARKERS LA
SIMON EVANS CL
1 CATHERTON CL
2 HEATH CL
3 LACON CL
4 FRYERS CL
LEA VW
CHILDE RD
CHURCH STREET
LION LANE
Cemy
HIGH STREET
Mill Farm
A4117 Ludlow
LUDLOW ROAD
PO
VAUGHAN RD
CURDALE CL
LARKS RISE
EAGLE LANE
Cleobury Mortimer
Works
Curdale Farm
BARNFIELDS
WHITCOMB'S ORCHARD
Oakwood
TENBURY ROAD
Newhouse Farm
Mawley Hall
Rowley Brook
Upper Reaside Farm
The Rookery
Weir
Gardeners Bank
Rookery Farm
Sundayshill Coppice
Southwood Covert
Barnslands Farm
Reaside Manor Farm
Houghtonspole Bridge

24

Shropshire STREET ATLAS
A
B
C
D
E
F
Maxfields Coppice
Cleobury Lodge Farm
Whiteleasowe Coppice
Pond Bay
Malpass Wood
Meaton Farm
MEATON LANE
Silligrove Fishery
Silligrove
DY12
Mad Brook
Cleobury Mortimer Golf Course
CH
Neenshill Coppice
Baveney Brook
Breakneck Bank
Coachroad Coppice
Weston Plantation
Furnace Coppice
DY14
Nailings Coppice
Weston Farm
Weston Plantation
Bell Coppice
Hungry Hill
Hungry Hill Farm
Catswell Farm
Lem Brook
A4117
B4202
The Coppice
PH
Lodge Coppice
Woodredon
Oak Farm
PH
A4117
Works
Fletchers Farm
Sturt Coppice
Prizeley Farm
Cleobury Coppice
Fletchers Coppice
Bayton Pool
Tanner's Coppice
Beach Hay
Norgrovesend Farm
Woodside Farm
B4202
Ankretts Farm
Teddon Farm
8
7
77
6
5
76
4
3
75
2
1
74
70
71

40

24

23

A
B
C
D
E
F
Shropshire STREET ATLAS
Orchard Farm
Bens Coppice
Earnwood Copse
Corbets Park
8
Upper Wood
Winwoods Farm
DY12
Sturt Common
7
Woodlands
Ford
Manor Farm
Kingswood
Kingswood Farm
Longdon Orchard
Sturt Farm
77
Lower Kingswood Farm
Brand Wood
6
Wyre Forest
Dowles Brook
Wimperhill Wood
KINLET ROAD
The Woodlands
5
Nature Reserve
Railway Farm
STATION ROAD
Goodmoor Grange
Goodmoor Hill Farm
76
Round Hill Farm
Wyre Farm
Hedgewick Farm
STATION ROAD
4
Cherry Side
Fields Farm
Worralls Farm
Lynalls Farm
Cook's Green Farm
Lynall's Coppice
Sugars Farm
Yarrons Farm
3
New Parks
The Tynings
Yew Tree Farm
Lodge Coppice
The Woodland
Brandlodge Coppice
A4117
CHURCH LANE
75
The Lemmings
DY14
Oxbind Coppice
Far Forest
1 NEW FOREST CL
2 OAKLEAF RI
Lem Hill
Lem Hill Farm
Farthings
Five
Woodfield
NEW ROAD
Inniscarra
2
Doveys Farm
Key Farm
Lea Memorial CE Fst Sch
Coppice Bank
PLOUGH LANE
PO
Doghanging Coppice
Tree Tops
PH
Rousebind Coppice
1
Buckridge
Whitehouse Farm
Alton Lodge Farm
Yew Tree Farm
Fingerpost
Buckeridge Farm
Woodcroft
CHAPEL LANE
The Bramblings
The Blue Ball Farm
A4117
Visitor Centre
74
72
A
B
73
C
D
74
E
F

23

41

10
26

42
26

F2
1 PINETREE RD
2 BRANCHES CL
3 BIRCH TREE RD

F3
1 BRAMLEY WY
2 ELLESMERE DR
3 LANCASTER RD
4 YEW TREE CL
5 EARLY RIVER PL
6 ELTON RD
7 MERRICKS LA
8 FORT-MAHON PL
9 OAKWOOD RD
10 FOREST CL
11 MERRICKS CL
12 GROSVENOR WOOD
13 MORELLA CL
14 HALES PARK
15 HORNBEAM CL
16 CHERRY CL
17 IRONSIDE CL
18 WHITE HEART CL

25
11

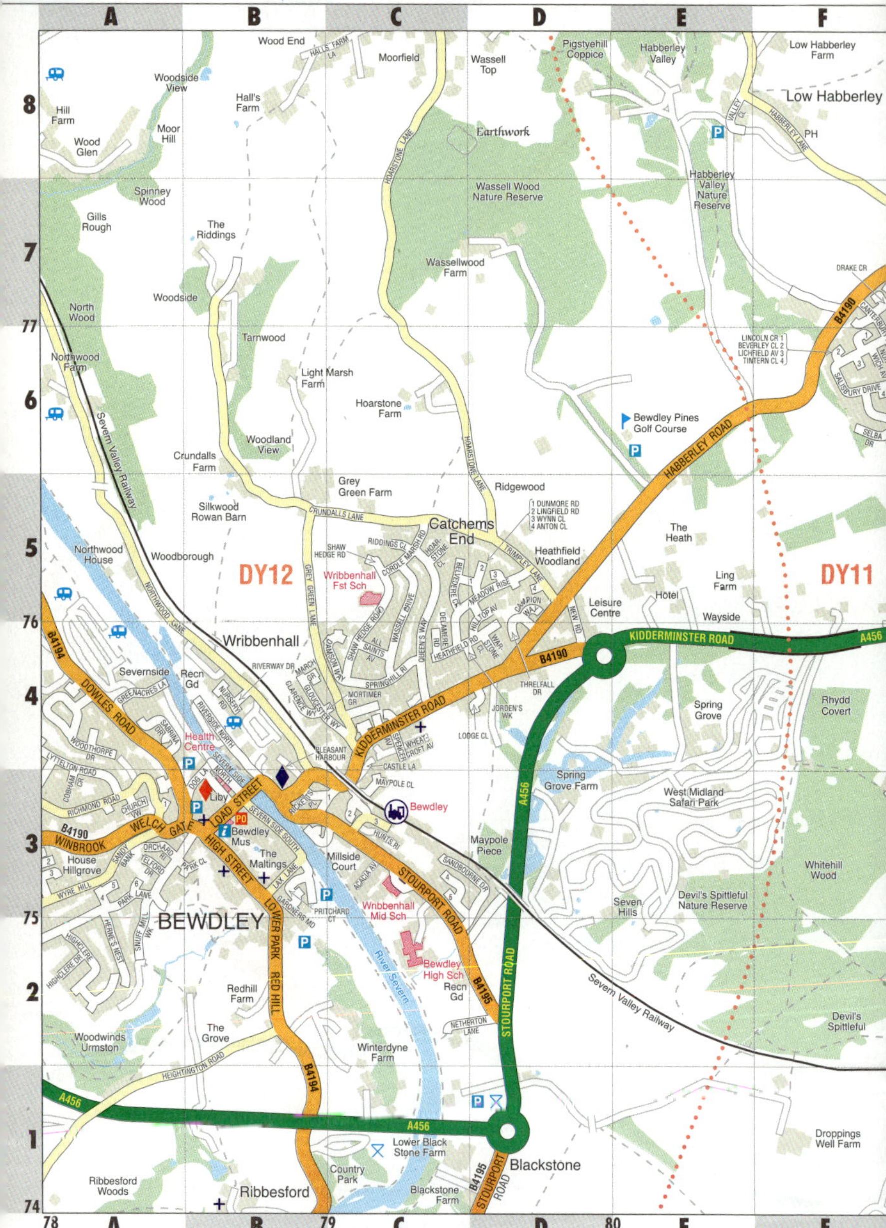

A3
1 VENUS BANK
2 OAKWOOD RD
3 FOREST CL
4 BARRATTS STILE LA
5 BARRATTS CL
6 ROSENHURST DR

C3
1 WESTBOURNE ST
2 STEPHENSON PL
3 STATION ROAD
4 BROOK VALE
5 SANDSTONE RD

25
43

C6
1 HABBERLEY ST
2 BENNETT ST
3 ADAMS HO
4 WOODFIELD ST
5 ST JOHN'S ST
6 ST JOHN'S CL

D6
1 MILLERS CT
2 MILLFIELD GDNS
3 RUTH CHAMBERLAIN CT
4 PATERNOSTER ROW
5 PERRETT WLK
6 ROCK COTTS
7 IDEAL BLDGS

E5
1 BRIDGE ST
2 MARLBOROUGH ST
3 WORCESTER CROSS

12

E6
1 BLACK HORSE LA
2 CALLOWS LA
3 FREDA EDDY CT
4 KING CHARLES SQ
5 DERICK BURCHER'S MALL
6 SIR GEORGE'S MALL

28

E6
7 SWAN CTR
8 SIR WALTER'S MALL
9 ROWLAND HILL CTR
10 ST GEORGES CT

F6
1 TRINITY CT
2 VICTORIA CT
3 SOUTH ST

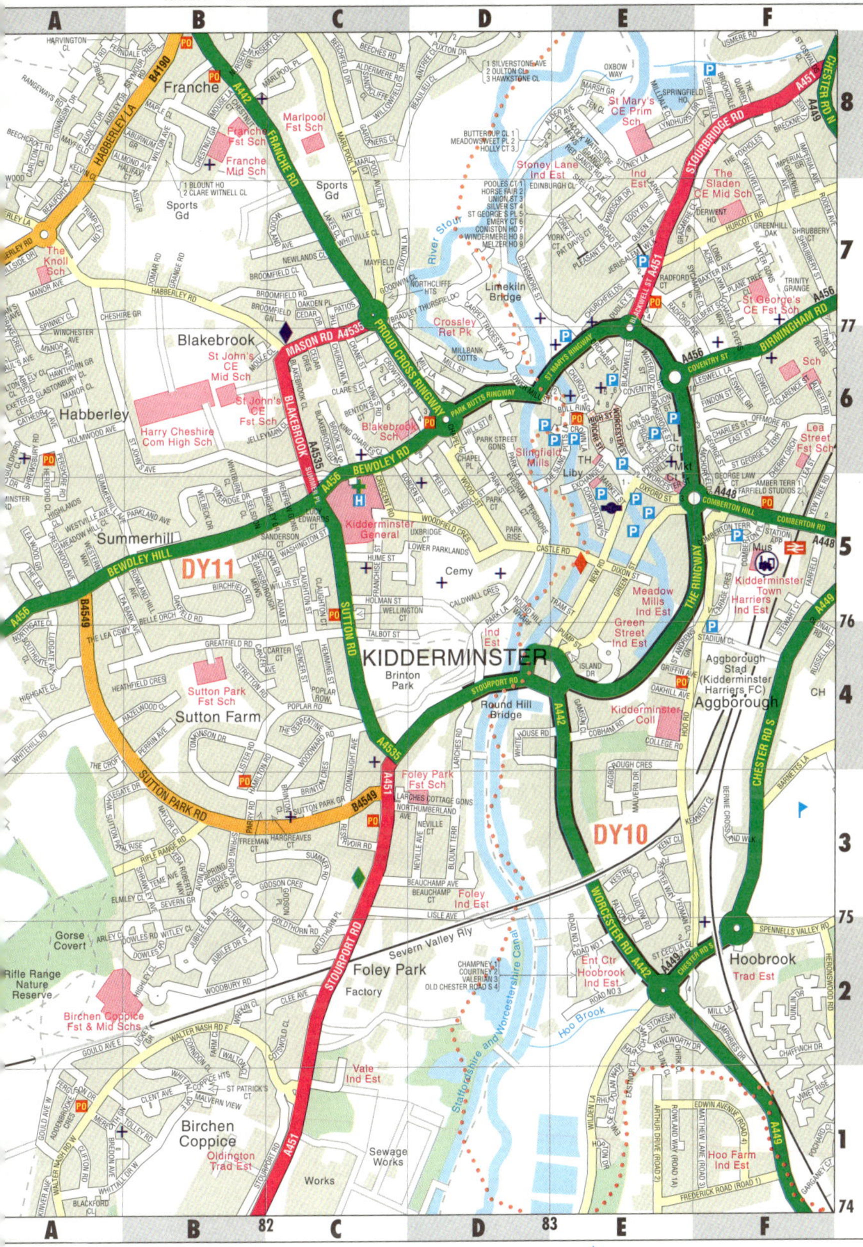

A5
1 THE HAWTHORNS
2 CHADDESLEY GDNS
3 SOMERLEYTON CT
4 COMBERTON MANS
5 COMBERTON CT

B6
1 MASEFIELD GDNS
2 GEORGE DANCE CL
3 KIPLING WLK
4 CHATTERTON WLK

27
13

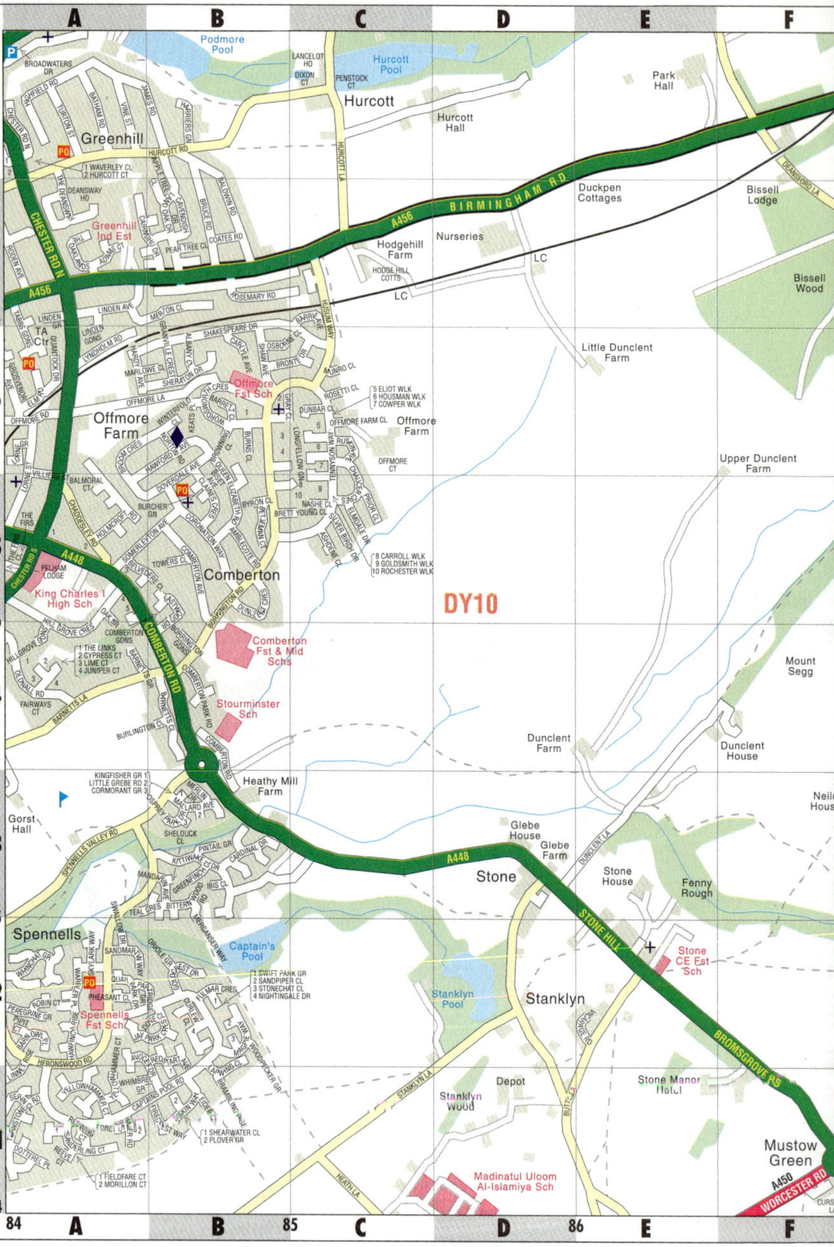

27
45

14
30

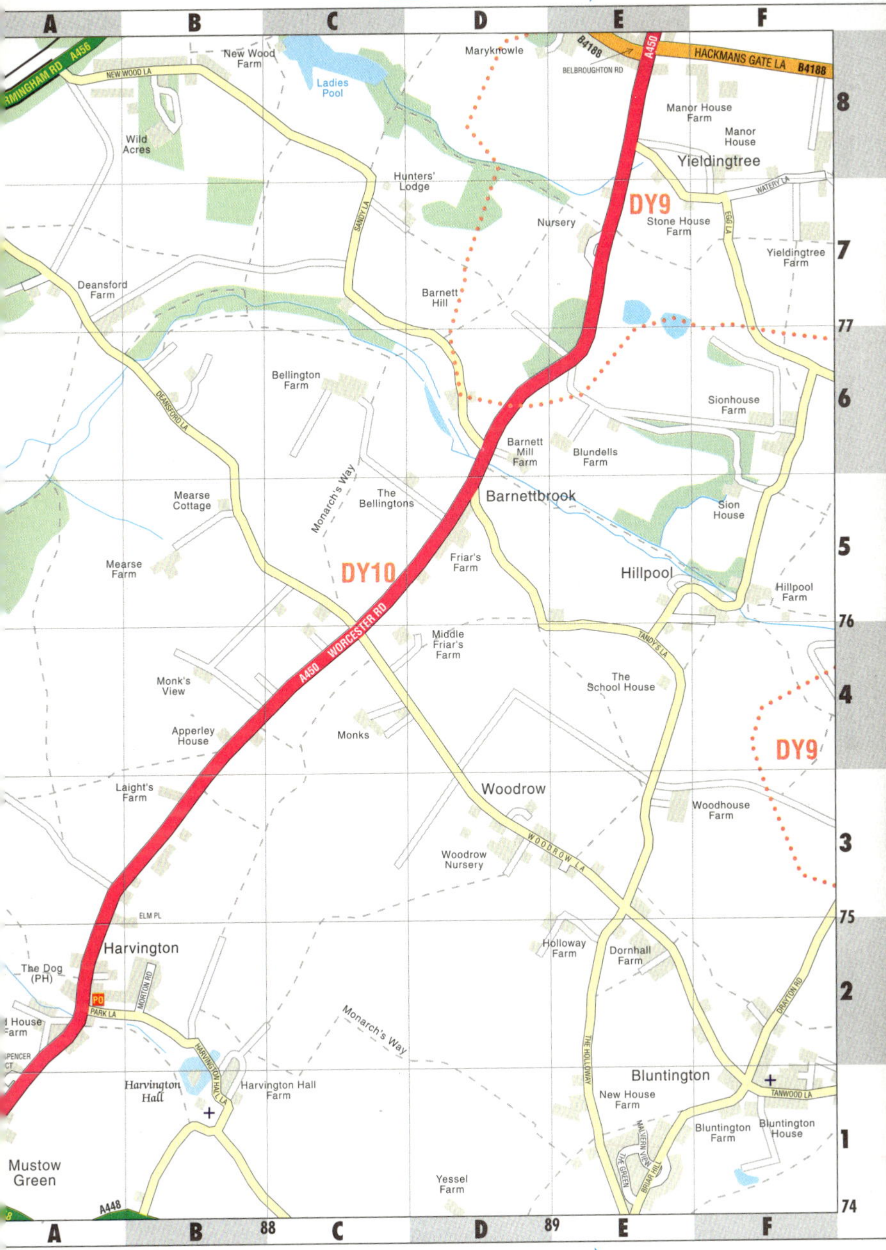
A
B
C
D
E
F
BIRMINGHAM RD A456
NEW WOOD LA
New Wood Farm
Ladies Pool
Maryknowle
B4188
BELBROUGHTON RD
A450
HACKMANS GATE LA B4188
8
Manor House Farm
Manor House
Yieldingtree
Wild Acres
Hunters' Lodge
WATERY LA
DY9
Stone House Farm
EGG LA
SANDY LA
Nursery
7
Yieldingtree Farm
Deansford Farm
Barnett Hill
77
Bellington Farm
6
Sionhouse Farm
DEANSFORD LA
Barnett Mill Farm
Blundells Farm
Mearse Cottage
Monarch's Way
The Bellingtons
Barnettbrook
Sion House
5
Mearse Farm
DY10
Friar's Farm
Hillpool
Hillpool Farm
76
WORCESTER RD
Middle Friar's Farm
TANDY'S LA
Monk's View
A450
The School House
4
Apperley House
Monks
DY9
Laight's Farm
Woodrow
Woodhouse Farm
WOODROW LA
3
Woodrow Nursery
ELM PL
75
Harvington
Holloway Farm
Dornhall Farm
The Dog (PH)
MORTON RD
2
PO
PARK LA
House Farm
Monarch's Way
DRAYTON RD
SPENCER CT
HARVINGTON HALL LA
THE HOLLOWAY
Harvington Hall
Harvington Hall Farm
Bluntington
New House Farm
TANWOOD LA
MALVERN VIEW
Bluntington Farm
Bluntington House
1
Mustow Green
THE GREEN
BRIAR HILL
Yessel Farm
A448
74
A
B
88
C
D
89
E
F

46
30

29
15

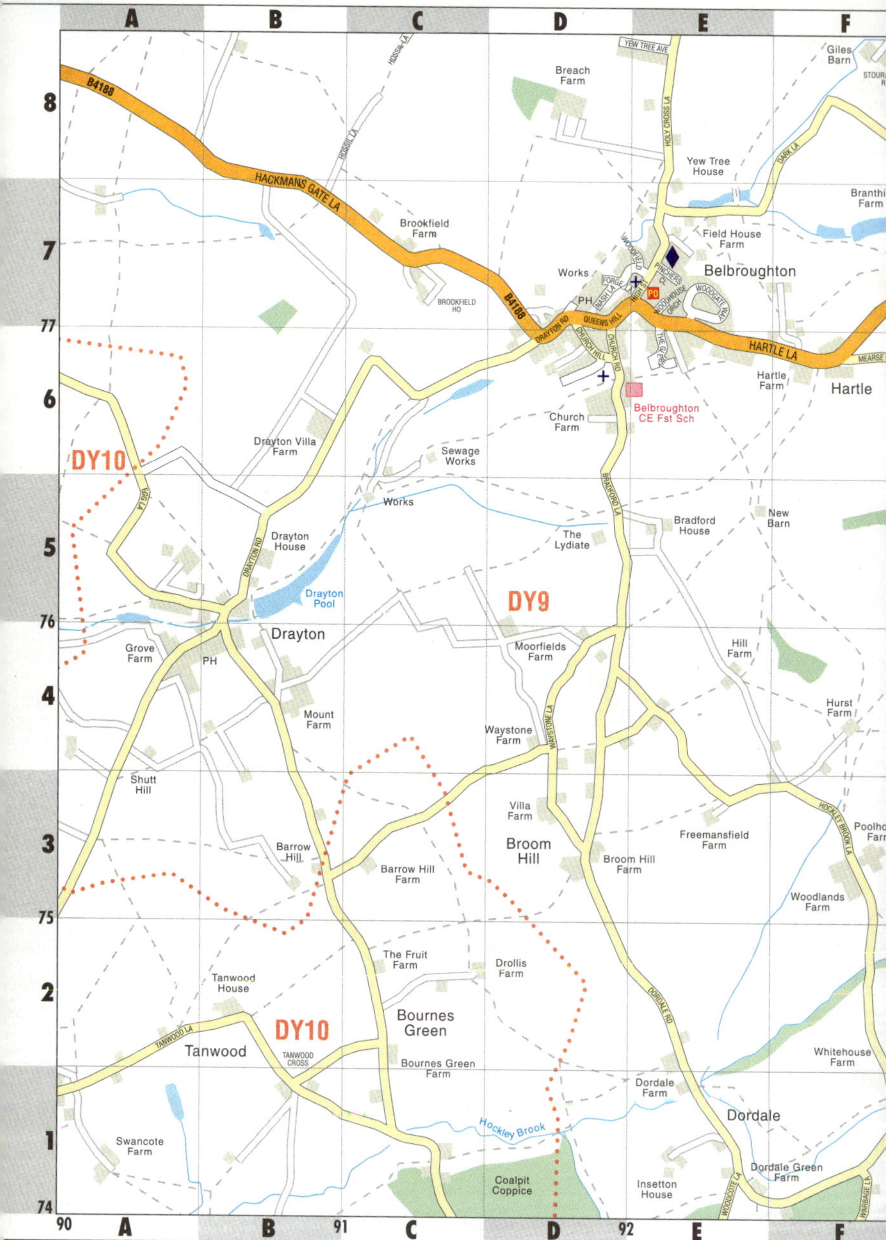
A B C D E F
8 7 77 6 5 76 4 3 75 2 1 74
90 91 92
B4188
HACKMANS GATE LA
HOSSIL LA
Breach Farm
YEW TREE AVE
HOLY CROSS LA
Giles Barn
STOUR
Yew Tree House
DARK LA
Branthi Farm
Brookfield Farm
Field House Farm
Works
Belbroughton
WOODFIELD
FORGE LA
NASH LA
HIGH ST
PINCHERS CL
PO
WOODHOUSE ORCH
WOODGATE WAY
PH
BROOKFIELD HO
QUEENS HILL
DRAYTON RD
CHURCH HILL
CHURCH RD
THE GLEBE
HARTLE LA
MEARSE
Hartle Farm
Hartle
Belbroughton CE Fst Sch
Church Farm
DY10
Drayton Villa Farm
Sewage Works
Works
BRADFORD LA
New Barn
Bradford House
The Lydiate
Drayton House
DRAYTON RD
Drayton Pool
DY9
Drayton
Grove Farm
PH
Moorfields Farm
Hill Farm
Mount Farm
Hurst Farm
Waystone Farm
WAYSTONE LA
Shutt Hill
Villa Farm
Broom Hill
Barrow Hill
Barrow Hill Farm
Freemansfield Farm
Broom Hill Farm
HOCKLEY BROOK LA
Poolho Farr
Woodlands Farm
The Fruit Farm
Drollis Farm
Tanwood House
DORDALE RD
Bournes Green
DY10
TANWOOD LA
Tanwood
TANWOOD CROSS
Bournes Green Farm
Whitehouse Farm
Dordale Farm
Dordale
Hockley Brook
Swancote Farm
Coalpit Coppice
Insetton House
Dordale Green Farm
WOODCOTE LA
WARBAGE LA

29
47

16
32

A
B
C
D
E
F
8
7
77
6
5
76
4
3
75
2
1
74
94
95
MOOR HALL DR
Holly Bush (PH)
Gorse Farm
GORSE GREEN LA
Sling Common
WOODFIELD LA
B62
Hayes Farm
FARLEY LA
Bell Heath
NEWTOWN LA
Newtown
GALTONS LA
Gorse Grove
QUANTRY LA
Study Ctr
Mill Pond
Bell End
HEATH END RD
THE GUTTER
Upper Madeley Farm
STOURBRIDGE RD
HARTLE LA
Bell Inn (PH)
Coalyard Farm
CHAPEL LA
Madeley Heath
Bell Hall
Fenn Brook
CHADWICH LA
Bell Hall Farm
Fenn Farm
BONFIRE HILL
Lower Madeley Farm
DY9
Lawn Barn House
Castle Bourne
MADELEY RD
MEARSE LA
Stoneybridge Farm
HARBOURS HILL
Hagley Hill Farm
Mearse Farm
Stoneybridge
A491
Fairfield Court
SANDY LA
B4091
Sand Pit
MIDDLE RD
Wildmoor
Wildmoor Farmhouse
Cross Coppice
THIRD RD
Crabtree Coppice
Swan Inn (PH)
Fairfield House
Wildmoor Mill Farm
Fairfield
SWAN LA
New Barn Farm
PEPPERWOOD CL
Poolhouse Dingle
Gorsey Piece
Fairfield Fst Sch
MILL LA
Monarch's Way
WOOD LA
PO
Glovers Meadow Farm
B61
Pepper Wood
ORCHARD VILLAS
Meadow Farm
YEW TREE LA
Fir Tree Farm
BOURNHEATH RD
Yewtree Farm
BROOK RD
Merchants Farm
MOUNT RD
NEW RD
M5
P
DORDALE RD
Snuff Hill
Mayfield Farm
MAYFIELD CL
WOODROW CL
Little Royal Farm
PARISH HILL
Nursery
SPRINGS AVE
CHADCOTE WAY
FAIRFIELD RD
Hilltop Farm
CLAYPIT LA
Royal Content Farm
Hillborough
DOCTORS HILL
YARNOLD LA
DODFORD RD
PH
MARSH WAY

48
32

31
17

A
B
C
D
E
F
8
7
77
6
5
76
4
3
75
2
1
74
96
97
98
DY9
B62
B45
B61
B60
PH
B4551
M5
A491
A38
A456
Waste Site
Thistle Grove Farm
QUANTRY LA
CHAPMAN'S HILL
Chapman's Hill Farm
Chapman's Hill
Windmill Hill
Waseley Hills Country Park
Waseley Hill
Waseleyhill Farm
Segbourne Coppice
Barnes Close
Chadwich Grange Farm
CHADWICH LA
MONEY LA
ROUND SAW CROFT 1
OLD QUARRY CL 2
MADLEY CL
GRANGE CRES
CLENT RD
WASELEY RD
ROMSLEY CL
WINDMILL AVE
SEGBOURNE RD
LEASOWE RD
LEOMINSTER CT
REA AVE
WINDMILL AVE
NEW INNS LA
RUBERY LA S
THE DOWERIES
WELLMEAD WLK
LEOMINSTER WLK
DEELANDS RD
THE PIKES
LEA WLK
RUBERY LA
BROOKEND DR
PINEWOOD CL
HILLVIEW RD
BEECHES CL
CLEVES RD
CLEVES DR
WOODLANDS RD
BOWES RD
BARRINGTON RD
LASHBROOKE HO
THE AVENUE
BROOK RD
HERON WAY
CALLOWBROOK LA
CALLOWBRIDGE RD
GUNNER LA
RICHMOND RD
KINETON RD
ROCKFORD CL
LYNDON RD
LIBRARY WAY
NEW RD
Holywell Prim Sch
Waseley Hills High Sch
North Worcestershire Path
Monarch's Way
DODFORD CL
HOMBMEAD GR
SHRAWLEY CL
Liby
COPPICE CL
ST CHAD'S RD
WHETTY LA
LEACH
GANNOW RD
GANNOW WLK
SCHOOL RD
WHETTYBRIDGE RD
LEGION RD
BIRCH RD
CHAPELFIELD MEWS
MAPLE RD
HOLMES DR
EACHWAY
Hollywell Farm
HOLYWELL LA
L Ctr
Beaconside Prim Sch
HAZEL RD
Eachway
SHEARWATER CL
WHITEHOUSE PL
COTTAGE GDNS
HEATHER DR
FAIRWAY DR
Chadwich Manor Estate
REDHILL LA
Redwell Farm
Yewtree Farm
Money Lane Farm
BEACON HILL
Chadwick Wood
Chadwich Manor
Spring Pools
SANDY LA
Brookhouse Farm
Keys Hill Farm
BIRMINGHAM RD
MANOR LA
Stock Hill
Beacon Hill
Heanor
Beaconwood
TOP RD
Wildmoor Oak (PH)
4
Beacon Farm
MONUMENT LA
High House Farm
Chadwich Farm
Sand Pit
BEACON LA
Lydiate Ash
LYDIATE ASH RD
MILL LA
WILDMOOR LA
HALESOWEN RD
HIGH RD
Lickey Hills Prim Sch
ALVECHURCH HIGHWAY
Upper Cottage Farm
Bellevue
WOODROW LA
ASCOT WAY 1
REDCAR CL 2
Upper Catshill
Lower Marlbrook
Upper Marlbrook
MARLBROOK LA
COBNALL RD
MAYFIELD CL
MONTGOMERY CL
ALEXANDER CL
CHURCHILL RD
WELCOME DR
CHELTENHAM RD
THIRSK WAY
HAYDOCK RD
CHEPSTOW DR
NEWBURY AVE
EPSOM RD
GOODWOOD RD
AINTREE CL
AINTREE RD
SANDOWN DR
SEDGEFIELD WLK
LINGFIELD WLK
MARLBROOK GDNS
SPRINGS AVE
BRACKEN GR
FERNDALE CL
BEEHIVE CL
GREEN LA
KEMPTON CT
ASH RD
GOLDEN CROSS LA
B4185
OAK RD
ACORN RD
CAVENDISH CL
BELLE VUE CL
HAZELTON RD
BROOKFIELDS CL
REDLAND CL
GLENDALE CL
GLADE CRES
COTTAGE LA
COTTAGE FARM LA
MERRILL GDNS
BEAUMONT LAWNS
FIRS CL
COTTAGE DR
BRACES LA
OLD BIRMINGHAM RD
B4096
PO
LINEHOUSE LA
GREENFIELD AVE
LICKEY ROCK
ASHGROVE CL
OLD HOUSE DR
HERBERT AUSTIN DR
LORD AUSTIN DR
GRANGE DR
LICKEY RD
Firs Farm
GOLDEN CROSS LA

31
49

18
34

A
B
C
D
E
F
8
7
77
6
5
76
4
3
75
2
1
74
00
01
Birmingham Great Pk
Callow Brook
Schs
Superstore
The Leys
L Ctr
A38
BRISTOL RD S
Rubery
Rednal Hill Jun & Inf Schs
St Columba's RC Prim Sch
Works
Longbridge
B31
B4120
LICKEY RD
Rednal
Nursery
Cofton Park
GROVELEY LA
B4096
Coft Common
The Grove
Albert Bradbeer Schs
Stacey Grange Gdns
Rednal Hill
Lickey Hills Country Park
Hillside
Lickey Hills
Hotel
CH
Beacon Hill
ROSE HILL
B45
BARNT GREEN RD
Bilberry Hill
Cofton Richards Farm
North Worcestershire Path
Lickey
Mast
Mon
Visitor Ctr
Lickey Hills Country Pk
Cofton Hill
Cofton Hackett
Cofton Hall Farm
COFTON CHURCH LA
Cofton Hall
Tower House
Upper Bittell Resr
BIRMINGHAM RD
Lickey Warren
Mill Shrub
River Arrow
Cofton Plantation
Kendal End
KENDAL END RD
Pinfields Wood
Bittell Farm House
Lower Bittell Resr
BITTELL RD
PH
B4120

50
34

33
19

E8
1 BEECH HURST
2 CAMPION HO
3 SAFFRON HO
4 SEDGEBERROW COVERT
5 LYNBROOK COVERT
6 TARRINGTON COVERT
7 REDBROOK COVERT

F8
1 COWSLIP CL
2 MANITOBA CROFT
3 CAMPION CL
4 WILLMORE CL

33
51

20
36

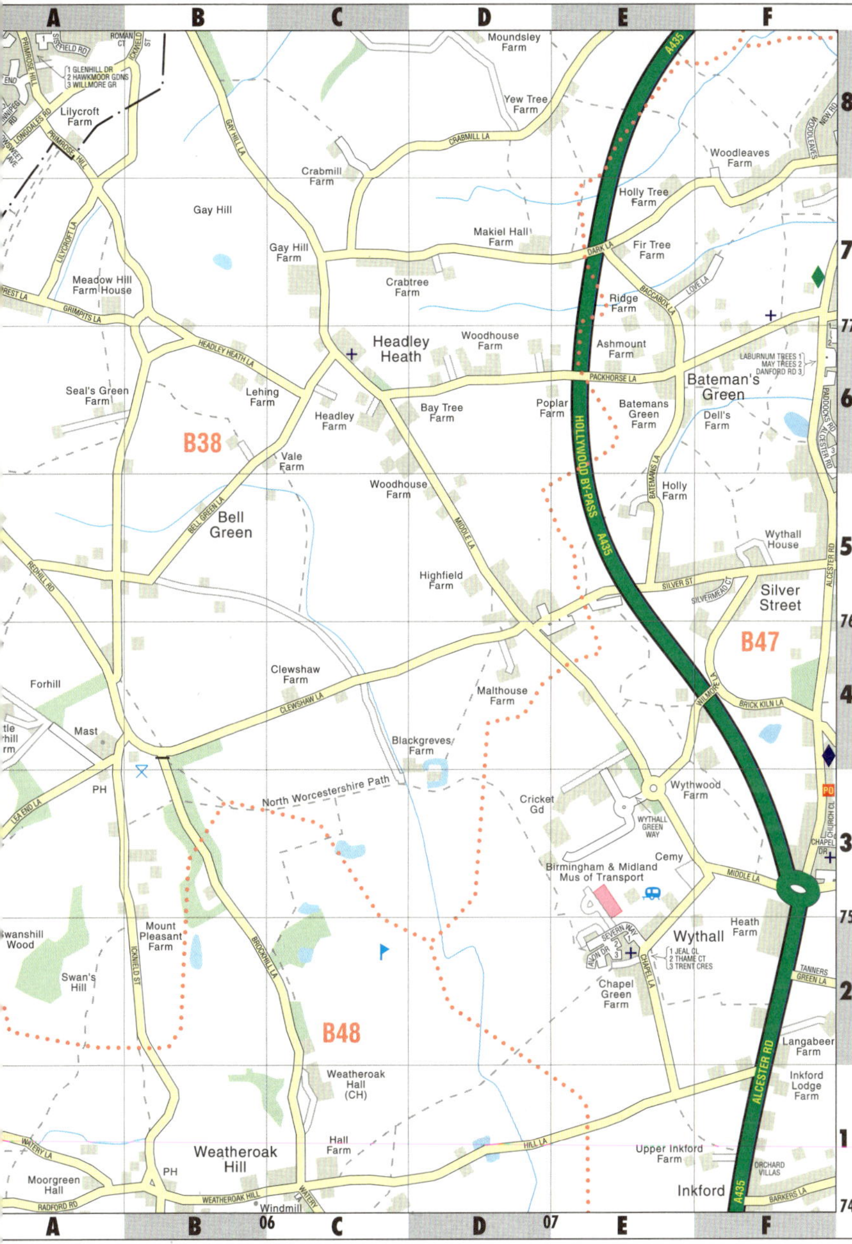
A
B
C
D
E
F
8
7
77
6
5
76
4
3
75
2
1
74
06
07
Moundsley Farm
Yew Tree Farm
CRABMILL LA
Crabmill Farm
Lilycroft Farm
PRIMROSE HILL
LONGDALES RD
1 GLENHILL DR
2 HAWKMOOR GDNS
3 WILLMORE GR
ROMAN CT
ICKNIELD ST
GAY HILL LA
Gay Hill
Gay Hill Farm
LILYCROFT LA
Meadow Hill Farm House
GRIMPITS LA
Makiel Hall Farm
Crabtree Farm
Holly Tree Farm
Woodleaves Farm
WOODLEAVES
NEW RD
DARK LA
Fir Tree Farm
BACCABOX LA
LOVE LA
Ridge Farm
Ashmount Farm
HEADLEY HEATH LA
Headley Heath
Woodhouse Farm
Seal's Green Farm
Lehing Farm
Headley Farm
Bay Tree Farm
Poplar Farm
PACKHORSE LA
Batemans Green Farm
Bateman's Green
LABURNUM TREES 1
MAY TREES 2
DANFORD RD 3
Dell's Farm
PADDOCKS RD
ALCESTER RD
B38
Vale Farm
Woodhouse Farm
HOLLYWOOD BY-PASS
A435
BATEMANS LA
Holly Farm
BELL GREEN LA
Bell Green
MIDDLE LA
Wythall House
REDHILL RD
Highfield Farm
SILVER ST
SILVERMEAD CT
Silver Street
B47
Forhill
Clewshaw Farm
CLEWSHAW LA
Malthouse Farm
WILMORE LA
BRICK KILN LA
Mast
Blackgreves Farm
PH
LEA END LA
North Worcestershire Path
Cricket Gd
Wythwood Farm
WYTHALL GREEN WAY
PO
CHURCH CL
CHAPEL DR
Cemy
Birmingham & Midland Mus of Transport
MIDDLE LA
Heath Farm
SEVERN WAY
AVON DR
Wythall
1 JEAL CL
2 THAME CT
3 TRENT CRES
CHAPEL LA
Mount Pleasant Farm
BROCKHILL LA
Swan's Hill
Chapel Green Farm
TANNERS GREEN LA
ICKNIELD ST
B48
Langabeer Farm
Weatheroak Hall (CH)
Inkford Lodge Farm
ALCESTER RD
WATERY LA
Hall Farm
HILL LA
Upper Inkford Farm
Moorgreen Hall
PH
Weatheroak Hill
ORCHARD VILLAS
Inkford
RADFORD RD
WEATHEROAK HILL
Windmill
WATERY LA
BARKERS LA

52
36

35
21

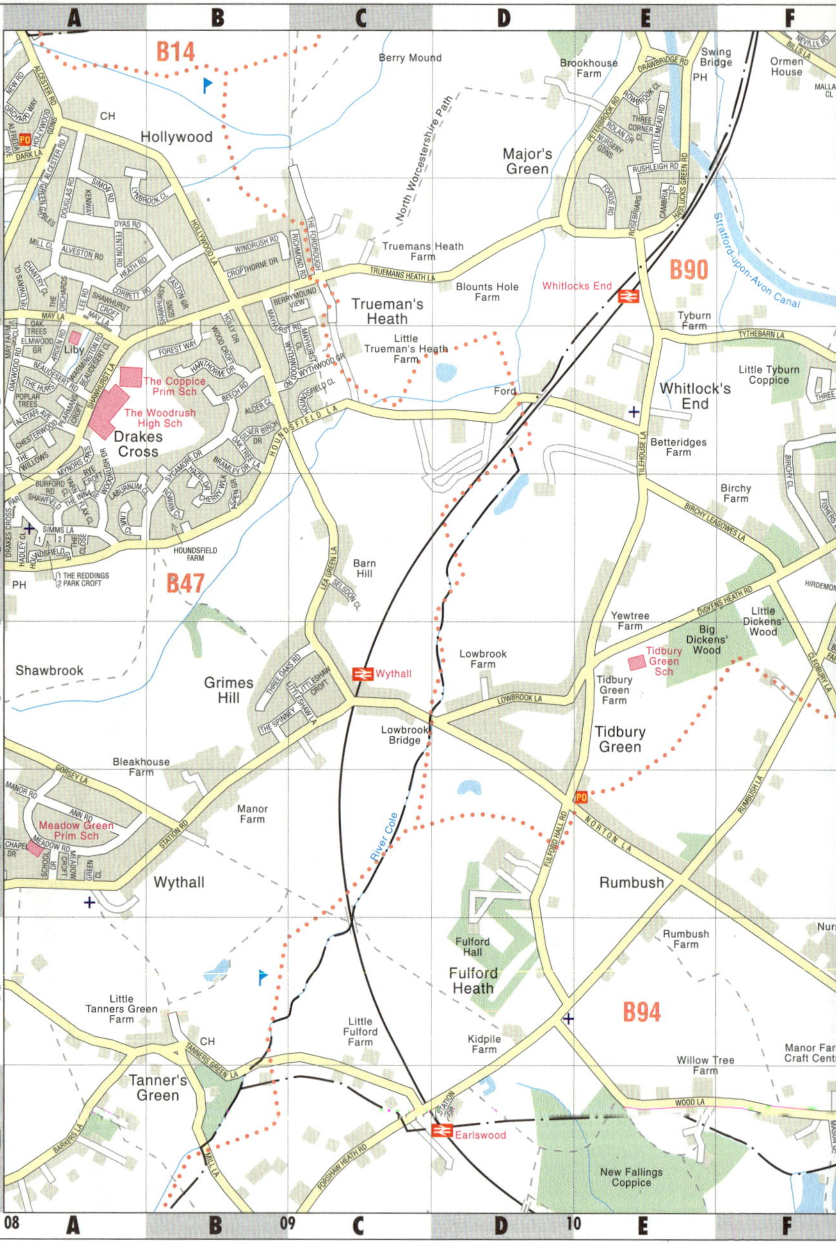
A
B
C
D
E
F
8
7
77
6
5
76
4
3
75
2
1
74
08
09
10
B14
Berry Mound
Brookhouse Farm
Swing Bridge
PH
Ormen House
Hollywood
CH
PO
North Worcestershire Path
Major's Green
Truemans Heath Farm
Trueman's Heath
Blounts Hole Farm
Whitlocks End
B90
Stratford-upon-Avon Canal
Tyburn Farm
TYTHEBARN LA
Little Trueman's Heath Farm
Little Tyburn Coppice
The Coppice Prim Sch
The Woodrush High Sch
Liby
Ford
Whitlock's End
Betteridges Farm
Drakes Cross
Birchy Farm
BIRCHY LEASOWES LA
HOUNDSFIELD LA
HOUNDSFIELD FARM
B47
PH
Barn Hill
Shawbrook
Grimes Hill
Wythall
Lowbrook Farm
Yewtree Farm
Big Dickens' Wood
Little Dickens' Wood
Tidbury Green Sch
Tidbury Green Farm
Tidbury Green
LOWBROOK LA
Lowbrook Bridge
Bleakhouse Farm
Manor Farm
Meadow Green Prim Sch
River Cole
NORTON LA
Wythall
Rumbush
Rumbush Farm
Fulford Hall
Fulford Heath
B94
Little Tanners Green Farm
CH
Little Fulford Farm
Kidpile Farm
Willow Tree Farm
Tanner's Green
WOOD LA
Earlswood
New Fallings Coppice
TRUEMANS HEATH LA
HOLLYWOOD LA
MAY LA
STATION RD
GORSEY LA
TANNERS GREEN LA
FORSHAW HEATH RD
BARKERS LA
MILL LA
FULFORD HALL RD
RUMBUSH LA
TILEHOUSE LA
DICKENS HEATH RD
LEA GREEN LA
ALCESTER RD

35
53

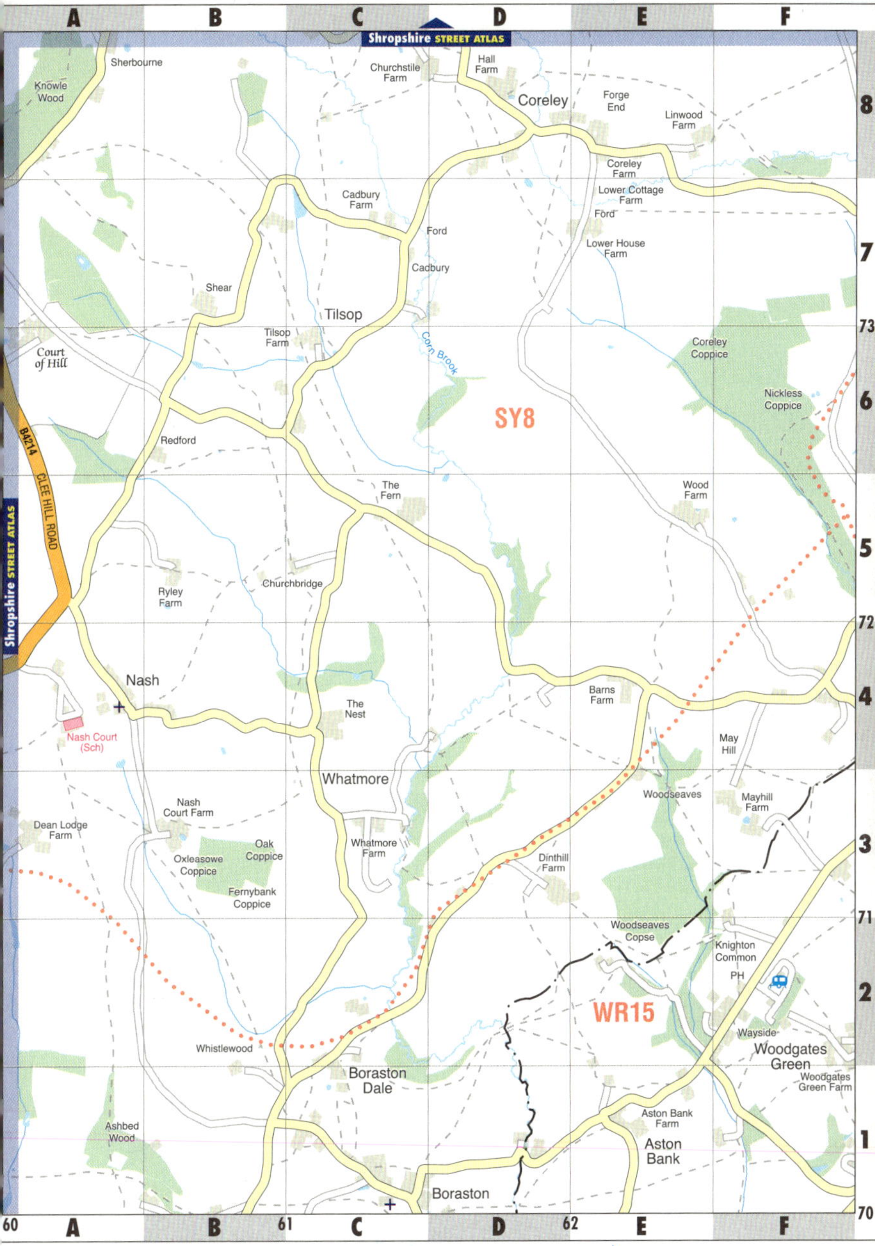
A B C D E F
Shropshire STREET ATLAS
Sherbourne
Knowle Wood
Churchstile Farm
Hall Farm
Coreley
Forge End
Linwood Farm
8
Coreley Farm
Lower Cottage Farm
Ford
Cadbury Farm
Ford
Lower House Farm
Cadbury
7
Shear
Tilsop
Tilsop Farm
73
Court of Hill
Corn Brook
Coreley Coppice
Nickless Coppice
6
SY8
B4214
CLEE HILL ROAD
Redford
The Fern
Wood Farm
5
Shropshire STREET ATLAS
Ryley Farm
Churchbridge
72
Nash
The Nest
Barns Farm
4
Nash Court (Sch)
May Hill
Whatmore
Woodseaves
Mayhill Farm
Dean Lodge Farm
Nash Court Farm
Oak Coppice
Oxleasowe Coppice
Whatmore Farm
Dinthill Farm
3
Fernybank Coppice
71
Woodseaves Copse
Knighton Common
PH
2
WR15
Wayside
Woodgates Green
Whistlewood
Boraston Dale
Woodgates Green Farm
Ashbed Wood
Aston Bank Farm
1
Aston Bank
Boraston
70
60 A B 61 C D 62 E F

37

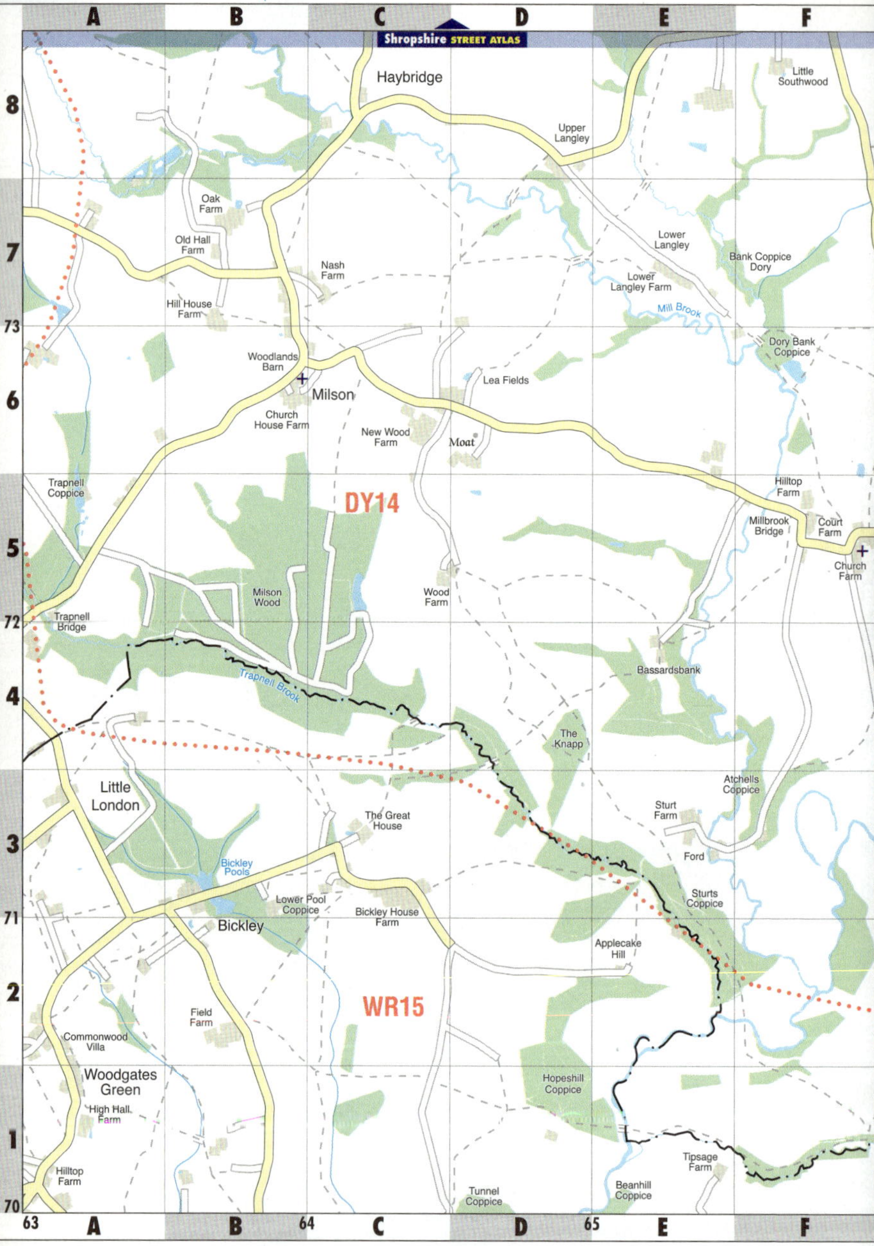

A
B
C
D
E
F
Shropshire STREET ATLAS
8
7
73
6
5
72
4
3
71
2
1
70
63
64
65
Haybridge
Little Southwood
Upper Langley
Oak Farm
Old Hall Farm
Nash Farm
Lower Langley
Bank Coppice Dory
Lower Langley Farm
Hill House Farm
Mill Brook
Dory Bank Coppice
Woodlands Barn
Milson
Lea Fields
Church House Farm
New Wood Farm
Moat
Trapnell Coppice
DY14
Hilltop Farm
Millbrook Bridge
Court Farm
Church Farm
Milson Wood
Wood Farm
Trapnell Bridge
Trapnell Brook
Bassardsbank
The Knapp
Little London
Atchells Coppice
Sturt Farm
The Great House
Ford
Bickley Pools
Lower Pool Coppice
Sturts Coppice
Bickley
Bickley House Farm
Applecake Hill
WR15
Field Farm
Commonwood Villa
Woodgates Green
Hopeshill Coppice
High Hall Farm
Tipsage Farm
Hilltop Farm
Tunnel Coppice
Beanhill Coppice

37

57

22
40
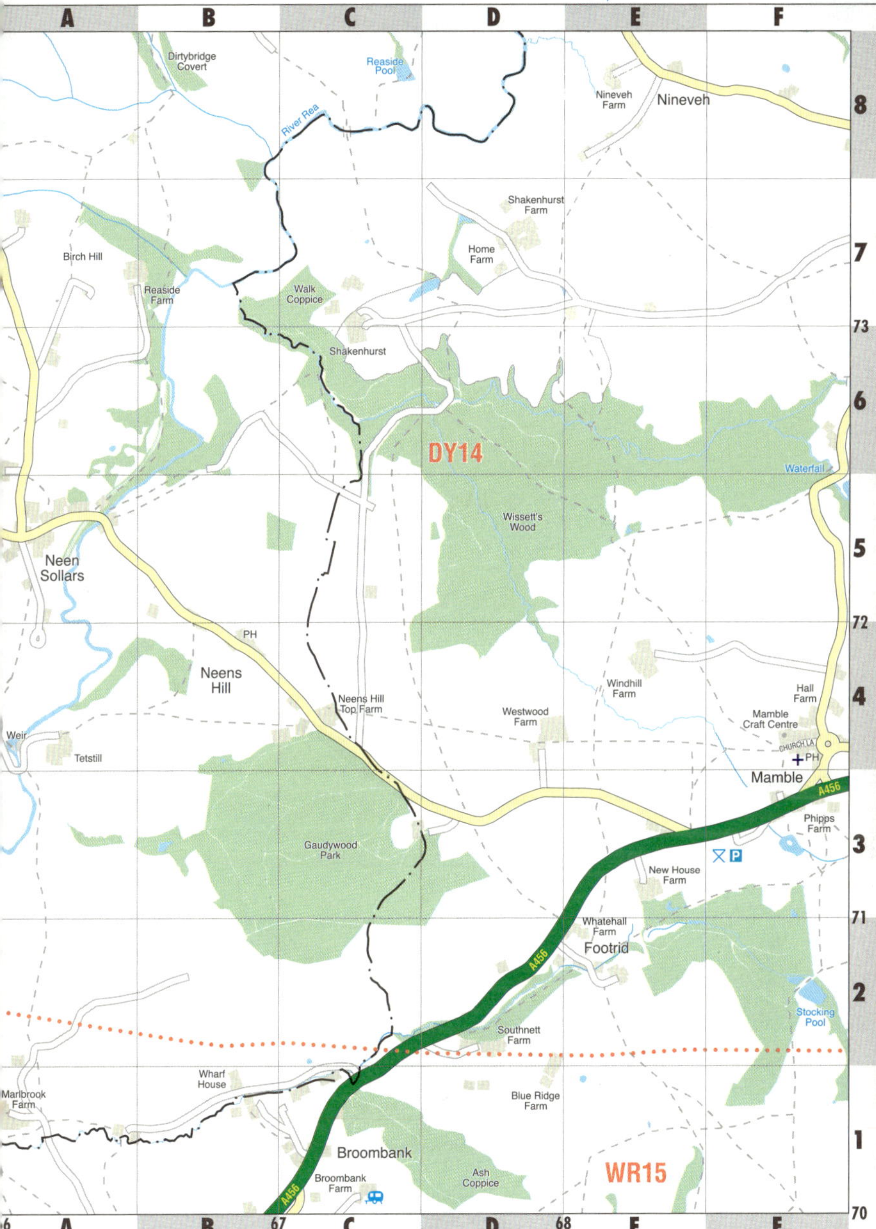
A
B
C
D
E
F
Dirtybridge Covert
Reaside Pool
River Rea
Nineveh Farm
Nineveh
Shakenhurst Farm
Home Farm
Birch Hill
Reaside Farm
Walk Coppice
Shakenhurst
DY14
Waterfall
Wissett's Wood
Neen Sollars
PH
Neens Hill
Neens Hill Top Farm
Windhill Farm
Westwood Farm
Hall Farm
Mamble Craft Centre
CHURCH LA
PH
Weir
Tetstill
Mamble
A456
Phipps Farm
Gaudywood Park
New House Farm
Whatehall Farm
Footrid
A456
Stocking Pool
Southnett Farm
Wharf House
Marlbrook Farm
Blue Ridge Farm
Broombank
Ash Coppice
WR15
Broombank Farm
A456
8
7
73
6
5
72
4
3
71
2
1
70
6
67
68
58
40

39
23

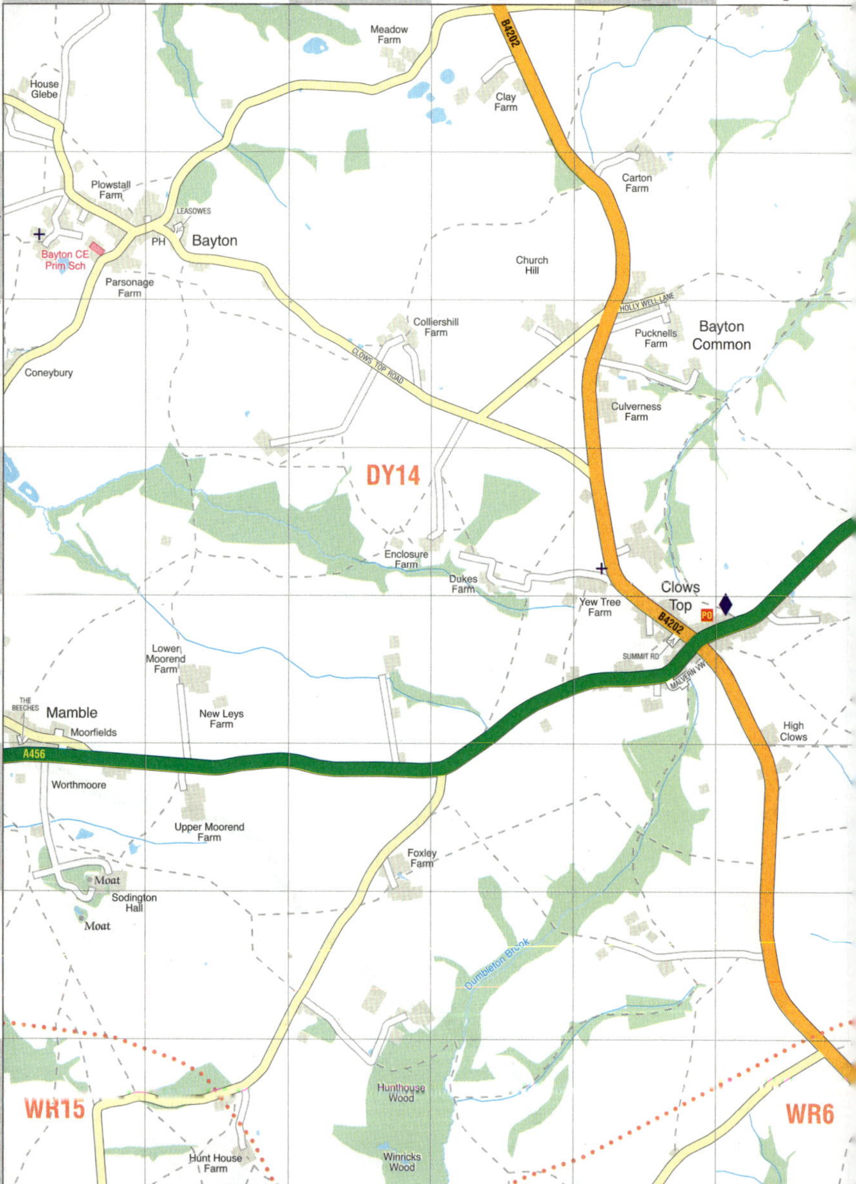
A
B
C
D
E
F
8
7
73
6
5
72
4
3
71
2
1
70
69
70
71
Meadow Farm
House Glebe
Clay Farm
B4202
Carton Farm
Plowstall Farm
LEASOWES
PH
Bayton
Bayton CE Prim Sch
Church Hill
Parsonage Farm
HOLLY WELL LANE
Colliershill Farm
Pucknells Farm
Bayton Common
Coneybury
CLOWS TOP ROAD
Culverness Farm
DY14
Enclosure Farm
Dukes Farm
Clows Top
Yew Tree Farm
PO
SUMMIT RD
MALVERN VW
Lower Moorend Farm
THE BEECHES
Mamble
New Leys Farm
Moorfields
High Clows
A456
Worthmoore
Upper Moorend Farm
Foxley Farm
Moat
Sodington Hall
Dumbleton Brook
WR15
Hunthouse Wood
WR6
Hunt House Farm
Winricks Wood

39
59

24
42

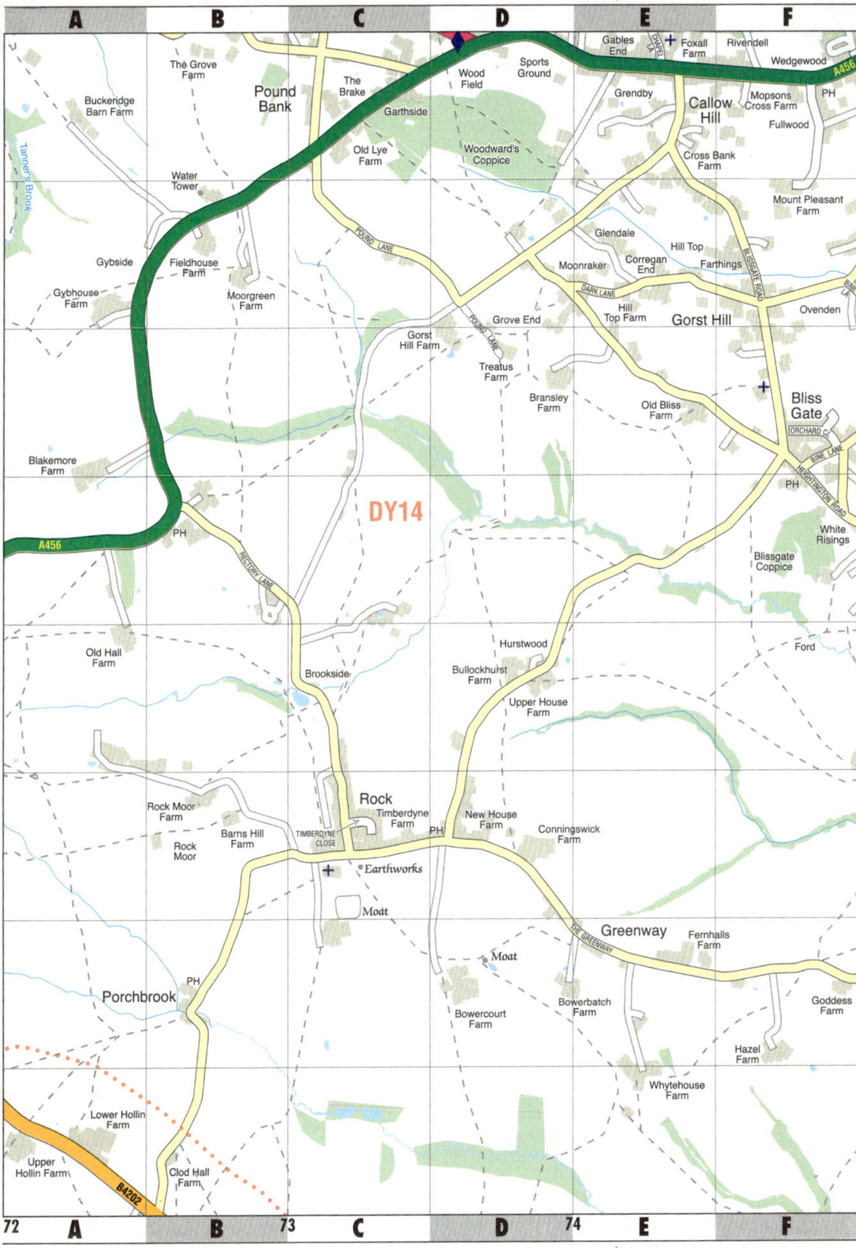
A
B
C
D
E
F
Buckeridge Barn Farm
Tanner's Brook
The Grove Farm
Pound Bank
The Brake
Garthside
Wood Field
Sports Ground
Gables End
CHAPEL LA
Foxall Farm
Rivendell
Wedgewood
A456
Grendby
Callow Hill
Mopsons Cross Farm
PH
Fullwood
Old Lye Farm
Woodward's Coppice
Cross Bank Farm
Water Tower
Mount Pleasant Farm
POUND LANE
Glendale
Hill Top
BLISSGATE ROAD
Gybside
Fieldhouse Farm
Moonraker
Corregan End
Farthings
Gybhouse Farm
Moorgreen Farm
DARK LANE
Hill Top Farm
Gorst Hill
Ovenden
BINE LA
Grove End
Gorst Hill Farm
POUND LANE
Treatus Farm
Bransley Farm
Old Bliss Farm
Bliss Gate
ORCHARD CL
BINE LANE
HEIGHTINGTON ROAD
PH
Blakemore Farm
DY14
White Risings
PH
A456
RECTORY LANE
Blissgate Coppice
Old Hall Farm
Hurstwood
Ford
Bullockhurst Farm
Brookside
Upper House Farm
Rock
Rock Moor Farm
Timberdyne Farm
New House Farm
Conningswick Farm
PH
Barns Hill Farm
TIMBERDYNE CLOSE
Rock Moor
Earthworks
Moat
Greenway
THE GREENWAY
Fernhalls Farm
Moat
PH
Porchbrook
Bowerbatch Farm
Goddess Farm
Bowercourt Farm
Hazel Farm
Whytehouse Farm
Lower Hollin Farm
Upper Hollin Farm
Clod Hall Farm
B4202
8
7
73
6
5
72
4
3
71
2
1
70
72
73
74

60
42

41
25

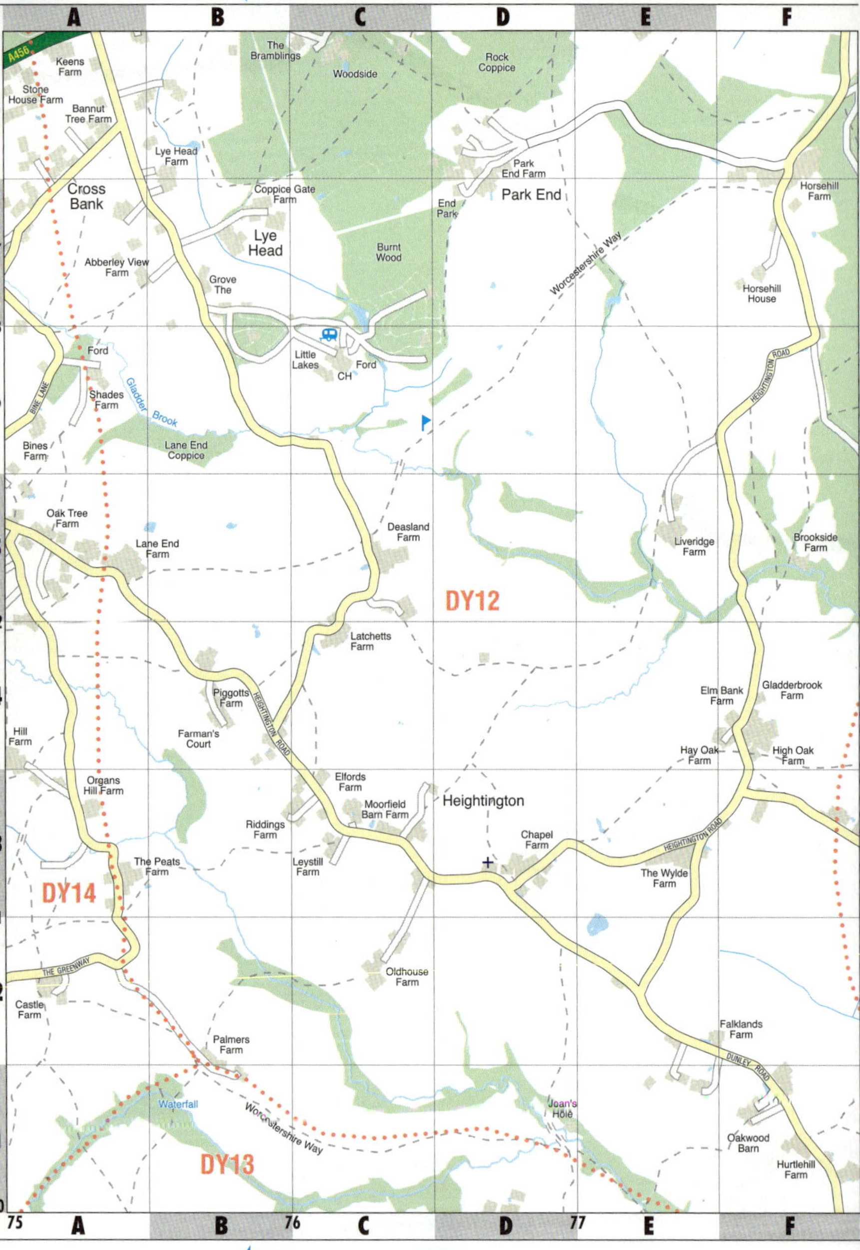
A456
Keens Farm
Stone House Farm
Bannut Tree Farm
Cross Bank
Lye Head Farm
The Bramblings
Woodside
Rock Coppice
Coppice Gate Farm
Lye Head
Park End Farm
End Park
Park End
Horsehill Farm
Abberley View Farm
Grove The
Burnt Wood
Worcestershire Way
Horsehill House
Ford
Little Lakes
Ford
CH
BINE LANE
Shades Farm
Gladder Brook
Lane End Coppice
Bines Farm
HEIGHTINGTON ROAD
Oak Tree Farm
Deasland Farm
Lane End Farm
Liveridge Farm
Brookside Farm
DY12
Latchetts Farm
Piggotts Farm
HEIGHTINGTON ROAD
Elm Bank Farm
Gladderbrook Farm
Hill Farm
Farman's Court
Hay Oak Farm
High Oak Farm
Organs Hill Farm
Elfords Farm
Moorfield Barn Farm
Heightington
Riddings Farm
Chapel Farm
HEIGHTINGTON ROAD
The Peats Farm
Leystill Farm
The Wylde Farm
DY14
THE GREENWAY
Oldhouse Farm
Castle Farm
Palmers Farm
Falklands Farm
DUNLEY ROAD
Waterfall
Worcestershire Way
Joan's Hole
Oakwood Barn
DY13
Hurtlehill Farm
A B C D E F
8 7 6 5 4 3 2 1
73 72 71 70
75 76 77

41
61

26

44

E5
1 WINDERMERE WY
2 BALA CL
3 DORSETT RD

E4
1 ELMFIELD WLK
2 PINE WLK
3 CRANBERRY DR
4 ROWANBERRY CL
5 MAYBERRY CL
6 ELDERBERRY CZ
7 FIELD END
8 SNOWBERRY CL
9 DEWBERRY CL

62

10 YEW TREE WLK
11 MAPLE CL
12 ROSE DENE
13 MOFFIT WY
14 ASH GR
15 CEDAR RI
16 BRIAR WY
17 LILAC GR

44

F1
1 ERNELEY CL
2 BARNFIELD RD
3 WILLIAM COLEY PL
4 WINDMILL CL

F2
1 HAROLD DAVIES DR
2 RYVERE CL

F4
1 GIBBONS CRES
2 TAN LA
3 COURT DR
4 DANESCROFT
5 MOOR HILL DR
6 GHELUVELT CT

43
27

A3
1 SION GDN
2 PARKES PAS
3 PARKES QUAY
4 STOUR LA
5 LODGE RD
6 BELL ROW
7 ENGINE LA

A4
1 BEWDLEY RD
2 BULLUS RD
3 PULLMAN CL
4 MINSTER RD
5 ST MICHAEL'S CL
6 GIBBONS CR
7 FOUNDRY ST
8 CHURCH DR
9 WORCESTER ST

B1
1 BRITANNIA GDN
2 WARD RD

B4
1 SAXILBY PL
2 SUMMERFIELD RD
3 ORCHARD CL
4 MILL CL

43
63

28
46

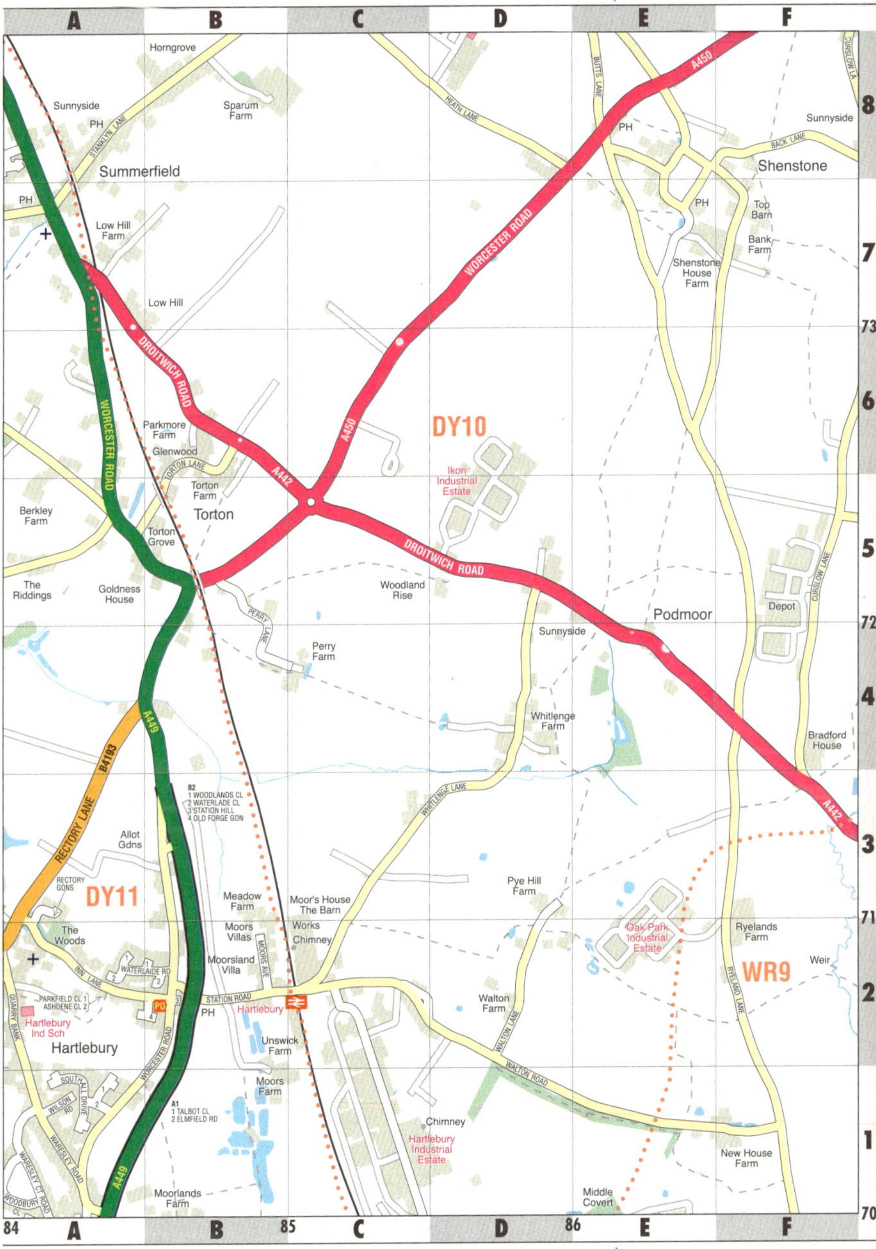
A
B
C
D
E
F
8
7
73
6
5
72
4
3
71
2
1
70
84
85
86
Horngrove
Sparum Farm
Sunnyside
PH
STANKLYN LANE
Summerfield
PH
Low Hill Farm
Low Hill
DROITWICH ROAD
WORCESTER ROAD
Parkmore Farm
Glenwood
TORTON LANE
Torton Farm
Torton
Torton Grove
Berkley Farm
The Riddings
Goldness House
A442
A450
HEATH LANE
WORCESTER ROAD
A450
BUTTS LANE
PH
BACK LANE
Sunnyside
Shenstone
PH
Top Barn
Bank Farm
Shenstone House Farm
CURSLOW LA
DY10
Ikon Industrial Estate
DROITWICH ROAD
Woodland Rise
PERRY LANE
Perry Farm
Podmoor
Sunnyside
Depot
CURSLOW LANE
Whitlenge Farm
Bradford House
A442
A449
B4193
RECTORY LANE
B2
1 WOODLANDS CL
2 WATERLADE CL
3 STATION HILL
4 OLD FORGE GDN
Allot Gdns
RECTORY GDNS
DY11
The Woods
Meadow Farm
Moor's House The Barn
Works
Chimney
Moors Villas
MOORS AVE
Moorsland Villa
WHITLENGE LANE
Pye Hill Farm
Oak Park Industrial Estate
Ryelands Farm
Weir
WR9
RYELAND LANE
INN LANE
WATERLAIDE RD
PARKFIELD CL
ASHDENE CL
PO
STATION ROAD
PH
Hartlebury
Hartlebury Ind Sch
Hartlebury
QUARRY BANK
WORCESTER ROAD
Unswick Farm
Walton Farm
WALTON LANE
WALTON ROAD
SOUTHALL DRIVE
WILSON RD
WARESLEY ROAD
WARESLEY CT ROAD
WOODBURY CL
Moors Farm
A1
1 TALBOT CL
2 ELMFIELD RD
A449
Chimney
Hartlebury Industrial Estate
New House Farm
Moorlands Farm
Middle Covert

64
46

45
29

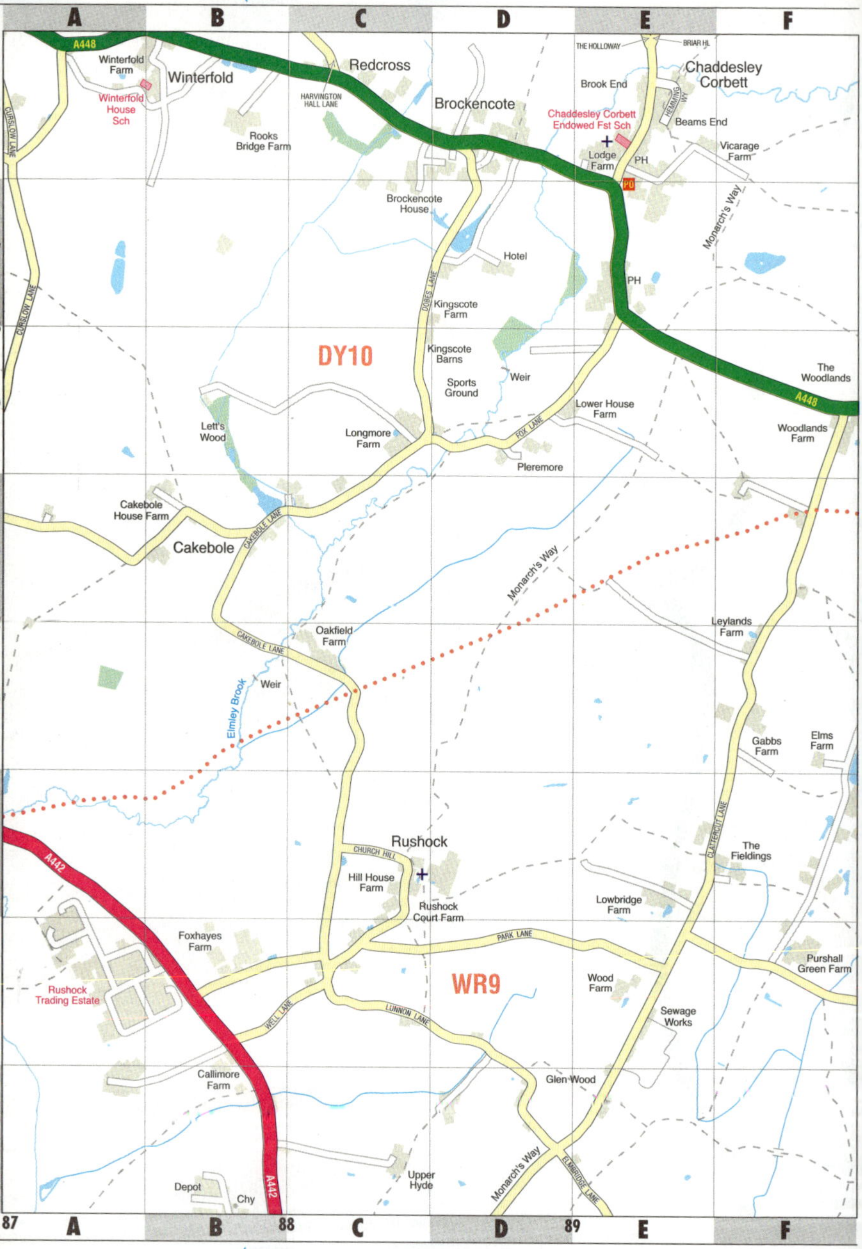
A
B
C
D
E
F
8
7
73
6
5
72
4
3
71
2
1
70
87
88
89
A448
Winterfold Farm
Winterfold
Winterfold House Sch
Rooks Bridge Farm
Redcross
HARVINGTON HALL LANE
Brockencote
Brockencote House
THE HOLLOWAY
BRIAR HL
Chaddesley Corbett
Brook End
HEMMING WAY
Beams End
Chaddesley Corbett Endowed Fst Sch
Lodge Farm
PH
PO
Vicarage Farm
Monarch's Way
Hotel
PH
CURSLOW LANE
DOBES LANE
Kingscote Farm
Kingscote Barns
DY10
Sports Ground
Weir
The Woodlands
Lower House Farm
Woodlands Farm
Lett's Wood
Longmore Farm
FOX LANE
Pleremore
Cakebole House Farm
Cakebole
CAKEBOLE LANE
Monarch's Way
Leylands Farm
Oakfield Farm
Weir
Elmley Brook
Gabbs Farm
Elms Farm
CLATTERCUT LANE
Rushock
CHURCH HILL
Hill House Farm
Rushock Court Farm
The Fieldings
Lowbridge Farm
A442
Foxhayes Farm
PARK LANE
Purshall Green Farm
Rushock Trading Estate
WR9
Wood Farm
WELL LANE
LUNNON LANE
Sewage Works
Callimore Farm
Glen Wood
Upper Hyde
Monarch's Way
ELMBRIDGE LANE
Depot
Chy
A442

45
65

30
48

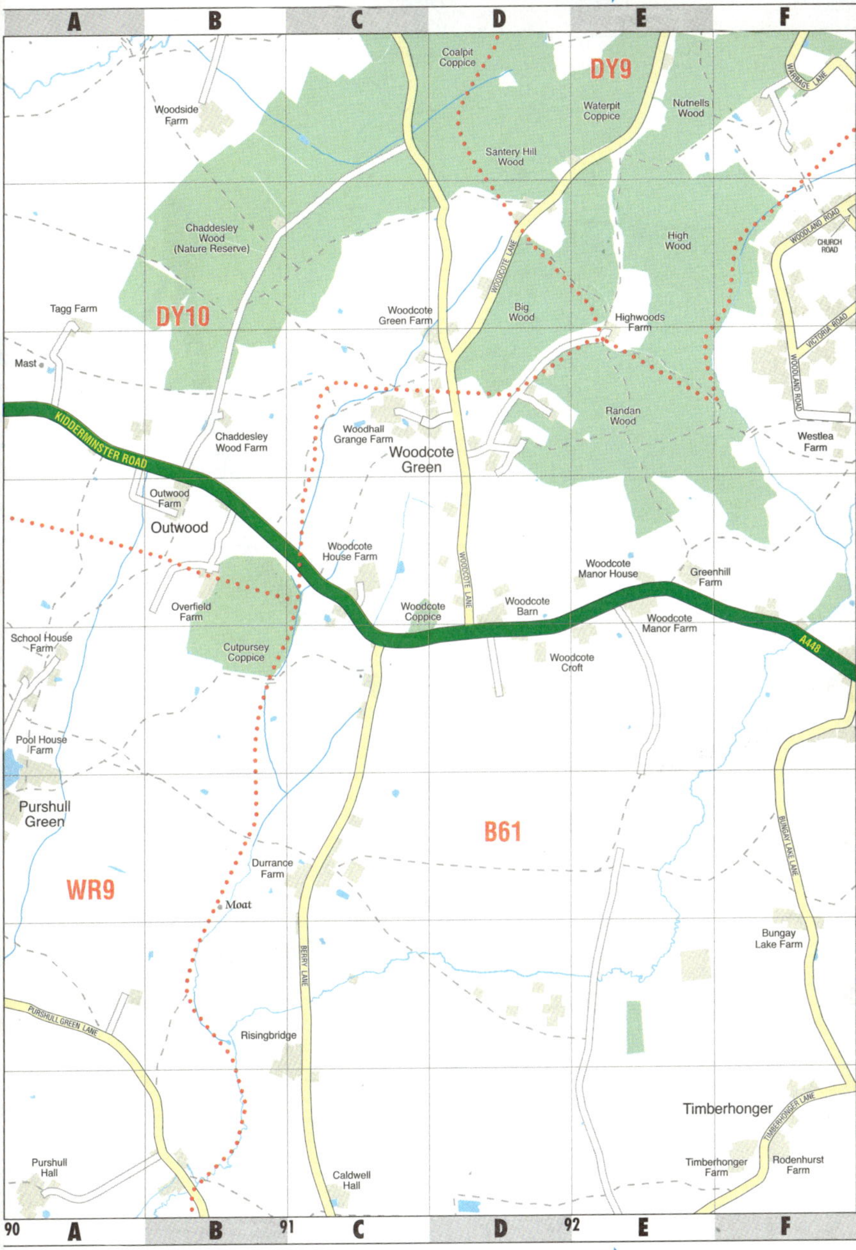
A
B
C
D
E
F
8
7
73
6
5
72
4
3
71
2
1
70
90
91
92
Coalpit Coppice
DY9
Waterpit Coppice
Nutnells Wood
WARBAGE LANE
Woodside Farm
Santery Hill Wood
Chaddesley Wood (Nature Reserve)
High Wood
WOODLAND ROAD
CHURCH ROAD
WOODCOTE LANE
Tagg Farm
DY10
Woodcote Green Farm
Big Wood
Highwoods Farm
VICTORIA ROAD
Mast
WOODLAND ROAD
KIDDERMINSTER ROAD
Randan Wood
Westlea Farm
Chaddesley Wood Farm
Woodhall Grange Farm
Woodcote Green
Outwood Farm
Outwood
Woodcote House Farm
Woodcote Manor House
Greenhill Farm
WOODCOTE LANE
Overfield Farm
Woodcote Coppice
Woodcote Barn
Woodcote Manor Farm
A448
School House Farm
Cutpursey Coppice
Woodcote Croft
Pool House Farm
Purshull Green
B61
BUNGAY LAKE LANE
Durrance Farm
WR9
Moat
Bungay Lake Farm
BERRY LANE
PURSHULL GREEN LANE
Risingbridge
Timberhonger
TIMBERHONGER LANE
Purshull Hall
Caldwell Hall
Timberhonger Farm
Rodenhurst Farm

66
48

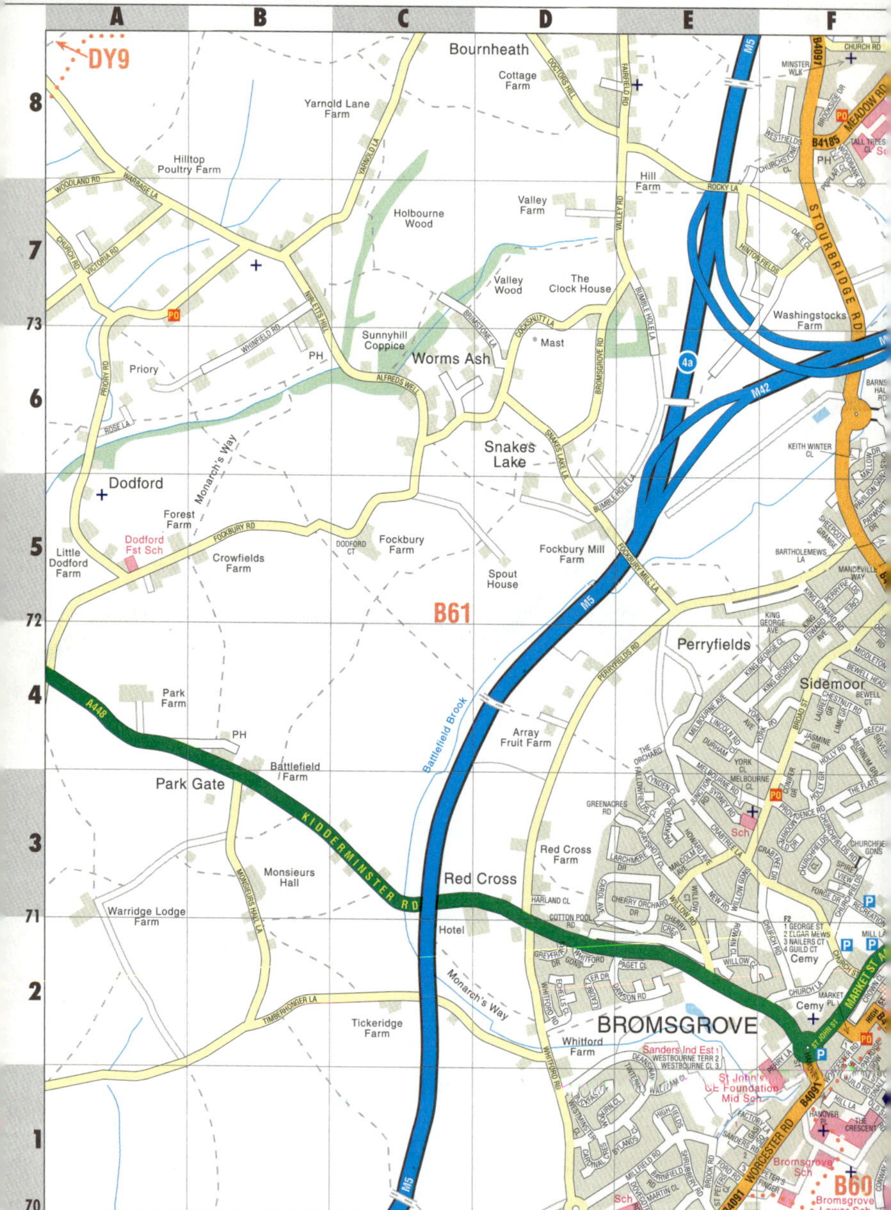
DY9
Bournheath
Cottage Farm
Yarnold Lane Farm
Hilltop Poultry Farm
Hill Farm
Valley Farm
Holbourne Wood
Valley Wood
The Clock House
Washingstocks Farm
Sunnyhill Coppice
Worms Ash
Mast
Priory
PH
Snakes Lake
Dodford
Forest Farm
Monarch's Way
Dodford Fst Sch
Little Dodford Farm
Crowfields Farm
Fockbury Farm
Fockbury Mill Farm
Spout House
B61
Perryfields
Sidemoor
Park Farm
Battlefield Brook
Array Fruit Farm
Battlefield Farm
Park Gate
Red Cross Farm
Monsieurs Hall
Red Cross
Warridge Lodge Farm
Hotel
Cemy
BROMSGROVE
Whitford Farm
Tickeridge Farm
Sanders Ind Est
St John's CE Foundation Mid Sch
Bromsgrove Sch
B60
Bromsgrove Lower Sch
Sch
KIDDERMINSTER RD
A448
M5
M42
B4091
B4185
STOURBRIDGE RD
WORCESTER RD
MARKET ST
4a

32
50

PHLETT CT
STMINSTER CT
RDIAN CT

68
50

49
33

A
B
C
D
E
F
8
7
73
6
5
72
4
3
71
2
1
70
99
00
01
Brook House
Barnt Green
Fiery Hill
Barnt Green
St Andrew's Fst Sch
The Paddocks
Sandhills Farm
B45
Linthurst Court
M42
Pike Hill
Masts
Uplands
High Croft
Linthurst Fst Sch
Linthurst
Blackwell
Withybed Green
B48
Foxhill House
Gorsey Lane Farm
Scarfield Farm
Wheeley Farm
Blackwell Court
Scarfields Dingle
Cobley Hill
Mast
Cobley Hill Farm
Andrew's Coppice
B60
Vigo
Hollow Tree Farm
Cattespool
Robin Hill Farm
Stoney Lane Farm
Sunny Bank Farm
Stoney Lane Cottage
Worcester & Birmingham Canal
Shortwood Rough Ground
The Lower House
Tunnel
Little Shortwood
Bromsgrove Private
Broad Green
Works
Oxleasows Farm
B9
B4120
BITTELL RD
B4096
HEWELL LA
BROOKHOUSE RD
SHEPLEY RD
BILLY LA
LINTHURST RD
PLYMOUTH RD
TWATLING RD
CHERRY HILL RD
FIERY HILL RD
HEWELL LA
SANDHILLS RD
SANDHILLS LA
SANDHILLS GN
AQUEDUCT LA
COOPERS HILL
LINTHURST NEWTOWN
STATION RD
BLACKWELL RD
WHEELEY RD
FOXHILL LA
SCARFIELD HILL
COBLEY HILL
GRANGE LA
HOLLOWTREE LA
AGMORE RD
STONEY LA
AGMORE LA
WHARF LA
BROCKHILL LA
TUTNALL LA
PLYMOUTH DR 1
GORSE MEADOW DR 2
WILLOW TREE DR 1
ROSE TERR 2
COACH COTTS 3
VICTORIA MEWS 4
STATION COTTS
LOCK KEEPERS REACH
REAR COTTS
FRONT COTTS
FORWARD COTTS
FOXHILL BARNS

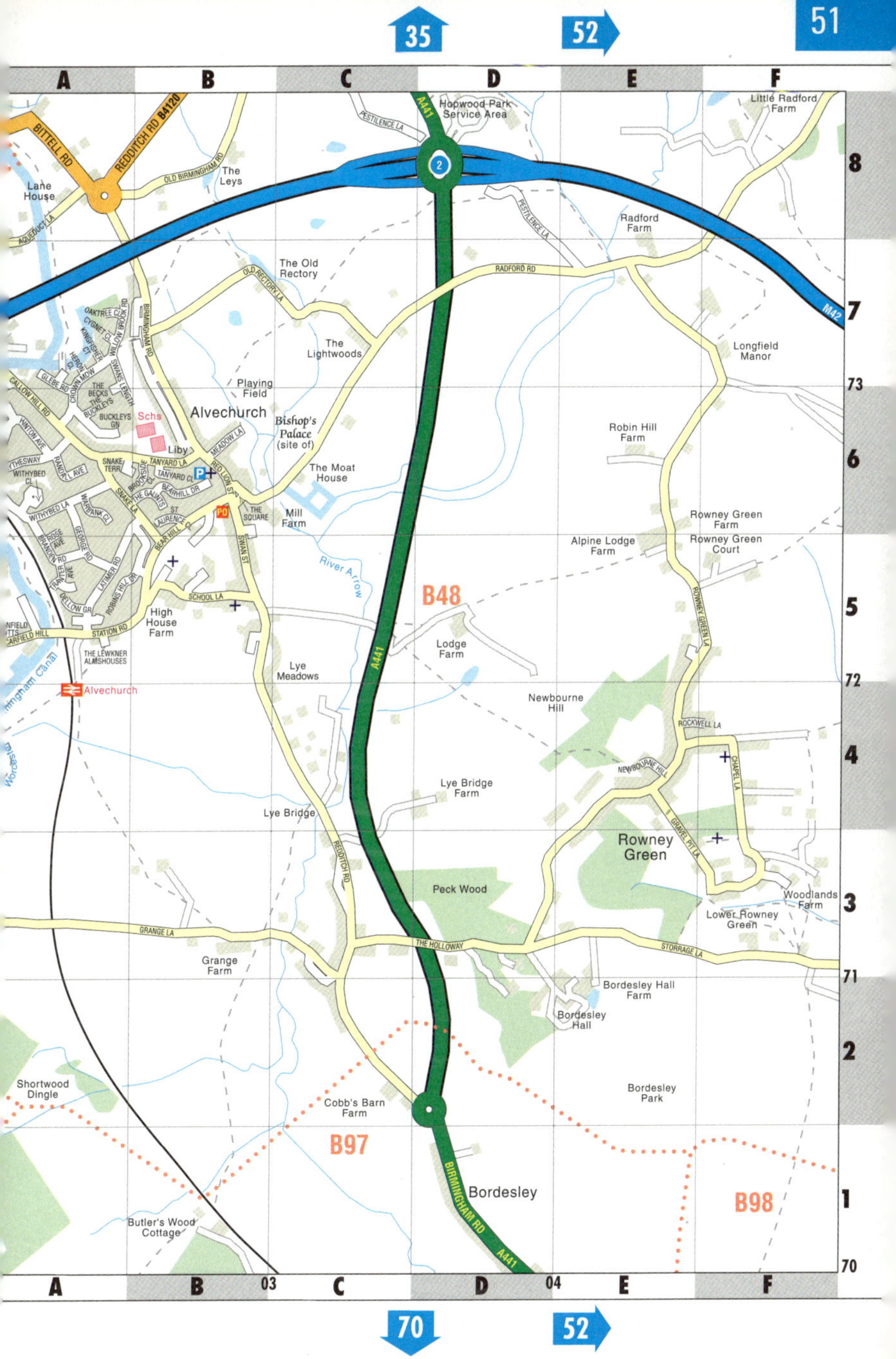
35
52
A
B
C
D
E
F
8
7
73
6
5
72
4
3
71
2
1
70
03
04
Little Radford Farm
Hopwood Park Service Area
PESTILENCE LA
A441
BITTELL RD
REDDITCH RD B4120
OLD BIRMINGHAM RD
The Leys
Lane House
AQUEDUCT LA
Radford Farm
RADFORD RD
The Old Rectory
OLD RECTORY LA
M42
The Lightwoods
Longfield Manor
Playing Field
Alvechurch
Schs
Liby
Bishop's Palace (site of)
Robin Hill Farm
The Moat House
Mill Farm
THE SQUARE
TANYARD LA
TANYARD CL
MEADOW LA
RED LION ST
SWAN ST
SCHOOL LA
STATION RD
Rowney Green Farm
Rowney Green Court
Alpine Lodge Farm
River Arrow
B48
High House Farm
THE LEWKNER ALMSHOUSES
Lodge Farm
Lye Meadows
ROWNEY GREEN LA
Alvechurch
Newbourne Hill
ROCKWELL LA
NEWBOURNE HILL
CHAPEL LA
Lye Bridge Farm
Lye Bridge
GRAVEL PIT LA
Rowney Green
REDDITCH RD
Peck Wood
Woodlands Farm
Lower Rowney Green
GRANGE LA
THE HOLLOWAY
STORRAGE LA
Grange Farm
Bordesley Hall Farm
Bordesley Hall
Shortwood Dingle
Bordesley Park
Cobb's Barn Farm
B97
Bordesley
BIRMINGHAM RD
B98
Butler's Wood Cottage
70
52

51
35

A
B
C
D
E
F
Newhouse Farm
Lanehouse Farm
Lower Inkford Farm
Brook Priory Farm
A435
PH
B47
WATERY LA
HILLCREST PK
DUMBLE PIT LA
ALCESTER RD
Birch Acre
Birch Acre Farm
Alcott Farm
M42
Moorfield Coppice
3
Seechem Lodge
Seechem Farm
ICKNIELD ST
Moorfield Farm
PH
Billesley Farm
BILLESLEY LA
Brookside
HOLLY LA
Hob Hill Farm
Newlands
LILLEY GREEN RD
Hob Hill
Old House Farm
Lilley Green Hall Farm
B48
Woodlands Farm
Rose Cottage Farm
SEAFIELD LA
WHITEPITS LA
Hill Farm
Storrage Wood
Barton Farm
OLD LA
Old Farm
Dump House Farm
DUMPHOUSE LA
Chapel Farm
Storrage House
STORRAGE LA
Heath Green Poultry Farm
Heath Green
BROCKHILL LA
Lower Park Farm
B98
Poplars Farm
Carpenters Wood
Brook Farm
Carpenters Hill Farm
Hall Farm
Beoley Hall
Carpenter's Hill
8
7
73
6
5
72
4
3
71
2
1
70
05
06
07

51
71

36

A
B
C
D
E
F
River Cole
Terry's Pool
Earlswood
MILL LA
FORSHAW HEATH RD
The Poplars
Clowes Wood
8
CLOWESWOOD LA
Pound Close Farm
The Lakes
Forshaw Heath
Terry's Green
SPRINGBROOK LA
Graves Coppice
POOLHEAD LA
MALTHOUSE LA
White House Farm
7
JUGGINS LA
OAKTREE FARM MOBILE HOMES PK
FORSHAW HEATH LA
Yew Tree Farm
Forshaw Park Farm
Glebe Farm
Springbrook Farm
Checkley's Coppice
73
SMALL LA
The Plantation
The Lyndons
Small Lane Farm
Earlswood Trad Est
BIDDLES HILL
Sewage Works
Spring Brook
6
Rugby Football Ground
M42
Tyler's Grove
B48
Windmill Naps
Portway
POOLHEAD LA
5
House Farm
Ladbrookpark Coppice
Poolhead Farm
WOOD END LA
B94
Holly Farm
72
Cottage Farm
ALCESTER RD
Little Ladbrooke Farm
Ladbrooke Hall
Ladbrooke Hall Farm
Wood End
PH
4
B4101
Lion Wood
PENN LA
CH
BROCKHILL LA
ALCESTER RD
Wood End
Hill Barn
WOODCOCK CL
3
RUSHBROOK LA
Rushbrook
Rushbrook Farm
High Park Farm
BROAD LA
VICARAGE HILL
Gilbert's Green
71
Highpark Wood
Spring Brook
B98
SEAFIELD LA
2
ARDEN LEYS
ASPLEY HEATH LA
Park Farm
Branson's Cross
Aspley Heath
B4101
River Alne
PH
ASPLEY HEATH
Tanworth-in-Arden
Baylis Green
BLIND LA
BEOLEY LA
BROAD LA
CHERRY PIT LA
Pinkfield Wood
1
BATES LA
Branson's Cross Farm
Aspley Farm
A435
B4101
Alderhanger Wood
70
09
10
M42 Birmingham N.E.C., Warwick (M40)
Birmingham & W. Midlands STREET ATLAS

72

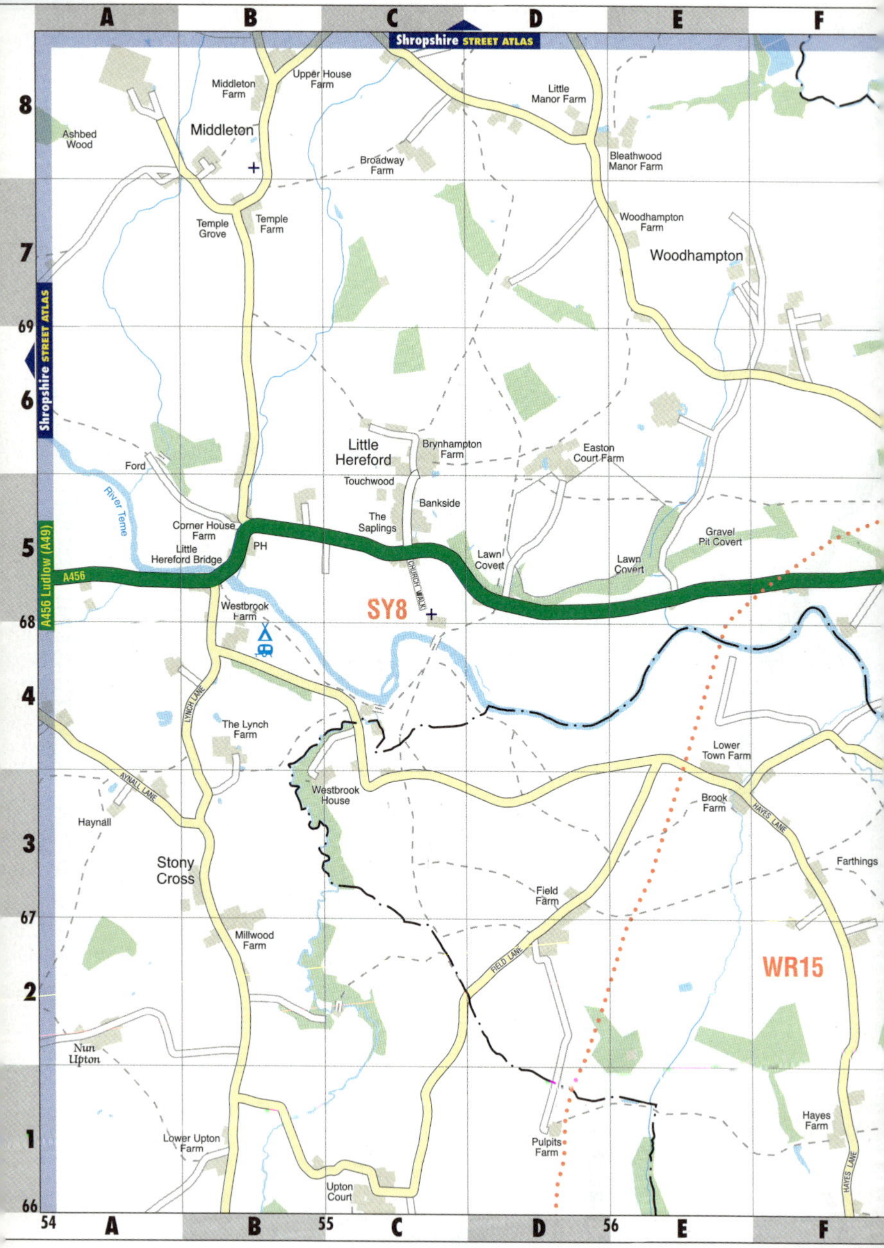
A
B
C
D
E
F
Shropshire STREET ATLAS
8
7
69
6
5
68
4
3
67
2
1
66
54
55
56
Middleton Farm
Upper House Farm
Little Manor Farm
Ashbed Wood
Middleton
Broadway Farm
Bleathwood Manor Farm
Temple Grove
Temple Farm
Woodhampton Farm
Woodhampton
Little Hereford
Brynhampton Farm
Easton Court Farm
Ford
Touchwood
Bankside
River Teme
The Saplings
Corner House Farm
Gravel Pit Covert
PH
Little Hereford Bridge
Lawn Covert
Lawn Covert
A456
A456 Ludlow (A49)
CHURCH WALK
SY8
Westbrook Farm
LYNCH LANE
The Lynch Farm
Lower Town Farm
AYNALL LANE
Westbrook House
Brook Farm
HAYES LANE
Haynall
Stony Cross
Farthings
Field Farm
Millwood Farm
FIELD LANE
WR15
Nun Upton
Hayes Farm
Lower Upton Farm
Pulpits Farm
HAYES LANE
Upton Court

73

56

F6
1 DEAN CL
2 MEADOW RI
3 SPRING CL
4 OAK TREE CL
5 LONGMEADOW DR
6 IVERLEY CT
7 PENLU RD
8 SWAN CT
9 SWAN CL
10 TEMESIDE CL

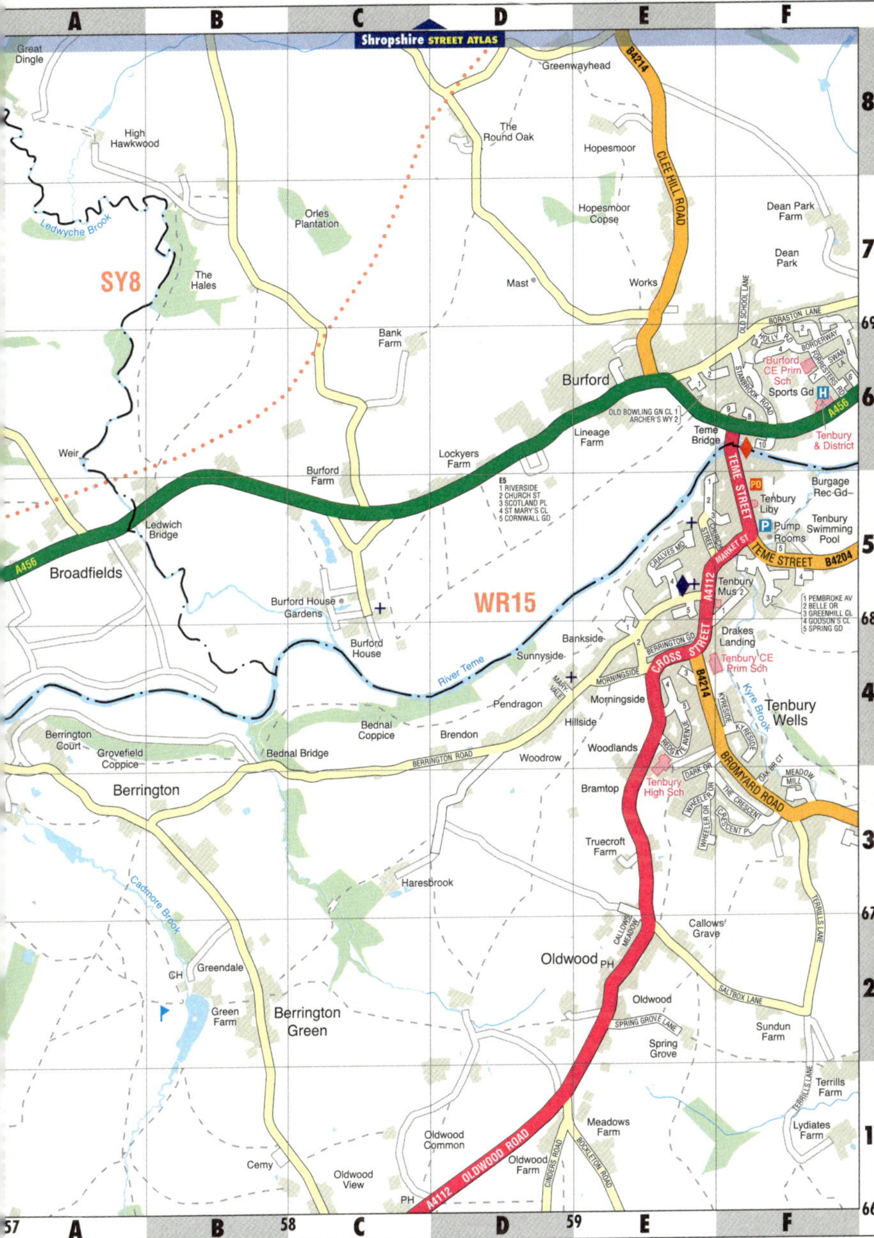

74

56

E4
1 COLLEGE CT
2 BOG LA
3 MOUNT PLEASANT
4 MOUNT OR
5 BURLEIGH CL

55
37

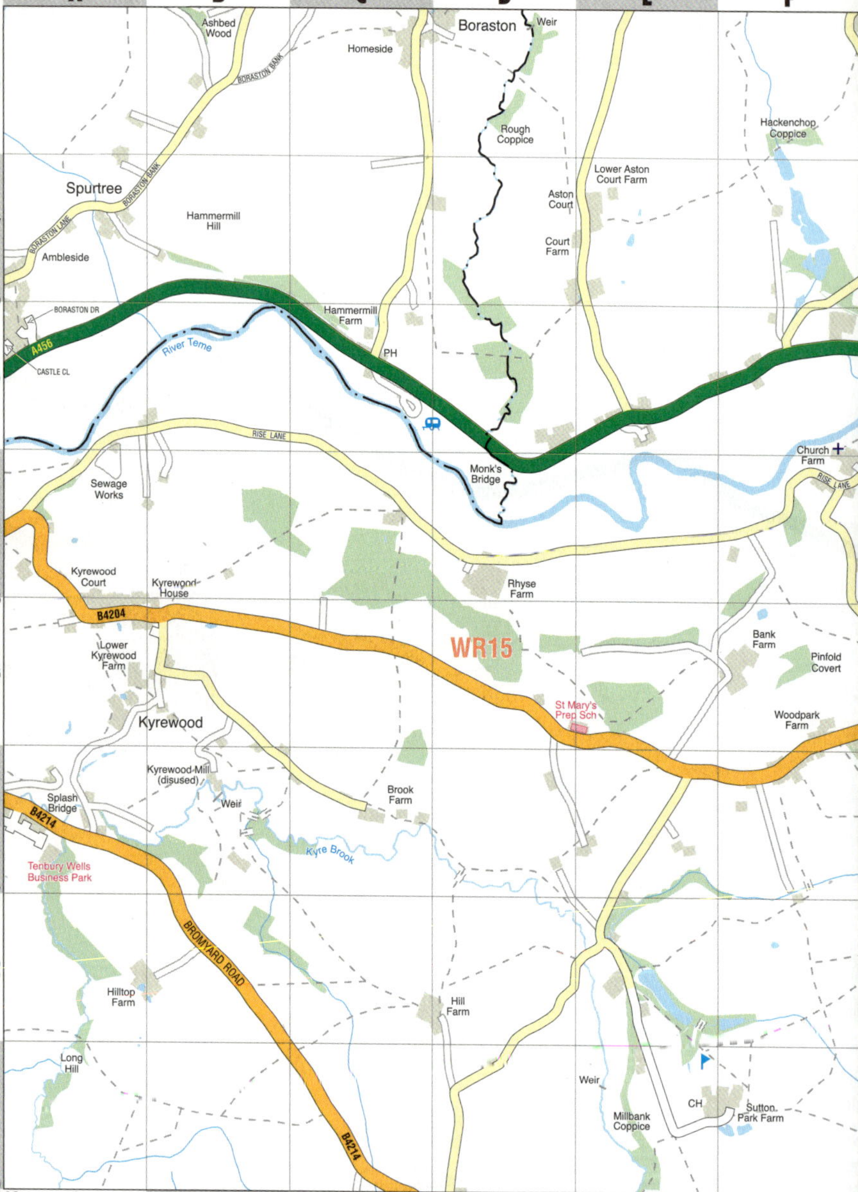
A
B
C
D
E
F
8
7
69
6
5
68
4
3
67
2
1
66
60
61
62
Ashbed Wood
BORASTON BANK
Boraston
Weir
Homeside
Rough Coppice
Hackenchop Coppice
Spurtree
Hammermill Hill
Lower Aston Court Farm
Aston Court
Court Farm
BORASTON LANE
Ambleside
BORASTON DR
A456
CASTLE CL
River Teme
Hammermill Farm
PH
RISE LANE
Sewage Works
Monk's Bridge
Church Farm
Kyrewood Court
Kyrewood House
Rhyse Farm
B4204
WR15
Lower Kyrewood Farm
Bank Farm
Pinfold Covert
St Mary's Prep Sch
Woodpark Farm
Kyrewood
Kyrewood Mill (disused)
Splash Bridge
B4214
Weir
Brook Farm
Kyre Brook
Tenbury Wells Business Park
BROMYARD ROAD
Hilltop Farm
Hill Farm
Long Hill
Weir
CH
Sutton Park Farm
Millbank Coppice

55
75

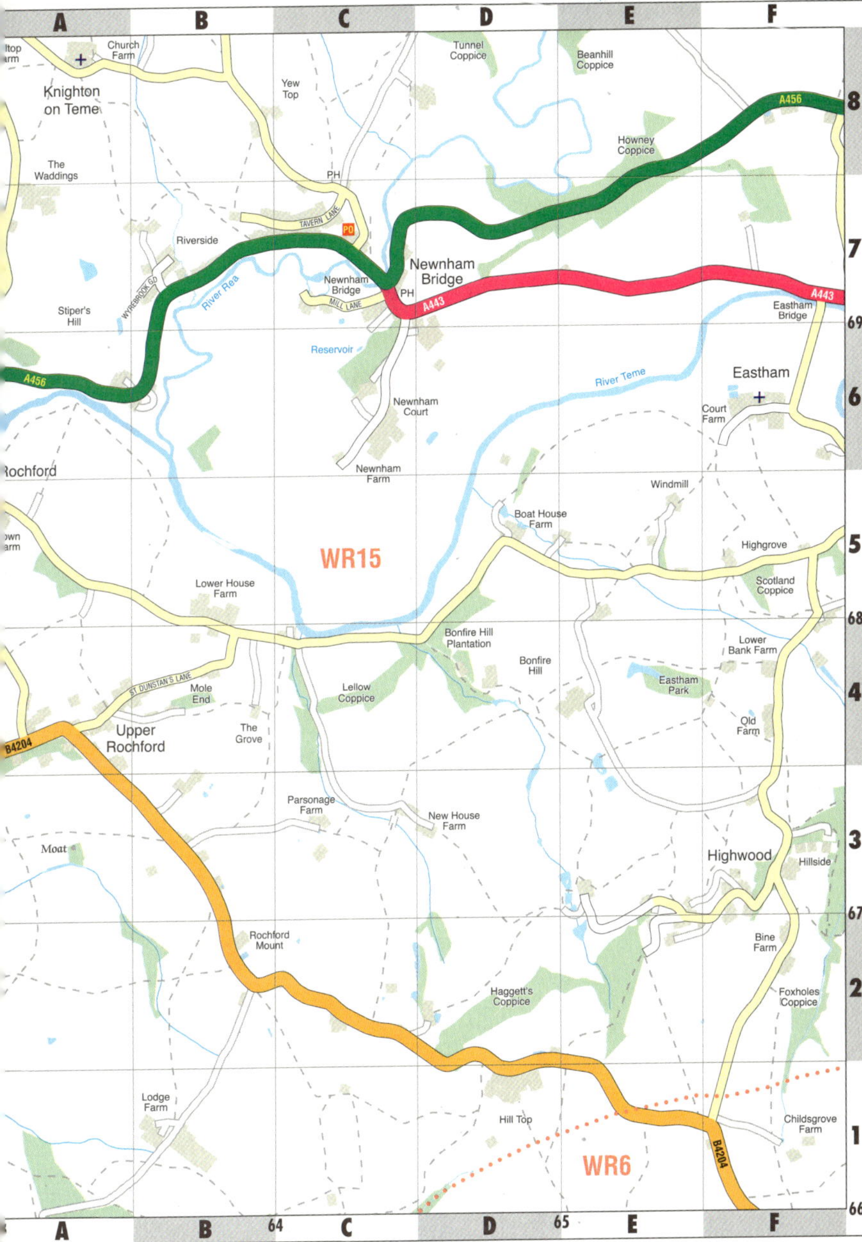
A
B
C
D
E
F
Church Farm
Knighton on Teme
Yew Top
Tunnel Coppice
Beanhill Coppice
A456
8
The Waddings
PH
Howney Coppice
Tavern Lane
PO
Riverside
7
Wyrebrook Gd
River Rea
Newnham Bridge
Newnham Bridge
Mill Lane
PH
A443
A443
Stiper's Hill
Eastham Bridge
69
Reservoir
Eastham
A456
River Teme
6
Newnham Court
Court Farm
Rochford
Newnham Farm
Windmill
Boat House Farm
5
WR15
Highgrove
Lower House Farm
Scotland Coppice
68
Bonfire Hill Plantation
Lower Bank Farm
Bonfire Hill
St Dunstan's Lane
Mole End
Lellow Coppice
Eastham Park
4
B4204
Upper Rochford
The Grove
Old Farm
Parsonage Farm
New House Farm
3
Moat
Highwood
Hillside
67
Rochford Mount
Bine Farm
Haggett's Coppice
Foxholes Coppice
2
Lodge Farm
Hill Top
Childsgrove Farm
1
WR6
B4204
66
64
65

57
39

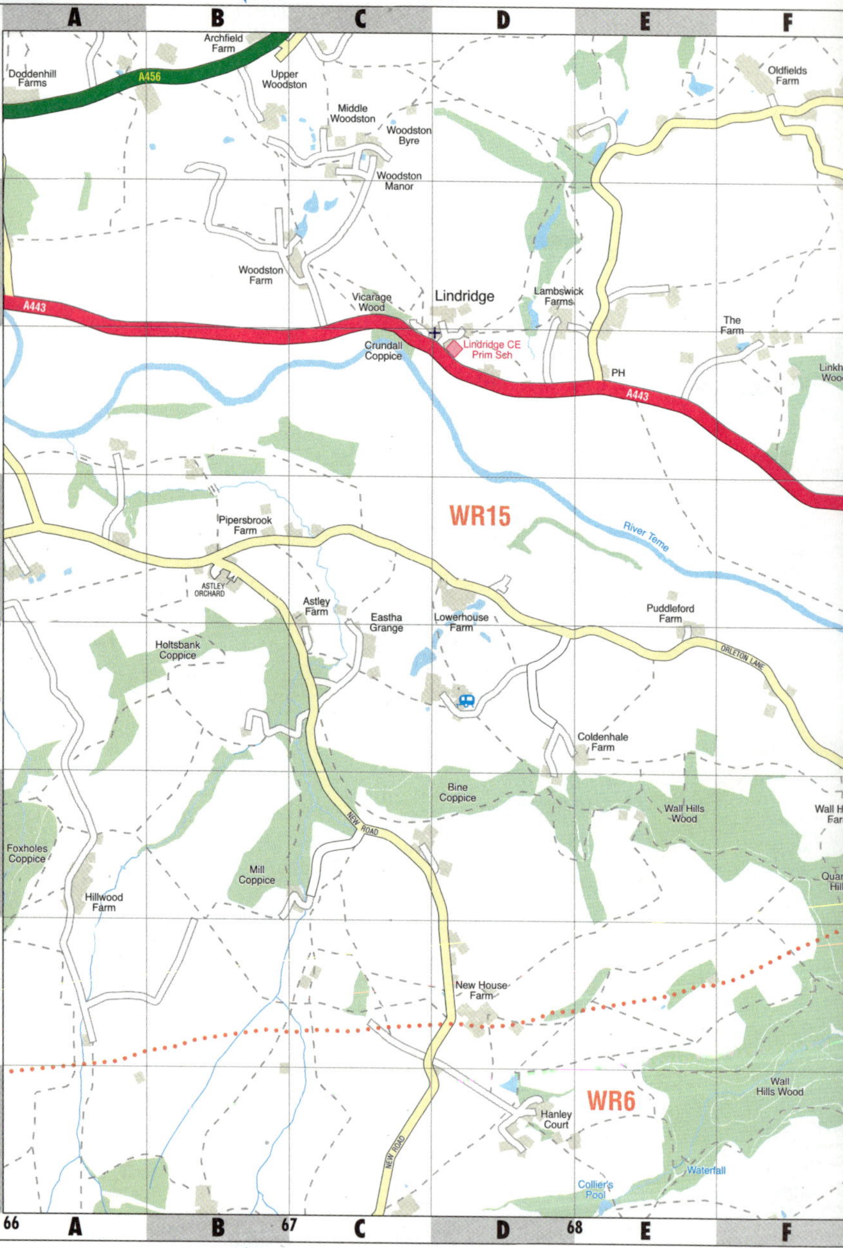
A
B
C
D
E
F
8
7
69
6
5
68
4
3
67
2
1
66
Archfield Farm
Doddenhill Farms
A456
Upper Woodston
Middle Woodston
Woodston Byre
Woodston Manor
Oldfields Farm
Woodston Farm
Lindridge
Lambswick Farms
Vicarage Wood
A443
Crundall Coppice
Lindridge CE Prim Sch
The Farm
PH
Linkh Wooc
A443
WR15
River Teme
Pipersbrook Farm
ASTLEY ORCHARD
Astley Farm
Eastha Grange
Lowerhouse Farm
Puddleford Farm
ORLETON LANE
Holtsbank Coppice
Coldenhale Farm
Bine Coppice
Wall Hills Wood
Wall H Farr
NEW ROAD
Foxholes Coppice
Mill Coppice
Quar Hill
Hillwood Farm
New House Farm
WR6
Wall Hills Wood
Hanley Court
NEW ROAD
Waterfall
Collier's Pool
66
67
68

57
77

40
60

A
B
C
D
E
F
8
7
69
6
5
68
4
3
67
2
1
66
70
71
THE PRY CLOSE
Woodside
Frith Common
The Grove
Hunthouse Wood
Winricks Wood
Brockhill Wood
Cothercraft Wood
Stildon Manor
DUMBLETON LANE
Dumbleton Farm
Menith Wood
CHAPEL LANE
FOX LANE
Stilehouse Farm
Menithwood Millennium Green
Rifle Coppice
Hollow Linkhill
Menithwood
PENN HALL LANE
Woodlands
Mill End
PH
Penn Hall
DUMBLETON LANE
WR15
Jacob's Wood
Upper Claywood
Mary's Wood
White House Farm
Bough Farm
Yeldon Farm
Eardiston
The Claywood
Claywood Farm
Pensax Wood
SUTHILL BRIDGE
Moor Farm
A443
MILL LANE
WR6
The Lowe Farm
Meadows Mill
Lower Ridney Farm
PO
PENSAX ROAD
Stockton on Teme
A443
STOCKTON ROAD
Upper Ridney Farm
Court Farm
Orleton Court Farm
Orleton
Upper House Farm
Lowerhouse Farm
River Teme
Weir
Brickbarns Coppice
Round Hill
Weir
B4203
Bickenham Wood
78
60

59
41

A
B
C
D
E
F
8
7
69
6
5
68
4
3
67
2
1
66
72
73
74
B4202
Lower Snead Farm
DY14
Hawkley Farm
New England Farm
Snead Common
Rowley Coppice
PENN HALL LANE
PH
The Bell
Pensax
Pensax CE Prim Sch
Fartown Farm
Worles Common
Kingswood
New Inn Farm
Field Farm
Beehive Farm
Jacob's Well
SUFFOLK LANE
Pensax Wood
Ridding Coppice
St Clairs Farm
PENSAX ROAD
Hall Wood
CLOWS TOP ROAD
WR6
Church Farm
Woodhouse Farm
Poolhouse Farm
Quarry (dis)
Walshes Farm
Abberley Parochial Prim Sch
MILLERS GN
Wharf Farm
STUD LANE
The Woodlands
Nurton's Farm
Abberley
Boddington Coppice
ROSEDALE
CLOWS TOP RD
CHURCHFIELD TR
Catchems End
THE COMMON
B4202
Aniceford Coppice
Orchard House Stud Farm
PO
A443
The Elms (Hotel)
Westlyn Old Farm
Quarry (dis)
STOCKTON ROAD
WYNNIATTES WAY
Hill Farm
Upper Crundle Farm
Westwood Home Farm
Bowling Green Farm
Elms Green
CRUNDELEND LANE
Old Yeates Farm
Clock Tower
A443
Upper Crundelend Farm
Ellbatch Wood
Worcestershire Way
Abberley Hall
Lower Crundelend Farm
STANFORD ROAD
Meneatt Wood
B4203
Kingswood Hollow
CAMP LA
Quarry (dis)

59
79

42
62

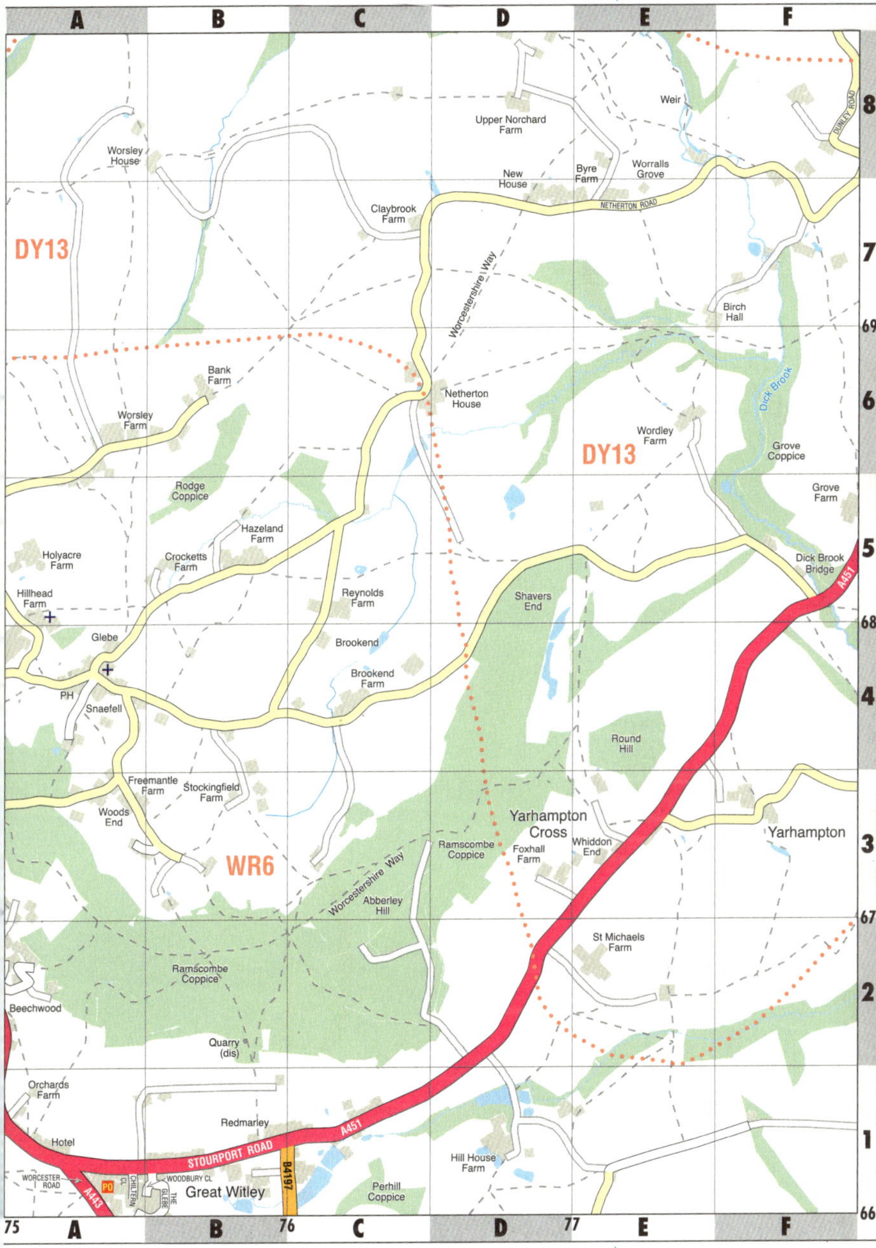
A
B
C
D
E
F
8
7
69
6
5
68
4
3
67
2
1
66
75
76
77
DY13
DY13
WR6
Weir
Upper Norchard Farm
DUNLEY ROAD
Worsley House
New House
Byre Farm
Worralls Grove
NETHERTON ROAD
Claybrook Farm
Worcestershire Way
Birch Hall
Bank Farm
Netherton House
Dick Brook
Worsley Farm
Wordley Farm
Grove Coppice
Rodge Coppice
Grove Farm
Hazeland Farm
Holyacre Farm
Crocketts Farm
Dick Brook Bridge
Hillhead Farm
Reynolds Farm
Shavers End
A451
Glebe
Brookend
Brookend Farm
PH
Snaefell
Round Hill
Freemantle Farm
Stockingfield Farm
Yarhampton Cross
Yarhampton
Woods End
Ramscombe Coppice
Foxhall Farm
Whiddon End
Worcestershire Way
Abberley Hill
St Michaels Farm
Ramscombe Coppice
Beechwood
Quarry (dis)
Orchards Farm
Redmarley
A451
Hotel
STOURPORT ROAD
Hill House Farm
B4197
WORCESTER ROAD
A443
PO
CHILTERN CL
WOODBURY CL
THE GLEBE
Great Witley
Perhill Coppice

80
62

61
43

E8
1 VAWDREY CL
2 YARRANTON CL
3 SEEDGREEN CL
4 CHESSHIRE CL
5 CHAPEL LA
6 HILLSIDE CL
7 SUMMERCFT
8 ASTLEY CT
9 MEADOW VW

F8
1 WINDMILL CL
2 HERMITAGE WA
3 CHEQUERS CL
4 REDSTONE LA
5 HANSTONE RD
6 WOODHAMPTON CL

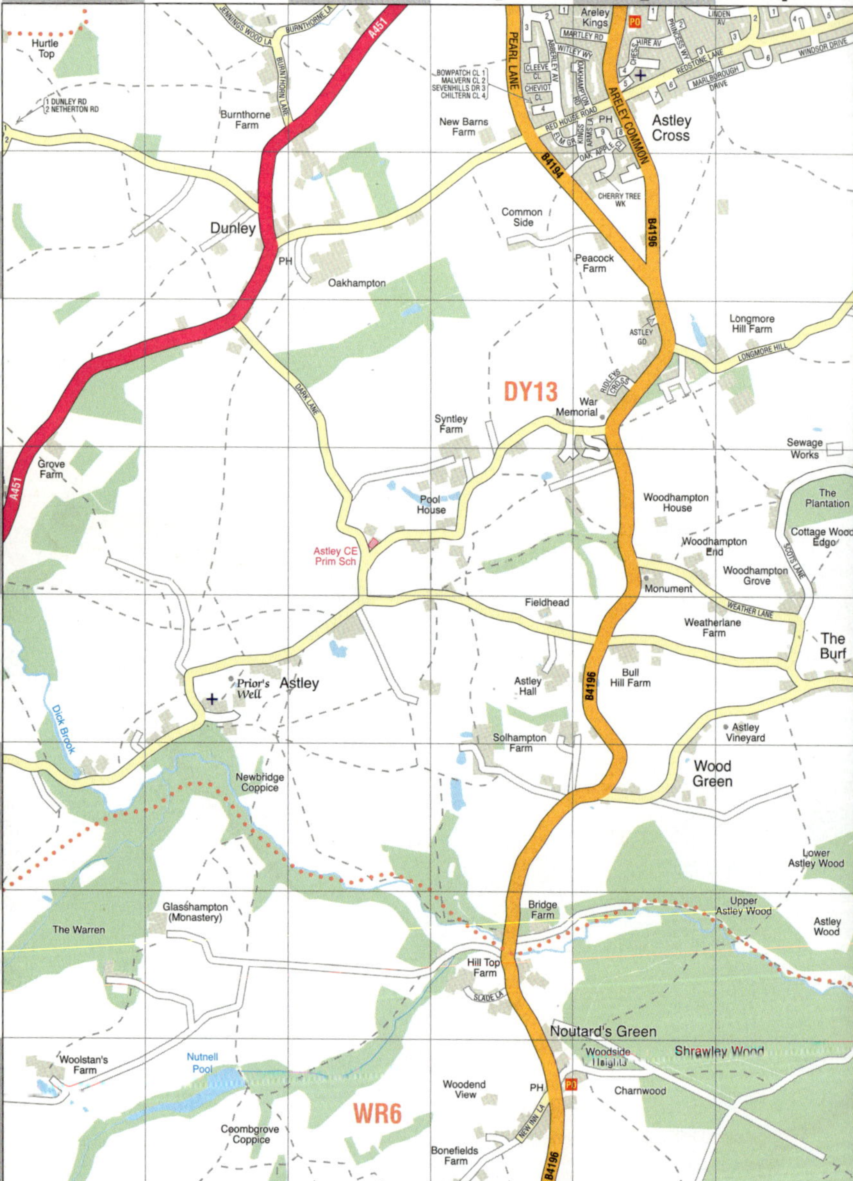

61
81

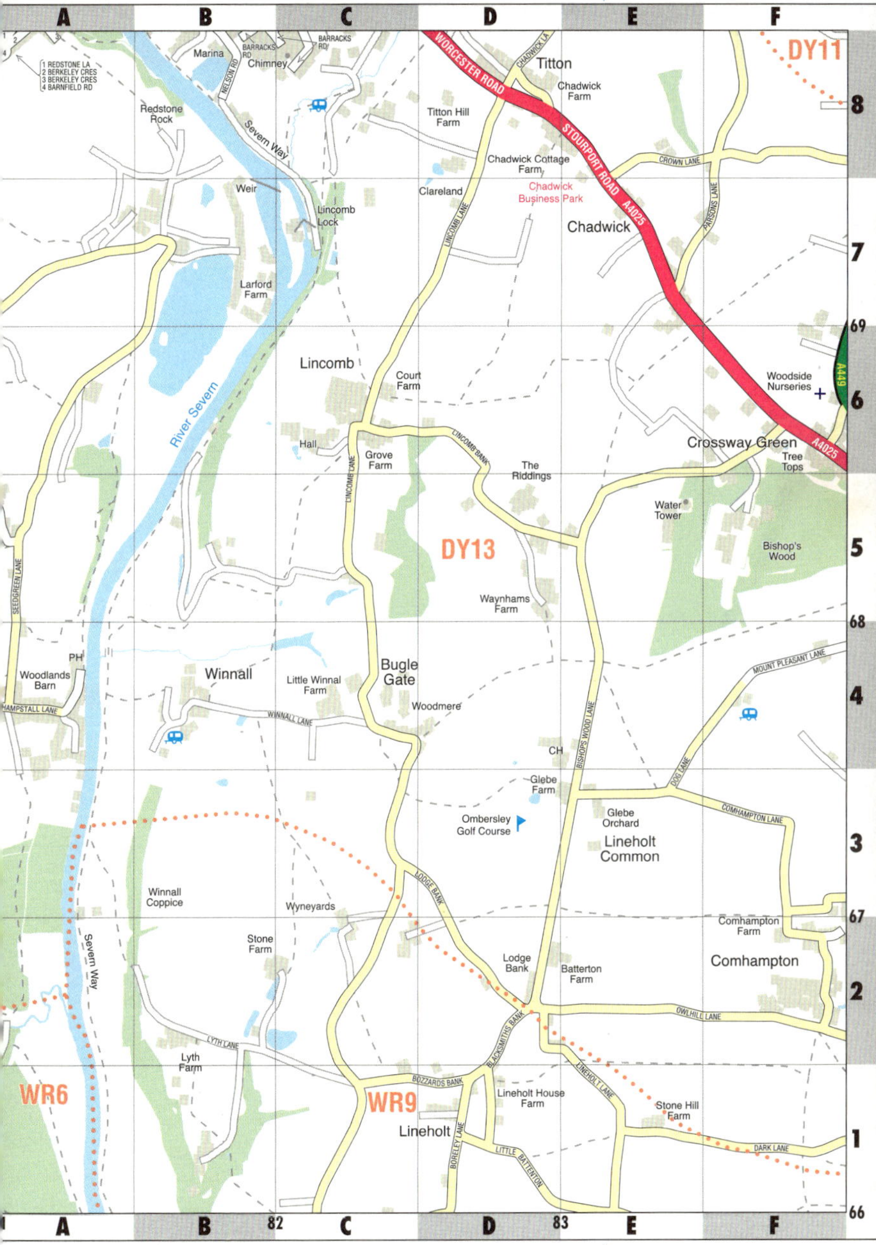
A
B
C
D
E
F
1 REDSTONE LA
2 BERKELEY CRES
3 BERKELEY CRES
4 BARNFIELD RD
Marina
NELSON RD
BARRACKS RD
Chimney
BARRACKS RD
WORCESTER ROAD
CHADWICK LA
Titton
Chadwick Farm
DY11
8
Redstone Rock
Severn Way
Titton Hill Farm
STOURPORT ROAD
Chadwick Cottage Farm
CROWN LANE
Weir
Clareland
Chadwick Business Park
PARSONS LANE
Lincomb Lock
LINCOMB LANE
A4025
Chadwick
7
Larford Farm
69
Lincomb
Court Farm
River Severn
A449
Woodside Nurseries
6
Hall
LINCOMB BANK
Crossway Green
Grove Farm
LINCOMB LANE
The Riddings
Tree Tops
Water Tower
DY13
Bishop's Wood
5
SEEDGREEN LANE
Waynhams Farm
68
PH
Woodlands Barn
Winnall
Little Winnal Farm
Bugle Gate
MOUNT PLEASANT LANE
HAMPSTALL LANE
WINNALL LANE
Woodmere
BISHOPS WOOD LANE
4
CH
DOG LANE
Glebe Farm
COMHAMPTON LANE
Glebe Orchard
Ombersley Golf Course
Lineholt Common
3
Winnall Coppice
LODGE BANK
Wyneyards
67
Comhampton Farm
Stone Farm
Severn Way
Lodge Bank
Batterton Farm
Comhampton
2
BLACKSMITHS BANK
OWLHILL LANE
LYTH LANE
Lyth Farm
LINEHOLT LANE
BOZZARDS BANK
Lineholt House Farm
Stone Hill Farm
WR6
WR9
Lineholt
BORELEY LANE
LITTLE BATTENTON
DARK LANE
1
66
82
83

63
45

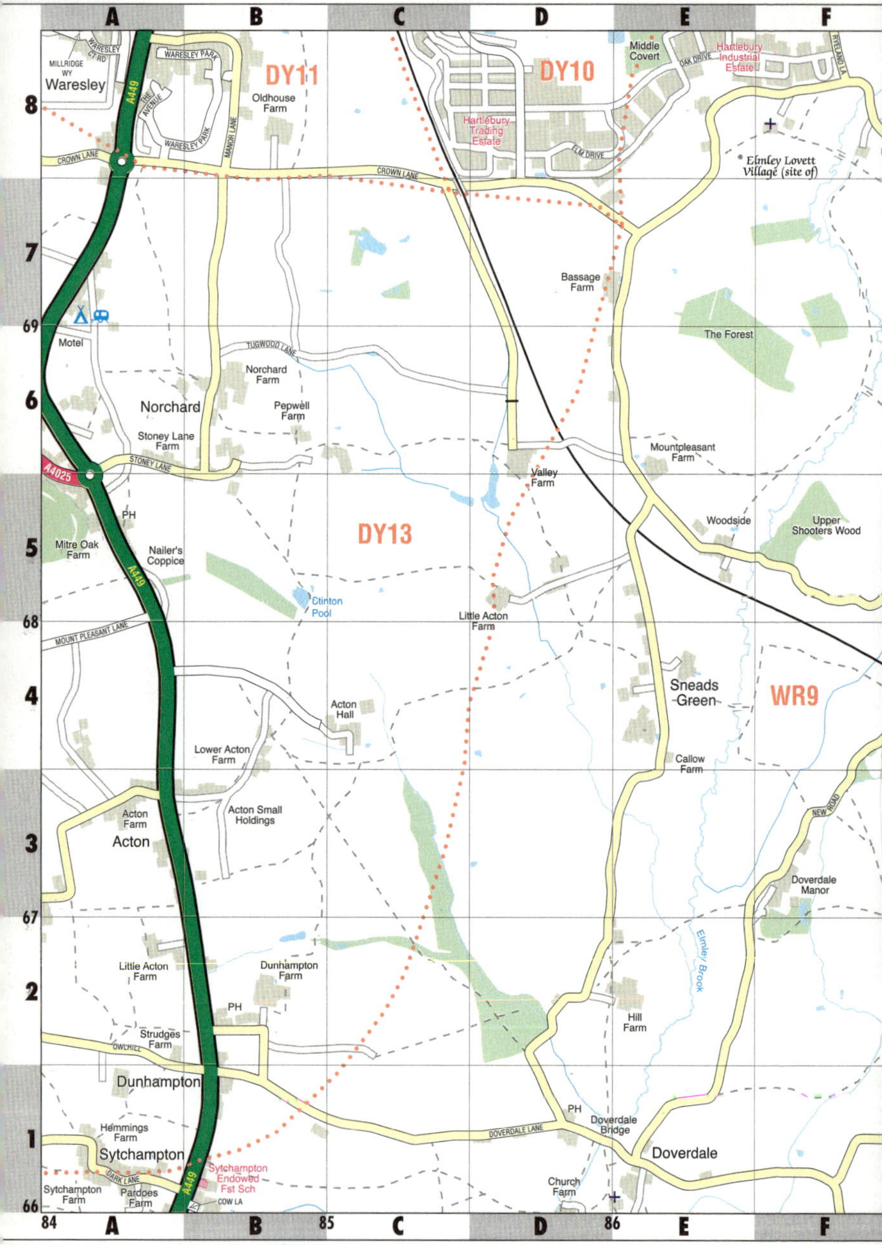
A
B
C
D
E
F
Waresley
WARESLEY CT RD
MILLRIDGE WY
WARESLEY PARK
THE AVENUE
MANOR LANE
DY11
Oldhouse Farm
DY10
Middle Covert
OAK DRIVE
Hartlebury Industrial Estate
RYELAND LA
Hartlebury Trading Estate
ELM DRIVE
Elmley Lovett Village (site of)
A449
CROWN LANE
8
7
69
6
5
68
4
3
67
2
1
66
Bassage Farm
The Forest
Motel
TUGWOOD LANE
Norchard Farm
Pepwell Farm
Norchard
Stoney Lane Farm
STONEY LANE
A4025
Mountpleasant Farm
Valley Farm
Woodside
Upper Shooters Wood
PH
DY13
Mitre Oak Farm
Nailer's Coppice
Ctinton Pool
Little Acton Farm
MOUNT PLEASANT LANE
Sneads Green
WR9
Acton Hall
Lower Acton Farm
Callow Farm
Acton Farm
Acton
Acton Small Holdings
NEW ROAD
Doverdale Manor
Elmley Brook
Little Acton Farm
Dunhampton Farm
Hill Farm
Strudges Farm
OWLHILL
Dunhampton
Hemmings Farm
Sychampton
DOVERDALE LANE
Doverdale Bridge
Doverdale
DARK LANE
Sytchampton Endowed Fst Sch
Church Farm
Sytchampton Farm
Pardoes Farm
COW LA
84
85
86

63
83

46
66

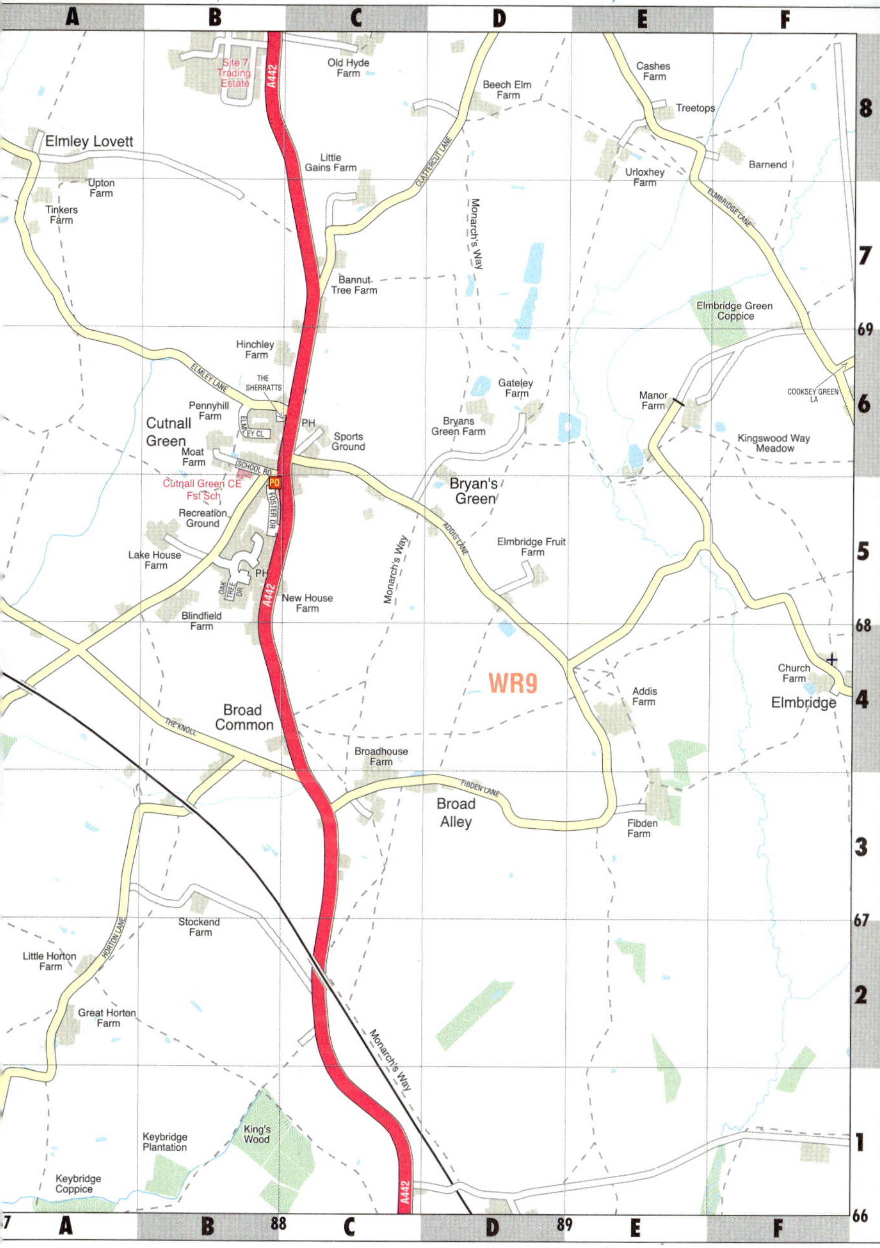
A
B
C
D
E
F
8
7
69
6
5
68
4
3
67
2
1
66
88
89
Site 7 Trading Estate
A442
Old Hyde Farm
Beech Elm Farm
Cashes Farm
Treetops
Elmley Lovett
Upton Farm
Tinkers Farm
Little Gains Farm
CLATTERCUT LANE
Urloxhey Farm
Barnend
ELMBRIDGE LANE
Monarch's Way
Bannut Tree Farm
Elmbridge Green Coppice
Hinchley Farm
ELMLEY LANE
THE SHERRATTS
Gateley Farm
Manor Farm
COOKSEY GREEN LA
Pennyhill Farm
Cutnall Green
ELMLEY CL
PH
Sports Ground
Bryans Green Farm
Kingswood Way Meadow
Moat Farm
SCHOOL RD
Cutnall Green CE Fst Sch
PO
FOSTER DR
Bryan's Green
Recreation Ground
ADDIS LANE
Elmbridge Fruit Farm
Lake House Farm
OAK TREE DR
New House Farm
Blindfield Farm
WR9
Church Farm
Addis Farm
Elmbridge
Broad Common
THE KNOLL
Broadhouse Farm
FIBDEN LANE
Broad Alley
Fibden Farm
Stockend Farm
HORTON LANE
Little Horton Farm
Great Horton Farm
Keybridge Plantation
King's Wood
Keybridge Coppice

84
66

65
47

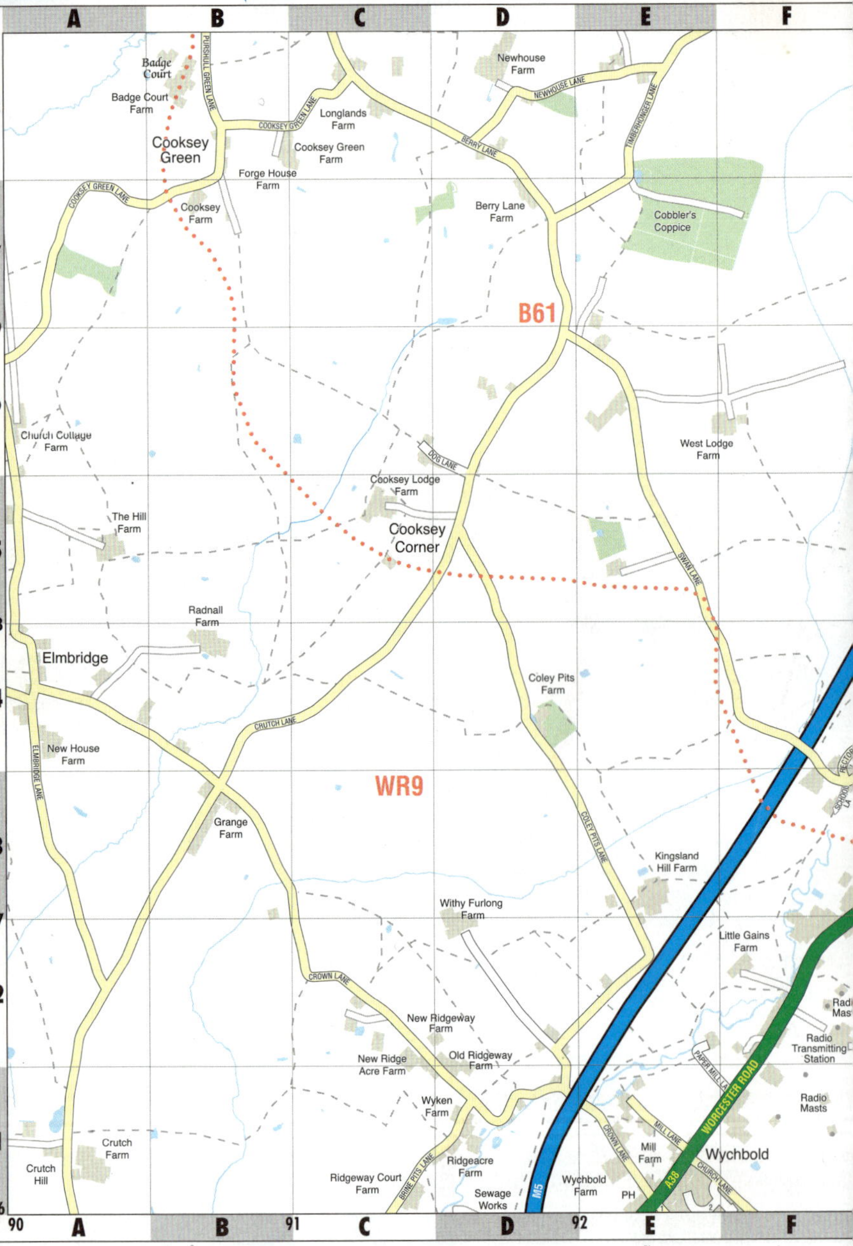

E1
1 CHEQUERS LA
2 PEAR TREE WY

65
85

F6
1 SUGARBROOK CT
2 Aston Fields Trad Est
3 Silver Birches Bsns Pk

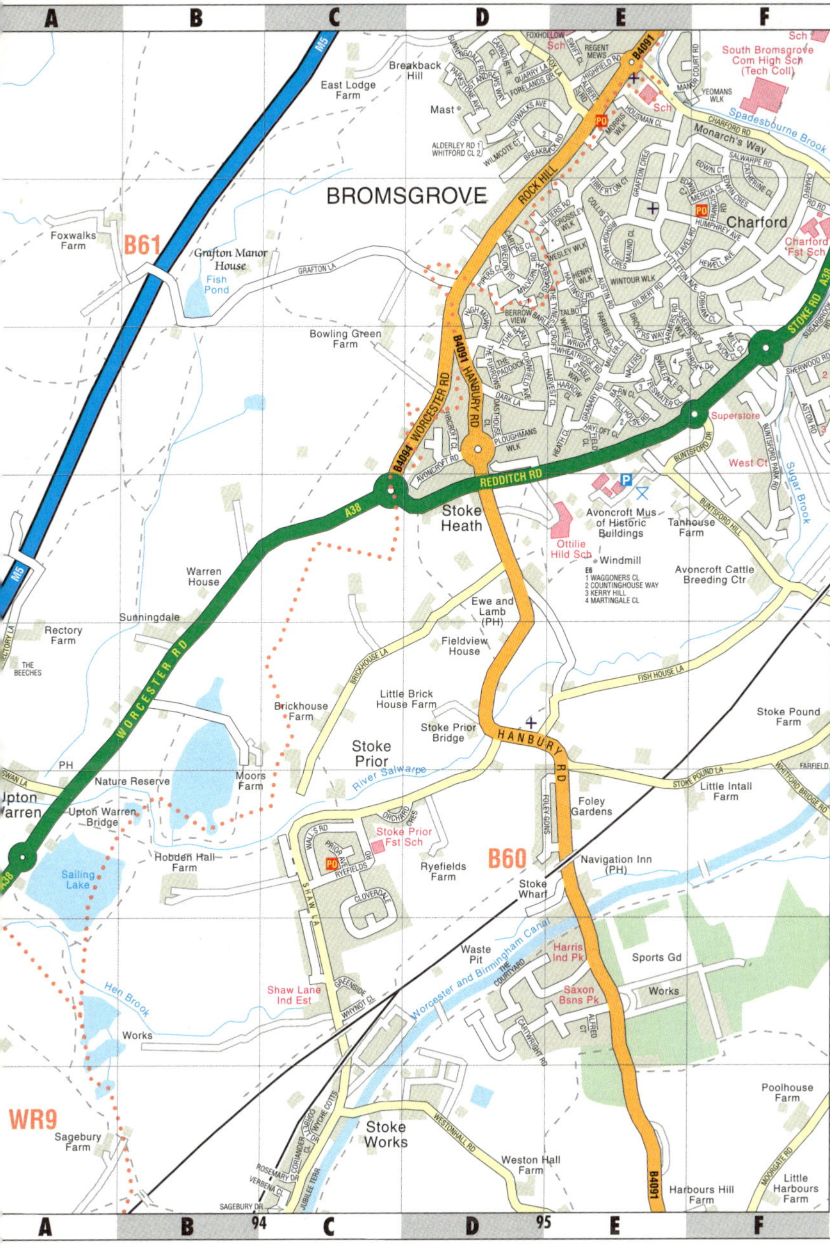

67
49

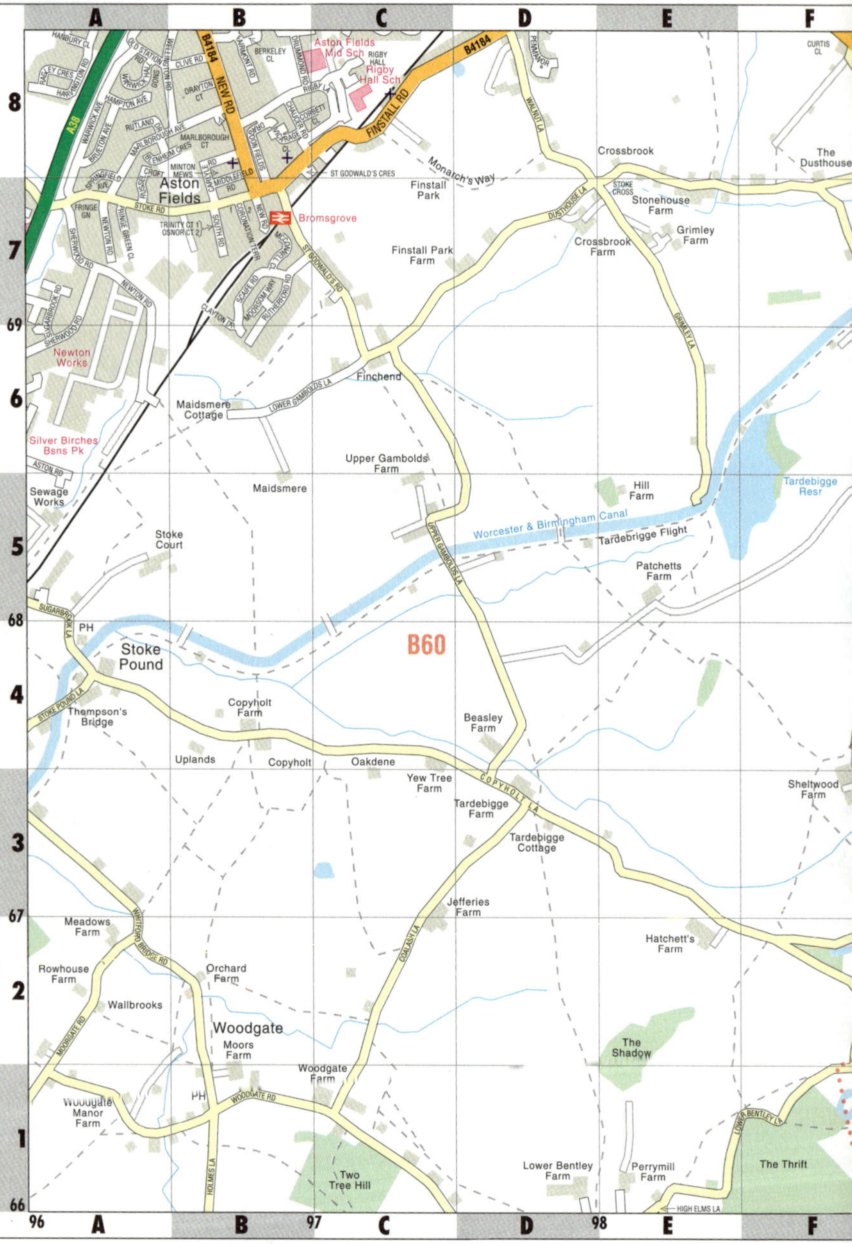
A
B
C
D
E
F
8
7
69
6
5
68
4
3
67
2
1
66
96
97
98
A38
B4184
NEW RD
FINSTALL RD
HANBURY CL
RAGLEY CRES
HARVINGTON RD
WARWICK AVE
BRUETON AVE
HAMPTON AVE
RUTLAND DR
MARLBOROUGH AVE
MARLBOROUGH CT
BLENHEIM CRES
SPRINGFIELD AVE
CROFT
MINTON MEWS
CARLYLE RD
MIDDLEFIELD RD
CLIVE RD
DRAYTON CT
WELLINGTON RD
OLD STATION RD
BERKELEY CL
DRUMMOND RD
CHAUCER RD
CORBETT CL
VICARAGE CL
Aston Fields Mid Sch
RIGBY HALL
Rigby Hall Sch
PENNAMOR
Aston Fields
STOKE RD
FRINGE GN
NEWTON RD
SOUTH RD
CORONATION TERR
TRINITY CT 1
OSNOR CT 2
ST GODWALD'S CRES
Bromsgrove
ST GODWALD'S RD
SHERWOOD RD
SUGARBROOK RD
CLAYTON DR
SCAIFE RD
MOORSOM WAY
RUTHERFORD RD
Newton Works
Silver Birches Bsns Pk
ASTON RD
Sewage Works
Monarch's Way
Finstall Park
Finstall Park Farm
WALNUT LA
DUSTHOUSE LA
Crossbrook
STOKE CROSS
Stonehouse Farm
Crossbrook Farm
Grimley Farm
GRIMLEY LA
CURTIS CL
The Dusthouse
Finchend
LOWER GAMBOLDS LA
Maidsmere Cottage
Upper Gambolds Farm
Maidsmere
Hill Farm
Tardebigge Resr
Worcester & Birmingham Canal
Tardebigge Flight
Stoke Court
UPPER GAMBOLDS LA
Patchetts Farm
SUGARBROOK LA
PH
Stoke Pound
B60
STOKE POUND LA
Thompson's Bridge
Copyholt Farm
Beasley Farm
Uplands
Copyholt
Oakdene
Yew Tree Farm
COPYHOLT LA
Tardebigge Farm
Tardebigge Cottage
Sheltwood Farm
Jefferies Farm
Meadows Farm
WHITFORD BRIDGE RD
Hatchett's Farm
Rowhouse Farm
Orchard Farm
COALASH LA
Wallbrooks
Woodgate
MOORGATE RD
Moors Farm
The Shadow
Woodgate Farm
PH
WOODGATE RD
Woodgate Manor Farm
LOWER BENTLEY LA
The Thrift
HOLMES LA
Two Tree Hill
Lower Bentley Farm
Perrymill Farm
HIGH ELMS LA

67
87

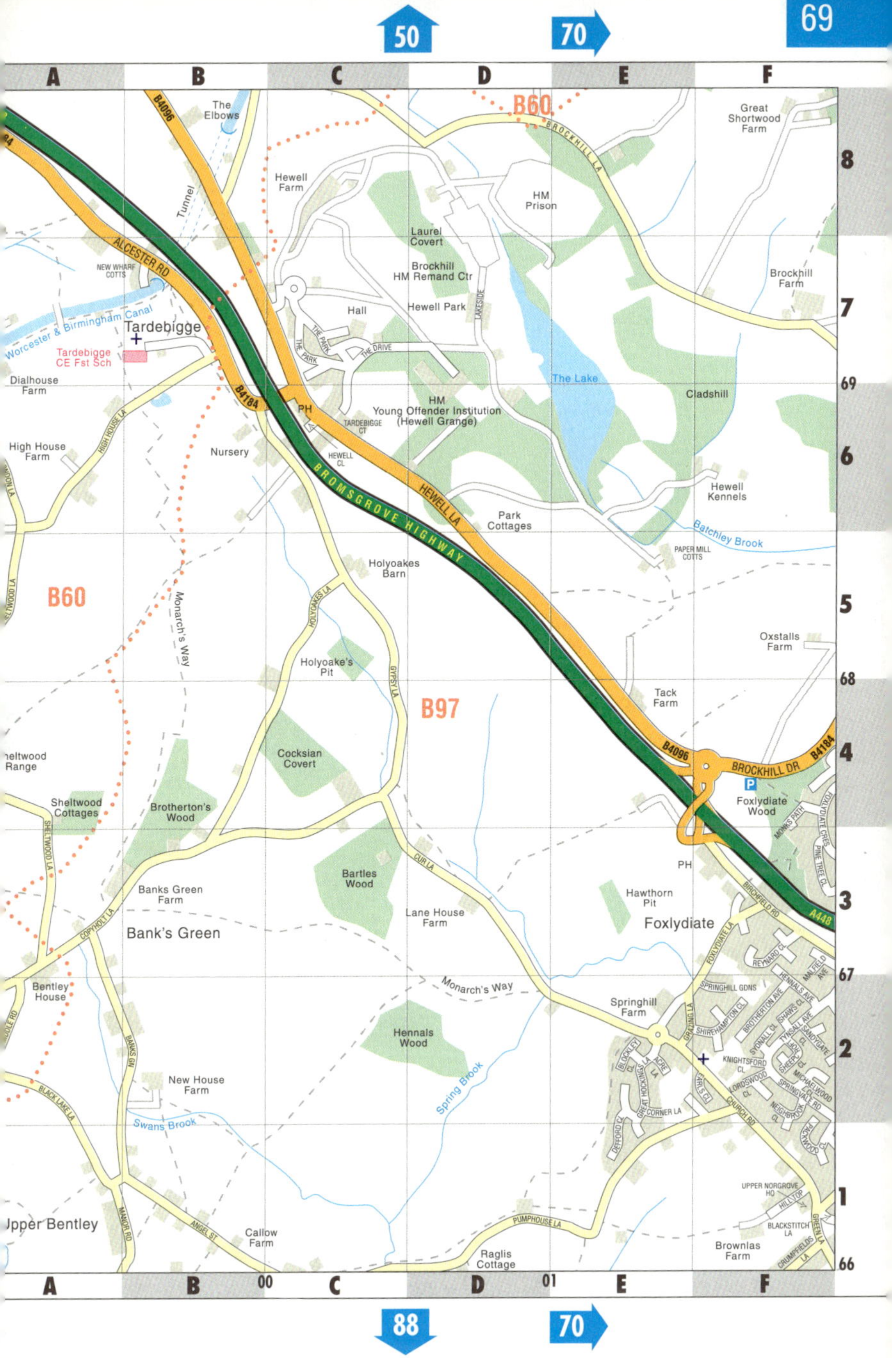
50
70
A
B
C
D
E
F
8
7
69
6
5
68
4
3
67
2
1
66
00
01
88
70
B4096
The Elbows
Tunnel
B60
BROCKHILL LA
Great Shortwood Farm
Hewell Farm
HM Prison
Laurel Covert
Brockhill HM Remand Ctr
Brockhill Farm
ALCESTER RD
NEW WHARF COTTS
Worcester & Birmingham Canal
Tardebigge
Tardebigge CE Fst Sch
Hall
Hewell Park
LAKESIDE
THE PARK
THE DRIVE
The Lake
Cladshill
Dialhouse Farm
B4184
PH
HM Young Offender Institution (Hewell Grange)
TARDEBIGGE CT
HEWELL CL
High House Farm
HIGH HOUSE LA
Nursery
BROMSGROVE HIGHWAY
HEWELL LA
Park Cottages
Hewell Kennels
Batchley Brook
PAPER MILL COTTS
Holyoakes Barn
B60
Monarch's Way
HOLYOAKES LA
Holyoake's Pit
Oxstalls Farm
GYPSY LA
B97
Tack Farm
Sheltwood Range
Cocksian Covert
B4096
BROCKHILL DR
B4184
Foxlydiate Wood
Sheltwood Cottages
Brotherton's Wood
SHELTWOOD LA
Bartles Wood
CUR LA
PH
Banks Green Farm
Lane House Farm
Hawthorn Pit
Foxlydiate
A448
COPYHOLT LA
Bank's Green
Bentley House
Monarch's Way
Springhill Farm
Hennals Wood
BANKS GN
Spring Brook
New House Farm
BLACK LAKE LA
Swans Brook
CORNER LA
CHURCH RD
Upper Bentley
MANOR RD
ANGEL ST
Callow Farm
PUMPHOUSE LA
Raglis Cottage
Brownlas Farm
UPPER NORGROVE HO
BLACKSTITCH LA
HILLTOP
GREEN LA
CRUMPFIELDS LA

69
51

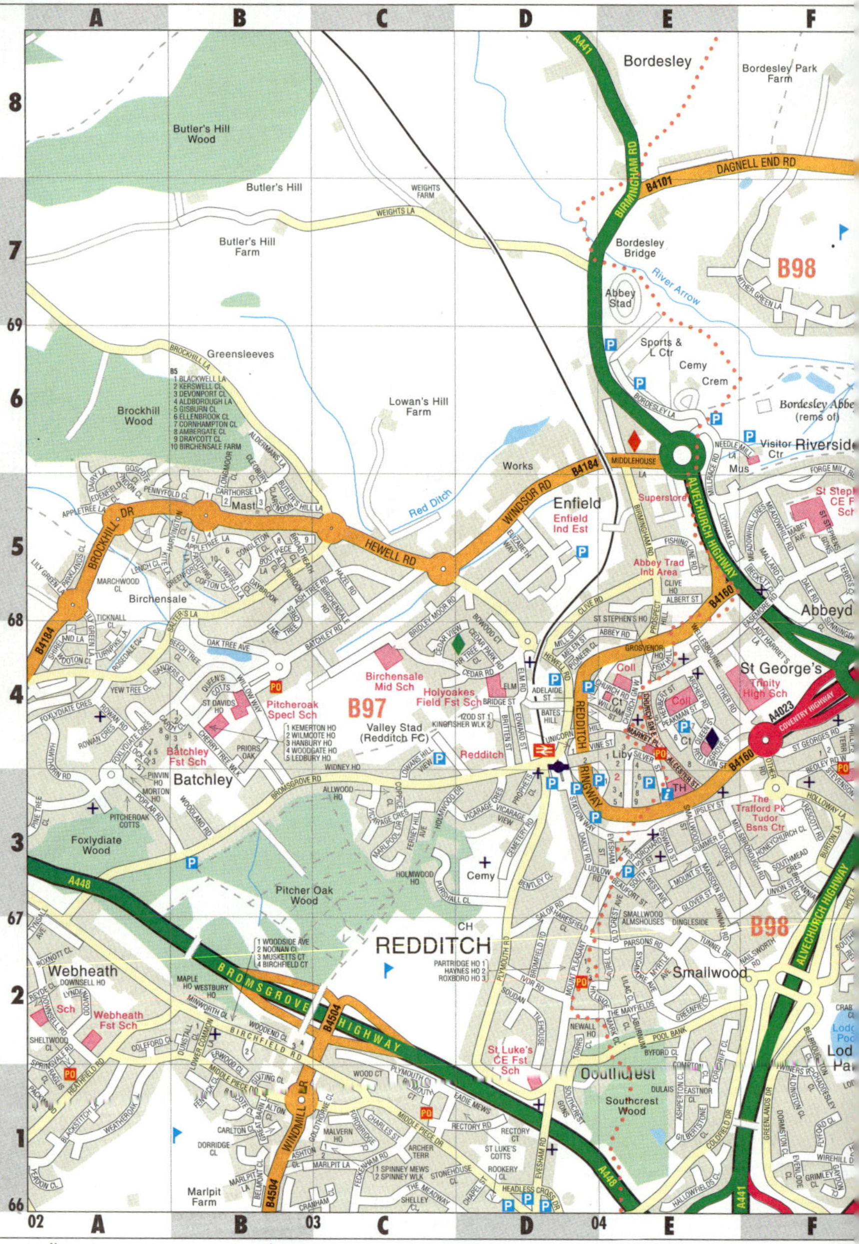

A4
1 CLADSWORTH HO
2 RADFORD HO
3 FOXLYDIATE MEWS
4 ABBERTON HO
5 HADZOR HO
6 WEETHLEY HO
7 STRETTON HO
8 RAGLEY HO
9 ELMLEY HO

69
89

E3
1 CLARKE ST
2 Kingfisher Sh Ctr
3 EVESHAM SQ
4 PARK WLK
5 GEORGE WLK
6 ROYAL SQ
7 WALFORD WLK
8 MILWARD SQ
9 EVESHAM MEWS

E4
1 WORCESTER SQ
2 EVESHAM WLK
3 NEW WLK
4 MARKET WLK
5 SMALLWOOD ARCH
6 WELLINGTON ST
7 VICTORIA ST
8 SOUTH EAST QUADRANT

F4
1 GRANGE CT
2 GRANGE RD
3 ST GEORGE'S

52 72

A
B
C
D
E
F
8
7
69
6
5
68
4
3
67
2
1
66
06
07
The Rose Cottage
Perrymill Farm
B4101
ICKNIELD ST
St Leonard's Grange
Clevedon Farm
Beoley Fst Sch
PH
BEOLEY LA
BEACHFIELD RD
HOLT HILL
MOSS LA
Holt End
THE GLEBE
CHURCH HILL
Church Hill Farm
Beoley
Dagnell End Farm
DAGNELL END RD
B4497
The Dagnell Brook
RAVENS BANK DR
JERSEY CL
HARTLEBURY CL
IMPNEY CL
NASEBY CL
HOME MEADOW LA
HILLMORTON CL
LATCHFORD CL
MOORGATE CL
NORTHFIELD CL
THORNHILL RD
ACANTHUS RD
HEDERA RD
Schs
Marlfield Farm Fst Sch
Church Hill
CHURCH HILL WAY
MENDIP HO
PO
Sch
LOXLEY CL
KNOWLE CL
HAWKESBURY CL
Moons Pk
Ind Est
Oak Tree Pk
Manor Side Ind Est
WALKERS RD
EAGLE RD
Moons Moat
TA Ctr
Paper Mill Hill
Papermill Farm
BROOKLANDS LA
PARK WAY
PAPER MILL DR
MARLFIELD LA
EDGEWORTH CL
EXHALL CL
CLEEVE CL
Moon's Moat
Moons Moat Fst Sch
BARNWOOD CL
ACTON CL
ARLEY CL
MOONS MOAT DR
BLACK SOLLS RD
A4023
PALMERS RD
OXLEASOW RD
KINGHAM CL
Abbeydale
B4497
COVENTRY HIGHWAY
Beoley Mill
Peltland Trad Ctr
B98
South Moons Moat Ind Est
PADGETS LA
Ind Est
Arrow Valley Park
PROCTORS BARN LA
HOLLOWAY DR
1 PROSPECT RD S
2 ARROW RD S
BEOLEY RD E
HARRY TAYLOR HO
Arrow Valley Countryside Ctr
Arrow Valley Lake
Lakeside Ind Est
River Arrow
BATTENS DR
Ipsley Alders Marsh Nature Reserve
ALDERS DR
Victor Bsns Ctr
Lakeside
Kingfisher Ent Pk
SHAWBANK RD
ARROWDALE RD
CLEARWELL RD
WINYATES CRAFTS CTR
PO
WINYATES CTR
Tenacres Fst Sch
Sch
Winyates
HOLLY OAKS
WARWICK HIGHWAY
A4189
Ipsley
Ipsley Ct
Arrow Vale Com High Sch
L Ctr
ICKNIELD STREET DR
IPSLEY CHURCH LA
Ipsley Mill Farm
POLESWORTH CL
Schs
WATERY LA
RAVENSMERE RD
STUDLEY RD
Works
HARPORT RD
PO
Securehold Bsns Ctr
Greenlands Bsns Ctr
NASH RD
OLD FORGE DR
PO
Matchborough
Sch
Sch
Sch
MATCHBOROUGH CTR
CLAYBROOK DR
B4497

90 72

71
53

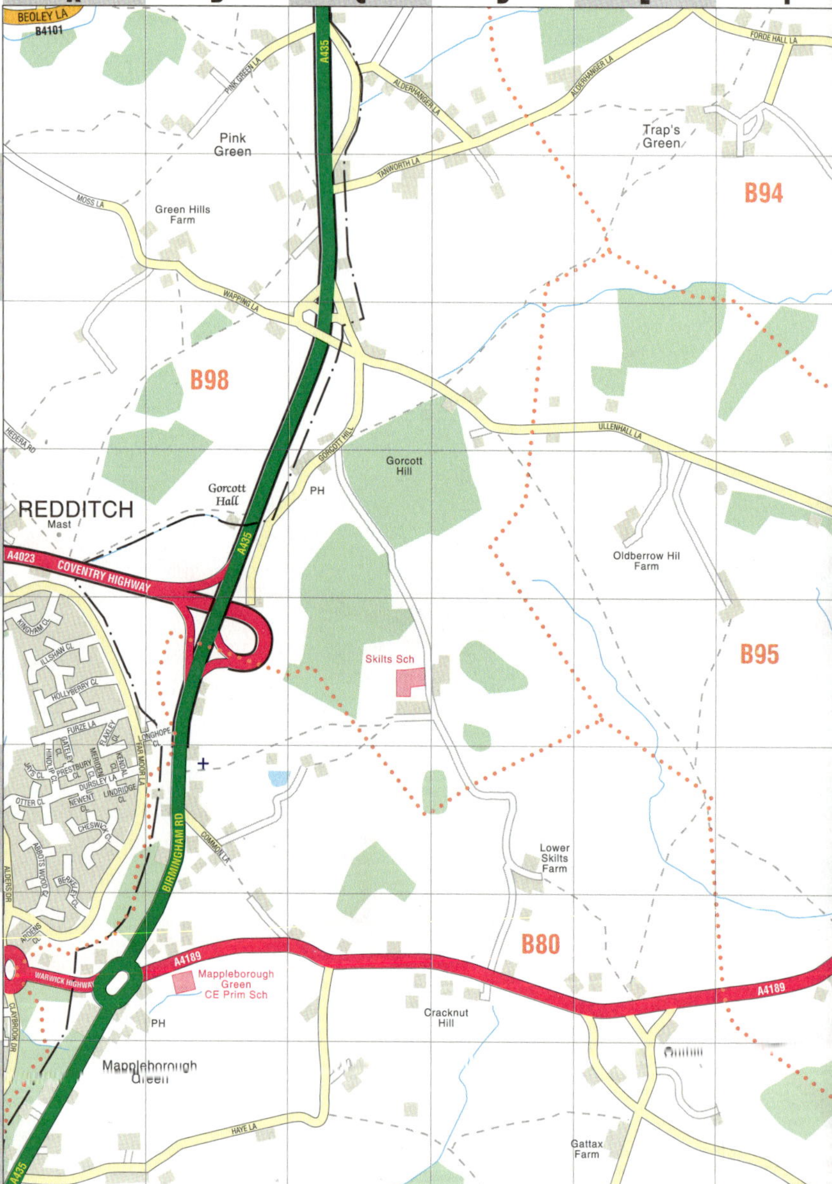
A
B
C
D
E
F
8
7
69
6
5
68
4
3
67
2
1
66
08
09
10
BEOLEY LA
B4101
PINK GREEN LA
A435
ALDERHANGER LA
FORDE HALL LA
Pink
Green
Trap's
Green
TANWORTH LA
MOSS LA
Green Hills
Farm
B94
WAPPING LA
B98
HEDERA RD
GORCOTT HILL
ULLENHALL LA
Gorcott
Hill
Gorcott
Hall
PH
REDDITCH
Mast
A4023
COVENTRY HIGHWAY
Oldberrow Hil
Farm
KINGHAM CL
ILLSHAW CL
HOLLYBERRY CL
Skilts Sch
B95
FURZE LA
LONGHOPE CL
FAR MOOR LA
PRESTBURY CL
DURSLEY LA
LINDRIDGE CL
NEWENT CL
OTTER CL
CHESWICK CL
BIRMINGHAM RD
COMMON LA
ABBOTS WOOD CL
BERKELEY CL
ALDERS DR
Lower
Skilts
Farm
ARDENS CL
B80
A4189
WARWICK HIGHWAY
Mappleborough
Green
CE Prim Sch
CLAYBROOK DR
PH
Cracknut
Hill
Mappleborough
Green
HAYE LA
Gattax
Farm

71
91

54
74

A
B
C
D
E
F
8
7
65
6
5
64
4
3
63
2
1
62
55
56
Upton Brook
HAYES LANE
WR15
Redwood
Ford Farm
Dugdale Farm
SY8
Nurton Court
Wood Sutton
Lane End Barn
Valley Farm
Middleton on the Hill
Raddle Bank
Lower Easton Farm
Church House Farm
Five Ashes
Easton
A4112
Ash Farm
Pole Farm
Hills Farm
The Hills
Leysters Pole
PO
Leysters
Little Pole Farm
Pool Farm
PH
Lane End
Moor Abbey
Moat
HR6
Church House
Ghorst Farm
Motte
New House Farm
Lodge Farm
Starch Field Covert
Pound Farm
Great Heath
Leysters Farm
Woonton Court
Woonton Court Farm
Woonton
Cornford Brake

92
74

73
55

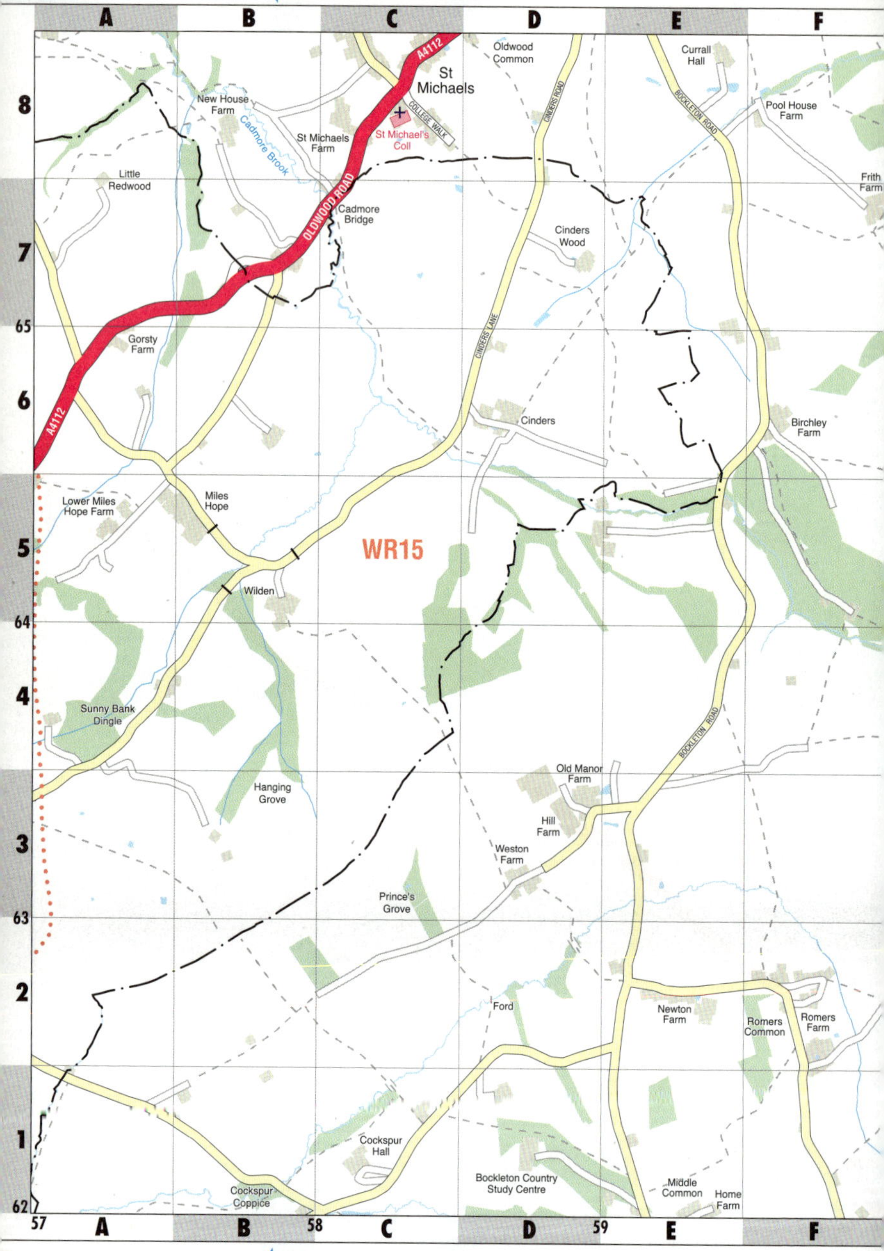
A
B
C
D
E
F
8
7
65
6
5
64
4
3
63
2
1
62
57
58
59
A4112
St Michaels
Oldwood Common
Currall Hall
New House Farm
Cadmore Brook
St Michaels Farm
COLLEGE WALK
St Michael's Coll
CINDERS ROAD
BOCKLETON ROAD
Pool House Farm
Little Redwood
Frith Farm
OLDWOOD ROAD
Cadmore Bridge
Cinders Wood
Gorsty Farm
CINDERS LANE
Cinders
Birchley Farm
Lower Miles Hope Farm
Miles Hope
WR15
Wilden
Sunny Bank Dingle
Old Manor Farm
Hanging Grove
Hill Farm
Weston Farm
Prince's Grove
Ford
Newton Farm
Romers Common
Romers Farm
Cockspur Hall
Bockleton Country Study Centre
Middle Common
Home Farm
Cockspur Coppice

73
93

56
76

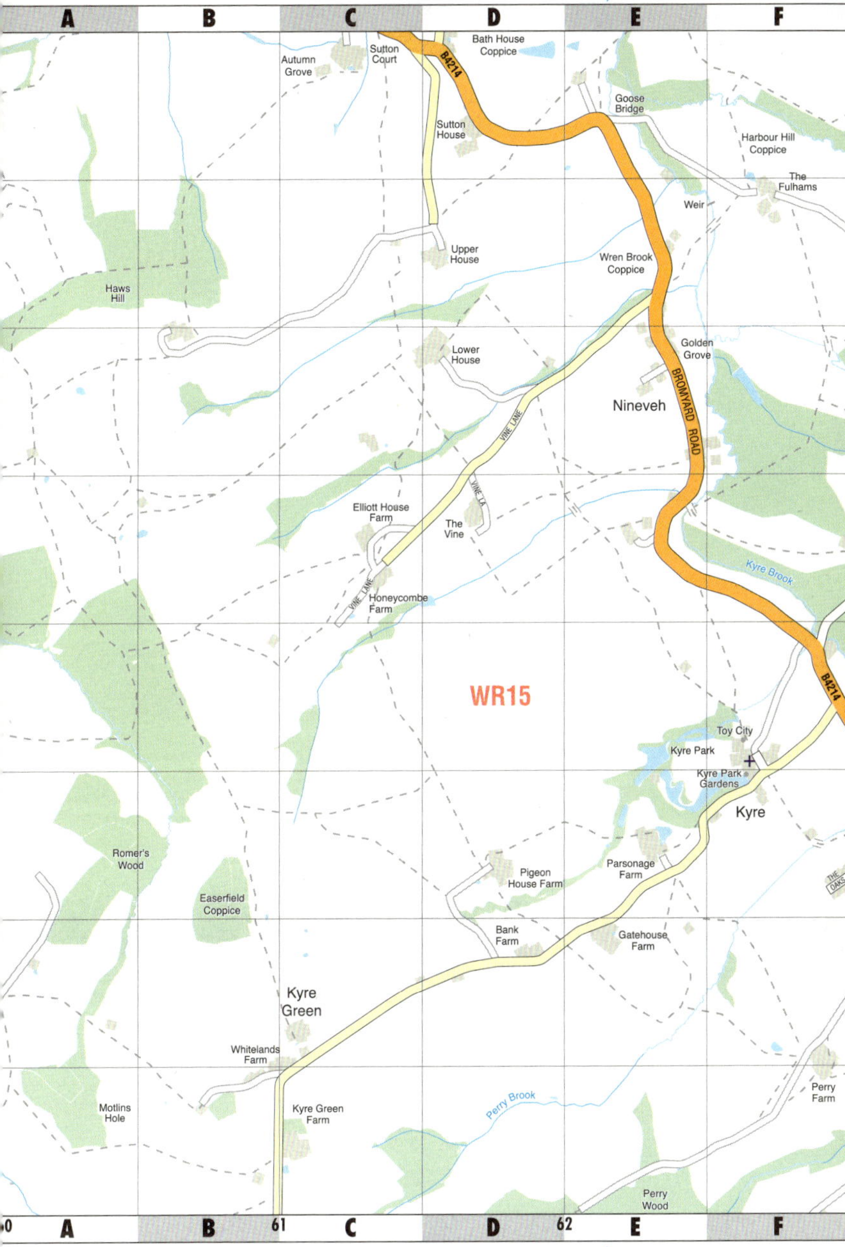

A
B
C
D
E
F
8
7
65
6
5
64
4
3
63
2
1
62
61
62
Bath House Coppice
Autumn Grove
Sutton Court
B4214
Goose Bridge
Harbour Hill Coppice
Sutton House
The Fulhams
Weir
Upper House
Wren Brook Coppice
Haws Hill
Golden Grove
Lower House
Nineveh
BROMYARD ROAD
VINE LANE
VINE LA
Elliott House Farm
The Vine
Kyre Brook
Honeycombe Farm
WR15
Toy City
Kyre Park
Kyre Park Gardens
Kyre
Romer's Wood
Pigeon House Farm
Parsonage Farm
THE OAKS
Easerfield Coppice
Bank Farm
Gatehouse Farm
Kyre Green
Whitelands Farm
Perry Farm
Motlins Hole
Kyre Green Farm
Perry Brook
Perry Wood

94
76

75
57

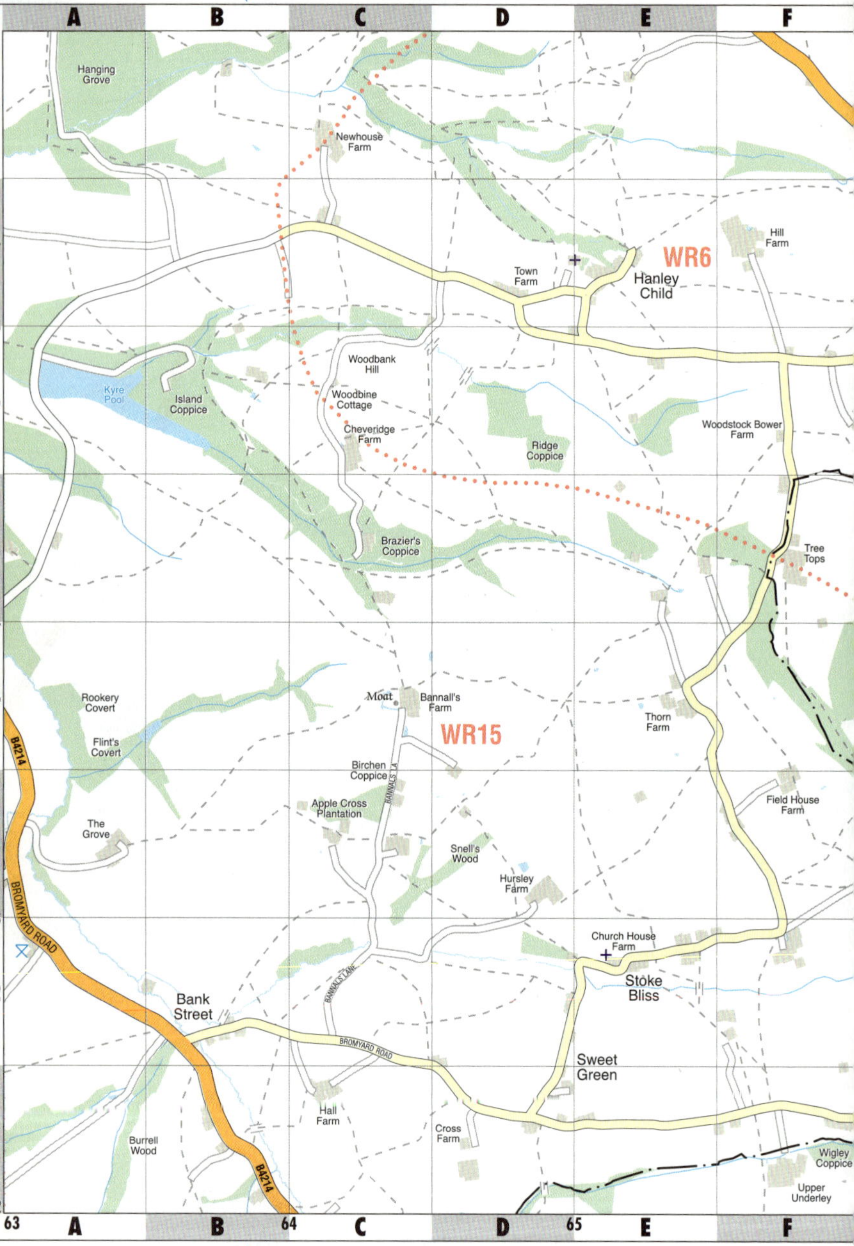
A
B
C
D
E
F
8
7
65
6
5
64
4
3
63
2
1
62
63
64
65
Hanging Grove
Newhouse Farm
WR6
Hill Farm
Town Farm
Hanley Child
Kyre Pool
Island Coppice
Woodbank Hill
Woodbine Cottage
Cheveridge Farm
Ridge Coppice
Woodstock Bower Farm
Brazier's Coppice
Tree Tops
Rookery Covert
Moat
Bannall's Farm
WR15
Flint's Covert
Thorn Farm
B4214
Birchen Coppice
BANNALS LA
Apple Cross Plantation
Field House Farm
The Grove
Snell's Wood
Hursley Farm
BROMYARD ROAD
Church House Farm
Stoke Bliss
Bank Street
BANNALS LANE
BROMYARD ROAD
Sweet Green
Hall Farm
Cross Farm
Burrell Wood
B4214
Wigley Coppice
Upper Underley

75
95

A B C D E F
Hanley William
Church Farm
The Broach Farm
NEW ROAD
Belt Plantation
Broomy Fields Farm
Dovetree Farm
8
B4204
Water Tower
Holly Farm
BELL LANE
Ash Grove
Lodge Farm
7
High House Farm
PH
Adamswood Farm
Broad Heath
KINTHALL LANE
POUK LANE
65
Pouk Lane Coppice
6
Kinthall Farm
WR6
B4204
Dudshill Court
High House
Lea Farm
5
Park Farm
Whistlewood Farm
Lea Green
64
Wolferlow Park
B4203
4
Horse Pasture Plantation
Stoke Hill
CHURCH CL
CHURCH LANE
PO
Brook Farm
ORCHARD GD
Upper Sapey
PH
Stoke Hill
3
Upper House Farm
Tippens Farm
Poswick Farm
63
WR15
Sapey Golf Course
Weir
CH
2
South Batch Farm
Heath Farm
1
HR7
B4203
Heath End
62
66 A B 67 C D 68 E F

77
59

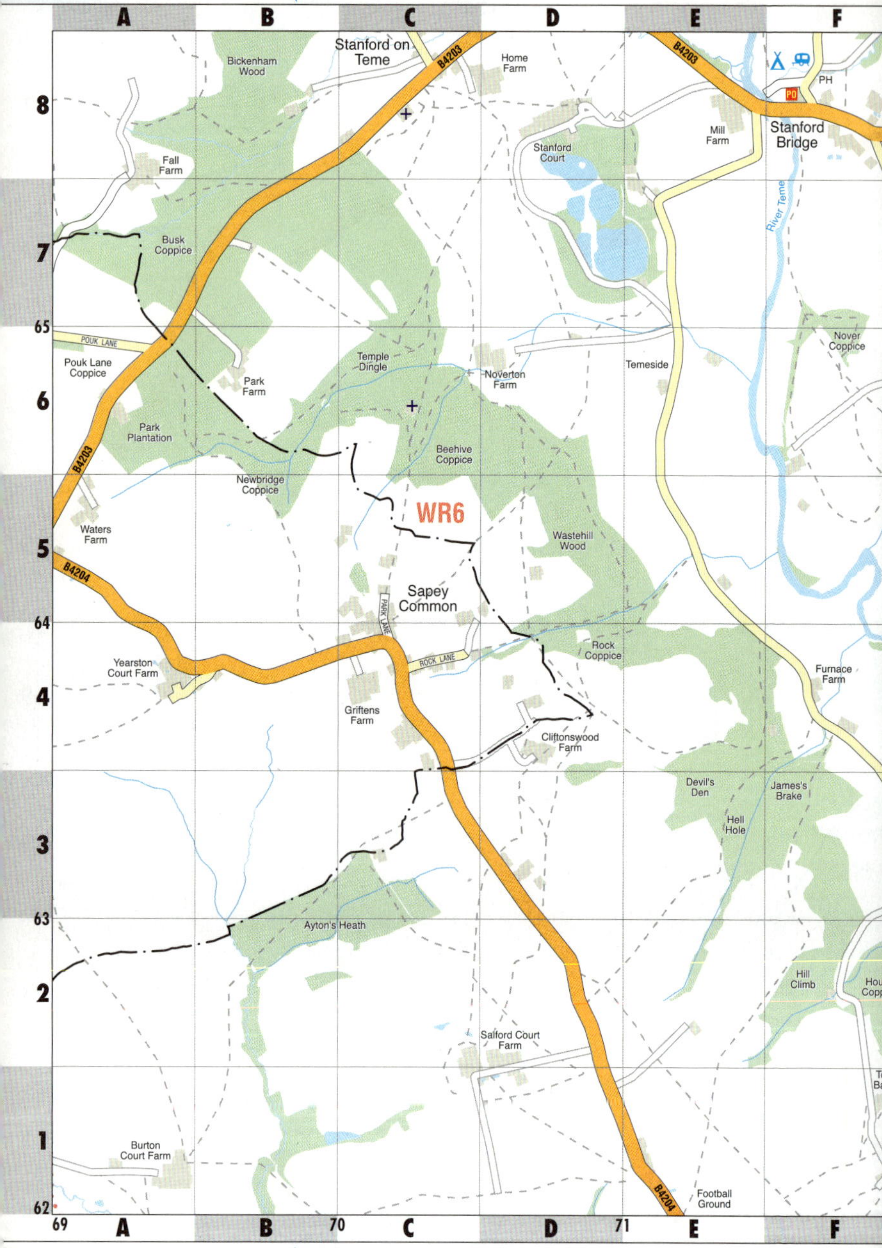
A
B
C
D
E
F
8
7
65
6
5
64
4
3
63
2
1
62
69
70
71
Stanford on Teme
Bickenham Wood
B4203
Home Farm
PH
PO
Mill Farm
Stanford Bridge
Stanford Court
Fall Farm
River Teme
Busk Coppice
POUK LANE
Pouk Lane Coppice
Temple Dingle
Noverton Farm
Temeside
Nover Coppice
Park Farm
Park Plantation
Beehive Coppice
Newbridge Coppice
WR6
Waters Farm
Wastehill Wood
B4204
Sapey Common
PARK LANE
ROCK LANE
Rock Coppice
Yearston Court Farm
Griftens Farm
Furnace Farm
Cliftonswood Farm
Devil's Den
James's Brake
Hell Hole
Ayton's Heath
Hill Climb
Salford Court Farm
Burton Court Farm
Football Ground

77
97

60
80

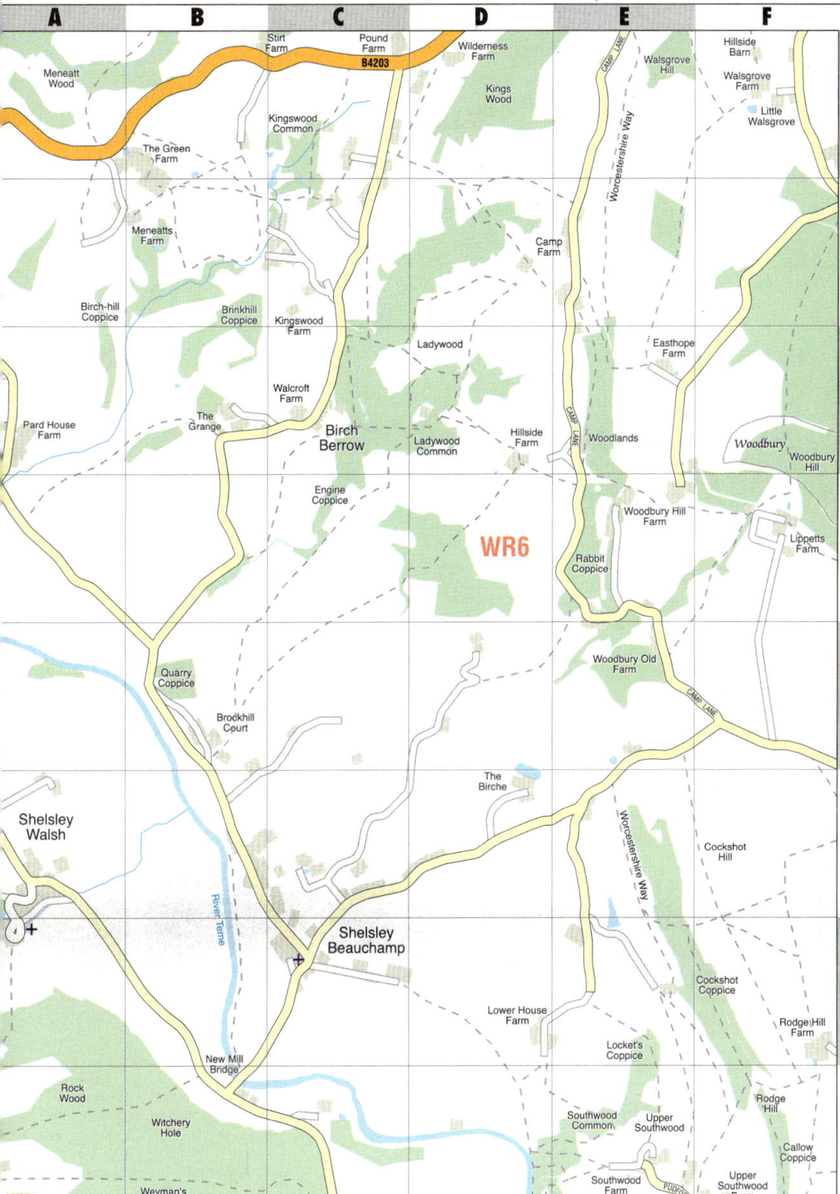
A
B
C
D
E
F
8
7
65
6
5
64
4
3
63
2
1
62
73
74
Meneatt Wood
Stirt Farm
Pound Farm
B4203
Wilderness Farm
Kings Wood
Walsgrove Hill
Hillside Barn
Walsgrove Farm
Little Walsgrove
Kingswood Common
The Green Farm
Meneatts Farm
Camp Farm
Worcestershire Way
CAMP LANE
Birch-hill Coppice
Brinkhill Coppice
Kingswood Farm
Ladywood
Easthope Farm
Walcroft Farm
Pard House Farm
The Grange
Birch Berrow
Ladywood Common
Hillside Farm
Woodlands
Woodbury
Woodbury Hill
Engine Coppice
Woodbury Hill Farm
Lippetts Farm
WR6
Rabbit Coppice
Woodbury Old Farm
Quarry Coppice
Brockhill Court
The Birche
Shelsley Walsh
Cockshot Hill
River Teme
Shelsley Beauchamp
Cockshot Coppice
Lower House Farm
Rodge Hill Farm
Locket's Coppice
New Mill Bridge
Rock Wood
Witchery Hole
Southwood Common
Upper Southwood
Rodge Hill
Callow Coppice
Weyman's Wood
Southwood Farm
PUDFORD LANE
Upper Southwood Farm

98
80

A
B
C
D
E
F
8
7
65
6
5
64
4
3
63
2
1
62
75
76
77
Great Witley
THE GLEBE
Great Witley CE Prim Sch
P
WORCESTER ROAD
A443
B4197
MARTLEY ROAD
Perhill Coppice
The Plantations
Lodge Plantation
Meadow Farm
Heath Farm
Structon's Heath
Hillhampton Farm
Moat
Home Farm
Hundred Pool
Weir
Front Pool
Witley Court
New Wood
Lodge Pool
Woodbury Hill
Woodbury
Washing Pool
Warford Pool
Deer Barn Farm
WR6
Deerbarn Covert
Wallhouse Plantation
Park Farm
Woodbury Farm
Fetterlocks Farm
Applewood Barn
Bank Farm
BANK ROAD
Prickley Farm
Dundridge Coppice
Hockham's Farm
HOCKHAM'S LANE
Birches Coppice
Laughern Brook
Brookfield Coppice
Quarry (dis)
Uckeridge
Birchend Farm
Witton Hill
Pughs Rough Farm
Lower Farm

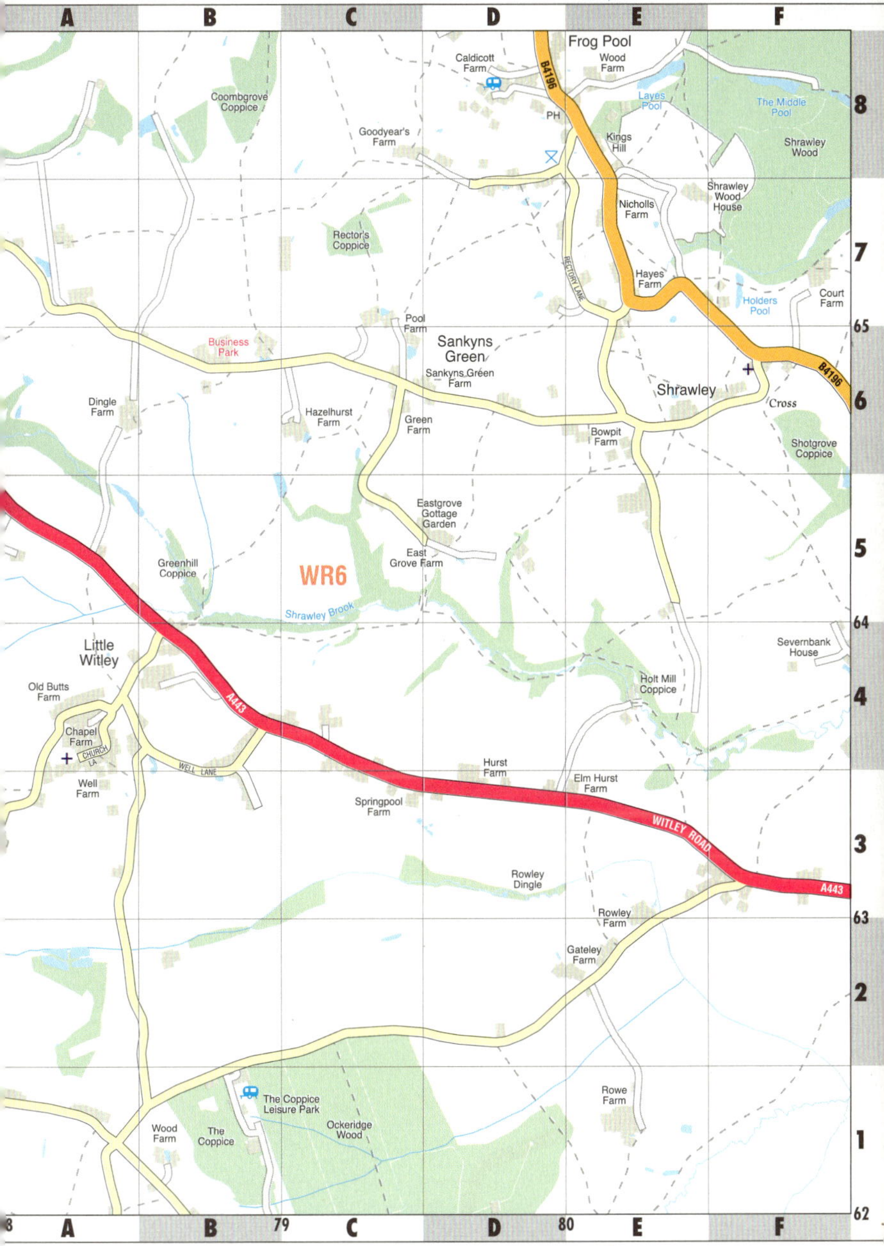
A
B
C
D
E
F
Frog Pool
Caldicott Farm
Wood Farm
B4196
Coombgrove Coppice
Layes Pool
The Middle Pool
PH
Goodyear's Farm
Kings Hill
Shrawley Wood
Shrawley Wood House
Nicholls Farm
Rector's Coppice
RECTORY LANE
Hayes Farm
Holders Pool
Court Farm
Pool Farm
Sankyns Green
Business Park
Sankyns Green Farm
Shrawley
B4196
Cross
Dingle Farm
Hazelhurst Farm
Green Farm
Bowpit Farm
Shotgrove Coppice
Eastgrove Cottage Garden
East Grove Farm
Greenhill Coppice
WR6
Shrawley Brook
Little Witley
Severnbank House
Old Butts Farm
Holt Mill Coppice
A443
Chapel Farm
CHURCH LA
WELL LANE
Well Farm
Hurst Farm
Elm Hurst Farm
Springpool Farm
WITLEY ROAD
A443
Rowley Dingle
Rowley Farm
Gateley Farm
The Coppice Leisure Park
Ockeridge Wood
Rowe Farm
Wood Farm
The Coppice
8
7
65
6
5
64
4
3
63
2
1
62
8
79
80

81
63
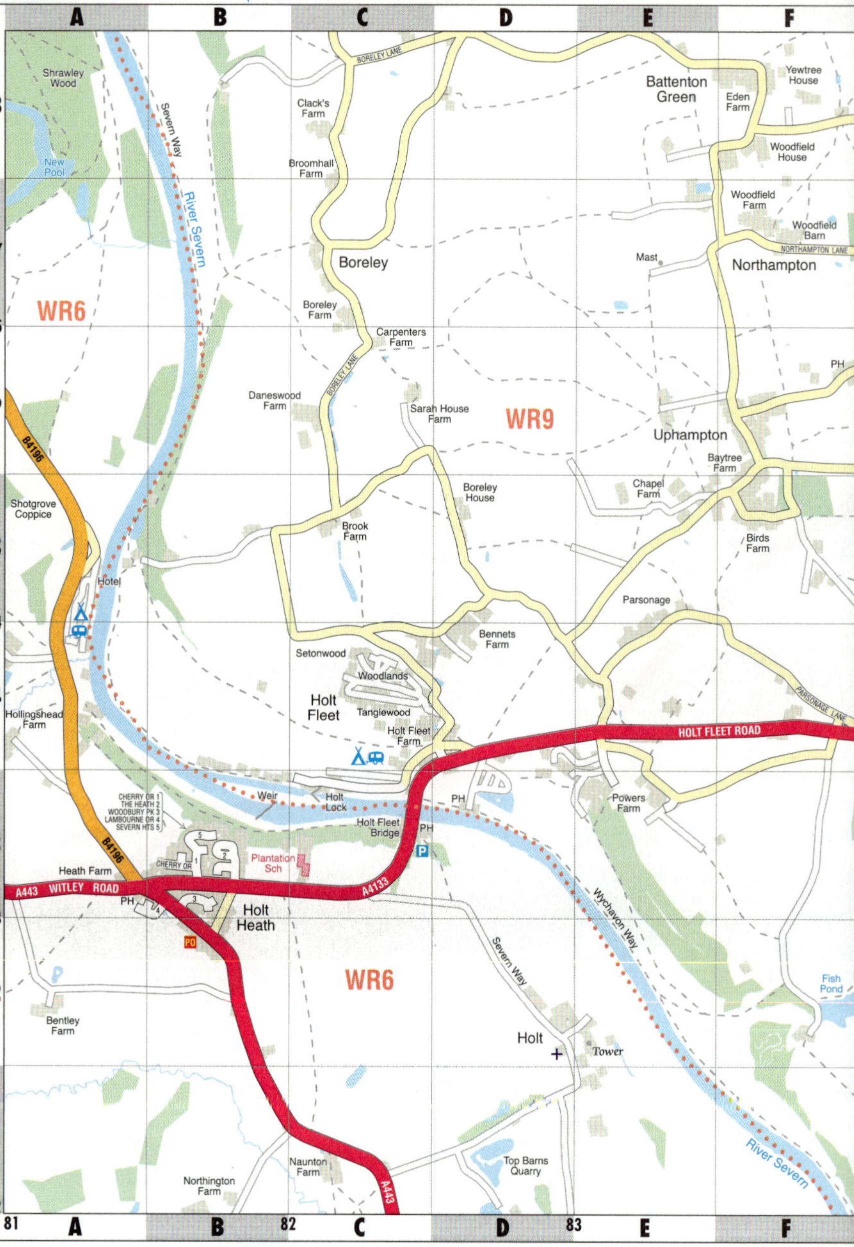
A
B
C
D
E
F
8
7
65
6
5
64
4
3
63
2
1
62
81
82
83
Shrawley Wood
New Pool
Severn Way
River Severn
WR6
Clack's Farm
Broomhall Farm
BORELEY LANE
Boreley
Boreley Farm
Carpenters Farm
Battenton Green
Eden Farm
Yewtree House
Woodfield House
Woodfield Farm
Woodfield Barn
NORTHAMPTON LANE
Mast
Northampton
PH
Daneswood Farm
Sarah House Farm
WR9
Uphampton
Baytree Farm
Chapel Farm
Boreley House
Brook Farm
Birds Farm
Parsonage
B4196
Shotgrove Coppice
Hotel
Bennets Farm
Setonwood
Woodlands
Holt Fleet
Tanglewood
Holt Fleet Farm
HOLT FLEET ROAD
PARSONAGE LANE
Hollingshead Farm
Weir
Holt Lock
Holt Fleet Bridge
PH
Powers Farm
CHERRY DR 1
THE HEATH 2
WOODBURY PK 3
LAMBOURNE DR 4
SEVERN HTS 5
CHERRY DR
Plantation Sch
Heath Farm
A443 WITLEY ROAD
A4133
PH
Holt Heath
PO
WR6
Severn Way
Wychavon Way
Fish Pond
Bentley Farm
Holt
Tower
Naunton Farm
Northington Farm
Top Barns Quarry
A443
River Severn
81
101

64
84

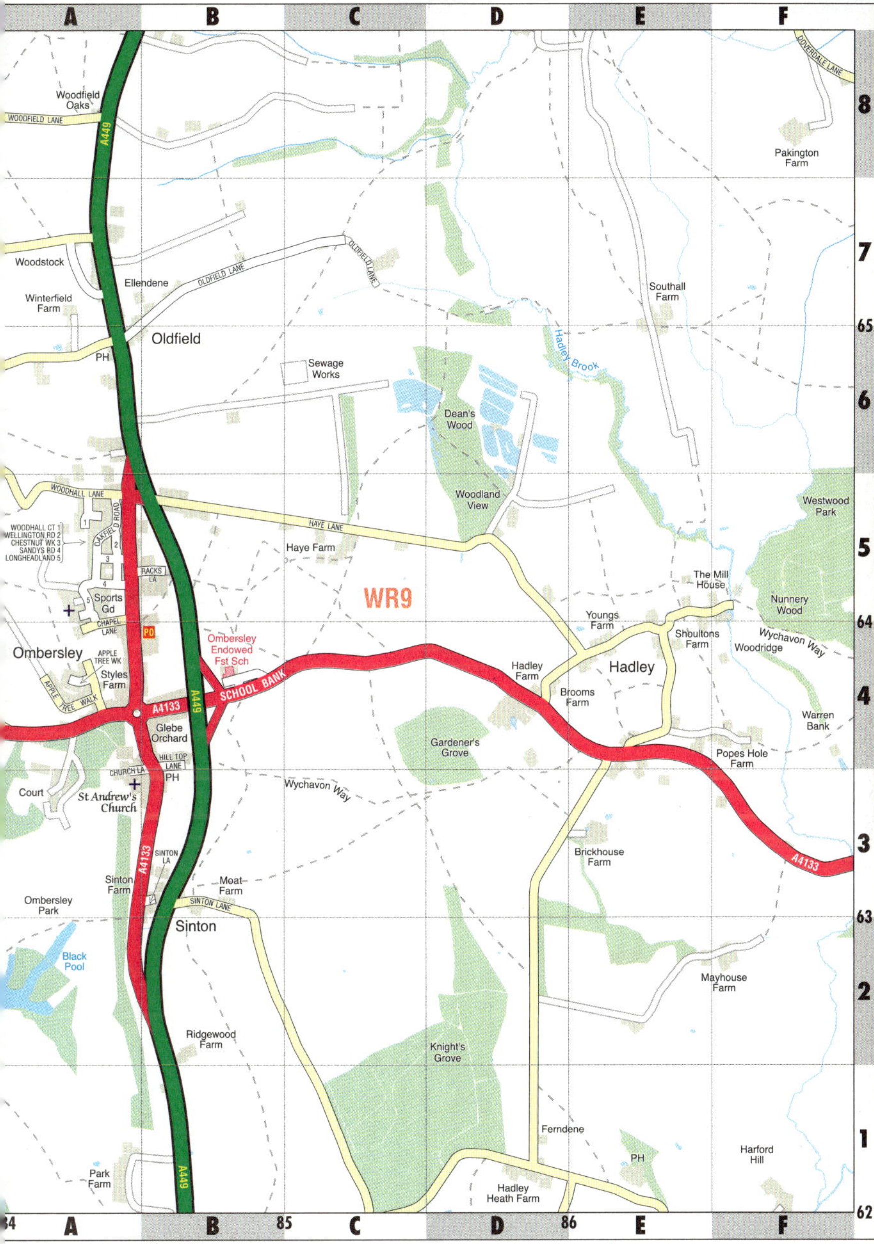
A
B
C
D
E
F
8
7
65
6
5
64
4
3
63
2
1
62
84
85
86
Woodfield Oaks
WOODFIELD LANE
A449
Woodstock
Winterfield Farm
Ellendene
OLDFIELD LANE
OLDFIELD LANE
Oldfield
PH
Sewage Works
Pakington Farm
DOVERDALE LANE
Southall Farm
Hadley Brook
Dean's Wood
Woodland View
WOODHALL LANE
OAKFIELD ROAD
HAYE LANE
Haye Farm
WOODHALL CT 1
WELLINGTON RD 2
CHESTNUT WK 3
SANDYS RD 4
LONGHEADLAND 5
RACKS LA
Sports Gd
CHAPEL LANE
PO
WR9
Westwood Park
The Mill House
Nunnery Wood
Youngs Farm
Shoultons Farm
Wychavon Way
Woodridge
Ombersley
APPLE TREE WK
Styles Farm
APPLE TREE WALK
Ombersley Endowed Fst Sch
SCHOOL BANK
A4133
Hadley Farm
Hadley
Brooms Farm
Warren Bank
Glebe Orchard
Gardener's Grove
Popes Hole Farm
HILL TOP LANE
CHURCH LA
PH
Court
St Andrew's Church
Wychavon Way
Brickhouse Farm
A4133
SINTON LA
Sinton Farm
Moat Farm
SINTON LANE
Ombersley Park
Sinton
Black Pool
Mayhouse Farm
Ridgewood Farm
Knight's Grove
Ferndene
PH
Harford Hill
Park Farm
Hadley Heath Farm

102
84

83
65

D5
1 PLOUGHMANS WY
2 DROVERS WY
3 DROVERS PL
4 SHEPHERDS HL
5 SHEPHERDS CL
6 FARMERS CT

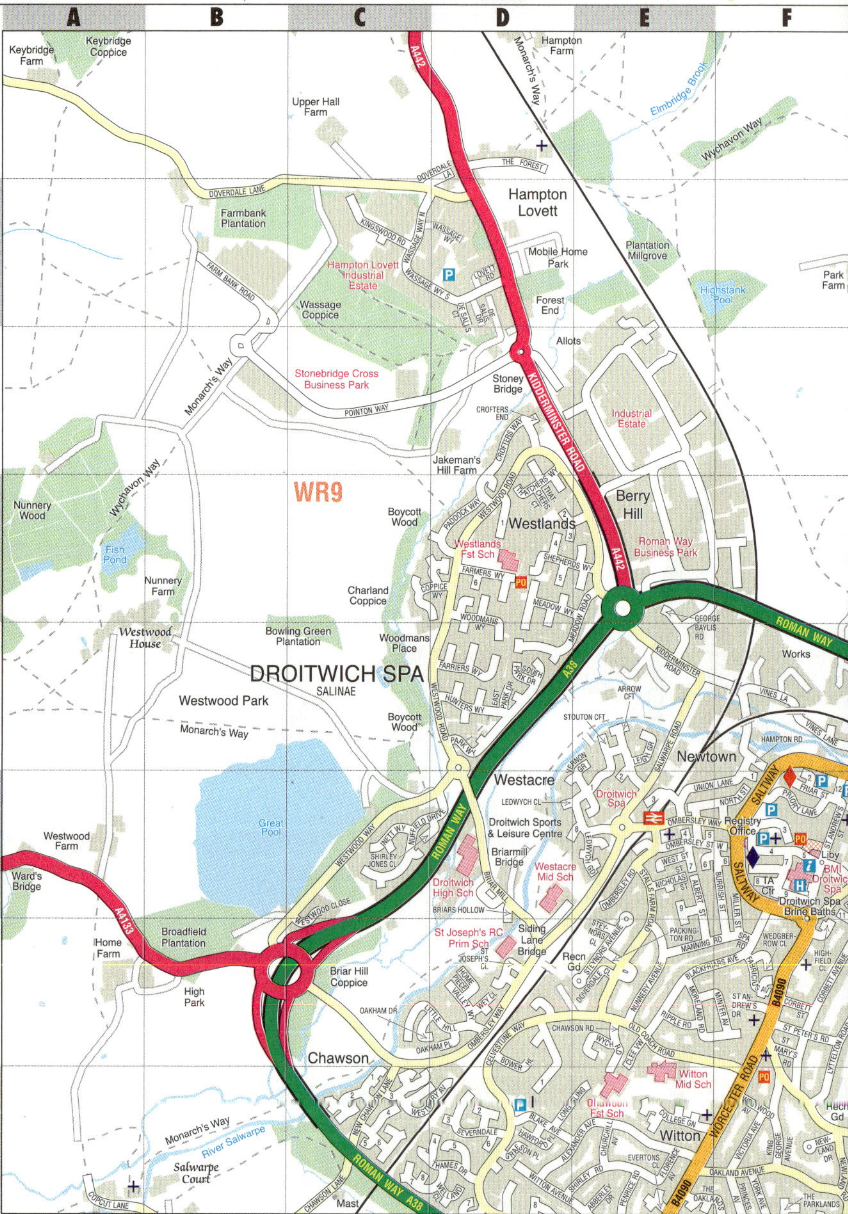

83
103

C1
1 ALDERBROOK RD
2 OAKLEIGH RD
3 COLFORD CL
4 OLD CHAWSON LA
5 BRECON CL
6 BARNS CFT WY
7 WHARFEDALE CR
8 DERWENT GR

D1
1 PADGEWELL HL
2 WENSLEYDALE
3 GLENDALE
4 TEESDALE CL
5 WAVENEY RD
6 AVONDALE
7 TEME CR
8 CALDER CL

E3
1 LEDWYCH RD
2 DOWLES CFT
3 ACRE LA
4 STATION ST
5 WESTCROFT ST
6 HARRIS CL
7 ALBERT ST
8 ARCHERS CL
9 ST RICHARD'S GD

F3
1 PRIORY GD
2 CHORLEY RD
3 COVERCROFT
4 OMBERSLEY ST E
5 VICTORIA SQ
6 BOURNE CL
7 HERITAGE WY
8 ST ANDREW'S CL
9 ST ANDREWS RD
10 SEVERN CT
11 COBHAM CT
12 RICKETT'S LA

66
86

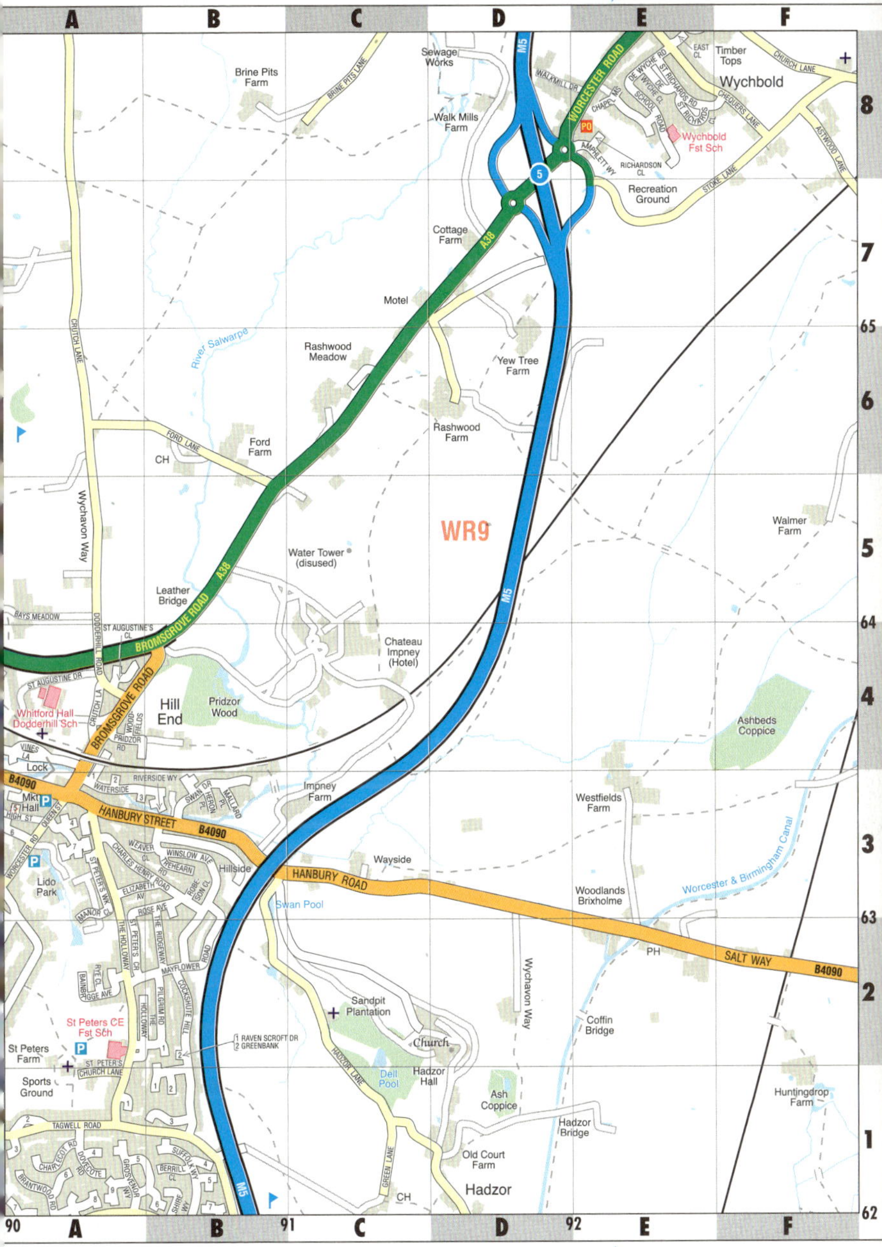

A1
1 THE ORCHARD LEA
2 TAGWELL RD
3 ADRIAN CL
4 LANGLEY RD
5 GROSVENOR CR
6 BRANTWOOD CL
7 HENLEY DR
8 CLAYHALL RD
9 HAMMOND CL

A3
1 WOODFIELD RD
2 WATERSIDE CL
3 RIVERSIDE RD
4 ST GEORGE'S CR
5 GURNEYS LA
6 TOWER HL
7 HERIOTTS CT

B1
1 PORTLAND RD
2 CHERRY CL
3 PRIMSLAND DR
4 LEYCROFT
5 MARHON CL
6 GROSVENOR CL
7 PERCHERON WY

104
86

85
67

A
B
C
D
E
F
8
7
65
6
5
64
4
3
63
2
1
62
93
94
95
SAGEBURY DR
PH
ASTWOOD CL
New Elms Farm
WESTONHALL ROAD
B4091
MOORGATE ROAD
Harbours Hill
Redhouse Farm
Astwood Bridge
Auchmillan Farm
SHAW LANE
Pipers Hill Farm
Causeway Meadows Farm
PH
ASTWOOD LANE
Sharpway Gate Farm
SHARPWAY GATE
PH
The Firs
Astwood Court Farm
Poplars Farm
Locks
Hillfields Farm
Sharpway Gate
ASTWOOD LANE
Astwood
Astwood Manor Farm
Farthings Green
P
Old Astwood Farm
Lock
Knotts Farm
Astwood Lane Bridge
Astwood Newhouse Farm
Webbhouse Farm
Rectory Farm
B60
Lock
Goodwins Hill Coppice
Church Coppice
Ridge End
Worcester & Birmingham Canal
Cross
Old Bell Farm
Brick Kiln Pool
Hanbury CE Fst Sch
Hanbury Park
Summerhill Wood
Hanbury Hall (NT)
P
Beck's Farm
Summerhill Farm
The Moorlands
Summer Hill
Belt Covert
Whitehouse Farm
PUMPHOUSE LANE
Lady Wood
Pumphouse Farm
WR9
SCHOOL ROAD
The Hareings
Gallows Green
B4090
Howning's Farm
SALT WAY
SALT WAY
GOOSEHILL LANE
Mere Green Farm
B4090
Sewage Works
Mere Green

68
88

A
B
C
D
E
F
8
7
65
6
5
64
4
3
63
2
1
62
96
97
98
Bentley Common
Vicarage Farm
Lower Bentley
The Thrift
Keys Farm
WOODGATE ROAD
HIGH ELMS LANE
Commonbarn Farm
High Elms Farm
HOLMES LANE
Pipers Hill Farm
Piper's Hill
FOSTERS GREEN
Foster's Green
Holmes Farm
Ash Plantation
Tyrells Lane Farm
HILL LANE
Forest Hill
B60
Forest Farm
HANBURY ROAD
Valley Farm
FOREST LANE
Crossways Farm
WALLHOUSE LANE
The Mount
Ditchford Bank
SCHOOL ROAD
Deerpen Thorns
Brickley Brake
Jinney Ring Craft Centre
Resr
Orchardside
Ditchford Bank Farm
Woodrow Farm
Hanbury
Recreation Ground
Great Lodge Farm
Badgers Brake
Oxpasture Bank
Carter's Hill
B4091
COURTS CL
Woolmere Green
PH
BERROWHILL LA
SALT WAY
Seeley Brook
Kinswood Rozell
Cottage Monkwood
B96
Middle Hill
Monkwood Farm
WR9
Red House Farm
Cart House Farm
Park Farm
Skirgens Farm
B4090
Fishpool Hill

106
88

87
69

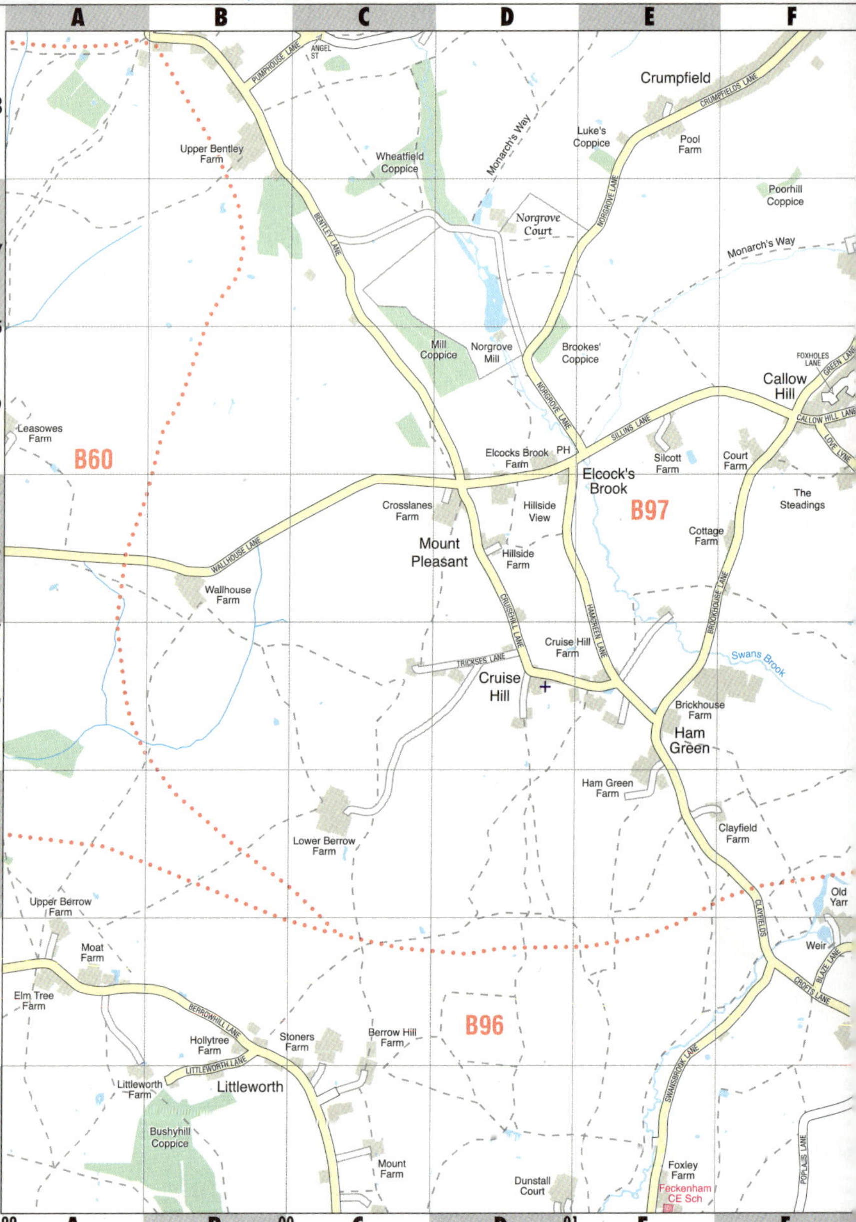
A
B
C
D
E
F
8
7
65
6
5
64
4
3
63
2
1
62
99
00
01
PUMPHOUSE LANE
ANGEL ST
Crumpfield
CRUMPFIELDS LANE
Luke's Coppice
Pool Farm
Upper Bentley Farm
Wheatfield Coppice
Monarch's Way
NORGROVE LANE
Poorhill Coppice
Norgrove Court
BENTLEY LANE
Monarch's Way
Mill Coppice
Norgrove Mill
Brookes' Coppice
FOXHOLES LANE
GREEN LANE
Callow Hill
Leasowes Farm
NORGROVE LANE
SILLINS LANE
CALLOW HILL LANE
LOVE LYNE
B60
Elcocks Brook Farm
PH
Silcott Farm
Court Farm
Elcock's Brook
The Steadings
Crosslanes Farm
Hillside View
B97
Mount Pleasant
Hillside Farm
Cottage Farm
WALLHOUSE LANE
Wallhouse Farm
CRUISEHILL LANE
HAMGREEN LANE
BROOKHOUSE LANE
Cruise Hill Farm
Swans Brook
TRICKSES LANE
Cruise Hill
Brickhouse Farm
Ham Green
Ham Green Farm
Lower Berrow Farm
Clayfield Farm
Old Yarr
Upper Berrow Farm
CLAYFIELDS
Weir
Moat Farm
BLAZE LANE
CROFTS LANE
Elm Tree Farm
BERROWHILL LANE
Hollytree Farm
Stoners Farm
Berrow Hill Farm
B96
LITTLEWORTH LANE
Littleworth Farm
Littleworth
SWANSBROOK LANE
Bushyhill Coppice
POPLARS LANE
Mount Farm
Dunstall Court
Foxley Farm
Feckenham CE Sch

87
107

70
90

A
B
C
D
E
F
REDDITCH
Headless Cross
Oakenshaw
Crabbs Cross
Walkwood
Callow Hill
Hunt End
Weavers Hill
Dagtail End
Eastern Hill
Astwood Bank
Downsell Wood
Morton Stanley Park
Walkwood Coppice
Oakenshaw Wood
Superstore
Mid Sch
The Vaynor Fst Sch
The Harry Taylor Fst Sch
St Augustine's RC High Sch
Astwood Bank Fst Sch
Ridgeway Trad Est
Stonepits Copse
New Coppice
Slough Farm
The Moors
Lanehouse Farm
Lovelyne Farm
Chapel House Farm
Upper Huntend Farm
Astwood Hill Farm
The Wren's Nest Farm
Yew Tree House
Hole Farm
Astwood Court
Sewage Works
Doebank House
Eastern Hill Farm
Sambourne Lane Farm
Foxpits
Thickwithey Brook
Wixon Brook
Monarch's Way
ALCESTER HIGHWAY
BROMSGROVE HIGHWAY
WARWICK HIGHWAY
EVESHAM RD
ROUGH HILL DR
THE SLOUGH
WINDMILL DR
B4504
B97
B98
B96
A441
A448
A4189
B4092
FECKENHAM RD
DAGTAIL LA
ASTWOOD LA
CROFTS LA
DARK LA
SAMBOURNE LA
JILL LA
BLAZE LA
LOVE LYNE
WALKWOOD RD
1 EASTWOOD CT
2 DEWSBURY CL
3 POST OFFICE WLK
4 NEW RD
BROOKHAMPTON CL 1
ALDERMINSTER CL 2
8
7
65
6
5
64
4
3
63
2
1
62
03
04

108
90

89
71

A
B
C
D
E
F
8
7
65
6
5
64
4
3
63
2
1
62
05
06
07
Greenlands
The Io Ctr
Park Farm
Arrow Valley Park
Dingleside Mid Sch
Old Forge Bsns Ctr
Washford Ind Est
The Old Forge
Ipsley Brook
Park Farm Ind Est
Washford
Woodrow
Woodrow Fst Sch
B98
Red Hill
BIRMINGHAM RD
ICKNIELD STREET DR
B4497
B4093
STUDLEY RD
Hill Crest
L Ctr
Kingsley Coll
Washford Farm
River Arrow
Green Lane
The Alexandra
Tanhouse Farm
Poplars Trad Est
Washford Bridge
Wirehill Wood
Wirehill
Green Lane Farm
REDDITCH RD
Priory Farm and remains of Priory
Rough Hill Wood
Wapping
B97
Studley Common
Renshaw Ind Est
Studley Bridge
A448
THE SLOUGH
HIGH ST
B4092
Works
STATION RD
St Mary's RC Prim Sch
B80
Studley
Studley High Sch
Thomas Town
Studley St Mary's CE Jun Sch
The Park
Troy Ind Est
ALCESTER RD
A435
JILL LA
BROMSGROVE RD
Littlewood Green
PH
Littlewood Green Farm
Spinney Cottage
B96
Reins Farm
Holt Farm
Sambourne Reins
Middletown
Elmdale House
Perrymill Farm
Sperndal Ash
Sambourne
Haydon Way Farm

72

A
B
C
D
E
F
8
7
65
6
5
64
4
3
63
2
1
62
09
10
Clarke's Green
Summerhouse Hill
Morton Bagot Manor
MANOR DR
Hardwick House
HARDWICK LA
Field Farm
Castle Farm
Arden Way
Mars Hill
B80
Warwickshire STREET ATLAS
CASTLE RD
Cemy
Netherstead
Morton Common Farm
Priory Earthworks
River Arrow
Arden Way
St Giles Farm
Spernall Park
B49
Works
Round Hill
BURFORD LA
SPERNAL LA
Spernall
49
Warwickshire STREET ATLAS

73

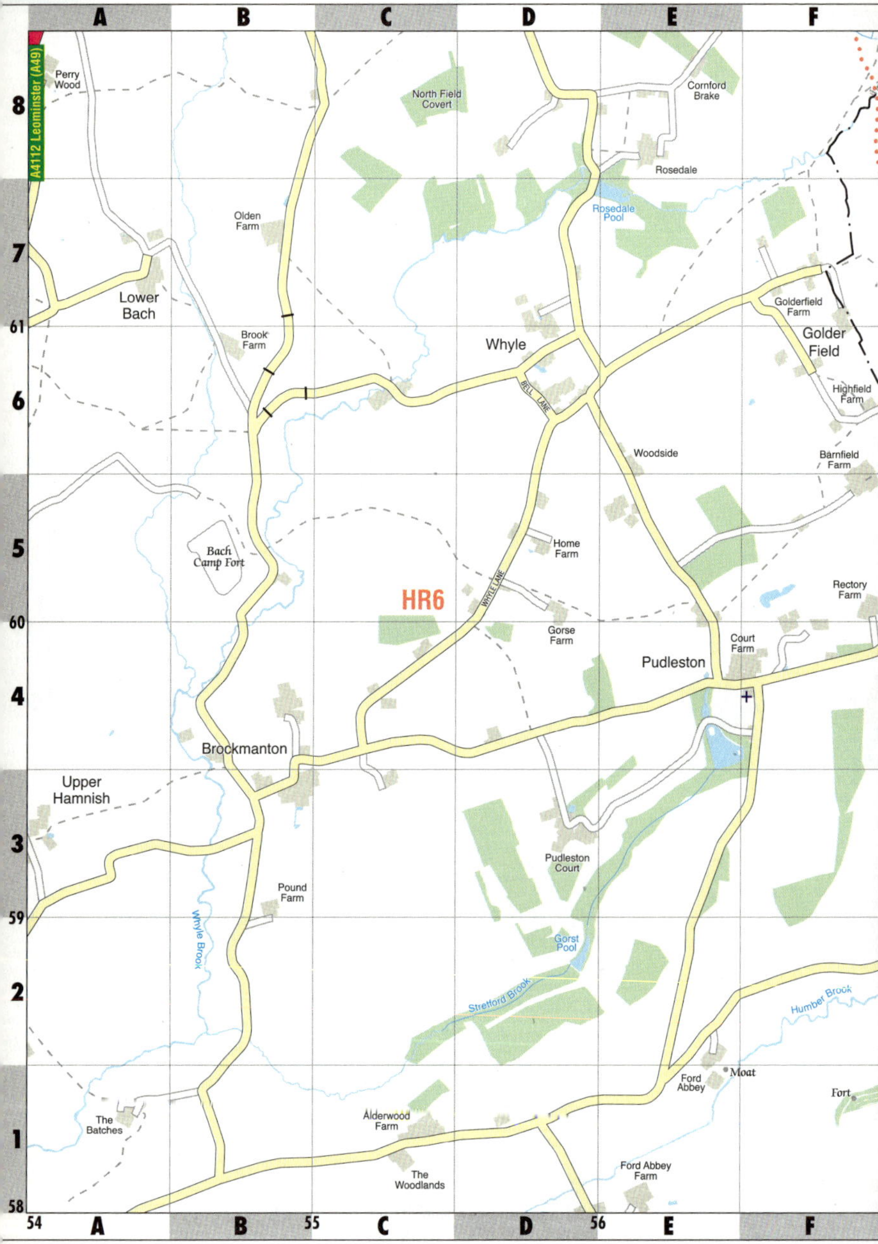
A
B
C
D
E
F
8
7
61
6
5
60
4
3
59
2
1
58
54
55
56
A4112 Leominster (A49)
Perry Wood
North Field Covert
Cornford Brake
Rosedale
Rosedale Pool
Olden Farm
Lower Bach
Brook Farm
Whyle
Bell Lane
Golderfield Farm
Golder Field
Highfield Farm
Woodside
Barnfield Farm
Bach Camp Fort
Home Farm
HR6
Whyle Lane
Rectory Farm
Gorse Farm
Court Farm
Pudleston
Brockmanton
Upper Hamnish
Pudleston Court
Pound Farm
Whyle Brook
Gorst Pool
Stretford Brook
Humber Brook
Moat
Ford Abbey
Fort
The Batches
Alderwood Farm
The Woodlands
Ford Abbey Farm

74
94

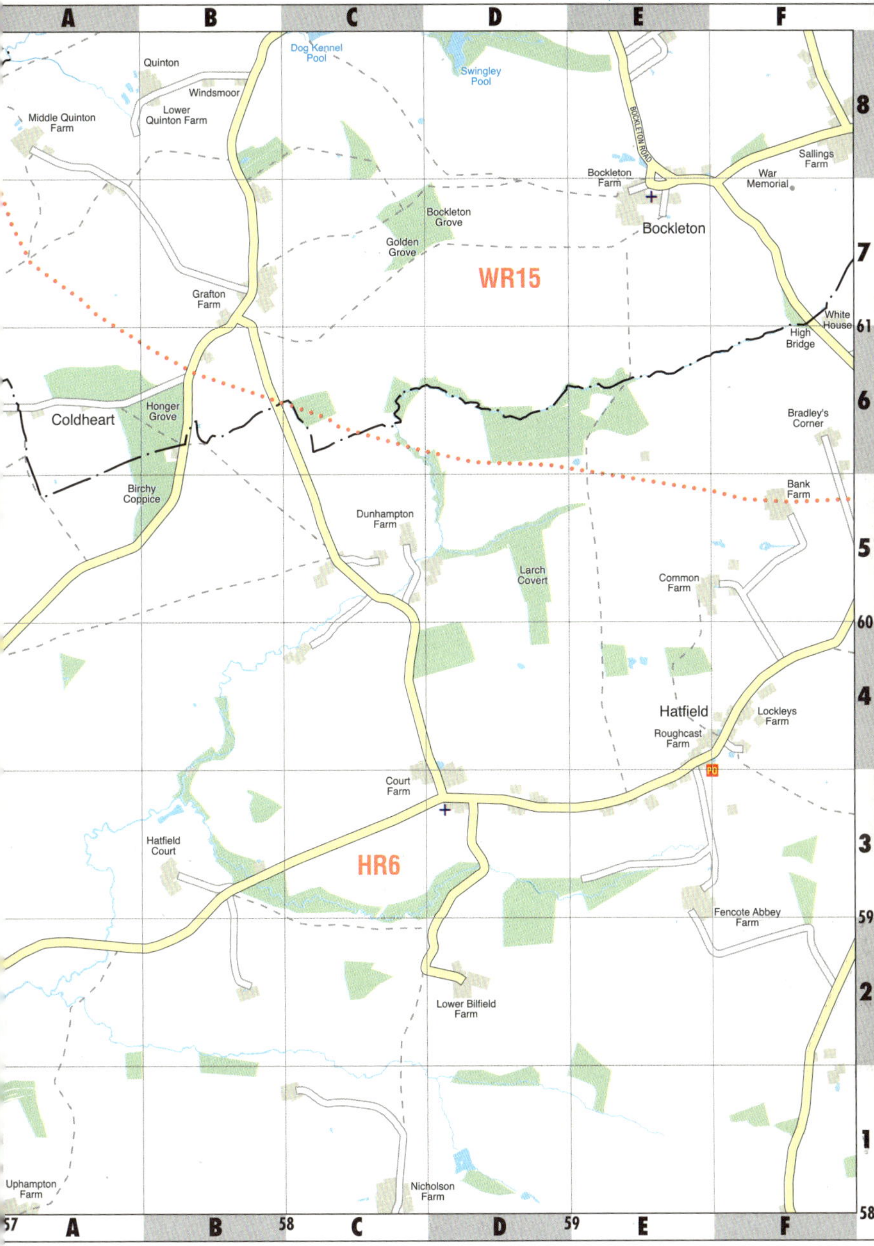

Quinton
Windsmoor
Lower Quinton Farm
Middle Quinton Farm
Dog Kennel Pool
Swingley Pool
BOCKLETON ROAD
Bockleton Farm
Bockleton
Sallings Farm
War Memorial
Bockleton Grove
Golden Grove
WR15
Grafton Farm
White House
High Bridge
Coldheart
Honger Grove
Bradley's Corner
Birchy Coppice
Bank Farm
Dunhampton Farm
Larch Covert
Common Farm
Hatfield
Lockleys Farm
Roughcast Farm
Court Farm
Hatfield Court
HR6
Fencote Abbey Farm
Lower Bilfield Farm
Uphampton Farm
Nicholson Farm
A
B
C
D
E
F
8
7
61
6
5
60
4
3
59
2
1
58
57
58
59

94

93
75

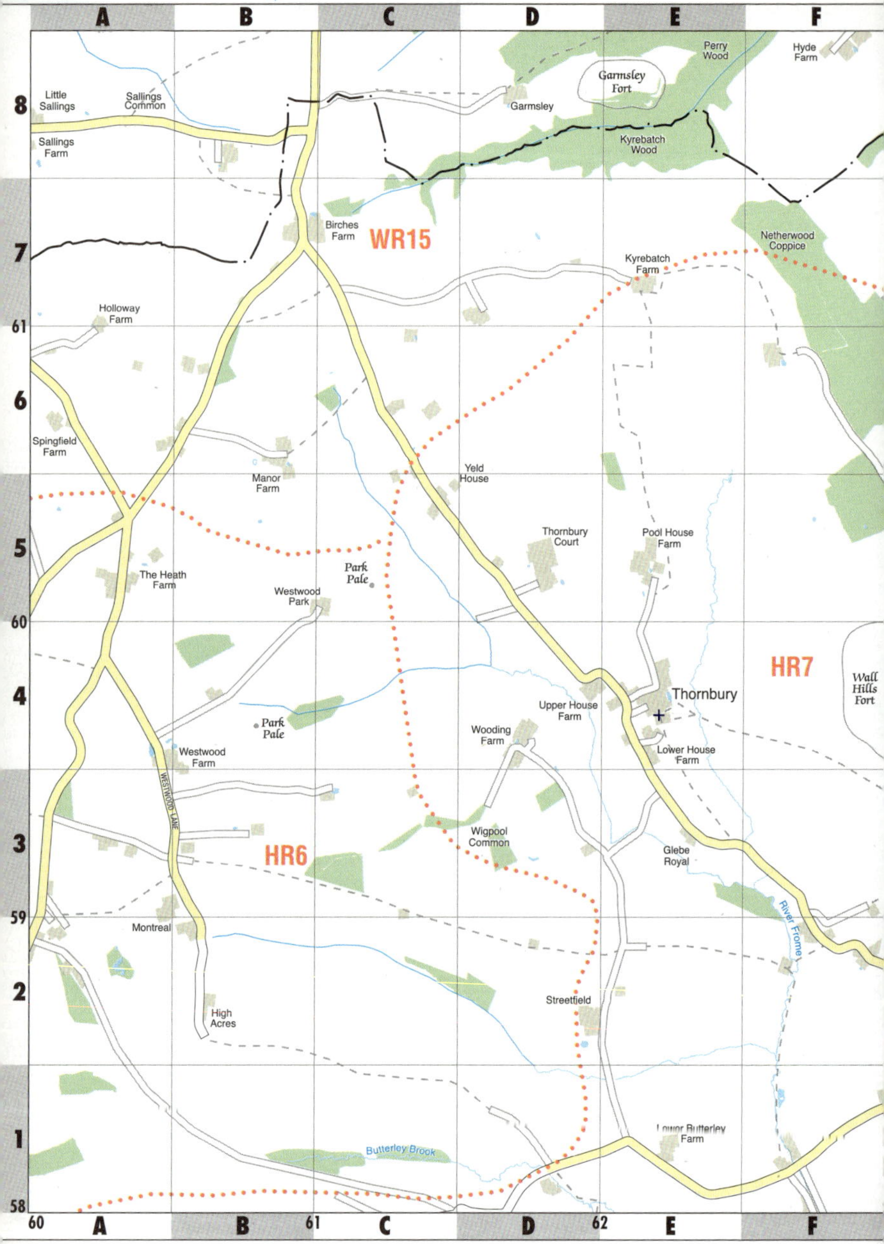
A
B
C
D
E
F
8
7
61
6
5
60
4
3
59
2
1
58
60
61
62
Little Sallings
Sallings Common
Sallings Farm
Garmsley
Garmsley Fort
Perry Wood
Hyde Farm
Kyrebatch Wood
Birches Farm
WR15
Kyrebatch Farm
Netherwood Coppice
Holloway Farm
Spingfield Farm
Manor Farm
Yeld House
Thornbury Court
Pool House Farm
The Heath Farm
Park Pale
Westwood Park
Thornbury
HR7
Wall Hills Fort
Upper House Farm
Wooding Farm
Lower House Farm
Park Pale
Westwood Farm
WESTWOOD LANE
Wigpool Common
Glebe Royal
HR6
River Frome
Montreal
Streetfield
High Acres
Lower Butterley Farm
Butterley Brook

93

76
96

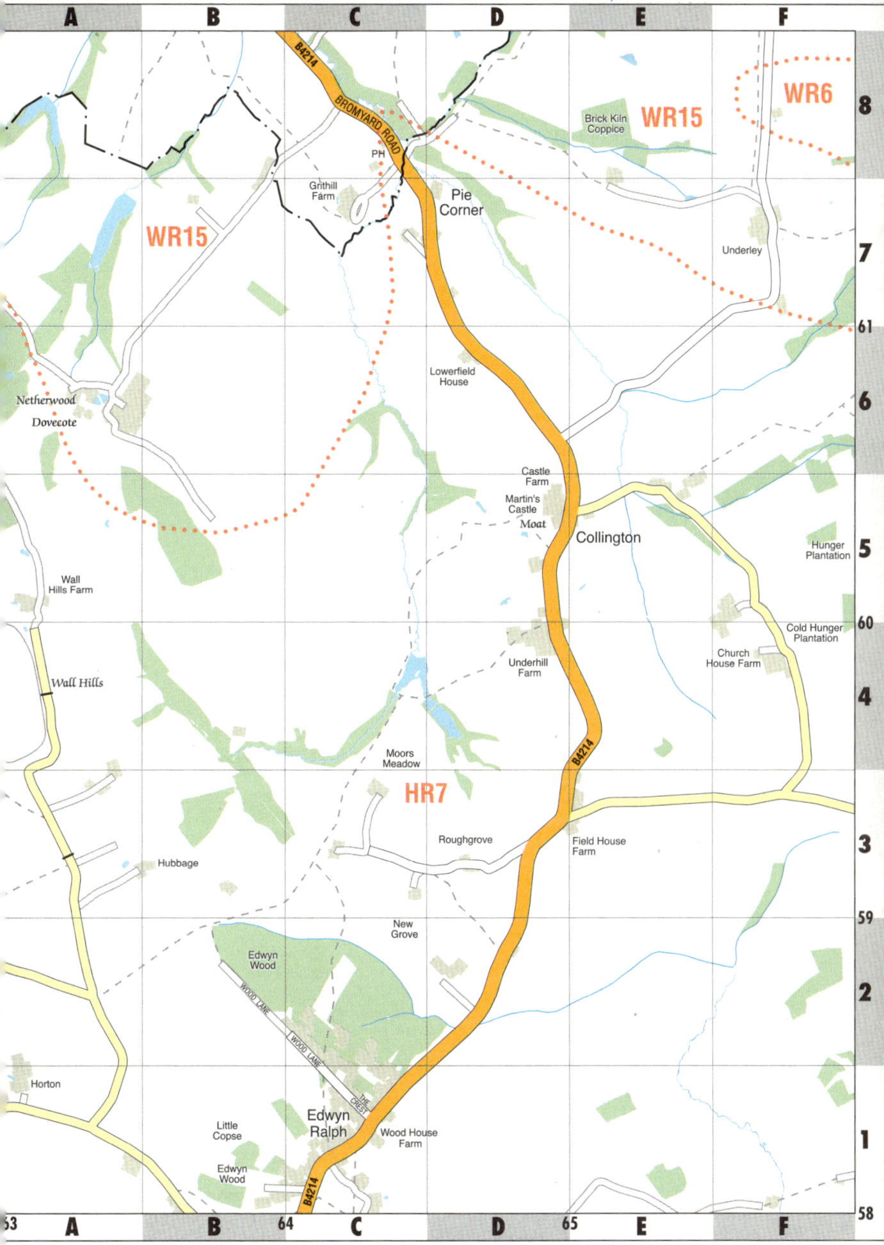
A
B
C
D
E
F
B4214
BROMYARD ROAD
PH
Grithill Farm
Pie Corner
Brick Kiln Coppice
WR15
WR6
Underley
WR15
Lowerfield House
Netherwood
Dovecote
Castle Farm
Martin's Castle
Moat
Collington
Hunger Plantation
Wall Hills Farm
Cold Hunger Plantation
Church House Farm
Underhill Farm
Wall Hills
Moors Meadow
B4214
HR7
Roughgrove
Field House Farm
Hubbage
New Grove
Edwyn Wood
WOOD LANE
WOOD LANE
THE CREST
Horton
Little Copse
Edwyn Ralph
Wood House Farm
Edwyn Wood
B4214
8
7
61
6
5
60
4
3
59
2
1
58
63
64
65

96

95
77

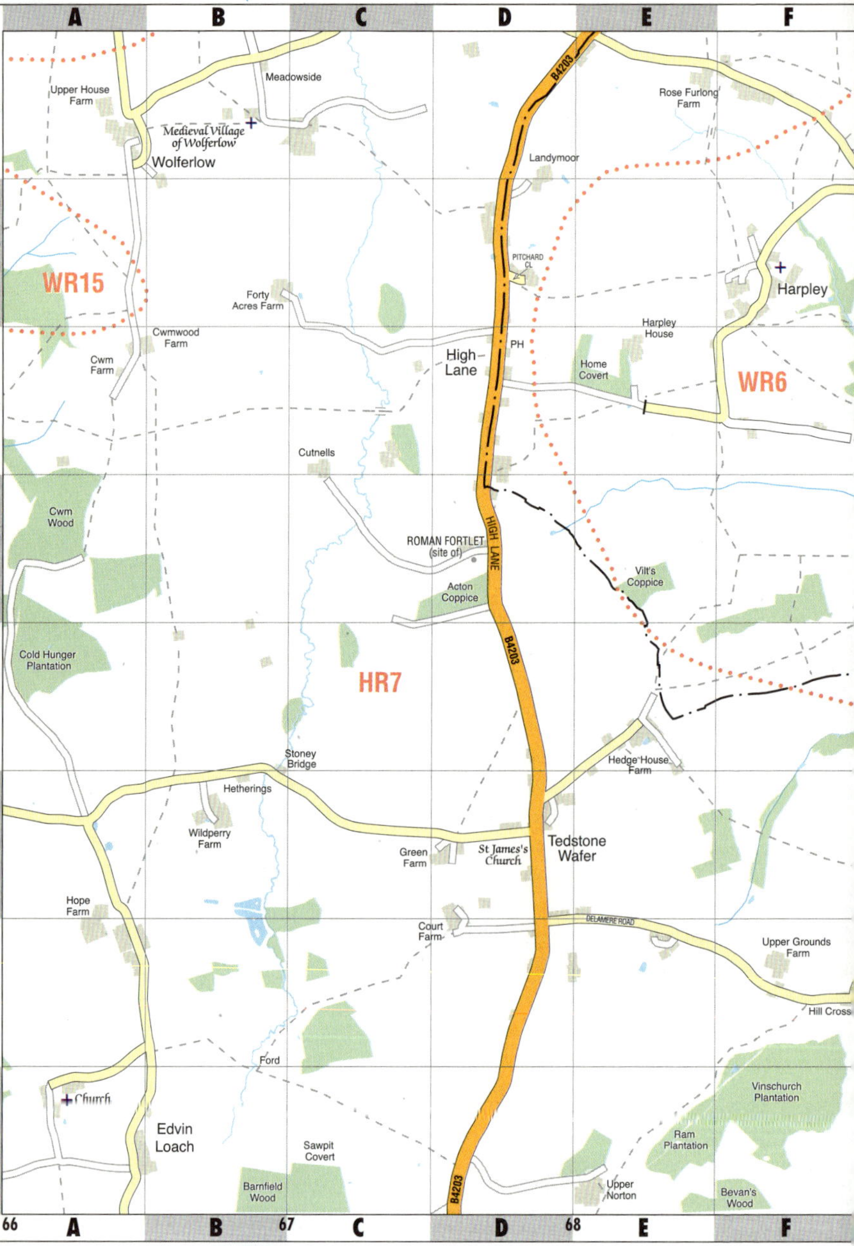
A
B
C
D
E
F
8
7
61
6
5
60
4
3
59
2
1
58
66
67
68
Upper House Farm
Meadowside
Medieval Village of Wolferlow
Wolferlow
B4203
Rose Furlong Farm
Landymoor
PITCHARD CL
WR15
Forty Acres Farm
Harpley
Cwmwood Farm
Cwm Farm
PH
High Lane
Harpley House
Home Covert
WR6
Cutnells
Cwm Wood
HIGH LANE
ROMAN FORTLET (site of)
Vilt's Coppice
Acton Coppice
Cold Hunger Plantation
HR7
Stoney Bridge
Hedge House Farm
Hetherings
Wildperry Farm
Green Farm
St James's Church
Tedstone Wafer
Hope Farm
Court Farm
DELAMERE ROAD
Upper Grounds Farm
Hill Cross
Ford
Church
Vinschurch Plantation
Edvin Loach
Sawpit Covert
Ram Plantation
Barnfield Wood
Upper Norton
Bevan's Wood

95

78
98

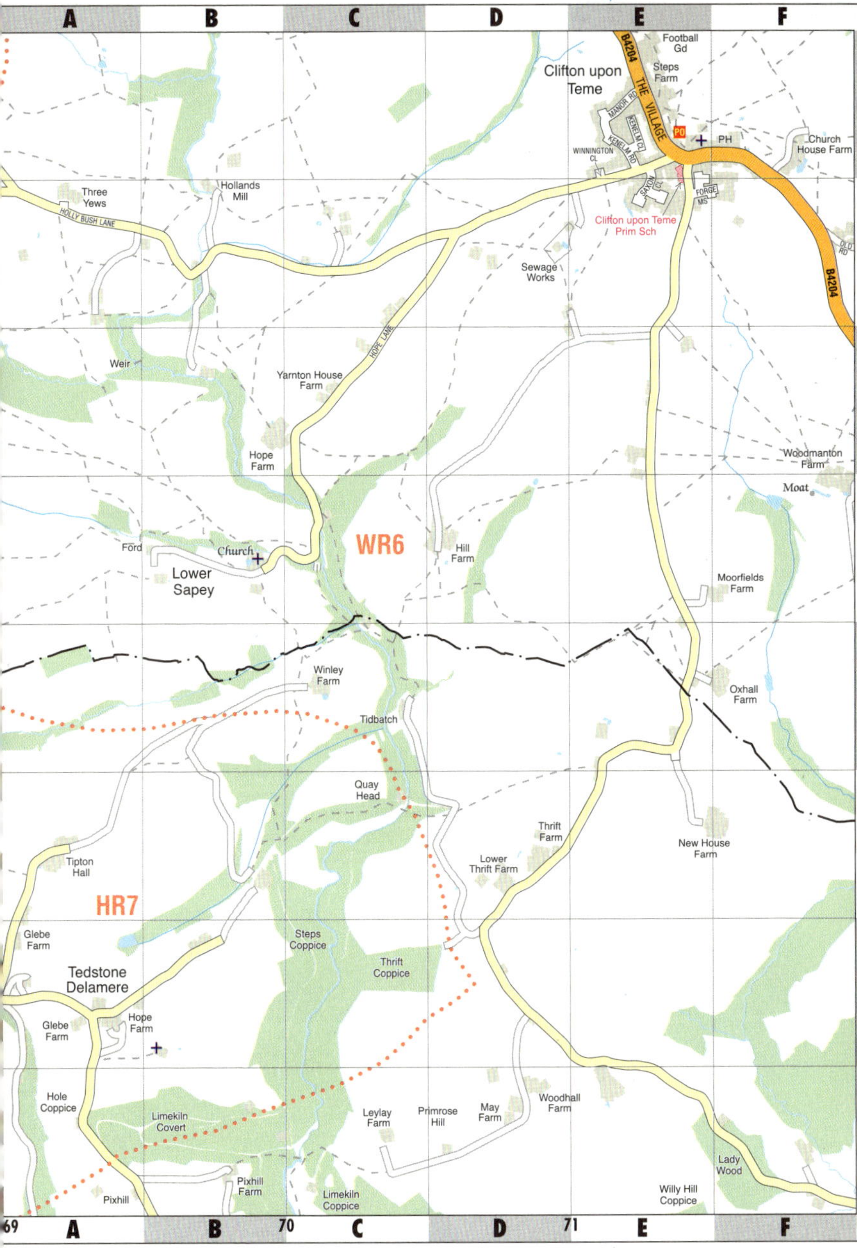
A
B
C
D
E
F
Football Gd
B4204
Clifton upon Teme
Steps Farm
THE VILLAGE
MANOR RD
KENELM CL
KENELM RD
WINNINGTON CL
PO
PH
Church House Farm
Three Yews
Hollands Mill
HOLLY BUSH LANE
SAXON CL
FORGE MS
Clifton upon Teme Prim Sch
OLD RD
Sewage Works
Weir
Yarnton House Farm
HOPE LANE
Hope Farm
Woodmanton Farm
Moat
Ford
Church
Lower Sapey
WR6
Hill Farm
Moorfields Farm
Winley Farm
Oxhall Farm
Tidbatch
Quay Head
Thrift Farm
Tipton Hall
Lower Thrift Farm
New House Farm
HR7
Glebe Farm
Steps Coppice
Thrift Coppice
Tedstone Delamere
Hope Farm
Glebe Farm
Hole Coppice
Limekiln Covert
Leylay Farm
Primrose Hill
May Farm
Woodhall Farm
Lady Wood
Pixhill Farm
Pixhill
Limekiln Coppice
Willy Hill Coppice
8
7
61
6
5
60
4
3
59
2
1
58
69
70
71

110
98

97
79

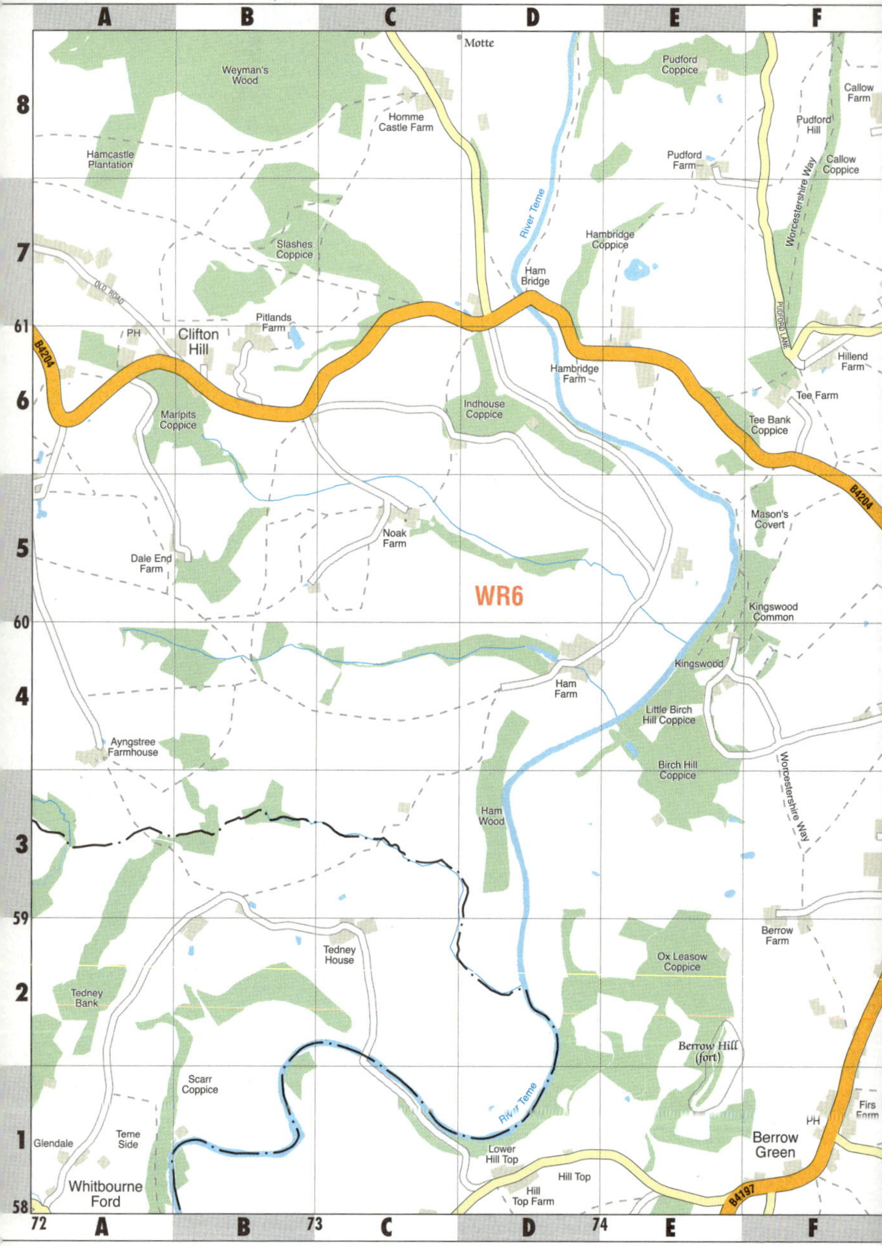
A
B
C
D
E
F
Motte
Weyman's Wood
Pudford Coppice
Callow Farm
Homme Castle Farm
Pudford Hill
Hamcastle Plantation
Pudford Farm
Callow Coppice
River Teme
Worcestershire Way
Hambridge Coppice
Slashes Coppice
Ham Bridge
OLD ROAD
PUDFORD LANE
Pitlands Farm
PH
Clifton Hill
B4204
Hambridge Farm
Hillend Farm
Tee Farm
Indhouse Coppice
Marlpits Coppice
Tee Bank Coppice
B4204
Mason's Covert
Noak Farm
Dale End Farm
WR6
Kingswood Common
Kingswood
Ham Farm
Little Birch Hill Coppice
Ayngstree Farmhouse
Birch Hill Coppice
Worcestershire Way
Ham Wood
Berrow Farm
Tedney House
Ox Leasow Coppice
Tedney Bank
Berrow Hill (fort)
Scarr Coppice
River Teme
Firs Farm
PH
Teme Side
Glendale
Berrow Green
Lower Hill Top
Hill Top
Whitbourne Ford
Hill Top Farm
B4197
8
7
61
6
5
60
4
3
59
2
1
58
72
73
74

97
111

80
100
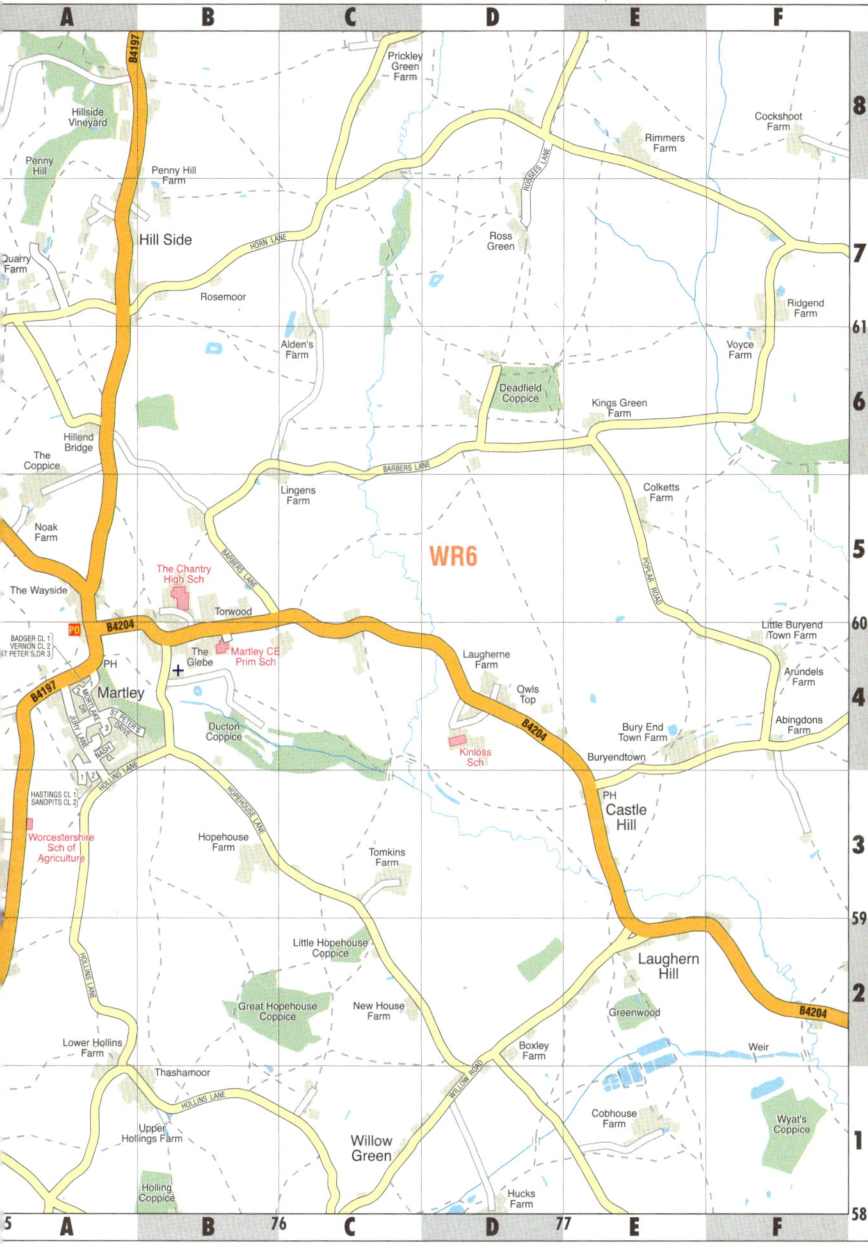

112
100

99
81

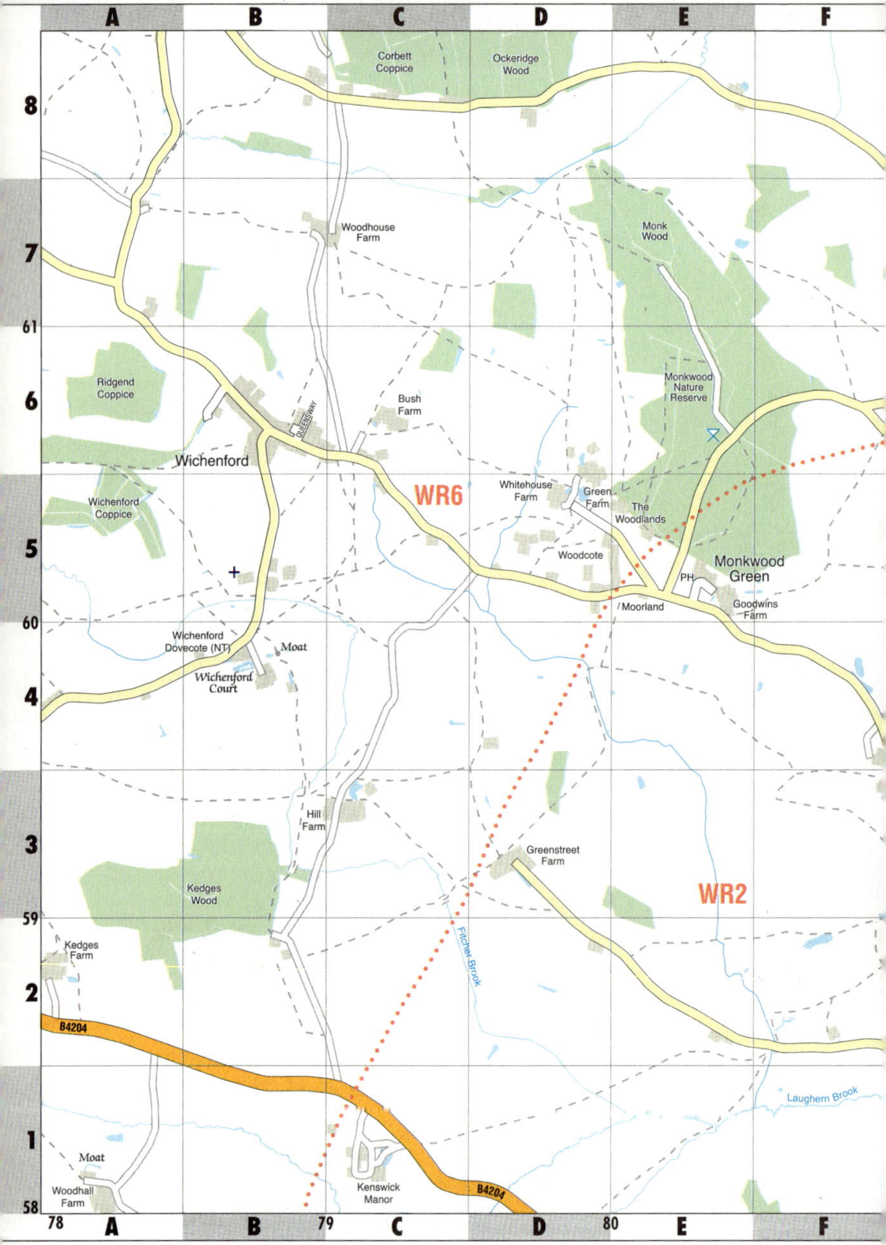
A
B
C
D
E
F
8
7
61
6
5
60
4
3
59
2
1
58
78
79
80
Corbett Coppice
Ockeridge Wood
Woodhouse Farm
Monk Wood
Ridgend Coppice
Bush Farm
Monkwood Nature Reserve
QUEENSWAY
Wichenford
WR6
Whitehouse Farm
Green Farm
The Woodlands
Wichenford Coppice
Woodcote
Monkwood Green
PH
Moorland
Goodwins Farm
Wichenford Dovecote (NT)
Moat
Wichenford Court
Hill Farm
Greenstreet Farm
Kedges Wood
WR2
Kedges Farm
Fitcher Brook
B4204
Laughern Brook
Moat
Woodhall Farm
Kenswick Manor
B4204

99
113

82
102

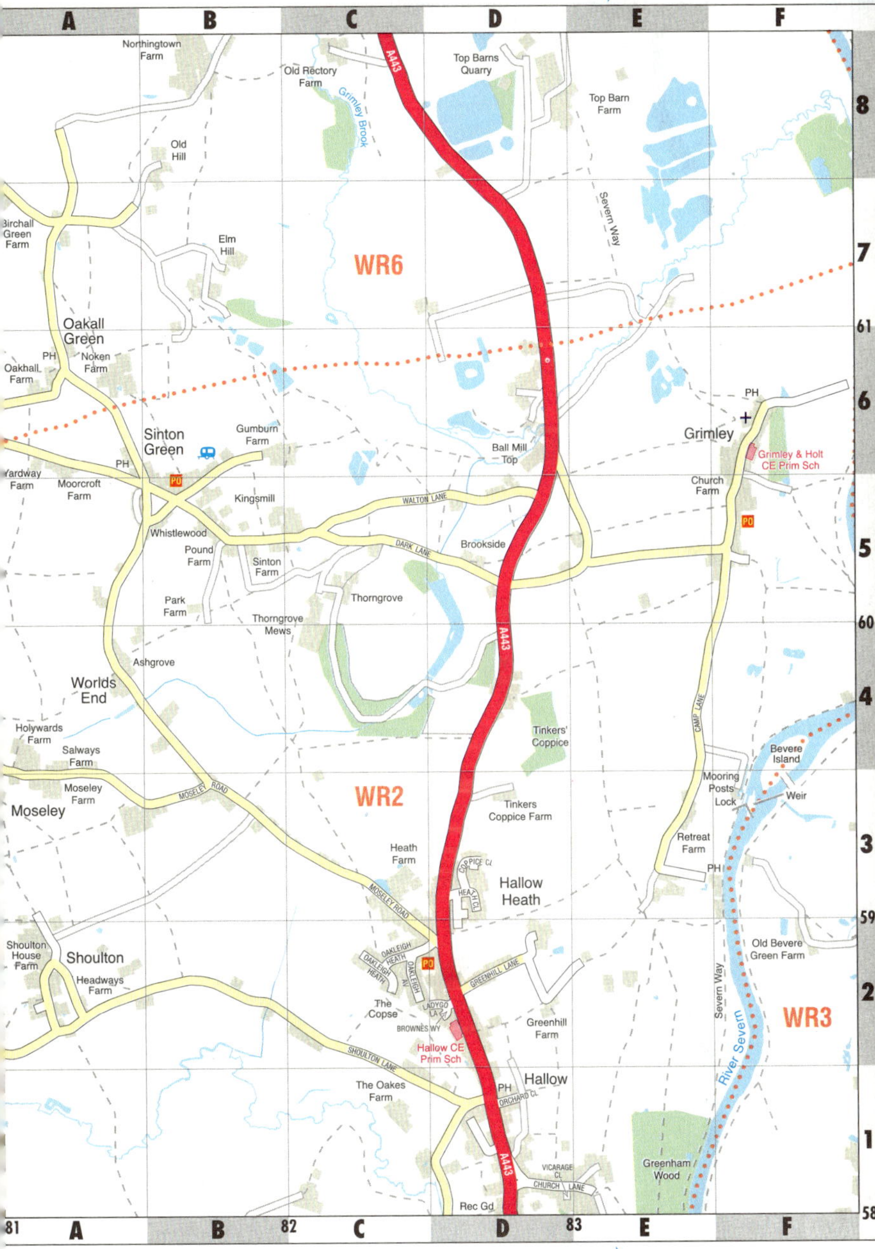

114
102

101
83

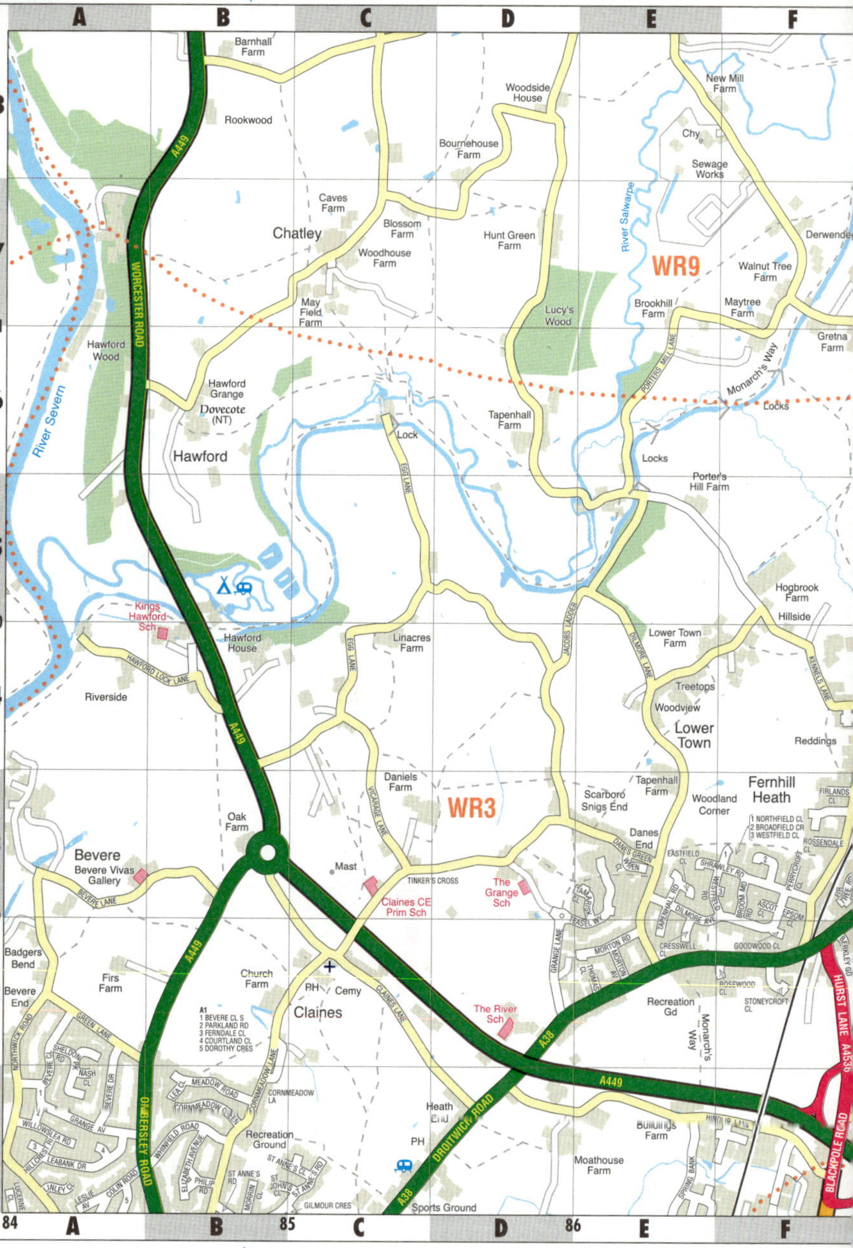

101
115

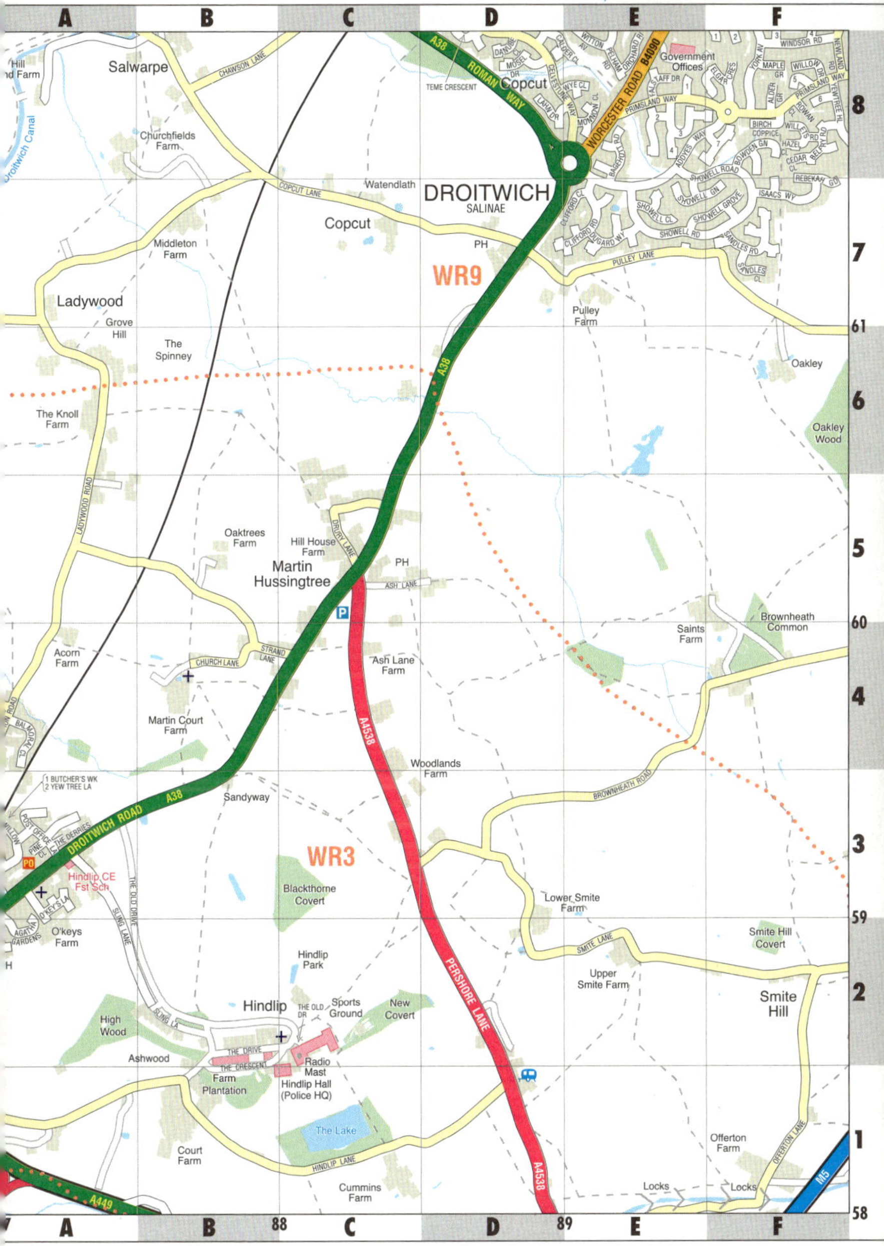
A
B
C
D
E
F
Salwarpe
Droitwich Canal
Churchfields Farm
CHAWSON LANE
COPCUT LANE
Watendlath
DROITWICH
SALINAE
Copcut
TEME CRESCENT
A38
ROMAN WAY
WORCESTER ROAD
B4090
Government Offices
PRIMSLAND WAY
SHOWELL ROAD
SHOWELL GROVE
SHOWELL CL
SHOWELL RD
SHOWELL GN
ISAACS WY
CLIFFORD CL
CLIFFORD RD
PULLEY LANE
SANDLES RD
SANDLES CL
Middleton Farm
PH
WR9
Ladywood
Grove Hill
The Spinney
Pulley Farm
Oakley
Oakley Wood
The Knoll Farm
LADYWOOD ROAD
Oaktrees Farm
Hill House Farm
DRURY LANE
Martin Hussingtree
ASH LANE
Brownheath Common
Saints Farm
Acorn Farm
CHURCH LANE
STRAND LANE
Ash Lane Farm
Martin Court Farm
A4538
Woodlands Farm
1 BUTCHER'S WK
2 YEW TREE LA
Sandyway
DROITWICH ROAD
BROWNHEATH ROAD
WR3
Hindlip CE Fst Sch
Blackthorne Covert
Lower Smite Farm
O'keys Farm
THE OLD DRIVE
SLING LANE
SMITE LANE
Smite Hill Covert
Hindlip Park
Upper Smite Farm
PERSHORE LANE
Smite Hill
High Wood
Hindlip
Sports Ground
New Covert
Ashwood
THE DRIVE
THE CRESCENT
Radio Mast
Farm Plantation
Hindlip Hall (Police HQ)
The Lake
HINDLIP LANE
Court Farm
Cummins Farm
Offerton Farm
OFFERTON LANE
Locks
M5
A449
8
7
61
6
5
60
4
3
59
2
1
58
88
89

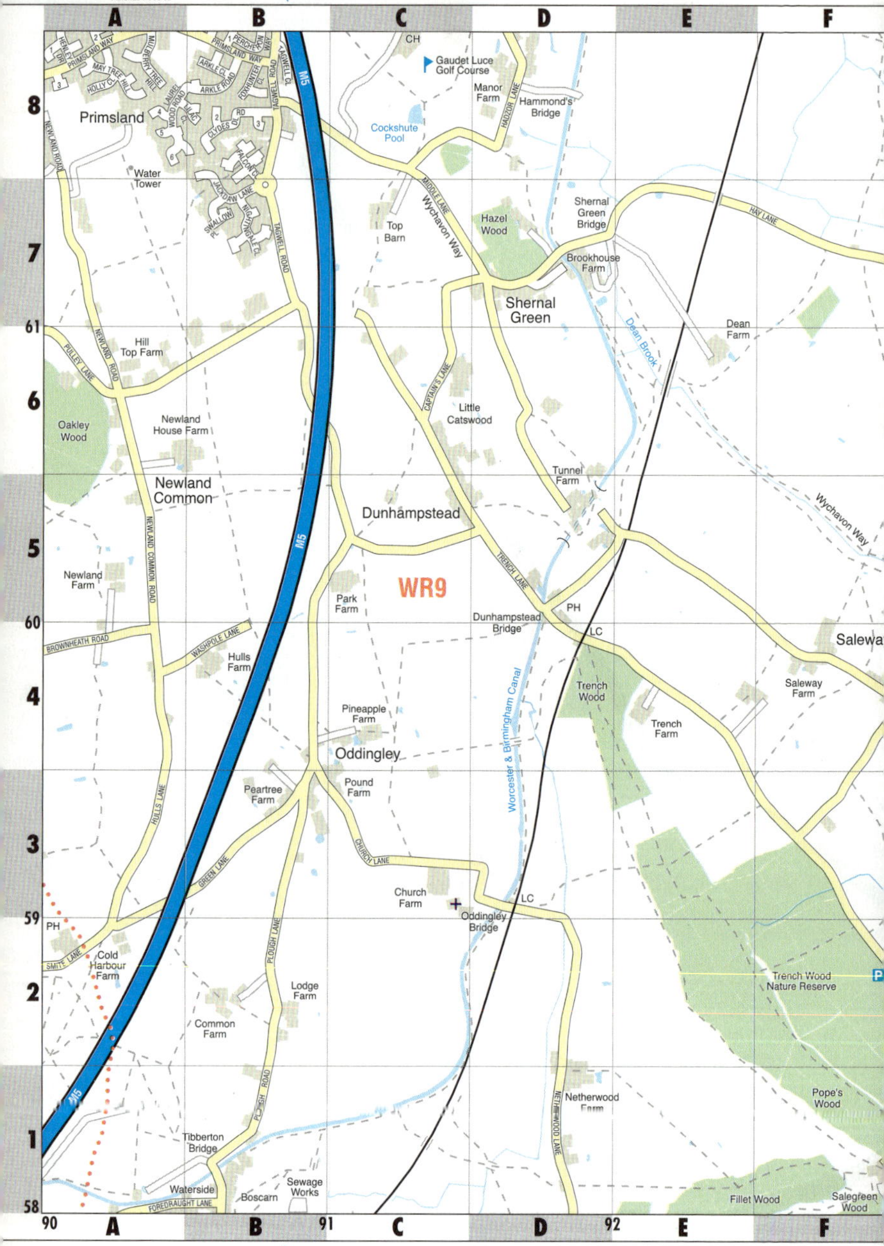
A
B
C
D
E
F
8
7
61
6
5
60
4
3
59
2
1
58
90
91
92
Primsland
PRIMSLAND WAY
MAY TREE HILL
HOLLY CL
MULBERRY TREE HILL
PERCHERON WAY
ARKLE CL
ARKLE ROAD
FOXHUNTER CL
TAGWELL ROAD
TAGWELL CL
LAUREL WOOD ROAD
LILAC CL
CLYDES DL
FALCON CL
JACKDAW LANE
SWALLOW PL
NIGHTINGALE CL
NEWLAND ROAD
Water Tower
M5
CH
Gaudet Luce Golf Course
Manor Farm
HADZOR LANE
Hammond's Bridge
Cockshute Pool
MIDDLE LANE
Wychavon Way
Top Barn
Hazel Wood
Shernal Green Bridge
Brookhouse Farm
HAY LANE
Shernal Green
Dean Brook
Dean Farm
PULLEY LANE
Hill Top Farm
CAPTAIN'S LANE
Little Catswood
Oakley Wood
Newland House Farm
Newland Common
Tunnel Farm
Dunhampstead
NEWLAND COMMON ROAD
Newland Farm
WR9
TRENCH LANE
Park Farm
PH
Dunhampstead Bridge
LC
Salewa
BROWNHEATH ROAD
WASHPOLE LANE
Hulls Farm
Trench Wood
Saleway Farm
Worcester & Birmingham Canal
Pineapple Farm
Trench Farm
Oddingley
Peartree Farm
Pound Farm
HULLS LANE
CHURCH LANE
GREEN LANE
Church Farm
Oddingley Bridge
PH
SMITE LANE
Cold Harbour Farm
PLOUGH LANE
Lodge Farm
Trench Wood Nature Reserve
P
Common Farm
PLOUGH ROAD
Netherwood Farm
NETHERWOOD LANE
Pope's Wood
Tibberton Bridge
Waterside
FOREDRAUGHT LANE
Boscarn
Sewage Works
Fillet Wood
Salegreen Wood

86
106

118
106

105
87

105
119

88
108

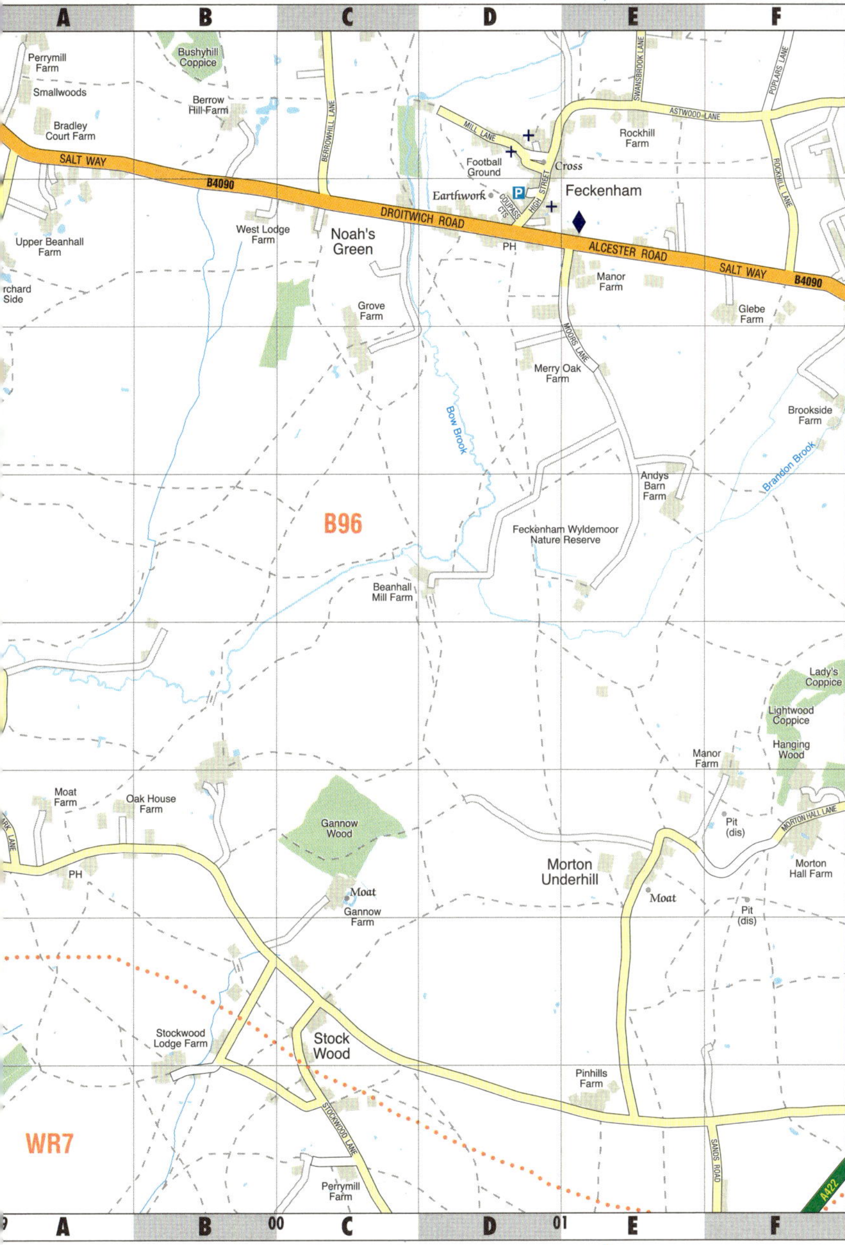

120
108

107
89

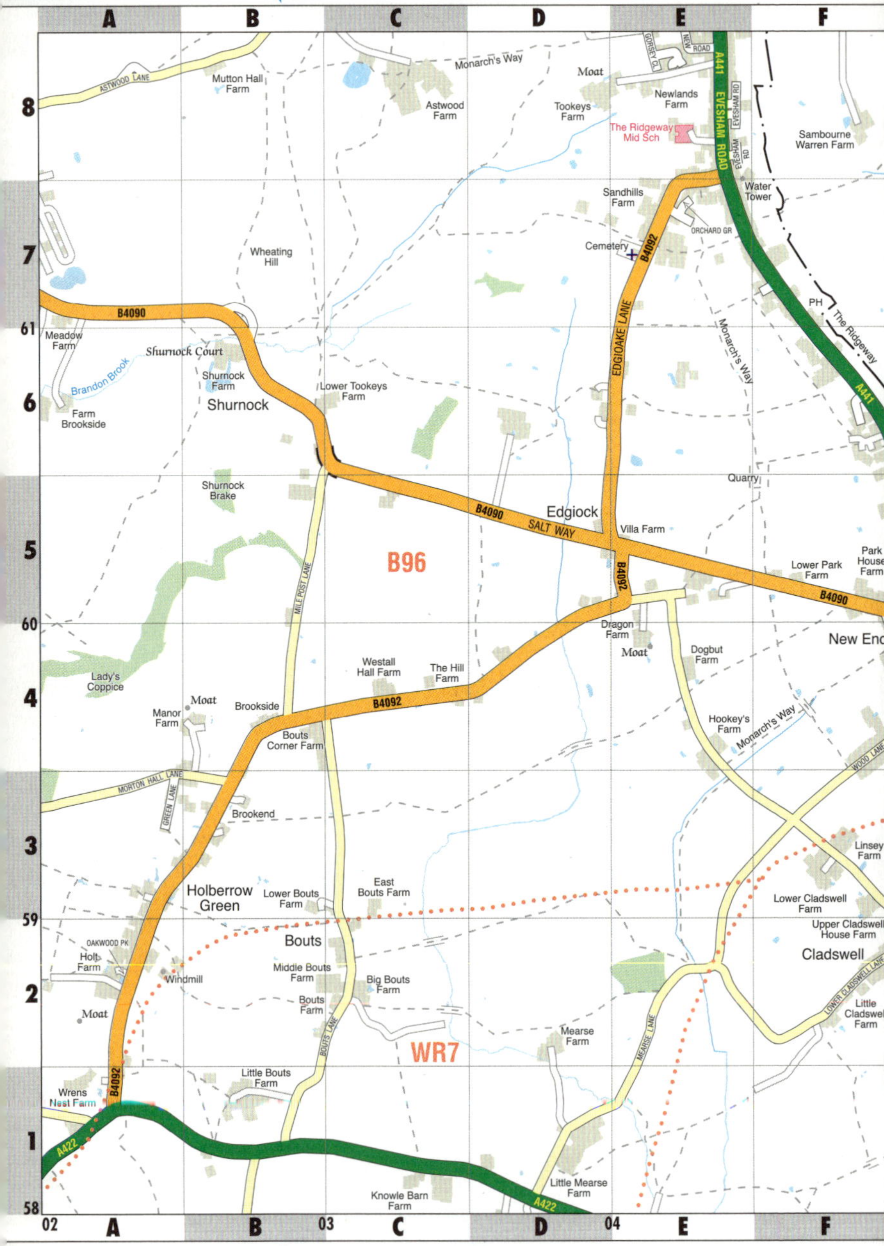

107
121

90

A
B
C
D
E
F
SAMBOURNE-PK
Sambourne
SAMBOURNE LA
MIDDLETOWN LANE
PH
PO
Glebe Farm
Hall
Whitemoor Farm
Sambourne Hall Farm
WIKE LANE
Cain Brook
A435
HAYDON WAY
Thundering Ditch
WHITEMOOR LANE
Saddlers Hill Coppice
Alcester Warren Farm
BIRMINGHAM ROAD
Watching Hill Spinneys
SAMBOURNE LANE
A435 Alcester
B96
Coughton Park
Moat
RIDGEWAY
B4090
Butler's Coppice
Coughton
Coughton CE Prim Sch
Coughton Lodge Farm
Coughton Lodge Farm
Warwickshire STREET ATLAS
PH
BRANDHEATH LA
Billingsborough Wood
COUGHTON LANE
ALCESTER HEATH
Alcester Park Farm
B49
Coppice View
Chicken Meadow Barn
Alcester Lodge
Alcester Heath Farm
A441
Ford
CHURCH DR
KINGS COUGHTON LA
Asplands Husk Coppice
CLADSWELL LANE
CHURCH LANE
Spittle Brook
DSWELL CL
B4090
EVESHAM ROAD
Monarch's Way
Cladswell Hall Farm
CHAMBERLAIN LANE
Cookhill
OAK TREE LANE
Coldcomfort Wood
Forge Farm
The Springs
Three Oak Hill Wood
A441
8
7
61
6
5
60
4
3
59
2
1
58
06
07

122

97

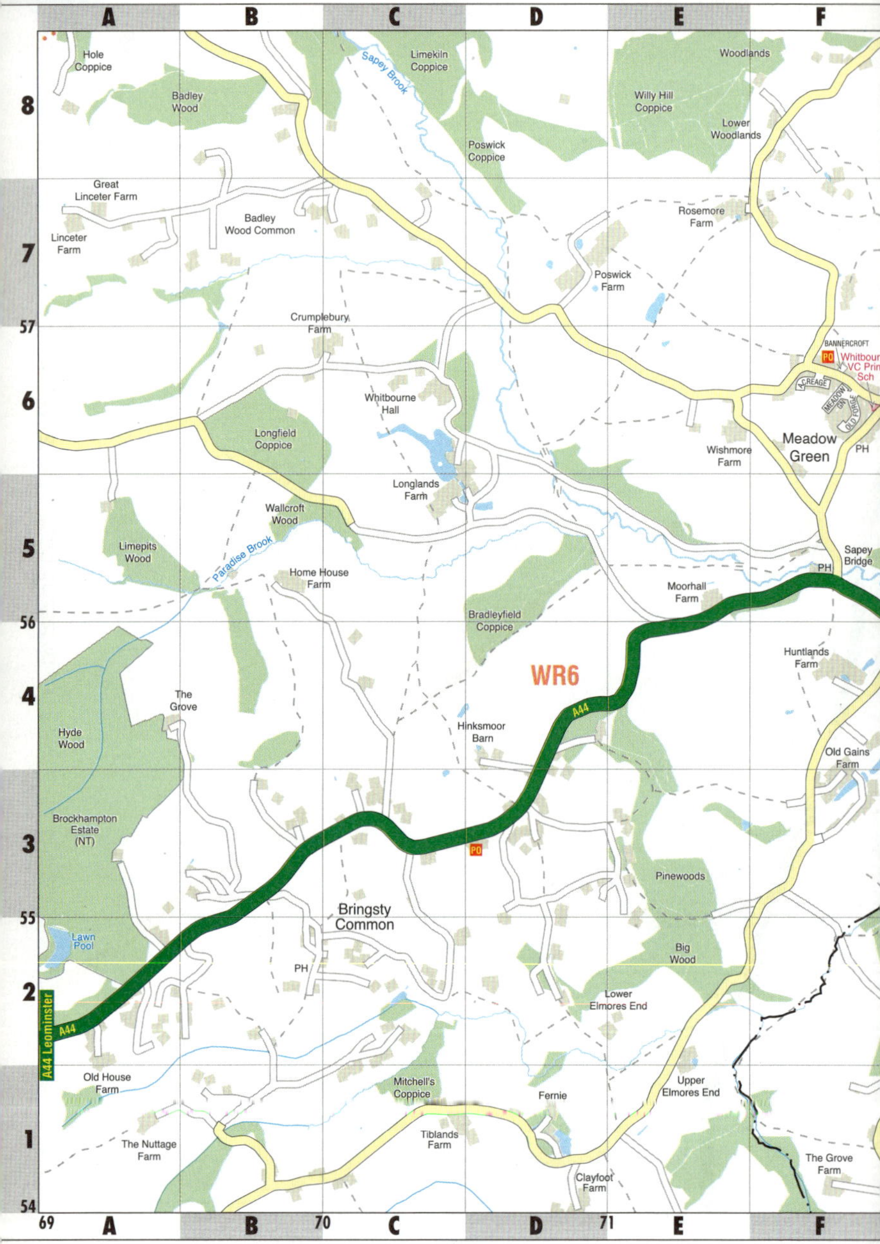

A
B
C
D
E
F
8
7
57
6
5
56
4
3
55
2
1
54
69
70
71
Hole Coppice
Badley Wood
Limekiln Coppice
Sapey Brook
Woodlands
Willy Hill Coppice
Lower Woodlands
Poswick Coppice
Great Linceter Farm
Badley Wood Common
Linceter Farm
Rosemore Farm
Poswick Farm
Crumplebury Farm
BANNERCROFT
PO
Whitbourne VC Prim Sch
ACREAGE
MEADOW GN
OLD FORGE
Whitbourne Hall
Longfield Coppice
Meadow Green
Wishmore Farm
PH
Longlands Farm
Wallcroft Wood
Limepits Wood
Paradise Brook
Home House Farm
Sapey Bridge
PH
Moorhall Farm
Bradleyfield Coppice
Huntlands Farm
WR6
The Grove
A44
Hyde Wood
Hinksmoor Barn
Old Gains Farm
Brockhampton Estate (NT)
PO
Pinewoods
Bringsty Common
Lawn Pool
Big Wood
PH
A44 Leominster
A44
Lower Elmores End
Old House Farm
Mitchell's Coppice
Fernie
Upper Elmores End
The Nuttage Farm
Tiblands Farm
Clayfoot Farm
The Grove Farm

123

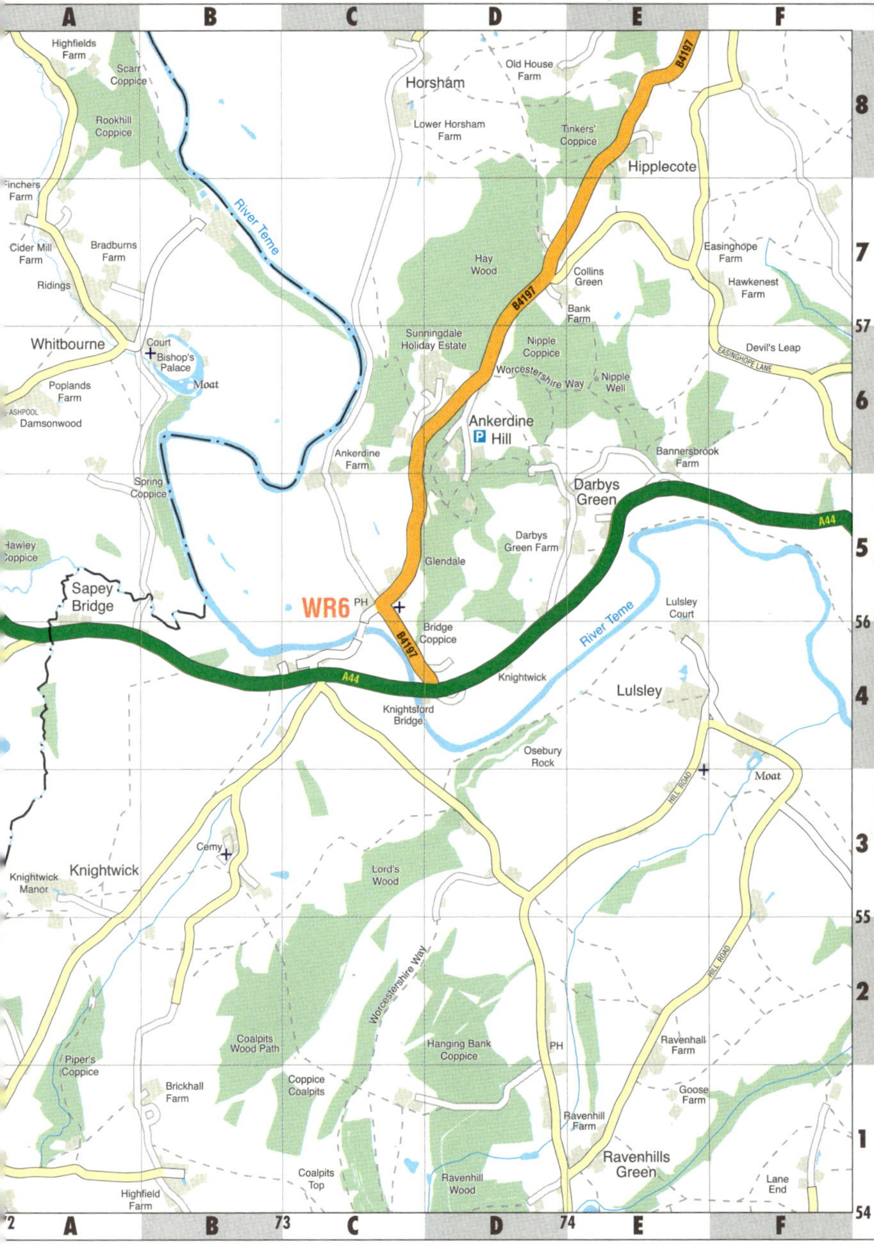
Highfields Farm
Scarr Coppice
Rookhill Coppice
Finchers Farm
Cider Mill Farm
Bradburns Farm
Ridings
Whitbourne
Court
Bishop's Palace
Moat
Poplands Farm
ASHPOOL
Damsonwood
River Teme
Horsham
Old House Farm
Lower Horsham Farm
Tinkers' Coppice
Hipplecote
B4197
Hay Wood
Collins Green
Bank Farm
Easinghope Farm
Hawkenest Farm
Devil's Leap
EASINGHOPE LANE
Sunningdale Holiday Estate
Nipple Coppice
Worcestershire Way
Nipple Well
Ankerdine Hill
Ankerdine Farm
Bannersbrook Farm
Spring Coppice
Darbys Green
Darbys Green Farm
Hawley Coppice
Sapey Bridge
Glendale
A44
WR6
PH
Bridge Coppice
Lulsley Court
Knightwick
Lulsley
Knightsford Bridge
Osebury Rock
HILL ROAD
Moat
Cemy
Knightwick Manor
Knightwick
Lord's Wood
Worcestershire Way
Coalpits Wood Path
Hanging Bank Coppice
PH
Ravenhall Farm
Piper's Coppice
Brickhall Farm
Coppice Coalpits
Goose Farm
Ravenhill Farm
Ravenhills Green
Coalpits Top
Ravenhill Wood
Lane End
Highfield Farm
A
B
C
D
E
F
8
7
57
6
5
56
4
3
55
2
1
54
72
73
74

A
B
C
D
E
F
8
7
57
6
5
56
4
3
55
2
1
54
75
76
77
Holling Coppice
Woodside
HOLLINS LA
Hucks Farm
Hypsmoor Farm
The Grove
Hollings End
WILLOW ROAD
Grove Farm
Newtown
Barn House Farm
Wants Green Farm
Hill Top
Wants Green
Peghouse Wood
Woodend Farm
Moat
Shooter's Coppice
Woodland Venture
Peg House Farm
Cobbler's Corner
Woodacre
Haynes Green Farm
Upper Doddenham Farm
Woodlands
Lower Gurnox Farm
Groveley Coppice
EASINGHOPE LANE
Broadley Coppice
Baggotts Coppice
A44
Doddenham
Ridgeacre Farm
WR6
Landymoor Coppice
Forest Farm
Broad Green
Moat
Hill Farm
WESTON HILL
Cedars Farm
Stoney Ley Farm
Noxons Farm
Stone Farm
Broadwas
PH
PO
Butts Farm
Hilltop Farm
Broadwas Court
CHURCH LANE
Broadwas CE Prim Sch
Brook Farm
TABBERNESS CL
Hilltop Barn
Salvendale
River Teme
Red Cliff
Folly Farm
TEME LANE

100
114

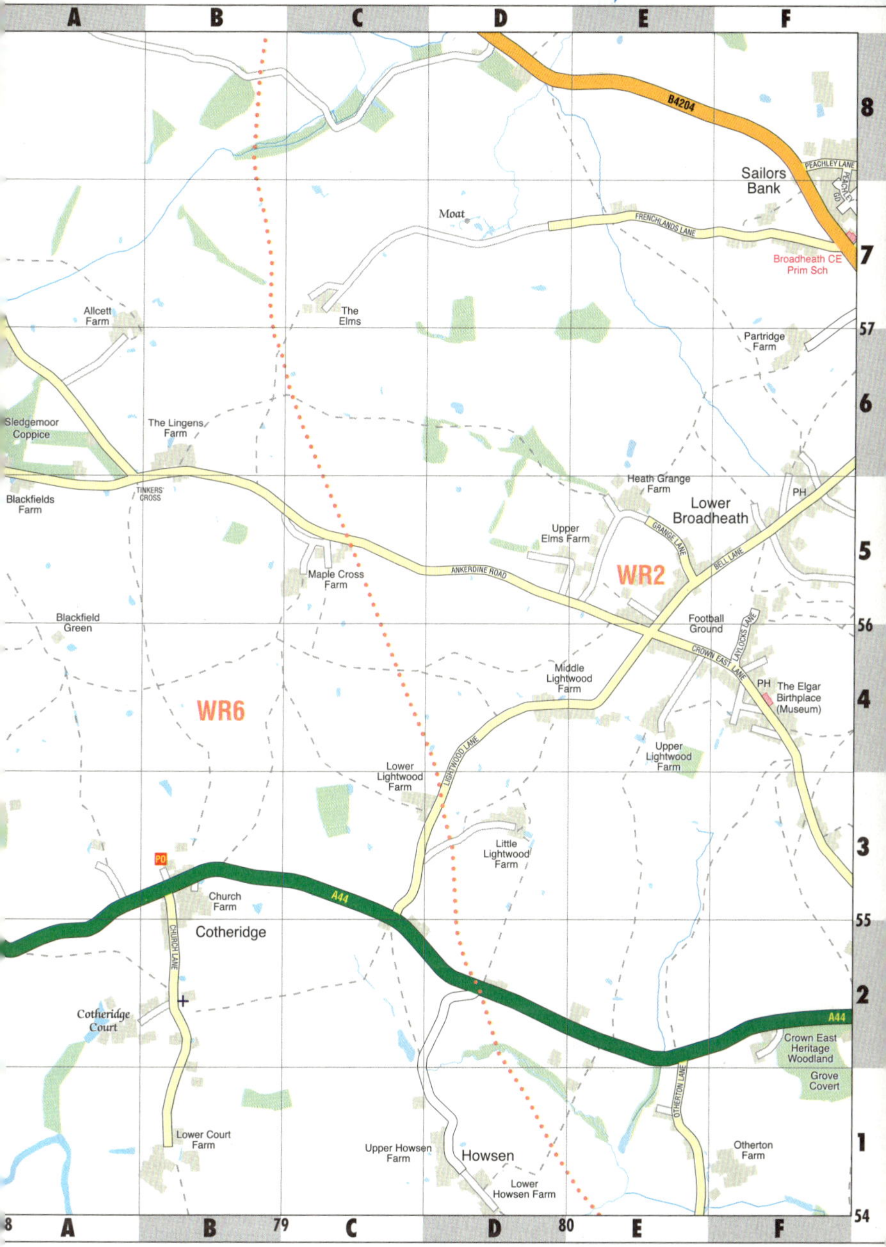

126
114

113
101

E5
1 RUSSET CL
2 RIBSTON CL
3 PACKINGTON RD
4 EVERARD CL
5 EVERARD PL
6 LANGLEY CL
7 MONARCH PL
8 WESTHAVEN PL

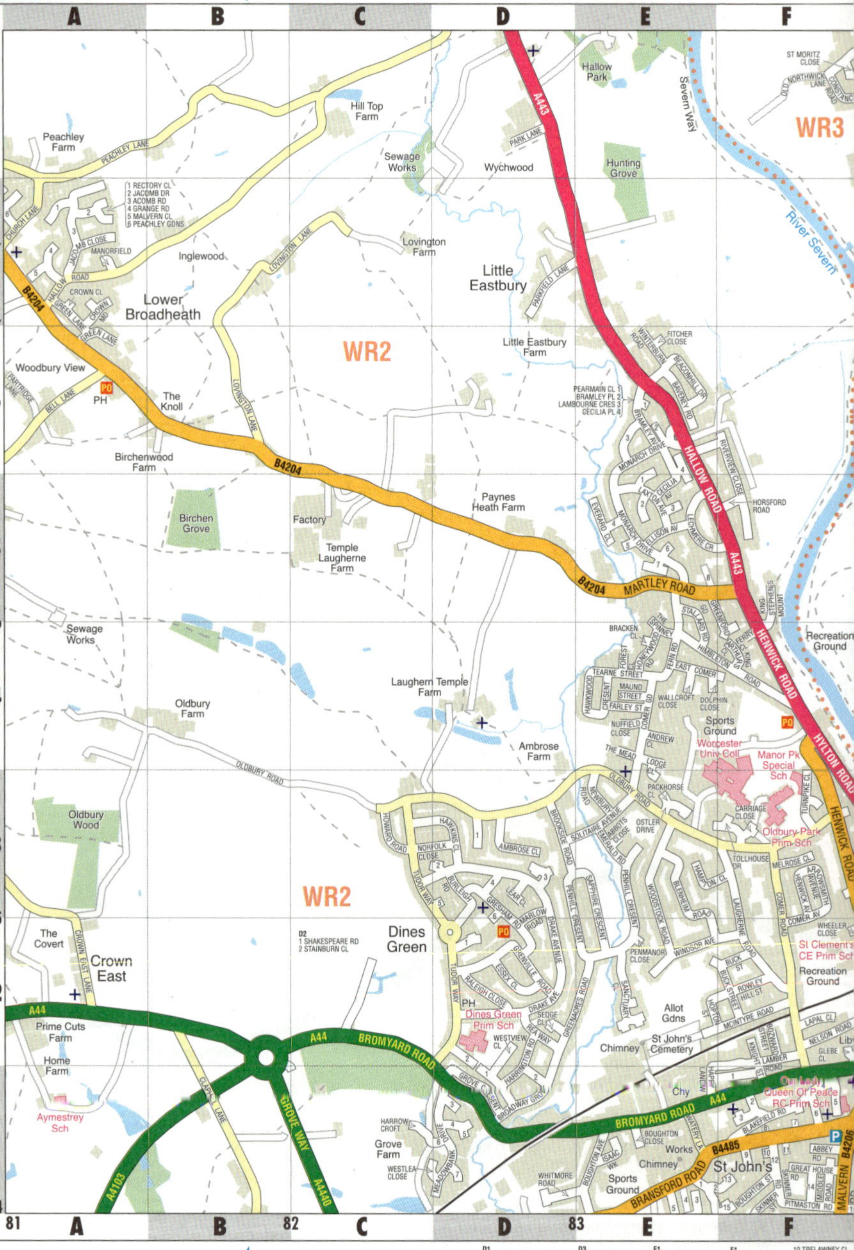

113
127

D1
1 STAINBURN AVE
2 ROSEMARY AVE
3 FIELDHEAD CL
4 LOW FOLDCL
5 LEASOWE CL
6 FARMBROOK CL
7 HAYFIELD CL

D3
1 DUDLEY CL
2 FITZWILLIAM C
3 DOWLAND GRDS
4 SPENSER RD
5 HATHAWAY CL
6 SHAKESPEARE RD

E1
1 SMITHS AVE
2 PALMERS GRN
3 SWINTON CL
4 LITTLE BOUGHTON STR
5 SWINTON LA

F1
1 HAPPY LAND N
2 BLAKEFIELD WK
3 SINTON TER
4 BLAKEFIELD GDNS
5 CHURCH TER
6 GRAHAM RD
7 STAR LANE
8 BLAKEFIELD WK
9 AVENUE RD
10 TRELAWNEY CL
11 NARROW WK
12 SCHOOL RD
13 PALMERS GRN
14 BEDWARDINE RD
15 NURSERY WK
16 VERNON PK RD

A5
1 BARBOURNE LA
2 BARBOURNE WK
3 BERKELEY ST
4 LYTTELTON ST
5 TOWNSEND ST
6 WOODBINE RD
7 SELBORNE RD
8 LOWER BARBOURNE TER
9 BARBOURNE CRES
10 LANGDALE RD
11 THORNELOE RD
12 FOUNTAIN PL
13 SABRINA TER

B6
1 ST STEPHEN'S TER
2 SUMMER ST
3 BLANQUETTES ST
4 CYPRESS ST
5 ST STEPHEN'S ST
6 BROMSGROVE ST
7 MELBOURNE ST
8 OFFLEY ST
9 SYDNEY ST
10 WAKEMAN ST
11 ADELAIDE CL
12 NORTHCOTE ST
13 NEW BANK ST
14 PRICE ST

102

C4
1 LANSDOWNE RI
2 LITTLE CHESTNUT ST
3 WASHINGTON ST

116

F6
1 BARBERS CL
2 DRAPERS CL
3 JOINERS CL
4 MASONS DR
5 VINTNERS CL
6 SHIP WRIGHTS CL
7 TANNERS CL
8 GARDNERS CL
9 COOPERS CL
10 CARTERS CL
11 PLOUGHMANS CL
12 MILLERS CL
13 GAMEKEEPERS DR
14 RANDWICK CL
15 HARESFIELD CL

A B C D E F

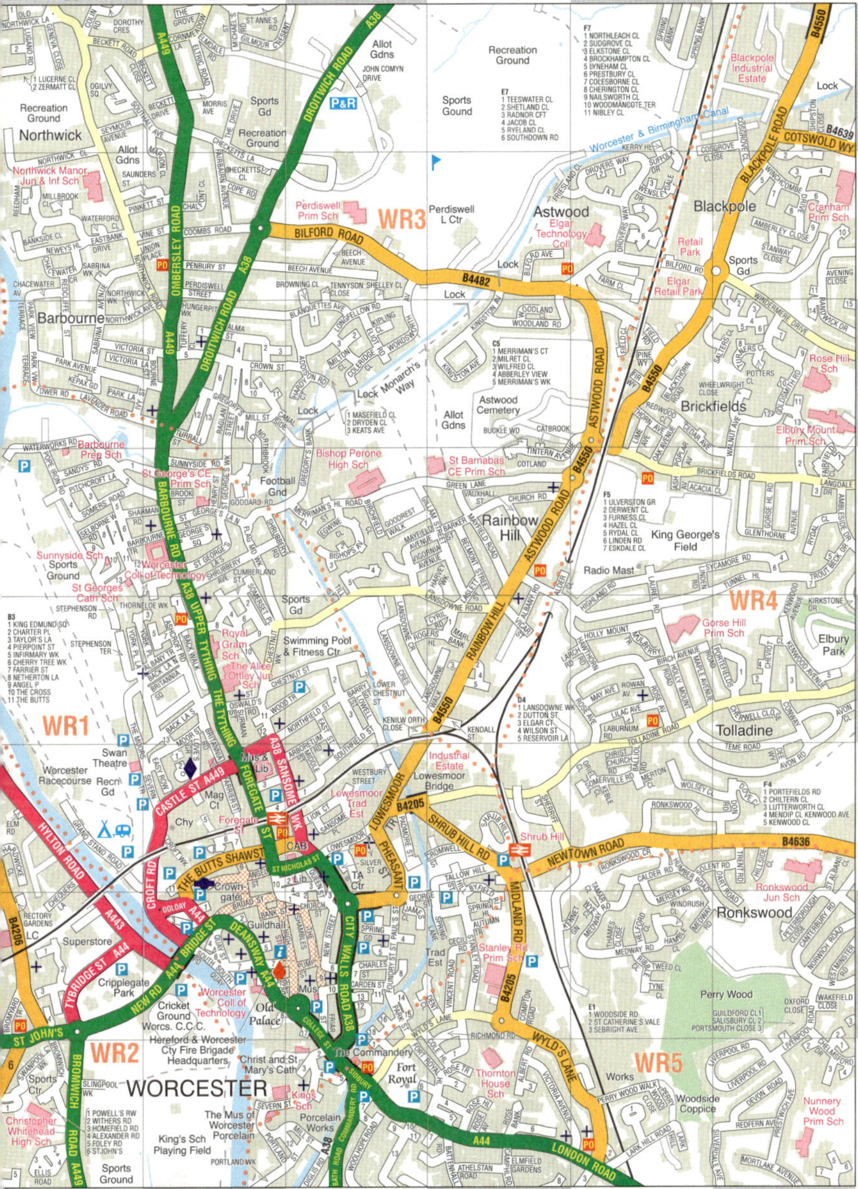

84 A B 85 C D 86 E F

A2
1 ST CLEMENT'S CT
2 ST CLEMENT'S GD
3 ST CLEMENT'S CL
4 BUSH WK

B2
1 MORETON PL
2 MALTHOUSE PL
3 NEWPORT ST
4 WARMSTRY CT
5 LOWER BULL ENTRY
6 HOOD ST
7 COPENHAGEN ST
8 COLLEGE YD

B4
1 BREWERY WK
2 LANDSDOWNE ST
3 WINDMILL CL
4 WHITE LADIES CL
5 LEICESTER ST
6 WHITE LADIES WK
7 HEBB ST
8 LITTLE LONDON
9 LANSDOWNE RD
10 TENNIS WK
11 SANSOME WK
12 MCNAUGHT PL
13 BRAYMOOR RD

C1
1 DERBY RD
2 EDGAR ST
3 CASTLE PL
4 KING ST
5 ST PETERS ST
6 ROYAL ALBERT CL
7 BATH RD
8 GREEN HL BATH RD
9 PROSPECT PL
10 GREEN HILL LONDON RD
11 GREEN HILL PL
12 WILLOW ST
13 ST DUNSTAN'S CRES

128

C2
1 ST SWITHIN'S ST
2 TRINITY ST
3 CORN MARKET
4 WELLINGTON CL
5 PROVIDENCE ST
6 CHARLES ST
7 TEMPERANCE ST
8 BLOCKHOUSE CL
9 FRIAR ST
10 UNION ST
11 CARDEN CL
12 CLARE ST
13 SOUTH ST
14 LOCK ST
15 LITTLE PK ST
16 PRINCE RUPERT RD
17 COLL PRECINCTS
18 HAMILTON RD

116

C3
1 LITTLE SOUTHFIELD ST
2 THE AVENUE
3 THE TRINITY
4 TRINITY PASSAGE

D1
1 ST WULSTAN'S CRES
2 FORT ROYAL LA
3 EDWARD CL
4 UPPER PK ST
5 VICTORIA PL
6 ST CATHERINE'S HL
7 BATTENHALL P
8 CAMP HILL AVE

F1
1 CHESTER CL
2 LINCOLN GN
3 NEWCASTLE CL
4 SHEFFIELD CL
5 NUNNERY LA
6 BRENT WOOD CL
7 HAZEWOOD CL

B7
1 CIRENCESTER PL
2 SNOWSHILL CL
3 WASHBROOK CL
4 WOOD PIECE CL
5 TIVERTON CL
6 DUNSTER CL
7 AMROTH GD

115

B5
1 MIDDLETON GD
2 TREACLE NOOK
3 RACE FIELD
4 LORD'S HEATH
5 WATER CFT
6 WAGGON PL
7 LITTLE PIECE
8 WINDLES ROW
9 ROUGH MD
10 STANAGE CL
11 TOWN ACRES
12 PLOUGH CFT
13 QUISTERS

103

C6
1 BODIAM CL
2 CASTELL PL
3 CONISBOROUGH
4 CHILHAM PL
5 STOKESAY LA
6 WALKWORTH AV
7 PICKERING GR
8 SUDELEY AV
9 SKENFRITH PL
10 FARNHAM GR
11 LAUNCESTON PL
12 TAMWORTH AV
13 LYDFORD TER AV
14 BEESTON GARDENS
15 HARLECH CL
16 CARISBROOKE AV

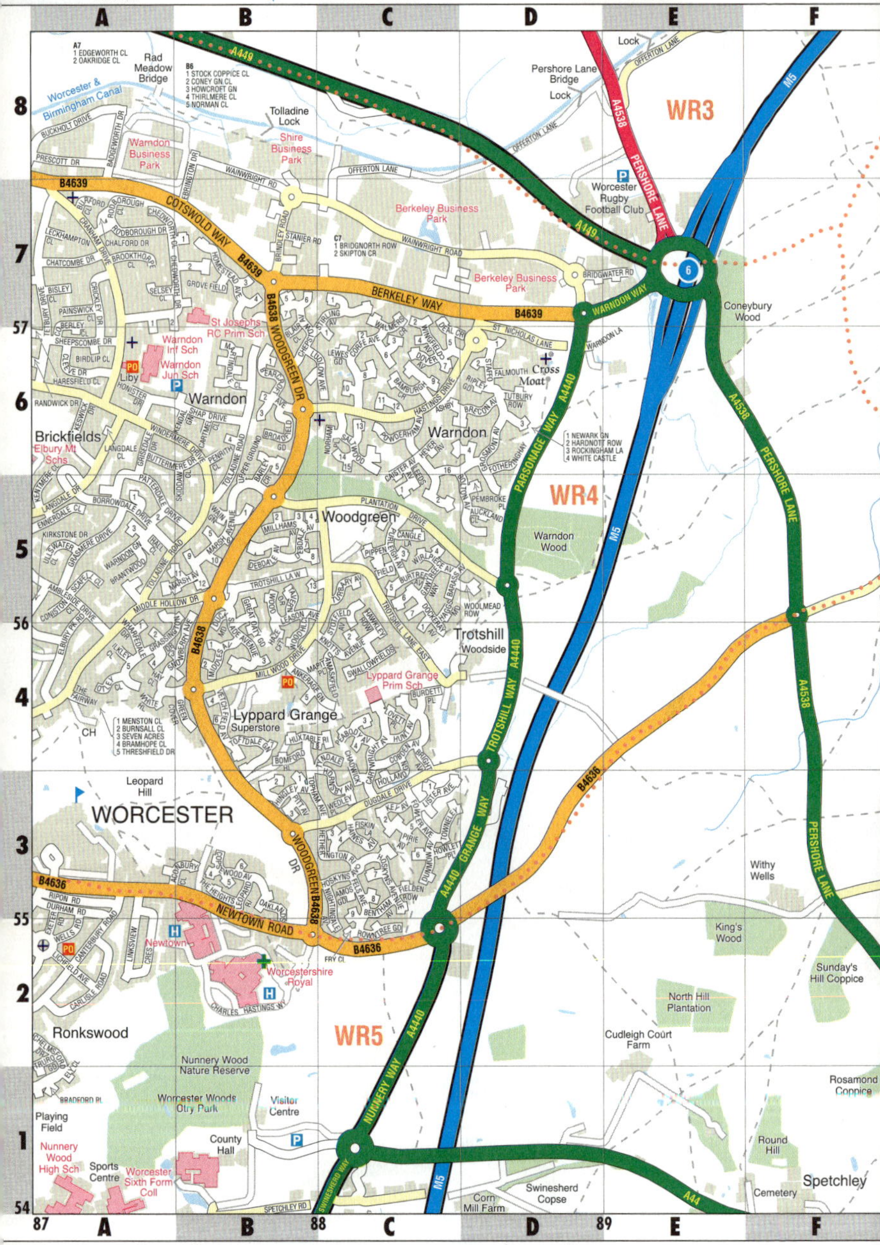

A5
1 CARROCK FELL
2 BOWNESS DR
3 GLENRIDDING CL

B3
1 ORWIN GN
2 TATTERSALL
3 TWARNLEY RI
4 BLOSSOM CL
5 BRAMBLE GD
6 VIEWFIELDS

B4
1 SPRING MD
2 GREENFIELD CL
3 SIX ACRES CFT
4 HOCK COPPICE
5 WITHINCROFT
6 NINE ACRES GN
7 WISELACK PL
8 NEASON CL

115

C3
1 SHERIDAN ROW
2 MCCORMICK AV
3 PINKUS CL
4 COLLINGSAV
5 FOWLER AV
6 HOBHOUSE GD
7 IDLETON
8 SHAFTESBURY GN
9 WILBERFORCE PI

129

C4
1 WATCHETTS GN
2 DRUMBLES LA
3 CLARKSON GD
4 TREVITHICK CL

C5
1 WARDOUR PL
2 EGREMONT GD
3 WRYFLATT
4 BACCHURST PL
5 HERNE FIELD
6 GAWTREE WY
7 THACKHOLME

104
118

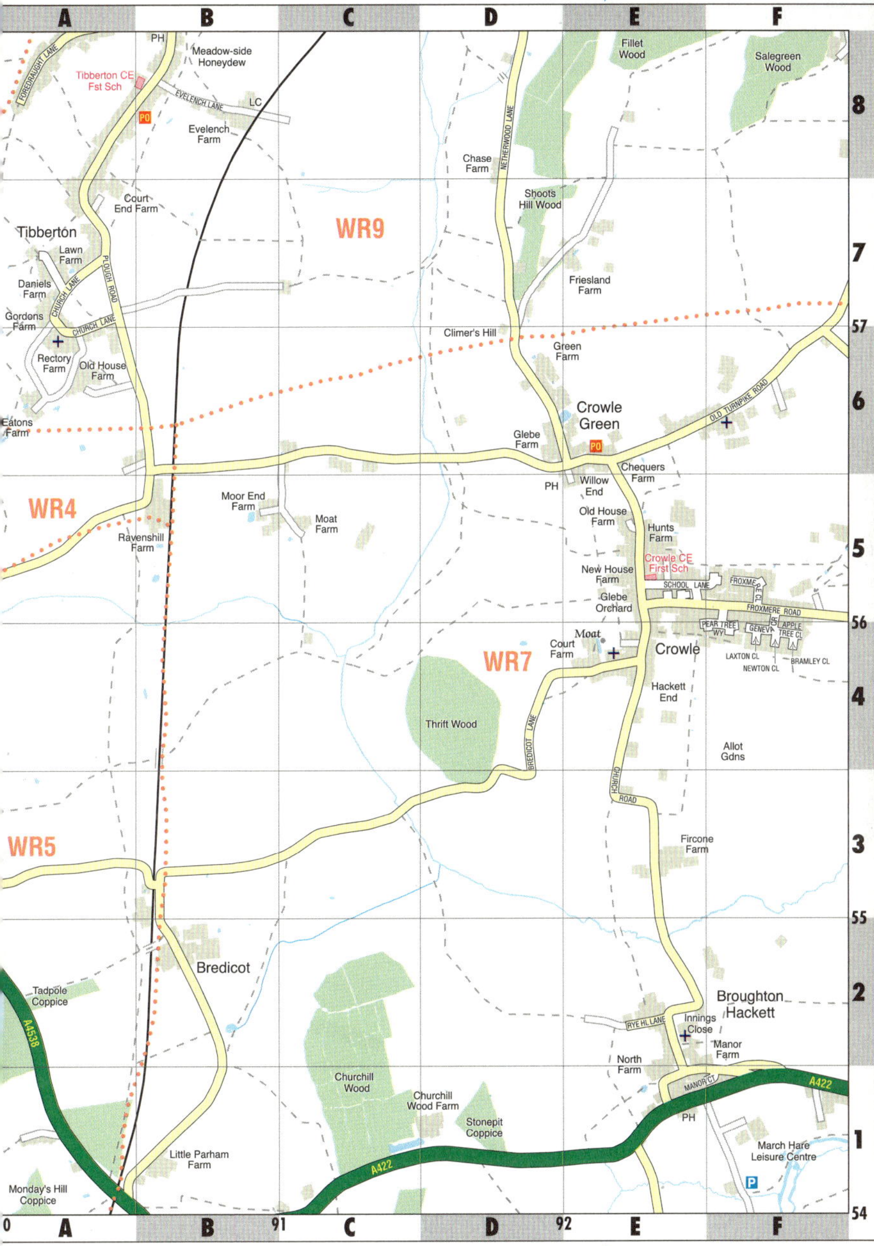

130
118

117
105

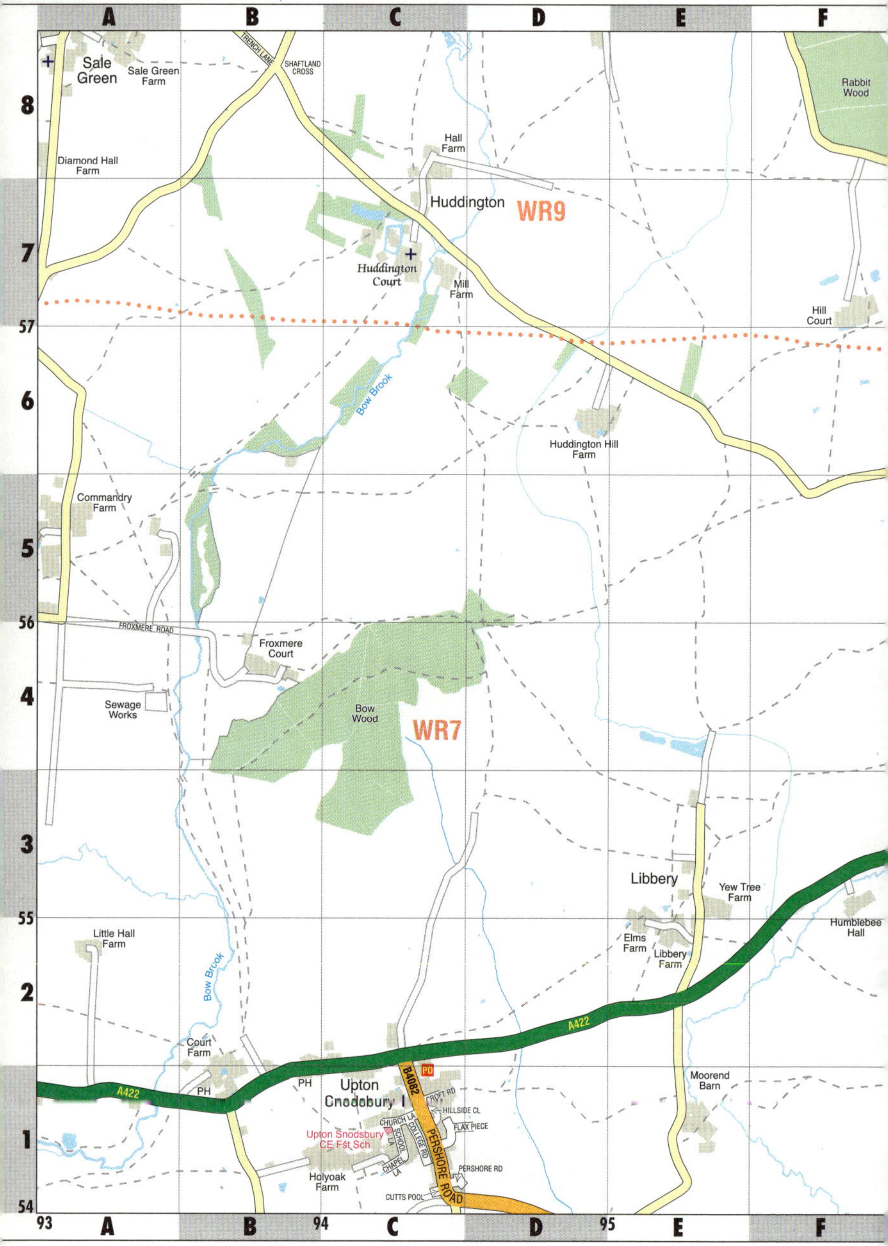

117
131

106
120

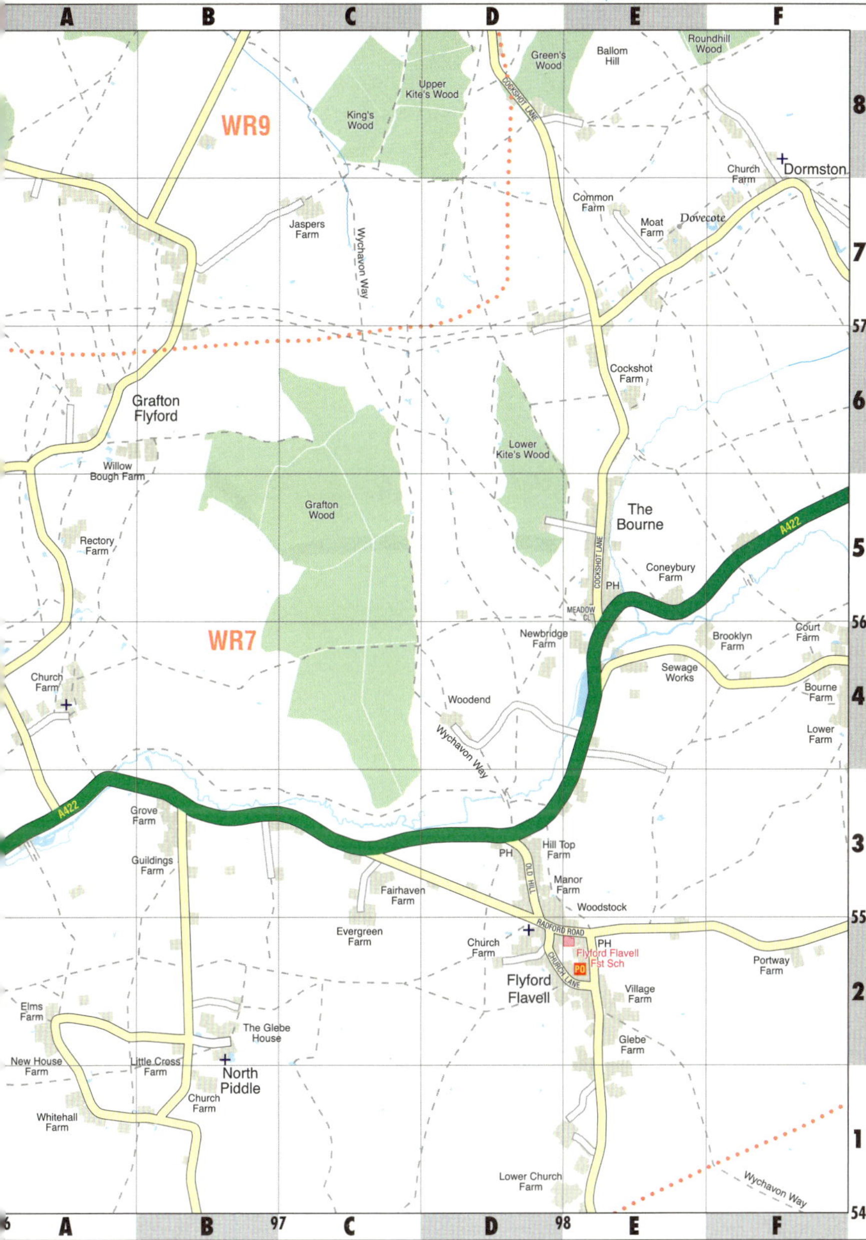
A
B
C
D
E
F
WR9
Green's Wood
Ballom Hill
Roundhill Wood
Upper Kite's Wood
King's Wood
COCKSHOT LANE
Dormston
Church Farm
Common Farm
Moat Farm
Dovecote
Jaspers Farm
Wychavon Way
Cockshot Farm
Grafton Flyford
Lower Kite's Wood
Willow Bough Farm
Grafton Wood
The Bourne
Rectory Farm
A422
Coneybury Farm
PH
MEADOW CL
Newbridge Farm
Brooklyn Farm
Court Farm
WR7
Sewage Works
Church Farm
Bourne Farm
Woodend
Wychavon Way
Lower Farm
Grove Farm
Hill Top Farm
Guildings Farm
PH
OLD HILL
Manor Farm
Fairhaven Farm
Woodstock
RADFORD ROAD
Evergreen Farm
Church Farm
PH
Flyford Flavell Fst Sch
PO
CHURCH LANE
Portway Farm
Flyford Flavell
Village Farm
Elms Farm
The Glebe House
Glebe Farm
New House Farm
Little Cross Farm
North Piddle
Church Farm
Whitehall Farm
Lower Church Farm
Wychavon Way
8
7
57
6
5
56
4
3
55
2
1
54
96
97
98

119
107

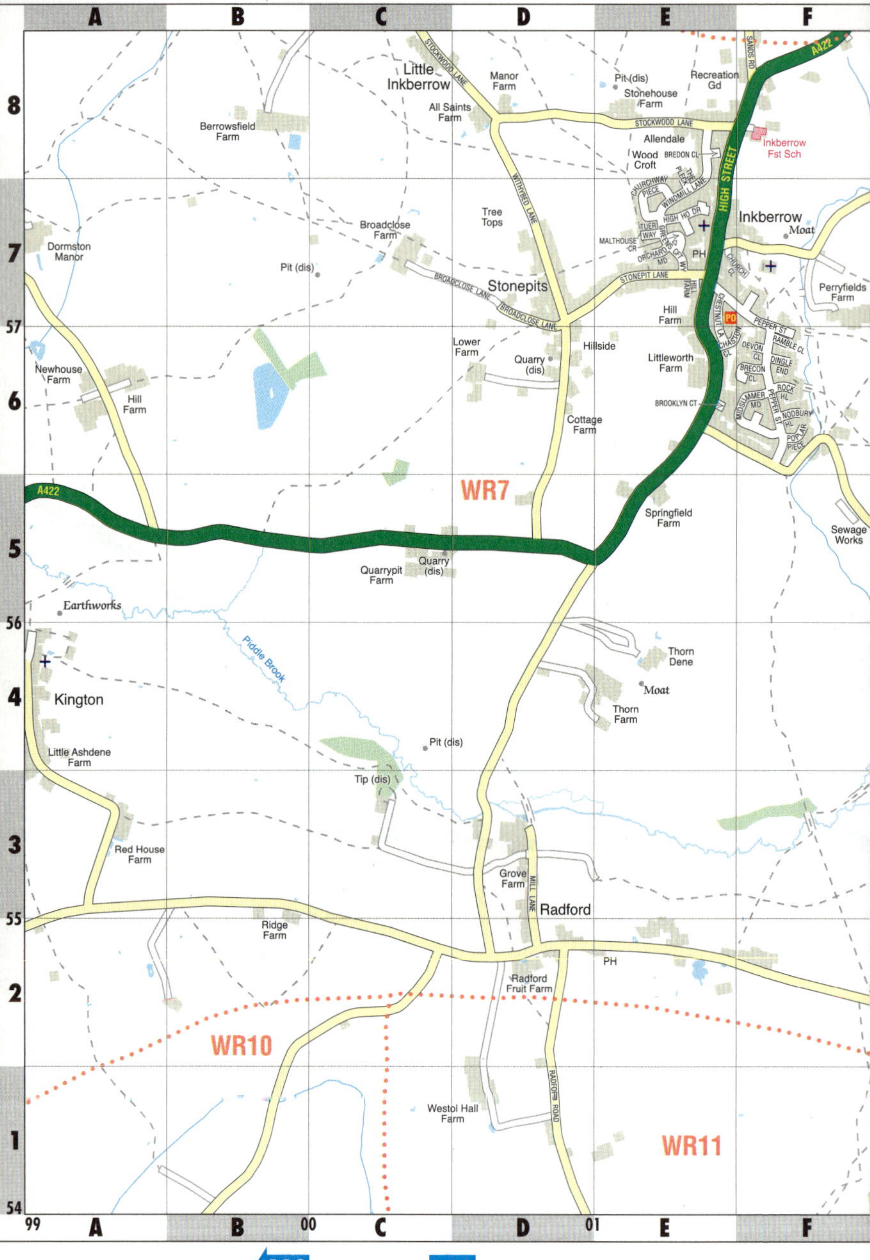
A
B
C
D
E
F
8
7
57
6
5
56
4
3
55
2
1
54
99
00
01
Little Inkberrow
STOCKWOOD LANE
Manor Farm
All Saints Farm
Pit (dis)
Stonehouse Farm
Recreation Gd
SANDS RD
A422
STOCKWOOD LANE
Allendale
Wood Croft
BREDON CL
Inkberrow Fst Sch
Berrowsfield Farm
CHURCHWAY PIECE
THE PLECK
WINDMILL LANE
HIGH HO DR
HIGH STREET
Inkberrow
Moat
TUER WAY
GREENS CFT WY
MALTHOUSE CR
ORCHARD MD
PH
CHURCH CL
Tree Tops
Broadclose Farm
WITHYBED LANE
Dormston Manor
Pit (dis)
BROADCLOSE LANE
Stonepits
BROADCLOSE LANE
STONEPIT LANE
HILL FARM
Hill Farm
Perryfields Farm
CHESTNUT LA
PO
CHASTON CL
PEPPER ST
RAMBLE CL
DEVON CL
DINGLE END
BRECON CL
Lower Farm
Quarry (dis)
Hillside
Littleworth Farm
Newhouse Farm
Hill Farm
ROCK HL
BROOKLYN CT
MIDSUMMER MD
PEPPER ST
NODBURY HL
POPLAR PIECE
Cottage Farm
WR7
A422
Springfield Farm
Sewage Works
Quarrypit Farm
Quarry (dis)
Earthworks
Piddle Brook
Thorn Dene
Moat
Kington
Thorn Farm
Little Ashdene Farm
Pit (dis)
Tip (dis)
Red House Farm
Grove Farm
MILL LANE
Radford
Ridge Farm
PH
Radford Fruit Farm
WR10
RADFORD ROAD
Westol Hall Farm
WR11

108
122

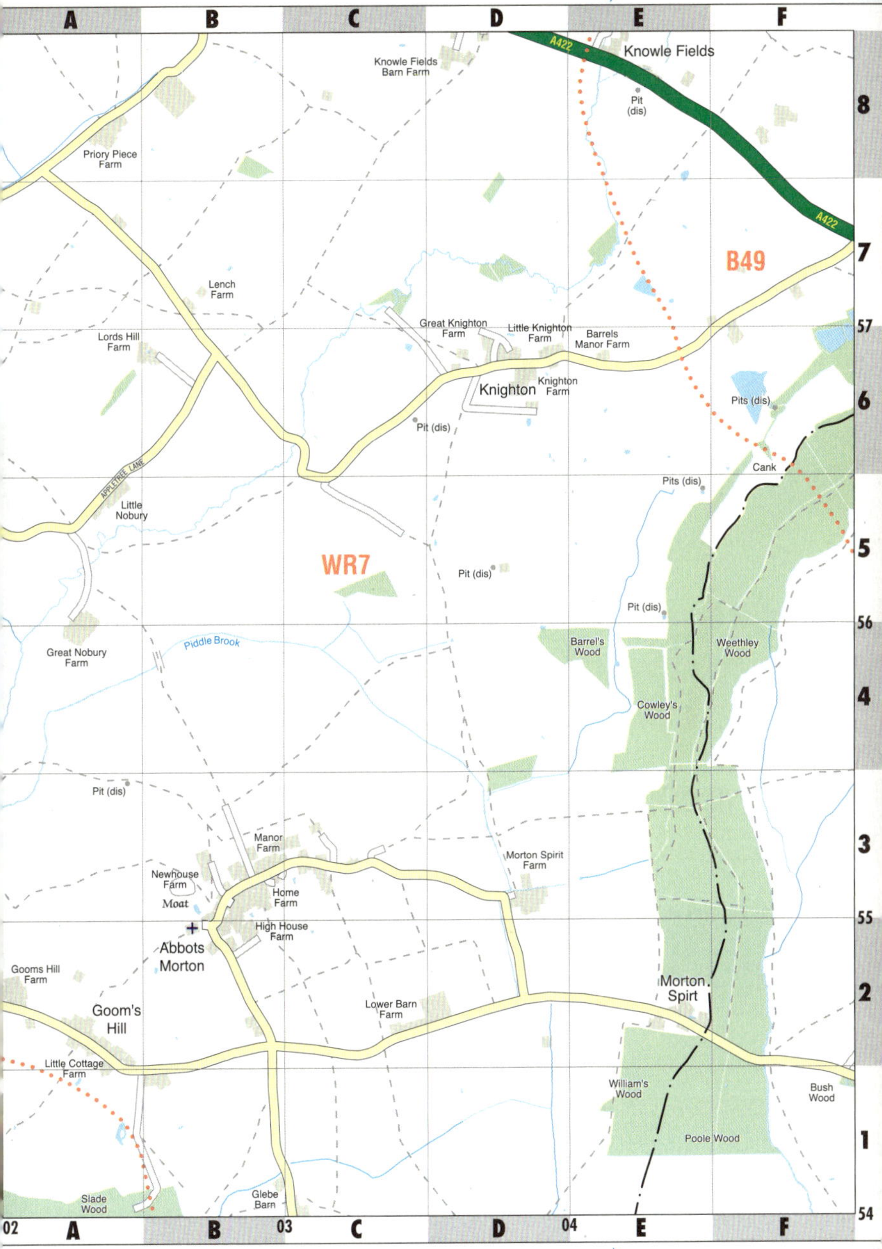

134
122

121
109

121
135

110
124

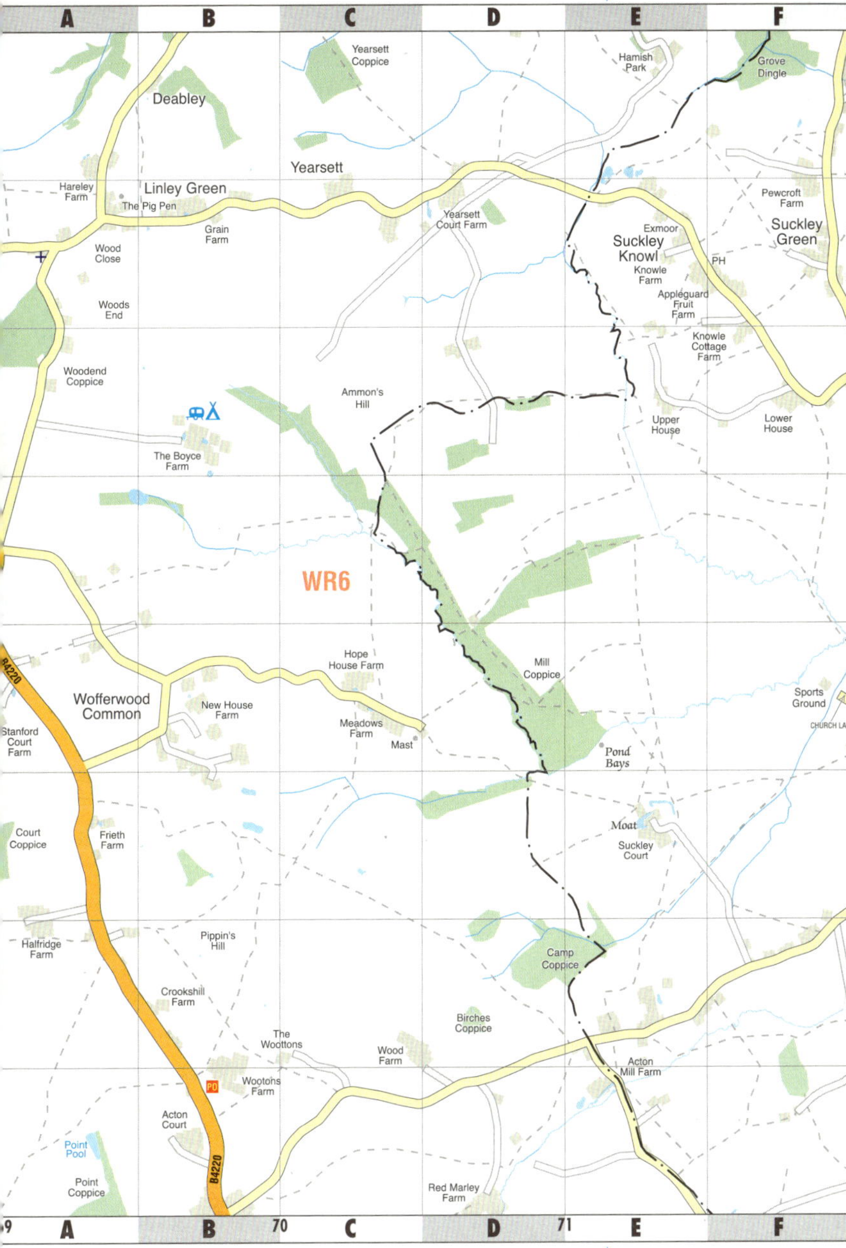
A
B
C
D
E
F
Yearsett Coppice
Hamish Park
Grove Dingle
Deabley
Yearsett
Hareley Farm
Linley Green
The Pig Pen
Grain Farm
Yearsett Court Farm
Pewcroft Farm
Exmoor
Suckley Knowl
Suckley Green
PH
Wood Close
Knowle Farm
Appleguard Fruit Farm
Woods End
Knowle Cottage Farm
Woodend Coppice
Ammon's Hill
Upper House
Lower House
The Boyce Farm
WR6
Hope House Farm
Mill Coppice
Sports Ground
CHURCH LA
Wofferwood Common
New House Farm
Stanford Court Farm
Meadows Farm
Mast
Pond Bays
B4220
Moat
Court Coppice
Frieth Farm
Suckley Court
Halfridge Farm
Pippin's Hill
Camp Coppice
Crookshill Farm
Birches Coppice
The Woottons
Wood Farm
Acton Mill Farm
PO
Wootons Farm
Acton Court
Point Pool
Point Coppice
Red Marley Farm
8
7
53
6
5
52
4
3
51
2
1
50
69
70
71

124

123
111

A
B
C
D
E
F
8
7
53
6
5
52
4
3
51
2
1
50
72
73
74
Almshouse Wood
Worcestershire Way
Visitor Centre
Ravenshill Wood Nature Reserve
Round Hill
High Wood
Green Street Farm
Court
Fieldend Rose Wood
FOLLY ROAD
Crews Hill
Football Ground
Ravenwood Place
Alfrick
PO
UPPER HOUSE
White House
WHITE HOUSE CT
Woodfield Barn
Patches Farm
Yarringtons Farm
Whitehouse Farm
Blackhouse Farm
Alfrick Pound
Barley Farm
WR6
Weir
Woodland View
Rundells End
Suckley Hills
STOCKS ROAD
Nature Reserve
Lower Court
CHURCH LANE
Worcestershire Way
Catterhall Farm
Mousehole Farm
Papermill Coppice
Suckley Prim Sch
Weir
Mousehole Bridge
Old Storridge Common
Suckley
WOODLAND RD
Sewage Works
NEW RD ESTATE
Sheephill Coppice
Stocks Farm
Lower Tundridge Farm
Upper Tundridge Farm
Watchwood
Grove Hill Court
Grove Hill
Fincher's Farm
Coneygore Coppice
Sindons Mill Farm
Weir
Works
Weir
Lower Mosewick Farm
The Beck
Birchwood
PO
PH
Batchelor's Bridge
Riddings Farm
Quarry Side
Longley Green
Halesend Wood
Worcestershire Way
Shuttifield Coppice
Birchwood Hall
Birchwood Common
The Riddings
Batchcombe Fruit Farm
Woodhouse Dingle

123

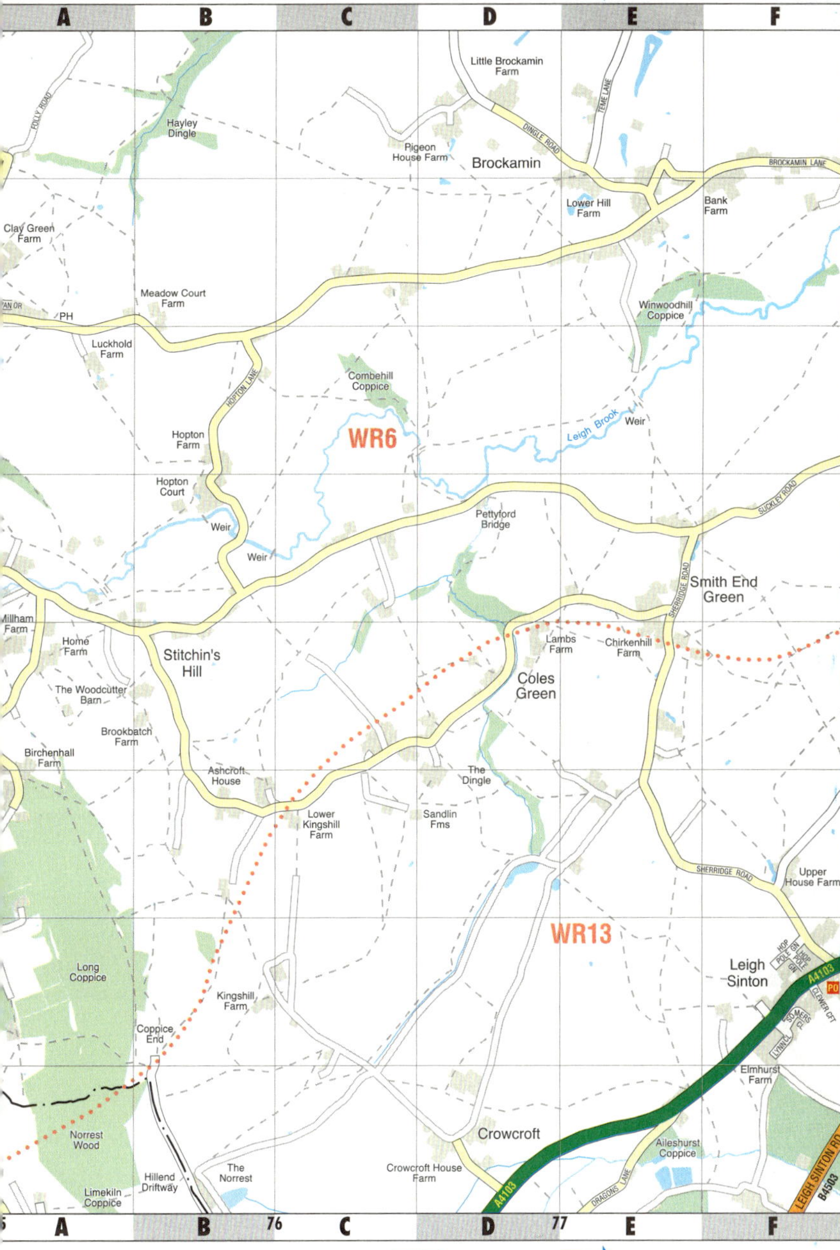
A
B
C
D
E
F
Little Brockamin Farm
TEME LANE
FOLLY ROAD
Hayley Dingle
Pigeon House Farm
Brockamin
DINGLE ROAD
BROCKAMIN LANE
Lower Hill Farm
Bank Farm
Clay Green Farm
Meadow Court Farm
PH
Luckhold Farm
Winwoodhill Coppice
Combehill Coppice
HOPTON LANE
Hopton Farm
WR6
Leigh Brook
Weir
Hopton Court
Weir
Weir
Pettyford Bridge
SUCKLEY ROAD
Smith End Green
SHERRIDGE ROAD
Millham Farm
Home Farm
Stitchin's Hill
Lambs Farm
Chirkenhill Farm
Coles Green
The Woodcutter Barn
Brookbatch Farm
Birchenhall Farm
Ashcroft House
The Dingle
Lower Kingshill Farm
Sandlin Fms
SHERRIDGE ROAD
Upper House Farm
WR13
Long Coppice
Leigh Sinton
HOP POLE GN
A4103
PO
CLEWER CFT
SOMERS CL
LYNN CL
Kingshill Farm
Coppice End
Elmhurst Farm
Norrest Wood
Crowcroft
Aileshurst Coppice
Limekiln Coppice
Hillend Driftway
The Norrest
Crowcroft House Farm
A4103
DRAGONS LANE
LEIGH SINTON RD
B4503
8
7
53
6
5
52
4
3
51
2
1
50
76
77

125
113

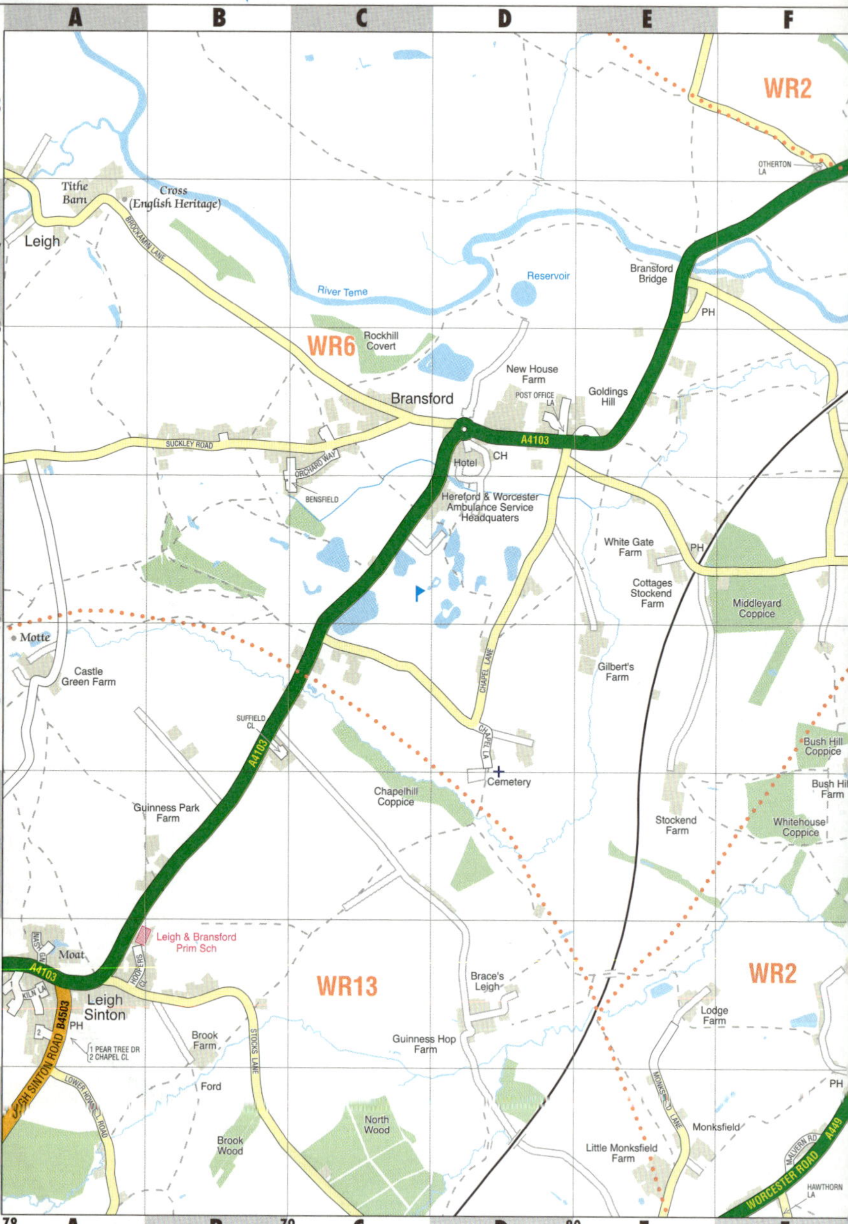

125
139

114
128

F7
1 ELM LINK CL
2 WHITES RD
3 CHARNWOOD CL
4 ST LAWRENCE CL
5 JASPER RD

F6
1 FRANKLIN CL
2 WESTMOUNT CL
3 DAWSON CL
4 BRUNSWICK CL
5 LABRADOR RD
6 EDMONTON CL

7 BAFFIN RD

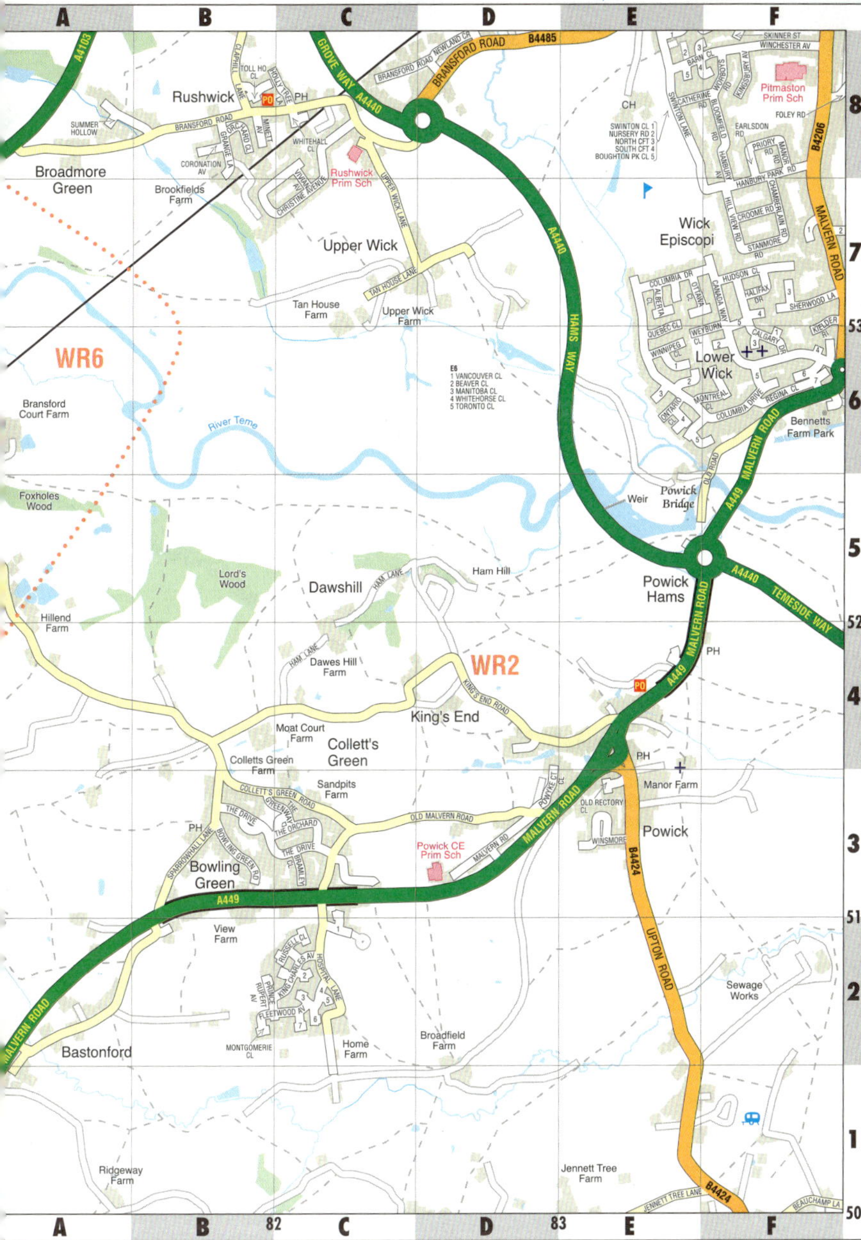

C2
1 HAMILTON CL
2 BYRON CL
3 ESSEX CL
4 CROMWELL CL
5 DEANE CL
6 BERRY CL
7 AUSTEN CL

140
128

C5
1 THORNEY WLK
2 CAMPION WLK
3 BREAM CL
4 EAGLE CL
5 FALCON CL
6 KESTREL DR
7 DACE RD
8 MARIGOLD CL

127

D5
1 SWALLOW CL
2 DRAYCOTE CL
3 PARTRIDGE CL
4 QUEENSWOOD DR
5 HIDCOTE CL
6 BULLFINCH CL
7 JASMINE CL
8 LARKSPUR RD
9 MAGNOLIA CL
10 PRIMROSE DR
11 THISTLE CL
12 TREFOIL CL

115

D6
1 BARNES PL
2 SPRINGFIELD CL
3 BURNHAM CL
4 BLAKENEY CL
5 HUNSTANTON CL
6 SOUTHWOLD CL
7 FRAMLINGHAM CL
8 COLTISHALL CL
9 HEMSBY CL
10 ALDERSEY CL
11 CONNAUGHT CL

E6
1 MALHAM PL
2 BOWOOD LA
3 RAINTHORPE AV
4 HAYLING CL
5 ROSEMOOR GDNS
6 SANDPIPER CL
7 KNAPP PL
8 BICTON AV
9 RUTLAND PL
10 RANNOCH AV
11 LISMORE GN
12 BLAGDON CL
13 STROMA AV

E8
1 MIDHURST CL
2 WYCHELM CL
3 LANCING CL
4 MARLBOROUGH ST
5 GOODWOOD CL
6 CANNON ST
7 LIVINGSTONE
8 HAILSHAM CL
9 PEVENSEY CL

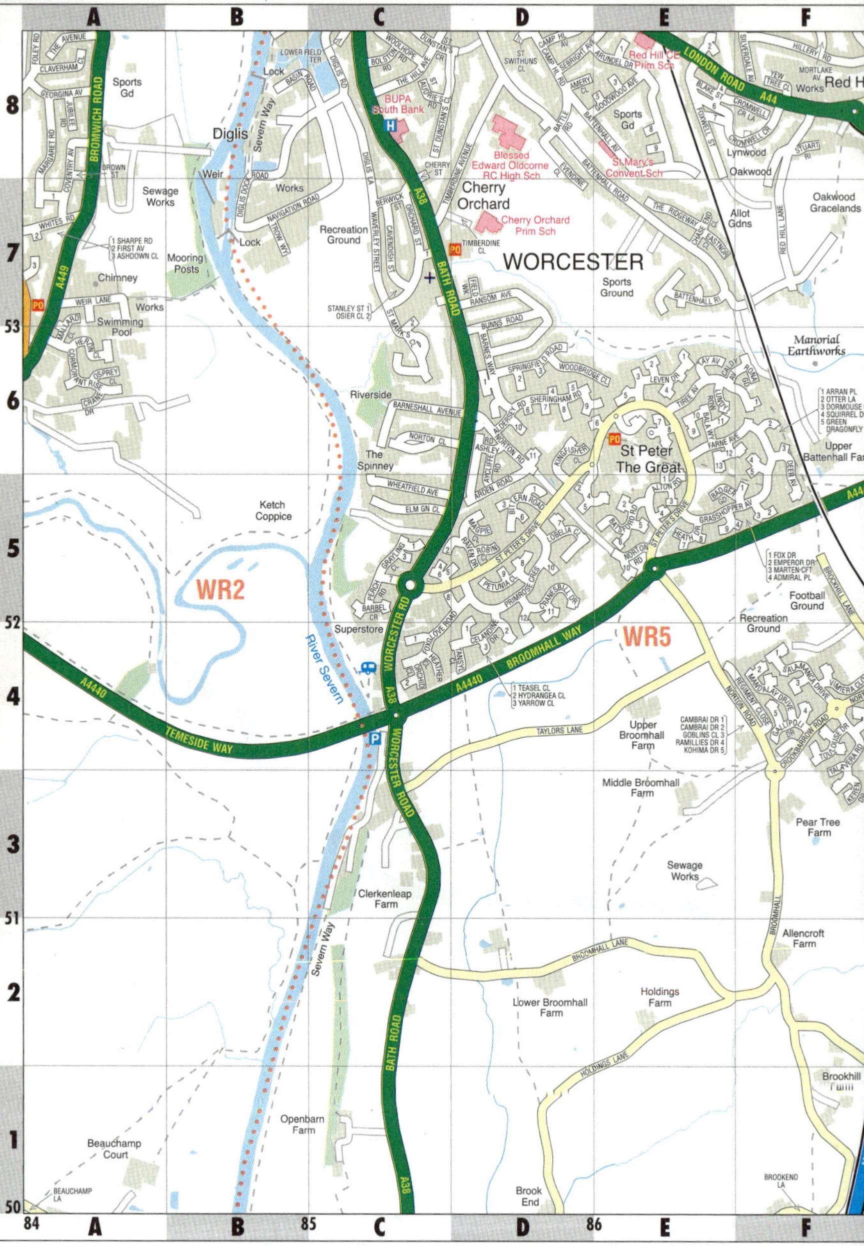

C4
1 HYACINTH CL
2 BEGONIA CL

127

141

E5
1 WESTONBIRT CL
2 RAVENSHILL CL
3 WASELEY CL
4 DINMORE CL
5 SLIMBRIDGE CL
6 STONELEIGH CL
7 BRIMSTONE CL
8 PEACOCK CL
9 CAMBERWELL DR
10 BROOMHALL GR

116
130

142
130

129
117

129
143

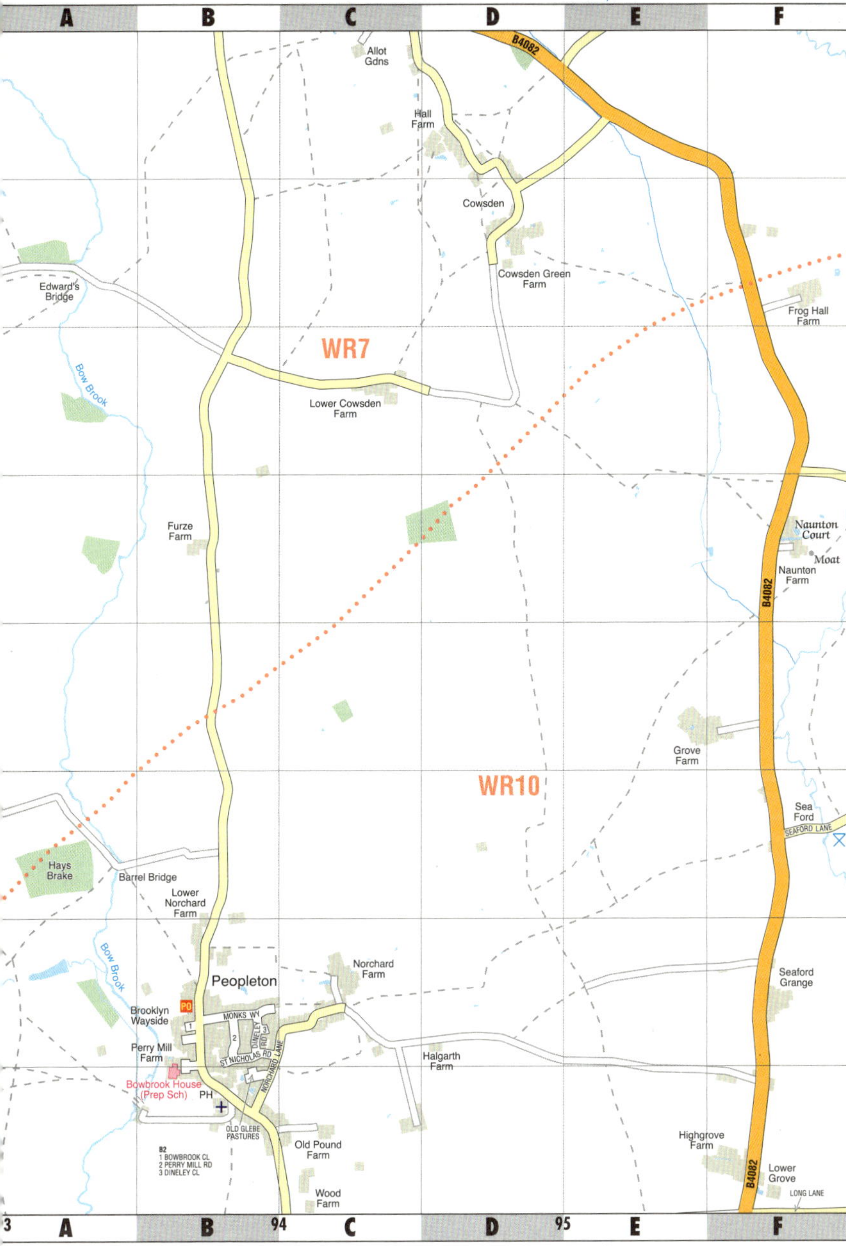
A
B
C
D
E
F
8
7
53
6
5
52
4
3
51
2
1
50
3
94
95
B4082
Allot Gdns
Hall Farm
Cowsden
Cowsden Green Farm
Frog Hall Farm
Edward's Bridge
WR7
Bow Brook
Lower Cowsden Farm
Furze Farm
Naunton Court
Moat
Naunton Farm
Grove Farm
WR10
Sea Ford
SEAFORD LANE
Hays Brake
Barrel Bridge
Lower Norchard Farm
Peopleton
Norchard Farm
Seaford Grange
PO
Brooklyn Wayside
MONKS WY
DINELEY RD
ST NICHOLAS RD
NORCHARD LANE
Perry Mill Farm
Halgarth Farm
Bowbrook House (Prep Sch)
PH
OLD GLEBE PASTURES
Old Pound Farm
Wood Farm
Highgrove Farm
Lower Grove
LONG LANE
B2
1 BOWBROOK CL
2 PERRY MILL RD
3 DINELEY CL

131
119

131
145

120
134

146
134

133
121

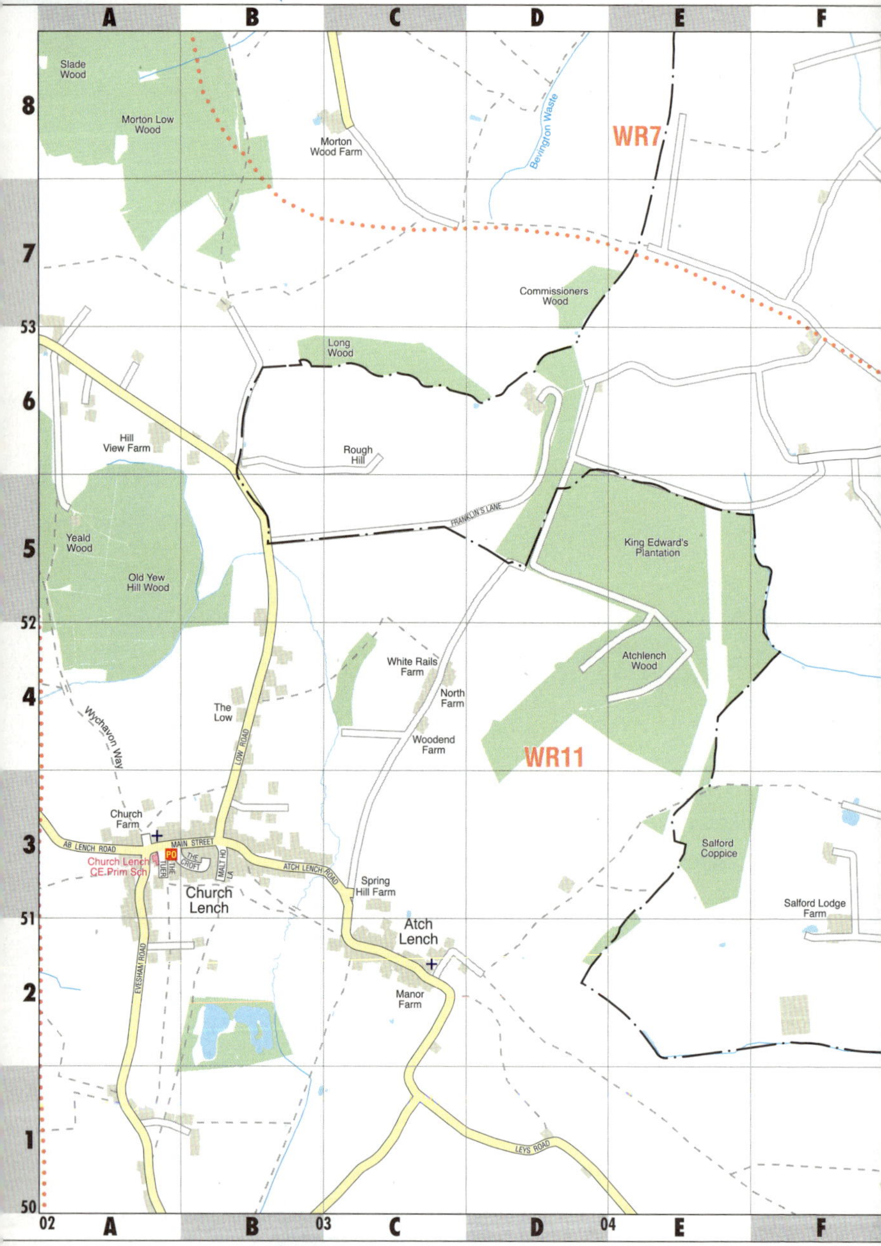

133
147

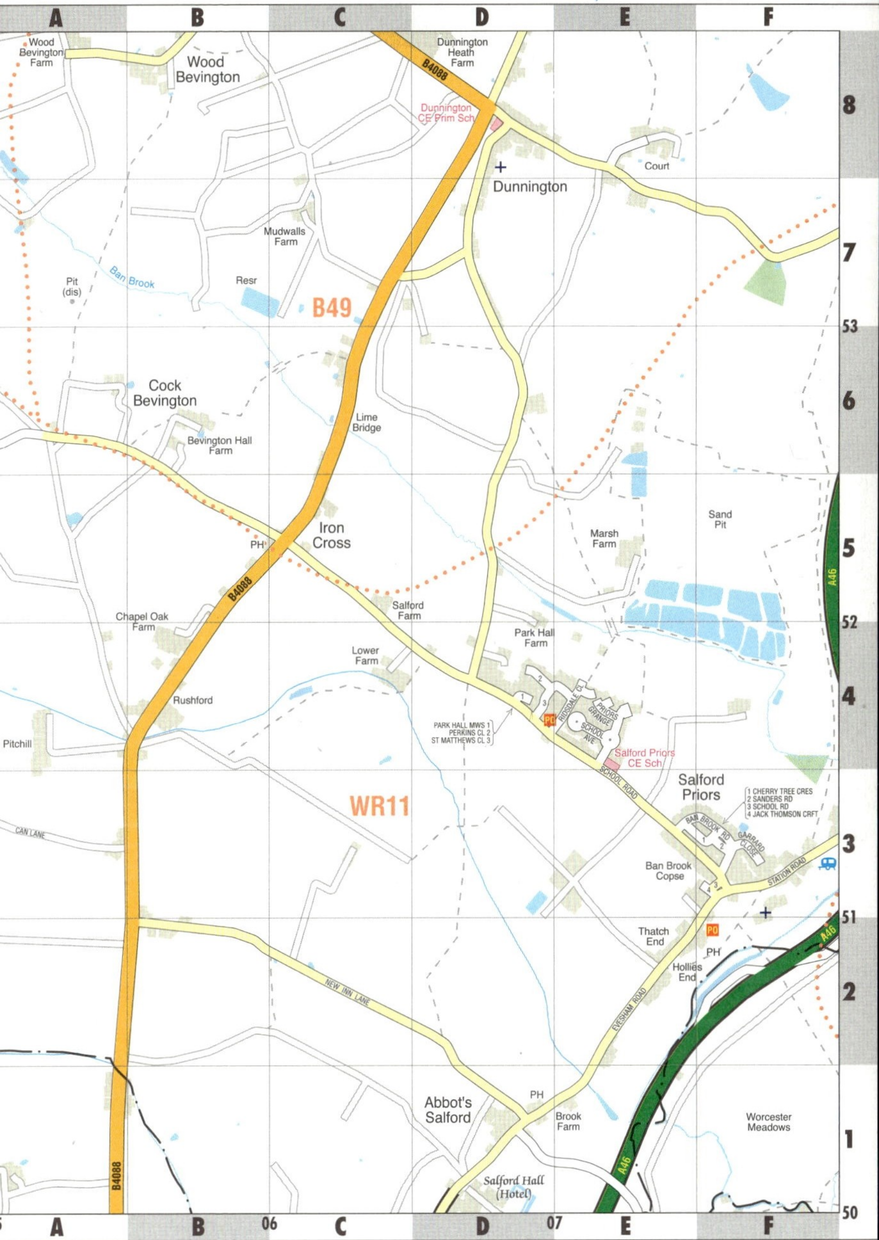
A
B
C
D
E
F
8
7
53
6
5
52
4
3
51
2
1
50
06
07
Wood Bevington Farm
Wood Bevington
Dunnington Heath Farm
B4088
Dunnington CE Prim Sch
Dunnington
Court
Mudwalls Farm
Pit (dis)
Ban Brook
Resr
B49
Cock Bevington
Lime Bridge
Bevington Hall Farm
Iron Cross
PH
Sand Pit
Marsh Farm
A46
Salford Farm
Chapel Oak Farm
Park Hall Farm
Lower Farm
Rushford
Pitchill
RIDSDALE CL
PRIORS GRANGE
SCHOOL AVE
PO
PARK HALL MWS 1
PERKINS CL 2
ST MATTHEWS CL 3
Salford Priors CE Sch
SCHOOL ROAD
Salford Priors
WR11
1 CHERRY TREE CRES
2 SANDERS RD
3 SCHOOL RD
4 JACK THOMSON CRFT
BAN BROOK RD
GARRARD CLOSE
CAN LANE
Ban Brook Copse
STATION ROAD
Thatch End
Hollies End
NEW INN LANE
EVESHAM ROAD
Abbot's Salford
Brook Farm
Worcester Meadows
Salford Hall (Hotel)

135

D5
1 LAMBOURNE CL
2 LAMBOURNE CL
3 ST LAURENCE WY
4 EBSDORF CL
5 WATLEYS CLPIPPIN CL
6 FRIDAY CLBLENHEIM CL
7 FRIDAY CL
8 BLENHEIM CL
9 WILKES WY
10 HOLDER CL

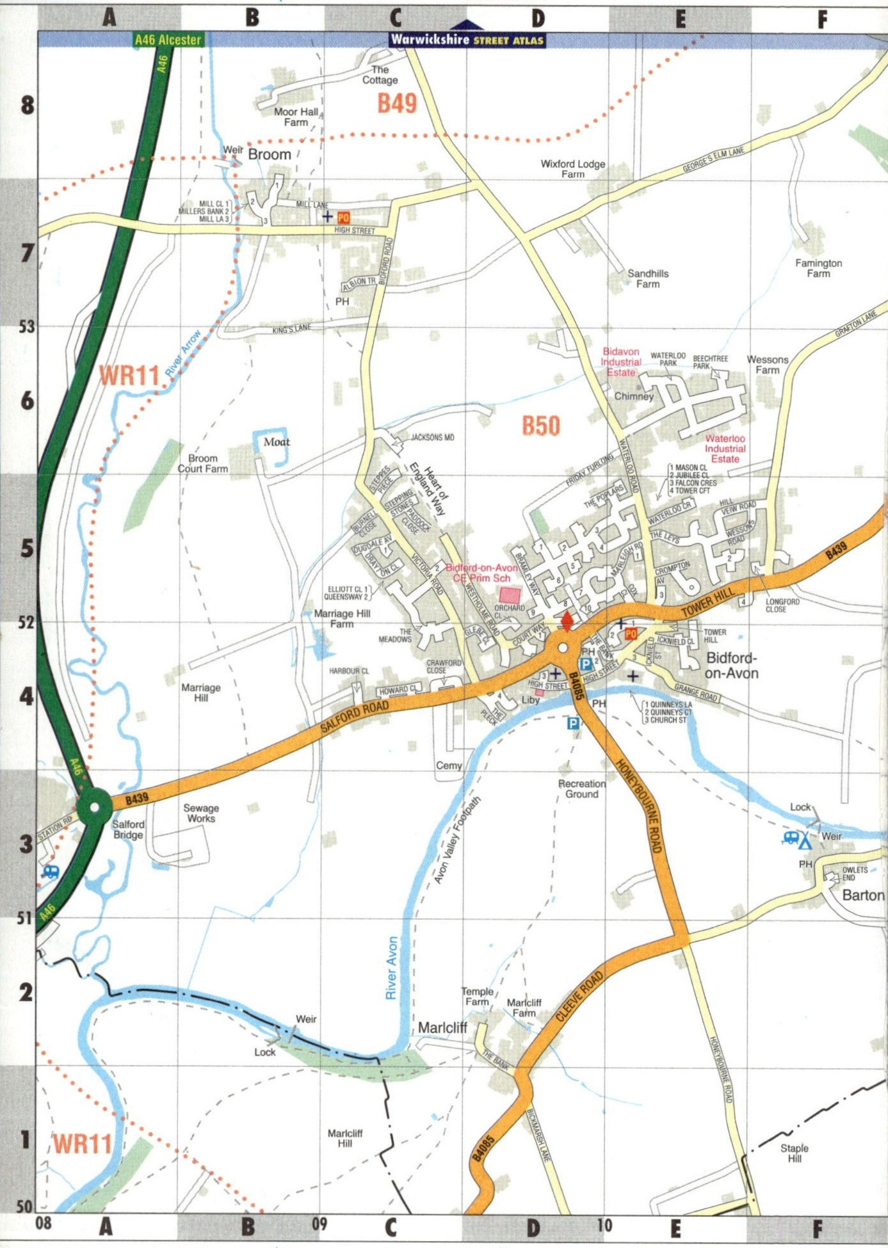

135

149

D4
1 TRAFALGAR CT
2 SAXONFIELDS
3 CHAPEL CL
4 HOLLAND CL

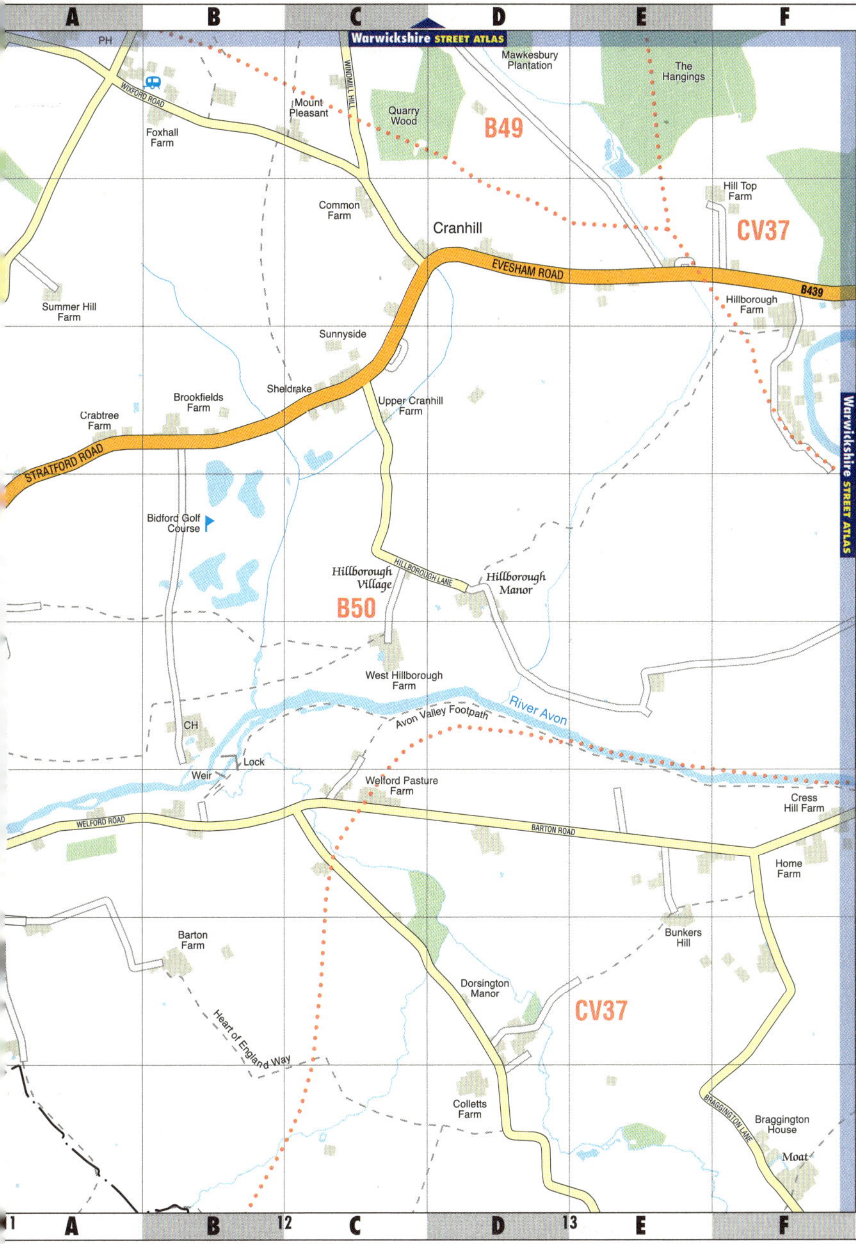
A
B
C
D
E
F
Warwickshire STREET ATLAS
PH
Wixford Road
Foxhall Farm
Mount Pleasant
Windmill Hill
Quarry Wood
Mawkesbury Plantation
The Hangings
B49
Hill Top Farm
Common Farm
Cranhill
CV37
Evesham Road
B439
Summer Hill Farm
Hillborough Farm
Sunnyside
Sheldrake
Brookfields Farm
Crabtree Farm
Upper Cranhill Farm
Stratford Road
Bidford Golf Course
Hillborough Village
Hillborough Lane
Hillborough Manor
B50
West Hillborough Farm
River Avon
Avon Valley Footpath
CH
Lock
Weir
Welford Pasture Farm
Cress Hill Farm
Welford Road
Barton Road
Home Farm
Bunkers Hill
Barton Farm
Dorsington Manor
CV37
Heart of England Way
Colletts Farm
Braggington Lane
Braggington House
Moat
8
7
53
6
5
52
4
3
51
2
1
50
11
12
13

150

125

F5
1 SPRINGFIELD GLADE
2 TAYSON WY
3 GREENFIELDS RD
4 UPPER HOWSELL CL
5 ST KITTS CL
6 LECHMERE CR

152

F4
1 BEAUCHAMP RD
2 CHESTER PL
3 LOWER QUEST HILLS RD
4 LANSDOWNE RD
5 DALBURY CL

126
140

B5
1 BEECH CL
2 BROOKFIELD
3 REGENCY RD
4 THE HOLLIES MS
5 CORONATION RD
6 QUEEN ELIZABETH RD

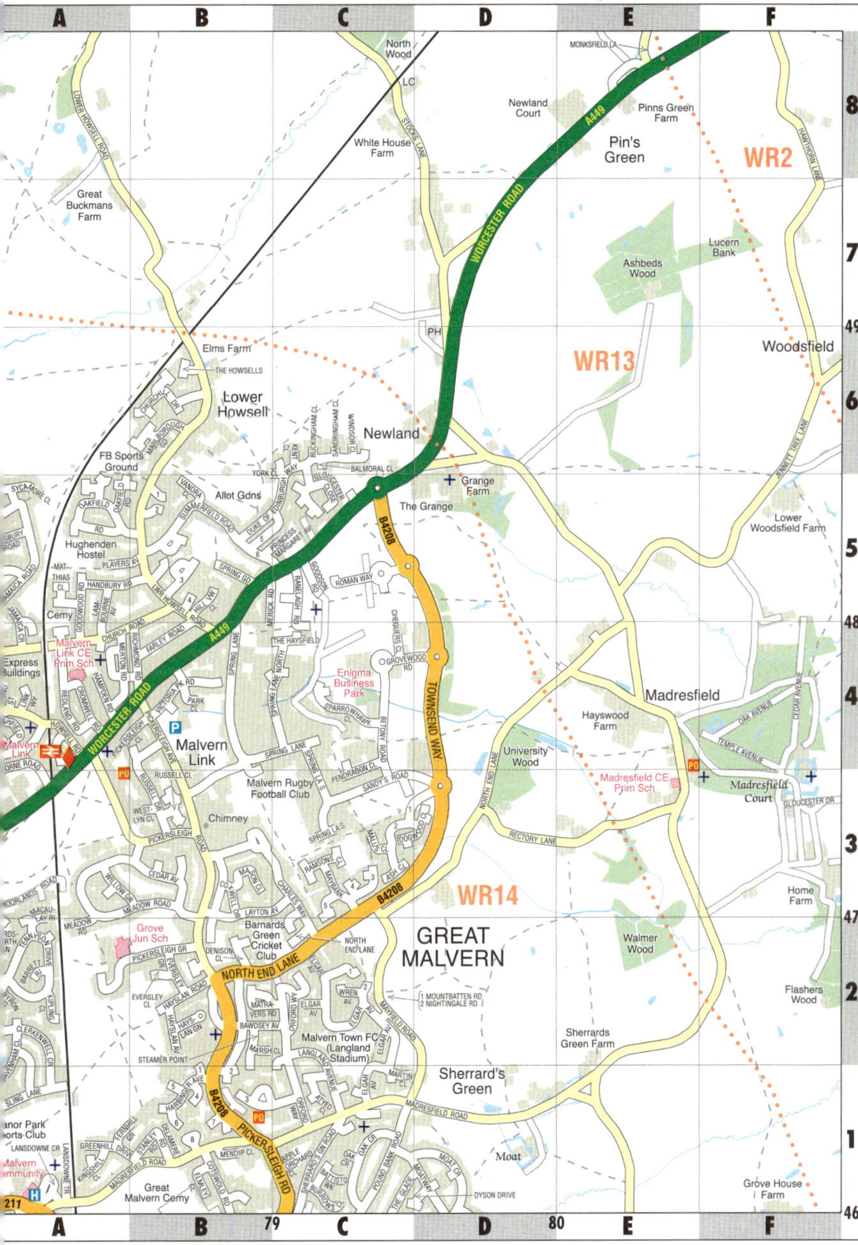

B1
1 ALICANTE CL
2 EDITH BERRY CT
3 CLARE RD
4 SHIRLEY CL
5 CHALLENGER CL
6 SUNRISE
7 ASHDOWN CL
8 LANSDOWNE CL

C3
1 MANSFIELD RD
2 SPINDLE RD
3 WHITETHORN GROVE
4 ARUM CL
5 BRAMBLE CL

153
140

139
127

F8
1 BEAUCHAMP LA
2 POLE ELM CL
3 ABBEY CL
4 STANBROOK HOUSE RD

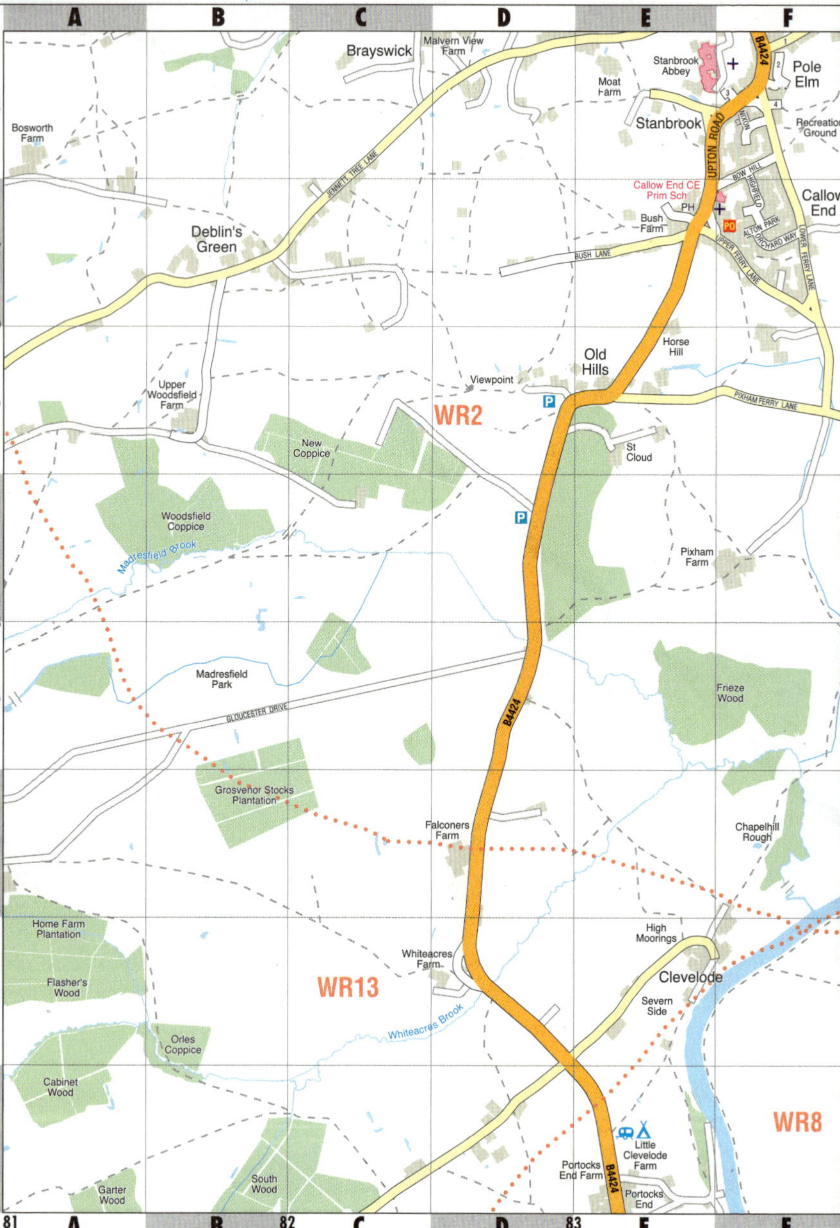

C7
1 ASTON CL
2 HETHERINGTON CL
3 CHRISTINA CL

C6
1 THE OAKS
2 FARLIE CL
3 OLD VICARAGE CL
4 FLORENCE CL
5 BYEFIELDS
6 DARWIN CL
7 PLOVERS RI
8 ADELAIDE CL

128
142

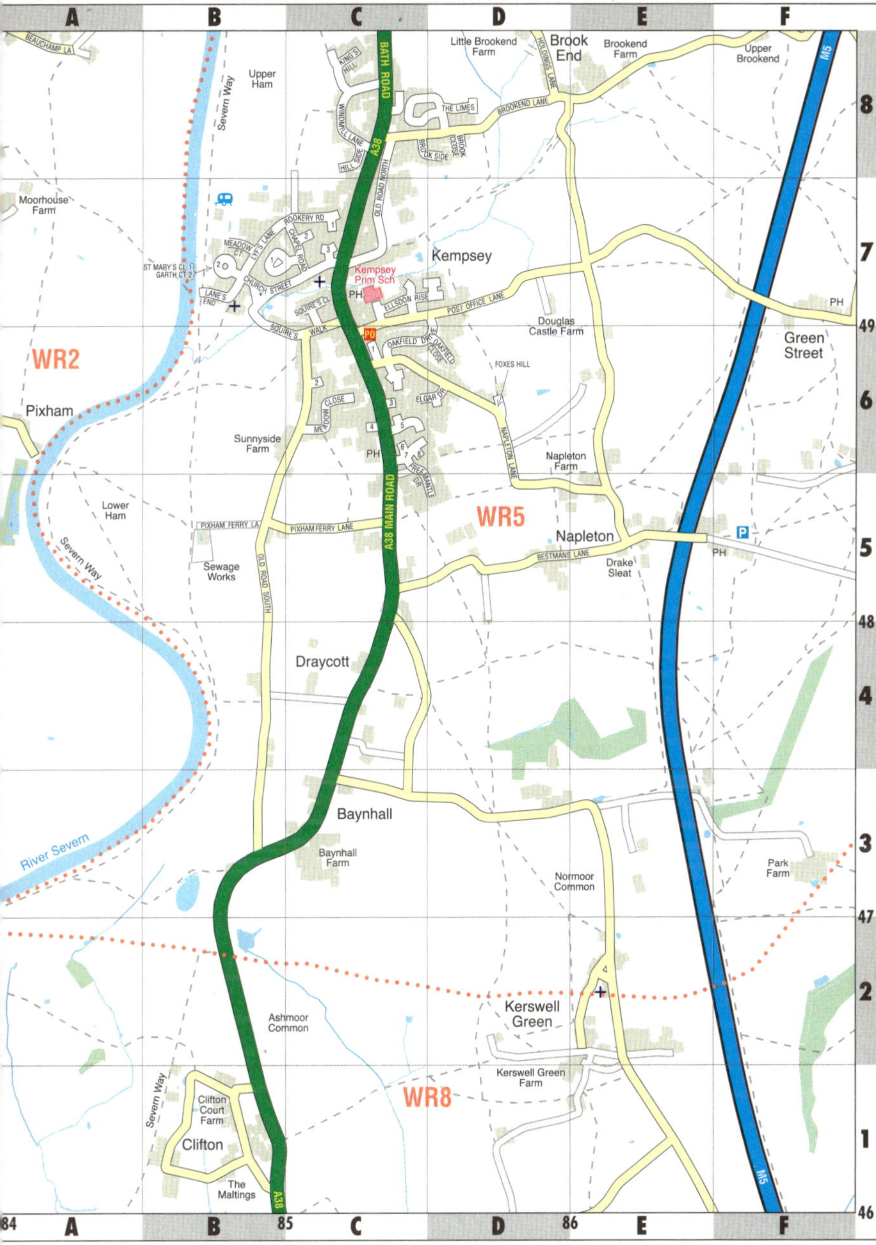

155
142

141
129

141
156

A
B
C
D
E
F
B4084
A44
Manor Farm
Pond Bay
MANOR FARM
CHURCH LANE
FROGGERY LA
BOXBUSH RD
Stoulton
WR7
Sewage Works
STATION CL
EGDON LANE
Hazel Farm
LC
Windmill Hill Farm
WINDMILL LANE
Tagg Coppice
Weir
Windmill Hill
Thorndon Farm
WADBOROUGH ROAD
Hawbridge
Hawbridge Bungalow Farm
CLAVERTON
PH
Sewage Works
Thorndon Grove
Drakes Broughton
STONEBOW ROAD
HAWTHORNE CL
LAUREL CL
MAGNOLIA CL
LEWIS CL
PH
STONEBOW RD
PO
BEECH AV
SHRUBBERY ROAD
KEEPERS CL
PH
Applegrove
Orchard's End
St Barnabas CE Fst & Mid Sch
Caldewell House
WOODLEIGH
WALCOT LANE
Teal Farm
Dufty Coppice
Great Blaythorn Wood
Mill Rough
Wadborough Hall Farm
MILL LANE
WR10
Coppice View
Blaythorn Wood
Lodge Wood
Wadborough
Deerfold Wood
WR8
Merrilands Farm
Caddicroft Farm
Ufnell Bridge
Two Springs
Callan's Wood
CRABBE LANE
CHEVINGTON LANE
Croome Perry Wood
Crabbe Farm
Ramsden
New Farm
Besford Bridge Farm
Wrights Farm
Besford Bridge
SALTERS LANE
Tiddesley Wood
8
7
49
6
5
48
4
3
47
2
1
46
90
91
92

143
131

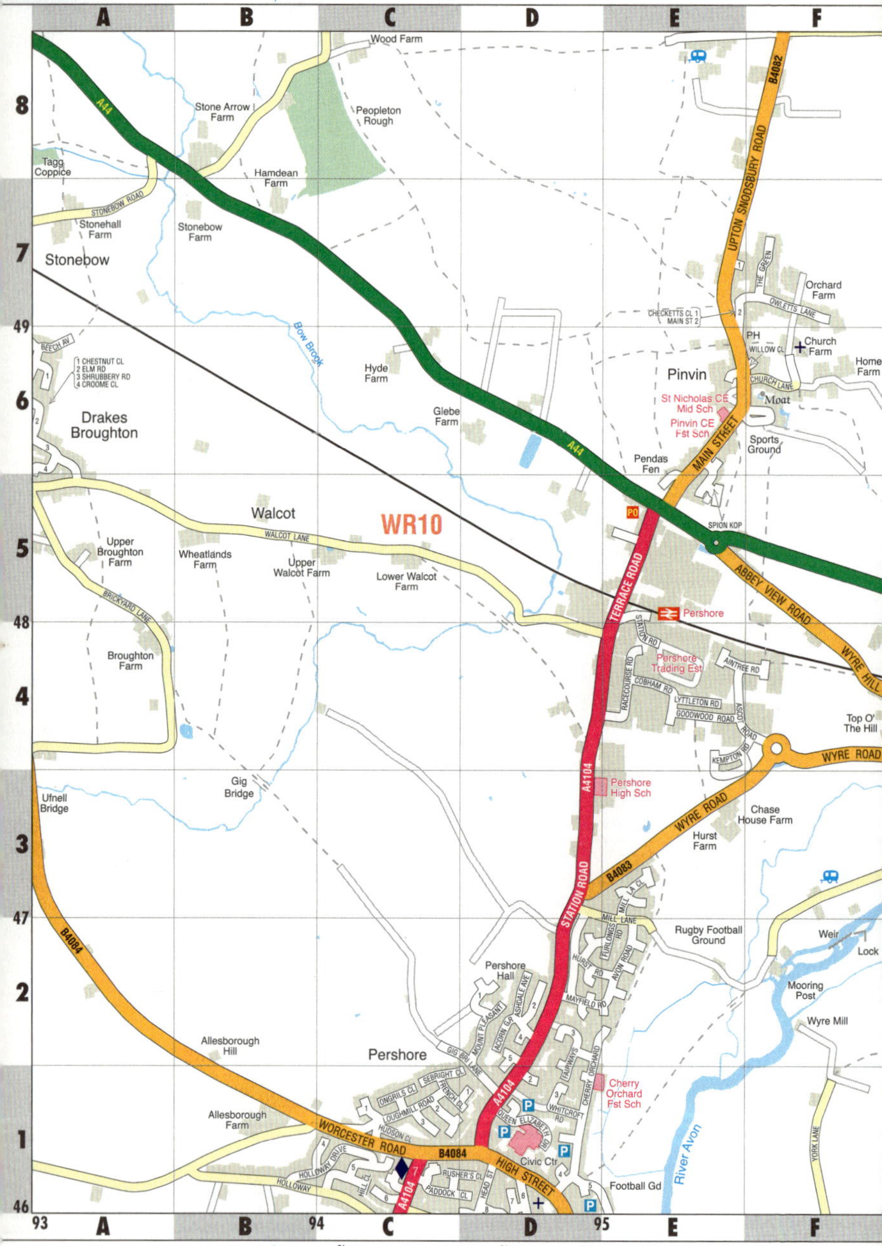

143
158

C1
1 SHELDON CL
2 BEDFORD CL
3 SCOBELL CL
4 WILLOW CL
5 ALLESBOROUGH DR
6 RAIL GROUND
7 THREE SPRINGS RD

D1
1 WHITTAKERS CL
2 NURSERY CL
3 FAIRWAYS WLK
4 REDLANDS
5 KING GEORGE'S WY
6 PRIEST LA
7 ST AGATHA'S CL
8 ST AGATHAS RD

D2
1 MOUNT PLEASANT BARNS
2 BEECHCOMBE CL
3 APPLE TREE RD
4 BIRCHTREE GR
5 MAPLE AV

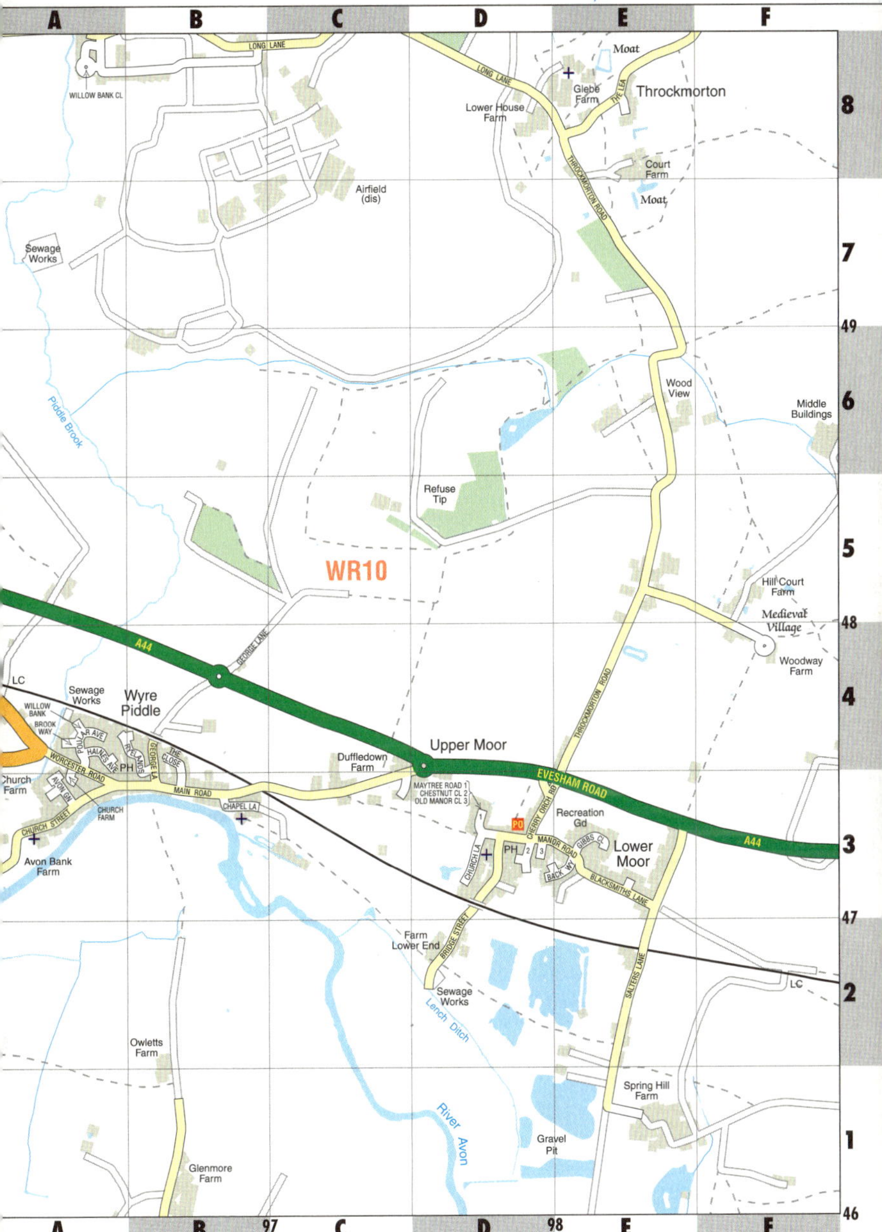
A
B
C
D
E
F
LONG LANE
WILLOW BANK CL
Moat
Throckmorton
Glebe Farm
THE LEA
Lower House Farm
Court Farm
Moat
THROCKMORTON ROAD
Airfield (dis)
Sewage Works
Wood View
Middle Buildings
Piddle Brook
Refuse Tip
WR10
Hill Court Farm
Medieval Village
Woodway Farm
A44
GEORGE LANE
LC
Sewage Works
Wyre Piddle
WILLOW BANK
BROOK WAY
Upper Moor
Duffledown Farm
Church Farm
WORCESTER ROAD
MAIN ROAD
CHAPEL LA
CHURCH FARM
CHURCH STREET
Avon Bank Farm
MAYTREE ROAD
CHESTNUT CL
OLD MANOR CL
EVESHAM ROAD
CHERRY ORCH RD
Recreation Gd
PO
PH
MANOR ROAD
GIBBS CL
Lower Moor
BACK WY
BLACKSMITHS LANE
CHURCH LA
Farm Lower End
BRIDGE STREET
SALTERS LANE
LC
Sewage Works
Lench Ditch
Owletts Farm
Spring Hill Farm
River Avon
Gravel Pit
Glenmore Farm
8
7
49
6
5
48
4
3
47
2
1
46
97
98

145
133

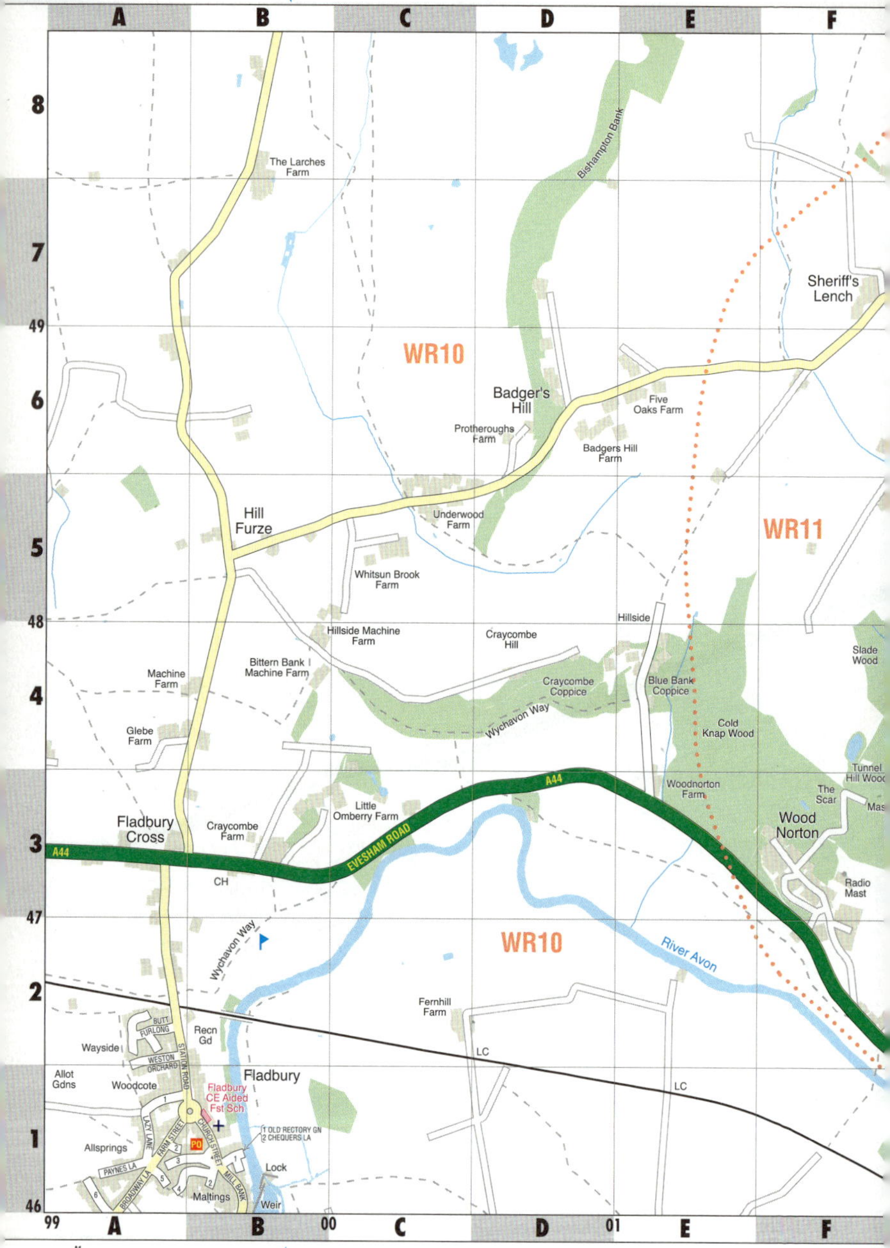

A1
1 COACH DR
2 SANDYS CL
3 ANCHOR LA
4 THE CHANTRY
5 WOODWARD PK
6 BROADWAY CL

145
160

A
B
C
D
E
F
Handgate Farm
Handgate Farm
Wychavon Way
Harvington Hill
BROOKDALE
LEYS ROAD
BLAKENHURST
OAK TREE RD
Leys Barn Farm
LEYSFIELD 1
ORCHARD PL 2
Harvington
Harvington Brook
Cottars End
B4088
EVESHAM ROAD
Tythe Barn Farm
Resr
Sheriff's Lench Farm
HIPTON HILL
Hipton Hill
WR11
Hotel
Grange Farm
Ashmore's Farm
A46
Coppice Farm
Hipton Hill Wood
CHURCH LA
Swines Hill Wood
Lenchwick Coppice
Tunnel Hill
Half Moon Coppice
Manor Farm
Norton
New Farm
THE PADDOCKS
KING'S LANE
HEATHFIELD ROAD
Lenchwick
LLOYD CL
Woodland View
ST EGWIN'S CL
Shepherd's Plantation
CHADBURY ROAD
Heliport
River Avon
Chadbury
Chadbury Farm
Vale Wildlife Visitor Centre
Evesham Country Park
Manor Farm
Twyford
A44
Weir
Chadbury Lock
8
7
49
6
5
48
4
3
47
2
1
46
02
03
04

147
135

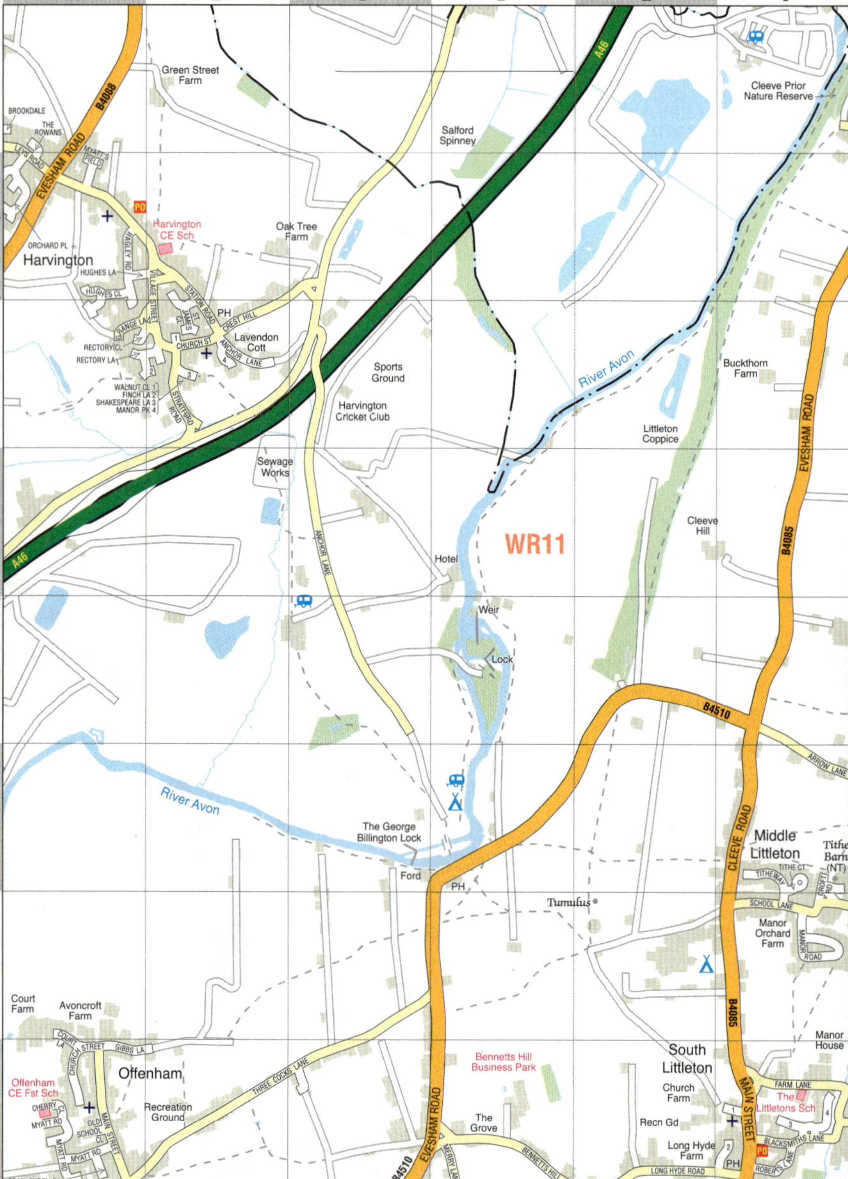

F1
1 CHURCH LA
2 ST MICHAEL'S CL
3 HATHAWAY CL
4 BLACKSMITHS CL

147
162

A
B
C
D
E
F
Greystones
Bickmarsh
Froglands Farm
FROGLANDS LANE
MILL LANE
NIGHTINGALE LA 1
WEST END 2
BACK LA 3
Bay Tree Farm
Wings Wellington
B4085
BICKMARSH LANE
SIXTEEN ACRES LA
Bickmarsh Hall
Clay Hall Farm
Manor House
MANOR CT
CLEEVE ROAD
MAIN STREET
THE CLOSE
QUARRY LANE
Cleeve Prior
Cleeve Prior CE Fst Sch
PH
HODEN LA
B50
Buckle Street
CV37
Kingmoor Farm
The Rough
BUCKLE STREET
HODEN LANE
Moor Barn
Hoden
Woodlands Farm
WR11
Lower Farm
WEST SIDE
EAST SIDE
Middle Farm
North Littleton
ARROW END
Blakes Hill Farm
Football Ground
Amery Lodge Farm
SCHOOL LANE
Ullington
Cross
BLAKE'S HILL
Honeybrook Farm
SHINEHILL LANE
LEVEDON GN
Norval Farm
8
7
49
6
5
48
4
3
47
2
1
46
09
10

149
137

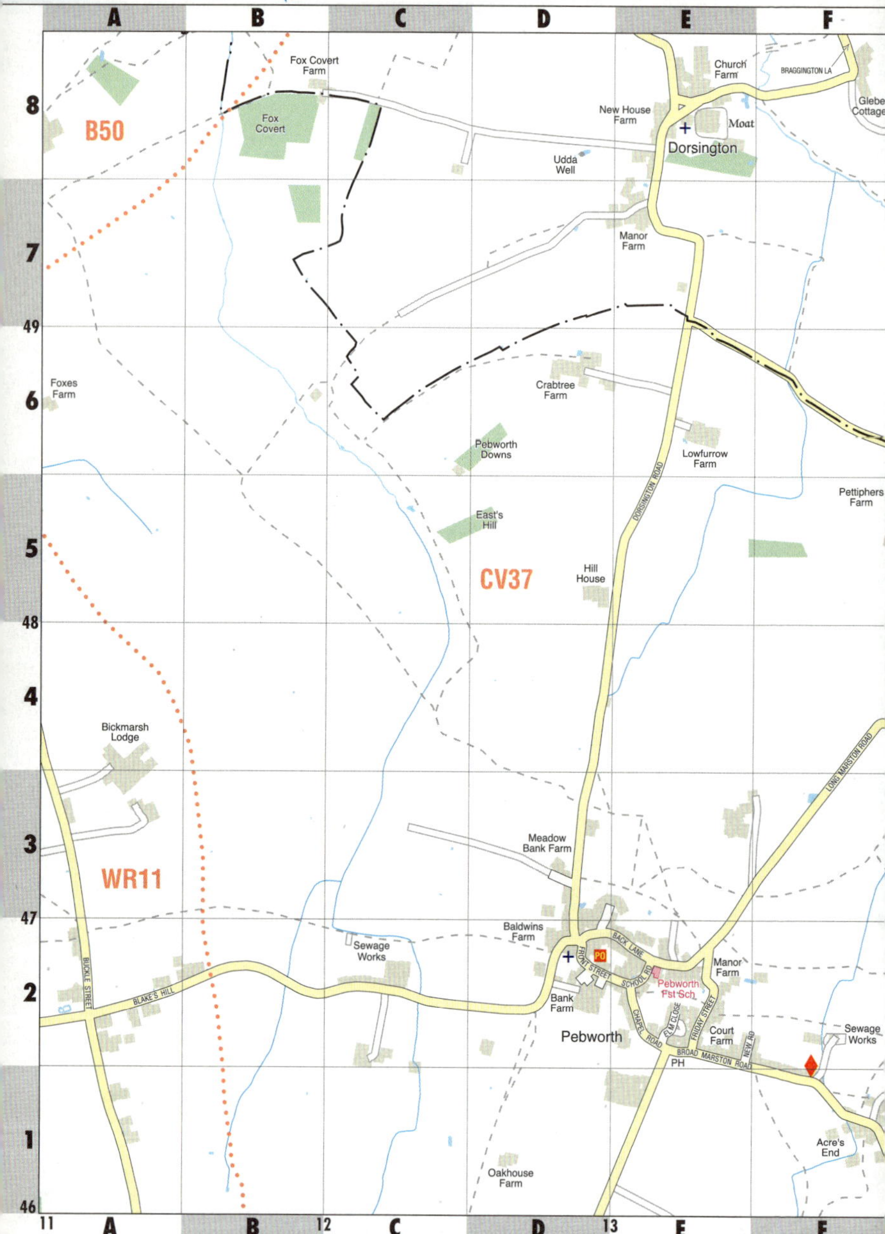

149
164

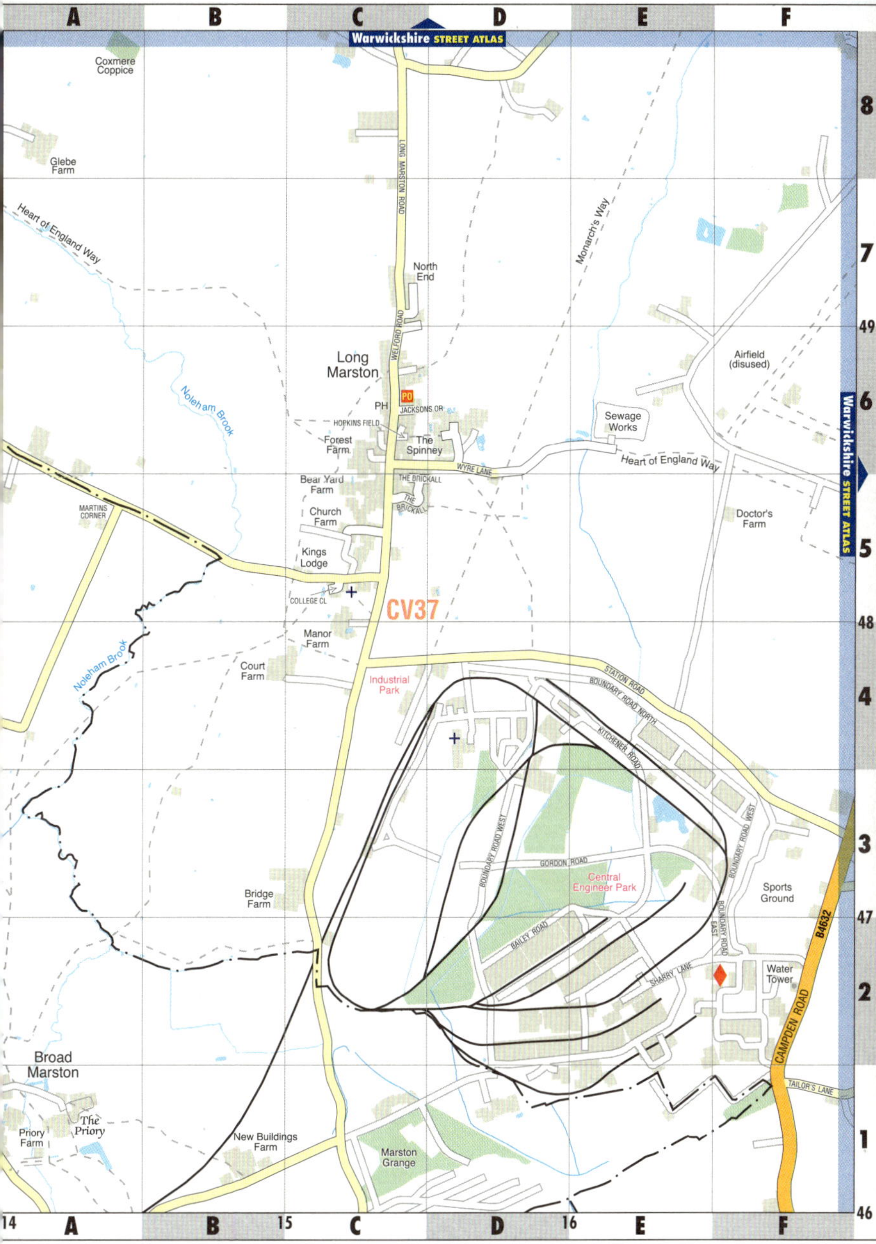
A
B
C
D
E
F
Warwickshire STREET ATLAS
Coxmere Coppice
Glebe Farm
8
7
49
6
5
48
4
3
47
2
1
46
Heart of England Way
Monarch's Way
LONG MARSTON ROAD
North End
WELFORD ROAD
Long Marston
PH
PO
JACKSONS DR
HOPKINS FIELD
Forest Farm
The Spinney
WYRE LANE
Sewage Works
Airfield (disused)
Noleham Brook
MARTINS CORNER
Bear Yard Farm
THE BRICKALL
Church Farm
Kings Lodge
Doctor's Farm
COLLEGE CL
CV37
Manor Farm
Court Farm
Industrial Park
STATION ROAD
BOUNDARY ROAD NORTH
KITCHENER ROAD
BOUNDARY ROAD WEST
GORDON ROAD
Central Engineer Park
Bridge Farm
Sports Ground
BAILEY ROAD
BOUNDARY ROAD EAST
SHARRY LANE
Water Tower
B4632
CAMPDEN ROAD
Broad Marston
TAILOR'S LANE
The Priory
Priory Farm
New Buildings Farm
Marston Grange
14
15
16

138

F8
1 BACK LA
2 VICTORIA RD
3 GRANGE RD
4 ORCHARD RD

A1
1 CRESCENT RD
2 ALBERT RD
3 CHEVENHAM CL
4 BROOKSIDE
5 BROOKMILLCL

B2
1 INGHAM PEDL CL
2 SPRING CL
3 HILL VW CL
4 MEADOW WK
5 HARBOUR DR
6 OAK DR
7 ACORN CL
8 BALLARD CL
9 SILVER ST

166

A8
1 LAWNSIDE
2 THORNGROVE RD
3 MANBY RD
4 CHRIST CHURCH RD

B8
1 GILBERT RD
2 LOWER WILTON RD
3 COTSWOLD RD
4 MAYFLOWER CL
5 LYDES RD
6 LOWER CH RD

139
154

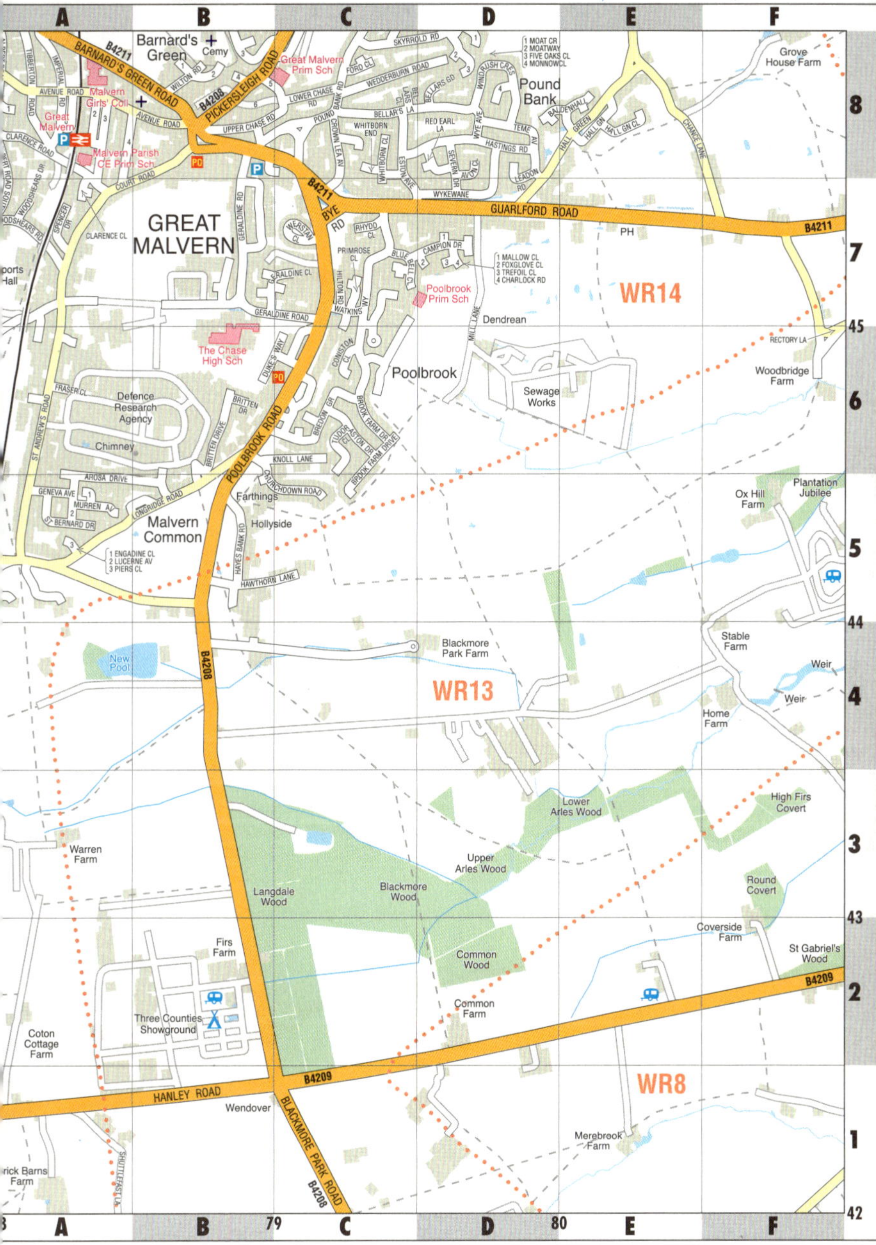

167
154

153
140

153
168

141
156

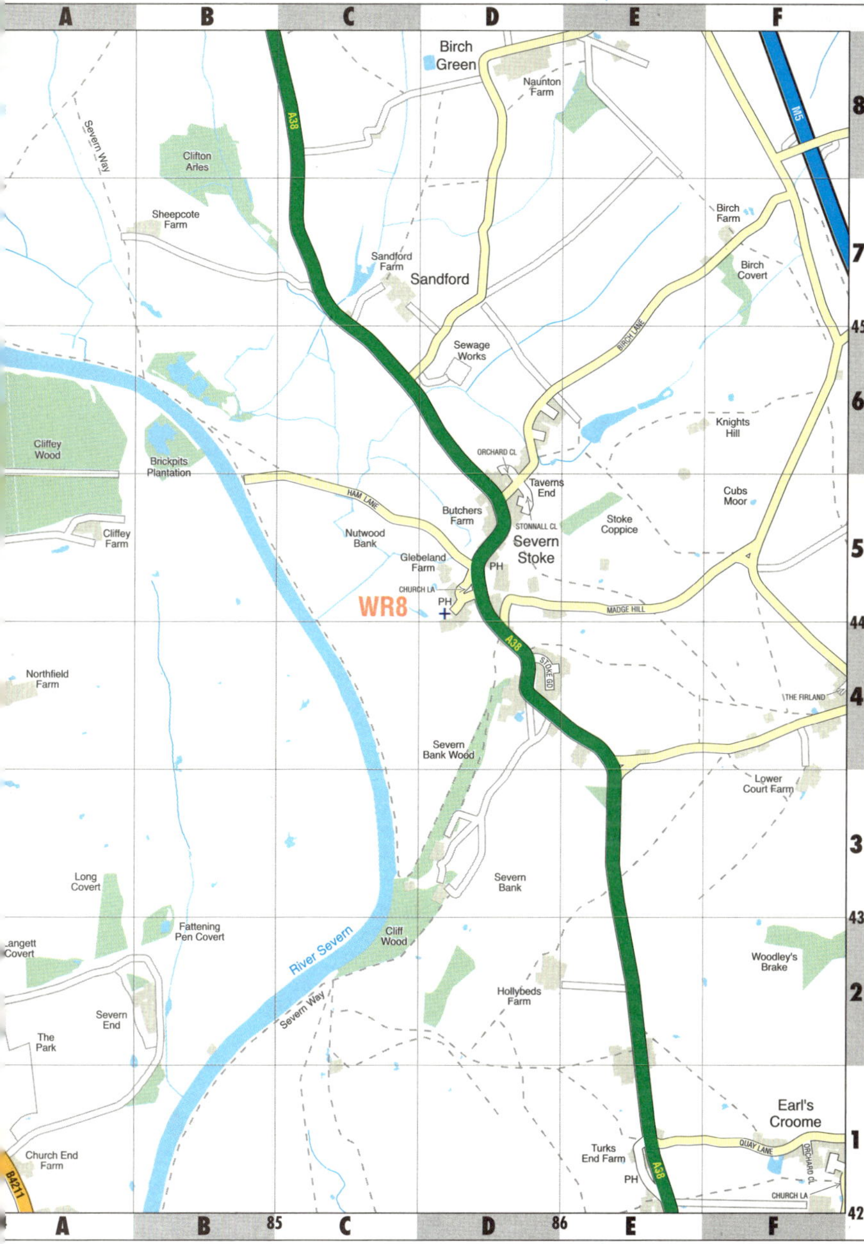

169
156

155
142

155
170

143
158

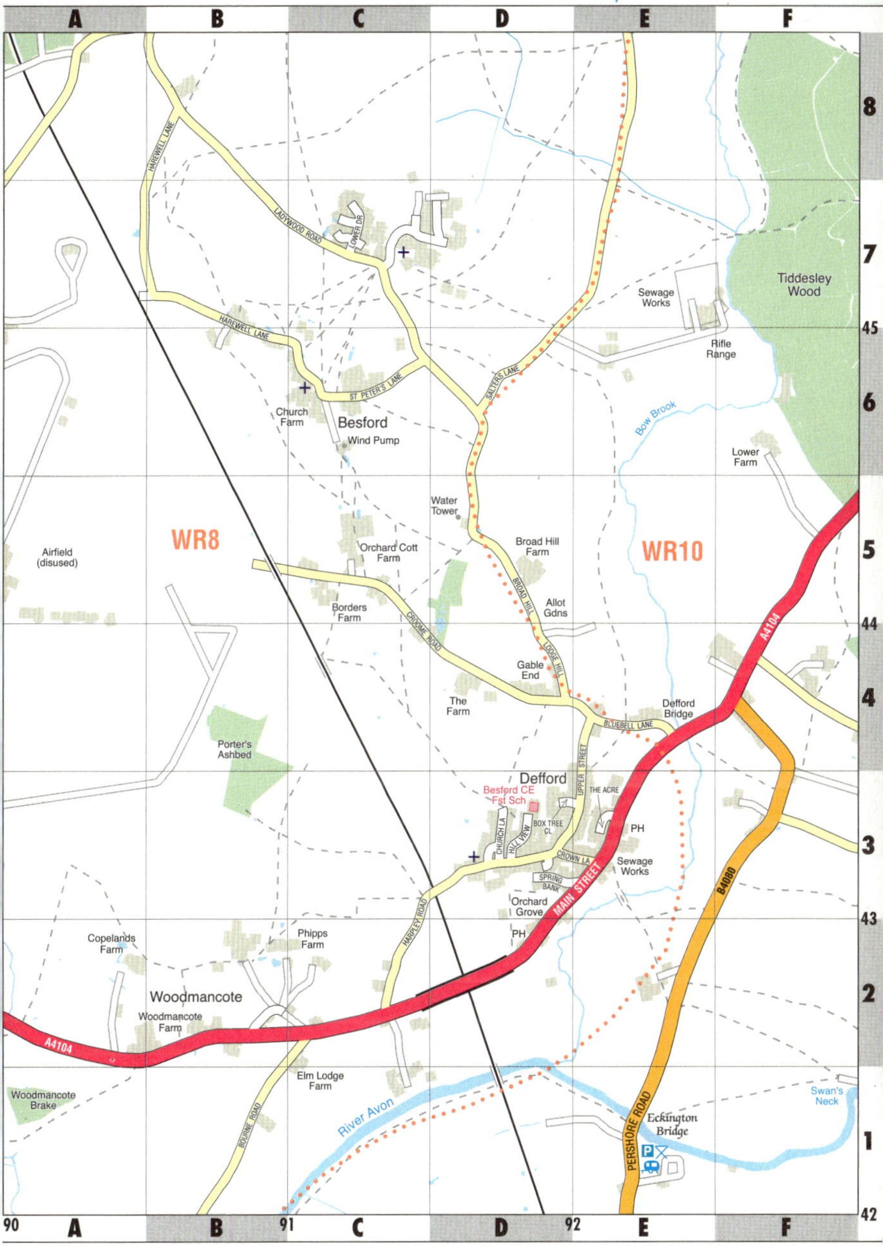

171
158

157
144

C8
1 HOLLOWAY
2 ABBOTS GRANGE
3 ORCHARD CL

D8
1 HEAD ST
2 ST AGATHAS RD
3 ST AGATHA'S CL
4 MONKS CL
5 LITTLE PRIEST LA
6 LOWER PRIEST LA
7 CHURCH ST
8 CHURCH ROW
9 BETJEMAN CL
10 CHURCH WK
11 MASONS RYDE

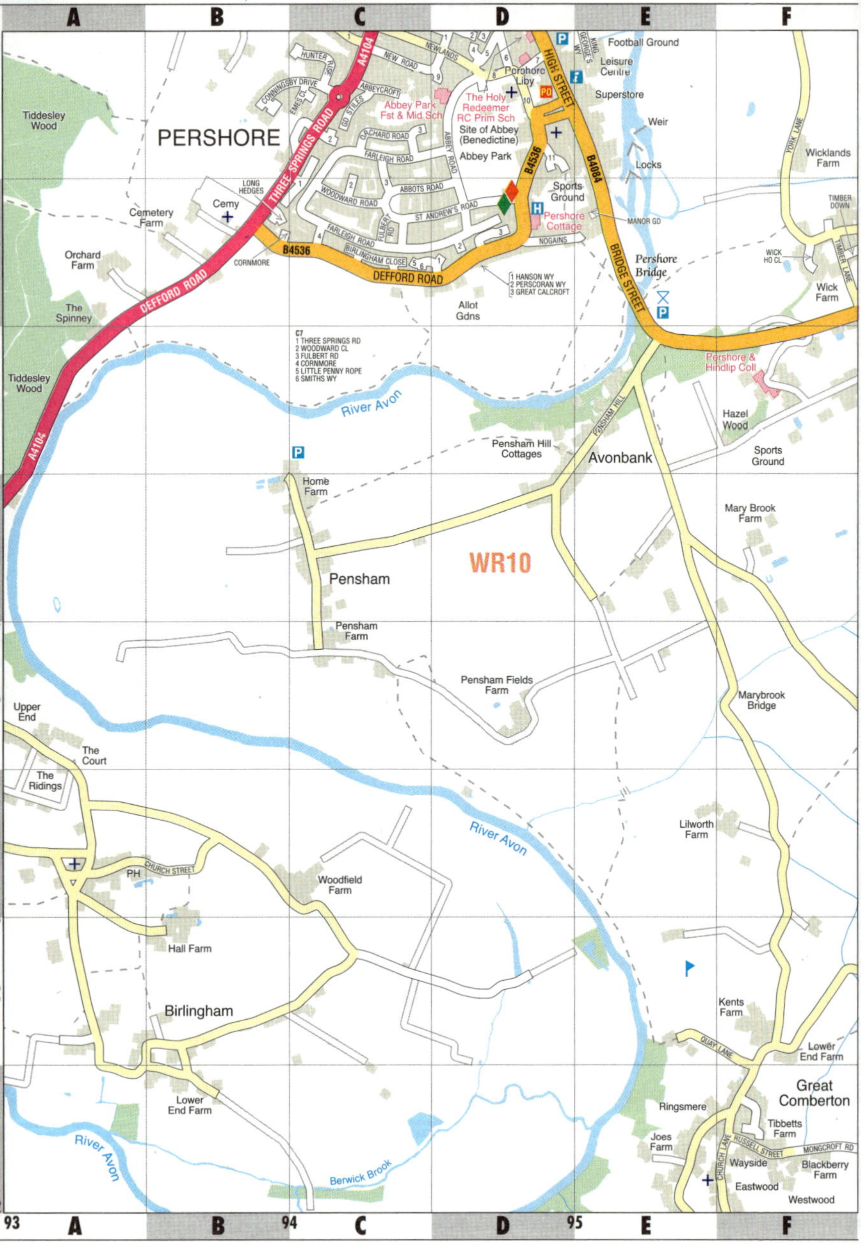

157
172

145
160

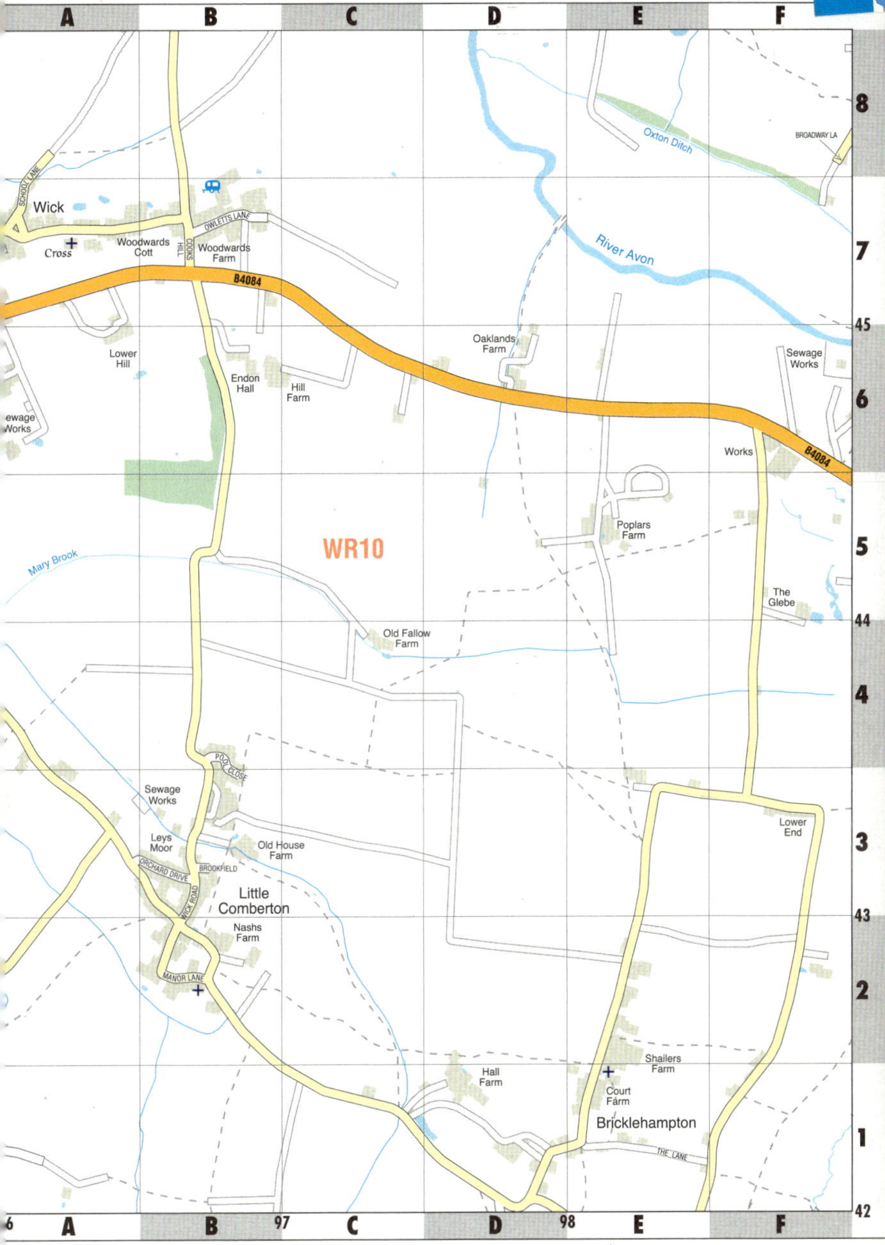

173
160

159
146

159
174

D5
1 SHEPHERDS POOL
2 HENRY FOWLER CL
3 RUDGE RD
4 TERRILL CT
5 RIGHTONS CT
6 ST EGWIN'S RD
7 THE HODGES
8 DE LA BERE CL

D1
1 ORLEANS CL
2 ST CATHERINES RD
3 ST JAMES DR
4 ST MARGARETS RD
5 JASMINE WLK
6 ST MARKS CL
7 ST LUKES CL
8 ST PHILIPS DR
9 ST PATRICKS CL
10 BLACKBERRY WY

E1
1 SPRINGFIELD DR
2 ST MATTHEWS CL
3 ST JOHNS CL
4 FOUR POOLS LA
5 ST GEORGES CL
6 ST WULSTANS CL

E2
1 ANNE CR
2 BATTLETON RD
3 FOUR POOLS LA

F2
1 ROWAN CL
2 ALMOND CL
3 CHERRY CL
4 LAUREL AV
5 MAPLE CL
6 OAK TREE CL
7 POPLAR CL
8 HOLLY CL
9 HOLMWOOD GDN
10 LINDEN CL
11 LARCH RD

F3
1 CEDARWOOD GDN
2 BUTTERFLY CR
3 DONNEY BROOK
4 WINDMERES
5 HILL CREST

Offenham
PH
PO
Field Farm
Bennetts Hill Farm
BOAT LANE
FERRY LANE
MAIN STREET
NEW RD
LEASOWES ROAD
LAURELS AV
LAURELS ROAD
MILL LANE
Offenham Cross
B4510
MERRY LANE
STATION ROAD
Broadway Brook
EVESHAM ROAD
Boltons Farm
Blackminster Mid Sch
B4085
High Cross Farm
BLACKMINSTER
A46
Parks Farm
THE PARKS
LC
Blackminster
WR11
OFFENHAM ROAD
CHESTNUT CL 1
CHAPEL LA 2
THE HOP GDN 3
MANOR GDN 4
Aldington
MAIN STREET
MILL LA
VILLAGE STREET
Claybrook Farm
BIRMINGHAM ROAD
Stone Cottage
Sherwood Cott
Sherwood Farm
1 LICHFIELD AV
2 OFFENHAM RD
Endborough
HORSEBRIDGE ROAD
PACKS CL
BANKS RD
PH
B4035
BADSEY ROAD
OAK CLOSE
BRETFORTON RD
Ashdown Farm
SYNEHURST AV
SYNEHURST CR
HITHER GN
BADSEY LANE
TYNE DR
SHANNON WY
MANOR CL
Manor House
HIGH STREET
GREENLEYS
1 THE DRIFT
2 OLD POST OFFICE LA
3 ST JAMES CL
THE LANKETS
Badsey
Sports Ground
SEWARD ROAD
MANOR SIDE 1
THE POPLARS 2
THE KNAPP 3
BREWERS LANE
1 WARDS CL
2 CONWY DR
3 CLYDE AV
4 MOUNT RD
5 HILL CREST
Pine Tops
CHAPEL STREET
BADSEY FIELDS LANE
BROADWAY RD
SCHOOL LA
Glebe Cott
MILL LA
FIELDS CLOSE
BINYON CL
Badsey Fst Sch
ALLESBROOK GD
SANDS LANE
1 HAWTHORN RD
2 BLACKTHORN CL
3 THORN LEA
BROADWAY ROAD
Badsey Brook
WILLERSEY ROAD
BROADWAY RD
A44
Manor House
Orchard Farm
LONGDON HILL
GOLDEN LANE
Ropers Farm
Twr View Farm
MANOR RD
WILLERSEY ROAD
A B C D E F
8 7 6 5 4 3 2 1
45 44 43 42
05 06 07

149 164

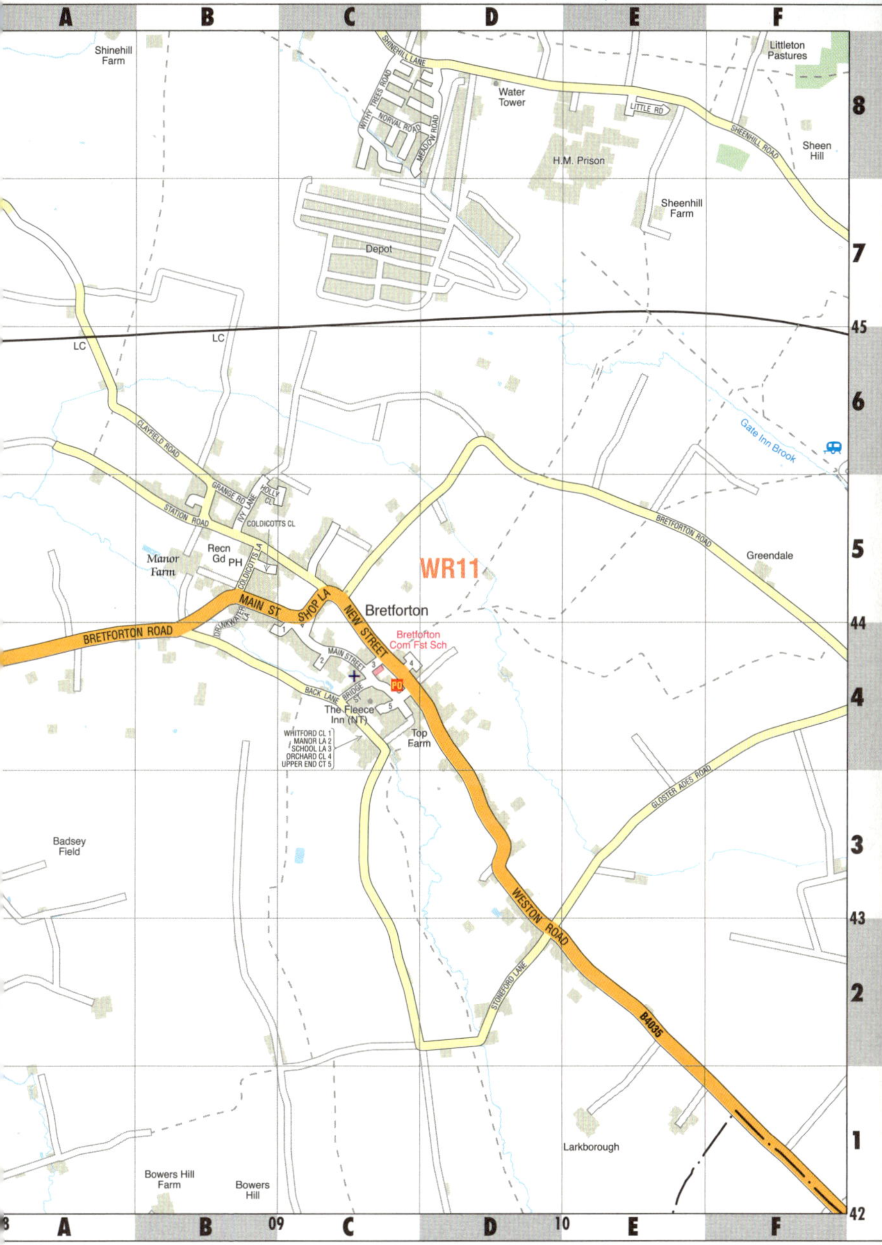

Shinehill Farm
Littleton Pastures
SHINEHILL LANE
WITHY TREES ROAD
NORVAL ROAD
MEADOW ROAD
Water Tower
LITTLE RD
H.M. Prison
SHEENHILL ROAD
Sheen Hill
Sheenhill Farm
Depot
LC
LC
CLAYFIELD ROAD
GRANGE RD
IVY LANE
HOLLY CL
STATION ROAD
COLDICOTTS CL
COLDICOTTS LA
Recn Gd
PH
Manor Farm
WR11
MAIN ST
SHOP LA
NEW STREET
Bretforton
DRINKWATER LA
BRETFORTON ROAD
Bretforton Com Fst Sch
MAIN STREET
BACK LANE
BRIDGE ST
PO
The Fleece Inn (NT)
WHITFORD CL 1
MANOR LA 2
SCHOOL LA 3
ORCHARD CL 4
UPPER END CT 5
Top Farm
Gate Inn Brook
BRETFORTON ROAD
Greendale
GLOSTER ADES ROAD
Badsey Field
WESTON ROAD
STONEFORD LANE
B4035
Larkborough
Bowers Hill Farm
Bowers Hill
09
10

163
150

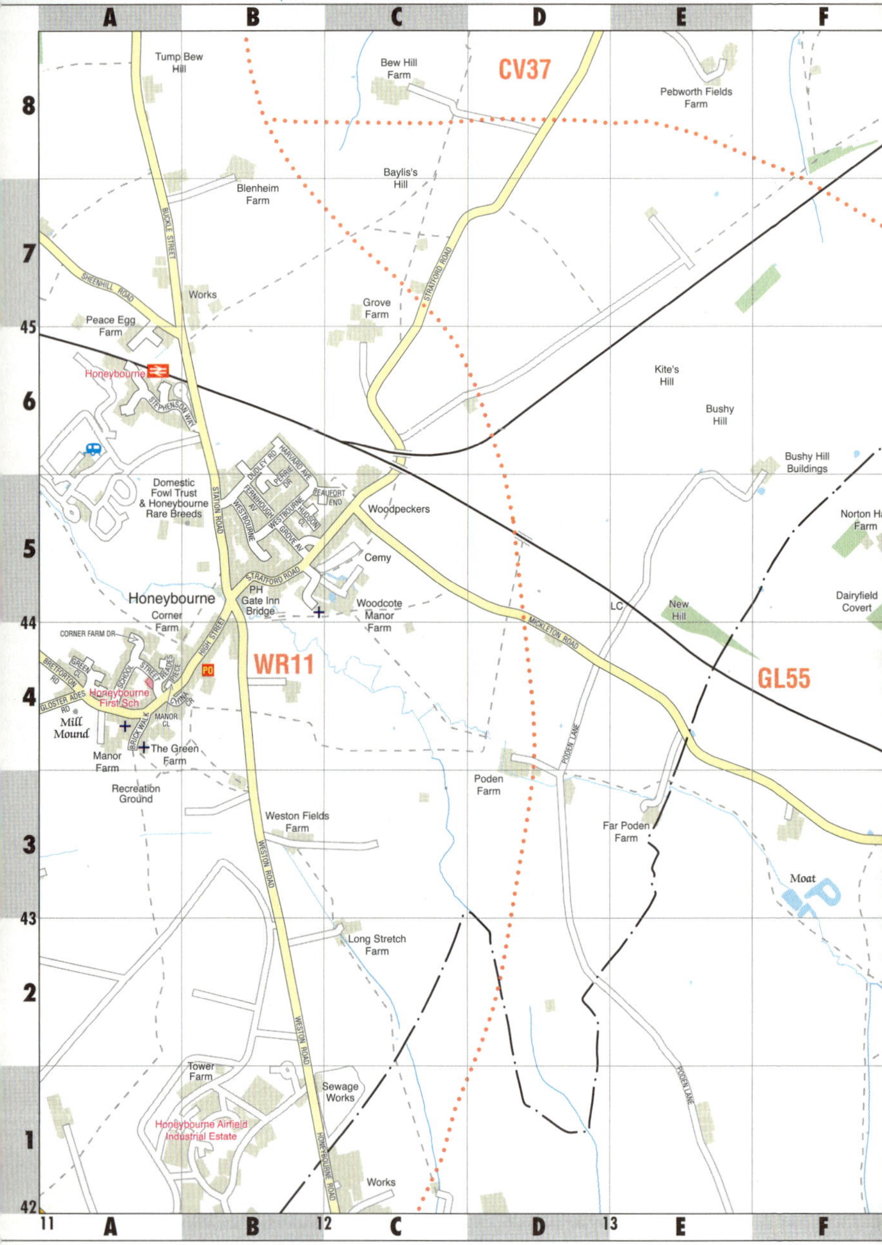

163
178

151

A
B
C
D
E
F
8
7
45
6
5
44
4
3
43
2
1
42
4
15
16
CV37
GL55
Pitchall Farm
Finches Meadow Farm
Lower Clopton Farm
CAMPDEN ROAD
B4632
LONG MARSTON ROAD
BROAD MARSTON ROAD
STRATFORD ROAD
Gran Brook
Warwickshire STREET ATLAS
Heart of England Way
Allot Gdns
ORCHARD CL
MEON ROAD
NURSERY CL
GRANBROOK LANE
CEDAR RD
CEDAR ROAD
BEARCROFT GD 1
WHEATFIELD CT 2
INVERLEA CT 3
GLOUCESTER LA 4
Granbrook Farm
Mickleton
Monument
BACK LANE
Hotel
Mickleton Prim Sch
CHAPEL LANE
OLD MANOR GD
PH
COTSWOLD EDGE
MILL LA
HIGH STREET
PO
Cemy
ALVESTON GRANGE 1
GARDEN CL 2
NORTON VIEW
POUND LANE
ARBOUR CLOSE
BALLARDS CLOSE
Mickleton Wood Farm
Norton Hall
Fox Covert
Norton Brook
Thistley Hill Coppice
Thistley Hill
Flower Farm
Draycott Farm
Darling Farm
BROADWAY ROAD
Bath Coppice
Kiftsgate Court Garden
BAKER'S HILL
Old Coppice
Norton Grounds Farm
Ninevah Bridge Farm
Longhills Farm
Ninevah Farm
Baker's Hill Wood
Harvest Piece Farm
Baker's Hill
Monarch's Way
Railway Plantation
Cottage Farm
Dairy Hills
B4081
Leys Coppice
Gloucestershire STREET ATLAS

E7
1 RICHMONDS PITCH
2 KINGS RD
3 WOODLANDS CL
4 WELLS CL
5 HEATHLANDS CL

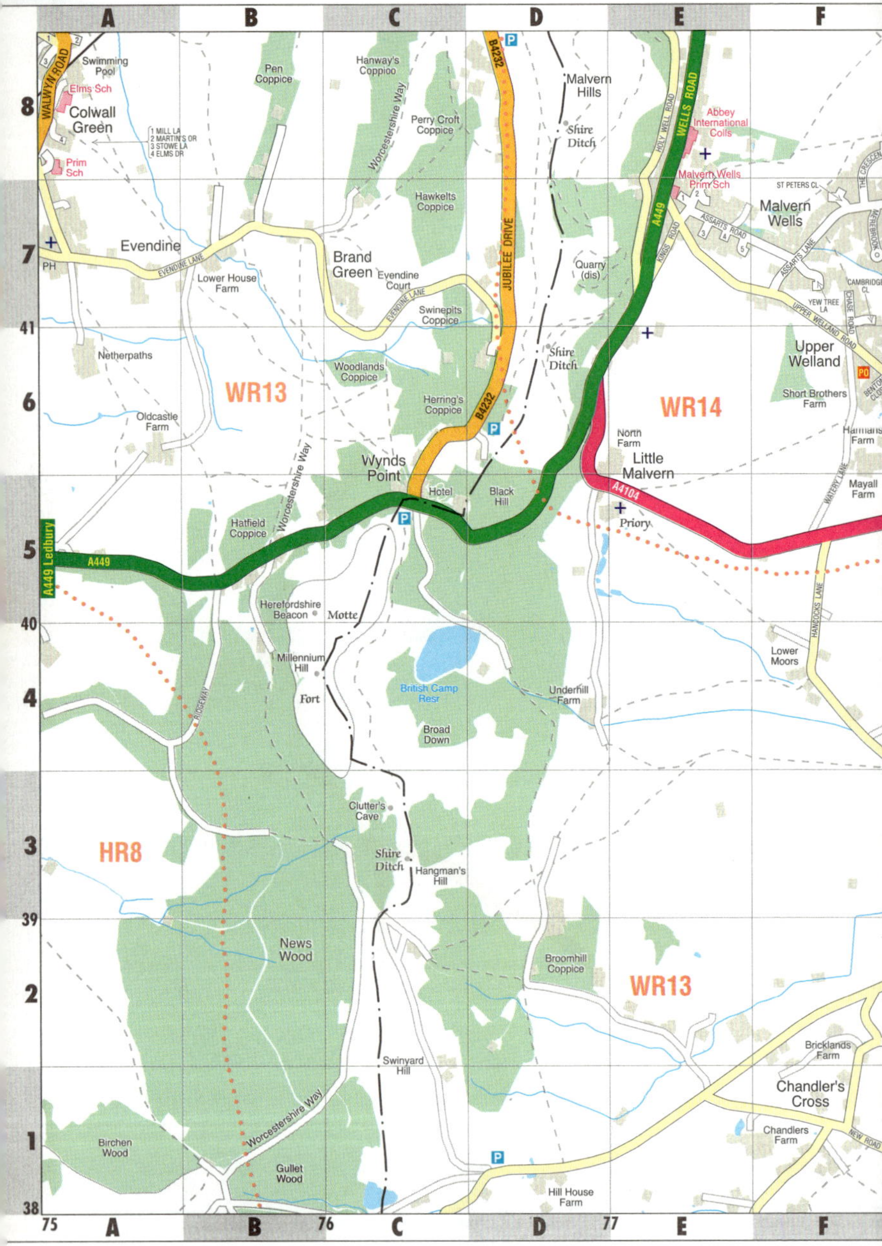

153
168

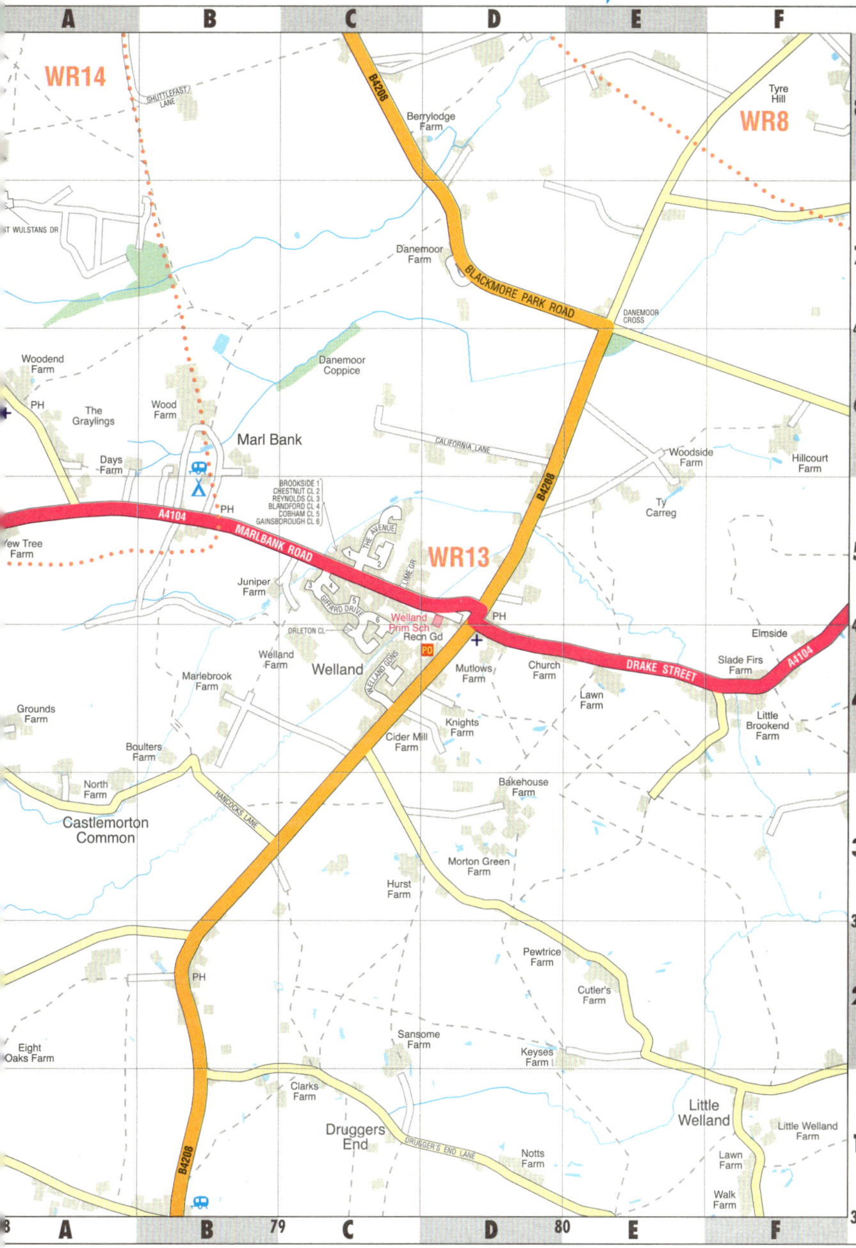

180
168

167
154

167
181

155
170

C6
1 HIGH ST
2 LONDON LA
3 RIVERSIDE CL
4 COURT ST

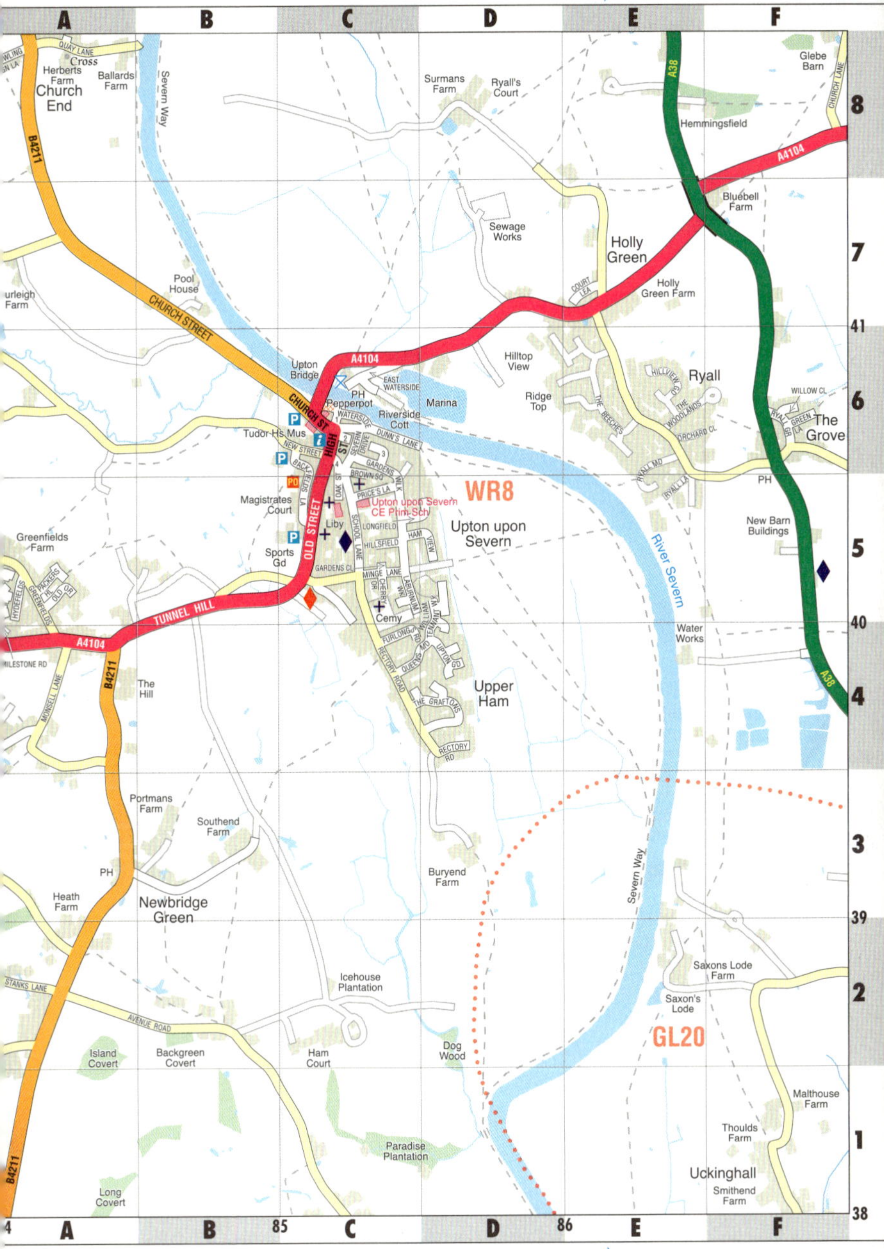

182
170

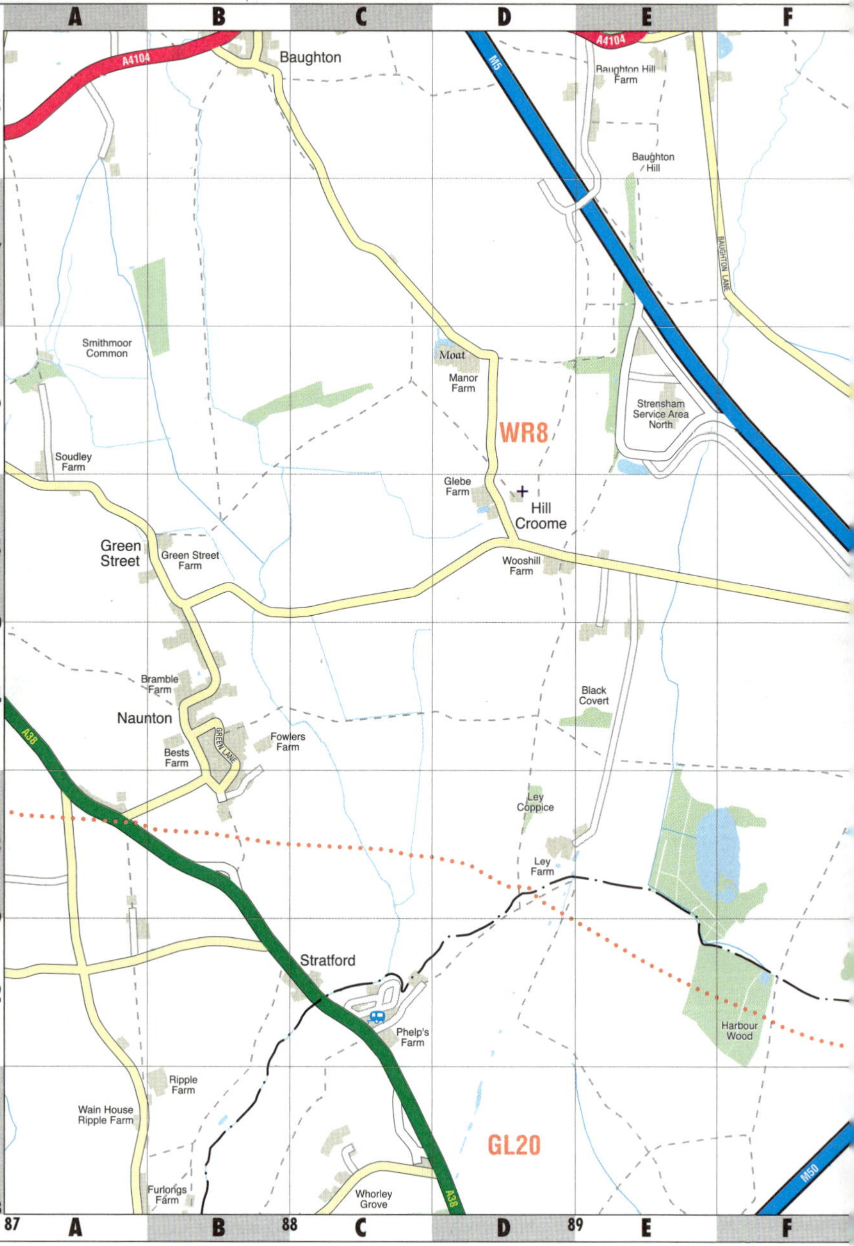
A B C D E F
8
7
41
6
5
40
4
3
39
2
1
38
87
88
89
A4104
Baughton
M5
Baughton Hill Farm
Baughton Hill
BAUGHTON LANE
Smithmoor Common
Moat
Manor Farm
Strensham Service Area North
WR8
Soudley Farm
Glebe Farm
Hill Croome
Green Street
Green Street Farm
Wooshill Farm
Bramble Farm
Black Covert
Naunton
A38
GREEN LANE
Fowlers Farm
Bests Farm
Ley Coppice
Ley Farm
Stratford
Phelp's Farm
Harbour Wood
Ripple Farm
Wain House Ripple Farm
GL20
M50
Furlongs Farm
Whorley Grove

157
172

184
172

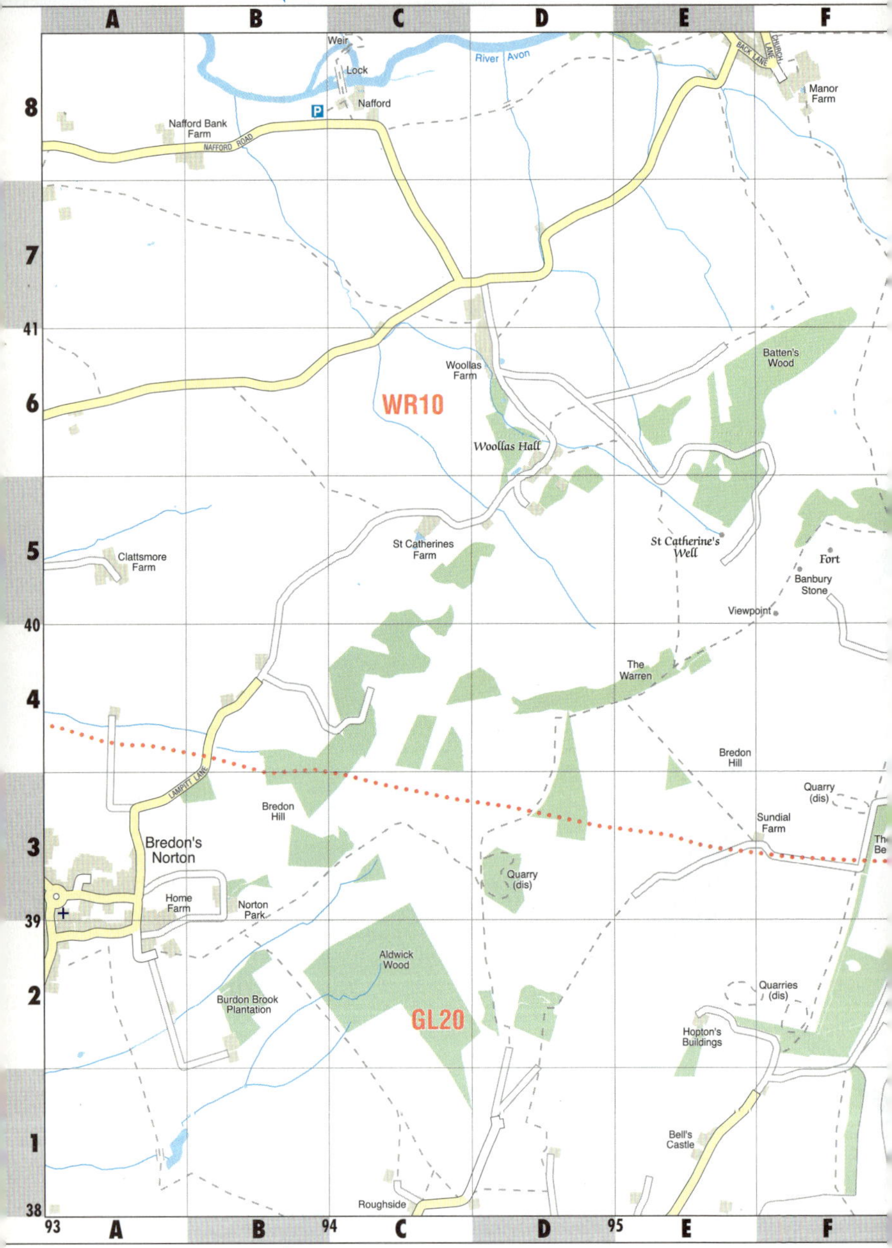
A
B
C
D
E
F
Weir
Lock
River Avon
Nafford
Nafford Bank Farm
NAFFORD ROAD
BACK LANE
CHURCH LANE
Manor Farm
8
7
41
6
5
40
4
3
39
2
1
38
Batten's Wood
Woollas Farm
WR10
Woollas Hall
St Catherine's Well
St Catherines Farm
Clattsmore Farm
Fort
Banbury Stone
Viewpoint
The Warren
Bredon Hill
Quarry (dis)
Sundial Farm
LAMPITT LANE
Bredon Hill
Bredon's Norton
Quarry (dis)
Home Farm
Norton Park
Aldwick Wood
Quarries (dis)
Burdon Brook Plantation
GL20
Hopton's Buildings
Bell's Castle
Roughside
93
94
95

159
174

186
174

173
160

173
187

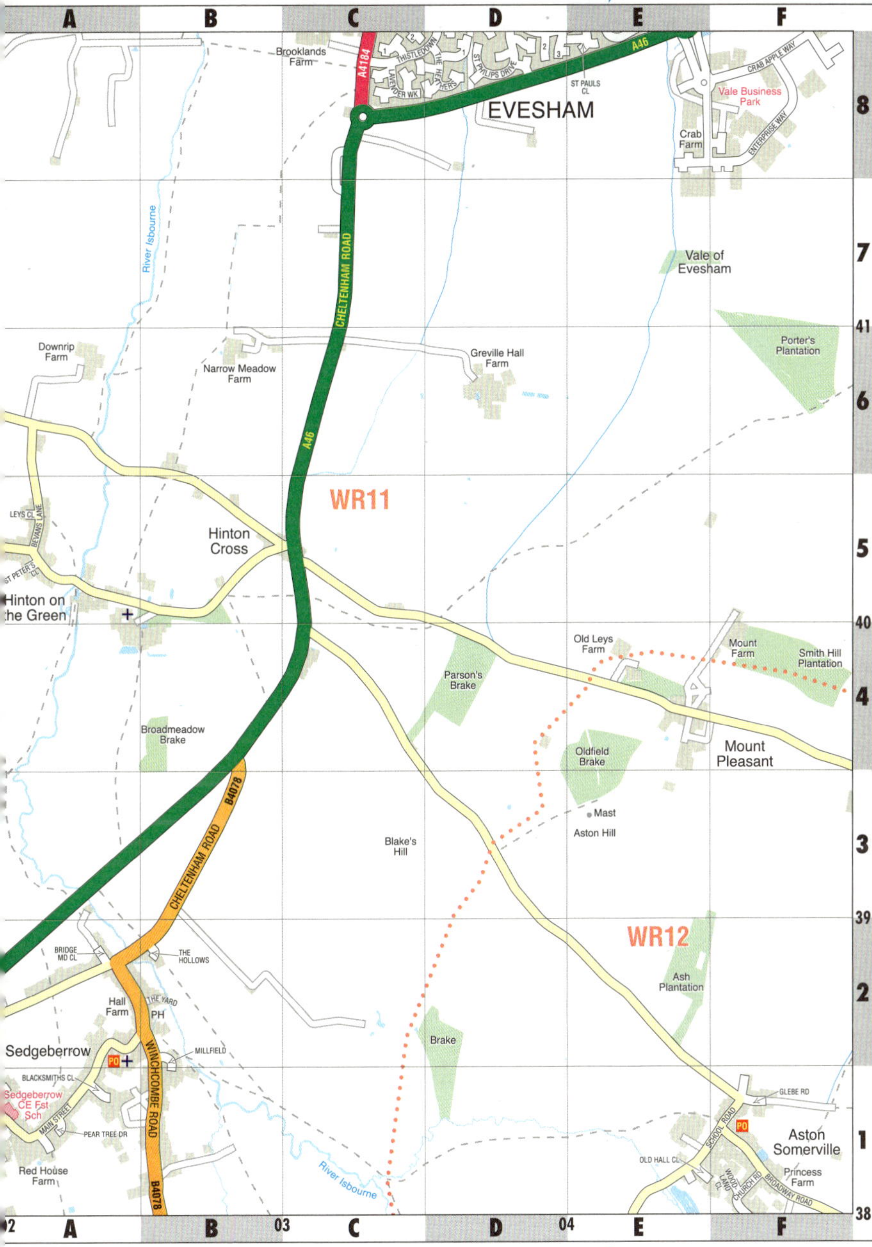
A
B
C
D
E
F
8
7
41
6
5
40
4
3
39
2
1
38
03
04
Brooklands Farm
A4184
THISTLEDOWN
THE HEATHERS
LAVENDER WK
ST PHILIPS DRIVE
ST PAULS CL
A46
EVESHAM
CRAB APPLE WAY
Vale Business Park
Crab Farm
ENTERPRISE WAY
River Isbourne
CHELTENHAM ROAD
Vale of Evesham
Porter's Plantation
Downrip Farm
Narrow Meadow Farm
Greville Hall Farm
WR11
LEYS CL
BEVANS LANE
ST PETER'S CL
Hinton Cross
Hinton on the Green
Old Leys Farm
Mount Farm
Smith Hill Plantation
Parson's Brake
Broadmeadow Brake
Oldfield Brake
Mount Pleasant
B4078
Mast
Aston Hill
Blake's Hill
WR12
BRIDGE MD CL
THE HOLLOWS
Ash Plantation
Hall Farm
THE YARD
PH
Sedgeberrow
PO
MILLFIELD
Brake
WINCHCOMBE ROAD
BLACKSMITHS CL
Sedgeberrow CE Fst Sch
MAIN STREET
PEAR TREE DR
GLEBE RD
SCHOOL ROAD
Aston Somerville
OLD HALL CL
WOODLAND CL
CHURCH RD
BROADWAY ROAD
Princess Farm
Red House Farm
River Isbourne

175
162

175
189

163
178

190
D1
1 TYTHE RD
2 AVERILL CL
3 SANDS CL
4 THE SANDS
178
E1
1 LIME TREE AVE
2 BRIDGEMANS CL

177
164

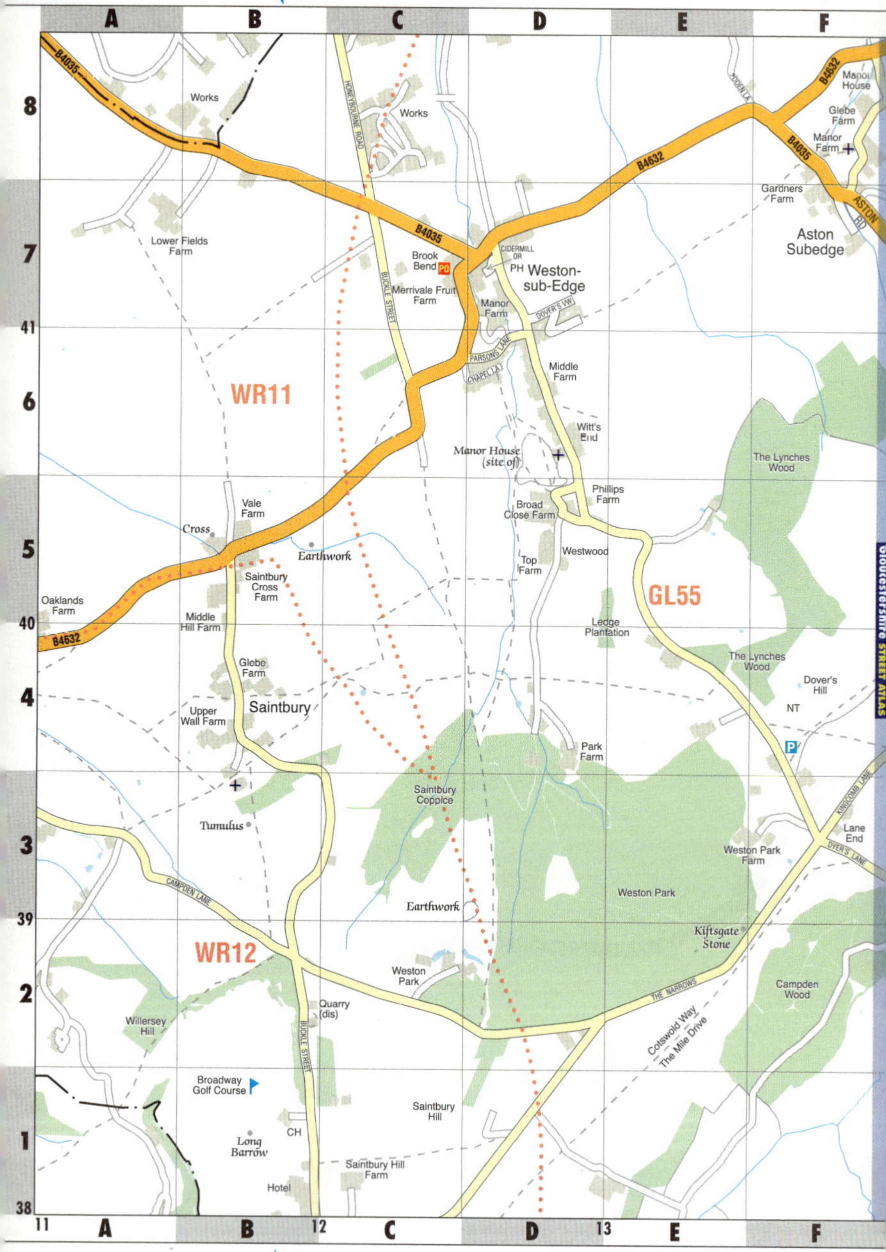

177
191

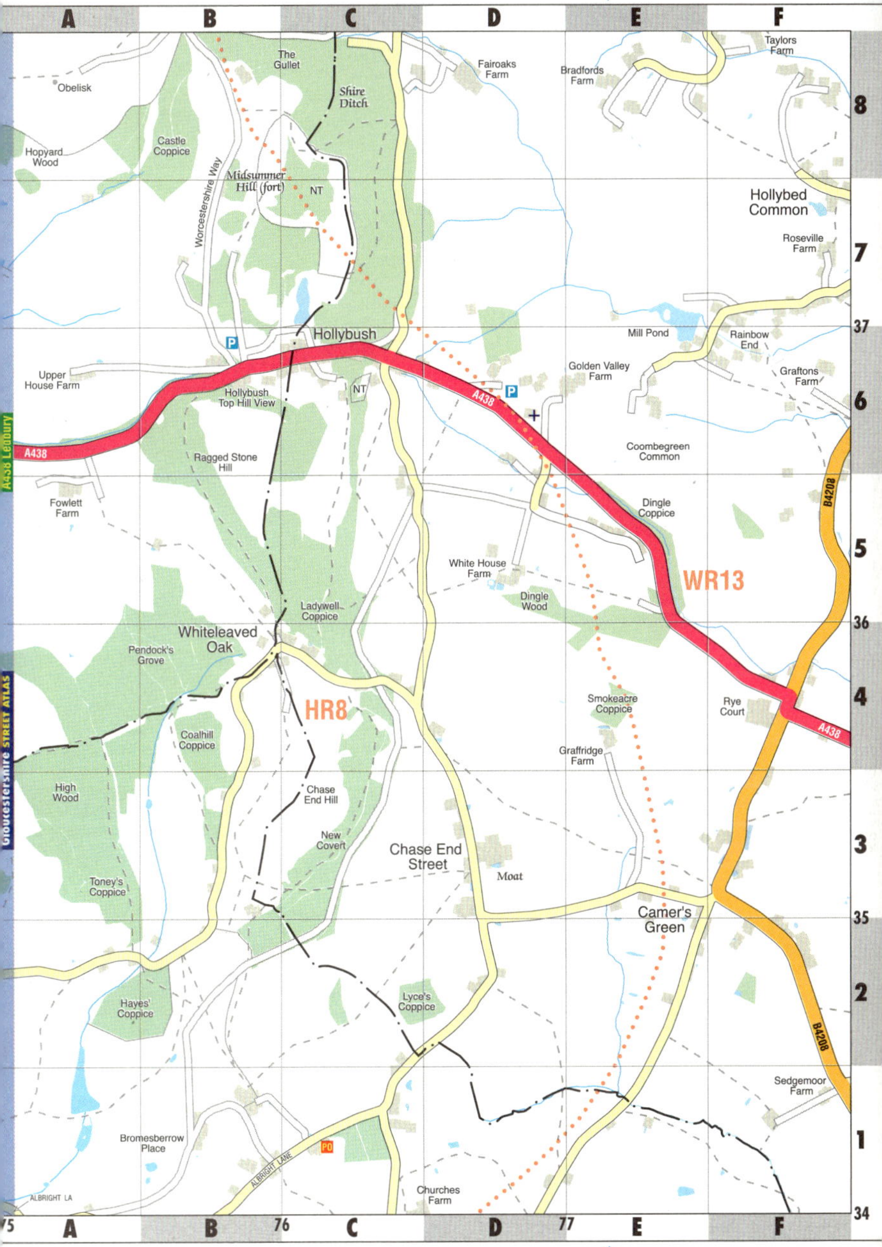
A B C D E F
8 7 37 6 5 36 4 3 35 2 1 34
75 76 77
Obelisk
Hopyard Wood
Castle Coppice
The Gullet
Shire Ditch
Midsummer Hill (fort)
NT
Worcestershire Way
Fairoaks Farm
Bradfords Farm
Taylors Farm
Hollybed Common
Roseville Farm
Mill Pond
Rainbow End
Graftons Farm
Golden Valley Farm
Hollybush
Upper House Farm
Hollybush Top Hill View
A438
A438 Ledbury
Ragged Stone Hill
Fowlett Farm
Coombegreen Common
Dingle Coppice
B4208
White House Farm
Dingle Wood
WR13
Ladywell Coppice
Whiteleaved Oak
Pendock's Grove
HR8
Smokeacre Coppice
Rye Court
Coalhill Coppice
Graffridge Farm
Gloucestershire STREET ATLAS
High Wood
Chase End Hill
New Covert
Chase End Street
Moat
Toney's Coppice
Camer's Green
Hayes' Coppice
Lyce's Coppice
Sedgemoor Farm
Bromesberrow Place
PO
ALBRIGHT LANE
ALBRIGHT LA
Churches Farm

179
167

179
193

A
B
C
D
E
F
WR8
Drinkwater's Farm
Coneyburrow Hill
Worcestershire Way Link
Beesoni Farm
Weir
Hillworth
B4211
8
7
37
6
5
4
36
3
35
2
1
34
Yard Bridge
New House
Churchend Farm
Longdon
St Marys CE Prim Sch
Manor Farm
ORCHARD RIDGE
THE BADHAMS
MOAT
BANK
PH
Moat
BEAR LANE
GL20
Longdon Marsh
Brook Farm
Lower Swell Farm
Rectory Farm
Parsonage Farm
Marsh End Farm
Red House Farm
WR13
Moor Court Farm
Pendock Moor
Sledge Green
Hill Court Farm
M50
Robertsend
A438
GL19
81
82
83

181 169

181 195

170
184

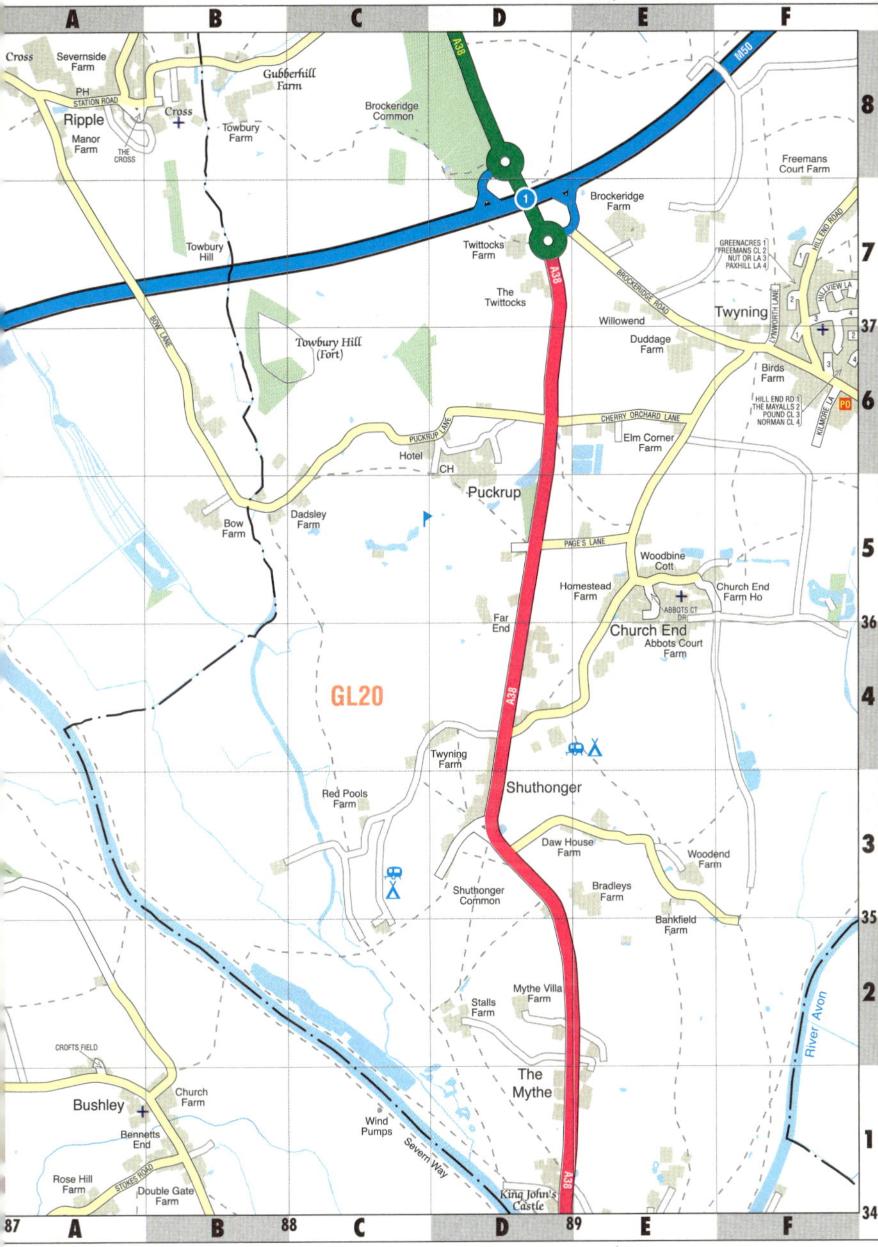
A
B
C
D
E
F
8
7
37
6
5
36
4
3
35
2
1
34
87
88
89
Cross
Severnside Farm
Gubberhill Farm
PH
STATION ROAD
Ripple
Cross
Manor Farm
THE CROSS
Towbury Farm
Brockeridge Common
A38
M50
1
Freemans Court Farm
Brockeridge Farm
Towbury Hill
Twittocks Farm
GREENACRES 1
FREEMANS CL 2
NUT OR LA 3
PAXHILL LA 4
HILL END ROAD
HILLVIEW LA
The Twittocks
BROCKERIDGE ROAD
LYNWORTH LANE
Twyning
Willowend
Duddage Farm
BOW LANE
Towbury Hill (Fort)
Birds Farm
HILL END RD 1
THE MAYALLS 2
POUND CL 3
NORMAN CL 4
KILMORE LA
PO
CHERRY ORCHARD LANE
PUCKRUP LANE
Elm Corner Farm
Hotel
CH
Puckrup
Bow Farm
Dadsley Farm
PAGE'S LANE
Woodbine Cott
Homestead Farm
Church End Farm Ho
ABBOTS CT DR
Far End
Church End
Abbots Court Farm
GL20
Twyning Farm
Shuthonger
Red Pools Farm
Daw House Farm
Woodend Farm
Shuthonger Common
Bradleys Farm
Bankfield Farm
Mythe Villa Farm
Stalls Farm
River Avon
CROFTS FIELD
The Mythe
Church Farm
Bushley
Wind Pumps
Severn Way
Bennetts End
Rose Hill Farm
STOKES ROAD
Double Gate Farm
King John's Castle

183
171

F6
1 BREDON LODGE
2 GRAVEL PITS CL
3 PLANTATION CRES
4 RUSSET CL
5 BROADACRE CL
6 HOMESTEAD CL
7 THE CROFTLANDS
8 GLEBELAND DR
9 BRICKNELL AV
10 COTSWOLD CL

183
197

E1
1 GEORGE DOWTY DR
2 THE PEAR OR
3 THE APPLE OR
4 BEVAN GDN
5 WHEATSTONE CL
6 MONKEY MD
7 CROMERS CL
8 SPRINGWATER CL
9 FARM CL
10 REDWOOD CT
11 SYCAMORE RD

A
B
C
D
E
F
The Farm
Westmancote
FARM LA
CHAPEL LANE
Lower Westmancote
HILL CL
Wayside Bing
Moreton's Farm
KEMERTON ROAD
Allot Gdns
Ashbury Farm
WING LANE
BAYLISS RD
PH
PO
JOB'S LANE
Home Farm
Kemerton
Overbury Park
Woodlands
Overbury
Court
Recreation Gd
Overbury CE First Sch
SCHOOL LANE
QUEENSMEAD
Thurstan's Wood
WELLINGTON LODGE CL
WATERLOO WY
ORCHARD CL
B4079
Gravel Pit
KINSHAM LANE
Weir
Lowermill Farm
GL20
CRASHMORE LANE
CHELTENHAM ROAD
Sewage Works
CHAPEL LANE
Clows Top
True Blue Farm
Kinsham
Wells Farm
Home Farm
Gravel Pit
Reservoir
Aston on Carrant
Upper Farm
Upper Oaks Farm
Carrant Gardens
Aston Fields Farm
Depot
B4079
8
7
37
6
5
36
4
3
35
2
1
34
3
94
95

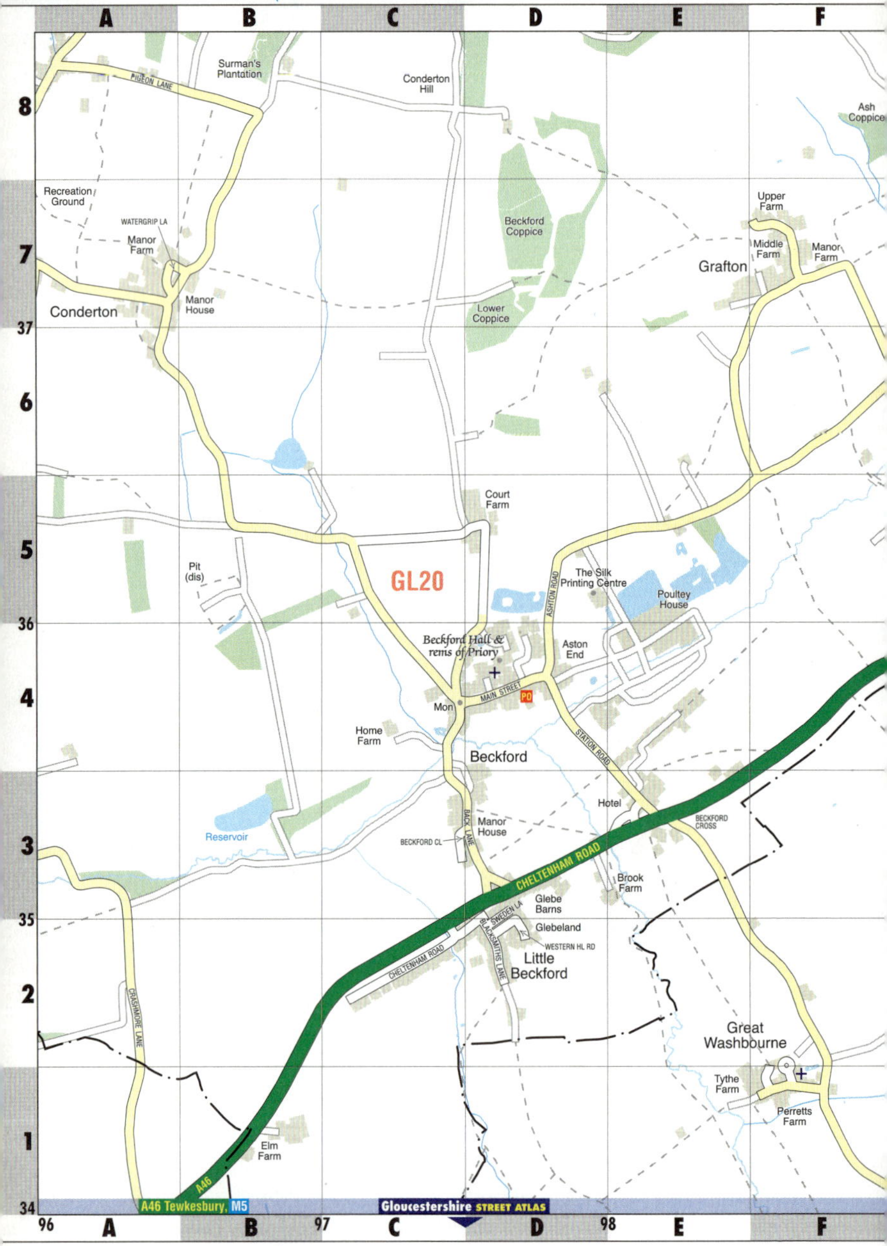
A
B
C
D
E
F
8
7
37
6
5
36
4
3
35
2
1
34
96
97
98
Surman's Plantation
PIGEON LANE
Conderton Hill
Ash Coppice
Recreation Ground
WATERGRIP LA
Manor Farm
Beckford Coppice
Upper Farm
Middle Farm
Manor Farm
Grafton
Conderton
Manor House
Lower Coppice
Court Farm
Pit (dis)
GL20
ASHTON ROAD
The Silk Printing Centre
Poultey House
Beckford Hall & rems of Priory
Aston End
MAIN STREET
PO
Mon
Home Farm
Beckford
STATION ROAD
Hotel
Reservoir
BACK LANE
Manor House
BECKFORD CL
BECKFORD CROSS
CHELTENHAM ROAD
Brook Farm
Glebe Barns
SWEDEN LA
Glebeland
WESTERN HL RD
CHELTENHAM ROAD
BLACKSMITHS LANE
Little Beckford
CRASHMORE LANE
Great Washbourne
Tythe Farm
Perretts Farm
Elm Farm
A46

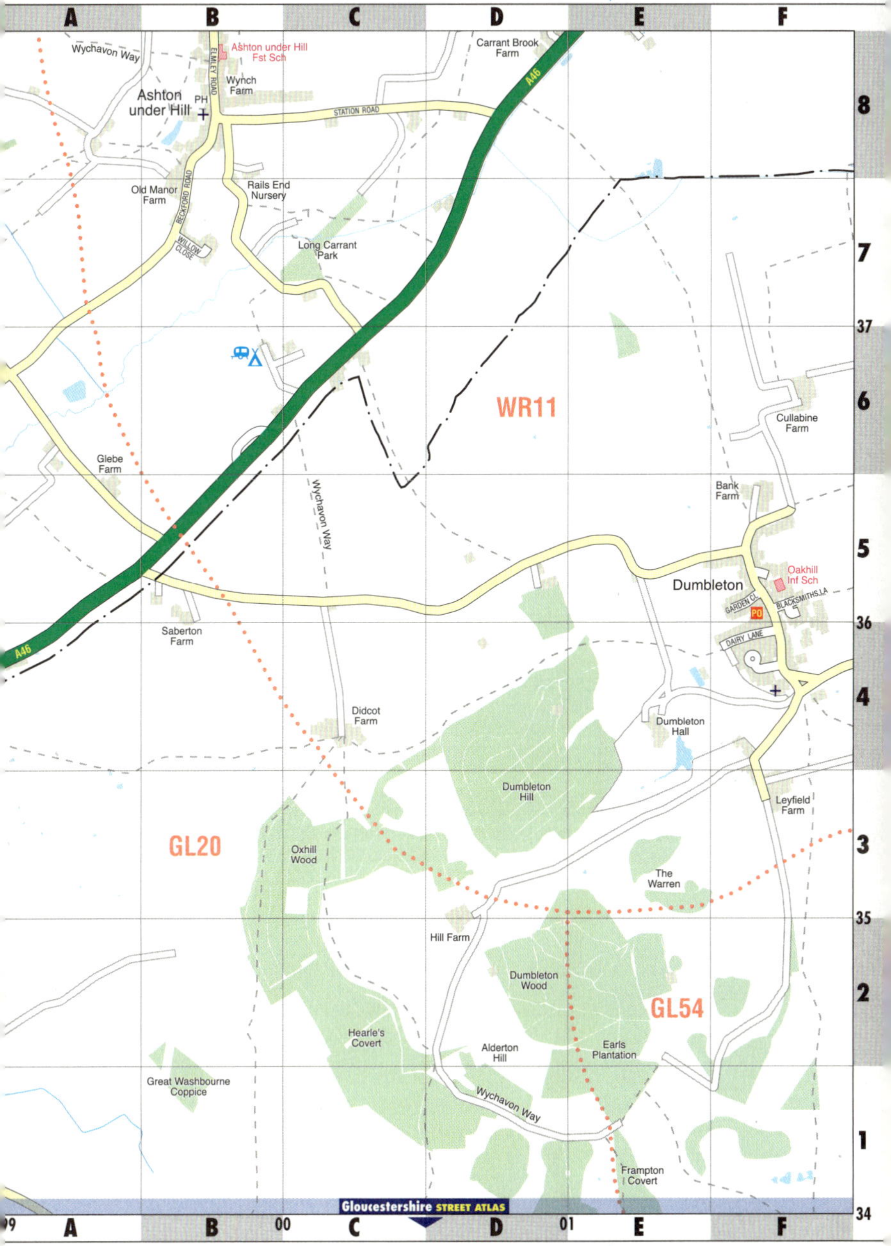
A
B
C
D
E
F
Wychavon Way
Ashton under Hill Fst Sch
Carrant Brook Farm
ELMLEY ROAD
Wynch Farm
Ashton under Hill
PH
A46
STATION ROAD
8
Old Manor Farm
BECKFORD ROAD
Rails End Nursery
WILLOW CLOSE
Long Carrant Park
7
37
WR11
6
Cullabine Farm
Glebe Farm
Wychavon Way
Bank Farm
5
Oakhill Inf Sch
Dumbleton
GARDEN CL
BLACKSMITHS LA
PO
Saberton Farm
36
DAIRY LANE
4
Didcot Farm
Dumbleton Hall
Dumbleton Hill
Leyfield Farm
GL20
Oxhill Wood
3
The Warren
35
Hill Farm
Dumbleton Wood
2
GL54
Hearle's Covert
Alderton Hill
Earls Plantation
Great Washbourne Coppice
Wychavon Way
1
Frampton Covert
34
99
00
01

187
175

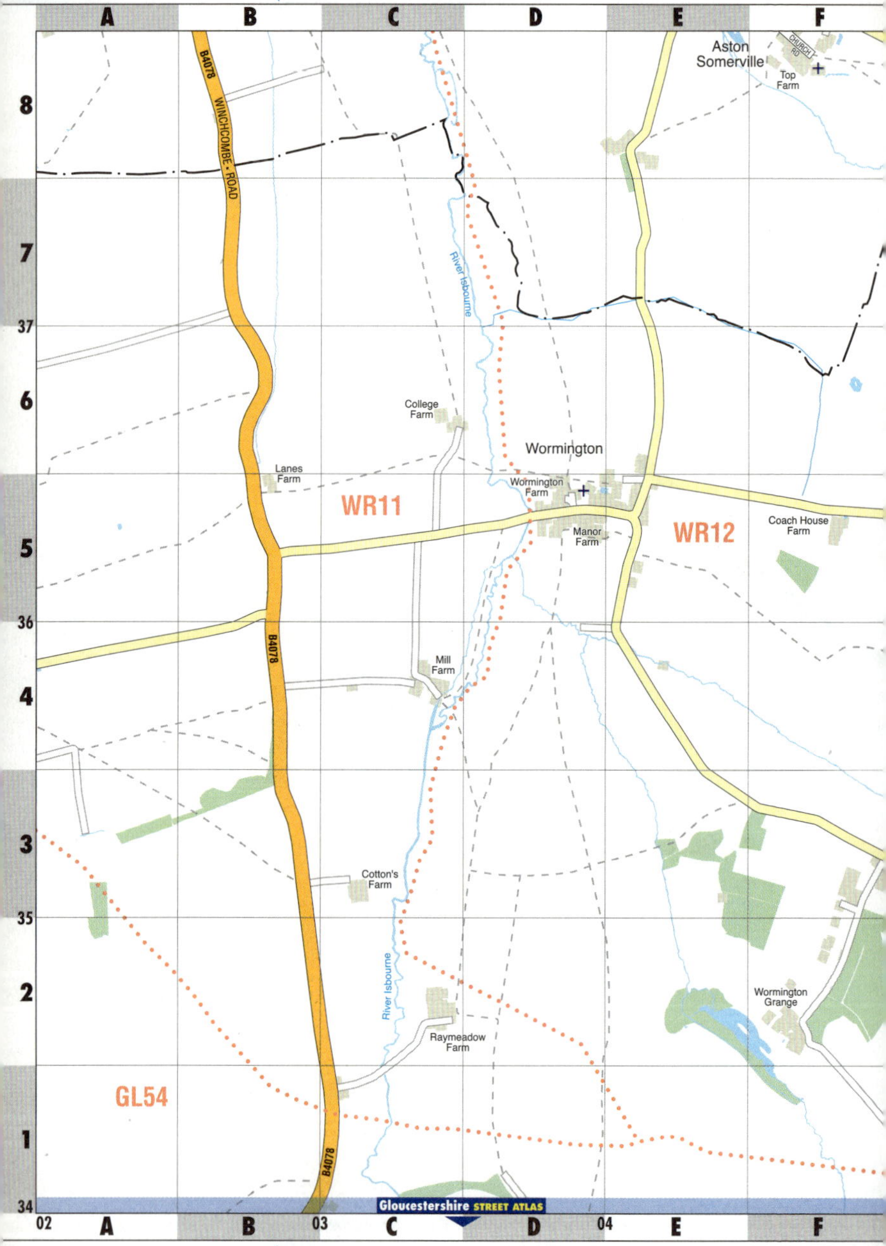
A
B
C
D
E
F
8
7
37
6
5
36
4
3
35
2
1
34
02
03
04
Aston
Somerville
CHURCH RD
Top
Farm
B4078
WINCHCOMBE ROAD
River Isbourne
College
Farm
Wormington
Lanes
Farm
Wormington
Farm
WR11
Manor
Farm
WR12
Coach House
Farm
Mill
Farm
Cotton's
Farm
River Isbourne
Wormington
Grange
Raymeadow
Farm
GL54
B4078
Gloucestershire STREET ATLAS

187

A
B
C
D
E
F
8
7
6
5
4
3
2
1
37
36
35
34
05
06
07
Mocho Farm
Buckland Fields Farm
Little Mocho Farm
Coppice Mocho
Peasebrook Farm
B4632
Mast
Rushbrooke Wood
Little Buckland
Archer Farm
CHELTENHAM ROAD
Slingate Brake
Wormington Brake
Leasow House
WR12
Rudfel House
Football Ground
Willow Farm
THE LANE
Bull Corner Brake
Wynniatt's Brake
B4632
Green Meadow Farm
PO
Potters Farm
Bowmeadow Farm
Hill Farm
Laverton
Hoo Farm
Top Farm
Stanton Fields
Ryefield Farm
East Lodge Farm
Laverton Hill Plantation
Stanton
CHURCH LA
Charity Farm
PH
Manorway
HIGH STREET
HIGH ST
STANWAY ROAD
B4632

189
177

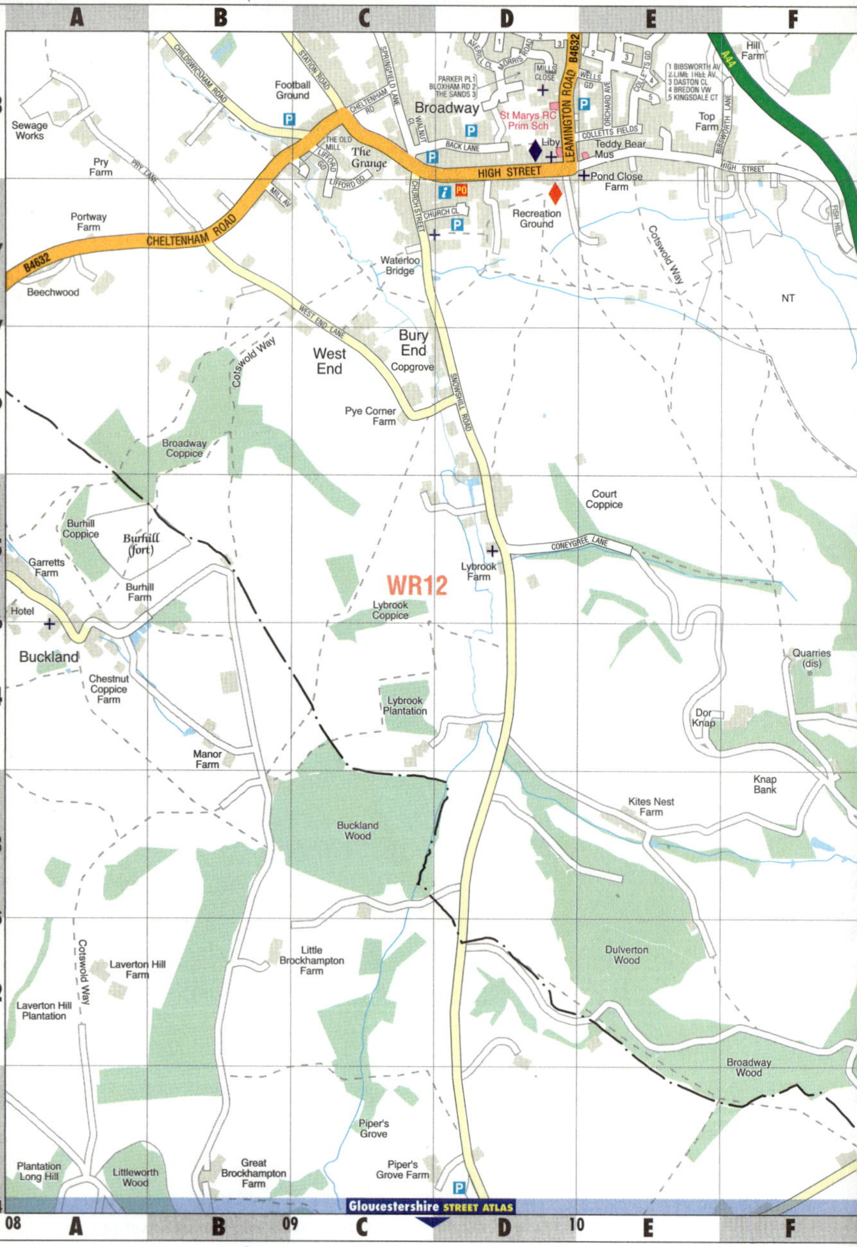
A
B
C
D
E
F
8
7
37
6
5
36
4
3
35
2
1
34
08
09
10
Broadway
Football Ground
Sewage Works
Pry Farm
PRY LANE
Portway Farm
Beechwood
B4632
CHELTENHAM ROAD
CHILDSWICKHAM ROAD
STATION ROAD
SPRINGFIELD LANE
CHELTENHAM RD
THE OLD MILL
LIFFORD GD
The Grange
MILL AV
WALNUT CL
BACK LANE
HIGH STREET
CHURCH STREET
CHURCH CL
AVERILL CL
MORRIS ROAD
MILLS CLOSE
PARKER PL 1
BLOXHAM RD 2
THE SANDS 3
St Marys RC Prim Sch
Liby
LEAMINGTON ROAD
WELLS GD
ORCHARD AVE
COLLETTS GD
COLLETTS FIELDS
Teddy Bear Mus
Pond Close Farm
Recreation Ground
1 BIBSWORTH AV
2 LIME TREE AV
3 DASTON CL
4 BREDON VW
5 KINGSDALE CT
Top Farm
BIBSWORTH LANE
Hill Farm
A44
FISH HILL
PO
Waterloo Bridge
Cotswold Way
NT
WEST END LANE
West End
Bury End
Copgrove
Pye Corner Farm
SNOWSHILL ROAD
Broadway Coppice
Burhill Coppice
Burhill (fort)
Garretts Farm
Burhill Farm
Hotel
Buckland
Chestnut Coppice Farm
Court Coppice
CONEYGREE LANE
Lybrook Farm
WR12
Lybrook Coppice
Lybrook Plantation
Quarries (dis)
Dor Knap
Knap Bank
Manor Farm
Kites Nest Farm
Buckland Wood
Little Brockhampton Farm
Dulverton Wood
Laverton Hill Farm
Laverton Hill Plantation
Broadway Wood
Piper's Grove
Piper's Grove Farm
Plantation Long Hill
Littleworth Wood
Great Brockhampton Farm

189

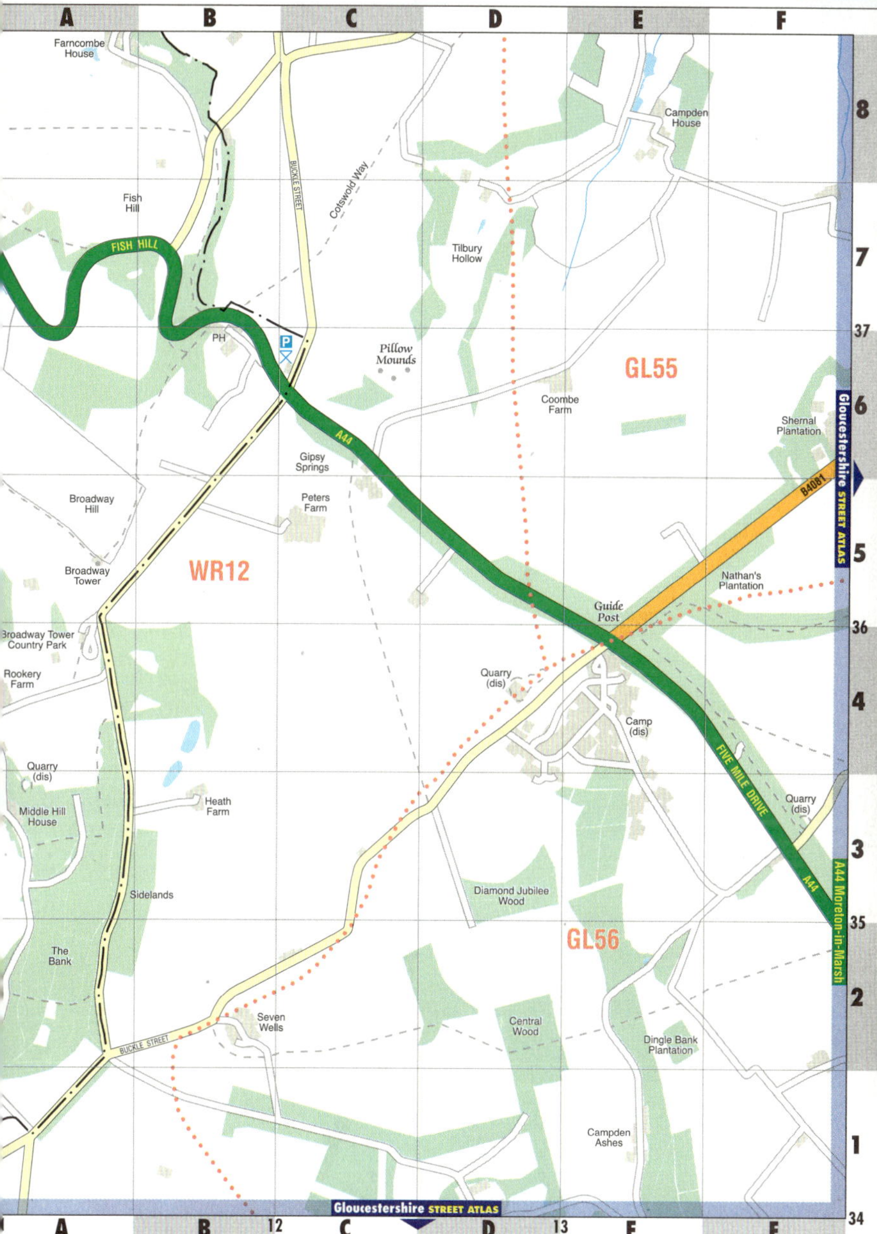
A B C D E F
Farncombe House
Fish Hill
FISH HILL
BUCKLE STREET
Cotswold Way
Campden House
Tilbury Hollow
PH
Pillow Mounds
GL55
Coombe Farm
Shernal Plantation
A44
Gipsy Springs
Peters Farm
Broadway Hill
B4081
Broadway Tower
WR12
Nathan's Plantation
Guide Post
Broadway Tower Country Park
Rookery Farm
Quarry (dis)
Camp (dis)
Quarry (dis)
Middle Hill House
Heath Farm
FIVE MILE DRIVE
Quarry (dis)
Sidelands
Diamond Jubilee Wood
GL56
The Bank
Seven Wells
Central Wood
Dingle Bank Plantation
BUCKLE STREET
Campden Ashes
Gloucestershire STREET ATLAS
A44 Moreton-in-Marsh
8 7 37 6 5 36 4 3 35 2 1 34
12 13

179

A
B
C
D
E
F
8
7
33
6
5
32
4
3
31
2
1
30
75
76
77
ALBRIGHT LANE
Aubreys Farm
Churches Farm
Eggs Tump
King's Green
Kingsgreen Farm
Carpenters Farm
WR13
HR8
B4208
Berrends Farm
Cobb's Cross
Glebe View
COOK'S LANE
Lake Farm
WYNDBROOK LANE
A417 Ledbury
A417
M50
2
M50 Ross-on-Wye
Russellsend Coppice
Bury Court
Park Farm
Combe Gill
Gloucestershire STREET ATLAS
Reservoir
Grimers Farm
May Farm
Glynch Brook
Hazeldine Wood
Hanover Green Farm
Blackford Mill Farm
Mast
Pfera Hall
Camp Farm
DRURY LANE
The Twynings
Playley Green
Lowbands Old Farm
CHARTIST LANE
GL19
LITTLE GN
PO
MILL LANE
PHILLIPS LANE
PH
Lowbands
Cherry Tree Farm
HYDE PARK CORNER
Playley Green Farm
PARSONS LANE
TOWER HO DRIVE
Redmarley D'Abitot
Hillview Farm
Redmarley CE Prim Sch
PHILLIPS LANE
Weir
Downhouse Coppice
RED DITCH LANE
Heath Farm
Glynch Farm
Caravan Scar Farm
Mellow Farm
The Down House
Hawcross
CHAPEL LANE
INNERSTONE LA
Princehill Wood
Brangwells Farm
Gloucestershire STREET ATLAS
A417 Gloucester

A
B
C
D
E
F
8
7
33
6
5
32
4
3
31
2
1
30
79
80
WR13
GL19
Oak Meadow Farm
Portway
Portway Farm
Berrow Wood
Underhill Farm
Grove Farm
M50
NETHERLEY LANE
GROVEFIELD
Pendock CE Prim Sch
Grafton Farm
Cleeve Farm
Rye Coppice
Drakes Pit
Brentwood
Pendock
GRAFTON LANE
Moat
New House Farm
PO
Pendock
Villa Farm
Cromer Farm
Grove Farm
Frogsmarsh
Hill Court Farm
Ash Farm
Marsh Court
Hill Top Farm
B4208
New Barn Farm
Dobs Hill Farm
Fort
Gadbury Plantation
Cole's Farm
Bridge End
Parsonage Farm
Gadfield Elm
Eldersfield
LIME STREET
Glebe Barn
MILL LANE
Berth Hill
Shotts Farm
The Hill
Vynes Farm
Moorend Farm
MOOREND ROAD
The Hawthorns
Staunton Coppice
Gloucestershire STREET ATLAS

193
181

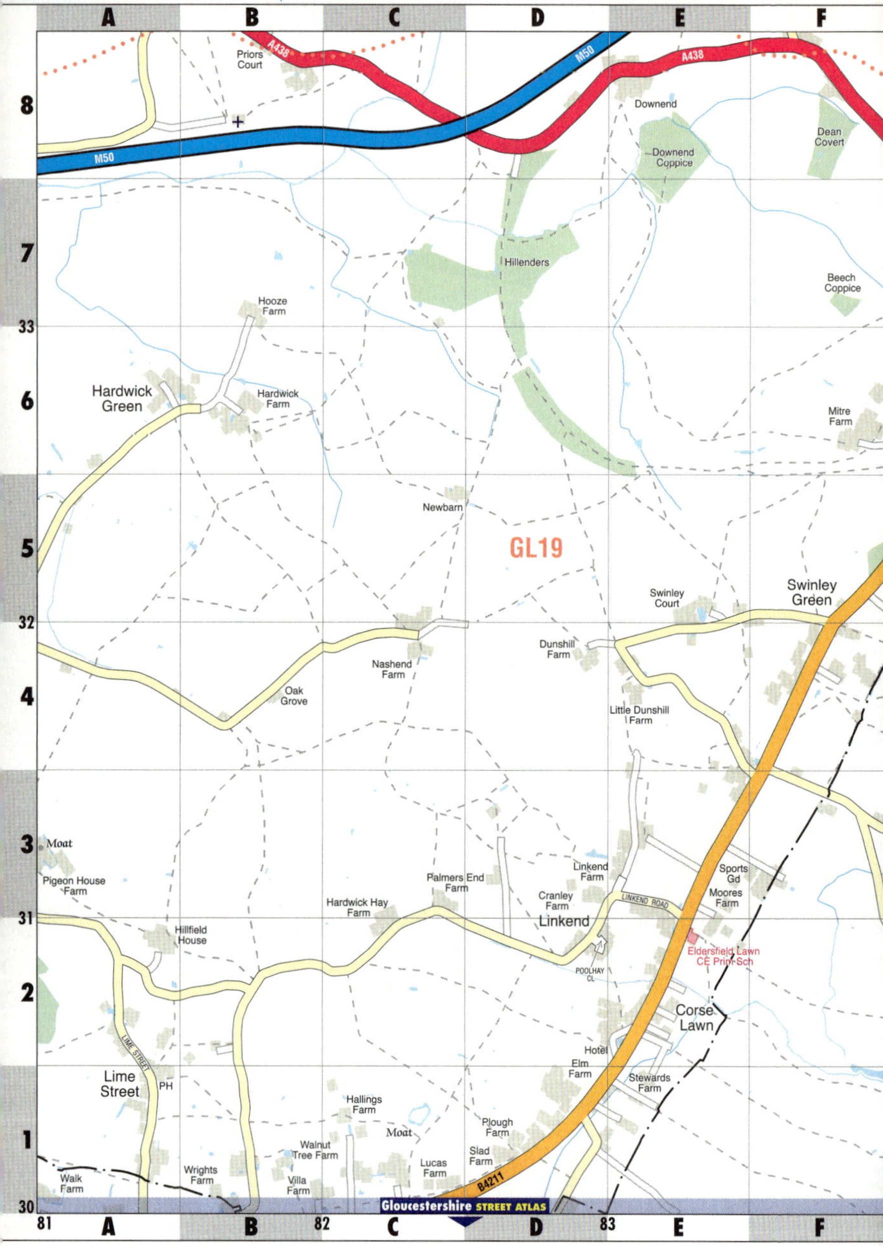
A
B
C
D
E
F
8
7
33
6
5
32
4
3
31
2
1
30
81
82
83
A438
M50
Priors Court
Downend
Downend Coppice
Dean Covert
Hillenders
Beech Coppice
Hooze Farm
Hardwick Green
Hardwick Farm
Mitre Farm
Newbarn
GL19
Swinley Court
Swinley Green
Dunshill Farm
Nashend Farm
Oak Grove
Little Dunshill Farm
Moat
Pigeon House Farm
Palmers End Farm
Linkend Farm
Sports Gd
Moores Farm
Cranley Farm
Linkend
LINKEND ROAD
Hardwick Hay Farm
Hillfield House
Eldersfield Lawn CE Prim Sch
POOLHAY CL
Corse Lawn
Hotel
Elm Farm
Stewards Farm
LIME STREET
Lime Street
PH
Hallings Farm
Moat
Plough Farm
Walnut Tree Farm
Slad Farm
Lucas Farm
Wrights Farm
Walk Farm
Villa Farm
B4211

193

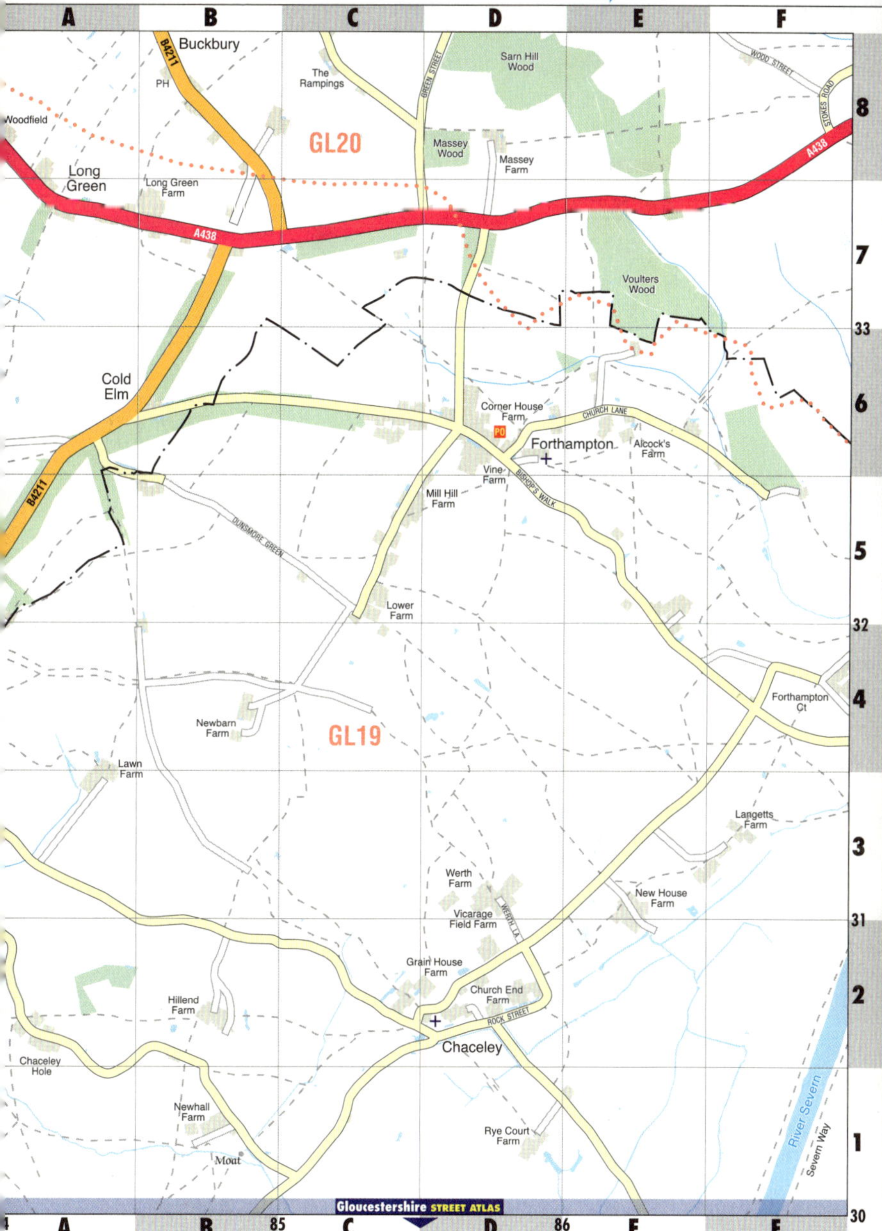
A
B
C
D
E
F
8
7
33
6
5
32
4
3
31
2
1
30
85
86
Buckbury
B4211
PH
The Rampings
GREEN STREET
Sarn Hill Wood
WOOD STREET
STOKES ROAD
Woodfield
GL20
Massey Wood
Massey Farm
A438
Long Green
Long Green Farm
Voulters Wood
Cold Elm
Corner House Farm
PO
CHURCH LANE
Forthampton
Alcock's Farm
Vine Farm
BISHOP'S WALK
Mill Hill Farm
DUNSMORE GREEN
Lower Farm
Forthampton Ct
Newbarn Farm
GL19
Lawn Farm
Langetts Farm
Werth Farm
New House Farm
Vicarage Field Farm
WERTH LA
Grain House Farm
Church End Farm
Hillend Farm
ROCK STREET
Chaceley
Chaceley Hole
Newhall Farm
Moat
Rye Court Farm
River Severn
Severn Way

195
183

E6
1 QUAY ST
2 SMITH'S LA
3 TRINITY ST
4 SHAKESPEARE CT
5 TOLSEY LA
6 NELSON ST
7 SAFFRON RD
8 POST OFFICE LA
9 ST MARY'S LA
10 SMITHS CT

F6
1 WYNYARDS CL
2 WATLEDGE CL
3 BACK OF MOUNT PLEASANT
4 CHANCE ST
5 ORCHARD CT
6 BARTON MS

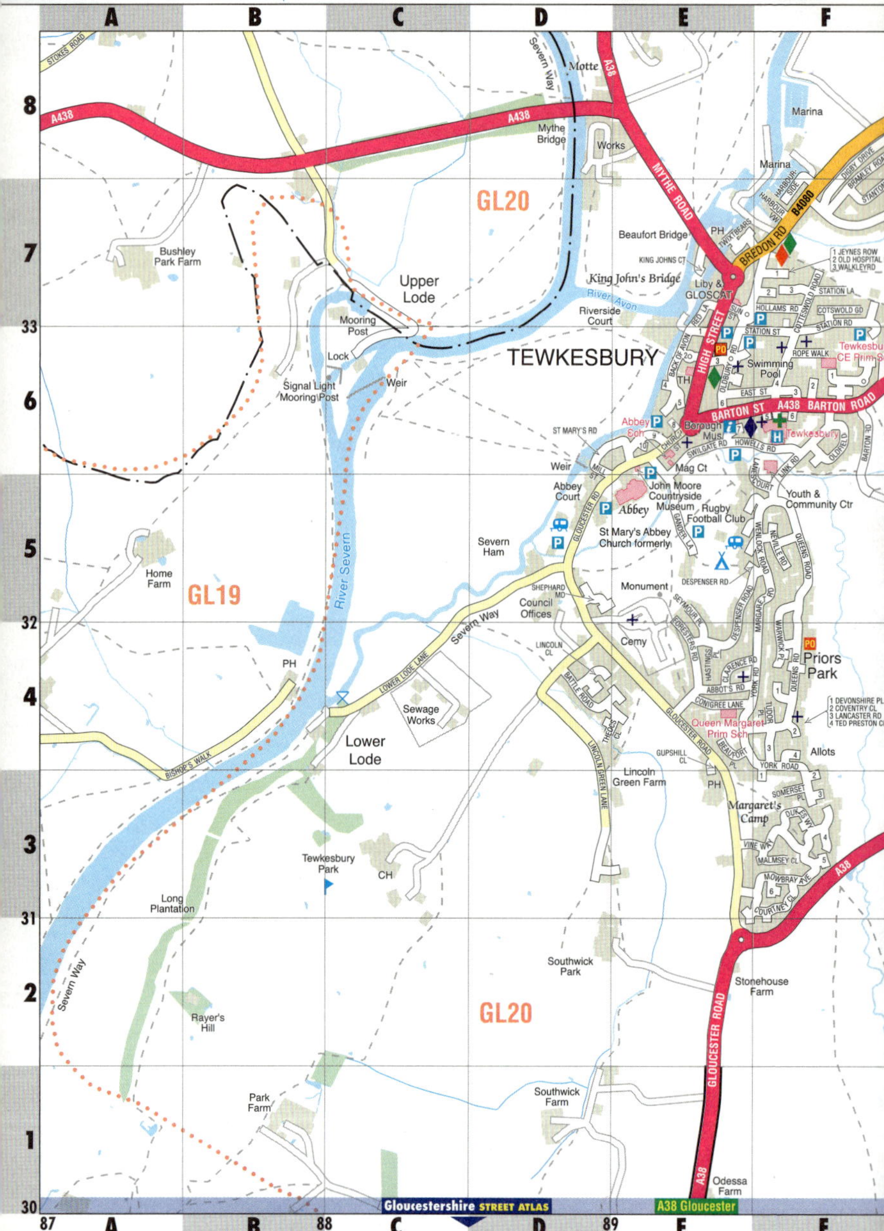

F3
1 MANOR PL
2 RICHARD PL
3 EDWARD PL
4 ABBEY MD
5 WOODVILLE RD
6 HOLME RD

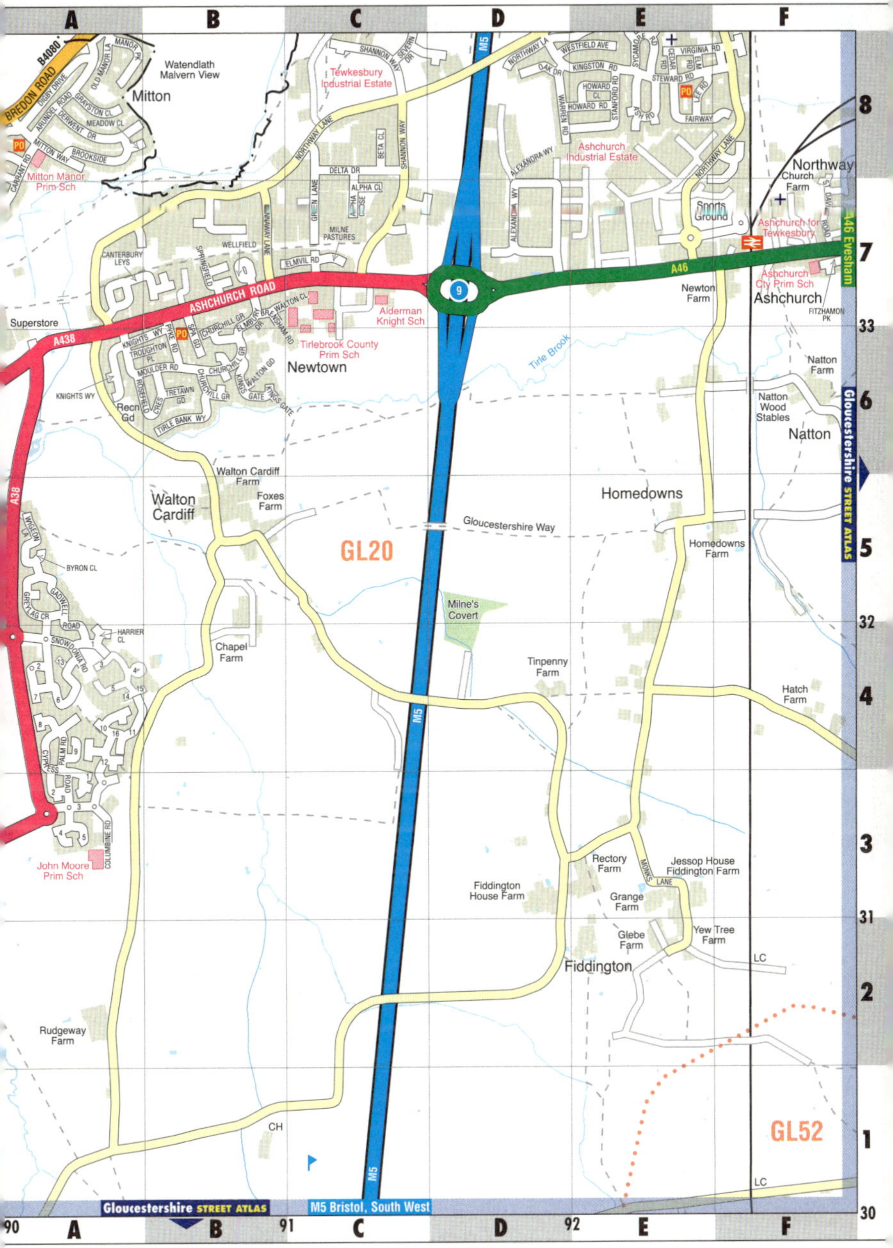

A4
1 CAMBRIAN RD
2 MILLENNLUM CL
3 BUCKINGHAM CL
4 LEXINGTON CL
5 ARLINGTON RD
6 CLIFFORD AVE
7 LONGTOWN RD
8 HOLMOAK CL
9 LAUREL AV
10 HAWKMOTH CL
11 CAMBRIAN RD
12 BELLFLOWER RD
13 HEVER CL
14 MUSKET CL
15 CHARLES CL
16 WOODRUSH RD

A3
1 PEACH CL
2 LIME RD
3 MONTEREY RD
4 THATCHAM RD
5 RICHMOND RD

Ludlow

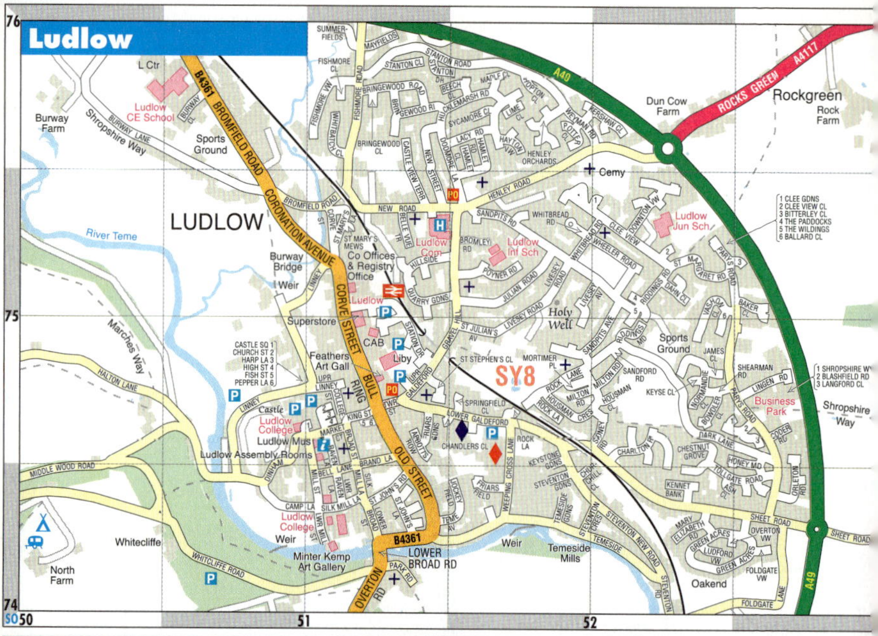

Stratford-upon-Avon

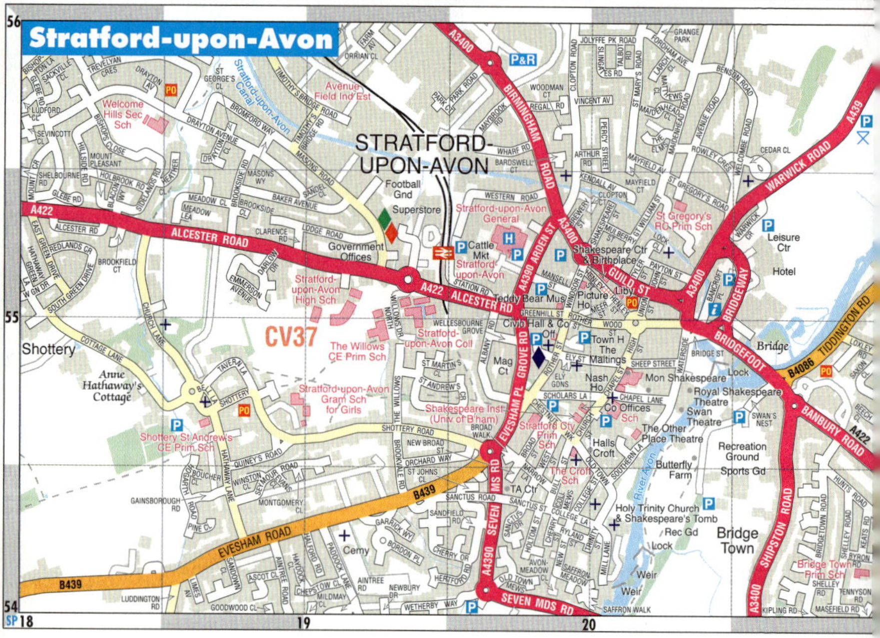

Index

Church Rd **6** Beckenham BR2..........**53** C6

Place name	Location number	Locality, town or village	Postcode district	Page and grid square
May be abbreviated on the map	Present when a number indicates the place's position in a crowded area of mapping	Shown when more than one place has the same name	District for the indexed place	Page number and grid reference for the standard mapping

Public and commercial buildings are highlighted in magenta. Places of interest are highlighted in blue with a star★

Abbreviations used in the index

Acad	**Academy**	Comm	**Common**	Gd	**Ground**	L	**Leisure**	Prom	**Prom**
App	**Approach**	Cott	**Cottage**	Gdn	**Garden**	La	**Lane**	Rd	**Road**
Arc	**Arcade**	Cres	**Crescent**	Gn	**Green**	Liby	**Library**	Recn	**Recreation**
Ave	**Avenue**	Cswy	**Causeway**	Gr	**Grove**	Mdw	**Meadow**	Ret	**Retail**
Bglw	**Bungalow**	Ct	**Court**	H	**Hall**	Meml	**Memorial**	Sh	**Shopping**
Bldg	**Building**	Ctr	**Centre**	Ho	**House**	Mkt	**Market**	Sq	**Square**
Bsns, Bus	**Business**	Ctry	**Country**	Hospl	**Hospital**	Mus	**Museum**	St	**Street**
Bvd	**Boulevard**	Cty	**County**	HQ	**Headquarters**	Orch	**Orchard**	Sta	**Station**
Cath	**Cathedral**	Dr	**Drive**	Hts	**Heights**	Pal	**Palace**	Terr	**Terrace**
Cir	**Circus**	Dro	**Drove**	Ind	**Industrial**	Par	**Parade**	TH	**Town Hall**
Cl	**Close**	Ed	**Education**	Inst	**Institute**	Pas	**Passage**	Univ	**University**
Cnr	**Corner**	Emb	**Embankment**	Int	**International**	Pk	**Park**	Wk, Wlk	**Walk**
Coll	**College**	Est	**Estate**	Intc	**Interchange**	Pl	**Place**	Wr	**Water**
Com	**Community**	Ex	**Exhibition**	Junc	**Junction**	Prec	**Precinct**	Yd	**Yard**

Index of localities, towns and villages

A

Abberley 60 F4
Abberton 133 A8
Abbeydale 70 F5
Abbots Morton 121 B2
Abbot's Salford 135 D1
Abbotswood 142 E7
Ab Lench 133 E4
Acton 64 A3
Aggborough 27 F4
Aldington 162 D5
Alfrick 124 F7
Alfrick Pound 124 E5
Alvechurch 51 B6
Alveley 1 C5
Amblecote 5 F7
Ankerdine Hill 111 D6
Areley Kings 43 E1
Arrow 122 F6
Arrowfield Top 34 C2
Ashchurch 197 F7
Ashton under Hill 174 B1
Aspley Heath 53 D2
Astley 62 C4
Astley Cross 62 E8
Aston Bank 37 E1
Aston Fields 68 A7
Aston on Carrant 185 C1
Aston Somerville 175 F1
Aston Subedge 178 F7
Astwood Dodderhill 86 A7
Astwood Worcester 115 D7
Astwood Bank 89 F1
Atch Lench 134 C2
Avonbank 158 E6

B

Badger's Hill 146 D6
Badsey 162 E3
Bank's Green 69 B3
Bank Street 76 B2
Barbourne 115 A6
Barnard's Green 153 B8
Barnettbrook 29 D5
Barnt Green 50 A7
Bartley Green 18 E8
Barton 136 F3
Bastonford 127 A2
Batchley 70 B3
Bateman's Green 35 E6
Battenton Green 82 E8
Baughton 170 B8
Baynhall 141 C3
Bayton 40 B7
Bayton Common 40 E6
Beach Hay 23 F1
Beckford 186 D4
Beech Lanes 9 E6
Belbroughton 30 B7
Bell End 31 C7
Belle Vale 7 E5
Bell Heath 31 E8
Bengeworth 161 F3
Beoley 71 D7
Berrington 55 B3
Berrington Green 55 C2
Berrow 180 C1
Berrow Green 98 F1
Berry Hill 84 E5
Besford 157 C6
Bevere 102 A3
Bewdley 26 B2
Bickley 38 B2
Bickmarsh 149 E8
Bidford-on-Avon 136 E4
Billesley 21 C6
Billesley Common 21 A5
Birch Acre 52 D7
Birch Berrow 79 C6
Birchen Coppice 27 B1
Birch Green 155 D8
Birchwood 124 E1
Birdsgreen 1 D7
Birlingham 158 B2
Birmingham 20 C5
Birtsmorton 180 D4
Birts Street 180 A6
Bishampton 132 F3
Blackheath 7 E8
Blackminster 162 E6
Blackmore End 154 B5
Blackpole 115 F7
Blackstone 26 D1
Blackwell 50 A5
Blakebrook 27 B6
Blakedown 14 C2
Blakeshall 12 E7
Bliss Gate 41 F6
Bluntington 29 E1
Bockleton 93 E7
Boraston 37 D1
Boraston Dale 37 C1
Boreley 82 C7
Bournes Green 30 C2
Bourneville 19 E7
Bournheath 48 D8
Bouts 108 B2
Bowling Green 127 B3
Bradley Green 106 F6
Brand Green 166 C7
Brandwood End 20 D4
Bransford 126 C6
Branson's Cross 53 C2
Brayswick 140 C8
Bredicot 117 B2
Bredon 184 F6
Bredon's Hardwick 184 C4
Bredon's Norton 172 A3
Bretforton 163 C5
Brickfields 115 F6
Bricklehampton 159 E1
Bridge End 193 F4
Brierley Hill 6 F8
Bringsty Common 110 C3
Broad Alley 65 D3
Broad Common 65 B4
Broadfields 55 A5
Broad Green 50 A1
Broad Green Broadwas 112 E4
Broad Heath 77 A7
Broad Marston 151 A2
Broadmore Green 127 A8
Broadwas 112 C3
Broadwaters 13 B1
Broadway 190 D8
Brockamin 125 D8
Brockencote 46 D8
Brockmanton 92 B4
Bromsgrove 67 D7
Brook End 141 D8
Broom 136 B8
Broombank 39 C1
Broome 15 A2
Broom Hill 30 D3
Brotheridge Green 168 C7
Broughton Green 105 F7
Broughton Hackett 117 F2
Bryan's Green 65 D5
Buckbury 182 A1
Buckland 190 A4
Buckridge 24 A1
Bugle Gate 63 C4
Burcot 49 E4
Burford 55 E6
Burlish Park 43 F6
Bury End 190 C6
Bushley 183 A1
Bushley Green 182 E2
Buttonoak 10 A1

C

Cakebole 46 B5
California 9 F2
Callow End 140 F7
Callow Hill 89 A7
Callow Hill Rock 41 E8
Camer's Green 179 E3
Carpenter's Hill 52 F1
Castle Hill 99 E3
Castlemorton 180 C7
Castlemorton Common 167 A3
Catchems End 26 C5
Catshill 49 A8
Caunsall 13 B7
Chaceley 195 D2
Chadbury 147 A2
Chaddesley Corbett 46 E8
Chadwick 63 E7
Chandler's Cross 166 F1

Charford 67 F7
Charlton 160 E8
Charlton Hartlebury 44 E3
Chase End Street 179 D3
Chatley 102 C7
Chawson 84 C2
Cherry Orchard 128 D7
Childswickham 176 E2
Church End Hanley Castle 169 A8
Church End Twyning 183 E4
Church Hil 71 C6
Churchill 14 C3
Churchill 130 E7
Church Lench 134 B3
Cladswell 108 F2
Claines 102 C2
Clanbrook 4 A7
Cleeve Prior 149 A7
Clent 15 F3
Cleobury Mortimer 22 C4
Clevelode 140 E2
Clifton 141 B1
Clifton Hill 98 B6
Clifton upon Teme 97 E8
Cobbler's Corner 112 F7
Cobley Hill 50 E4
Cock Bevington 135 B6
Cofton Hackett 33 C3
Cold Elm 195 A6
Coldheart 93 A6
Coles Green 125 D4
Collett's Green 127 C4
Collington 95 E5
Colwall Green 166 A8
Colwall Stone 152 A2
Comberton 28 B5
Comhampton 63 F2
Compton 3 B6
Conderton 186 A7
Cookhill 109 A1
Cookley 13 A6
Cooksey Corner 66 C5
Cooksey Green 66 B8
Coombeswood 8 C7
Copcut Droitwich 103 D8
Copcut Salwarpe 103 C7
Coreley 37 D8
Corse Lawn 194 E2
Cotheridge 113 B2
Cotteridge 19 E5
Coughton 109 F5
Crabbs Cross 89 A6
Cradley 7 D6
Cradley Heath 7 D8
Cranhill 137 D7
Cropthorne 160 B6
Cross Bank 42 A7
Crossway Green 63 F6
Crowcroft 125 D1
Crowle 117 E4
Crowle Green 117 E6
Crown East 114 A2
Cruise Hill 88 D4
Crumpfiled 88 E8
Crumpton Hill 138 B6
Cutnall Green 65 B6

D

Dagtail End 89 E3
Darbys Green 111 E5
Dawshill 127 C5
Dayhouse Bank 17 A1
Deabley 123 B8
Deblin's Green 140 B7
Defford 157 D3
Diglis 128 B8
Dines Green 114 C2
Ditchford Bank 87 E5
Doddenham 112 A5
Dodford 48 A5
Dordale 30 E1
Dormston 119 F8
Dorsington 150 E8
Doverdale 64 E1
Dowles 25 F6
Drakelow 12 B5
Drakes Broughton 144 A6
Drakes Cross 36 A6
Draycott 141 C4
Drayton 30 B4
Droitwich Spa 84 C4
Druggers End 167 C1
Duckswich 168 E4
Dumbleton 187 F5
Dunhampstead 104 C5
Dunhampton 64 A1
Dunley 62 B7
Dunnington 135 D7
Dunsley 4 C4
Dunstall Common 156 C3

E

Eachway 32 F6
Eardiston 59 B5
Earl's Common 105 F3
Earl's Croome 155 F1
Earlswood 53 F8
Eastham 57 F6
Eckington 171 F7
Edgiock 108 D5
Edvin Loach 96 B1
Edwyn Ralph 95 C1
Egdon 130 D3
Eggs Tump 192 C8
Elcock's Brook 88 E5
Eldersfield 193 E3
Elmbridge 65 F4
Elmley Castle 173 E7
Elmley Lovett 65 A8
Elms Green 60 B2
Enfield 70 D5
Evendine 166 A7
Evesham 161 B5

F

Fairfield 31 D3
Fairfield Evesham 161 D2
Fairfield Wolverley and Cookley 12 B3
Far Forest 24 B2
Feckenham 107 E7
Fenn Green 1 E3
Fernhill Heath 102 F3
Fiddington 197 E2
Fingerpost 24 D1
Finstall 49 D1
Fladbury 146 B1
Fladbury Cross 146 A3
Flyford Flavell 119 D2
Foley Park 27 C2
Footrid 39 E2
Forshaw Heath 53 C7
Forthampton 195 E6
Foster's Green 87 D7
Four Pools 161 E1
Foxlydiate 69 F3
Franche 12 C1
Frankley 18 B2
Frankley 18 B5
Frankley Green 18 A5
Frankley Hill 17 F3
Frith Common 59 A8
Frog Pool 81 E8
Frogsmarsh 193 C5

G

Gadfield Elm 193 B3
Gallows Green 86 B2
Gallowstree Elm 4 A6
Gilbert's End 154 C1
Gilver's Lane 168 B7
Golder Field 92 F6
Good's Green 11 A7
Goom's Hill 121 A2
Goosehill Green 105 B7
Gorst Hill 41 E7
Grafton 186 E7
Grafton Flyford 119 B5
Great Comberton 158 F1
Great Malvern 139 D2
Great Washbourne 186 E2
Great Witley 61 B1
Greenhill 28 A8
Greenhill Evesham 161 E7
Greenlands 90 A8
Green Lane 90 C6
Green Street Kempsey 141 F6
Green Street Ripple 170 A5
Greenway 41 E2
Greystones 149 D8
Griffin's Hill 19 D8
Grimes Hill 36 B4
Grimley 101 F6
Guarlford 154 A7
Guller's End 182 C3

H

Habberley 27 A6
Haden Cross 8 A8
Hadley 83 E4
Hadzor 85 D1
Hagley 15 D6
Halesowen 8 D4
Hales Park 25 F3
Hall Flat 49 C7
Hall Green 21 E8
Hallow 101 D1
Hallow Heath 101 D3
Ham Green 88 E4
Hampton 161 A3
Hampton Lovett 84 D7
Hanbury 87 A4
Hanley Castle 154 F1
Hanley Child 76 E7
Hanley Swan 154 A2
Hanley William 77 C8
Harbours Hill 86 F8
Hardwick Green 194 A6
Harpley 96 F7
Hartle 30 F6
Hartlebury 45 A2
Hartlebury Common 44 C2
Hartsgreen 2 C4
Harvington 29 B2
Harvington 148 A7
Hasbury 7 E3
Hasluck's Green 21 F2
Hatfield Hatfield and Newhampton 93 E4
Hatfield Norton Juxta Kempsey 129 B1
Hawbridge 143 A7
Hawcross 192 C1
Hawford 102 B6
Hawkesley 34 F8
Hawne 8 A5
Haybridge 38 C8
Hayley Green 7 C1
Headless Cross 89 D8
Headley Heath 35 C6
Heath Green 52 F3
Heightington 42 D3
High Green 156 A7
High Lane 96 D6
Highter's Heath 21 B2
Highwood 57 F3
Hill Croome 170 D5
Hill End Droitwich Spa 85 B4
Hill End Twyning 184 A8
Hill Furze 146 B5
Hillpool 29 E5
Hill Side 99 B7
Himbleton 105 C2
Hindlip 103 B2
Hinton Cross 175 B5
Hinton on the Green 175 A5
Hipplecote 111 E8
Hoden 149 D4
Holbeache 11 A2
Holberrow Green 108 B3
Holdfast 182 C8
Hollow Court 106 D1
Hollybed Common 179 F7
Hollybush 179 C6
Holly Green 169 E7
Hollywood 36 B8
Holt 82 D2
Holt End 71 F8
Holt Fleet 82 C4
Holt Heath 82 B3
Holy Cross 15 E2
Homedowns 197 E5
Homer Hill 7 B6
Honeybourne 164 A5
Hoobrook 27 F2
Hook Bank 168 A5
Hopwood 34 B3
Horsham 111 C8
Howsen 113 D1
Huddington 118 C7
Hunnington 17 B8
Hunt End 89 C5
Hurcott 28 C8
Hurst Green 8 F8

I

Illey 17 E8
Inkberrow 120 F7
Inkford 35 F1
Interfield 138 F8
Ipsley 71 C2
Iron Cross 135 C5
Iverley 14 B7

K

Kemerton 185 D7
Kempsey 141 D7
Kendal End 33 C2
Kersoe 174 A5
Kerswell Green 141 D2
Kidderminster 27 D4
King's End 127 D4
Kingsford 12 B8
King's Green 192 D8
King's Heath 20 E7
King's Norton 19 E2
Kingswood Lower 24 C7
Kington 120 A4
Kinnersley 156 A3
Kinsham 185 A3
Kinver 3 F4
Kitwell 18 A7
Knighton 121 D6
Knighton on Teme 57 A8
Knightwick 111 A3
Knowle Fields 121 E8
Kyre 75 F3
Kyre Green 75 C2
Kyrewood 56 B4

L

Ladywood 103 A7
Lakeside 71 A3
Lapal 8 F3
Laughern Hill 99 E2
Laverton 189 E3
Lea End 34 F3
Leapgate 44 E5
Leigh 126 A7
Leigh Sinton 125 F2
Leigh Sinton House Farm 126 A2
Lem Hill 24 A2
Lenchwick 147 C3
Leysters 73 E4
Libbery 118 E3
Lickey 33 A3
Lickey End 49 C6
Lickhill 43 E5
Lifford 20 B5
Lime Street 194 A1
Lincomb 63 C6
Lindridge 58 D7
Lineholt 63 D1
Lineholt Common 63 E3
Linkend 194 D2
Linley Green 123 B7
Linthurst 50 A6
Little Beckford 186 D2
Little Comberton 159 B3
Little Eastbury 114 D7
Little Hereford 54 C6
Little Inkberrow 120 C8
Little London 38 A3
Little Malvern 166 E6
Little Welland 167 F1
Little Witley 81 A4
Littleworth Feckenham 88 B1
Littleworth Norton Juxta Kempsey 129 D1
Lodge Park 70 F2
Long Bank 25 C1
Longbridge 33 D7
Longdon 181 F5
Longdon Heath 168 F2
Longdon Hill End 168 C2
Long Green 195 A8
Longley Green 124 C1
Long Marston 151 C6
Lowbands 192 E3
Lower Bach 92 A7
Lower Bentley 87 E8
Lower Broadheath 113 E5
Lower Clent 15 D4
Lower Hook 168 B5
Lower Howsell 139 B6
Lower Illey 17 D7
Lower Lode 196 C4
Lower Moor 145 E3
Lower Sapey 97 B5
Lower Strensham 171 A6
Lower Town 102 E4
Lower Westmancote 185 B7
Lower Wick 127 F6
Lower Wolverton 130 F2
Lower Wyche 152 F5
Low Habberley 26 F8
Lulsley 111 E4
Lydiate Ash 32 C3
Lye 6 E6
Lye Head 42 B7
Lyppard Grange 116 B4

M

Madeley Heath 31 E7
Madresfield 139 E4
Major's Green 36 D8
Malvern Common 153 B5
Malvern Link 139 B4
Malvern Wells 152 F1
Mamble 39 F3
Mappleborough Green 72 A1
Marl Bank 167 B6
Marlbrook 32 C1
Marlcliff 136 C2
Marsh Common 156 E1
Martin Hussingtree 103 C5
Martley 99 A4
Matchborough 71 E1
Meadow Green 110 F6
Menithwood 59 D7
Mere Green 86 D1
Mickleton 165 E4
Middle Littleton 148 F3
Middleton 54 B8
Middleton on the Hill 73 A6
Middletown 90 D1
Milson 38 C6
Mitton 197 B8
Monkwood Green 100 F5
Moons Moat 71 F5
Morton Spirt 121 E2
Morton Underhill 107 E3
Moseley 101 A3
Mount Pleasant 88 D5
Murcot 176 C5
Mustow Green 28 F1

N

Napleton 141 E5
Nash 37 A4
Nash End 10 E8
Natton 197 F6
Naunton 170 B4
Naunton Beauchamp 132 B5
Neen Savage 22 D7
Neens Hill 39 B4
Neen Sollars 39 A5
Netherton 174 A8
Newbridge Green 169 B3
New End 108 F4
Newland 139 C6
Newland Common 104 A5
Newnham Bridge 57 D7
Newtown Ashchurch 197 C6
Newtown Droitwich 84 E4
Newtown Martley 112 B8
Nineveh Bayton 39 E8
Nineveh Kyre 75 E6
Noah's Green 107 C7
Norchard 64 A6
Northfield 19 B4
North Littleton 149 B3
North Piddle 119 B1
Northway 184 E2
Northwick 115 A8
Norton 5 D2
Norton Norton and Lenchwick 147 D4
Norton Norton Juxta Kempsey 129 C2
Noutard's Green 62 E2

O

Oakall Green 101 A6
Oakenshaw 89 E6
Ockeridge 80 F1
Oddingley 104 C4
Offenham 148 A1
Offenham Cross 162 C8
Offmore Farm 28 A6
Oldbury 9 C7
Oldfield 83 B6
Old Hills 140 E6
Old Storridge Common 124 F3
Old Swinford 6 A2
Oldwood 55 E2

Ombersley 83 A4
Orleton 59 B2
Outhill 72 E1
Outwood 47 B5
Overbury 185 F8
Overend 7 E6

P

Park End 42 D7
Park Farm 90 C8
Park Gate 48 B3
Pebworth 150 D2
Pedmore 6 B1
Pendock 193 B6
Pensax 60 B6
Pensham 158 C5
Peopleton 131 B2
Perryfields 48 E4
Pershore 144 C2
Phepson 105 C4
Picken End 154 B2
Pie Corner 95 D7
Pin's Green 139 E8
Pinvin 144 E6
Piper's End 182 B3
Piper's Hill 87 A7
Pirton 142 C3
Pixham 141 A6
Playley Green 192 C4
Podmoor 45 E5
Pole Elm 140 F8
Poolbrook 153 D6
Porchbrook 41 B2
Portway 53 A5
Portway Pendock 193 A8
Potter's Cross 4 A5
Pound Bank Malvern 153 D8
Pound Bank Rock 41 B8
Pound Green 10 B2
Powick 127 E3
Powick Hams 127 E5
Priestfield 154 C6
Primsland 104 A8
Priors Park 196 F4
Puckrup 183 D5
Pudleston 92 E4
Purshull Green 47 A3

Q

Quarry Bank 7 A8
Queenhill 182 D6
Quinton 8 F5

R

Radford 120 D3
Rainbow Hill 115 D5
Ramsden 143 E2
Ravenhills Green 111 E1
Redcross 46 C8
Redditch 70 C2
Red Hill 128 F8
Redmarley D'Abitot 192 A3
Rednal 33 C6
Rhydd 154 F6
Rhydd Green 154 E7
Ribbesford 26 B1
Ridgeacre 9 D6
Ripple 183 A8
Riverside 70 F6
Rochford 57 A6
Rock 41 C3
Romsley 17 A4
Romsley 2 A2
Romsley Hill 17 A2
Ronkswood 115 F2
Rous Lench 133 E7
Rowney Green 51 E3
Rubery 33 B7
Rumbush 36 E3
Rushbrook 53 D3
Rushock 46 C3
Rushwick 127 B8
Ryall 169 E6
Rye Street 180 A4

S

Sailors Bank 113 F8
Saintbury 178 B4
St George's 70 F4
St John's 114 F1
St Michaels 74 C8
St Peter The Great 128 E6
Sale Green 105 A1
Saleway 104 F4
Salford Priors 135 F3
Salwarpe 103 B8
Sambourne 90 B1
Sandford 155 D7
Sankyns Green 81 D6
Sapey Bridge 111 A5
Sapey Common 78 C5
Sedgeberrow 175 A2
Selly Oak 19 B8
Severn Stoke 155 D5
Sharpway Gate 86 E7
Shatterford 11 C7
Shell 105 E4
Shelsley Beauchamp 79 C2
Shelsley Walsh 79 A3
Shenley Fields 18 E7
Shenstone 45 F8
Sheriff's Lench 146 F7
Shernal Green 104 D7
Sherrard's Green 139 D1
Shoulton 101 A2
Shrawley 81 E6
Shurnock 108 B6
Shuthonger 183 D3
Sidemoor 48 F4
Silver Street 35 F5
Sinton 83 B2
Sinton Green 101 B6
Slades Green 182 C2
Sledge Green 181 A1
Smallwood 70 E2
Smethwick 9 E8
Smite Hill 103 F2
Smith End Green 125 F5
Sneachill 130 B7
Snead Common 60 C7
Sneads Green 64 E4
Snuff Hill 31 D1
Solihull 21 E2
Solihull Lodge 21 E2
Southcrest 70 D1
South Littleton 148 E1
Spennells 28 A2
Spernall 91 B1
Spetchley 116 F1
Springfield 21 E5
Spurtree 56 A7
Stakenbridge 14 E3
Stambermill 6 C6
Stanbrook 140 E8
Stanford Bridge 78 F8
Stanford on Teme 78 C8
Stanklyn 28 D2
Stanley 1 A3
Stanton 189 D1
Staple Hill 49 C8
Stirchley 20 B7
Stitchin's Hill 125 B4
Stock Green 106 F2
Stockton on Teme 59 E3
Stock Wood 107 C2
Stoke Bliss 76 E2
Stoke Heath 67 D5
Stoke Pound 68 A4
Stoke Prior 67 C4
Stoke Wharf 67 D3
Stoke Works 67 C1
Stone 28 D3
Stonebow 144 A7
Stonehall 142 C6
Stonepits 120 D7
Stoney Hill 49 A2
Stony Cross 54 B3
Storridge 138 A6
Stoulton 143 B8
Stourbridge 5 D4
Stourport-on-Severn 43 C6
Stourton 4 F7
Stratford 170 C2
Strensham 171 C6
Structon's Heath 80 E8
Studley 90 F4
Suckley 124 A3
Suckley Green 123 F7
Suckley Knowl 123 E7
Summerfield 45 A8
Summerhill 27 A5
Sutton Farm 27 B4
Sweet Green 76 E2
Swinesherd 129 B8
Swinley Green 194 F5
Sytchampton 64 A1

T

Tanner's Green 36 A1
Tanwood 30 B2
Tanworth-In-Arden 53 F2
Tardebigge 69 B7
Tedstone Delamere 97 A2
Tedstone Wafer 96 D3
Ten Acres 20 B8
Tenbury Wells 55 F4
Terry's Green 53 F7
Tewkesbury 196 D6
The Bourne 119 E5
The Burf 62 F4
The Grove 169 F6
The Hook 168 C6
The Hyde 168 F5
The Lakes 25 F4
The Mythe 183 D1
The Ramplings 182 C1
The Walshes 43 F1
Thomas Town 90 E3
Thornbury 94 E4
Throckmorton 145 E8
Tibberton 117 A7
Tidbury Green 36 E4
Tilsop 37 C7
Timberhonger 47 F1
Titton 63 D8
Tolladine 115 F4
Torton 45 B5
Trimpley 11 C1
Trotshill 116 D4
Tunnel Hill 168 F5
Turleygreen 1 C7
Turves Green 19 A1
Twyford 147 E1
Twyning 183 F7
Twyning Green 184 B6

U

Uckinghall 169 F1
Ullington 149 F3
Uphampton 82 E6
Upper Arley 10 D5
Upper Bentley 69 A1
Upper Catshill 32 B2
Upper Colwall 152 D4
Upper Ham 169 D4
Upper Hamnish 92 A3
Upper Haselor 174 E8
Upper Howsell 138 F6
Upper Lode 196 C7
Upper Moor 145 C4
Upper Rochford 57 A4
Upper Sapey 77 E3
Upper Strensham 171 A4
Upper Welland 166 F6
Upper Wick 127 C7
Upper Wolverton 130 C2
Upper Wyche 152 E4
Upton Snodsbury 118 C1
Upton upon Severn 169 D5
Upton Warren 67 A3

W

Wadborough 143 A4
Walcot 144 B5
Walker's Heath 20 B1
Walkwood 89 B6
Walton Cardiff 197 B5
Walton Pool 16 A2
Wants Green 112 C7
Wapping 90 E5
Waresley 64 A8
Warley Woods 9 E8
Warndon 116 B6
Warstock 21 C3
Washford 90 E7
Weatheroak Hill 35 B1
Weavers Hill 89 C4
Webheath 70 A2
Weethley 122 A4
Weethley Bank 122 B2
Weethley Gate 122 B1
Welland 167 C4
Welland Stone 168 B2
Weoley Castle 19 A8
Westacre 84 D3
West End 190 C6
West Hagley 15 A5
West Heath 34 B7
Westlands 84 D5
West Malvern 138 C1
Westmancote 185 B8
Weston-sub-Edge 178 D7
Whatmore 37 C3
Whitbourne 111 A6
Whitbourne Ford 98 A1
White End 180 B1
White Ladies Aston 130 E6
Whiteleaved Oak 179 B4
Whitlock's End 36 E6
Whittington Kinver 4 D2
Whittington 129 B6
Whyle 92 D6
Wichenford 100 B6
Wick 159 A7
Wick Episcopi 127 E7
Wickhamford 176 E8
Wilden 44 D6
Wildmoor 31 F4
Willersey 177 F4
Willow Green 99 C1
Windmill Hill 143 D7
Winnall 63 B4
Winterfold 46 B8
Winyates 71 E2
Wirehill 90 B5
Withybed Green 50 F6
Withymoor Village 6 C8
Witnells End 11 C8
Witton 84 E1
Witton Hill 80 D1
Wofferwood Common 123 A4
Wolferlow 96 B8
Wollaston 5 E6
Wollescote 6 E4
Wolverley 12 E4
Wood Bevington 135 B8
Woodcock Hill 18 E8
Woodcote Green 47 C6
Wood End 53 F3
Woodgate 68 B2
Woodgate 9 A1
Woodgates Green 38 A1
Woodgate Valley 9 C3
Woodgreen 116 C5
Wood Green 62 E3
Woodhampton 54 E7
Woodmancote 157 B2
Wood Norton 146 F3
Woodrow 29 D3
Woodrow 90 B7
Woodsfield 139 F6
Woolmere Green 87 A3
Woonton 73 B1
Worcester 115 B1
Worlds End 101 A4
World's End 9 D5
Worles Common 60 B6
Wormington 188 D6
Worms Ash 48 C6
Wribbenhall 26 B4
Wychbold 66 E1
Wynds Point 166 C6
Wyre Piddle 145 B4
Wythall 36 B3

Y

Yardley Wood 21 E5
Yarhampton 61 F3
Yarhampton Cross 61 D3
Yearsett 123 C8
Yieldingtree 29 F8

A

Ab Lench Rd WR10 133 F4
Abberley Ave DY13 43 D1
Abberley Cl
Halesowen B63 7 F2
Redditch B98 71 C5
Abberley Dr WR9 84 E1
Abberley Hall WR6 60 F1
Abberley Parochial Prim Sch WR6 60 F4
Abberley Rd B68 9 B8
Abberley View 4 WR3 115 C5
Abberton Cl B63 8 C3
Abberton House 4 B97 70 A4
Abberton Rd WR10 133 A4
Abbey Cl
Bromsgrove B60 49 C2
3 Callow End WR2 140 F8
Abbey Cres B63 7 D4
Abbey Int Colleges WR14 166 E8
Abbey La WR11 161 C3
Abbey Mdw 4 GL20 196 F3
Abbey Pk Fst & Mid Sch WR10 158 C8
Abbey Rd
Evesham WR11 161 C3
Great Malvern WR14 152 F8
Halesowen B63 7 C4
Kidderminster DY11 27 A6
Pershore WR10 158 D8
Redditch B97 70 E4
Worcester WR2 114 F1
Abbey Sch GL20 196 E6
Abbey Trad Ind Area B97 70 E5
Abbey View Rd WR10 144 E5
Abbeycroft WR10 158 C8
Abbeydale Rd B31 19 A2
Abbeyfields Dr B80 90 E6
Abbot Chyryton's Pl 7 WR11 161 C4
Abbot Rd B63 16 C8
Abbot's Rd GL20 196 E4
Abbots Cl WR2 114 E3
Abbots Ct Dr GL20 183 E5
Abbots Grange 2 WR10 158 C8
Abbots Rd
Birmingham B14 20 E7
Pershore WR10 158 C7
Abbots Wood Cl B98 72 A3
Abbotswood WR11 161 D8
Abbotts Cl DY13 44 D6
Abdon Ave B29 19 C7
Acacia Ave DY12 26 C3
Acacia Cl WR4 115 E5
Acacia Ct DY8 5 E6
Acacia Rd B30 19 E8
Acanthus Rd B98 71 F6
Acheson Rd B28, B90 21 F3
Ackleton Gr B29 9 F1
Aconbury Cl WR5 116 B3
Acorn Cl
Birmingham, Bournville B30 19 E8
2 Colwall Stone WR13 152 B2
Acorn Ct B45 33 D7
Acorn Gdns B30 20 A7
Acorn Gr WR10 144 D2
Acorn Rd Catshill B61 49 B8
Halesowen B62 8 C8
Acorns The B61 49 A8
Acre La 3 Droitwich WR9 84 E3
Redditch B97 69 E2
Acre The WR8 157 E3
Acreage WR6 110 F6
Acres Rd DY5 6 E8
Acton Cl B98 71 D5
Adam St DY11 27 C5
Adam's Hill DY9 15 E4
Adams Brook Dr B32 9 B1
Adams Cl DY10 28 A7
Adams Hill B32 9 B1
Adams House 3 DY11 27 C6
Addenbrooke House B64 7 F8
Addenbrooke Cres DY11 27 A1
Addison Rd
Birmingham, King's Heath B14 20 F7
Worcester WR3 115 C6
Addyes Way WR9 103 E8
Adelaide Cl
8 Kempsey WR5 141 C6
11 Worcester WR3 115 B6
Adelaide St B97 70 D4
Admiral Pl WR5 128 F5
Adrian Cl 3 WR9 85 A1
Adstone Gr B31 19 A1
Agatha Gdns WR3 103 A2
Agenoria Dr DY8 5 F5
Aggborough Cres DY10 27 E3
Aggborough Stadium (Kidderminster Harriers FC) DY10 27 F4
Agmore La B60 50 B3
Agmore Rd B60 50 B4
Ainsdale Cl DY8 5 F2
Ainsdale Gdns B63 7 D2
Aintree Cl Catshill B61 32 A1
Kidderminster DY11 27 D8
Aintree Rd WR10 144 E4
Aire Croft B31 19 B1
Albany Cl DY10 28 B6
Albany Ct 1 B62 9 A7
Albany Rd WR3 115 D4
Albany Terr WR1 115 B4
Albemarle Rd DY8 5 F2
Albert Bradbeer Inf Sch B31 33 F7
Albert Bradbeer Jun Sch B31 33 F7
Albert Cl B80 90 E4
Albert Dr B63 7 F2
Albert Pk Mews WR14 138 F3
Albert Pk Rd WR14 138 F4
Albert Rd
Birmingham, King's Heath B14 20 F7
Bromsgrove B61 67 E8
2 Colwall Stone WR13 152 A1
Evesham WR11 161 C5
Halesowen B63 7 F3
Kidderminster DY10 27 F6
Oldbury B68 9 C8
Worcester WR5 115 D1
Albert Rd N WR14 138 F2
Albert Rd S WR14 153 A8
Albert St
7 Droitwich WR9 84 E3
Redditch B97 70 E5
Stourbridge DY8 5 F5
Stourbridge, Lye DY9 6 E5
Alberta Cl WR2 127 E7
Albion Rd WR14 138 E4
Albion Terr B50 136 C7
Alborn Cres B38 34 D8
Albright & Wilson House B68 9 E7
Albright La HR8 179 A1
Albrighton Rd B63 7 F3
Albury Rd B80 90 E4
Alcester Gdns B14 20 F7
Alcester Heath B49 109 C4
Alcester Highway B98 89 F8
Alcester Rd
Feckenham B96 107 E7
Finstall B60 49 F1
Hollywood B47 35 F5
Lickey End B60 49 D5
Portway B48 52 F7
Studley B80 90 E3
Tardebigge B60, B97 69 B7
Alcester Rd S
Birmingham, Alcester Lane's End B14 20 E6
Birmingham, Highter's Heath B14 20 F2
Alcester St B98 70 E4
Aldborough La 4 B97 70 B5
Aldbourne Way B38 34 E7
Aldbury Rd B14 21 A3
Aldeford Dr DY5 6 D8
Alder Ave DY10 27 E8
Alder Cl Hollywood B47 36 B6
Worcester WR4 115 D4
Alder Gr Droitwich WR9 103 F8
Evesham WR11 161 F2
Halesowen B62 8 E6
Alder La B30 19 C6
Alder Way B60 49 B2
Alderbrook Cl B97 70 B5
Alderbrook Rd 1 WR9 84 C1
Alderhanger La B98 72 C8
Alderlea Cl DY8 6 A2
Alderley Rd B61 67 D8
Alderman Knight Sch GL20 197 C7
Aldermans La B97 70 B6
Aldermere Rd DY11 27 C8
Alderminster Cl B97 89 E4
Alderney Gdns B38 19 D1
Alders Cl B98 71 A3
Alders Dr B98 71 F4
Alders The B62 16 F4
Aldersey Cl 10 WR5 128 D6
Aldersey Rd WR5 128 D6
Aldersmead Rd B31 19 C1
Aldgate Dr DY5 6 C7
Aldington Cl B98 70 F1
Aldridge Rd B68 9 B8
Alexander Ave WR9 84 D1
Alexander Cl B61 32 A1
Alexander Hill DY5 6 F8
Alexander Patterson Specl Sch The DY10 13 C2
Alexander Rd WR2 115 A1
Alexandra Hospl The B98 90 C6
Alexandra La WR14 138 F3
Alexandra Rd
Birmingham, Stirchley B30 20 A7
Evesham WR11 161 A3
Great Malvern WR14 138 F3
Halesowen B63 7 F4
Alexandra Way GL20 197 D7
Alford Cl B45 33 C7
Alfred Ct B60 67 E2
Alfred St B14 20 F7
Alfreda Ave B47 36 A8
Alfreds Well B61 48 C6
Alhambra Rd B60 49 C1
Alicante Cl 1 WR14 139 B1
Alice Ottley Jun Sch The WR1 115 B4
Alison Dr DY8 5 E3
Alison Rd B62 8 F3
All Saints Ave DY12 26 C4
All Saints Rd B14 20 E7
All Saints' CE Sch DY13 44 D5
All Saints' Rd B61 49 A3
Allardene WR11 161 E3
Allen Cl B80 90 E3
Allendale Ave B80 90 E3
Allendale Cres B80 90 E3
Allendale Ct B80 90 E3
Allens Croft Prim Sch B14 20 C5
Allens Croft Rd B14 20 C6
Allens Farm Rd B31 18 E3
Allensmore Cl B98 71 F2
Allesborough Dr 5 WR10 144 C1
Allesbrook Gdns WR11 162 D2
Allwell Dr B14 20 F2
Allwood Gdns B32 9 A2
Allwood House B97 70 C3
Alma St Halesowen B63 7 C5
Worcester WR3 115 B6
Almond Ave DY11 27 B8
Almond Cl
Birmingham B29 19 A6
2 Evesham WR11 161 F2
Almond Way DY13 43 D5
Almonry Her Ctr* WR11 161 D4
Alperton Dr DY9 6 E2
Alpha Cl GL20 197 C7
Alton Cl B97 70 B1
Alton Pk WR2 140 F7
Alton Rd WR5 128 E5
Alvechurch CE Fst & Mid Sch B48 51 B6
Alvechurch Highway
Lydiate Ash B60 32 D2
Redditch B98 70 F3
Alvechurch House B60 49 B3
Alvechurch Rd
Birmingham B31 34 B7
Halesowen B63 7 F2
Alvechurch Sta B48 51 A4
Alveley Cl B98 71 D4
Alveley Prim Sch WV15 1 C6
Alveston Cl B98 71 C2
Alveston Grange GL55 165 D3
Alveston Rd B47 36 A7
Alwold Ct B29 9 F2
Alwold Rd B29 9 F2
Amber Terr DY10 27 F5
Amber Way B62 8 C6
Ambergate Cl 8 B97 70 B5
Amberley Cl WR4 115 F7
Amblecote Prim Sch DY8 5 F7
Amblecote Rd
Brierley Hill DY5 6 D8
Kidderminster DY10 28 B5
Ambleside B32 9 C1
Ambleside Dr
Brierley Hill DY5 6 C8
Worcester WR4 115 F5
Ambleside Way B60 49 B1
Ambrose Cl WR2 114 D3
Amersham Cl B32 9 E5
Amery Cl WR5 128 D8
Amos Gdns WR4 116 C3
Amos Rd DY9 6 F2
Amphlett Ct 1 B60 49 A2
Amphlett Way WR9 85 E8
Amroth Cl B45 33 B7
Amroth Gdns 7 WR4 116 B7
Amwell Gr B14 20 F3
Anchor La
3 Fladbury WR10 146 A1
Harvington WR11 148 B6
Anchorfields DY10 27 F6
Andressy Mews B61 49 A5
Andrew Cl WR2 114 E4
Andrew Rd B63 8 A3
Andrews Cl DY5 6 E8
Andrews Dr 2 WR11 161 C2
Angel Pas DY8 6 A5
Angel Pl 9 WR1 115 B3
Angel St
Bentley Pauncefoot B97 88 C8
Upper Bentley B97 69 B1
Worcester WR1 115 B3
Angelo House B13 21 D7
Ankadine Rd DY8 6 B6
Ankerage Gn WR4 116 B4
Ankerdine Ave 1 DY13 43 D1
Ankerdine Ct B63 8 A3
Ankerdine Rd WR2 113 D5
Ann Rd B47 36 A3
Anne Cres 1 WR11 161 E2
Annscroft B38 19 D2
Ansley Cl B98 71 F1
Anton Cl DY12 26 D5
Apley Rd DY8 5 E7
Apollo Rd DY9 7 A5
Apperley Way B63 7 B7
Appian Cl B14 20 E5
Apple Orch Cl WR14 139 C1
Apple Orch The 3 GL20 184 E1
Apple Tree Cl
Crowle WR7 117 F4
Kidderminster DY10 28 B7
Apple Tree Rd 3 WR10 144 D2
Apple Tree Wlk WR9 83 A4
Appleby Cl B14 20 D5
Appleton Ave DY8 6 A2
Appleton Cl B30 19 E8
Appleton House B31 18 E5
Appletree Cl B31 18 F1
Appletree La
Inkberrow WR7 121 A5
Redditch B97 70 B5
Appletrees Cres B61 49 A5
Apsley Cl B68 9 A7
Apsley Croft B38 20 B2
Apsley Rd B68 9 A7
Aqueduct La B48 50 F7
Aqueduct Rd B90 21 E1
Arboretum Rd WR1 115 C3
Arbour Cl GL55 165 D3
Archer Cl
Great Malvern WR14 138 E4
Studley B80 90 D4
Archer Ct DY9 6 E2
Archer Rd
Birmingham B14 21 C4
Redditch B98 70 E4
Archer Terr B97 70 C1
Archer's Way WR15 55 E6
Archers Cl 8 WR9 84 E3
Ardarth Rd B38 20 A2
Arden Cl DY8 5 E7
Arden House B60 49 B3
Arden Leys B94 53 D2
Arden Rd
Birmingham, Rubery B45 18 A1
Hollywood B47 36 A6
Worcester WR5 128 D5
Arden Way WV15 1 C5
Ardencote Rd B13 21 A6
Ardens Cl B98 72 A2
Ardingley Wlk DY5 6 B7
Ardley Rd B14 21 A5
Areley Comm DY13 43 E1
Areley Comm Fst Sch DY13 43 E1
Areley Ct DY13 43 E2
Areley La DY13 43 E3
Arkle Cl WR9 104 B8
Arkle Rd WR9 104 B8
Arkwright Rd B32 9 C5
Arley Arboretum* DY12 10 C6
Arley Cl
Kidderminster DY11 27 A2
Redditch B98 71 D5
Arley Dr DY8 5 E3
Arley La DY12 10 F6
Arley Sta DY12 10 C5
Arlington Ct DY8 6 B4
Arlington Gr B14 21 B2
Arlington Rd
Birmingham B14 21 B3
5 Walton Cardiff GL20 197 A4
Armstrong Cl DY8 6 B6
Arnold Gr B30 19 D4
Arosa Dr WR14 153 A5
Arran Pl WR5 128 F6
Arrow Croft WR9 84 E4
Arrow End WR11 149 A3
Arrow House 1 B68 9 B8
Arrow La WR11 148 F3
Arrow Rd N B98 71 A4
Arrow Rd S B98 71 A4
Arrow Vale Com High Sch B98 71 E2
Arrow Valley Pk* B98 71 B4
Arrow Wlk B38 20 B1
Arrowdale Rd B98 71 A3
Arrowfield Gn B38 34 D7
Arrowsmith Ave WR2 114 F3
Arthur Dr (Road 2) DY11 27 E1
Arthur Dr DY11 44 E8
Arthur St B98 71 B3
Artingstall House B30 20 B8
Arum Cl 4 WR14 139 C3
Arundel Ct 13 B29 19 C7
Arundel Dr WR5 128 E8
Arundel Rd
Birmingham B14 21 A1
Bromsgrove B60 49 B1
Tewkesbury GL20 197 A8
Ascot Cl WR3 102 F3
Ascot Ct 11 B29 19 C7
Ascot Rd WR10 144 E4
Ascot Way B61 32 B1
Ash Ave WR4 115 E5
Ash Cl WR14 139 C3
Ash Ct DY8 6 A4
Ash Dr B61 32 B1
Ash Gr Evesham WR11 161 E2
Kidderminster DY11 27 B7
Stourbridge DY9 6 D3
14 Stourport-on-Severn DY13 43 E4
Ash La Alvechurch B48 34 D2
Martin Hussingtree WR3 103 C5
Ash Lea WR8 156 B1
Ash Rd GL20 197 E8
Ash Tree Rd
Birmingham B30 20 A6
Redditch B97 70 B5
Ashbourne Ridge B63 7 D5
Ashbrook Dr B45 33 B8
Ashbrook Gr B30 20 C8
Ashbrook Rd B30 20 C8
Ashburton Rd B14 20 D5
Ashbury Covert 3 B30 20 C3
Ashby WR4 116 C6
Ashchurch Cty Prim Sch GL20 197 F7
Ashchurch for Tewkesbury Sta GL20 197 F7
Ashchurch Ind Est GL20 197 E8
Ashchurch Rd GL20 197 B7
Ashcott Cl B38 19 D2
Ashcroft Rd WR1 115 B4
Ashdale Ave WR10 144 D2
Ashdale Dr B14 21 A1
Ashdene Cl
Hartlebury DY11 45 A2
Kidderminster DY10 28 C5
Ashdown Cl
Birmingham, Frankley B45 18 A2
7 Great Malvern WR14 139 B1
Worcester WR2 128 A7
Ashenden Cl 4 WR9 103 F8
Ashfield Cres DY9 7 A3
Ashfield Ct B38 19 E4
Ashfield Gr B63 7 E2
Ashfield House B28 21 E3
Ashgrove Cl B60 32 D1
Ashill Rd B45 33 B7
Ashley Cl DY8 5 D2
Ashley Ct B45 33 A1
Ashley Rd
Kidderminster DY10 13 B1
Worcester WR5 128 D6
Ashmead Dr B45 33 C4
Ashmead Rise B45 33 C4
Ashmore Rd B30 19 F5
Ashmores Cl B97 89 D5
Ashorne Cl B98 90 D8
Ashperton Cl B98 70 E1
Ashpool WR6 111 A6
Ashton Cl B97 70 B1
Ashton Rd GL20 186 D5
Ashton under Hill Fst Sch WR11 187 B8
Ashville Dr B63 8 A5
Ashwater Dr B14 20 D2
Aspen Cl 3 WR11 161 F1
Aspen Gr B47 36 B5
Aspen Wlk DY13 43 E5
Aspens Way B61 49 A6
Aspley Heath B94 53 D2
Aspley Heath La B94 53 D2
Assarts La WR14 166 F7
Assarts Rd WR14 166 E7
Astbury Ct 4 B68 9 B7
Aster Ave DY11 12 D1
Astles Rock Wlk DY7 3 F3
Astley Ave B62 8 F6
Astley CE Prim Sch DY13 62 C5
Astley Cl B98 90 A7
Astley Cres B62 8 F5
Astley Ct 8 DY13 62 E8
Astley Gdns DY13 62 E6
Astley Orch WR15 58 B5
Astley Rd B60 49 C1
Astley Vineyard* DY13 62 F4
Aston Cl 1 WR5 141 C7
Aston Dr WR14 153 C6
Aston Fields Mid Sch B60 68 C8
Aston Fields Trad Est 2 B60 67 F6
Aston Rd
Aston Subedge GL55 178 F7
Bromsgrove B60 67 F6
Astons Cl DY5 6 D7
Astons Fold DY5 6 D7
Astwood Bank Fst Sch B96 89 E2
Astwood La
Astwood Bank B96 89 C2
Dodderhill WR9 85 F8
Feckenham B96 107 E8
Inkberrow B96 108 A8
Astwood Rd WR3 115 D5
Atch Lench Rd WR11 134 B3
Atcham Cl B98 71 F3
Atcheson Cl B80 90 E4
Athelstan Rd WR5 115 D1
Atherstone Cl
Redditch B98 71 F1
Solihull B90 21 E2
Athol Cl B32 18 D8
Atkinson St WR12 176 E2
Attwood Bsns Ctr 2 DY9 6 F5
Attwood St
Halesowen B63 7 F5
Stourbridge DY9 6 F5
Atworth Cl B98 90 B5
Atyed Cl WR14 139 C1
Aubrey Rd B32 9 E7
Auckland Cl WR4 116 D5
Auckland House B32 9 F4
Audley Dr DY11 27 A8
Audnam DY8 5 F8
Augustine Ave B80 90 D4
Austcliff Cl B97 89 D6
Austcliffe La DY10 13 C5
Austcliffe Rd DY10 13 A5
Austen Cl 7 WR2 127 C2
Austin Rd B60 67 E7
Austin Rise B31 33 F7
Austrey Gr B29 19 A8
Autumn Terr WR5 115 D2
Auxerre Ave B98 90 B8
Auxerre House B98 90 B8
Avalon Rd B60 49 C2
Avebury Gr B30 20 C7
Avebury Rd B30 20 C8
Avenbury Cl B98 71 F1
Avening Cl WR4 115 F7
Avenue Rd
Astwood Bank B96 89 E1

Avenue Rd *continued*
Birmingham, King's Heath B14 .....20 D8
Great Malvern WR14 .....153 A8
Upton upon Severn WR8 .....169 A2
9 Worcester WR2 .....114 F1
Avenue The
Birmingham, Eachway B45 .....32 E7
Blackwell B60 .....50 A6
Blakedown DY10 .....14 B2
Hartlebury DY11 .....64 A8
Summerfield DY11 .....44 F8
Welland WR13 .....167 C5
2 Worcester WR1 .....115 C3
Worcester WR2 .....128 A8
Averill Cl
2 Broadway WR12 .....177 D1
Broadway WR12 .....190 D8
Aversley Rd B38 .....34 E8
Avery Ct 6 B68 .....9 B7
Avery Dell Ind Est B30 .....20 A6
Avill Gr DY11 .....27 C7
Avocet Dr
Kidderminster DY10 .....28 A2
4 Stourport-on-Severn DY13 .....44 B2
Avon Cl Bromsgrove B60 .....67 F6
Great Malvern WR14 .....153 D8
Worcester WR4 .....115 F4
Avon Dr
4 Eckington WR10 .....171 E7
Wythall B47 .....35 E2
Avon Gn WR10 .....145 A3
Avon House 3 B68 .....9 B8
Avon Rd Halesowen B63 .....7 B5
Kidderminster DY11 .....27 B3
Pershore WR10 .....144 E2
Stourbridge DY8 .....5 F3
Worcester WR4 .....115 F3
Avon St WR11 .....161 D5
Avon View GL20 .....184 A1
Avonbank Cl B97 .....89 C6
Avoncroft Mus of Historic Bldgs* B60 .....67 E5
Avoncroft Rd B60 .....67 D6
Avondale 6 WR9 .....84 D1
Axborough La DY10 .....13 D4
Aycliffe Rd WR5 .....128 D5
Aylesmore Cl B32 .....9 C1
Aymestrey Sch WR2 .....114 A1
Aynall La SY8 .....54 A3

B

Babylon La WR10 .....132 F3
Baccabox La B47 .....35 E7
Bacchurst Pl 4 WR4 .....116 C5
Bach Camp Fort* HR6 .....92 B5
Bach Mill Dr B28 .....21 D3
Back La Beckford GL20 .....186 C3
Bredon GL20 .....184 E7
Bretforton WR11 .....163 C4
Broadway WR12 .....190 D8
Cleeve Prior WR11 .....149 A8
Great Comberton WR10 .....172 E8
1 Great Malvern WR14 .....152 F8
Mickleton GL55 .....165 D4
Pebworth CV37 .....150 E2
Stone DY10 .....45 F8
Back La N WR1 .....115 B4
Back La S WR1 .....115 B4
Back of Avon GL20 .....196 E6
Back of Mount Pleasant 3 GL20 .....196 F6
Back Rd B38 .....19 F2
Back Way WR10 .....145 D3
Back Wlk WR1 .....115 B4
Backfields La WR8 .....169 C6
Badbury Cl B80 .....90 D4
Badbury Gdns B80 .....90 D4
Badger Brook La B96 .....89 D1
Badger Cl Martley WR6 .....99 A4
Redditch B98 .....71 D3
Badger Gdns WR5 .....128 E5
Badger St DY9 .....6 E6
Badger Way B60 .....50 B5
Badgers Croft B62 .....8 B7
Badgers The B45 .....33 A2
Badgeworth Dr WR4 .....116 A8
Badhams The GL20 .....181 F5
Badland Ave DY10 .....12 F1
Badon Covert B14 .....20 D2
Badsey Cl B31 .....19 C4
Badsey Fields La WR11 .....162 E3
Badsey Fst Sch WR11 .....162 E2
Badsey La
Evesham WR11 .....161 F4
Willersey WR11 .....177 D6
Badsey Rd WR11 .....162 A4
Baffin Rd 7 WR2 .....127 F6
Bagehott Rd WR9 .....103 E8
Bagley Rd DY5 .....6 D6
Bagley St DY9 .....6 C6
Bagnell Rd B13 .....20 F7
Bailey Rd CV37 .....151 D2
Bainbrigge Ave WR9 .....85 A2
Baker's Hill GL55 .....165 E2
Baker's La WR11 .....174 B1
Bala Cl 2 DY13 .....43 F5
Bala Way WR5 .....128 E6
Balaams Wood Dr B31 .....18 B1
Balaclava Rd B14 .....20 E8
Bald's La DY9 .....6 F5
Balden Rd B32 .....9 F7
Baldenhall WR14 .....153 D8
Baldwin Rd
Bewdley DY12 .....25 F4
Birmingham B30 .....20 A3
Kidderminster DY10 .....28 B7
Stourport-on-Severn DY13 .....44 B4
Baldwins La B28 .....21 F4
Balholm B62 .....8 D5
Ballarat Wlk DY8 .....5 F5
Ballard Cl 8 WR13 .....152 B2
Ballards Cl GL55 .....165 D3
Balliol Rd WR4 .....115 E3
Balmoral Cl
Evesham WR11 .....161 E6
Fernhill Heath WR3 .....103 A4
Great Malvern WR14 .....139 C6
Halesowen B62 .....8 B7
Balmoral Ct DY10 .....28 A5
Balmoral Rd B32 .....18 B7
Bamburgh Cres WR4 .....116 C6
Bamford Cl WR13 .....154 A7
Ban Brook Rd WR11 .....135 E3
Bangham Pit Rd B31 .....18 E6
Bank Farm Cl DY9 .....6 C1
Bank Rd WR6 .....80 E3
Bank St
Great Malvern WR14 .....138 F2
Stourbridge DY9 .....6 F5
Worcester WR1 .....115 B2
Bank The B50 .....136 D2
Banks Gn B97 .....69 B2
Banks Rd WR11 .....162 E4
Bankside Cl WR3 .....115 A7
Bannals La WR15 .....76 C2
Bannercroft WR6 .....110 F6
Banners La
Halesowen B63 .....7 D6
Redditch B97 .....89 E5
Banners St B63 .....7 D6
Bannut Tree La DY7 .....3 C5
Bant Mill Rd B60 .....49 A1
Barass Ave WR4 .....116 C5
Barbara Rd B28 .....21 E4
Barbel Cres WR5 .....128 C5
Barberry House B38 .....19 F1
Barbers Cl 1 WR4 .....115 F6
Barbers La WR6 .....99 B5
Barbourne Cres 9 WR1 .....115 A5
Barbourne La WR1 .....115 A5
Barbourne Prep Sch WR1 .....115 A6
Barbourne Rd WR1 .....115 B5
Barbourne Terr WR1 .....115 A5
Barbourne Wlk 2 WR1 .....115 A5
Barbrook Dr DY5 .....6 B7
Barclay Rd B67 .....9 F8
Bardenholme Gdns DY9 .....6 D3
Barford Cl B98 .....71 F1
Barford Cres 5 B38 .....20 C2
Bark Piece B32 .....9 C3
Barker St WR3 .....115 D5
Barkers La
Cleobury Mortimer DY14 .....22 D4
Wythall B47 .....36 A1
Barley Cres WR4 .....116 B5
Barley Croft B60 .....67 E6
Barley Mow La B61 .....49 B8
Barlich Way B98 .....71 A2
Barlow Cl B45 .....17 E2
Barn Cl Birmingham B30 .....20 B6
Blackheath B64 .....7 E6
Halesowen B63 .....7 E2
Stoke Heath B60 .....67 E6
Stourbridge DY9 .....6 C4
Worcester WR2 .....127 E8
Barn Croft B32 .....9 E1
Barn La
Birmingham, King's Heath B13 .....21 A7
Sedgeberrow WR11 .....174 F1
Barn Owl Pl DY10 .....28 A2
Barn Owl Wlk DY5 .....6 C6
Barn Piece B32 .....9 B4
Barnard Cl WR11 .....161 E2
Barnard's Gn Rd WR14 .....153 A8
Barnes Hill B29 .....9 F2
Barnes Pl 1 WR5 .....128 D6
Barnes Way WR5 .....128 D6
Barneshall Ave WR5 .....128 C6
Barnetts Cl DY10 .....28 B4
Barnetts Gr DY10 .....28 A4
Barnetts La DY10 .....28 A4
Barnfield Cider & Wine Mill* WR12 .....177 A1
Barnfield Rd
Bromsgrove B61 .....48 E1
Halesowen B62 .....8 D7
2 Stourport-on-Severn DY13 .....43 F1
Barnfields DY14 .....22 B3
Barnpark Covert 9 B14 .....20 C2
Barns Croft Way 6 WR9 .....84 C1
Barnsdale Cres B31 .....18 E4
Barnsley Hall Rd B61 .....49 A6
Barnsley Rd B61 .....49 B4
Barnswood Cl B63 .....7 C5
Barnt Gn Junc B45 .....50 D8
Barnt Gn Rd B45 .....33 C3
Barnwood Cl B98 .....71 D5
Barnwood Rd B32 .....9 F4
Baron Bsns Ctr DY9 .....6 E5
Barrack La B63 .....7 B6
Barracks Rd DY13 .....44 C1
Barrar Cl DY8 .....5 E8
Barratts Cl 5 DY12 .....26 A3
Barratts House B14 .....20 E2
Barratts Rd B38 .....20 A1
Barratts Stile La 4 DY12 .....26 A3
Barrett Cl DY10 .....28 B6
Barrett Rise WR14 .....139 A2
Barrie Ave DY10 .....28 C7
Barrington Rd B45 .....32 E7
Barron Rd B31 .....19 B3
Barrow Cl B98 .....71 F3
Barrs Cres B64 .....7 F8
Barrs Rd B64 .....7 E8
Barry St WR1 .....115 C4
Barsham Dr DY5 .....6 C8
Barston Rd B68 .....9 B7
Bartestree Cl B98 .....71 F1
Bartholemews La B61 .....48 F5
Bartleet Rd B98 .....90 E8
Bartley Dr B31 .....18 E8
Bartley Gn Tech Coll B32 .....9 C1
Bartley House B32 .....18 D8
Bartley Woods B32 .....9 B2
Barton Croft B28 .....21 F4
Barton Lodge Rd B28 .....21 E4
Barton Mews 6 GL20 .....196 F6
Barton Rd
Tewkesbury GL20 .....196 F6
Welford-on-Avon CV37 .....137 D3
Barton St GL20 .....196 E6
Bascote Cl B97 .....70 B1
Basil Gr B31 .....18 E4
Basil Rd B31 .....18 E4
Basin Rd WR5 .....128 B8
Baskerville Rd DY10 .....12 F1
Bassett Rd B63 .....7 A6
Bassnage Rd B63 .....7 E2
Batchelor Cl DY8 .....5 F8
Batchley Fst Sch B97 .....70 B4
Batchley Rd B97 .....70 C4
Batemans La B47 .....35 E5
Bates Hill B97 .....70 D4
Bates La B94 .....53 F1
Bath Ct 4 B29 .....19 B7
Bath La DY7 .....3 D5
Bath Mdw B63 .....7 E5
Bath Mews DY8 .....5 F5
Bath Rd Kempsey WR5 .....128 C1
Stourbridge DY8 .....5 F5
7 Worcester WR5 .....115 C1
Batham Rd DY10 .....28 A8
Batheaston Cl B38 .....34 D7
Batsford Cl B98 .....90 B5
Batsford Rd WR5 .....128 E5
Batson Rise DY5 .....6 A8
Battenhall Ave WR5 .....128 D8
Battenhall Pl 7 WR5 .....115 D1
Battenhall Rd WR5 .....115 D1
Battenhall Rise WR5 .....128 E7
Battens Cl B98 .....70 F3
Battens Dr B98 .....71 D3
Battisto Wlk WR14 .....139 C1
Battle Rd
Tewkesbury GL20 .....196 D4
Worcester WR5 .....128 D8
Battle Well* WR11 .....161 D8
Battleton Rd 2 WR11 .....161 E2
Baughton La
Earl's Croome WR8 .....156 E1
Hill Croome WR8 .....170 F7
Baveney Rd WR2 .....114 E6
Baverstock Rd B14 .....20 E2
Baverstock Sch B14 .....20 E2
Bawdsey Ave WR14 .....139 B2
Baxter Ave DY10 .....27 F7
Baxter Gdns DY10 .....27 F7
Bay Tree Cl B38 .....34 D8
Bayford Ave B31 .....33 E6
Baylie Ct DY8 .....5 F5
Baylie St DY8 .....5 F4
Bayliss Cl B31 .....19 B5
Bayliss Rd GL20 .....185 D7
Bayly Cl WR11 .....161 E2
Baynham Dr WR5 .....129 A8
Bays Mdw WR9 .....85 A5
Bayston Rd B14 .....20 E3
Bayton CE Prim Sch DY14 .....40 A7
Beach Cl
Birmingham B31 .....19 C1
1 Evesham WR11 .....161 E3
Beach Dr B63 .....8 A5
Beach Rd DY13 .....43 E1
Beach St B63 .....8 A5
Beacon Cl B45 .....33 A6
Beacon Hill B45 .....32 F5
Beacon La Kinver DY7 .....2 F3
Marlbrook B60, B45 .....32 E4
Upper Arley WV15 .....2 D3
Beacon Rd WR14 .....152 D4
Beacon Rise DY9 .....6 D4
Beacon View B45 .....33 A6
Beaconhill Dr WR2 .....114 E6
Beaconside Prim Sch B45 .....32 E6
Beaks Hill Rd B38 .....19 E2
Beale St DY8 .....5 F5
Bean Croft B32 .....9 C2
Bear Hill B48 .....51 B5
Bear La GL20 .....181 F4
Bearcroft Ave WR4 .....116 B6
Bearcroft Gdn GL55 .....165 D4
Bearhill Dr B48 .....51 B6
Beauchamp Ave DY11 .....27 D3
Beauchamp Ct DY11 .....27 D3
Beauchamp La
Callow End WR2 .....127 F1
Powick WR2 .....128 A1
Beauchamp Rd
Birmingham B13 .....21 C5
1 Great Malvern WR14 .....138 F4
Beaudesert Cl B47 .....36 A6
Beaudesert Rd B47 .....36 A6
Beaufort Ave DY11 .....27 A7
Beaufort End WR11 .....164 C5
Beaufort Pl GL20 .....196 E4
Beaufort St B98 .....70 E3
Beaulieu Cl DY11 .....27 D8
Beaumaris House B31 .....18 D6
Beaumont Dr DY5 .....6 B7
Beaumont Lawns B60 .....32 D1
Beaumont Rd
Birmingham B30 .....19 F6
Halesowen B62 .....8 E8
Beauty Bank B64 .....8 A8
Beauty Bank Cres DY8 .....5 F6
Beauty Bank Prim Sch DY8 .....5 F6
Beaver Cl 2 WR2 .....127 E6
Beaver Pk B63 .....7 F6
Beckett Cl Redditch B98 .....70 F5
Worcester WR3 .....115 A8
Beckett Dr WR3 .....115 B8
Beckett Rd WR3 .....115 A8
Beckfield Cl B14 .....20 E2
Beckford Cl GL20 .....186 C3
Beckford Cross GL20 .....186 E3
Beckford Hall* GL20 .....186 C4
Beckford Rd WR11 .....187 B7
Beckman Rd DY9 .....6 C2
Becks The B48 .....51 A7
Bedcote Pl DY8 .....6 B5
Bedford Cl 2 WR10 .....144 C1
Bedlam Wood Rd B31 .....18 C1
Bedwardine Rd 14 WR2 .....114 F1
Beech Ave
Birmingham, Quinton B32 .....9 D7
Drakes Broughton WR10 .....143 F6
Halesowen B62 .....8 C8
Worcester WR3 .....115 C7
Beech Ave N WR3 .....115 C7
Beech Cl
1 Great Malvern WR14 .....139 B5
Kinver DY7 .....4 B4
Beech Ct
Birmingham B45 .....33 D7
Birmingham, Bournville B30 .....19 E4
Beech Farm Croft B31 .....19 A3
Beech Gr B14 .....21 A5
Beech Hill House B32 .....18 C8
Beech Hurst 1 B38 .....34 E8
Beech Pk Dr B45 .....50 C8
Beech Rd
Birmingham, Bournville B30 .....19 E6
Bromsgrove B61 .....48 F4
Hollywood B47 .....36 B6
Stourbridge DY8 .....5 F3
Beech Tree Cl B97 .....70 B4
Beech Wlk B38 .....34 F8
Beechcombe Cl 2 WR10 .....144 D2
Beechcote Ave DY11 .....12 D2
Beechcroft Dr B61 .....49 B4
Beechcroft Est B63 .....7 C6
Beechcroft Rd DY11 .....27 A8
Beechdale B68 .....9 B7
Beecher Pl B63 .....7 D5
Beecher Rd B63 .....7 D5
Beecher Rd E B63 .....7 D5
Beecher St B63 .....7 C5
Beeches Cl B45 .....32 D8
Beeches Ct B45 .....33 B7
Beeches Farm Dr B31 .....34 A7
Beeches Inf Sch The B45 .....18 B2
Beeches Mews DY9 .....14 F4
Beeches Rd DY11 .....12 C1
Beeches The
Mamble DY14 .....40 A4
Ryall WR8 .....169 E6
Upton Warren B61 .....67 A4
Beeches View Ave B63 .....7 C4
Beeches Way B31 .....34 A7
Beechfield Cl B62 .....8 C8
Beechfield Dr
2 Kidderminster DY11 .....12 C1
Kidderminster DY11 .....27 C8
Beechlawn Dr DY7 .....4 E7
Beechtree La DY10 .....13 E6
Beechtree Pk B50 .....136 E6
Beechwood Ct
1 Birmingham B30 .....20 C3
Blackheath B64 .....8 A7
Beechwood Rd
Birmingham, King's Heath B14 .....20 F5
Smethwick B67 .....9 F8
Beehive Cl B61 .....32 A1
Beeston Cl DY5 .....6 D8
Beeston Gdns 14 WR4 .....116 C6
Beeston Rd DY10 .....13 A5
Begonia Cl 2 WR5 .....128 C4
Beilby Rd B30 .....20 B5
Belbroughton CE Fst Sch DY9 .....30 E6
Belbroughton Cl B98 .....70 F2
Belbroughton Rd
Blakedown DY10 .....14 D1
Clent DY9 .....15 E2
Halesowen B63 .....7 F2
Stourbridge DY8 .....5 E3
Belfont Trad Est B62 .....8 C4
Belfry Dr DY8 .....5 E6
Belfry Rd WR9 .....103 F8
Belgrave Rd B62 .....8 D8
Bell Gn La B38 .....35 B5
Bell Heath Way B32 .....9 B2
Bell Hill B31 .....19 A5
Bell Holloway B31 .....18 F5
Bell La
Birmingham, Northfield B31 .....19 A4
Broadheath WR2 .....113 F5
Hanley WR6 .....77 A7
Studley B80 .....90 E4
Bell Mdw DY9 .....15 B8
Bell Mdw Way B14 .....20 E1
Bell Mead B80 .....90 E4
Bell Row 6 DY13 .....44 A3
Bell Sh Ctr The B31 .....19 A4
Bell St DY8 .....6 A5
Bellar's La WR14 .....153 C8
Bellars Cl WR14 .....153 C8
Bellars Gdns WR14 .....153 D8
Belle Orch
Kidderminster DY11 .....27 B5
Tenbury Wells WR15 .....55 F5
Belle Vale B63 .....7 E5
Belle Vue Cl B61 .....32 C1
Belle Vue Dr B62 .....8 E6
Belle Vue Terr WR14 .....152 E8
Bellfield B31 .....18 F4
Bellfield House B14 .....20 D1
Bellfield Jun & Inf Sch B31 .....18 F4
Bellflower Rd 12 GL20 .....197 A4
Bellman's Cross DY12 .....11 B7
Bells Farm Cl B14 .....20 C2
Bells Farm Inf & Jun Sch B14 .....20 C2
Bells La B14 .....20 D2
Bellwood Rd B31 .....18 F4
Belmont Cl B97 .....70 B1
Belmont Covert B31 .....19 B6
Belmont Rd
Birmingham, Rubery B45 .....33 A6
Great Malvern WR14 .....138 E4
Stourbridge DY9 .....6 F4
Belmont St WR3 .....115 D5
Belstone Cl B14 .....20 D6
Belton Gr B45 .....33 C8
Belvedere Cl DY10 .....28 A5
Belvedere Cres DY12 .....26 C5
Belvedere Dr B61 .....49 A4
Belvide Gr B29 .....19 B8
Belvoir Bank WR14 .....138 E3
Belvoir Rd B60 .....49 C1
Ben Nevis Way DY8 .....6 A6
Benbow Cl WR14 .....152 E2
Bengeworth Fst Sch WR11 .....161 E4
Bengrove Cl B98 .....90 A7
Bennett St 2 DY11 .....27 C6
Bennetts Farm Pk* WR2 .....127 F6
Bennetts Hill WR11 .....148 D1
Bennetts Hill Bsns Pk WR11 .....148 D1
Bensfield WR6 .....126 C5
Benson Rd B14 .....21 B1
Bent Ave B32 .....9 D6
Bentham Ave WR4 .....116 C3
Bentham Ct B31 .....18 F5
Bentley Cl B97 .....70 D3
Bentley Gr B29 .....18 F8
Bentley La B97 .....88 C7
Bentmead Gr B38 .....20 A1
Benton Cl WR14 .....166 F6
Benton's Ct DY11 .....27 C6
Beoley Fst Sch B98 .....71 E8
Beoley Gr B45 .....33 A7
Beoley La Beoley B98 .....71 F8
Portway B98 .....53 B1
Beoley Rd E B98 .....71 A4
Beoley Rd W B98 .....70 F4
Berberry Cl B30 .....19 D6
Berkeley Bsns Pk WR4 .....116 C7
Berkeley Cl
Bromsgrove B60 .....68 B8
Redditch B98 .....72 A3
Whittington WR5 .....129 B7
Berkeley Cres DY13 .....44 A1
Berkeley Prec B14 .....20 F2
Berkeley Rd B90 .....21 F3
Berkeley St 3 WR1 .....115 A5
Berkeley Way WR4 .....116 C7
Berkeswell Cl B98 .....71 C7
Berkley Gdns WR3 .....102 F2
Bernie Crossland Wlk DY10 .....27 F3
Bernwall Cl DY8 .....5 F4
Berrill Cl WR9 .....85 B1
Berrington Cl B98 .....71 D2
Berrington Gdns WR15 .....55 E4
Berrington Rd WR15 .....55 C4
Berrow Hill (fort)* WR6 .....98 E2
Berrow Hill Rd 3 DY11 .....12 B1
Berrow View B61 .....67 D7
Berrowhill La B96 .....88 B2
Berry Cl 6 WR2 .....127 C2
Berry Dr B45 .....33 A1
Berry La B61 .....47 C2
Berryfield Rd WR11 .....161 A3
Berrymound View B47 .....36 C7
Berwick Gr B31 .....18 D3
Berwick St WR5 .....128 C7
Besford CE Fst Sch WR8 .....157 D3
Besford Gr B31 .....18 D3

Bestmans La WR5 141 D5
Beta Cl GL20 197 C8
Beta Gr B14 21 C4
Betjeman Cl 9 WR10 158 D8
Betjeman Ct DY10 28 B5
Betony Rd WR14 139 C4
Bettle Cl 4 WR10 143 F6
Betton Rd B14 20 E5
Bevan Gdns 4 GL20 184 E1
Bevans La WR11 175 A5
Bevere Cl WR3 102 A1
Bevere Cl S 1 WR3 102 A1
Bevere Dr WR3 102 A1
Bevere La WR3 102 A3
Bevere Vivas Gall* WR3 102 A3
Beverley Cl
Astwood Bank B96 89 E2
Kidderminster DY11 26 F6
Beverley Ct 1 B62 9 A6
Beverley Ct Rd B32 9 C6
Beverley Rd B45 33 A7
Beverley Way WR14 138 E6
Bewdley High Sch DY12 26 C2
Bewdley Hill DY11 27 B5
Bewdley La WR11 161 C4
Bewdley Mus* DY12 26 B3
Bewdley Rd
Birmingham B30 20 B8
Kidderminster DY11 27 C6
1 Stourport-on-Severn DY13 44 A4
Bewdley Rd N DY13 43 D7
Bewdley St WR11 161 C4
Bewdley Sta DY12 26 C3
Bewell Ct B61 48 F4
Bewell Head B61 48 F4
Bewlay Cl DY5 6 B7
Bibsworth Ave
Birmingham B13 21 D8
Broadway WR12 190 E8
Bibsworth La WR12 177 D2
Bibury Rd B28 21 E7
Bickington Rd B32 9 D1
Bickmarsh La B50 136 D1
Bicknell Croft B14 20 E2
Bicton Ave 8 WR5 128 E6
Bidavon Ind Est B50 136 E6
Biddles Hill B94 53 C6
Bidford Rd
Bidford-on-Avon B50 136 C7
Birmingham B31 18 E3
Bidford-on-Avon CE Prim Sch B50 136 D5
Bigbury La DY13 44 D6
Bight The WR10 160 E8
Bigwood Dr B32 9 D1
Bilberry Cl DY13 43 E5
Bilberry Dr B45 33 A6
Bilberry Rd B14 20 C6
Bilbrook Gr B29 9 F2
Bilbury Cl B97 89 C6
Bilford Ave WR3 115 D7
Bilford Rd WR3 115 C7
Billesley La
Birmingham B13 21 A8
Portway B48 52 E6
Billesley Prim Sch B13 21 C6
Bills La B90 36 F8
Billy La B45, B60 50 A7
Bilton Ind Est B38 34 E8
Bine La DY14 41 F6
Binswood Rd B62 9 A7
Binton Cl B98 71 F1
Binton Croft B13 20 F8
Binton Rd B90 21 F1
Binyon Cl WR11 162 E2
Birch Ave
Birmingham B31 18 C1
Evesham WR11 161 F2
Worcester WR4 115 E4
Birch Cl B30 19 E6
Birch Coppice WR9 103 F8
Birch Ct B30 19 E4
Birch Dr DY8 5 E6
Birch Gr Alveley WV15 1 C6
Oldbury B68 9 D7
Birch La Oldbury B68 9 D7
Severn Stoke WR8 155 E6
Birch Rd
Birmingham, Eachway B45 32 E6
Oldbury B68 9 D7
Birch Tree Rd 3 DY12 25 F2
Birch Wlk B68 9 D8
Birchen Coppice Fst Sch DY11 27 B2
Birchen Coppice Mid Sch DY11 27 B2
Birchensale Farm B97 70 B5
Birchensale Mid Sch B97 70 C4
Birchensale Rd B97 70 C5
Birches La B48 50 F6
Birches The DY13 44 B3
Birchfield Cl
Halesowen B63 7 E2
Worcester WR3 115 C5
Birchfield Cres DY9 6 F3
Birchfield Ct B97 70 B2
Birchfield Dr DY13 43 E5
Birchfield Rd
Kidderminster DY11 27 B5
Redditch B97 70 B2
Birchfield Rd *continued*
Stourbridge DY9 6 F3
Birchgate DY9 6 F4
Birchtree Gr 4 WR10 144 D2
Birchwood Cl DY11 27 A7
Birchwood Rd WR14 138 E6
Birchwoods B32 9 B2
Birchy Cl B90 36 F6
Birchy Leasowes La B90 36 E5
Bird Cage Wlk B38 19 F2
Bird's Barn La DY7 3 C2
Birdie Cl B38 19 D1
Birdlip Cl WR4 116 A6
Birdlip Gr B32 9 C6
Birdwell Croft B13 20 F6
Birkdale Ave B60 50 A5
Birkdale Cl DY8 5 F2
Birkdale Gr B29 20 A8
Birley Gr B63 7 C1
Birlingham Cl WR10 158 C7
Birlingham House B60 49 B3
Birmingham & Midland Mus of Transport* B47 35 E3
Birmingham Great Pk B45 33 B8
Birmingham Rd
Alvechurch B48 51 B7
Badsey WR11 162 E5
Blakedown DY10 14 C2
Hagley DY9 15 D7
Halesowen B63 8 B4
Hopwood B31, B48 34 B4
Kidderminster DY10 28 D7
Lickey End B60, B61 49 B6
Lydiate Ash B45, B61 32 D5
Marlbrook B61 32 B1
Redditch B97, B98 70 E8
Sambourne B49 109 F7
Studley B80, B98 90 E7
Birmingham St
Halesowen B63 8 D3
Stourbridge DY8 6 B5
Birstall Way B38 34 C8
Bisell Way DY5 6 C6
Biset Ave DY10 28 B5
Bishop Challoner RC Sch B14 20 F8
Bishop Cl B45 17 E1
Bishop Hall Cres B60 67 E7
Bishop Perowne High Sch WR3 115 C5
Bishop St DY13 44 A5
Bishop's Ct B31 19 B3
Bishop's Wlk GL19 195 D6
Bishops Ave WR3 115 C5
Bishops Gate B31 19 A2
Bishops Wlk B64 8 A6
Bishops Wood La DY13 63 E4
Bishopstone Cl B98 71 F2
Bisley Cl WR4 116 A7
Bissell Cl B28 21 F6
Bissell St B32 9 A6
Bittell Cl B31 33 F7
Bittell Ct B31 33 F7
Bittell Farm Rd B48 34 A2
Bittell La B45 50 E8
Bittell Rd
Alvechurch B48 51 A8
Barnt Green B45 50 E8
Bittern Rd WR5 128 D5
Bittern Wlk DY5 6 C6
Bittern Wood Rd DY10 28 B3
Black Haynes Rd B29 19 A6
Black Horse La 1 DY10 27 E6
Black Lake La B60, B97 69 A2
Black Soils Rd B98 71 F5
Black Thorne Cl 4 WR9 104 A8
Blackberry La B63 8 A2
Blackberry Way 10 WR11 161 D1
Blackburne Rd B28 21 F6
Blackbushe Cl B17 9 F7
Blackdown Cl B45 18 A2
Blackford Cl
Halesowen B63 7 D2
Kidderminster DY11 27 A1
Blackfriars Ave WR9 84 E2
Blackheath Way WR14 152 C8
Blackminster WR11 162 E6
Blackminster Cty Mid Sch WR11 162 E7
Blackmore La B60 49 A3
Blackmore Pk Rd
Malvern Wells WR13 153 C1
Welland WR13 167 D7
Blackmore Rd WR14 138 E3
Blackpole Ind Est WR4 115 F8
Blackpole Rd WR4 102 F1
Blacksmiths Bank WR9 63 D1
Blacksmiths Cl
Sedgeberrow WR11 175 A1
4 South Littleton WR11 148 F1
Blacksmiths La
Beckford GL20 186 D2
Childswickham WR12 176 E2
Cropthorne WR10 160 C7
Dumbleton WR11 187 F5
Hill & Moor WR10 145 E3
South Littleton WR11 148 F1
Blackstitch La B97 70 A1
Blackstone Mdws Ctry Pk* DY12 43 C8
Blackthorn Cl
Birmingham B30 19 C6
Evesham WR11 162 A2
Blackthorn Ct B98 71 E1
Blackthorn Rd
Birmingham, Bournville B30 19 D6
Worcester WR4 115 E6
Blackwell La 1 B97 70 B5
Blackwell Rd B45, B60 50 B5
Blackwell St DY10 27 E6
Blackwood Rd B60 49 B2
Blaenwern Dr B63 7 B7
Blagdon Cl 12 WR5 128 E6
Blagdon Rd B63 8 A6
Blair Cl WR4 116 B6
Blake Ave WR9 84 D1
Blake Hall Cl DY5 6 C7
Blake Rd B61 49 B8
Blake St WR5 128 E8
Blake's Hill
North & Middle Littleton WR11 149 D2
Pebworth WR11 150 A2
Blakebrook DY11 27 C6
Blakebrook Cl DY11 27 C6
Blakebrook Day Specl Sch DY11 27 C6
Blakebrook Gdns DY11 27 C6
Blakedown CE Prim Sch DY10 14 C1
Blakedown Rd B63 7 F1
Blakefield Gdns WR2 114 F1
Blakefield Rd WR2 114 F1
Blakefield Wlk
8 Worcester WR2 114 F1
2 Worcester WR2 114 F1
Blakemere Cl B98 71 F3
Blakemore Cl B32 9 F3
Blakeney Ave DY8 5 D6
Blakeney Cl 4 WR5 128 D6
Blakenhurst WR11 147 F8
Blakes Field Dr B45 33 A1
Blakes La WR13 154 C8
Blakeshall La DY11 12 D5
Blandford Cl WR13 167 C5
Blandford Rd B32 9 F5
Blanquettes Ave WR3 115 C6
Blanquettes St 3 WR3 115 B6
Blayneys La WR11 161 E8
Blaze La
Astwood Bank B96, B97 89 A3
Feckenham B96 88 F2
Bleachfield Rd B98 71 F8
Blenheim Cl 8 B50 136 D5
Blenheim Cres B60 68 A8
Blenheim Dr GL20 184 F6
Blenheim Rd WR2 114 E3
Blessed Edward Oldcorne RC High Sch WR5 128 D8
Blind La
Evesham WR11 161 C5
Tanworth-In-A B94 53 D1
Blissgate Rd DY14 41 F7
Blithe Cl DY8 6 A8
Blithfield Dr DY5 6 B7
Blockhouse Cl 8 WR1 115 C2
Blockley Cl B97 69 E2
Bloomfield Rd WR2 127 F8
Bloomfield St N B63 7 F5
Bloomfield St W B63 7 F4
Bloomsbury Gr B14 20 C7
Blossom Cl 4 WR5 116 B3
Blossom Dr B61 49 A5
Blossomfield Cl
Birmingham B38 34 D8
Evesham WR11 161 B2
Blossomfield Ct B38 34 D8
Blount House DY11 27 B8
Blount Terr DY11 27 D3
Bloxham Rd WR12 177 D1
Blue Ball La B63 7 C7
Blue Bell Cl WR14 153 C7
Blue Bird Pk B62 17 B7
Blue Cedars DY8 5 C6
Bluebell Croft B31 18 F4
Bluebell La WR8 157 E4
Bluebell Way 1 WR11 175 D8
Blythe Cl B97 89 D7
Blythesway B48 51 A6
Blythsford Rd B28 21 F4
BMI Droitwich Spa WR9 84 F3
Boat La
8 Evesham WR11 161 C4
Offenham WR11 162 A8
Bobs Coppice Wlk DY5 6 F7
Bockleton Rd
Bockleton WR15 93 E8
Tenbury WR15 55 E1
Bodenham Cl B98 71 D3
Bodenham Rd
Birmingham B31 18 E1
Oldbury B68 9 B8
Bodiam Cl 1 WR4 116 C6
Bog La 2 WR15 55 E4
Boleyn Rd B45 17 E2
Bolney Rd B32 9 E4
Bolston Rd WR5 128 C8
Bolton Ave WR4 116 C5
Bomers Field B45 33 C7
Bomford Hill WR4 116 B4
Bond St
Birmingham, Stirchley B30 20 A7
Great Malvern WR14 139 A4
Bondfield Rd B13 21 B6
Bonfire Hill DY9 31 E6
Boon St WR10 171 D7
Boot Piece La B97 70 B5
Booton Ct DY10 13 A1
Boraston Bank WR15 56 A7
Boraston Dr WR15 56 A6
Boraston La
Burford WR15 56 A7
Tenbury Wells WR15 55 F6
Borderway WR15 55 F6
Bordesley Abbey* B98 70 F6
Bordesley La B98 70 F6
Boreley La WR9 63 D1
Borough Cres DY8 5 E5
Borough Ct B63 8 B4
Borrington Gdns DY10 28 B4
Borrington Rd DY10 28 B5
Borrowdale Cl DY5 6 B8
Borrowdale Dr WR4 116 A5
Borrowdale Gr B31 18 D3
Borrowdale Rd B31 18 C3
Bosbury Rd WR14 139 A5
Bosbury Terr B30 20 B7
Bosmere Ct B31 18 F3
Boston La WR11 160 E5
Bott La DY9 6 E6
Boughton Ave WR2 114 E1
Boughton Cl WR2 114 E1
Boughton Pk Cl WR2 127 E8
Boughton St WR2 114 F1
Boultons La B97 89 D6
Boundary Rd E CV37 151 F2
Boundary Rd N CV37 151 E4
Boundary Rd W CV37 151 D3
Bourlay Cl B45 17 E2
Bourne Ave Catshill B61 31 F1
Halesowen B62 8 F4
Bourne Cl
Birmingham B13 21 D6
6 Droitwich WR9 84 F3
Bourne Gn B32 9 E6
Bourne Rd
Defford WR8 157 B1
Strensham WR8 171 A6
Bourne St WR3 115 B6
Bourne Way Gdns B29 20 A8
Bourne's Pl 2 WR11 161 C4
Bournebrook Cres B62 9 A4
Bournes Cl B63 7 F3
Bournes Cres B63 7 E4
Bournes Hill B63 7 E4
Bournheath Rd B61 31 D2
Bournville Coll of F Ed B30 19 C7
Bournville Inf Sch B30 19 E7
Bournville Jun Sch B30 19 E7
Bournville La B30 19 E6
Bournville Mews B30 19 E5
Bournville Sch & Sixth Form B30 19 C6
Bournville Sta B30 20 A7
Bouts La WR7 108 B2
Bow Hill WR2 140 F7
Bow La GL20 183 B7
Bowbrook Cl 1 WR10 131 B2
Bowbrook House (Preparatory Sch) WR10 131 B1
Bowden Gn WR9 103 F8
Bower Bank 2 DY13 43 E2
Bower Hill WR9 84 D2
Bower Hill Dr 4 DY13 43 E2
Bower La DY5 7 A8
Bowes Rd B45 32 E7
Bowler Rd GL20 184 E1
Bowling Gn La WR8 169 A8
Bowling Gn Rd
Bowling Green WR2 127 B3
Stourbridge DY8 5 E5
Bowmore Rd B60 49 B1
Bowness Dr 2 WR4 116 A5
Bowood Cres B31 19 B2
Bowood Ct B97 70 D4
Bowood La 2 WR5 128 E6
Bowpatch Cl DY13 62 D8
Bowpatch Rd DY13 43 D1
Box Tree Cl WR8 157 D3
Boxbush Dr WR7 143 A8
Boxnott Cl B97 70 A2
Bozward St WR2 114 F2
Bozzards Bank WR9 63 C1
Brabham Cl DY11 12 D1
Braceby Ave B13 21 C6
Braces La B60 32 C1
Bracken Cl WR2 114 E4
Bracken Gr B61 32 A1
Bracken Way B38 34 D6
Brackendale Way DY9 6 D4
Brackenfield Rd B63 7 E3
Brades Cl B63 7 B7
Bradford La DY9 30 D5
Bradford Pl WR5 116 A1
Bradley Dr WR14 138 E5
Bradley Rd DY8 5 F6
Bradley Thursfield Ct DY11 27 C7
Bradleys Cl B64 7 E7
Bradmore Gr B29 19 A8
Bradnock Cl B13 21 C7
Bradshaw Ave B38 19 D1
Bradshawe Cl B28 21 D3
Bradstock Rd B30 20 C4
Bradwell House B31 18 D5
Braggington La CV37 137 E1
Braggs Farm La B90 36 F4
Braid Cl B38 19 D1
Brake La DY8 14 E6
Brake The DY8 14 F6
Bramber Way DY8 5 F2
Bramble Cl
Birmingham, Shenley Fields B31 18 F6
5 Great Malvern WR14 139 C3
Bramble Gdns 5 WR5 116 B3
Brambles The DY9 6 D3
Brambling Rise DY10 28 B1
Brambling Wlk DY5 6 C6
Bramcote Rd B32 9 C5
Bramhope Cl WR4 116 A4
Bramley Ave WR2 114 E6
Bramley Cl
Bowling Green WR2 127 C3
Crowle WR7 117 F4
Bramley Dr B47 36 B6
Bramley Pl WR2 114 E6
Bramley Rd GL20 196 F7
Bramley Way
1 Bewdley DY12 25 F3
Bidford-on-Avon B50 136 D5
Brampton Cl DY10 13 B4
Bramshaw Cl B14 20 F2
Branch Rd B38 34 E8
Branches Cl 2 DY12 25 F2
Branden Rd B48 51 A5
Brandheath La B96 109 A4
Brandon Ct B31 19 B1
Brandon Gr B31 33 F7
Brandon Way DY5 6 E8
Brandwood Gr B14 20 D5
Brandwood House B14 20 D7
Brandwood Pk Rd B14 20 C4
Brandwood Rd B14 20 D5
Branscombe Cl B14 20 D5
Bransford Rd WR2 114 E1
Brantwood WR4 116 A5
Brantwood Cl 6 WR9 85 A1
Brantwood Rd 2 WR9 104 A8
Brasenose Rd GL20 184 E6
Brassie Cl B38 19 D1
Brayford Ave DY5 6 B7
Braymoor Rd WR1 115 B4
Breaches La B98 90 D8
Breakback Rd B61 67 D8
Bream Cl 3 WR5 128 C5
Brecknell Rise DY10 27 F8
Brecon Ave
Bromsgrove B61 49 A5
Warndon WR4 116 D6
Brecon Cl
5 Droitwich WR9 84 C1
Inkberrow WR7 120 F6
Brecon Dr DY8 6 B6
Breden Barn (NT)* GL20 184 D6
Bredicot La WR7 117 D4
Bredon Ave
Kidderminster DY11 27 A1
Stourbridge DY9 6 C5
Bredon Cl WR7 120 E8
Bredon Cres WR11 161 A2
Bredon Ct B63 8 A3
Bredon Gr WR14 153 C6
Bredon Hancocks Endowed CE Fst Sch GL20 184 E7
Bredon Hill Mid Sch WR11 174 C2
Bredon House B98 90 B7
Bredon Lodge 1 GL20 184 F6
Bredon Rd
Bromsgrove B61 67 D7
Stourbridge DY8 6 B6
Tewkesbury GL20 196 E7
Bredon Sch (Pull Court) GL20 182 E5
Bredon View
Broadway WR12 190 E8
Redditch B97 89 D8
Bredon Way 4 DY13 43 D1
Breedon Gdns B98 71 A3
Breedon Rd B30 20 A5
Brennand Cl B68 9 C8
Brennand Rd B68 9 B8
Brensham Rd GL20 197 B7
Brent Rd B30 20 D8
Brent Wood Cl 6 WR5 115 F1
Brentford Rd B14 21 A5
Bretforton Com Fst Sch WR11 163 C4
Bretforton Rd WR11 162 E4
Brett Dr B32 18 C8
Brett Young Cl DY10 28 B5
Brettell La DY8 5 F8
Brewers La WR11 162 E3
Brewery Wlk 1 WR1 115 B4
Briar Cl Evesham WR11 161 D5
Lickey End B60 49 C6
Briar Hill
Bluntington DY10 29 E1
Chaddesley Corbett DY10 46 E8
Briar Mill WR9 84 D3
Briar Way 16 DY13 43 E4
Briars Hollow WR9 84 D3
Briars The DY9 14 F4
Brick Kiln La B47 35 F4
Brick Kiln St DY5 7 A8
Brick Wlk WR11 164 A4
Brickall The CV37 151 C5
Brickfields Rd WR4 115 E5
Brickhouse La B60 67 C4
Brick-kiln St WR11 161 D4
Bricknell Ave 9 GL20 184 F6
Brickyard La
Drakes Broughton & Wadborough WR10 144 A5
Studley B80 90 C4
Bridewell Dr WR11 174 F1
Bridge Mdw Cl WR11 175 A2

Bridge Piece B31 ... 19 B2
Bridge Rd Alveley WV15 ... 1 D6
Cookley DY11 ... 13 A6
Bridge St
Bretforton WR11 ... 163 C4
Evesham WR11 ... 161 D4
Halesowen B63 ... 7 C7
Hill & Moor WR10 ... 145 D2
1 Kidderminster DY10 ... 27 E5
Pershore WR10 ... 158 E7
Redditch B97 ... 70 D4
Stourport-on-Severn DY13 ... 43 F3
Worcester WR1 ... 115 B2
Bridge Trad Ctr The B64 ... 7 D8
Bridgeburn Rd B31 ... 18 E8
Bridgemans Cl WR12 ... 177 E1
Bridgnorth Rd
Kidderminster Foreign DY11 ... 11 F4
Kinver DY7 ... 4 B7
Stourbridge DY7 ... 5 C6
Bridgnorth Row 1 WR4 ... 116 C7
Bridgwater Rd WR4 ... 116 D7
Bridle Mead B38 ... 34 D8
Bridle Rd DY8 ... 5 D6
Bridley Moor Rd B97 ... 70 C5
Bridport House B31 ... 18 E7
Brier Mill Rd B63 ... 8 C3
Briery Cl B64 ... 7 F7
Briery Rd B63 ... 7 E3
Brigfield Cres B13 ... 21 B5
Brigfield Rd B13 ... 21 B5
Bright Ave WR4 ... 116 C4
Bright St DY8 ... 5 D6
Brightstone Rd B45 ... 18 B2
Brimstone Cl 7 WR5 ... 128 E5
Brimstone La B61 ... 48 D7
Brindley Brae DY7 ... 4 C4
Brindley Ct 1 B68 ... 9 B7
Brindley Heath Jun Sch DY7 ... 4 A5
Brindley Rd WR4 ... 116 B7
Brindley St DY13 ... 43 F5
Brine Pits La WR9 ... 66 C1
Bringewood Gr B32 ... 18 B8
Brinklow Cl B98 ... 90 D8
Brinklow Rd B29 ... 9 F2
Brinton Cl DY11 ... 27 C3
Brinton Cres DY11 ... 27 C3
Briseley Cl DY5 ... 6 D8
Bristol Ct 15 B29 ... 19 C7
Bristol Rd B29 ... 19 D8
Bristol Rd S
Birmingham B31 ... 18 F2
Birmingham, Longbridge B31, B45 ... 33 C7
Briston Cl DY5 ... 6 C8
Britannia Cl B98 ... 70 F3
Britannia Gdns 1 DY13 ... 44 B1
Britannia Rd WR1 ... 115 B4
Britannia Sq WR1 ... 115 B4
Britford Cl B14 ... 20 F3
Britten Dr WR14 ... 153 B6
Britten St B97 ... 70 D4
Broach Rd DY13 ... 44 B1
Broad Acres B31 ... 18 E6
Broad Gd Rd B98 ... 71 B2
Broad Heath Cl B97 ... 70 B5
Broad Hill WR10 ... 157 D5
Broad La
Birmingham B14 ... 20 E4
Bishampton WR10 ... 133 A3
Tanworth-In-A B98 ... 53 E3
Broad Marston Rd
Mickleton GL55 ... 165 B6
Pebworth CV37 ... 150 E2
Broad Mdw La B30 ... 20 B3
Broad St
Bromsgrove B61 ... 48 F4
Kidderminster DY10 ... 27 E7
Worcester WR1 ... 115 B2
Broadacre Cl 5 GL20 ... 184 F6
Broadclose La WR7 ... 120 C7
Broadcott Ind Est B64 ... 8 A8
Broadfield Cres WR3 ... 102 F3
Broadfield Gdns WR4 ... 116 B6
Broadfields DY9 ... 15 A6
Broadheath CE Prim Sch WR2 ... 113 F7
Broadheath Cl 1 WR9 ... 103 E8
Broadhidley Dr B32 ... 9 B1
Broadlands Dr WR14 ... 138 D4
Broadmeadow Cl B30 ... 20 B3
Broadmeadow House B32 ... 18 D8
Broadmeadow Inf Sch B30 ... 20 B2
Broadmeadow Jun Sch B30 ... 20 B2
Broadstone Ave B63 ... 7 B4
Broadwas CE Prim Sch WR6 ... 112 B3
Broadwas Cl B98 ... 71 C5
Broadwaters Dr
Hagley DY9 ... 15 B4
Kidderminster DY10 ... 28 A8
Broadway Ave B63 ... 8 A2
Broadway Cl 6 WR10 ... 146 A1
Broadway Fst Sch WR12 ... 177 E1
Broadway Gr WR2 ... 114 D1
Broadway La WR10 ... 146 A1
Broadway Rd
Aston Somerville WR12 ... 175 F1
Broadway WR12 ... 177 A2
Evesham WR11 ... 161 F3
Weston Subedge GL55 ... 165 C2
Broadway Rd *continued*
Willersey WR12 ... 177 E3
Broadway Teddy Bear Mus* WR12 ... 190 E8
Broadway The DY8 ... 5 D3
Broadwood Dr WR13 ... 152 B2
Brockamin La WR6 ... 125 F8
Brockeridge Rd GL20 ... 183 E7
Brocket Cl 6 DY13 ... 43 E6
Brockhampton Cl 4 WR4 ... 115 F7
Brockhampton Est (NT)* WR6 ... 110 A3
Brockhill Dr B97 ... 70 A5
Brockhill La
Alvechurch B48 ... 35 B2
Beoley B98 ... 52 F2
Norton Juxta Kempsey WR5 ... 128 F5
Tardebigge B97 ... 69 E8
Brockhill Rd WR13 ... 152 C3
Brockley's Wlk DY7 ... 4 C3
Brockmoor Cl DY9 ... 6 C2
Brockton Pl 2 DY13 ... 43 E1
Brockworth Rd B14 ... 20 C2
Bromfield Rd B97 ... 70 D2
Bromford Ct B31 ... 19 B1
Bromford Dell B31 ... 19 C4
Bromley St DY9 ... 6 F6
Brompton Dr DY5 ... 6 B7
Brompton Pool Rd B28 ... 21 E3
Bromsgrove Highway
Bromsgrove B60 ... 49 D1
Redditch B97 ... 70 B2
Tardebigge B60, B97 ... 69 C6
Bromsgrove Lower Sch B60 ... 48 F1
Bromsgrove Mus* B61 ... 49 A3
Bromsgrove Private Hospl B60 ... 50 B1
Bromsgrove Rd
Clent DY9 ... 15 D4
Dodford B61 ... 48 D6
Droitwich WR9 ... 85 A4
Halesowen B63 ... 8 C4
Kidderminster DY10 ... 28 F2
Redditch B97 ... 70 B3
Romsley B62 ... 17 A5
Studley B80 ... 90 D2
Bromsgrove Sch B61 ... 48 F1
Bromsgrove St
Halesowen B63 ... 8 C4
Kidderminster DY10 ... 27 E6
Worcester WR3 ... 115 B6
Bromsgrove Sta B60 ... 68 B7
Bromwall Rd B13 ... 21 B6
Bromwich La
Stourbridge DY9 ... 15 B8
Worcester WR2 ... 115 A1
Bromwich Rd WR2 ... 115 A1
Bromyard Rd
Kyre WR15 ... 75 E6
Stoke Bliss WR15 ... 76 A3
Tenbury WR15 ... 56 B2
Tenbury Wells WR15 ... 55 F4
Worcester WR2 ... 114 E1
Bromyard Terr WR2 ... 115 A2
Bronsil Cl WR5 ... 129 A8
Bronsil Dr WR14 ... 138 F6
Bronte Dr DY10 ... 28 C6
Brook Cl Kempsey WR5 ... 141 D8
Solihull B90 ... 21 F1
Brook Cres Hagley DY9 ... 15 B5
Stourbridge DY9 ... 6 F3
Brook Dr B32 ... 9 D1
Brook Farm Dr WR14 ... 153 C5
Brook Fields Cl B60 ... 32 C1
Brook Holloway DY9 ... 6 F4
Brook La
Birmingham, Billesley B13 ... 21 B7
Birmingham, Harborne B32 ... 9 F5
Charlton WR10 ... 160 E8
Cropthorne WR10 ... 160 B6
Brook Pk Trad Est 4 DY9 ... 6 F5
Brook Rd
Birmingham, Eachway B45 ... 32 E7
Bromsgrove B61 ... 48 E1
Fairfield B61 ... 31 C2
Stourbridge DY8 ... 6 B3
Brook Side WR5 ... 141 C8
Brook St Brierley Hill DY5 ... 7 A8
Kidderminster DY11 ... 27 C6
Redditch B98 ... 71 A4
Stourbridge DY8 ... 5 E5
Stourbridge, Lye DY9 ... 6 F5
Worcester WR1 ... 115 B5
Brook Vale 4 DY12 ... 26 C3
Brook Wlk B32 ... 9 D2
Brookdale
Harvington WR11 ... 147 F8
Kidderminster DY10 ... 27 F8
Brookdale Cl B45 ... 18 A1
Brookend Dr B45 ... 32 F7
Brookend La WR5 ... 128 F1
Brookfield
2 Great Malvern WR14 ... 139 B5
Little Comberton WR10 ... 159 B3
Brookfield Cl B97 ... 89 D4
Brookfield House DY9 ... 30 C7
Brookhampton Cl B97 ... 89 E4
Brookhouse La B97 ... 88 E4
Brookhouse Rd B45 ... 49 F7
Brookland Rd DY9 ... 15 A4
Brooklands Dr
Birmingham B14 ... 20 E5
Brooklands Dr *continued*
Kidderminster DY11 ... 12 D1
Brooklands La B98 ... 71 B5
Brooklea Gr B38 ... 20 A1
Brooklyn Ct WR7 ... 120 E6
Brookmans Ave B32 ... 9 D4
Brookmeadow Ct B28 ... 21 D6
Brookmill Cl 5 WR13 ... 152 A1
Brookpiece House B14 ... 20 E2
Brookside
Birmingham, Northfield B31 ... 18 F5
4 Colwall Stone WR13 ... 152 A1
Tewkesbury GL20 ... 197 A8
Welland WR13 ... 167 C5
Brookside Ave B13 ... 21 B7
Brookside Cl
Alvechurch B48 ... 51 B6
Halesowen B63 ... 7 D3
Brookside Dr B61 ... 48 F8
Brookside Rd WR2 ... 114 D3
Brookside Way DY10 ... 14 B2
Brookthorpe Cl WR4 ... 116 A7
Brookvale Cl B61 ... 49 B4
Brookwillow Rd B63 ... 7 E1
Brookwood Ave B28 ... 21 D5
Brookwood Dr B45 ... 50 C8
Broom Cl B60 ... 49 B2
Broom Cres DY10 ... 28 A6
Broom Dr B14 ... 20 E4
Broom Mdw Rd WR3 ... 102 F3
Broome Cl 5 B63 ... 8 A3
Broome La
Blakedown DY9 ... 14 F2
Hagley DY9 ... 15 B2
Broomehill Cl DY5 ... 6 C7
Broomfield Cl DY11 ... 27 C7
Broomfield Gn DY11 ... 27 C7
Broomfield Rd DY11 ... 27 C7
Broomhall WR5 ... 128 F2
Broomhall Gn 10 WR5 ... 128 E5
Broomhall La WR5 ... 128 D2
Broomhall Way WR5 ... 128 D4
Broomy Cl DY13 ... 43 D5
Broseley Ave B31 ... 34 B8
Brotherton Ave B97 ... 69 F2
Broughton Cres B31 ... 33 D8
Broughton Rd DY9 ... 6 D3
Brown Sq WR8 ... 169 C6
Brown St WR2 ... 128 A8
Brown Westhead Pk DY10 ... 12 F3
Brownes Way WR2 ... 101 C2
Brownheath Rd
Martin Hussingtree WR3 ... 103 E3
Salwarpe WR9 ... 104 A4
Browning Cl
Kidderminster DY10 ... 28 B6
Worcester WR3 ... 115 B7
Browning Twr B31 ... 19 C3
Brownsea Cl B45 ... 17 F1
Bruce Rd DY10 ... 28 B7
Brueton Ave B60 ... 68 A8
Brueton Dr B98 ... 71 A3
Brunel Cl 4 DY13 ... 44 A5
Brunswick Cl 4 WR2 ... 127 F6
Brunswick Gate DY8 ... 6 A1
Bryher Wlk B45 ... 17 E1
Bryndale Ave B14 ... 20 C4
Brynside Cl B14 ... 20 D2
Bryony Rd B29 ... 19 B7
Buck St WR2 ... 114 F2
Buckbury Cl DY9 ... 6 D2
Buckfast Cl B61 ... 48 D1
Buckholt Dr WR4 ... 116 A8
Buckingham Cl
Great Malvern WR14 ... 139 C6
3 Walton Cardiff GL20 ... 197 A4
Buckingham Ct B29 ... 19 D8
Buckle St
Bickmarsh WR11 ... 149 F6
Chipping Campden WR12 ... 191 A2
Honeybourne WR11 ... 164 A7
Pebworth WR11 ... 150 A2
Saintbury GL55 ... 178 C7
Willersey WR12 ... 178 B2
Buckle Wood WR3 ... 115 D6
Buckleys Gn B48 ... 51 A6
Buckleys The B48 ... 51 A6
Bucknall Cres B32 ... 18 A8
Bucknall House B14 ... 20 E6
Buckridge Cl B38 ... 34 D7
Bulford Cl B14 ... 20 F2
Bull Ring 4 Halesowen B63 ... 8 B3
Kidderminster DY10 ... 27 E6
Bullfinch Cl 6 WR5 ... 128 D5
Bullus Rd 3 DY13 ... 44 A4
Bumble Hole La B61 ... 48 E7
Bunbury Gdns B30 ... 19 D4
Bunbury Rd B30, B31 ... 19 C4
Bundle Hill B63 ... 8 A4
Bungay Lake La B61 ... 47 F3
Bunns Rd WR5 ... 128 D6
Buntsford Dr B60 ... 67 F6
Buntsford Hill B60 ... 67 F5
Buntsford Pk Rd B60 ... 67 F6
BUPA S Bank Hospl WR5 ... 128 C8
Burcher Gn DY10 ... 28 B5
Burcot Ave B60 ... 49 B4
Burcot House B60 ... 49 B3
Burcot La
Bromsgrove, Burcot B60 ... 49 B3
Bromsgrove, Stoney Hill B60 ... 49 C4
Burdett Pl WR4 ... 116 C4
Burdock House B38 ... 19 F1
Burdock Rd B29 ... 19 A6
Burfield Rd B63 ... 7 C6
Burford CE Prim Sch WR15 ... 55 F6
Burford Cl WR4 ... 116 A7
Burford Ct DY8 ... 6 A4
Burford Gdns 5 WR11 ... 161 E4
Burford House Gdns* WR15 ... 55 C5
Burford La B49, B80 ... 91 E1
Burford Pk Rd B38 ... 34 E8
Burford Rd
Evesham WR11 ... 161 E4
Hollywood B47 ... 36 A6
Burgesses The DY7 ... 4 B3
Burghley Dr DY11 ... 27 C5
Burghley Wlk DY5 ... 6 B8
Burleigh Cl 5 WR15 ... 55 E4
Burleigh Rd WR2 ... 114 D3
Burley Cl B90 ... 21 F2
Burley Way B38 ... 34 C8
Burlingham Ave WR11 ... 161 F4
Burlington Cl DY10 ... 28 B4
Burlish Cl DY13 ... 43 F6
Burlish Crossing DY13 ... 43 E7
Burlish Mid Sch DY13 ... 43 F6
Burlish Top Nature Reserve* DY13 ... 43 F7
Burma Cl WR11 ... 161 E3
Burman Rd B90 ... 21 F2
Burnell Cl B50 ... 136 C5
Burnham Cl 3 WR5 ... 128 D6
Burnhill Gr B29 ... 19 A8
Burnlea Gr B31 ... 19 C1
Burns Cl
Kidderminster DY10 ... 28 B6
Redditch B97 ... 89 C8
Stourbridge DY8 ... 6 A8
Burnsall Cl WR4 ... 116 A4
Burnside Way B31 ... 33 F7
Burnt Mdw Rd B98 ... 71 F6
Burnt Oak Dr DY8 ... 6 B5
Burnthorn La DY13 ... 62 B8
Burnthorne La DY13 ... 43 C1
Burrington Rd B32 ... 18 A8
Burrish St WR9 ... 84 F3
Burrows Cl WR14 ... 139 C1
Burton Ind Est B64 ... 7 E8
Burton La B98 ... 70 F3
Burtree Ave WR4 ... 116 C5
Bury Mound Ct B90 ... 21 C2
Bush La WR2 ... 140 D7
Bush Wlk 4 WR2 ... 115 A2
Bushley Cl B98 ... 90 A7
Butcher's Wlk WR3 ... 103 A3
Butchers La B63 ... 7 C7
Bute Cl B45 ... 17 E1
Butler St B96 ... 89 E1
Butler's Hill La B97 ... 70 B5
Butt Furlong WR10 ... 146 A2
Butter Wlk B38 ... 34 C8
Buttercup Cl DY10 ... 27 E8
Buttercup Dr B60 ... 49 C6
Butterfly Cres 2 WR11 ... 161 F3
Buttermere Cl DY5 ... 6 B7
Buttermere Dr
Birmingham B32 ... 9 F3
Worcester WR4 ... 116 A6
Buttermere Rd DY13 ... 43 F6
Button Bridge La DY12 ... 10 A6
Butts La DY10 ... 28 D1
Butts The 11 WR1 ... 115 B2
Bye Rd WR14 ... 153 C7
Byefields 5 WR5 ... 141 C6
Byfield Rise WR5 ... 115 D2
Byford Cl B98 ... 70 E2
Bylands Cl B61 ... 48 E1
Byron Cl
2 Bowling Green WR2 ... 127 C2
Great Malvern WR14 ... 139 A2
Kidderminster DY10 ... 28 B5
Walton Cardiff GL20 ... 197 A5
Byron Rd B97 ... 89 D8
Byron Way B61 ... 49 A8

C

Caban Cl B31 ... 18 E5
Cadbury Coll B38 ... 19 F1
Cadbury World* B30 ... 19 F7
Cairndhu Dr DY10 ... 28 B7
Caister Ave WR4 ... 116 C5
Cakebole La DY10 ... 46 B5
Calder Cl
8 Droitwich WR9 ... 84 D1
Droitwich WR9 ... 103 D8
Calder Rd
Stourport-on-Severn DY13 ... 43 E7
Worcester WR5 ... 115 E3
Caldwall Cres DY11 ... 27 D5
Caldy Ave WR5 ... 128 E6
Caldy Wlk
5 Birmingham B45 ... 17 F1
7 Stourport-on-Severn DY13 ... 43 E6
Caledonia DY5 ... 6 D7
Cales Ave WR14 ... 138 E4
Calewood Rd DY5 ... 6 D7
Calgary Dr WR2 ... 127 F6
California House B32 ... 9 E2
California La WR13 ... 167 D6
California Way B32 ... 9 F3
Callcott Dr DY5 ... 6 D7
Callow Cl 7 DY13 ... 43 D1
Callow End CE Prim Sch WR2 ... 140 E7
Callow Hill La
Feckenham B97 ... 88 F6
Redditch B97 ... 89 B6
Callow Hill Rd B48 ... 51 A6
Callowbridge Rd B45 ... 32 F7
Callowbrook La B45 ... 32 F7
Callows La 2 DY10 ... 27 E6
Callows Mdw WR15 ... 55 E2
Calverley Rd B38 ... 34 D8
Camberwell Dr 9 WR5 ... 128 E5
Cambrai Dr
Birmingham B28 ... 21 F8
Worcester Norton WR5 ... 128 F4
Cambria Cl B90 ... 36 E7
Cambria Rd WR11 ... 161 D5
Cambrian Rd
11 Walton Cardiff GL20 ... 197 A4
1 Walton Cardiff GL20 ... 197 A4
Cambridge Cl WR14 ... 166 F7
Cameo Dr DY8 ... 5 F8
Camford Gr B14 ... 20 F3
Camino Rd B32 ... 9 F3
Camp Hill WR14 ... 138 C1
Camp Hill Ave
8 Worcester WR5 ... 115 D1
Worcester WR5 ... 128 D8
Camp Hill Rd WR5 ... 115 D1
Camp La
Birmingham, King's Norton B38 ... 19 F3
Grimley WR2 ... 101 E4
Shelsley Beauchamp WR6 ... 60 E1
Camp Wood Cl B30 ... 19 F8
Campden Cl B97 ... 89 D6
Campden La WR12 ... 177 F3
Campden Rd
Mickleton GL55 ... 165 D2
Quinton CV37 ... 151 F2
Campion Cl 3 B38 ... 34 F8
Campion Dr WR14 ... 153 D7
Campion Gr B63 ... 7 D3
Campion House 2 B38 ... 34 E8
Campion Way DY12 ... 26 D5
Can La WR11 ... 135 A3
Canada Bank WR10 ... 160 E7
Canada Way WR2 ... 127 F7
Canal Side Hopwood B48 ... 34 B2
Worcester WR3 ... 115 B6
Canal St DY8 ... 5 F6
Cangle La WR4 ... 116 C5
Cannon St WR5 ... 128 E8
Canterbury Cl B80 ... 90 C4
Canterbury Leys GL20 ... 197 A7
Canterbury Rd
Kidderminster DY11 ... 26 F7
Worcester WR5 ... 115 F2
Cantlow Rd B13 ... 21 A6
Canvey Cl B45 ... 17 E1
Capcroft Rd B13 ... 21 B6
Capern Gr B32 ... 9 F5
Captain's La WR9 ... 104 C6
Captains Pool Rd DY10 ... 28 A1
Carden Cl 11 WR1 ... 115 C2
Carden St WR1 ... 115 C2
Cardinal Cres B61 ... 48 D1
Cardinal Dr DY10 ... 28 B3
Cardington Cl B98 ... 71 F3
Cardy Cl B97 ... 70 B4
Careless Gn DY9 ... 6 F4
Carisbrooke Ave 16 WR4 ... 116 C6
Carisbrooke Dr B62 ... 8 D3
Carlisle Rd WR5 ... 116 A2
Carlton Ave DY9 ... 6 E3
Carlton Cl
Kidderminster DY11 ... 27 A8
Redditch B97 ... 70 B1
Carlton Rd WR14 ... 138 F3
Carlyle Ave DY10 ... 28 B6
Carlyle Rd B60 ... 68 B8
Carmel Gr B32 ... 9 B1
Carnforth Rd B60 ... 49 B1
Carnoustie Cl B61 ... 67 D8
Carol Ave B61 ... 48 D3
Carol Cres B63 ... 7 F5
Carol Gdns DY8 ... 5 F8
Carpenter Glade B63 ... 7 D5
Carpet Trades Way DY11 ... 27 D7
Carrant Brook Jun Sch GL20 ... 184 E1
Carrant Rd GL20 ... 197 A7
Carriage Cl WR2 ... 114 F3
Carrock Fell 1 WR4 ... 116 A5
Carroll Wlk DY10 ... 28 C5
Carter Ave DY11 ... 27 B4
Carter Ct DY11 ... 27 C4
Carter's La
Birmingham B62 ... 9 A3
Halesowen B62 ... 8 F4
Carters Cl
Bromsgrove B61 ... 67 D7
10 Worcester WR4 ... 115 F6
Carthorse La B97 ... 70 B5
Cartland Rd B14, B30 ... 20 C7
Cartmel Cl WR4 ... 116 B6
Cartwright Ave WR4 ... 116 C3
Cartwright Rd B60 ... 67 D2
Carver Gdns DY8 ... 5 E2
Caslon Cres DY8 ... 5 D4
Caslon Flats B63 ... 7 C4
Caslon Prim Sch B63 ... 7 C4
Caslon Rd B63 ... 7 C6
Castell Pl 2 WR4 ... 116 C6
Castle Cl WR15 ... 56 A6

Castle Croft B68 9 D8
Castle Gr DY8 6 B3
Castle Hts B64 8 B8
Castle La DY12 26 C4
Castle Pl WR1 115 C1
Castle Rd
Birmingham B29 19 B8
Birmingham, King's Norton B30 19 F4
Cookley DY10 13 A4
Kidderminster DY11 27 E5
Studley B80 90 F4
Castle Rd E B68 9 D8
Castle Rd W B68 9 C8
Castle St
Astwood Bank B96 89 E2
3 Evesham WR11 161 E4
Kinver DY7 4 A4
Worcester WR1 115 B3
Castle The DY8 6 B3
Castle Toot* DY14 22 E5
Castleditch La B98 89 E7
Castlemorton CE Prim Sch WR13 180 C7
Catbrook WR3 115 D6
Cathcart Rd DY8 5 E5
Cathedral Ave DY11 27 A6
Catherine Cl B60 67 F8
Catherine Rd WR2 127 E8
Catherton Cl DY14 22 B4
Catherton Rd DY14 22 B5
Catshill Fst Sch B61 49 A8
Catshill Mid Sch B61 48 F8
Caunsall Rd DY11 13 B6
Causey Farm Rd B63 16 C8
Cavendish Cl
Birmingham B38 20 B1
Marlbrook B60 32 C1
Cavendish Dr
Hagley DY9 14 F4
Kidderminster DY10 28 B7
Cavendish Rd B62 8 F4
Cavendish St WR5 128 C7
Caynham Cl B98 71 D4
Caynham Rd B32 18 B8
Cecil Rd WR5 115 D2
Cecil St DY8 5 F5
Cecilia Ave WR2 114 E5
Cecilia Pl WR2 114 E6
Cedar Ave
Great Malvern WR14 139 B3
Madresfield WR13 139 F4
Worcester WR4 115 E6
Cedar Cl Alveley WV15 1 C6
Birmingham B30 19 E6
Droitwich WR9 103 F8
Oldbury B68 9 C8
Stourbridge DY8 5 D2
Stourport-on-Severn DY13 43 F2
Cedar Cres DY11 27 C6
Cedar Dr
Birmingham, West Heath B31 34 B7
Bromsgrove B60 49 A1
Kidderminster DY11 27 C7
Cedar Gdns DY7 3 F6
Cedar Gr DY9 15 A6
Cedar Pk Rd B97 70 D4
Cedar Rd
Birmingham B30 19 E6
Mickleton GL55 165 E4
Northway GL20 197 E8
Redditch B97 70 D4
Cedar Rise 15 DY13 43 E4
Cedar Terr B60 49 A1
Cedar View B97 70 C4
Cedar Way B31 18 F1
Cedarwood Gdns 1 WR11 161 F3
Celandine Dr WR5 128 D4
Celandine Way WR11 175 C8
Celvestune Way WR9 84 D2
Cemetery Rd
Redditch B97 70 D3
Stourbridge DY9 6 E5
Centenary Cl 1 B31 19 A1
Central Ave
Birmingham B31 33 F8
Blackheath, Cradley Heath B64 7 D7
Stourbridge DY9 6 E3
Central Rd B60 49 A2
Centre Cl B63 8 B3
Centre La B63 8 B3
Centreway The B14 21 D4
Chaceley Ct B97 89 D8
Chacewater Ave WR3 115 A7
Chacewater Cres WR3 115 A7
Chadbury Rd
Halesowen B63 8 C3
Norton & Lenchwick WR11 147 B2
Chadcote Way B61 31 F1
Chaddersley Cl 2 B45 17 F1
Chaddesley Cl B98 70 F1
Chaddesley Corbett Endowed Fst Sch DY10 46 E8
Chaddesley Dr DY9 6 B1
Chaddesley Gdns 2 DY10 28 A5
Chaddesley Rd
Birmingham B31 19 D2
Halesowen B63 7 F2
Kidderminster DY10 28 A5
Chadsgrove Sch B61 48 F8
Chadwich La DY9 31 F7
Chadwick WR4 116 C4
Chadwick Ave B45 33 B6
Chadwick Bsns Pk DY13 63 D7
Chadwick La DY11 44 E2
Chadwick Mews B98 90 A7
Chaffinch Dr DY10 27 F2
Chaffinch Rd DY9 6 D3
Chale Gr B14 21 A3
Chalfont Cl WR3 115 B7
Chalfont Pl DY9 6 E2
Chalford Dr WR4 116 A7
Chalgrove Ave B38 19 E1
Challenger Cl 5 WR14 139 B1
Chalybeate Cl B45 17 F1
Chamberlain La B49 109 A2
Chamberlain Rd
Birmingham B13 21 A6
Worcester WR2 127 F7
Champney DY10 27 E2
Chance Croft B68 9 B8
Chance La WR14 153 E8
Chance St 4 GL20 196 F6
Chancel Way B62 8 C6
Chandler Ave DY7 3 F5
Chandlers Cl B97 89 D7
Channon Dr DY5 6 D8
Chanston Ave B14 20 E4
Chantry Cl B47 36 A7
Chantry Dr B62 9 A6
Chantry High Sch The WR6 99 B5
Chantry Rd DY7 5 C7
Chantry The 1 WR10 146 A1
Chapel Cl
3 Bidford-on-Avon B50 136 D4
Blackheath B64 8 B8
Leigh WR13 126 A2
Chapel Ct
Astwood Bank B96 89 E1
Kidderminster DY10 13 A1
Chapel Dr B47 35 F3
Chapel Hill DY10 13 A1
Chapel House La B63 7 C6
Chapel La
Aldington WR11 162 C5
Belbroughton DY9 31 D7
Beoley B98 71 F8
Bransford WR6 126 D4
Bredon GL20 185 A4
Childswickham WR12 176 F2
Lindridge WR6 59 D7
Mickleton GL55 165 D4
Ombersley WR9 83 A4
Redmarley D'abitot GL19 192 A1
Rock DY14 24 E1
Romsley B62 16 C6
Rowney Green B48 51 F4
5 Stourport-on-Severn DY13 62 E8
Upton Snodsbury WR7 131 C8
Weston-sub-Edge GL55 178 D6
Wyre Piddle WR10 145 B3
Wythall B47 35 E2
Chapel Mews WR9 85 E8
Chapel Pl DY11 27 D6
Chapel Rd Alveley WV15 1 C5
Astwood Bank B96 89 E1
Kempsey WR5 141 C7
Pebworth CV37 150 E2
Chapel St
Astwood Bank B96 89 E1
Badsey WR11 162 E3
Bromsgrove B60 49 A2
2 Evesham WR11 161 D4
Hagley DY9 15 A5
Halesowen B63 8 A3
Kidderminster DY11 27 D6
Redditch B97 70 D1
Stourbridge, Lye DY9 6 E5
Stourbridge, Wollaston DY8 6 A4
Chapel Wlk
Birmingham B30 20 A2
Bromsgrove B60 49 A2
Chapelfield Mews
Birmingham B45 32 F6
Stourbridge DY8 6 A4
Chapelfield Rd B45 33 A7
Chapman's Hill B62 17 B1
Charfield Cl B30 19 D7
Charford Fst Sch B60 67 F7
Charford Rd B60 67 F8
Charity Cres WR11 161 D1
Charlecot Rd WR9 85 A1
Charlecote Cl B98 71 D2
Charlecott Cl B13 21 D7
Charles Ave DY10 13 A1
Charles Cl
Evesham WR11 161 D3
15 Walton Cardiff GL20 197 A4
Charles Dickens Cl 2 WR9 103 E8
Charles Hastings Way WR5 116 B2
Charles Henry Rd WR9 85 A3
Charles Rd
Halesowen B63 7 F4
Stourbridge DY8 5 E4
Charles St
Kidderminster DY10 27 F6
Redditch B97 70 C1
6 Worcester WR1 115 C2
Charles Way WR14 139 C3
Charlock Rd WR14 153 D7
Charlotte Bronte Dr 3 WR9 103 E8
Charlotte Rd B30 20 A6
Charlton Cl WR11 161 A3
Charlton Dr B64 7 D7
Charlton La DY11 44 F4
Charnwood Cl
Birmingham B45 18 B3
Brierley Hill DY5 6 B8
3 Worcester WR2 127 F7
Charnwood Ct DY9 6 E2
Charter Cres B64 8 B8
Charter Pl 2 WR1 115 B3
Chartist La GL19 192 E4
Chartwell Grange B64 8 A7
Chase End Cl WR5 128 E7
Chase High Sch The WR14 153 B6
Chase Rd
Colwall WR14 152 D2
Great Malvern WR14 166 F7
Chaston Cl WR7 120 E6
Chatcombe Dr WR4 116 A7
Chatham Rd B31 19 A3
Chatsworth Rd B62 8 A7
Chatterton Wlk 4 DY10 28 B6
Chaucer Cl DY8 6 A8
Chaucer Cres DY10 28 C5
Chaucer House B63 7 B5
Chaucer Rd B60 68 B8
Chawn Hill DY9 6 C3
Chawn Pk Dr DY9 6 C3
Chawnhill Cl DY9 6 C3
Chawson Fst Sch WR9 84 E1
Chawson La WR9 84 C1
Chawson Rd WR9 84 E2
Cheapside 1 DY13 44 A2
Checketts Cl
Pershore/Pinvin WR10 144 E7
Worcester WR3 115 B7
Checketts La WR3 115 B8
Chedworth Cl
Birmingham B29 19 B6
Redditch B98 71 C5
Worcester WR4 116 A7
Chedworth Dr WR4 116 A7
Chells Gr B13 21 B5
Chelmarsh Cl B98 71 C7
Chelmsford Dr WR5 115 F1
Chelsea Cl B32 9 F4
Chelsea Ct 6 B29 19 B7
Chelston Rd B31 18 E2
Cheltenham Ave B61 32 B1
Cheltenham Rd
Beckford GL20 186 C2
Bredon GL20 185 A5
Broadway WR12 190 A7
Buckland WR12 189 F5
Evesham WR11 161 C1
Hinton on the Green WR11 175 B3
Sedgeberrow WR11 174 F1
Chelworth Rd B38 20 B2
Chepstow Ave WR4 116 B6
Chepstow Dr B61 32 B1
Chepstow Gr B45 33 B6
Chequers Cl
Great Malvern WR14 139 C5
3 Stourport-on-Severn DY13 62 F8
Chequers La
1 Dodderhill WR9 66 E1
Dodderhill WR9 85 F8
Fladbury WR10 146 B1
Worcester WR2 115 A2
Cherhill Covert 7 B14 20 C2
Cherington Cl
Redditch B98 71 F1
8 Worcester WR4 115 F7
Cherington Rd B29 20 A8
Cherrington Cl B31 18 F7
Cherrington Gdns DY9 15 C7
Cherry Cl
16 Bewdley DY12 25 F3
2 Droitwich WR9 85 B1
3 Evesham WR11 161 F2
Offenham WR11 148 A1
Cherry Cres B61 48 E2
Cherry Gr DY8 5 E4
Cherry Hill Ave B45 50 C8
Cherry Hill Dr B45 50 C8
Cherry Hill Rd B45 50 C8
Cherry Orch
Bredon GL20 184 E6
Holt WR6 82 B3
Kidderminster DY10 27 F6
Pershore WR10 144 D1
Upton upon Severn WR8 169 C5
Cherry Orch Ave B63 7 F5
Cherry Orch Cres B63 7 F6
Cherry Orch Dr B61 48 E3
Cherry Orch Fst Sch WR10 144 E1
Cherry Orch La GL20 183 E6
Cherry Orch Prim Sch WR5 128 D7
Cherry Orch Rd WR10 145 D3
Cherry Pit La B98 53 A1
Cherry St Halesowen B63 7 F5
Stourbridge DY8 5 E4
Worcester WR5 128 C8
Cherry Tree Cres WR11 135 F3
Cherry Tree Dr WR14 152 F4
Cherry Tree La B63 7 D1
Cherry Tree Wlk
Astley & Dunley DY13 62 E7
Redditch B97 70 B4
Cherry Tree Wlk *continued*
6 Worcester WR1 115 B3
Cherry Wlk B47 36 B5
Cherrytree Ct DY9 6 E3
Cherwell Cl WR4 115 F4
Cheshire Cl DY8 5 D8
Cheshire Gr DY11 27 A7
Cheslyn Gr B14 21 A3
Chessetts Gr B13 21 A6
Chesshire Ave DY13 62 E8
Chesshire Cl 4 DY13 62 E8
Chester Cl 1 WR5 115 F1
Chester Ct 5 B29 19 B7
Chester Pl 2 WR14 138 F4
Chester Rd
Blackheath B64 7 C8
Kinver DY7 3 F7
Chester Rd N DY10 28 A7
Chester Rd S DY10 27 F4
Chester Rise B68 9 B8
Chesterfield Cl B31 19 B2
Chesterfield Ct B38 19 E4
Chesterton Cl B97 89 D4
Chesterwood B47 36 A6
Chesterwood Rd B13 20 F6
Chestnut Cl
Aldington WR11 162 C5
Drakes Broughton WR10 144 A6
Evesham WR11 161 B2
Hill & Moor WR10 145 D3
Stourbridge DY8 5 D3
Welland WR13 167 C5
Chestnut Ct DY11 27 B8
Chestnut Dr
Birmingham, Rednall B45 33 D4
Great Malvern WR14 152 F4
Chestnut Gr
Kidderminster DY11 27 B8
Kinver DY7 3 F5
Chestnut La WR7 120 E7
Chestnut Pl B14 20 E8
Chestnut Rd
Astwood Bank B96 89 E1
Bromsgrove B61 48 F4
Oldbury B68 9 C7
Chestnut Spinney 5 WR9 103 F8
Chestnut St WR1 115 C4
Chestnut Wlk
Ombersley WR9 83 A5
Worcester WR1 115 B4
Cheswick Cl B98 72 A3
Chesworth Rd B60 49 B1
Cheveley Ave B45 33 B7
Chevenham Cl 3 WR13 152 A1
Cheverton Rd B31 18 E4
Chevington La WR10 143 E2
Cheviot Cl
Stourport-on-Severn DY13 62 D8
Worcester WR4 115 F4
Cheviot Rd DY8 6 A6
Cheviot Way B63 7 D2
Cheyne Gdns B28 21 E3
Cheyne Wlk DY5 6 C7
Chichester Ave DY11 12 C1
Chichester Dr B32 9 A5
Chilcote Cl B28 21 F4
Chilcote Prim Sch B28 21 F4
Childe Rd DY14 22 C4
Childswickham Rd WR12 190 B8
Chilham Pl 4 WR4 116 C6
Chiltern Cl
Great Witley WR6 61 A1
Halesowen B63 7 D1
Stourport-on-Severn DY13 62 D8
2 Worcester WR4 115 F4
Chiltern House B98 71 E1
Chiltern Rd DY8 6 B6
Chilton Rd B14 21 D4
China Cnr WR11 164 A4
Chinn Brook Rd B13 21 C5
Chip Cl B38 19 D2
Chirbury Gr B31 19 B1
Chirk Cl DY10 27 E2
Chirton Gr B14 20 D6
Chiseldon Croft B14 21 A3
Chorley Rd 2 WR9 84 F3
Christ & St Mary's Cath WR1 115 C1
Christ Church Rd
4 Great Malvern WR14 153 A8
Worcester WR4 115 E3
Christina Cl 3 WR5 141 C7
Christine Ave WR2 127 C7
Christopher Rd B62 8 E3
Christopher Whitehead High Sch WR2 115 A1
Church Ave Clent DY9 15 F3
Stourbridge DY8 6 A7
Stourport-on-Severn DY13 44 A4
Church Cl
Broadway WR12 190 C7
Inkberrow WR7 120 E7
Upper Sapey WR6 77 E4
Wythall B47 35 F3
Church Croft B63 8 A4
Church Ct
Astwood Bank B96 89 E2
Stourbridge DY8 6 A5
Church Down Cl B97 89 D6
Church Dr
Birmingham B30 20 B7
Church Dr *continued*
Cookhill B49 109 A2
10 Stourport-on-Severn DY13 44 A4
Church End 1 WR10 132 F4
Church Farm
Wick WR10 145 A3
Wyre Piddle WR10 145 A4
Wyre Piddle WR10 145 A4
Church Farm Barn & Cotts DY10 14 B3
Church Gn E B98 70 E4
Church Gn W B97 70 E4
Church Gr B13 21 C5
Church Hill
Belbroughton DY9 30 D6
Beoley B98 71 D8
Birmingham, Frankley Green B32 18 B6
Birmingham, Northfield B31 19 B3
Kinver DY7 3 F2
Rushock WR9 46 C3
Church Hill Mid Sch B98 71 D6
Church Hill Way B98 71 D6
Church La
2 Bishampton WR10 132 F4
Broadheath WR2 114 A7
Broadwas WR6 112 B3
Bromsgrove B61 48 F2
Cookhill B49 109 A2
Cotheridge WR6 113 B2
Defford WR8 157 D3
Dodderhill WR9 66 E1
Earl's Croome WR8 156 A1
Flyford Flavell WR7 119 D1
Forthampton GL19 195 E6
Great Comberton WR10 158 F1
Halesowen B63 8 B4
Hallow WR2 101 D1
Hill & Moor WR10 145 D3
Himbleton WR9 105 D2
Little Witley WR6 81 A4
Mamble DY14 39 F4
Martin Hussingtree WR3 103 B4
Norton & Lenchwick WR11 147 E4
Norton Juxta Kempsey WR5 129 B3
Oddingley WR9 104 C3
Ombersley WR9 83 A3
Pershore/Pinvin WR10 144 F6
Rock DY14 24 B2
Severn Stoke WR8 155 D5
1 South Littleton WR11 148 F1
Stanton WR12 189 D1
Stoulton WR7 143 B8
Suckley WR6 123 F4
Tibberton WR9 117 A6
Upper Sapey WR6 77 E4
Upton Snodsbury WR7 131 C8
Whittington WR5 129 B6
Church Lench CE Prim Sch WR11 134 A3
Church Leys WR10 160 C7
Church Rd Alveley WV15 1 C5
Aston Somerville WR12 175 F1
Astwood Bank B96 89 E2
Belbroughton DY9 30 D6
Birmingham, Northfield B31 19 A4
Bromsgrove B61 48 F2
Castlemorton WR13 180 D7
Catshill B61 48 F8
Crowle WR7 117 E4
Dodford B61 47 F7
Evesham WR11 161 B2
Great Malvern WR14 139 A4
Halesowen B63 7 C7
Redditch, St George's B97 70 E4
Redditch, Webheath B97 69 F2
Stock & Bradley B96 106 F7
Stourbridge, Lye DY9 6 E5
Stourbridge, Old Swinford DY8 6 B3
Worcester WR3 115 D5
Church Row 8 WR10 158 D8
Church St
Bidford-on-Avon B50 136 E4
Birlingham WR10 158 A3
Bredon GL20 184 E6
Broadway WR12 190 C7
Bromsgrove B61 48 F2
Cleobury Mortimer DY14 22 C4
Eckington WR10 171 E7
Evesham WR11 161 E3
Fladbury WR10 146 B1
Great Malvern WR14 152 F8
Hagley DY9 15 A5
Hanley Castle WR8 169 B7
Harvington WR11 148 B6
Kempsey WR5 141 B7
Kidderminster DY10 27 E6
Offenham WR11 148 A1
7 Pershore WR10 158 D8
Stourbridge DY8 6 A5
Studley B80 90 E3
2 Tenbury Wells WR15 55 E5
Tewkesbury GL20 196 E6
Upton upon Severn WR8 169 C6
Willersey WR12 177 F4
Worcester WR1 115 C2
Wyre Piddle WR10 145 A3
Church Terr 5 WR2 114 F1
Church View DY12 26 A3
Church View Gdns 2 DY7 4 A4

Church Wlk
Kidderminster DY11 ....27 C6
Little Hereford SY8 ....54 C5
10 Pershore WR10 ....158 D8
Stourport-on-Severn DY13 ....43 E2
Churchdown Rd WR14 ...153 B6
Churchfield Terr WR6 ....60 F4
Churchfields
Bromsgrove B61 ....48 F3
Kidderminster DY10 ....27 E7
Churchfields Cl B61 .....48 F3
Churchfields Gdns B61 ..48 F3
Churchfields Rd B61 ....48 F3
Churchill & Blakedown Sta DY10 ....14 C2
Churchill Ave WR9 ......84 E1
Churchill Dr
Great Malvern WR14 .....139 B6
Stourbridge DY8 ....6 A7
Churchill Gr GL20 ....197 B6
Churchill La DY10 ....14 B3
Churchill Rd
Catshill B61 ....32 A1
Halesowen B63 ....7 F2
Sedgeberrow WR11 ....174 F1
Churchstone Cl B61 .....48 F8
Churchward Cl DY8 ....6 B6
Churchway Piece WR7 ....120 E7
Churchwell Ct B63 ....8 B2
Cider Ave DY5 ....6 E8
Cidermill Orch GL55 ....178 D7
Cinders La WR15 ....74 D6
Cinders Rd WR15 ....55 D1
Cirencester Cl B60 ....49 B2
Cirencester Pl 1 WR4 ..116 B7
City Est B64 ....7 D8
City Walls Rd WR1 ....115 C2
Cladswell Cl B49 ....109 A2
Cladswell La B49 ....109 A2
Cladsworth House 1 B97 ....70 A4
Claerwen Ave DY13 ....43 E7
Claerwen Gr B31 ....18 E5
Claines CE Prim Sch WR3 ....102 C3
Claines Cres DY10 ....28 B5
Claines La WR3 ....102 C2
Claines Rd
Birmingham B31 ....19 C4
Halesowen B63 ....7 D5
Clanbrook Rd DY7 ....3 F7
Clandon Cl B14 ....20 C2
Clapgate La B32 ....9 C2
Claphill La
Rushwick WR2 ....114 B1
Worcester WR2 ....127 B8
Clarage House B62 ....8 D8
Clare Ct B90 ....21 D2
Clare Rd 3 WR14 ....139 B1
Clare St 12 WR1 ....115 C2
Clare Witnell Cl DY11 ....27 B8
Clare's Ct DY11 ....27 C6
Claremont Ct WR14 ....152 E1
Claremont Way B63 ....8 A3
Clarence Cl WR14 ....153 A7
Clarence Rd
Great Malvern WR14 ....153 A8
Tewkesbury GL20 ....196 E4
Clarence St DY10 ....27 F6
Clarence Way DY12 ....26 B4
Clarendon Cl B97 ....70 B5
Clarendon Pl B62 ....9 A6
Clark St DY8 ....5 E4
Clarke St 1 B97 ....70 E3
Clarks Hill Rise WR11 ...161 B3
Clarkson Gdns 3 WR4 ..116 C4
Clarkson Pl Ind Est DY5 ...6 E7
Clatterbach La DY9 ....16 A4
Clattercut La WR9 ....46 E3
Claughton Ct DY11 ....27 C5
Claughton St DY11 ....27 C5
Clavedon Cl B31 ....18 E7
Claverdon Cl B97 ....89 D4
Claverdon House B13 ...21 A7
Claverham Cl WR2 ....128 A8
Claverton WR7 ....143 B7
Clay Dr B32 ....9 A5
Claybrook Dr B98 ....90 F7
Claybrook Fst Sch B98 ...71 F1
Claycroft Pl DY9 ....6 E5
Claydon Gr 3 B14 ....21 A3
Clayfield Dr WR14 ....138 E4
Clayfield Rd WR11 ....163 B6
Clayfields B96 ....88 F3
Clayhall Rd 8 WR9 ....85 A1
Claypit La B61 ....31 E1
Clayton Dr B60 ....68 B7
Clayton Gdns B45 ....33 A2
Clearwell Rd B98 ....71 C3
Clee Ave DY11 ....27 C2
Clee Hill Rd
Burford WR15 ....55 E8
Nash SY8 ....37 A6
Clee Rd Birmingham B31 ..34 A8
Cookley DY10 ....13 B5
Stourbridge DY8 ....6 A6
Clee View WR9 ....84 E2
Cleeve Cl Redditch B98 ...71 D5
Stourport-on-Severn DY13 ....62 D8
Cleeve Dr WR4 ....116 A6
Cleeve Prior CE Fst Sch WR11 ....149 B7
Cleeve Rd
Bidford-on-Avon B50 .....136 D2
Birmingham B14 ....21 C4

Cleeve Rd *continued*
Cleeve Prior WR11 ....149 B7
South Littleton WR11 .....148 F3
Clensmore St DY10 ....27 D7
Clent Ave
Kidderminster DY11 ....27 B1
Redditch B97 ....89 D7
Clent Dr DY9 ....15 D6
Clent Fst Sch DY9 ....15 F2
Clent House
Bromsgrove B60 ....49 B3
Halesowen B63 ....8 A2
Clent Rd
Birmingham, Rubery B45 ....32 E8
Oldbury B68 ....9 D8
Stourbridge DY8 ....6 A6
Clent View Rd
Birmingham B32 ....9 A1
Halesowen B63 ....7 C5
Stourbridge DY8 ....5 C2
Clent Way B32 ....18 A8
Cleobury Cl B97 ....70 B5
Cleobury La B90 ....36 F4
Cleobury Mortimer Cty Prim Sch DY14 ....22 B4
Cleobury Rd DY12 ....25 E3
Clerkenwell Cres WR14 ....139 A2
Clevedon Gn WR11 .....149 A1
Cleveland Dr B45 ....33 A2
Cleveland St DY8 ....5 E4
Cleves Dr B45 ....32 E7
Cleves Rd B45 ....32 E8
Clewer Croft WR13 .....125 F2
Clewley Gr B32 ....9 B5
Clews Rd B98 ....89 F7
Clewshaw La B38 ....35 C4
Cliff Rock Rd B45 ....33 B7
Cliffey House Sch WR8 ....154 F7
Clifford Ave 6 GL20 ....197 A4
Clifford Cl WR9 ....103 E7
Clifford Rd WR9 ....103 E7
Clifton Cl B98 ....90 E8
Clifton Rd Halesowen B62 ..8 E8
Kidderminster DY11 ....27 A1
Wolverley & Cookley DY10 ....13 C3
Clifton St DY8 ....5 F4
Clifton upon Teme Prim Sch WR6 ....97 E7
Clinic Dr DY9 ....6 E5
Clive Rd Birmingham B32 ...9 D7
Bromsgrove B60 ....68 B8
Redditch B97 ....70 D5
Clivedon Way B62 ....8 B7
Cloister Dr B62 ....8 D3
Cloisters The B80 ....90 D4
Clonmel Rd B30 ....20 A6
Close The
Birmingham, Beech Lanes B17 ....9 F7
Birmingham, Griffin's Hill B29 ....19 D8
Cleeve Prior WR11 ....149 A7
Eckington WR10 ....171 F8
Halesowen B63 ....7 D6
Hollywood B47 ....36 A5
Hunnington B62 ....17 A7
Wyre Piddle WR10 ....145 B4
Clover Ct B38 ....19 D2
Clover Dr B32 ....9 D2
Clover Rd B29 ....19 A7
Cloverdale B60 ....67 C3
Cloweswood La B94 .....53 F8
Clows Top Rd
Abberley WR6 ....60 E5
Bayton DY14 ....40 C6
Club View B38 ....19 D2
Clun Rd B31 ....18 F6
Clunbury Rd B31 ....34 A8
Clusters The DY9 ....6 E5
Clyde Ave
Evesham WR11 ....161 F3
Halesowen B62 ....8 E8
Clydes Dale Rd WR9 .....104 B8
Clydesdale Cl 2 WR9 ...104 B8
Clydesdale Rd B32 ....9 B6
Coach Cotts B45 ....50 D8
Coalash La B60 ....68 C2
Coalbourn La DY8 ....5 F7
Coalbourne Gdns B63 .....7 C5
Coalbournhill Glassworks* DY8 ....5 F7
Coates Rd DY10 ....28 B7
Cob La B30 ....19 C6
Cobden Ave WR4 ....116 C4
Cobden St
Kidderminster DY11 ....27 D5
Stourbridge DY8 ....5 E5
Coberley Cl WR4 ....116 A6
Cobham Cl
Bromsgrove B60 ....67 F7
Welland WR13 ....167 C5
Cobham Cres DY12 ....26 A3
Cobham Ct 11 WR9 ....84 F3
Cobham Ct Mews DY9 ...15 D6
Cobham Rd
Halesowen B63 ....8 B4
Kidderminster DY10 ....27 E4
Pershore/Pinvin WR10 ....144 E4
Stourbridge DY8 ....6 B2
Cobley Hill B48 ....50 E4
Cobnall Rd B61 ....32 A2
Cobs Field B30 ....19 C6
Cochrane Cl DY9 ....15 C8
Cock Hill La B45 ....32 F8

Cocksheds La B62 ....8 C8
Cockshot La B96 ....106 D1
Cockshot Rd WR14 ....138 F2
Cockshute Hill WR9 .....85 B2
Cockshutt La B61 ....48 D7
Cocksmead Croft B14 ...20 D5
Cocksmoor House B14 ..20 D7
Cockthorpe Cl B17 ....9 F7
Codsall Rd B64 ....7 E8
Cofton Church La B45 ...33 D3
Cofton Cl B97 ....70 B5
Cofton Ct B45 ....33 D7
Cofton Gr B31 ....33 E6
Cofton Lake Rd B45 .....33 C3
Cofton Prim Sch B31 ....34 A6
Cofton Rd B31 ....34 B7
Cokeland Pl B64 ....7 D8
Cold Comfort La B49 ...122 F8
Coldbath Rd B13 ....21 B8
Coldfield Dr B98 ....89 E7
Coldicott Gdns 1 WR11 ....161 C2
Coldicotts Cl WR11 .....163 B5
Coldicotts La WR11 .....163 B5
Cole Bank Rd B28 ....21 E8
Cole Gn B90 ....21 F2
Cole Hill WR5 ....115 D1
Cole Valley Rd B28 ....21 D6
Colebourne Rd B13 ....21 D6
Colebrook Croft B90 .....21 F2
Colebrook Rd B90 ....21 F2
Coleford Cl B97 ....70 A2
Colemeadow Rd
Birmingham B13 ....21 B6
Redditch B98 ....71 F6
Coleridge Cl
Redditch B97 ....89 C8
Worcester WR3 ....115 C6
Colesborne Cl 7 WR4 ...115 F7
Colesbourne Ave B14 ...20 C2
Coleshill Cl B97 ....89 C5
Coleside Ave B13 ....21 D7
Coley Pits La WR9 ....66 E3
Coleys La B31 ....19 A2
Colford Cl 3 WR9 ....84 C1
Colin Rd WR3 ....102 A1
Colleen Ave B30 ....20 B3
College Cl
Cleobury Mortimer DY14 ...22 C5
Long Marston CV37 .....151 C5
College Ct 1 WR15 ....55 E4
College Gn WR9 ....84 E1
College Gr WR14 ....152 F6
College Precincts 17 WR1 ....115 C2
College Rd
Birmingham, Quinton B32 ....9 A6
Bredon GL20 ....184 D6
Bromsgrove B60 ....49 A2
Great Malvern WR14 .....152 F7
Kidderminster DY10 ....27 E4
Stourbridge DY8 ....6 A4
Upton Snodsbury WR7 ....131 C8
College St WR1 ....115 C2
College Wlk
Birmingham B29 ....19 D8
Bromsgrove B60 ....49 A2
Tenbury WR15 ....74 C8
College Yd 8 WR1 ....115 B2
Collett Cl DY8 ....6 A6
Collett's Gn Rd WR2 ....127 B3
Colletts Fields WR12 ....190 E8
Colletts Gdns WR12 .....190 E8
Colley Gate B63 ....7 C6
Colley La B63 ....7 C6
Colley La Prim Sch B63 ...7 C6
Colley Orch B63 ....7 C6
Collin Cl 4 WR12 ....177 E4
Collin La WR12 ....177 C3
Collings Ave 4 WR4 ....116 C3
Collins Cl B32 ....9 A5
Collinsfield WR11 ....161 E6
Collinson Cl B98 ....71 A1
Collis Cl B60 ....67 E7
Collis St DY8 ....5 F8
Colman Hill B63 ....7 D5
Colman Hill Ave B63 ......7 D6
Colmers Farm Inf Sch B45 ....33 B8
Colmers Farm Jun Sch B45 ....33 B8
Colmers Farm Sch B45 ..33 B8
Colmers Wlk B31 ....18 D1
Colmore Ave B14 ....20 D7
Colmore Inf Sch B14 ....20 D7
Colmore Jun Sch B14 ....20 D7
Colmore Rd B14 ....20 D7
Coln Cl B31 ....18 F6
Colonial Ind Pk B64 ......7 D7
Colshaw Rd DY8 ....5 E4
Coltishall Cl 8 WR5 ....128 D6
Colts La B98 ....71 D3
Columbia Dr WR2 ....127 E7
Columbine Gr WR11 .....161 C1
Columbine Rd GL20 .....197 A3
Colwall Gn CE Prim Sch WR13 ....166 A8
Colwall Sta WR13 ....152 B2
Colworth Rd B31 ....18 F4
Comber Croft B13 ....21 D8
Comber Gr DY7 ....4 A3
Comber Rd DY7 ....3 F2
Comberton Ave DY10 ....28 B5
Comberton Ct 5 DY10 ...28 A5
Comberton Fst Sch DY10 ....28 B4
Comberton Gdns DY10 ...28 B5
Comberton Hill DY10 ....27 F5

Comberton Mans 4 DY10 ....28 A5
Comberton Mid Sch DY10 ....28 B4
Comberton Pk Rd DY10 ..28 B4
Comberton Pl DY10 ....27 F5
Comberton Rd DY10 .....28 B4
Comberton Terr DY10 ....27 F5
Comer Ave WR2 ....114 F2
Comer Gdns WR2 ....114 E4
Comer Rd WR2 ....114 F3
Comhampton La DY13 ....63 F3
Commandery Civil War Ctr The* WR1 ....115 C1
Commandery Rd WR5 ...115 C1
Common Barn La DY10 ..13 D5
Common La
Mappleborough Green B80 ....72 B3
Neen Savage DY14 ....22 A2
Common Rd WR11 ....161 E5
Common The WR6 ....60 E3
Como Rd WR14 ....138 F1
Compa The DY7 ....4 A3
Compton Cl Kinver DY7 ....3 F4
Redditch B98 ....70 E2
Compton Gdns DY7 ....3 F4
Compton Gr B63 ....7 C4
Compton Grange B64 .....7 C8
Compton Rd
Halesowen B62 ....8 F5
Kinver DY7 ....3 E4
Stourbridge DY9 ....6 D2
Worcester WR5 ....115 D2
Condover Rd B31 ....34 B8
Conduit Hill 1 WR11 ....161 E4
Coney Gn DY8 ....6 B5
Coney Gn Cl 2 WR4 ....116 B6
Coney Gn Dr B31 ....33 F8
Coneygree La WR12 .....190 D5
Congleton Cl B97 ....70 B5
Conifer Cl DY5 ....6 C8
Conifer Dr B31 ....19 B3
Conifer Gr B61 ....48 F3
Conifer Paddock B62 .....8 E8
Conigree La GL20 ....196 E4
Coningsby Dr DY11 ....27 A8
Conisborough 3 WR4 ..116 C6
Coniston Cl
Birmingham B28 ....21 F7
Bromsgrove B60 ....49 B1
Great Malvern WR14 .....153 C6
Worcester WR4 ....116 A5
Coniston Cres DY13 ....43 F6
Coniston House DY10 ....27 E7
Coniston Way DY12 ....25 E3
Connaught Ave DY11 ....27 C4
Connaught Cl 11 WR5 ...128 D6
Connaught Rd B60 ....49 C1
Conningsby Dr WR10 ...158 B8
Connops Way DY9 ....6 E5
Conolly Dr B45 ....18 B1
Consort Rd B30 ....20 A3
Constance Rd WR3 .....114 F8
Conway WR4 ....115 F4
Conway Ave B32 ....9 B6
Conway House B31 ....18 D6
Conway Rd B60 ....48 F1
Conwy Dr WR11 ....162 A3
Cook's La WR13 ....192 E7
Cookes Croft B31 ....19 B2
Cookley Cl B63 ....7 F2
Cookley La DY7 ....4 B1
Cookley Sebright Endowed Fst Sch DY10 ....13 A5
Cooks Cross WV15 ....1 C6
Cooks Hill WR10 ....159 B7
Cooksey Gn La
Elmbridge WR9 ....65 F6
Upton Warren WR9 ....66 A7
Coombe Hill B64 ....8 B8
Coombefield Rd WR11 ....176 D7
Coombes La B31 ....33 F7
Coombes Rd B62 ....8 B7
Coombs Rd
Halesowen B62 ....8 B7
Worcester WR3 ....115 B7
Coombswood Way B65 ....8 B8
Cooper Cl B60 ....67 E6
Cooper's La WR11 ....161 E3
Coopers Cl 9 WR4 ....115 F6
Coopers Hill B48 ....50 E6
Copcut La WR9 ....84 A1
Cope Rd WR3 ....115 B7
Copelands The DY7 ....4 A3
Copenhagen St 7 WR1 ..115 B2
Copperbeech Cl B32 ....9 F5
Coppice Ave DY9 ....6 F3
Coppice Cl
Birmingham, Eachway B45 ....32 F7
Great Malvern WR14 .....138 E6
Hallow WR2 ....101 D3
Redditch B97 ....70 C3
Coppice Hollow B32 ....9 B1
Coppice Hts DY11 ....27 B1
Coppice Prim Sch The B47 ....36 A6
Coppice Rd B64 ....7 E7
Coppice The
Birmingham, Frankley B31 ....18 C2
Hagley DY8 ....14 F5
Coppice Trad Est DY11 ...44 B8
Coppice Way WR9 ....84 C5
Copse Cl B31 ....19 A2
Copsewood Ave WR5 ...116 B3

Copston Gr B29 ....19 B8
Copyholt La
Stoke Prior B60 ....68 D3
Upper Bentley B60, B97 ....69 A3
Corbett Ave WR9 ....84 F2
Corbett Cl B60 ....68 B8
Corbett Cres DY8 ....6 A7
Corbett Dr B60 ....67 C1
Corbett Hospl DY8 ....5 F7
Corbett House 8 DY8 .....5 F8
Corbett Rd
Hollywood B47 ....36 A7
Kidderminster DY11 ....27 A8
Corbett St WR9 ....84 F2
Corbizum Ave B80 ....90 D4
Cordle Marsh Rd DY12 ..26 C5
Corfe Ave WR4 ....116 C6
Corfe Cl B32 ....9 F5
Coriander Cl
Birmingham B45 ....18 B2
Stoke Prior B60 ....67 C1
Corinne Cl B45 ....33 A6
Corley Ave B31 ....19 B3
Corley Cl B90 ....21 E1
Cormorant Gr DY10 ....28 B3
Cormorant Rise WR2 ...128 A6
Corn Mill Cl B32 ....9 E1
Corn Mill Rd WR11 ....161 C1
Corn Mkt 3 WR1 ....115 C2
Cornbow Ctr B63 ....8 B3
Cornbrook Rd B29 ....18 F7
Corndon Cl DY11 ....27 B2
Corner Farm Dr WR11 ..164 A4
Corner La B97 ....69 E2
Corner Stone Ctry Club B31 ....19 B5
Cornerway B38 ....34 F7
Cornfield Ave B60 ....67 D6
Cornfield Rd B31 ....19 B4
Cornfield Way WR11 ....174 B2
Corngreaves Rd B64 ....7 E7
Corngreaves Trad Est B64 ....7 D7
Corngreaves Wlk B64 .....7 E7
Cornhampton Cl 7 B97 ..70 B5
Cornhill Gr B30 ....20 C7
Cornmeadow Gn WR3 ...102 B1
Cornmeadow La WR3 ...102 B1
Cornmill Cl WR10 ....173 E7
Cornmore WR10 ....158 B7
Cornwall Ave
Kidderminster DY11 ....12 C1
Oldbury B68 ....9 B8
Cornwall Gdns 5 WR15 ..55 E5
Cornwall Rd
Birmingham, Rubery B45 ....17 E1
Stourbridge DY8 ....5 D8
Cornwell Cl B98 ....90 B5
Coronation Ave WR2 ...127 B8
Coronation Rd 3 WR14 ..139 B5
Coronation St WR11 .....161 F4
Coronation Terr B60 .....68 B7
Coronation Way DY10 ....28 B5
Corporation St DY10 .....27 E5
Corrie Croft B32 ....18 B7
Corron Hill B63 ....8 B4
Corser St DY8 ....6 A3
Corvedale Rd B29 ....19 A6
Corville Rd B62 ....8 F6
Corwen Croft B31 ....18 E6
Cosford Cl B98 ....71 F1
Cosgrove Cl WR4 ....115 F8
Costers La B98 ....71 F2
Cote La Enville DY7 ....3 F8
Kinver DY7 ....4 A7
Cotford Rd B14 ....21 A2
Cotheridge Ct* WR6 ....113 A2
Cotheridge La WR10 ....171 E7
Cotland WR3 ....115 D5
Coton Gr B90 ....21 E2
Cotswold Ave 6 DY13 ....43 D1
Cotswold Cl
Birmingham B45 ....18 B2
10 Bredon GL20 ....184 F6
Kidderminster DY11 ....27 C2
Cotswold Croft B63 ....7 C1
Cotswold Edge GL55 ....165 D4
Cotswold Gdns GL20 ....196 F7
Cotswold House 6 B14 ..21 A3
Cotswold Rd
3 Great Malvern WR14 ...153 B8
Stourbridge DY8 ....6 B6
Cotswold Way
Bromsgrove B61 ....49 A5
Worcester WR4 ....115 F8
Cottage Dr B60 ....32 D1
Cottage Farm La B60 .....32 C1
Cottage Gdns B45 ....32 F6
Cottage La B60 ....32 C1
Cottages The B63 ....7 E6
Cotteridge Inf & Jun Sch B30 ....20 A5
Cotteridge Rd B30 ....20 A4
Cotteswold Rd GL20 ....196 F6
Cotton Pool Rd B61 ....48 E2
Cotton's La WR11 ....174 A1
Cottrells Cl B14 ....21 C4
Coughton CE Prim Sch B49 ....109 F5
Coughton La B49 ....109 E4
Countinghouse Way 2 B60 ....67 E6

County Cl
Birmingham, Stirchley B30 20 C6
Birmingham, Woodgate B32 9 D3
County La DY7 14 D8
County Pk Ave B62 8 D3
Coupass Cotts B96 107 D7
Court Cl DY11 12 B1
Court Dr 3 DY13 43 F4
Court La WR11 148 A2
Court Lea WR8 169 E7
Court Oak Gr B32 9 F6
Court Oak Rd B32 9 F6
Court Rd
Great Malvern WR14 153 A7
Strensham WR8 171 A3
Court St 7 Stourbridge DY8 6 A5
4 Upton upon Severn WR8 169 C6
Court Way B50 136 D4
Courtland Cl 4 WR3 102 A1
Courtney DY10 27 E2
Courtney Cl GL20 196 F3
Courtway Ave B14 21 B1
Courtyard The B60 67 D2
Coventry Ave WR2 128 A7
Coventry Cl GL20 196 F4
Coventry Highway B98 71 C4
Coventry St
Kidderminster DY10 27 F6
Stourbridge DY8 6 A5
Covercroft 3 WR9 84 F3
Coverfield WR8 154 A2
Covers The B80 90 E6
Covert La DY8 5 D2
Cow La WR9 64 B1
Cowl Barn La WR13 152 B3
Cowl St WR11 161 D4
Cowleigh Bank WR14 138 D4
Cowleigh Rd WR14 138 D3
Cowper Wlk DY10 28 C6
Cowslip Cl
1 Birmingham, Hawkesley B38 34 F8
Birmingham, Selly Oak B29 19 A7
Cowslip Wlk DY5 6 C6
Cox Cl B50 136 E5
Coxcroft Ave DY5 6 F8
Coxlea Cl WR11 161 C5
Coxwell Dr WR14 139 B3
Crab Apple Way
4 Evesham WR11 161 F1
Evesham WR11 175 F8
Crab Mill Cl B38 34 E7
Crabbe La WR8 143 C2
Crabbe St DY9 6 F5
Crabbs Cross La B97 89 E5
Crabmill La B38 35 D8
Crabtree Cl
Birmingham B31 19 C2
Hagley DY9 15 B6
Redditch B98 71 A2
Crabtree Dr B61 48 F3
Crabtree La B61 48 E3
Cradley CE Prim Sch B63 7 C7
Cradley Cl B98 71 F2
Cradley Fields B63 7 D5
Cradley Forge DY5 7 A8
Cradley Heath Factory Ctr B64 7 B8
Cradley Heath Sta B64 7 B8
Cradley High Sch B63 7 B6
Cradley Rd B64 7 C8
Cralves Mead WR15 55 E5
Cranberry Dr 3 DY13 43 E4
Cranbourne Cl B45 18 B2
Cranbourne Rd DY8 6 B4
Crane Dr WR2 128 A6
Crane St DY11 27 C6
Cranesbill Dr WR5 128 D5
Cranesbill Rd B29 19 A6
Cranham Cl B97 70 B1
Cranham Dr WR4 116 A7
Cranham Prim Sch WR4 115 F7
Cranmoor Cres B63 8 A5
Crashmore La
Beckford GL20 186 A2
Overbury GL20 185 F5
Craufurd Ct DY8 6 A3
Craufurd St DY8 6 A3
Crawford Cl B50 136 C4
Crendon Cl B80 90 E5
Crescent Grange Rd The DY9 6 C4
Crescent Pl WR15 55 F3
Crescent Rd
1 Colwall Stone WR13 152 A1
Kidderminster DY11 27 C5
Crescent The
Blackheath, Cradley Heath B64 8 A7
Bromsgrove B60 48 F1
Colwall Stone WR13 152 A2
Great Malvern WR14 166 F7
Hagley DY8 14 F5
Hindlip WR3 103 B1
Tenbury Wells WR15 55 F3
Wolverley & Cookley DY10 13 B4
Cressage Ave B31 19 A1
Cresswell Cl WR3 102 E2
Crest Hill WR11 148 B6
Crest The
Birmingham B31 34 C7
Edwyn Ralph HR7 95 C1
Crest View B14 21 B4
Crestwood Ave DY11 27 A5
Creswick Gr B45 33 C7
Cricketers Mdw B64 7 F7
Cricklewood Dr B62 8 D3
Crickley Dr WR4 116 A7
Crimmond Rise B63 7 E5
Croft Bank
Great Malvern WR14 138 C1
Mathon WR14 152 B8
Croft Cl B98 71 D3
Croft Farm Dr WR14 138 B1
Croft Farm Leisure & Water Pk* GL20 184 B3
Croft Rd
Evesham WR11 161 D6
South Littleton WR11 148 F2
Upton Snodsbury WR7 131 C8
Worcester WR1 115 B2
Croft The
Birmingham B31 19 B2
Blakedown DY10 14 C2
Church Lench WR11 134 A3
Kidderminster DY11 27 A4
Croft Wlk WR1 115 B3
Croftdown Rd B32 9 F6
Croftdown Sch WR14 152 F7
Crofters Cl DY8 6 B4
Crofters End WR9 84 D6
Crofters Way WR9 84 D6
Croftlands The 7 GL20 184 F6
Crofts Field GL20 183 A2
Crofts La
Astwood Bank B96 89 B2
Feckenham B96 88 F2
Croftwood Rd DY9 6 D4
Cromdale Dr B63 7 D3
Cromers Cl 7 GL20 184 F1
Crompton Ave B50 136 E5
Crompton Rd B45 17 D1
Cromwell Cres WR5 128 E8
Cromwell Cres La WR5 128 E8
Cromwell La B31 18 E8
Cromwell Rd
4 Bowling Green WR2 127 C2
Great Malvern WR14 139 A4
Cromwell St WR1 115 D3
Crookbarrow Rd WR5 128 F4
Crookbarrow Way WR5 129 A5
Crookham Cl B17 9 F7
Crooks La B80 90 D3
Croome Cl
Drakes Broughton WR10 144 A6
Redditch B98 71 F1
Croome Rd
Defford WR8 157 C5
Worcester WR2 127 F7
Cropredy Rd B31 34 B8
Cropthorne Cl B98 90 B7
Cropthorne Dr B47 36 B7
Cropthorne House B60 49 B3
Cropthorne With Charlton CE Fst Sch WR10 160 C6
Cross Farms La B45 17 F1
Cross St Halesowen B63 8 A3
Stourbridge DY8 5 E5
Tenbury Wells WR15 55 E4
Cross The Ripple GL20 183 A8
Stourbridge DY9 6 E6
10 Worcester WR1 115 B3
Cross Wlks DY9 6 E5
Crossgate Rd B98 90 C7
Crossley Ret Pk DY11 27 D6
Crossley Wlk B60 67 E7
Crossroads The WR7 130 B8
Crowhurst Rd B31 33 E7
Crowle CE Fst Sch WR7 117 E5
Crowle Dr DY9 6 C5
Crown Cl
Broadheath WR2 114 A7
Bromsgrove B61 48 F2
Crown Ctr The* 2 DY8 6 A5
Crown E Heritage Woodland* WR2 113 F2
Crown E La
Broadheath WR2 113 E4
Rushwick WR2 114 A2
Crown La Defford WR8 157 D3
Dodderhill WR9 66 C2
Hartlebury DY13 63 E8
Iverley DY10 14 C7
Kidderminster DY10 27 E6
Stourbridge DY8 5 F5
Crown Lea Ave WR14 153 C8
Crown Mdw
Alvechurch B48 51 A7
Broadheath WR2 114 A7
Crown Rd B30 20 A4
Crown St WR3 115 B6
Crowngate Sh Ctr WR1 115 B3
Crowther Gdns B63 7 C7
Crowther St DY11 27 C6
Cruisehill La B97 88 D5
Crumpfields La
Feckenham B97 88 E8
Redditch B97 69 F1
Crumpton Hill Rd WR13 138 B6
Crundalls La DY12 26 B5
Crundelend La WR6 60 B2
Crutch La
Dodderhill WR9 85 A7
Droitwich WR9 85 A4
Upton Warren WR9 66 B4
Crychan Cl B45 18 B2
Culford Dr B32 18 C8
Culmington Rd B31 33 F8
Cumberland Rd B68 9 B7
Cumberland St WR1 115 B5
Cumbrian Croft B63 7 D2
Cur La B97 69 D3
Curdale Cl DY14 22 B4
Curdale Rd B32 18 B8
Curlew Cl
Kidderminster DY10 28 B2
Northway GL20 184 D1
Curslow La
Chaddesley Corbett DY10 45 F5
Kidderminster DY10 28 F1
Stone DY10 45 F8
Curtis Cl B60 68 F8
Cutlers Rough Cl B31 18 F5
Cutnall Gn CE Fst Sch WR9 65 B5
Cutsdean Cl B31 18 F6
Cutts Pool WR7 131 C8
Cutty Sark Dr 2 DY13 44 B2
Cygnet Cl B48 51 A7
Cypress Cl 2 WR11 161 F1
Cypress Ct DY10 28 A4
Cypress Gr B31 18 E1
Cypress Rd GL20 197 A4
Cypress St WR3 115 B6
Cypress Way B31 33 F8
Cyprus Ave B96 89 D2
Cyprus Cl B29 19 A7
Cyril Rd WR3 115 D4

D

Dace Rd 7 WR5 128 C5
Dacer Cl B30 20 B5
Dad's La B13 20 D8
Daddlebrook Rd WV15 1 C6
Daffodil Way B31 33 E8
Dagnell End Rd B98 71 B7
Dagtail La B97 89 D3
Daimler Rd B14 21 D3
Dainton Gr B32 9 C1
Dairy Ct B68 9 D7
Dairy La
Dumbleton WR11 187 F4
Redditch B97 70 A5
Daisy Farm Rd B14 21 B3
Dalbury Cl 5 WR14 138 F4
Dalbury Rd B28 21 E5
Dale Cl B61 48 F7
Dale Hill B60 49 F6
Dale Rd Halesowen B62 8 F8
Redditch B98 70 F5
Stourbridge DY8 5 F2
Daleview Rd B14 21 C4
Damar Croft B14 20 D4
Damaskfield WR4 116 C4
Dame Elizabeth Cadbury Sch & Sixth Form B30 19 D7
Dame Ellen Pinsent Specl Sch B13 21 A7
Damson Cl B97 89 C6
Damson Way DY12 26 C4
Danbigh Ct 3 B29 19 C7
Dane Gr B13 20 D8
Danebury Pk WR14 138 D3
Danemoor Cross WR13 167 E7
Danes Gn WR3 102 E3
Danescroft 4 DY13 43 F4
Danford Cl DY8 6 A4
Danford Rd B47 35 F6
Danube Cl WR9 103 D8
Danzey Cl B98 90 B5
Danzey Gr B14 20 C3
Dark La
Astley & Dunley DY13 62 C6
Astwood Bank B96 89 D1
Belbroughton DY9 30 F8
Grimley WR2 101 C5
Hollywood B38, B47 35 E7
Kinver DY7 4 B3
Ombersley DY13 63 F1
Rock DY14 41 E7
Romsley B62 16 F4
Stock & Bradley B96 107 A3
Stoke Heath B60 67 D6
Dark Orch WR15 55 E3
Darris Rd B29 20 A8
Dart Rd WR5 115 F3
Dartmoor Cl B45 18 A2
Darwin Cl 6 WR5 141 C6
Daston Cl WR12 190 E8
Dauntsey Covert B14 20 D2
Davena Dr B29 9 E2
Davenham Cl WR14 139 A1
Davenham Rd B60 49 C1
Davenport Dr B60 49 B1
Daventry Gr B32 9 D6
Davids The B31 19 C5
Davies Rd WR11 161 D1
Dawberry Cl B14 20 D5
Dawberry Fields Rd B14 20 D5
Dawberry Rd B14 20 C6
Dawn Rd B31 18 E6
Dawson Cl 3 WR2 127 F6
Dawson Rd B61 48 E2
Daybrook Cl B97 70 B5
Dayhouse Bank B62 17 B1
De La Bere Cl 8 WR11 161 D5
De Salis Dr WR9 84 D7
De Salis Ct WR9 84 D7
De Walden Rd WR14 138 C1
De Wyche Cl WR9 85 E8
De Wyche Rd WR9 85 E8
Deacle Pl WR11 161 F4
Deal Cres WR4 116 C7
Deal Gr B31 19 A3
Dean Cl Stourbridge DY8 6 B6
1 Tenbury Wells WR15 55 F6
Deane Cl 5 WR2 127 C2
Deans Cl B98 71 D5
Deanscroft Dr B60 49 C6
Deansford La DY10 29 B6
Deansway
Bromsgrove B61 48 E2
Worcester WR1 115 B2
Deansway House DY10 28 A7
Deansway The DY10 28 A7
Dearmont Rd B31 33 E7
Debdale Ave WR4 116 B5
Dee Gr B38 34 E8
Dee Way WR4 115 F3
Deelands Rd B45 32 F8
Deeley Cl B64 7 E7
Deepwood Gr B32 18 B8
Deer Ave WR5 128 F6
Deer Barn Hill B98 71 A1
Deerhurst Cl B98 71 C7
Defford Cl B97 69 E1
Defford Rd WR10 158 A7
Delamere Rd
Bewdley DY12 26 C4
Birmingham B28 21 F7
Great Malvern WR14 139 B1
Tedstone Delamere HR7 96 E2
Dell Rd B30 20 A5
Dell The
Birmingham, Shenley Fields B31 18 D6
Bredon GL20 184 E7
Stourbridge DY8 5 E6
Della Dr B32 18 D8
Dellow Gr B48 51 A5
Dellows Cl B38 34 D7
Dellway Ct DY8 5 E5
Delph Dr DY5 6 E7
Delph La DY5 6 D8
Delphinium Cl 3 DY11 12 C1
Delrene Rd B28, B90 21 F3
Delta Dr GL20 197 C8
Denaby Gr B14 21 D4
Dencer Cl B45 33 A8
Dencil Cl B63 7 D5
Dene Hollow B13 21 C7
Dene Rd DY8 5 F3
Denehurst Cl B45 33 A1
Denford Gr B14 20 D5
Denholme Gr B14 21 A3
Denison Cl WR14 139 B2
Dennis Hall Rd DY8 6 A8
Dennis St DY8 5 F8
Denshaw Rd B14 20 D6
Dent Cl WR5 115 D2
Denton Rd DY9 7 A4
Denver Rd B14 21 A2
Derby Rd 1 WR5 115 C1
Derick Burcher's Mall 5 DY10 27 E6
Derries The WR3 103 A3
Derwent Ave DY13 43 F5
Derwent Cl 2 WR4 115 F5
Derwent Dr
6 Bewdley DY12 25 F4
Tewkesbury GL20 197 A8
Derwent Gr 8 WR9 84 C1
Derwent House DY10 27 F7
Derwent Rd B30 20 C8
Derwent Way B60 49 B1
Desborough House 8 B14 21 A3
Despenser Rd GL20 196 E4
Dettonford Rd B32 18 B8
Devil's Spittleful Nature Reserve* DY12 26 E3
Devon Cl
Inkberrow WR7 120 F6
Kidderminster DY11 12 C1
Devon Ct 3 B29 19 B7
Devon Rd
Birmingham B45 17 F1
Smethwick B67 9 E7
Stourbridge DY8 5 E7
Worcester WR5 115 F1
Devonport Cl 3 B97 70 B5
Devonshire Pl GL20 196 F4
Dewberry Cl 9 DY13 43 E4
Dewsbury Cl B96 89 E1
Dial Cl B14 20 F2
Dial La DY8 5 E8
Dice Pleck B31 19 C2
Dickens Gr 9 B14 21 A3
Dickens Heath Rd B90 36 F5
Didcot Cl B97 89 C5
Digby Dr GL20 196 F7
Digby Rd WR11 161 F3
Diglis Dock Rd WR5 128 B7
Diglis La WR5 128 C8
Diglis Rd WR5 115 C1
Dilmore Ave WR3 102 E3
Dilmore La WR3 102 E4
Dilwyn Cl B98 71 F1
Dimmingsdale Bank B32 9 C4
Dimsdale Gr B31 18 E3
Dimsdale Rd B31 18 D3
Dinchall Rd WR5 129 A8
Dinedor Cl B98 71 D3
Dineley Cl 3 WR10 131 B2
Dineley Rd WR10 131 B2
Dines Gn Prim Sch WR2 114 D2
Dingle Ave B64 7 E8
Dingle Cl B30 19 D7
Dingle End WR7 120 F6
Dingle Mead B14 20 C4
Dingle Rd Leigh WR6 125 D8
Stourbridge DY9 6 C2
Dingleside B98 70 E2
Dingleside Mid Sch B98 90 B8
Dinmore Ave B31 19 B4
Dinmore Cl
Redditch B98 71 D3
4 Worcester WR5 128 E5
Ditchford Cl B97 89 D4
Ditton Gr B31 33 F6
Dixon Ct DY10 28 C8
Dixon St DY10 27 E5
Dobbins Oak Rd DY9 6 E1
Dobes La DY10 46 C7
Dock La GL20 184 E7
Dock The Catshill B61 49 A8
Stourbridge DY9 6 F5
Dockar Rd B31 18 E2
Dockeray Ave WR4 116 C5
Doctors Hill
Bournheath B61 48 D8
Stourbridge DY9 6 C3
Dodderhill Rd WR9 85 A5
Doddington Gr B32 18 B8
Dodford Cl B45 32 F7
Dodford Ct B61 48 C6
Dodford Fst Sch B61 48 A5
Dodford House B60 49 B3
Dodford Rd B61 31 D1
Dog La Bewdley DY12 26 B3
Ombersley DY13 63 E3
Upton Warren B61 66 C6
Dogkennel La B63 8 B3
Dogwood Cl WR14 139 C3
Dolben La B98 71 D3
Dolday WR1 115 B2
Dolphin Cl WR2 114 E4
Dolphin Rd B98 71 A5
Domar Rd DY11 27 B7
Domestic Fowl Trust & Honeybourne Rare Breeds* WR11 164 A5
Dominic Dr B30 19 D4
Don Rd WR4 115 F3
Donney Brook 3 WR11 161 F3
Donnington Cl B98 71 C5
Doran Cl B63 7 D1
Dorchester Rd DY9 6 D2
Dordale Cl B31 18 C1
Dordale Rd DY9 30 E2
Dordon Cl B90 21 E1
Dormie Cl B38 19 D1
Dormouse Croft WR5 128 F6
Dormston Cl B98 70 F1
Dormston Dr B29 9 F2
Dormy Dr B31 34 A7
Dornie Dr B38 19 F1
Dornton Rd B30 20 C8
Dorothy Cres 5 WR3 102 A1
Dorrels Orch 3 WR10 132 F4
Dorridge Cl B97 70 B1
Dorset Cl B45 17 F2
Dorset Cotts B30 20 A6
Dorset Ct 2 B29 19 B7
Dorset Rd DY8 5 D8
Dorsett Rd 3 DY13 43 F5
Dorsington Rd CV37 150 E5
Dorstone Covert B14 20 C2
Dorville Cl B38 34 D8
Dotterel Pl DY10 28 A1
Double Hedges Rd WR10 173 A3
Douglas Rd B47 36 A7
Doulton Cl B32 9 F3
Dove Cl
Kidderminster DY10 28 B2
Worcester WR4 115 F3
Dove Dr DY8 6 A8
Dove Gdns B38 20 B2
Dove Ridge DY8 6 A7
Dovecote WR10 160 D8
Dovecote Rd
Bromsgrove B61 48 E1
Droitwich WR9 85 A1
Dovedale Ct 10 B29 19 C7
Dovedale Dr B28 21 F5
Dover Ave WR4 116 C6
Dover Cl B32 18 A7
Dover's View GL55 178 D7
Doverdale Ave DY10 28 B5
Doverdale Cl
Droitwich WR9 84 E2
Halesowen B63 7 E5
Redditch B98 90 B7
Doverdale La
Hampton Lovett WR9 83 F8
Ombersley WR9 64 D1
Doveridge Rd B28 21 E5
Doversley Rd B14 20 C5
Doveton House DY8 6 A3
Dowar Rd B45 33 C7
Doweries The B45 32 F8
Dowland Gdns 3 WR2 114 D3
Dowler's Hill Cres B98 90 A8
Dowles Cl B29 19 B6
Dowles Croft 2 WR9 84 E3
Dowles Manor* DY12 25 F5

Dowles Rd
Bewdley DY12 .... 26 A4
Kidderminster DY11 .... 27 B2
Upper Arley DY12 .... 25 F5
Downcroft Ave B38 .... 19 E2
Downfield La GL20 .... 184 B7
Downing Ct 5 B68 .... 9 B7
Downing St B63 .... 8 A5
Downland Cl B38 .... 19 F1
Downs Sch WR13 .... 152 B3
Downsell House B97 .... 70 A2
Downsell Rd B97 .... 70 A2
Dragons La WR13 .... 125 E1
Dragoon Fields B60 .... 68 B8
Drake Ave WR2 .... 114 D3
Drake Cres
Kidderminster DY11 .... 27 A7
Kidderminster Foreign DY11 .... 26 F7
Drake St WR13 .... 167 E4
Drakelow La DY11 .... 12 C5
Drakes Bridge Rd WR10 .... 171 D7
Drakes Cl B97 .... 89 C6
Drakes Cross Par B47 .... 36 A5
Drakes Hill Cl DY8 .... 5 C4
Drakes Lea WR11 .... 161 F5
Drapers Cl WR4 .... 115 F6
Drawbridge Rd B90 .... 36 E8
Draycote Cl 2 WR5 .... 128 D5
Draycott Cl 9 B97 .... 70 B5
Draycott Dr B31 .... 18 E7
Drayton Cl
Bidford-on-Avon B50 .... 136 C5
Redditch B98 .... 90 D8
Drayton Ct B60 .... 68 B8
Drayton Rd
Belbroughton DY9 .... 30 B5
Birmingham B14 .... 20 F8
Drew Cres DY9 .... 6 D2
Drew Rd DY9 .... 6 D3
Drews Holloway B63 .... 7 D5
Drews Holloway S B63 .... 7 D5
Drews House B14 .... 20 D1
Drews Mdw Cl 1 B14 .... 20 C2
Driffield Cl B98 .... 71 D2
Drift The WR11 .... 162 E3
Driftwood Cl B38 .... 34 D7
Drinkwater La WR11 .... 163 B4
Drive The
Bowling Green WR2 .... 127 B3
Halesowen B63 .... 8 A3
Halesowen, Cradley B63 .... 7 D5
Hindlip WR3 .... 103 B2
Hopwood B48 .... 34 B3
Redditch B97 .... 69 C7
Worcester WR3 .... 115 B8
Droitwich High Sch WR9 .... 84 D3
Droitwich Rd
Feckenham B96 .... 107 C7
Fernhill Heath WR3 .... 103 A3
Hartlebury DY10 .... 45 A6
Worcester WR3 .... 115 C8
Droitwich Spa Brine Baths* WR9 .... 84 F3
Droitwich Spa Lido Pk* WR9 .... 85 A3
Droitwich Spa Sta WR9 .... 84 E3
Droitwich Sports & Leisure Ctr WR9 .... 84 D3
Drovers Pl 3 WR9 .... 84 D5
Drovers Way
Bromsgrove B60 .... 67 E6
2 Droitwich WR9 .... 84 D5
Worcester WR3 .... 115 E7
Drugger's End La WR13 .... 167 C1
Druids La B14 .... 20 D1
Drumbles La 2 WR4 .... 116 C4
Drummond Rd
Bromsgrove B60 .... 68 B8
Stourbridge DY9 .... 6 F4
Drury La
Martin Hussingtree WR3 .... 103 C5
Redmarley D'abitot GL19 .... 192 B4
Stourbridge DY8 .... 6 A5
Dry Mill La DY12 .... 25 E4
Drybrook Cl B38 .... 34 E8
Dryden Cl WR3 .... 115 C6
Drysdale Cl WR11 .... 176 D7
Duck Mdw WR4 .... 116 B4
Dudley Cl WR2 .... 114 D3
Dudley Rd Halesowen B63 .... 8 B5
Honeybourne WR11 .... 164 B5
Stourbridge DY9 .... 6 E6
Dudley St DY10 .... 27 E7
Dudnill Gr B32 .... 18 A8
Dufton Rd B32 .... 9 E4
Dugard Way WR9 .... 103 E7
Dugdale Ave B50 .... 136 C5
Dugdale Dr WR4 .... 116 C3
Duke of Edinburgh Way WR14 .... 139 B5
Duke St DY8 .... 6 A6
Duke's Way WR14 .... 153 B6
Dukes Rd B30 .... 20 A3
Dukes Way GL20 .... 196 F3
Dulais Cl B98 .... 70 E1
Dulvern Gr B14 .... 20 D5
Dumble Pit La B48 .... 52 F7
Dumbleton La WR15 .... 59 B6
Dumphouse La B48 .... 52 C3
Dunard Rd B90 .... 21 F3
Dunbar Cl
Birmingham B32 .... 9 D1
Kidderminster DY10 .... 28 C6
Dunchurch Cl B98 .... 71 F1
Dunchurch Dr B31 .... 18 E7
Dunclent Cres DY10 .... 28 B5
Dunclent La DY10 .... 28 E3
Duncombe St DY8 .... 5 D5
Dunedin Dr B45 .... 33 B1
Dunedin House B32 .... 9 F4
Dunhampton Dr DY10 .... 13 B1
Dunkirk Dr WR5 .... 129 A4
Dunley Rd
Astley & Dunley DY13 .... 61 F8
Rock DY12 .... 42 F2
Dunlin Dr DY10 .... 27 F2
Dunlop Rd B97 .... 89 D5
Dunmore Rd DY12 .... 26 D5
Dunmow Ave WR4 .... 116 C3
Dunn's La WR8 .... 169 C6
Dunnigan Rd B32 .... 9 F3
Dunnington Ave DY10 .... 13 A1
Dunnington CE Prim Sch B49 .... 135 D8
Dunns Bank DY5 .... 6 F7
Dunsford Cl DY5 .... 6 B7
Dunslade Cres DY5 .... 6 F8
Dunsley Dr DY7 .... 4 C4
Dunsley Rd Kinver DY7 .... 4 B4
Stourbridge DY8 .... 5 C4
Dunsmore Dr DY5 .... 6 F8
Dunsmore Gn GL19 .... 195 B5
Dunstall Cl B97 .... 70 B2
Dunstall Gr B29 .... 18 F8
Dunstall Rd B63 .... 7 D3
Dunster Cl
Birmingham B30 .... 20 C4
6 Worcester WR4 .... 116 B7
Durant Cl B45 .... 17 D1
Durcott La WR11 .... 161 F3
Durcott Rd WR11 .... 161 E3
Durham Cl B61 .... 48 E4
Durham Rd
Stourbridge DY8 .... 5 D8
Worcester WR5 .... 116 A3
Durnford Croft B14 .... 20 E1
Dursley La B98 .... 72 A3
Dusthouse La B60 .... 68 D7
Dutton St 2 WR3 .... 115 D4
Duxford Cl B97 .... 89 B8
Dwellings La B32 .... 9 B5
Dyas Rd B47 .... 36 A7
Dyer's La GL55 .... 178 F3
Dyson Dr WR14 .... 139 D1
Dyson Perrins CE High Sch The WR14 .... 138 F5

E

Eachway B45 .... 32 F6
Eachway Farm Cl B45 .... 33 A6
Eachway La B45 .... 33 A6
Eadie Mews B97 .... 70 D1
Eagle Cl 4 WR5 .... 128 C5
Eagle Croft B14 .... 20 E2
Eagle La DY14 .... 22 C4
Eagle Rd B98 .... 71 E5
Eagle Trad Est B63 .... 8 A4
Eardisley Cl B98 .... 71 F1
Earls Cl B97 .... 69 F2
Earls Comm Rd WR9 .... 106 C1
Earls Ferry Gdns B32 .... 18 B7
Earls High Sch The B63 .... 8 B4
Earls Way B63 .... 8 B4
Earlsdon Rd WR2 .... 127 F8
Earlswood Sta B94 .... 36 D1
Earlswood Trad Est B94 .... 53 C6
Early River Pl 5 DY12 .... 25 F3
Easemore Rd B98 .... 70 F5
Easenhall La B98 .... 71 E1
Easinghope La WR6 .... 111 F6
Easmore Cl B14 .... 20 D2
East Cl WR9 .... 85 E8
East Comer WR2 .... 114 E4
East Pk Dr WR9 .... 84 D4
East Rd Bromsgrove B60 .... 49 A1
Stourport-on-Severn DY13 .... 44 B5
East Side WR11 .... 149 A3
East St Brierley Hill DY5 .... 7 A8
Kidderminster DY10 .... 27 F6
Tewkesbury GL20 .... 196 E6
Worcester WR1 .... 115 C4
East Waterside WR8 .... 169 C6
Eastbank Dr WR3 .... 115 A7
Eastern Hill B96 .... 89 F2
Easterton Croft B14 .... 20 E2
Eastfield Cl WR3 .... 102 E3
Eastgrove Cottage Gdn* WR6 .... 81 D5
Eastham Rd B13 .... 21 C6
Eastleigh Dr B62 .... 17 A4
Eastnor Cl
Kidderminster DY10 .... 27 E2
Redditch B98 .... 70 E1
Worcester WR5 .... 128 E7
Easton Gr B47 .... 36 B7
Eastville B31 .... 19 B3
Eastward Rd WR14 .... 138 F6
Eastwick Dr 3 WR11 .... 161 C2
Eastwood Ct B96 .... 89 E1
Eastwood Dr DY10 .... 28 B5
Easy Row WR1 .... 115 B3
Eathorpe Cl B98 .... 71 E1
Eaton Rd WR14 .... 152 E3
Ebmore Dr B14 .... 20 D2
Ebrington Cl B14 .... 20 D4
Ebrington Dr WR4 .... 116 B7
Ebrington Rd WR14 .... 138 C2
Ebsdorf Cl 4 B50 .... 136 D5
Ebury Rd B30 .... 20 B4
Echells Cl B61 .... 48 D2
Eckersall Rd B38 .... 19 E3
Eckington CE Fst Sch WR10 .... 171 F7
Eckington Cl B98 .... 90 B8
Eckington Wlk B38 .... 34 E7
Eddy Rd DY10 .... 27 E7
Eden Cl Birmingham B31 .... 33 E8
Studley B80 .... 90 D3
Edenfield Cl B97 .... 70 A5
Edenhall Rd B32 .... 9 B6
Edenhurst Rd B31 .... 33 F7
Edgar St 2 WR1 .... 115 C1
Edge Hill DY7 .... 3 F4
Edge View Cl DY7 .... 3 F5
Edge View Wlk DY7 .... 3 F5
Edgecliff High Sch DY7 .... 4 B5
Edgehill Rd B31 .... 19 B1
Edgewood Cl B64 .... 7 F8
Edgewood Dr B45 .... 33 B1
Edgewood Rd
Birmingham, King's Norton B38 .... 34 F7
Birmingham, Rednall B45 .... 33 B6
Edgeworth Cl
Redditch B98 .... 71 C5
1 Worcester WR4 .... 116 A7
Edgioake La B96 .... 108 E6
Edgmond Cl B98 .... 71 D4
Edinburgh Cl DY10 .... 27 E8
Edinburgh Rd B68 .... 9 B8
Edison Gr B32 .... 9 D5
Edith Berry Ct 2 WR14 .... 139 B1
Edith Wlk WR14 .... 138 F1
Edmonton Cl 6 WR2 .... 127 F6
Ednall La B60 .... 48 F1
Edward Cl 3 WR5 .... 115 D1
Edward Pl 3 GL20 .... 196 F3
Edward Rd
Birmingham, Highter's Heath B14 .... 21 A1
Halesowen B63 .... 7 F4
Oldbury B68 .... 9 C8
Edward St
Evesham WR11 .... 161 D5
Redditch B97 .... 70 D4
Edward's La WR7 .... 130 C6
Edwin Ave (Road 4) DY10 .... 27 F1
Edwin Cres B60 .... 67 F7
Edwin Ct B60 .... 67 F7
Edwin Rd B30 .... 20 B7
Effingham Rd B13 .... 21 C7
Egdon La WR7 .... 130 D2
Egg La
Belbroughton DY9, DY10 .... 30 A5
North Claines WR3 .... 102 C6
Egghill La B31, B45 .... 18 B3
Eggington Rd DY8 .... 5 D6
Egginton Rd B28 .... 21 E5
Egremond Gdns 2 WR4 .... 116 C5
Egret Ct DY10 .... 28 A1
Eider Cl DY10 .... 28 B1
Elan Ave DY13 .... 43 E7
Elan Cl Bewdley DY12 .... 25 F4
Cookley DY10 .... 13 B4
Elan Rd B31 .... 18 C2
Elbury Mount Prim Sch WR4 .... 115 F6
Elbury Mount Schools WR4 .... 116 A6
Elbury Pk Rd WR4 .... 116 A4
Elderberry Cl
Stourbridge DY8 .... 5 C3
6 Stourport-on-Severn DY13 .... 43 E4
Elderfield Rd B30 .... 20 B3
Eldersfield Cl B98 .... 71 E7
Eldersfield Lawn CE Prim Sch GL19 .... 194 E2
Eldon Rd
Birmingham, Woodgate B32 .... 9 A3
Halesowen B62 .... 8 F3
Eldorado Cl B80 .... 90 D4
Eleanor Harrison Dr DY10 .... 13 B5
Elford Cl B14 .... 20 E5
Elgar Ave WR14 .... 139 C1
Elgar Birthplace (Museum) The* WR2 .... 113 F4
Elgar Cres WR9 .... 103 F8
Elgar Ct 3 WR3 .... 115 D4
Elgar Dr WR5 .... 141 C6
Elgar Mews 2 B60 .... 48 F2
Elgar Ret Pk WR4 .... 115 E7
Elgar Tech Coll WR3 .... 115 D7
Elgin Cl DY8 .... 6 A7
Eliot Rd WR3 .... 115 C6
Eliot Wlk DY10 .... 28 C6
Elizabeth Ave
Droitwich WR9 .... 85 A3
Worcester WR3 .... 102 B1
Elizabeth House DY9 .... 6 E5
Elizabeth Rd
Evesham WR11 .... 161 D2
Halesowen B63 .... 7 F3
Elizabeth Way B97 .... 70 D5
Elkstone Cl 3 WR4 .... 115 F7
Elkstone Covert B14 .... 20 C2
Ellenbrook Cl 6 B97 .... 70 B5
Ellerdene Cl B98 .... 89 D8
Ellerside Gr B31 .... 18 F2
Ellerslie Cl DY5 .... 6 D8
Ellerslie Rd B13 .... 21 C7
Elliot Gdns B45 .... 33 B5
Elliott Cl 1 B50 .... 136 C5
Ellis Rd WR2 .... 115 A1
Ellison Ave WR2 .... 114 E5
Ellsdon Rise WR5 .... 141 C7
Elm Cl Cookley DY10 .... 13 B4
Pebworth CV37 .... 150 E2
Stourbridge DY8 .... 5 D2
Elm Croft B68 .... 9 C7
Elm Ct B97 .... 70 D4
Elm Dr Blakedown DY10 .... 14 B2
Hartlebury DY10 .... 64 D8
Elm Gn Cl WR5 .... 128 C5
Elm Gr Bromsgrove B61 .... 49 A4
Kinver DY7 .... 4 C3
Stourport-on-Severn DY13 .... 62 D8
Elm Link Cl 1 WR2 .... 127 F7
Elm Pl Cookley DY10 .... 13 B4
Harvington DY10 .... 29 B3
Elm Rd
Birmingham, Bournville B30 .... 19 F8
Drakes Broughton WR10 .... 144 A6
Evesham WR11 .... 161 F4
Kidderminster DY10 .... 28 A6
Northway GL20 .... 197 E8
Redditch B97 .... 70 D4
Worcester WR2 .... 115 A3
Elm Tree Gr B63 .... 7 D6
Elm Tree Rd B30 .... 20 A6
Elmbridge Cl B63 .... 7 D5
Elmbridge La
Elmbridge WR9 .... 66 A4
Rushock WR9 .... 46 D1
Elmbury Dr GL20 .... 197 B6
Elmcroft Ave B32 .... 9 A1
Elmdale B62 .... 9 A7
Elmdale Cres B31 .... 18 E4
Elmdale Dr DY10 .... 28 C5
Elmdale Gr B31 .... 18 E4
Elmdale Rd WR3 .... 115 B8
Elmfield Gdns WR5 .... 115 D1
Elmfield Rd 2 DY11 .... 45 A1
Elmfield Rudolf Steiner Sch DY8 .... 6 A3
Elmfield Wlk 1 DY13 .... 43 E4
Elmhurst Cl B97 .... 89 D4
Elmley Castle CE Fst Sch WR10 .... 173 E7
Elmley Cl
Elmley Lovett WR9 .... 65 B6
Great Malvern WR14 .... 139 B1
Kidderminster DY11 .... 27 B3
Elmley Gr B30 .... 20 B2
Elmley House 9 B97 .... 70 A4
Elmley La WR9 .... 65 B6
Elmley Rd WR11 .... 174 B1
Elms Cl B38 .... 34 C8
Elms Dr WR13 .... 166 A8
Elms Sch WR13 .... 166 A8
Elmside WR11 .... 161 F4
Elmstone Cl B97 .... 89 C5
Elmvil Rd GL20 .... 197 C7
Elmwood Gr B47 .... 36 A6
Elmwoods B32 .... 9 B2
Elsma Rd B68 .... 9 C8
Elton Rd 6 DY12 .... 25 F3
Eltric Rd WR3 .... 115 B8
Ely Cl
Kidderminster DY11 .... 27 A6
Worcester WR5 .... 116 A1
Ely Gr B32 .... 9 F4
Embassy Ind Est 1 DY9 .... 6 F5
Emerald Rd WR2 .... 114 E3
Emery Ct DY10 .... 27 E7
Emes Cl WR10 .... 158 C8
Emperor Dr WR5 .... 128 F5
Emsworth Gr B14 .... 20 D6
Endeavour Pl DY13 .... 44 A2
Enfield Ind Est B97 .... 70 D5
Enfield Rd B97 .... 89 D5
Engadine Cl WR14 .... 153 A5
Engadine Rd B60 .... 49 C1
Engine La
Stourbridge DY9 .... 6 D6
7 Stourport-on-Severn DY13 .... 44 A3
Enigma Bsns Pk WR14 .... 139 C4
Ennerdale Cl WR4 .... 116 A5
Ennerdale Dr B63 .... 7 D2
Ennerdale Rd DY13 .... 43 F6
Enterprise Dr DY9 .... 6 F6
Enterprise Way WR11 .... 175 F8
Enville Pl DY8 .... 5 E5
Enville Rd DY7 .... 3 F6
Enville St DY8 .... 5 F5
Epping Cl B45 .... 18 B2
Epsom Cl
Fernhill Heath WR3 .... 102 F3
Redditch B97 .... 89 C8
Epsom Ct 16 B29 .... 19 C7
Epsom Rd B61 .... 32 A1
Erica Cl Birmingham B29 .... 19 A8
Kidderminster DY11 .... 12 D1
Erneley Cl 1 DY13 .... 43 F1
Ernest Ct B38 .... 20 A1
Erwood Cl B97 .... 70 B2
Eskdale Cl 7 WR4 .... 115 F5
Eskdale Wlk DY5 .... 6 B8
Esmond Cl B30 .... 19 D5
Essex Cl
3 Bowling Green WR2 .... 127 C2
Worcester WR2 .... 114 D2
Essex Ct 5 B29 .... 19 C7
Essex Gdns DY8 .... 5 D7
Eston Ave WR14 .... 153 C8
Eton Dr DY8 .... 6 A3
Eton Wlk DY9 .... 15 A6
Ettingley Cl B98 .... 90 B5
Etwall Rd B28 .... 21 E6
Eunal Ct B97 .... 89 E5
Evans Cl DY11 .... 12 C3
Evelench La WR9 .... 117 B8
Evendene Rd WR11 .... 161 A3
Evendine Cl WR5 .... 128 D8
Evendine La WR13 .... 166 A7
Evenlode Cl 4 B98 .... 70 F1
Everard Cl 4 WR2 .... 114 E5
Everard Pl 5 WR2 .... 114 E5
Evers St DY5 .... 7 A8
Eversley Cl WR14 .... 139 B2
Eversley Gr WR14 .... 139 B2
Evertons Cl WR9 .... 84 E1
Eves Croft B32 .... 9 C1
Evesham Arts Ctr* WR11 .... 161 E6
Evesham Coll WR11 .... 161 D2
Evesham Com Hospl WR11 .... 161 D3
Evesham Ct DY11 .... 27 D5
Evesham Ctry Pk* WR11 .... 147 E1
Evesham High Sch WR11 .... 161 E2
Evesham House B60 .... 49 B3
Evesham Mews 9 B97 .... 70 E3
Evesham Rd
Astwood Bank B96 .... 108 E8
Broadway WR12 .... 177 B2
Childswickham WR12 .... 176 F5
Church Lench WR11 .... 134 A2
Cleeve Prior WR11 .... 148 F5
Cookhill B49 .... 122 B7
Fladbury WR10 .... 146 C3
Harvington WR11 .... 148 A7
Hill & Moor WR10 .... 145 D3
Norton & Lenchwick WR11 .... 147 F5
Redditch B96, B97 .... 89 E3
Salford Priors WR11 .... 135 E2
Stoulton WR7 .... 130 C6
Temple Grafton B50 .... 137 D7
Weethley B49 .... 122 B4
Evesham Sports & Leisure Ctr WR11 .... 161 D1
Evesham Sq 3 B97 .... 70 E3
Evesham St B97 .... 70 E3
Evesham Sta WR11 .... 161 D5
Evesham Wlk 2 B97 .... 70 E4
Eveson Rd DY8 .... 5 E2
Ewloe Cl DY10 .... 27 E1
Exchange St DY10 .... 27 E6
Exe Croft B31 .... 34 B8
Exeter Cl DY11 .... 27 A6
Exeter Rd WR5 .... 116 A2
Exford Cl DY5 .... 6 B7
Exhall Cl B98 .... 71 D5
Exmoor Ct B61 .... 49 A4
Exmoor Dr B61 .... 49 A4
Eymore Cl B29 .... 19 B6
Eyton Cl B98 .... 71 D3

F

Fabian Cl B45 .... 18 A2
Fabricius Ave WR9 .... 84 F2
Facet Rd B38 .... 20 A2
Factory La B61 .... 48 F1
Fairbairn Ave WR3 .... 115 B8
Fairbourne Gdns B97 .... 89 C7
Fairfax Rd B31 .... 34 A8
Fairfield Cl WR4 .... 115 F5
Fairfield Dr DY7 .... 4 A3
Fairfield Fst Sch B61 .... 31 D3
Fairfield House B60 .... 49 B3
Fairfield La DY11 .... 12 B3
Fairfield Pl WR11 .... 161 D2
Fairfield Rd
Birmingham B14 .... 20 E8
Bournheath B61 .... 31 D1
Evesham WR11 .... 161 D2
Halesowen B63 .... 8 A2
Fairfield Rise DY8 .... 5 D5
Fairford Cl B98 .... 71 E7
Fairlie Cres B38 .... 19 D1
Fairlight Dr B45 .... 33 A1
Fairmead Rise B38 .... 19 E1
Fairmile Rd B63 .... 8 A6
Fairmont Rd B60 .... 68 B8
Fairoak Dr B60 .... 67 F6
Fairway Birmingham B31 .... 18 E3
Northway GL20 .... 197 E8
Fairway Dr B45 .... 32 F6
Fairway Prim Sch B38 .... 19 D1
Fairway The
Birmingham B38 .... 19 D2
Worcester WR4 .... 116 A4
Fairways WR10 .... 144 D1
Fairways Ave DY8 .... 5 E2
Fairways Cl DY8 .... 5 E2
Fairways Dr B60 .... 50 B5
Fairways Wlk 3 WR10 .... 144 D1
Fakenham Croft B17 .... 9 F7
Falcon Cl
Droitwich Spa WR9 .... 104 B8
Kidderminster DY10 .... 27 E2
5 Worcester WR5 .... 128 C5
Falcon Cres B50 .... 136 E5

Falcon Rise DY8 .. 5 C6
Falcon View B30 .. 20 A4
Falconry Ctr* DY9 .. 14 F3
Falfield Gr B31 .. 33 E7
Falkland Croft B30 .. 20 B6
Falkland Rd WR11 .. 161 F1
Fallow Wlk B32 .. 9 A2
Fallowfield Ave B28 .. 21 F5
Fallowfield Rd B63 .. 7 D3
Fallowfields Cl B61 .. 48 E3
Falmouth WR4 .. 116 D6
Falstaff Ave B47 .. 36 A6
Falstaff Dr WR9 .. 103 E8
Falstaff House B13 .. 21 D7
Fancott Rd B31 .. 19 A5
Far Moor La B98 .. 72 A3
Far Wood Rd B31 .. 18 E8
Faraday Ave B32 .. 9 D5
Faraday Ct B32 .. 9 D5
Farfield
Kidderminster DY10 .. 27 F5
Stoke Prior B60 .. 67 F4
Farfield Cl B31 .. 19 B2
Farfield Studios DY10 .. 27 F5
Farlands Dr DY8 .. 6 A3
Farlands Rd DY8 .. 6 A3
Farleigh Rd WR10 .. 158 C8
Farley La B62 .. 16 F1
Farley Rd WR14 .. 139 B4
Farley St WR2 .. 114 E4
Farlie Cl 2 WR5 .. 141 C6
Farlow Cl B98 .. 71 D3
Farlow Rd B31 .. 19 C3
Farm Bank Rd WR9 .. 84 B7
Farm Cl
Kidderminster DY11 .. 27 B2
9 Northway GL20 .. 184 E1
Worcester WR3 .. 115 E7
Farm La Bredon GL20 .. 184 E6
South Littleton WR11 .. 148 F1
Farm Rd Redditch B98 .. 71 A3
Stourport-on-Severn DY13 .. 44 B4
Farm St WR10 .. 146 A1
Farmbrook Cl 6 WR2 .. 114 D1
Farmcote Cl B97 .. 89 D4
Farmcroft Rd DY9 .. 6 E2
Farmdale Gr B45 .. 33 A6
Farmers Ct
6 Droitwich WR9 .. 84 D5
Halesowen B63 .. 7 F4
Farmers La WR12 .. 176 E2
Farmers Rd B60 .. 67 E7
Farmers Way WR9 .. 84 D5
Farmside Cl DY9 .. 7 A3
Farnborough Cl B98 .. 71 F1
Farnbury Croft B38 .. 20 B2
Farndale Cl DY5 .. 6 B6
Farne Ave WR5 .. 128 A6
Farnham Gn 10 WR4 .. 116 C6
Farren Rd B31 .. 18 D1
Farrier Cl B60 .. 67 E6
Farrier St 7 WR1 .. 115 B3
Farriers Way WR9 .. 84 D4
Farthing La B97 .. 70 B5
Fastlea Rd B32 .. 9 D1
Fatherless Barn Cres B63 .. 7 D5
Faulkner Cl DY8 .. 5 F4
Fawley Gr B14 .. 20 B5
Fearnings Cotts B97 .. 89 D5
Featherbed La B97 .. 89 C5
Featherstone Rd B14 .. 20 E6
Feckenham CE Sch B96 .. 88 E1
Feckenham House B60 .. 49 B3
Feckenham Rd
Astwood Bank B96 .. 89 E2
Redditch, Headless Cross B97 .. 89 C8
Redditch, Hunt End B97 .. 89 C4
Feckenham Wyldemoor Nature Reserve* B96 .. 107 E5
Felbrigg Cl DY5 .. 6 D8
Feldon La B62 .. 8 E7
Fels Ave WR4 .. 116 C3
Felton Cl B98 .. 71 E1
Fen Cl DY10 .. 27 E8
Fennel Rd DY5 .. 6 C7
Fenton Rd B47 .. 36 A7
Fenwick Cl B97 .. 70 B1
Ferguson Dr DY11 .. 27 A1
Fern Rd WR2 .. 114 E4
Fernbank Cl B63 .. 7 E2
Ferndale Cl Catshill B61 .. 32 A1
Hagley DY9 .. 15 A5
Hartlebury DY13 .. 44 C3
3 Worcester WR3 .. 102 A1
Ferndale Cres DY11 .. 27 B8
Ferndale Pk DY9 .. 15 C8
Ferndale Rd B28 .. 21 F8
Ferney Hill Ave B97 .. 70 C3
Fernhill Gr WR14 .. 139 A1
Fernihough Ave WR11 .. 164 B5
Fernleigh B60 .. 49 A1
Fernwood Cl B98 .. 90 B5
Fernwood Croft B14 .. 20 E6
Fernwoods B32 .. 9 B2
Ferry Cl WR2 .. 114 F4
Ferry La
Offenham WR11 .. 162 A8
Ripple GL20 .. 182 F8
Field Ave B31 .. 18 F5
Field Barn La WR10 .. 160 C5
Field Cl Bromsgrove B60 .. 67 E6
Worcester WR4 .. 115 E6
Field Cottage Dr DY8 .. 6 B3
Field End 7 DY13 .. 43 E4
Field Farm La B98 .. 71 D2
Field La Birmingham B32 .. 18 B8
Clent DY9 .. 15 D4
Stourbridge DY8 .. 6 A3
Tenbury SY8 .. 54 D2
Field Rd WR4 .. 115 F6
Field Wlk WR5 .. 128 D7
Fielden Cl WR11 .. 161 E3
Fielden Row WR4 .. 116 C3
Fieldfare Cl WR14 .. 138 D6
Fieldfare Ct DY10 .. 28 A1
Fieldfare Rd DY9 .. 6 D4
Fieldhead Cl 3 WR2 .. 114 D1
Fieldhouse La B62 .. 16 E4
Fields Cl WR11 .. 162 E2
Fields La WR12 .. 177 E3
Fieldways Cl B47 .. 36 A7
Fiery Hill Dr B45 .. 50 C8
Fiery Hill Rd B45 .. 50 C8
Fimbrell Cl DY5 .. 6 A8
Finch La WR11 .. 148 B6
Finchfield Cl DY8 .. 5 C4
Findon Cl B97 .. 70 A5
Findon St DY10 .. 27 F6
Finmere Rd B28 .. 21 F8
Finsbury Dr DY5 .. 6 C7
Finstall Fst Sch B60 .. 49 B1
Finstall Rd
Bromsgrove B60 .. 68 C8
Finstall B60 .. 49 D1
Fir Croft DY5 .. 6 C8
Fir Gr Birmingham B14 .. 20 F5
Stourbridge DY8 .. 5 D6
Fir Tree Cl B97 .. 70 D4
Fir Tree Rd WR3 .. 102 F3
Fir Way WR4 .. 115 E6
Firbank Cl B30 .. 19 E7
Fircroft B31 .. 18 F8
Fircroft Cl B60 .. 67 D6
Fircroft Coll B29 .. 19 D8
Firecrest Way DY10 .. 28 B1
Firhill Croft B14 .. 20 D2
Firland The WR8 .. 155 F4
Firlands Cl WR3 .. 102 F3
Firmstone Ct DY8 .. 5 E7
Firmstone St DY8 .. 5 E7
Firs Cl
Great Malvern WR14 .. 152 F6
Marlbrook B60 .. 32 D1
Firs Cl The DY10 .. 28 A5
Firs Ind Est DY13 .. 44 B7
Firs The DY10 .. 28 A5
Firsby Rd B32 .. 9 E5
First Ave WR2 .. 128 A7
First Mdw Piece B32 .. 9 E4
Firth Dr Birmingham B14 .. 21 B5
Halesowen B62 .. 8 E8
Firth Pk Cres B62 .. 8 E8
Fish Hill
Broadway WR12 .. 190 F7
Redditch B97 .. 70 E4
Fish House La B60 .. 67 E4
Fish St WR1 .. 115 B2
Fisher Cl B45 .. 17 E2
Fishers Dr B90 .. 36 F5
Fishing Line Rd B97 .. 70 E5
Fiskin La WR4 .. 116 C3
Fitcher Cl WR2 .. 114 E6
Fitz Roy Ave B17 .. 9 F7
Fitzgerald Pl DY5 .. 6 B6
Fitzhamon Pk GL20 .. 197 F7
Fitzroy Rd B31 .. 18 D3
Fitzwilliam Cl 2 WR2 .. 114 D3
Five Mile Dr GL56 .. 191 F4
Five Oaks Cl WR14 .. 153 D8
Five Ways Blackheath B64 .. 7 C8
Churchill DY10 .. 14 A5
Fladbury CE Aided Fst Sch WR10 .. 146 B1
Fladbury Cl B98 .. 90 B8
Flag Mdw Wlk WR1 .. 115 B5
Flanders Cl B98 .. 71 D5
Flatlea B31 .. 18 F4
Flats The B61 .. 48 F3
Flavel Rd B60 .. 67 E7
Flavell Cl B32 .. 9 B1
Flax Cl B47 .. 36 A5
Flax Gdns B38 .. 34 F8
Flax Piece WR7 .. 131 C8
Flaxley Cl B98 .. 72 A4
Fleece Inn (NT) The* WR11 .. 163 C4
Fleece Rd WR12 .. 177 D1
Fleet La GL20 .. 184 B5
Fleet Rd GL20 .. 184 A6
Fleetwood Ave WR2 .. 127 B2
Fleming Rd B32 .. 9 D5
Fletcher St DY9 .. 6 F5
Fletton Gr B14 .. 21 A3
Flint Cl DY10 .. 27 E2
Florence Ave WR9 .. 84 E1
Florence Cl 4 WR5 .. 141 C6
Florence Rd B14 .. 20 F8
Flyford Cl B98 .. 70 F1
Flyford Croft B29 .. 9 F2
Flyford Flavell Fst Sch WR7 .. 119 E1
Fockbury Mill La B61 .. 48 E5
Fockbury Rd B61 .. 48 B5
Fold The B38 .. 20 A1
Foley Ave DY11 .. 44 C8
Foley Bsns Pk DY11 .. 44 C8
Foley Dr DY11 .. 44 B8
Foley Gdns B60 .. 67 E3
Foley Gr DY11 .. 44 B8
Foley Ind Est DY11 .. 27 D3
Foley Inf Sch DY7 .. 4 A3
Foley Pk Fst Sch DY11 .. 27 D3
Foley Rd Stourbridge DY9 .. 6 C2
Worcester WR2 .. 115 A1
Foley St DY7 .. 4 A4
Foley Terr WR14 .. 152 E8
Foley Wlk 3 WR2 .. 128 A8
Folkes Rd DY9 .. 7 A6
Folly Rd WR6 .. 124 F7
Folly The B97 .. 89 D8
Ford Abbey HR6 .. 92 E1
Ford Cl WR14 .. 153 C8
Ford La WR9 .. 85 B6
Ford Rd B61 .. 48 E1
Fordbridge Cl B97 .. 70 C1
Forde Hall La B94 .. 72 F8
Forde Way Gdns B38 .. 34 D7
Forder Gr B14 .. 21 A2
Fordhouse La B30 .. 20 B6
Fordhouse Rd B60 .. 49 B1
Fordraught La B62 .. 17 B1
Fordrough The
Birmingham B31 .. 19 C1
Hollywood B90 .. 36 C7
Fords Rd B90 .. 36 E7
Foredraft Cl B32 .. 9 C2
Foredraft St B63 .. 7 D5
Foredraught B80 .. 90 E4
Foredraught La WR9 .. 104 A1
Foredrift Cl B98 .. 70 E2
Foregate St
Astwood Bank B96 .. 89 E1
Worcester WR1 .. 115 B3
Foregate St Sta WR1 .. 115 B3
Forelands Gr B61 .. 67 D8
Forest Cl 10 Bewdley DY12 .. 25 F3
3 Bewdley DY12 .. 26 A3
Lickey End B60 .. 49 B6
Worcester WR2 .. 114 E4
Forest Dale B45 .. 33 B6
Forest Dr DY7 .. 3 F3
Forest Gate WR11 .. 161 E2
Forest La B60 .. 87 D5
Forest Rd B68 .. 9 C7
Forest The WR9 .. 84 D8
Forest View B97 .. 89 E6
Forest Way B47 .. 36 B6
Forester Way DY10 .. 27 E3
Foresters Rd GL20 .. 196 E5
Forfar Wlk B38 .. 19 D2
Forge Dr B61 .. 48 F3
Forge La
Belbroughton DY9 .. 30 D7
Blackheath B64 .. 7 B8
Blakedown DY10 .. 14 B1
Halesowen B62 .. 8 C5
Forge Mdws WR6 .. 97 E7
Forge Mill Needle Mus* B98 .. 70 F6
Forge Mill Rd B98 .. 70 F6
Forge Rd DY8 .. 5 F6
Forge The B63 .. 7 B8
Forge Trad Est B62 .. 8 C5
Forhill House B38 .. 34 F3
Forrell Gr B31 .. 34 B7
Forresters Rd WR15 .. 55 F6
Forshaw Heath La B94 .. 53 A7
Forshaw Heath Rd B94 .. 36 C1
Forsythia Cl B31 .. 18 F8
Fort Royal* WR5 .. 115 C1
Fort Royal Hill WR5 .. 115 C1
Fort Royal La 2 WR5 .. 115 D1
Forth Gr B38 .. 34 E8
Forth Way B62 .. 8 E8
Fort-Mahon Pl 8 DY12 .. 25 F3
Forward Cotts B48 .. 50 F6
Fossil Dr B45 .. 33 A7
Foster Ave B80 .. 90 E3
Foster Cres 3 DY7 .. 4 A4
Foster Dr WR9 .. 65 B5
Foster Pl DY8 .. 5 E6
Foster Rd WR11 .. 161 E3
Foster St Kinver DY7 .. 4 A4
6 Stourbridge DY8 .. 6 A5
Foster St E DY8 .. 6 A5
Fosters Gn B60 .. 87 D7
Fotheringhay WR4 .. 116 D6
Foundry St
9 Stourport-on-Severn DY13 .. 44 A4
Worcester WR1 .. 115 C2
Fountain Cl B31 .. 33 E6
Fountain Ct 1 WR11 .. 161 D3
Fountain Gdns 2 WR11 .. 161 D3
Fountain Pl 12 WR1 .. 115 A5
Four Acres B32 .. 9 C4
Four Dwellings High Sch B32 .. 9 B5
Four Dwellings Inf Sch B32 .. 9 C5
Four Dwellings Jun Sch B32 .. 9 B5
Four Oaks Cl B98 .. 89 D8
Four Pools Ind Est WR11 .. 161 D2
Four Pools La 3 WR11 .. 161 E2
Four Pools Rd WR11 .. 161 E2
Fourlands Rd B31 .. 18 E6
Fowler Ave 5 WR4 .. 116 C3
Fowler Pl 2 DY13 .. 44 A5
Fownhope Cl B98 .. 71 E3
Fox Covert DY8 .. 5 E5
Fox Dr WR5 .. 128 F5
Fox Hill B29 .. 19 C8
Fox Hill Cl B29 .. 19 C8
Fox Hollies Rd B28 .. 21 F7
Fox Hollow Cl B45 .. 33 C7
Fox La Bromsgrove B61 .. 67 E8
Chaddesley Corbett DY10 .. 46 D6
Kempsey WR5 .. 142 A8
Lindridge WR6 .. 59 D7
Norton Juxta Kempsey WR5 .. 129 A1
Foxcote Cl B98 .. 71 F4
Foxcote La B63, DY9 .. 7 A4
Foxes Cl B60 .. 50 B5
Foxes Hill WR5 .. 141 D6
Foxes Mdw B30 .. 19 F4
Foxes Ridge B64 .. 7 E8
Foxfield B31 .. 18 F4
Foxfield Dr DY8 .. 6 A3
Foxglove Cl
1 Evesham WR11 .. 161 F1
Great Malvern WR14 .. 153 D7
Foxglove Rd WR5 .. 128 C4
Foxglove Way B60 .. 49 C6
Foxhill Barns B48 .. 50 E5
Foxhill La B48 .. 50 E5
Foxholes La
Feckenham B97 .. 88 F6
Redditch B97 .. 89 A6
Foxholes The DY10 .. 27 F8
Foxhollies Dr B63 .. 7 E4
Foxhollow B61 .. 67 D8
Foxhope Cl B38 .. 20 B2
Foxhunt Rd B63 .. 7 E2
Foxhunter Cl WR9 .. 104 B8
Foxland Ave B45 .. 33 C7
Foxlea Rd B63 .. 7 D1
Foxlydiate Cres B97 .. 70 A4
Foxlydiate La B97 .. 69 F3
Foxlydiate Mews 3 B97 .. 70 A4
Foxwalks Ave B61 .. 67 D8
Foxwell St WR5 .. 128 E8
Foyle Rd B38 .. 19 F1
Fradley Cl B30 .. 19 D4
Framlingham Cl 7 WR5 .. 128 D6
Frampton Cl B30 .. 19 D7
Frampton Dr 3 WR12 .. 177 E4
Frances Rd B30 .. 20 A5
Franche Fst Sch DY11 .. 27 B8
Franche Mid Sch DY11 .. 27 B8
Franche Rd 6 DY11 .. 12 B1
Franchecourt Dr DY11 .. 12 B1
Franchise St DY11 .. 27 C5
Francis Rd
Bromsgrove B60 .. 67 F7
Stourbridge DY8 .. 5 C5
3 Stourport-on-Severn DY13 .. 43 E6
Francis Wlk B31 .. 34 A7
Frankley Ave B62 .. 8 F5
Frankley Beeches Rd B31 .. 18 D3
Frankley Com High Sch B45 .. 17 F1
Frankley Gn B32 .. 17 D5
Frankley Gn La B32 .. 17 E5
Frankley Hill La B32 .. 18 A4
Frankley Ind Pk B45 .. 18 B1
Frankley La B31, B32 .. 18 D6
Frankley Lodge Rd B31 .. 18 D4
Frankley Rd B68 .. 9 B8
Franklin Cl 1 WR2 .. 127 F6
Franklin Rd B30 .. 19 F5
Franklin Way B30 .. 19 F6
Franklin's La WR11 .. 134 C5
Frankton Cl B98 .. 90 E8
Fraser Cl WR14 .. 153 A6
Freda Eddy Ct 3 DY10 .. 27 E6
Frederick Eary House B98 .. 90 B7
Frederick Rd (Road 1) DY10 .. 27 F1
Frederick Rd
Great Malvern WR14 .. 138 F4
Oldbury B68 .. 9 D7
Fredericks Cl DY8 .. 5 E4
Freeman Ct DY11 .. 27 B3
Freemans Cl GL20 .. 183 F7
Freemantle Dr WR5 .. 141 C6
French Cl WR10 .. 144 C1
Frenchlands La WR2 .. 113 E7
Freshwater Dr DY5 .. 6 B8
Friar St Droitwich WR9 .. 84 F3
9 Worcester WR1 .. 115 C2
Friars Gorse DY7 .. 5 C8
Friday Cl 7 B50 .. 136 D5
Friday Furlong B50 .. 136 D5
Friday St CV37 .. 150 E2
Friesland Cl WR3 .. 115 D7
Fringe Gn B60 .. 68 A7
Fringe Gn Cl B60 .. 68 A7
Fringe Mdw Rd B98 .. 71 F6
Froggery La WR7 .. 143 A8
Froglands La WR11 .. 149 B8
Frogmill Com Jun Sch B45 .. 18 B2
Frogmill Rd B45 .. 18 B2
Frome Way B14 .. 20 D6
Front Cotts B48 .. 50 F6
Front St CV37 .. 150 D2
Froxmere Cl WR7 .. 117 F5
Froxmere Rd WR7 .. 117 F5
Fruitlands WR14 .. 152 E4
Fry Cl WR5 .. 116 C2
Fryer Rd B31 .. 34 B7
Fryers Cl DY14 .. 22 B4
Fugelmere Cl B17 .. 9 F7
Fulbert Rd WR10 .. 158 C7
Fulbrook Cl B98 .. 71 C5
Fulbrook Gr B29 .. 18 F8
Fulford Hall Rd B90, B94 .. 36 D3
Fulmar Cres DY10 .. 28 B2
Fulton Cl B60 .. 49 B1
Fulwood Ave B62 .. 8 F8
Furlong Ct B63 .. 7 C6
Furlong La B63 .. 7 D6
Furlong Mdw B31 .. 19 C2
Furlongs Cl 1 DY14 .. 22 D5
Furlongs Rd
Cleobury Mortimer DY14 .. 22 C5
Pershore WR10 .. 144 E2
Upton upon Severn WR8 .. 169 C4
Furlongs The DY8 .. 6 B3
Furnace Hill B63 .. 8 B5
Furnace La B63 .. 8 B5
Furness Cl 3 WR4 .. 115 F5
Furrows The B60 .. 67 D6
Furze La B98 .. 72 A4

G

Gaddesby Rd B14 .. 20 F8
Gadwell Rd GL20 .. 197 A5
Gainsborough Cl WR13 .. 167 C5
Gainsborough Hill DY8 .. 6 A3
Gainsborough Mews DY11 .. 27 B5
Gainsborough Trad Est DY9 .. 6 C4
Gainsford Dr B62 .. 8 B6
Galahad Way DY13 .. 43 F4
Gallipoli Dr WR5 .. 128 F4
Galton Rd B67 .. 9 F8
Galtons La DY9 .. 31 A7
Gamekeepers Dr 13 WR4 .. 115 F6
Gamson Cl DY10 .. 27 E4
Ganborough Cl B98 .. 71 E1
Gander La GL20 .. 196 E5
Gannaway La GL20 .. 197 B7
Gannow Gn La B45 .. 17 D1
Gannow Manor Cres B45 .. 17 E2
Gannow Manor Gdns B45 .. 17 F1
Gannow Rd B45 .. 32 E7
Gannow Wlk B45 .. 32 E7
Garden Cl
Birmingham, Frankley B45 .. 18 A2
Dumbleton WR11 .. 187 F5
Mickleton GL55 .. 165 D3
Garden Stiles WR10 .. 158 C8
Gardeners Cl DY11 .. 27 C8
Gardens Cl WR8 .. 169 C5
Gardens The WR11 .. 161 D6
Gardens Wlk WR8 .. 169 C6
Gardners Cl 8 WR4 .. 115 F6
Gardners Mdw DY12 .. 26 B3
Garganey Ct DY10 .. 27 F1
Garibaldi Terr B60 .. 49 A1
Garland Cres B62 .. 8 E8
Garland Rd DY13 .. 43 D6
Garland Way B31 .. 19 C4
Garrard Cl WR11 .. 135 F3
Garratts Wlk B14 .. 20 E1
Garth Ct WR5 .. 141 B7
Garth The B14 .. 21 D4
Garway Cl B98 .. 71 E1
Gas Sq B61 .. 48 F1
Gateley Cl B98 .. 72 A4
Gateley Rd B68 .. 9 D7
Gauden Rd DY9 .. 6 E2
Gaunts The B48 .. 51 B6
Gawtree Way 6 WR4 .. 116 C5
Gay Hill La B38 .. 35 B8
Gaydon Cl B98 .. 70 F1
Gayfield Ave DY5 .. 6 D8
Gaymore Rd DY10 .. 13 B5
Gazala Dr WR5 .. 129 A4
Gedney Cl B90 .. 21 C3
Geneva Ave WR14 .. 153 A5
Geneva Cl WR3 .. 115 A8
Geneva Cres WR7 .. 117 F4
Genners App B31 .. 18 D8
Genners La B31 .. 18 D7
Gentian Cl B31 .. 18 F6
Geoffrey Chaucer Wlk 4 WR9 .. 103 E8
Geoffrey Rd B90 .. 21 F3
George Baylis Rd WR9 .. 84 E5
George Dance Cl 2 DY10 .. 28 B6
George Dowty Dr 1 GL20 .. 184 E1
George La WR10 .. 145 B4
George Law Ct DY10 .. 27 F5
George Rd
Alvechurch B48 .. 51 A5
Halesowen B63 .. 7 F4
George St
1 Bromsgrove B61 .. 48 F2
Evesham WR11 .. 161 C5
Kidderminster DY10 .. 27 F6
Worcester WR1 .. 115 C2
George Wlk 5 B97 .. 70 E3
George's Elm La B50 .. 136 E8
Georgina Ave WR2 .. 128 A8
Gerald Rd DY8 .. 5 E7
Geraldine Cl WR14 .. 153 B7
Geraldine Rd WR14 .. 153 B7
Gheluvelt Ave DY10 .. 27 F7
Gheluvelt Ct 6 DY13 .. 43 F4
Gibb La B61 .. 49 A8
Gibbet La Kinver DY7 .. 4 E5

Gibbet La *continued*
Stourbridge DY7 .....5 B4
Gibbons Cres
1 Stourport-on-Severn DY13 .....43 F4
7 Stourport-on-Severn DY13 .....44 A4
Gibbs Cl WR10 .....145 E3
Gibbs Hill Rd B31 .....34 C7
Gibbs La WR11 .....148 A1
Gibbs Rd Redditch B98 .....71 A5
Stourbridge DY9 .....7 A5
Gibraltar DY7 .....4 B4
Gibson Gr WR14 .....138 E3
Giffard Dr WR13 .....167 C5
Gig Bridge La WR10 .....144 C2
Gig Mill Prim Sch DY8 .....5 E3
Gigmill Way DY8 .....5 E4
Gilbanks Rd DY8 .....5 D7
Gilbert Rd
Bromsgrove B60 .....67 E7
1 Great Malvern WR14 .....153 B8
Gilbert Scott Way DY10 .....27 F7
Gilbertstone Cl B98 .....70 E1
Gildas Ave B38 .....20 A1
Gilgal DY13 .....44 A4
Gillam St WR3 .....115 C5
Gilmour Cres WR3 .....102 C1
Gilt Edge Club Leisure Ctr DY13 .....44 A8
Gimble Wlk B17 .....9 F7
Gipsy La Kinver DY11 .....4 A1
Wolverley & Cookley DY11 .....3 F1
Gisburn Cl 5 B97 .....70 B5
GK Davies Trad Est DY9 .....7 A6
Glade The
Great Malvern WR14 .....139 C1
Stourbridge DY9 .....6 E5
Gladstone Dr DY8 .....5 D6
Gladstone Rd DY8 .....5 D6
Glasbury Croft B38 .....34 E7
Glasshouse Hill DY8 .....6 B3
Glastonbury Cl DY11 .....27 A6
Glastonbury Rd B14 .....21 C5
Gleads Croft B62 .....9 A3
Glebe Cl
Bidford-on-Avon B50 .....136 D4
Redditch B98 .....71 D2
Worcester WR2 .....114 F2
Glebe La DY8 .....5 E4
Glebe Rd Alvechurch B48 .....51 A7
Aston Somerville WR12 .....175 F1
Glebe The
Belbroughton DY9 .....30 E6
Beoley B98 .....71 F7
Great Witley WR6 .....61 B1
Glebeland Dr 8 GL20 .....184 F6
Glen Devon Cl B45 .....18 A2
Glen Rd DY8 .....5 F3
Glen Rise B13 .....21 C6
Glen Side B32 .....9 D2
Glen The B60 .....50 A5
Glenavon Rd B14 .....21 A3
Glencoe Rd 3 WR11 .....161 F4
Glendale 3 WR9 .....84 D1
Glendale Cl B63 .....8 B4
Glendene Cres B38 .....34 C7
Gleneagles Dr B60 .....50 A5
Glenelg Dr DY8 .....6 B2
Glenfield Cl B97 .....89 D6
Glengarry Cl B32 .....18 B7
Glenhill Dr B38 .....35 A8
Glenmoor WR10 .....171 F8
Glenmore Dr B38 .....19 D2
Glenridding Cl 3 WR4 .....116 A5
Glenroyde B38 .....34 E7
Glenthorne Ave WR4 .....115 F5
Glenwood Cl DY5 .....6 D8
Glenwood Rd B38 .....34 D8
Gloster Ades Rd WR11 .....163 E3
Gloucester Cl WR14 .....139 C5
Gloucester Dr WR13 .....139 F3
Gloucester La GL55 .....165 D4
Gloucester Rd GL20 .....196 D5
Gloucester Way DY12 .....26 B4
Glover Cl B28 .....21 F6
Glover St B98 .....70 E3
Glyn Farm Rd B32 .....9 C6
Glyn Rd B32 .....9 D6
Glynn Cres B63 .....7 B7
Glynside Ave B32 .....9 D6
Goblins Cl WR5 .....128 F4
Goddard Rd WR1 .....115 B5
Godson Cres DY11 .....27 C3
Godson Pl DY11 .....27 C3
Godson's Cl WR15 .....55 F5
Goffs Cl B32 .....9 F3
Goldcrest Dr DY10 .....28 B2
Golden Acres WV15 .....1 C5
Golden Cross La B61 .....32 B1
Golden Hind Dr DY13 .....44 A2
Golden La WR11 .....162 D1
Goldfinch Cl B30 .....19 D8
Goldfinch Rd DY9 .....6 C3
Goldsmith Rd
Birmingham B14 .....20 F8
Worcester WR4 .....115 F6
Goldsmith Wlk DY10 .....28 C5
Goldthorn Pl DY11 .....27 C2
Goldthorn Rd DY11 .....27 C2
Goldthorne Cl B97 .....70 C1
Goldthorne Wlk DY5 .....6 D8
Gomeldon Ave B14 .....20 F3
Gooch Cl DY8 .....6 B6
Goodalls Gr WR11 .....161 D6
Goodier's La GL20 .....184 A7
Goodleigh Ave B45 .....33 E6
Goodman Cl B28 .....21 F6
Goodrest Ave B62 .....9 A5
Goodrest Croft B14 .....21 C4
Goodrest La B38 .....34 F6
Goodrest Wlk WR3 .....115 C5
Goodrich Cl B98 .....71 F2
Goodrich Covert 10 B14 .....20 C2
Goodson Rd WR14 .....139 C5
Goodwin Cl B31 .....27 C7
Goodwood Ave WR5 .....128 E8
Goodwood Cl
7 Evesham WR11 .....161 C2
Fernhill Heath WR3 .....102 F2
5 Worcester WR5 .....128 E8
Goodwood Rd
Catshill B61 .....32 B1
Great Malvern WR14 .....139 A4
Pershore/Pinvin WR10 .....144 E4
Goodwyn Ave B68 .....9 C7
Goosehill Cl B98 .....71 E1
Goosehill La WR9 .....86 A2
Gorcott Hill B98 .....72 C5
Gordon Rd CV37 .....151 D3
Gordon Terr WR14 .....152 E4
Gorleston Gr B14 .....21 B2
Gorleston Rd B14 .....21 B2
Gorse Cl
Birmingham, Selly Oak B29 .....19 A8
5 Droitwich WR9 .....104 A8
Gorse Gn La DY9 .....31 C8
Gorse Hill WR11 .....174 B2
Gorse Hill Prim Sch WR4 .....115 F4
Gorse Hill Rd WR4 .....115 F5
Gorse Mdw Dr B45 .....50 B8
Gorsey Cl B96 .....108 E8
Gorsey La B47 .....36 A3
Gorsly Piece B32 .....9 C4
Gorsty Hill Rd B65 .....8 B8
Gorsy Rd B32 .....9 D5
Gorsymead Gr B31 .....18 C2
Goscote Cl B97 .....70 A5
Gould Ave E DY11 .....27 A2
Gould Ave W DY11 .....27 A1
Gould Dr GL20 .....184 E1
Gower House B62 .....8 F6
Gower Rd B62 .....8 F6
Gracemere Cres B28 .....21 E3
Gracewell Homes B13 .....21 D8
Grafson Pl WR9 .....84 D1
Grafton Cl
Great Malvern WR14 .....138 F3
Redditch B98 .....90 B7
Grafton Cres B60 .....67 E8
Grafton House B60 .....49 B3
Grafton La
Bidford-on-Avon B50 .....136 F6
Bromsgrove B61 .....67 C7
Pendock GL19 .....193 C6
Grafton Rd B90 .....21 C2
Graftons The WR8 .....169 C4
Graham Cres B45 .....33 A7
Graham Rd
Great Malvern WR14 .....138 F1
Halesowen B62 .....8 C8
6 Worcester WR2 .....114 F1
Grainger's La B64 .....7 D8
Graith Cl B28 .....21 E3
Grammar Sch La B63 .....8 A4
Grampian Rd DY8 .....6 A6
Granary Rd B60 .....67 E6
Granbrook La GL55 .....165 E4
Granby Cl B98 .....71 F4
Grand Stand Rd WR1 .....115 A3
Grange Ave WR3 .....102 A1
Grange Cres
Birmingham B45 .....32 F8
Halesowen B63 .....8 B3
Grange Ct
Northway GL20 .....184 F1
1 Redditch B98 .....70 F4
Stourbridge DY9 .....6 C3
Grange Farm Dr B38 .....34 D8
Grange Hill B62 .....8 C2
Grange Hill Rd B38 .....19 E1
Grange La
Alvechurch B48 .....51 B3
Broadheath WR2 .....113 E5
Fernhill Heath WR3 .....102 D2
Harvington WR11 .....148 A6
Stourbridge DY9 .....6 D4
Worcester WR2 .....127 B8
Grange Rd
Bidford-on-Avon B50 .....136 E4
Birmingham, King's Heath B14 .....20 E8
Blackheath B64 .....8 B8
Bretforton WR11 .....163 B5
Broadheath WR2 .....114 A7
3 Great Malvern WR14 .....152 F8
Halesowen B63 .....8 C3
Kidderminster DY11 .....27 B7
Northway GL20 .....184 E1
2 Redditch B98 .....70 F4
Stourbridge DY9 .....6 C4
Grange Rise B38 .....34 F7
Grange Sch The
North Claines WR3 .....102 D3
Stourbridge DY9 .....6 D4
Grange The B62 .....8 F6
Grange Way WR4 .....116 D3
Grangers La B98 .....89 F5
Granhill Cl B98 .....90 A8
Granshaw Cl B38 .....19 F1
Grant Ct B30 .....20 A5
Granton Cl B14 .....20 D5
Granton Rd B14 .....20 D5
Granville Cl B60 .....49 B1
Granville Crest DY10 .....28 B6
Granville Rd B64 .....8 B8
Grasmere Cl DY10 .....27 E6
Grasmere Dr WR4 .....116 A5
Grasmere Gr DY13 .....43 F6
Grasshopper Ave WR5 .....128 E5
Grassington Dr WR4 .....116 A4
Grassmere Dr DY8 .....5 F3
Grassmoor Rd B38 .....19 E2
Gratham Cl DY5 .....6 B7
Gravel Bank B32 .....9 D2
Gravel Pit La B48 .....51 E3
Gravel Pits Cl 2 GL20 .....184 F6
Gray Cl DY10 .....28 B6
Grayling Cl WR5 .....128 C5
Grayling Rd DY9 .....6 C6
Grayshott Cl B61 .....48 E3
Grayston Cl GL20 .....197 A8
Grayswood Pk Rd B32 .....9 C6
Grayswood Rd B31 .....33 F7
Grazebrook Croft B32 .....18 D8
Grazing La B97 .....69 F2
Grazings The DY7 .....4 C3
Great Barn La B97 .....70 B1
Great Calcroft WR10 .....158 D7
Great Cornbow 5 B63 .....8 B3
Great Farley Dr B31 .....18 C1
Great Hockings La B97 .....69 E2
Great House Rd WR2 .....114 F1
Great Malvern Prim Sch WR14 .....153 C8
Great Malvern Sta WR14 .....153 A8
Great Oaty Gdns WR4 .....116 B5
Great Stone Rd B31 .....19 A3
Great Western Way DY13 .....44 A5
Great Witley CE Prim Sch WR6 .....80 B8
Greatfield Rd DY11 .....27 B4
Greaves Gdns DY11 .....12 B1
Greaves Sq B38 .....20 B1
Green Acres Rd B38 .....34 D8
Green Bower Dr B61 .....49 A5
Green Cl
Childswickham WR12 .....176 E2
Honeybourne WR11 .....164 A4
Studley B80 .....90 E3
Wythall B47 .....36 A3
Green Cover WR4 .....116 B4
Green Ct B28 .....21 F8
Green Dr B32 .....9 C1
Green Dragonfly WR5 .....128 F6
Green Gables B47 .....36 A7
Green Hill Bath Rd 8 WR5 .....115 C1
Green Hill Cl B60 .....49 D6
Green Hill London Rd 10 WR5 .....115 C1
Green Hill Pl 11 WR5 .....115 C1
Green Hill Sch WR11 .....161 E6
Green La
Birmingham, Hawkesley B38 .....34 E8
Birmingham, Quinton B32 .....9 C6
Broadheath WR2 .....114 A6
Catshill B61 .....32 A1
Feckenham B97 .....88 F6
Great Malvern WR14 .....152 E1
Hadzor WR9 .....85 C1
Inkberrow B96 .....108 A3
Redditch B97 .....89 A7
Ripple WR8 .....170 B4
Ryall WR8 .....169 F6
Solihull B90 .....21 E1
Stourbridge DY9 .....6 E5
Studley B80 .....90 B5
Tewkesbury GL20 .....197 C7
Tibberton WR9 .....104 B3
Worcester WR3 .....102 A2
Green Leys WR10 .....133 A4
Green Leys Cres WV15 .....1 C5
Green Mdw DY9 .....15 B7
Green Mdw Prim Sch B29 .....18 F7
Green Mdw Rd B29 .....19 A7
Green Pk Rd
Birmingham B31 .....18 E2
Bromsgrove B60 .....49 B2
Green Slade Cres B60 .....32 C1
Green St Bushley GL20 .....182 D1
Kidderminster DY10 .....27 E5
Stourbridge DY8 .....5 F5
Green St Ind Est DY10 .....27 E4
Green Sward La B98 .....71 D1
Green The
Birmingham B31 .....18 C2
Birmingham, King's Norton B38 .....19 F2
4 Birmingham, Quinton B32 .....9 A6
Bluntington DY10 .....29 E1
Hagley DY9 .....14 F4
Pershore/Pinvin WR10 .....144 F7
Green Wickets B13 .....20 E6
Green Wlk B17 .....9 F7
Greenacres
Birmingham B32 .....9 E2
Twyning GL20 .....183 F7
Greenacres La DY12 .....26 A4
Greenacres Rd
Bromsgrove B61 .....48 E3
Worcester WR2 .....114 D2
Greenaleigh Rd B14 .....21 D3
Greenbank
Barnt Green B45 .....50 D8
Greenbank *continued*
2 Droitwich WR9 .....85 B2
Greenbank Rd DY12 .....25 E2
Greenbush Dr B63 .....8 A5
Greendale Cl B61 .....49 B8
Greenfield Ave
Marlbrook B60 .....32 D1
Stourbridge DY8 .....5 F5
Greenfield Cl 2 WR4 .....116 B4
Greenfield Cotts B48 .....51 A5
Greenfield Prim Sch DY8 .....5 F5
Greenfields
Redditch B98 .....70 E2
Upton upon Severn WR8 .....169 A5
Greenfields Cl 1 WR10 .....143 F6
Greenfields Rd 3 WR14 .....138 F5
Greenfinch Cl DY10 .....28 B3
Greenfinch Rd DY9 .....6 D3
Greenford Cl B97 .....70 B5
Greenford Gdns WR2 .....114 E5
Greenford Rd B14 .....21 C3
Greenhill Blackwell B60 .....49 F4
Evesham WR11 .....161 D6
Greenhill Ave DY10 .....27 F7
Greenhill Cl WR15 .....55 F5
Greenhill Ct B62 .....8 E7
Greenhill Dr WR14 .....139 A1
Greenhill Gdns B62 .....8 D6
Greenhill Ind Est DY10 .....28 A7
Greenhill La WR2 .....101 D2
Greenhill Oak DY10 .....27 F7
Greenhill Pk Rd WR11 .....161 D7
Greenhill Rd B62 .....8 D7
Greenhurst B45 .....33 A1
Greenlands Ave B98 .....71 A1
Greenlands Bsns Ctr B98 .....71 B2
Greenlands Dr B98 .....89 F8
Greenleas Gdns B63 .....8 C3
Greenleys WR11 .....162 E3
Greenoak Cres B30 .....20 C8
Greenroyde DY9 .....6 B1
Greens Croft Way WR7 .....120 E7
Greensforge La DY7 .....4 C7
Greenside B60 .....67 C2
Greenslade Croft B31 .....19 A2
Greenslade Rd B90 .....21 C2
Greenvale B31 .....18 F5
Greenway Ave WV15 .....1 C5
Greenway Gdns B38 .....34 E7
Greenway The
Bowling Green WR2 .....127 C3
Hagley DY9 .....14 F5
Rock DY14 .....41 D2
Greenways
Birmingham B31 .....18 F8
Halesowen B63 .....7 C6
Greenwood Cl B14 .....20 E5
Greenwoods The DY8 .....5 E5
Gregory Ave B29 .....19 A8
Gregory Rd DY8 .....5 D5
Gregory's Bank WR3 .....115 C5
Gregory's Mill St WR3 .....115 B6
Grendon Cl B98 .....71 D1
Grendon Rd B14 .....21 A3
Grendon Sch B14 .....21 A3
Grenville Rd WR2 .....114 D2
Gresham Rd
Birmingham B28 .....21 F6
Worcester WR2 .....114 D3
Grey Gn La DY12 .....26 B5
Grey's Rd B80 .....90 E3
Greyfriars Dr B61 .....48 D2
Greyhound La DY8 .....5 D2
Greylag Cres GL20 .....197 A5
Greystone Cl B98 .....71 C5
Griffin Cl B31 .....19 B6
Griffin Rd DY10 .....27 E4
Griffins Brook Cl B30 .....19 D7
Griffins Brook La B30 .....19 D6
Grigg Gr B31 .....18 E1
Grimley & Holt CE Prim Sch WR2 .....101 F6
Grimley Cl B98 .....70 F1
Grimley La B60 .....68 E6
Grimley Rd 2 B31 .....19 D2
Grimpits La B38 .....35 A7
Grisedale Dr WR4 .....116 A6
Gristhorpe Rd B29 .....20 A8
Grit La WR14 .....138 E6
Grizedale Cl B45 .....18 B2
Grosmont Ave WR4 .....116 D6
Grosvenor Ave DY10 .....28 A6
Grosvenor Cl 6 WR9 .....85 B1
Grosvenor Cres 5 WR9 .....85 A1
Grosvenor Ct DY9 .....6 B1
Grosvenor Gdns B61 .....49 B5
Grosvenor House B97 .....70 E4
Grosvenor Sh Ctr B31 .....19 A4
Grosvenor Sq B28 .....21 F5
Grosvenor Way
Brierley Hill DY5 .....6 E7
Droitwich WR9 .....85 A1
Grosvenor Wood 12 DY12 .....25 F3
Grove Ave Halesowen B63 .....7 F3
Honeybourne WR11 .....164 B5
Grove Cres WR2 .....114 D1
Grove Field WR4 .....116 B7
Grove Gdns B61 .....49 A6
Grove Jun Sch WR14 .....139 B2
Grove Mdw 4 DY14 .....22 D5
Grove Mews B31 .....34 B8
Grove Rd
Birmingham, King's Heath B14 .....20 D6
Stourbridge DY9 .....6 F3
Grove St B98 .....70 E4
Grove The
Birmingham, Rednall B45 .....33 D4
Birmingham, West Heath B31 .....34 B8
Stourport-on-Severn DY13 .....44 B2
Studley B80 .....90 D3
Worcester WR3 .....115 B8
Grove Villas B64 .....7 D7
Grove Way WR2 .....114 B1
Grovefield GL19 .....193 B7
Grovelley La B31, B45 .....33 E5
Grovewood Dr 2 B38 .....19 E1
Grovewood Rd WR14 .....139 C4
Grundy's La WR14 .....152 E1
Guardian Ct
Birmingham, Frankley B31 .....18 D3
3 Bromsgrove B60 .....49 A2
Guardian House B68 .....9 C7
Guardians Way B31 .....18 E8
Guarlford Rd
Great Malvern WR14 .....153 D7
Guarlford WR13 .....154 A7
Guild Ct 4 B60 .....48 F2
Guild Rd B60 .....48 F1
Guildford Cl
Kidderminster DY11 .....27 A6
Worcester WR5 .....115 F2
Guildford Ct 12 B29 .....19 C7
Guinness Cl B98 .....89 D8
Guiting Cl B97 .....70 B1
Guiting Rd B29 .....19 A7
Gullane Cl B38 .....19 D1
Gullswood Cl B14 .....20 D2
Gunbarrel Ind Ctr B63 .....7 F6
Gunner La B45 .....32 D7
Gunners La B80 .....90 E4
Gunnings La WR10 .....132 E4
Gupshill Cl GL20 .....196 E4
Gurneys La 6 WR9 .....85 A3
Gutter The DY9 .....31 E7
Guy's Wlk B61 .....49 A5
Gypsy La B97 .....69 C5

H

Habberley La
Kidderminster DY11 .....27 A8
Kidderminster Foreign DY11 .....26 F8
Habberley Rd
Bewdley DY12 .....26 E5
Kidderminster DY11 .....27 B7
Habberley St 1 DY11 .....27 C6
Habberley Valley Nature Reserve* DY11 .....26 E8
Hacketts La WR10 .....171 F7
Hackmans Gate La DY9 .....30 B7
Hadcroft Grange DY9 .....6 D4
Hadcroft Rd DY9 .....6 C4
Haddon Croft B63 .....7 C1
Haden Cl B64 .....8 A7
Haden Cross Dr B64 .....8 A7
Haden Hill Rd B63 .....8 B6
Haden Pk Rd B64 .....7 F7
Hadendale B64 .....8 A7
Hadley Cl B47 .....36 A5
Hadzor House 5 B97 .....70 A4
Hadzor La WR9 .....85 C2
Hadzor Rd B68 .....9 D8
Hafren Cl B45 .....18 B2
Hafren Way DY13 .....43 E4
Haggs Mdw WR4 .....116 C5
Hagley Cl DY9 .....15 C6
Hagley Cswy DY9 .....16 B8
Hagley Hill DY9 .....15 E7
Hagley House B60 .....49 B3
Hagley Mews DY9 .....15 D6
Hagley Pk Dr B45 .....33 A6
Hagley Prim Sch DY9 .....15 B5
Hagley RC High Sch DY8 .....14 F6
Hagley Rd Halesowen B63 .....7 E2
Stourbridge DY8 .....6 B3
Hagley Rd W B32, B68 .....9 D7
Hagley St 3 B63 .....8 B3
Hagley Sta DY9 .....15 A6
Hagley Wood La DY9, B62 .....16 B7
Haig Pl B13 .....21 A7
Hailsham Cl 8 WR5 .....128 E8
Haines Ave
Worcester WR4 .....116 C3
Wyre Piddle WR10 .....145 A4
Halas Ind Est B62 .....8 C5
Haldon Gr B31 .....33 E7
Hales Pk 14 DY12 .....25 F3
Hales Rd B63 .....8 A4
Halesbury Ct B63 .....7 F2
Halesbury Sch B62 .....8 E7
Halescroft Sq B31 .....18 E6
Halesmere Way B63 .....8 C3
Halesowen CE Prim Sch B63 .....8 B4
Halesowen Coll (e-commerce Ctr) B62 .....8 C8
Halesowen Coll (Walton Campus) B63 .....8 A3
Halesowen Coll (Whittingham main campus) B63 .....8 B5

Halesowen Ind Pk B62 ....8 B6
Halesowen Rd
Halesowen B62 ....8 F6
Lydiate Ash B61 ....32 C3
Halfcot Ave DY9 ....6 C3
Halfkey Rd WR13 ....138 D6
Halfshire La DY10 ....14 B1
Halifax Ct DY11 ....27 B8
Halifax Dr WR2 ....127 F7
Hall Cl WR4 ....116 A5
Hall Dale Cl B28 ....21 F5
Hall Dr DY9 ....15 D6
Hall Gn WR14 ....153 E8
Hall Gn Cl WR14 ....153 E8
Hall Gn Inf Sch B28 ....21 F7
Hall Gn Jun Sch B28 ....21 F7
Hall Gn Sch B28 ....21 E8
Hall La DY9 ....15 D6
Hall Mdw DY9 ....15 D7
Hall St DY8 ....6 A3
Halladale B38 ....19 F1
Hallow CE Prim Sch WR2 ....101 D2
Hallow Rd
Broadheath WR2 ....114 A7
Worcester WR2 ....114 E6
Hallowfields Cl B98 ....70 E1
Halls Farm La DY12 ....11 C1
Hallstead Rd B13 ....21 B5
Ham Dingle Prim Sch DY9 ....6 C2
Ham La Powick WR2 ....127 C4
Severn Stoke WR8 ....155 C5
Stourbridge DY9 ....6 C2
Ham View WR8 ....169 C5
Hamble Cl WR5 ....115 E2
Hambleton Rd B63 ....7 D2
Hambury Dr B14 ....20 D7
Hamgreen La B97 ....80 C5
Hamilton Ave
Halesowen B62 ....8 C3
Stourbridge DY8 ....5 D6
Hamilton Cl
1 Bowling Green WR2 ....127 C2
Lickey End B60 ....49 C6
Hamilton Dr
Birmingham B29 ....19 D8
Studley B80 ....90 D3
Hamilton Rd
Evesham WR11 ....161 C2
Kidderminster DY11 ....27 B3
Redditch B97 ....89 C8
18 Worcester WR5 ....115 C2
Hamlet Gdns B28 ....21 F8
Hamlet Rd B28 ....21 F8
Hammer Bank DY5 ....7 A8
Hammersley Cl B63 ....7 C7
Hammock Rd WR10 ....171 D7
Hammond Cl 9 WR9 ....85 A1
Hammond Way DY8 ....6 A7
Hampden Cl DY5 ....7 A8
Hampden Rd WR14 ....139 A4
Hampshire Ct 1 B29 ....19 B7
Hampstall La DY13 ....63 A4
Hampstead Glade B63 ....8 C2
Hampton Ave B60 ....68 A8
Hampton Cl
Redditch B98 ....90 B7
Worcester WR2 ....114 E3
Hampton Gdns DY9 ....6 D3
Hampton Gr DY7 ....4 B4
Hampton Lovett Ind Est WR9 ....84 C7
Hampton Rd WR9 ....84 F4
Hams Way WR2 ....127 E7
Hanbury Ave WR2 ....127 F8
Hanbury CE Fst Sch B60 ....86 F5
Hanbury Cl
Bromsgrove B60 ....68 A8
Halesowen B63 ....7 F1
Hanbury Ct DY8 ....6 A4
Hanbury Hall (NT)* B60 ....86 C4
Hanbury Hill DY8 ....6 A4
Hanbury House B97 ....70 B4
Hanbury Pk* B60 ....86 C4
Hanbury Pk Rd WR2 ....127 F7
Hanbury Rd Hadzor WR9 ....85 C3
Hanbury B60 ....87 A6
Stoke Heath B60 ....67 D4
Hanbury St WR9 ....85 A3
Hancocks La
Castlemorton WR13 ....167 B3
Welland WR13 ....166 F4
Handbury Rd WR14 ....139 A5
Handley Gr B31 ....18 C2
Hanging La B31 ....18 E2
Hangman's La WR8 ....154 E4
Hanley Castle High Sch WR8 ....154 F1
Hanley Cl B63 ....7 E4
Hanley Orch WR8 ....154 A2
Hanley Rd
Great Malvern WR14 ....152 F1
Malvern Wells WR13 ....153 B1
Hanley Terr WR14 ....152 E3
Hannon Rd B14 ....20 E5
Hanover Ct B97 ....89 D8
Hanover Pl B60 ....48 F1
Hanover St B61 ....48 F1
Hansom Rd B32 ....9 C5
Hanson Way WR10 ....158 D7
Hanstone Rd DY13 ....43 F1
Happy Land N WR2 ....114 F1
Happy Land W WR2 ....114 E1
Happy Valley
Great Malvern WR14 ....138 E1
Malvern WR14 ....152 E8
Harberrow Cl DY9 ....15 A6
Harbinger Ave WR14 ....139 B1
Harbinger Rd B38 ....20 B2
Harborne Rd B68 ....9 E8
Harborough Wlk DY9 ....6 B2
Harbour Cl B50 ....136 C1
Harbour Dr 5 WR13 ....152 B2
Harbour View GL20 ....196 F7
Harbours Cl B61 ....67 D7
Harbours Hill DY9 ....31 E6
Harbourside GL20 ....196 F7
Harbury Cl B98 ....71 D1
Harcourt Rd
Blackheath B64 ....7 F8
Mathon WR13 ....152 B6
Harden Ct B31 ....18 E1
Harden Manor Ct B63 ....8 C3
Harden Vale B63 ....7 E5
Hardnott Row WR4 ....116 D6
Hardwick Bank Rd GL20 ....184 D3
Hardwick Dr B62 ....8 A7
Hardwick La B80 ....91 B6
Hardwicke Cl WR2 ....115 A3
Hardwicke Way DY9 ....6 D5
Hardwike Wlk B14 ....20 D2
Hardy Ave DY10 ....28 A6
Hardy Ct WR3 ....115 C6
Hare Gr B31 ....18 D3
Harebell Gdns B38 ....34 F8
Haresfield Cl
Redditch B97 ....70 D3
15 Worcester WR4 ....115 F6
Harewell La WR8 ....157 B8
Harewood Cl B28 ....21 E5
Hargrave Rd B90 ....21 D1
Hargreaves Ct DY11 ....27 C3
Harland Cl B61 ....48 D3
Harlech Cl
Birmingham B32 ....18 A7
15 Worcester WR4 ....116 C6
Harlech Way DY10 ....27 E2
Harlestones House DY8 ....5 F7
Harlstones Cl DY8 ....6 A8
Harman's Hill WR9 ....105 E5
Harmon Rd DY8 ....5 C5
Harold Davies Dr 1 DY13 ....43 F2
Harold Evers Way DY10 ....27 F7
Harpers Rd
Birmingham, Highter's Heath B14 ....21 A1
Birmingham, Northfield B31 ....19 A2
Harpley Rd WR8 ....157 C2
Harport Rd B98 ....71 A1
Harrier Cl GL20 ....197 A4
Harriers Gn DY10 ....28 B8
Harriers Ind Est DY10 ....27 F5
Harringay Dr DY8 ....5 E3
Harrington Rd WR2 ....114 D1
Harris Cl 6 WR9 ....84 E3
Harris Ind Pk B60 ....67 E2
Harrison House B14 ....20 F3
Harrison Rd B97 ....89 C8
Harrop Way DY8 ....5 E8
Harrow Cl Hagley DY9 ....15 A6
Stoke Heath B60 ....67 E6
Harrow Croft WR2 ....114 C1
Harry Cheshire Com High Sch DY11 ....27 B6
Harry Taylor Fst Sch The B97 ....89 E6
Harry Taylor House B98 ....71 A4
Hartford Rd B60 ....49 B1
Hartland Rd B31 ....33 E6
Hartle La DY9 ....30 F6
Hartlebury Castle* DY11 ....44 F3
Hartlebury Cl B98 ....71 E7
Hartlebury Comm Nature Reserve* DY13 ....44 C2
Hartlebury Ind Est DY10 ....45 D1
Hartlebury Ind Sch DY11 ....45 A2
Hartlebury Rd
Halesowen B63 ....7 F2
Stourport-on-Severn DY13 ....44 C3
Hartlebury Sch DY11 ....44 F3
Hartlebury Sta DY11 ....45 B2
Hartlebury Trad Est DY10 ....64 D8
Hartmann Cl 7 DY14 ....22 C4
Harton Way B14 ....20 C5
Hartsbourne Dr B62 ....8 D4
Hartside Cl B63 ....7 D2
Hartswell Dr B13 ....20 F6
Harvard Ave WR11 ....164 B6
Harvest Cl
Birmingham B30 ....20 B6
Stoke Heath B60 ....67 E6
Harvey Mews B30 ....19 D7
Harvey Rd WR11 ....161 E4
Harvey Wlk WR3 ....115 D5
Harvey Works Ind Est B63 ....7 F6
Harvine Wlk DY8 ....5 E3
Harvington CE Sch WR11 ....148 B7
Harvington Cl
Kidderminster DY11 ....12 A1
Harvington Cl *continued*
Redditch B97 ....70 B5
Harvington Hall* DY10 ....29 B1
Harvington Hall La
Chaddesley Corbett DY10 ....46 C8
Harvington DY10 ....29 B1
Harvington Rd
Birmingham B29 ....19 A8
Bromsgrove B60 ....68 A8
Halesowen B63 ....7 F1
Oldbury B68 ....9 A8
Hasbury CE Prim Sch B63 ....7 F2
Hasbury Cl B63 ....7 E2
Hasbury Rd B32 ....18 B8
Haseley Cl B98 ....71 E1
Haselor La WR11 ....160 E2
Haslucks Gn Rd B90 ....36 E7
Hastings Cl WR6 ....99 A3
Hastings Dr WR4 ....116 C6
Hastings Pl GL20 ....196 E4
Hastings Rd
Bromsgrove B60 ....67 E7
Great Malvern WR14 ....153 D8
Haswell Rd B63 ....7 D4
Hatfield Bank WR5 ....129 A1
Hatfield Cl B98 ....71 E1
Hatfield La WR5 ....129 B2
Hatfield Rd DY9 ....6 C4
Hathaway Cl
3 South Littleton WR11 ....148 F1
5 Worcester WR2 ....114 D3
Hatherton Gr B29 ....9 F1
Haunch La B13 ....21 A5
Haven The B14 ....21 D4
Haverford Dr B45 ....33 B6
Havergal Wlk B63 ....7 B4
Hawfinch Rise DY10 ....28 A2
Hawford Ave DY10 ....28 B6
Hawford Dovecote (NT)* WR3 ....102 B6
Hawford Lock La WR3 ....102 A4
Hawford Pl WR9 ....84 D1
Hawkes Cl B30 ....20 A7
Hawkesbury Rd B90 ....21 F1
Hawkesley CE & Methodist Prim Sch B38 ....34 E7
Hawkesley Cres B31 ....19 A1
Hawkesley Dr B31 ....33 F8
Hawkesley End B38 ....34 E7
Hawkesley Mill La B31 ....18 F2
Hawkesley Sq B38 ....34 E7
Hawkestone Rd B29 ....19 A7
Hawkhurst Rd B14 ....20 F2
Hawkins Cl WR2 ....114 D3
Hawkley Row WR4 ....116 C5
Hawkmoor Gdns B38 ....35 A8
Hawkmoth Cl 10 GL20 ....197 A4
Hawksbury Cl B98 ....71 D5
Hawkstone Cl DY11 ....27 D8
Hawkswood Gr B14 ....21 B3
Hawkwood Cl WR14 ....138 E3
Hawkwood Cres WR2 ....114 E4
Hawne Cl B63 ....7 E6
Hawne La B63 ....7 F6
Hawnelands The B63 ....7 F5
Hawthorn Coppice DY9 ....15 A6
Hawthorn Cres DY12 ....25 E2
Hawthorn Croft B68 ....9 D7
Hawthorn Gr DY11 ....27 A6
Hawthorn La
Great Malvern WR13 ....153 B5
Newland WR2 ....139 F8
Powick WR2 ....126 F1
Hawthorn Rd
Brierley Hill DY5 ....6 E8
Bromsgrove B61 ....49 B4
Evesham WR11 ....161 F2
Redditch B97 ....70 A4
Worcester WR4 ....115 E4
Hawthorn Way GL20 ....184 F1
Hawthorne Cl WR10 ....143 F7
Hawthorne Dr B47 ....36 B6
Hawthorne Rd
Birmingham, King's Norton B30 ....19 D5
Halesowen B63 ....7 E2
Hawthorne Way DY7 ....4 C3
Hawthorne Wlk 6 WR9 ....103 F8
Hawthorns The
Hagley DY9 ....14 F4
1 Kidderminster DY10 ....28 A5
Oldbury B68 ....9 D7
Hay Cl
Kidderminster DY11 ....27 C7
Worcester WR4 ....116 A4
Hay Gn DY9 ....6 D5
Hay Gn Cl B30 ....19 D6
Hay Gn La B30 ....19 D6
Hay La WR9 ....104 E7
Haybridge Ave DY8 ....14 F5
Haybridge High Sch DY8 ....14 F6
Haydock Rd B61 ....32 B1
Haydon Way
Sambourne B49 ....109 F8
Studley B49 ....90 F1
Haye La
Mappleborough Green B80 ....72 B1
Ombersley WR9 ....83 C5
Hayes Bank Rd WR13 ....153 B5
Hayes Croft B38 ....34 F7
Hayes La Stourbridge DY9 ....7 A6
Tenbury WR15 ....54 F3
Hayes Rd DY11 ....12 C3
Hayes The
Birmingham B31 ....34 C7
Hayes The *continued*
Stourbridge DY9 ....7 A5
Hayes Trad Est DY9 ....7 A6
Hayfield Cl 7 WR2 ....114 D1
Hayford Cl B98 ....71 A5
Hayle Cl B38 ....20 B2
Hayley Gn Rd B32 ....18 B8
Hayley Pk Rd B63 ....16 C8
Hayling Cl
Birmingham B45 ....17 F1
4 St. Peter the Great County WR5 ....128 E6
Hayloft Cl B60 ....67 E6
Haylofts The B63 ....7 C1
Haynes Cl B61 ....49 B8
Haynes House B97 ....70 D2
Hays Cl WR12 ....177 E3
Hayseech B64 ....8 A7
Hayseech Rd B63 ....7 F6
Haysfield The WR14 ....139 C4
Hayslan Ave WR14 ....139 B2
Hayslan Gn WR14 ....139 B2
Hayslan Rd WR14 ....139 B2
Haytor Ave B14 ....20 D5
Haywood Dr B62 ....8 C8
Haze Croft WR4 ....116 B4
Hazel Ave WR11 ....161 F2
Hazel Cl
Droitwich Spa WR9 ....103 F8
4 Worcester WR4 ....115 F5
Hazel Croft B31 ....19 A3
Hazel Dr B47 ....36 B5
Hazel Gr DY8 ....5 C3
Hazel Rd
Birmingham B45 ....32 F6
Redditch B97 ....70 C5
Hazelbank B38 ....19 E2
Hazeldene DY13 ....44 C3
Hazeldene Rd B63 ....7 E2
Hazelgrove WV15 ....1 D6
Hazelhurst Rd B14 ....20 E7
Hazelmere Rd B28 ....21 F8
Hazels The DY9 ....14 F5
Hazelton Cl B61 ....49 C8
Hazelton Rd B61 ....32 C1
Hazelwell Cres B30 ....20 B6
Hazelwell Fordrough B30 ....20 B6
Hazelwell La B30 ....20 B7
Hazelwell Rd B30 ....20 A6
Hazelwell St B30 ....20 A7
Hazelwood Cl DY11 ....27 B4
Hazewood Cl 7 WR5 ....115 F1
Hazlitt Gr B30 ....19 D4
Head St 1 WR10 ....158 D8
Headless Cross Dr B97 ....70 D1
Headley Croft B38 ....34 D8
Headley Ct B97 ....89 D8
Headley Heath La B38 ....35 B6
Heale Cl B63 ....7 A7
Heath Cl
Birmingham B30 ....19 D5
Bromsgrove B60 ....67 E6
Cleobury Mortimer DY14 ....22 B4
Hallow WR2 ....101 D3
Heath Croft B31 ....34 A7
Heath Dr
Kidderminster DY10 ....13 B1
Worcester WR5 ....128 E5
Heath End Rd DY9 ....31 D7
Heath Farm Rd DY8 ....5 E3
Heath House B14 ....20 F2
Heath La
Kidderminster DY10 ....28 C1
Stone DY10 ....45 D8
Stourbridge DY8 ....6 A4
Heath Rd
Birmingham B30 ....19 D5
Hollywood B47 ....36 A7
Heath Rd S B31 ....19 B4
Heath Rise B14 ....21 A1
Heath St DY8 ....5 F4
Heath The WR6 ....82 B3
Heathcote Rd B30 ....20 A5
Heather Cl WR5 ....128 C4
Heather Dr
Birmingham B45 ....32 F6
Kinver DY7 ....3 F4
Heather House B38 ....19 F1
Heathers The WR11 ....175 D8
Heathfield Cres DY11 ....27 B4
Heathfield Gdns DY8 ....5 F4
Heathfield Rd
Bewdley DY12 ....26 C4
Birmingham, King's Heath B14 ....20 F8
Halesowen B63 ....7 E3
Hartlebury DY13 ....44 C1
Norton & Lenchwick WR11 ....147 D3
Redditch B97 ....70 A1
Heathfield Sch DY10 ....12 F2
Heathlands Cl 5 WR14 ....166 E7
Heathlands Gr B31 ....19 A1
Heathlands The
Stourbridge DY8 ....6 B4
Stourport-on-Severn DY13 ....44 B3
Heathleigh Rd B38 ....34 C8
Heathside Dr B38 ....20 B2
Heathy Farm Cl B32 ....9 B1
Heathy Rise B32 ....9 A2
Hebb St WR1 ....115 B4
Hebden Gr B28 ....21 E3
Hedera Rd B98 ....71 F6
Hedgefield Gr B63 ....7 C4
Hedgerows The B62 ....16 F4
Hedges Way B60 ....49 B1
Heightington Pl DY13 ....43 E1
Heightington Rd
Ribbesford DY12 ....25 F1
Rock DY14 ....41 F6
Heights The WR5 ....116 B3
Helford Cl WR5 ....115 E2
Helmsley Cl DY5 ....6 C8
Heming Rd B98 ....90 E8
Hemming St DY11 ....27 C4
Hemming Way DY10 ....46 E8
Hemmings Cl DY8 ....5 F5
Hemmingway 2 WR11 ....161 D2
Hemplands Rd DY8 ....5 F5
Hemsby Cl 9 WR5 ....128 D6
Hemyock Rd B29 ....19 B8
Henderson Ct 7 B68 ....9 B8
Henley Dr
7 Droitwich WR9 ....85 A1
Droitwich WR9 ....104 A8
Henley Pl WR14 ....138 F3
Henlow Rd B14 ....21 A2
Hennals Ave B97 ....69 F2
Henry Fowler Cl 2 WR11 ....161 D5
Henry St
1 Evesham WR11 ....161 C4
Worcester WR1 ....115 B5
Henry Wlk B60 ....67 E7
Hentland Cl B98 ....71 D4
Henwick Ave WR2 ....114 F3
Henwick Rd WR2 ....114 F3
Herbert Austin Dr B60 ....32 E1
Herbert St B98 ....70 E4
Hereford & Worcester Cty Mus* DY11 ....44 F3
Hereford Cl
Birmingham B45 ....18 A2
Kidderminster DY11 ....27 A5
Hereford Rd B68 ....9 B7
Hereward Rise B62 ....8 C5
Heriotts Ct 7 WR9 ....85 A3
Heritage Way 7 WR9 ....84 F3
Hermitage Way 2 DY13 ....62 F8
Hern Rd DY5 ....6 C6
Herne Field 5 WR4 ....116 C5
Herne's Nest DY12 ....26 A2
Hernehurst B32 ....9 C6
Heron Cl Alvechurch B48 ....51 A7
Worcester WR2 ....128 A6
Heron Pl WR9 ....85 B3
Heron Way B45 ....32 F7
Herondale Cres DY8 ....5 C4
Herondale Rd DY8 ....5 C4
Heronfield Cl B98 ....71 C5
Heronfield Dr B31 ....33 F6
Herons Gate Rd DY7 ....2 F5
Heronswood Rd
Birmingham B45 ....33 B6
Kidderminster DY10 ....28 A2
Hestia Dr B29 ....19 E8
Hetherington Cl 2 WR5 ....141 C7
Hetherington Rise WR4 ....116 C3
Hever Ave WR4 ....116 C6
Hever Cl 13 GL20 ....197 A4
Hewell Ave B60 ....67 F7
Hewell Cl
Birmingham B31 ....33 F7
Redditch B97 ....69 C6
Hewell La
Barnt Green B45 ....50 D8
Redditch B60, B97 ....69 D6
Hewell Rd
Barnt Green B45 ....50 D8
Redditch B97 ....70 D4
Hexton Cl B90 ....21 D2
Heycott Gr B38 ....20 C2
Heydon Rd B60 ....49 D1
Heythrop Gr B13 ....21 D8
Hickman St DY9 ....6 C6
Hickmans Cl 2 B62 ....9 A6
Hidage The WR5 ....142 D8
Hidcote Cl 5 WR5 ....128 D5
Higgins La B32 ....9 C5
High Ave B64 ....7 F8
High Clere B64 ....8 A7
High Elms La
Bentley Pauncefoot B60 ....87 E8
Upper Bentley B60 ....68 E1
High Farm Rd
Halesowen, Hasbury B63 ....7 F3
Halesowen, Hurst Green B62 ....8 F8
High Haden Cres B64 ....8 A8
High Haden Rd B64 ....8 A8
High Heath Cl B30 ....19 D5
High House Dr
Barnt Green B45 ....32 F3
Inkberrow WR7 ....120 E7
High House La B60 ....69 A6
High La HR7 ....96 D5
High Leasowes B63 ....8 A4
High Mdw Rd B38 ....20 A2
High Mdws B60 ....67 D7
High Pk Rd B63 ....7 C5
High St
Astwood Bank B96 ....89 E1
Badsey WR11 ....162 D3
Belbroughton DY9 ....30 E7
Bewdley DY12 ....26 B3
Bidford-on-Avon B50 ....136 C7
Birmingham, King's Heath B14 ....20 E8
Birmingham, Quinton B32 ....9 A6
Blackheath B64 ....7 C8
Bredon GL20 ....184 D6

High St *continued*
Brierley Hill, Quarry Bank DY5 7 A8
Broadway WR12 190 D8
Bromsgrove B61 49 A2
Cleobury Mortimer DY14 22 B4
Droitwich WR9 85 A3
Evesham WR11 161 D5
Feckenham B96 107 D7
1 Halesowen B63 8 B3
Honeybourne WR11 164 B4
Inkberrow WR7 120 E7
Kidderminster DY10 27 E6
Kinver DY7 4 B3
Mickleton GL55 165 D3
Pershore WR10 144 D1
Solihull B90 21 D2
Stanton WR12 189 D1
Stourbridge DY8 5 E7
Stourbridge, Amblecote DY8 5 F7
Stourport-on-Severn DY13 44 A3
Studley B80 90 E4
Tewkesbury GL20 196 E6
1 Upton upon Severn WR8 169 C6
Worcester WR1 115 C2
High Timbers B45 17 F1
High Trees Cl B98 89 E7
Highbury Ct B13 20 E7
Highbury Rd B14 20 D8
Highclere DY12 26 A2
Highclere Dr DY12 26 A2
Highcrest Cl B31 34 A7
Highfield WR2 140 F8
Highfield Ave B97 89 D8
Highfield Cl
Birmingham B28 21 D5
Droitwich WR9 84 F2
Great Malvern WR14 139 A4
Highfield Cres B63 7 D6
Highfield La
Birmingham B32 9 B4
Clent DY9 16 A3
1 Halesowen B63 8 A3
Highfield Mews B63 7 D6
Highfield Pl B14 21 D5
Highfield Rd
Birmingham, Yardley Wood B14, B28 21 D5
Bromsgrove B61 67 E8
Cookley DY10 13 A5
Evesham WR11 161 B4
Great Malvern WR14 138 F4
Halesowen B63 7 D5
Kidderminster DY10 28 A8
Redditch B97 89 D8
Studley B80 90 D4
Highfields B61 48 E1
Highfields Prim Sch B65 8 C8
Highgate Cl DY11 27 A4
Highgrove Ct DY10 13 A1
Highland House B62 8 C8
Highland Rd WR4 115 E4
Highland Ridge B62 8 E5
Highland Way B98 90 A7
Highlands Cl DY11 27 A5
Highley Cl
Kidderminster DY11 27 B2
Redditch B98 71 E4
Highlow Ave DY11 12 C1
Highmore Dr B32 18 C8
Highpark Ave DY8 5 D5
Highter's Heath Inf & Jun Sch B14 21 B3
Highter's Heath La B14 21 A2
Highters Cl B14 21 B2
Highters Rd B14 21 A3
Hightown B63 7 C6
Hightree Cl B32 9 B1
Highwood Croft B38 19 D1
Hilary Gr B31 18 F4
Hill Ave The WR5 128 C8
Hill Bank DY9 6 F5
Hill Bank Rd
Birmingham B38 20 A2
Halesowen B63 7 D6
Hill Cl Birmingham B31 19 C1
Bredon GL20 185 B7
Pershore WR10 144 C1
Hill Crest 5 WR11 161 F3
Hill Croft Rd B14 20 C6
Hill End Rd GL20 183 F6
Hill Farm WR7 120 E7
Hill Furze Rd WR10 133 C1
Hill Gr Cres DY10 28 A4
Hill La
Alvechurch B47, B48 35 D1
Bentley Pauncefoot B60 87 E6
Bromsgrove B60 48 F1
Clent DY9 15 E4
Elmley Castle WR10 173 D7
Hill Rd Lulsley WR6 111 E3
Pirton WR8 142 D3
Hill Rise View B60 49 C6
Hill Side WR5 141 C8
Hill St
Brierley Hill, Quarry Bank DY5 7 A8
Halesowen B63 8 A3
Kidderminster DY11 27 D6
Stourbridge DY8 5 F4
Stourbridge, Lye DY9 6 F5
Stourbridge, Amblecote DY8 5 F8
Worcester WR5 115 D3
Hill The B32 9 E2
Hill Top B97 69 F1
Hill Top Ave B62 8 E7
Hill Top La WR9 83 B4
Hill Top Rd B31 18 F3
Hill View WR8 157 D3
Hill View Cl
3 Colwall Stone WR13 152 B2
Great Malvern WR14 139 B5
Hill View Rd
Bidford-on-Avon B50 136 E5
Strensham WR8 171 A4
Worcester WR2 127 F7
Hillaire Cl B38 20 C2
Hillary Rd DY13 44 D7
Hillboro Rise DY7 4 A5
Hillborough La B50 137 C5
Hillbrow Cres B62 8 F8
Hillcrest Ave B63 7 B7
Hillcrest Ind Est B64 7 D8
Hillcrest Pk B47 52 F8
Hillcrest Rd B62 17 A4
Hillcrest Rise WR3 102 A1
Hillcrest Sch & Sixth Form Ctr B32 9 E3
Hillcroft House B14 20 F2
Hillditch La DY11 44 E2
Hillery Rd WR5 128 F8
Hillfields Rd DY5 6 B7
Hillgrove Gdns DY10 28 A4
Hillmeads Rd B38 20 A1
Hillmorton Cl B98 71 E6
Hillsfield WR8 169 C5
Hillside
Ashton under Hill WR11 174 B1
Redditch B98 70 D2
Hillside Ave
Blackheath B65 8 B8
Brierley Hill DY5 7 A8
Halesowen B63 7 D6
Hillside Cl
Birmingham B32 18 A8
Evesham WR11 161 A3
Kidderminster DY11 27 A7
6 Stourport-on-Severn DY13 62 E8
Upton Snodsbury WR7 131 C8
Worcester WR5 115 F3
Hillside Dr
Kidderminster DY11 27 A7
Lickey End B61 49 B6
Hillside Gr DY10 13 C3
Hillstone Sch WR14 152 F7
Hilltop DY9 6 F3
Hilltop Ave DY12 26 D4
Hillview Cl
Halesowen B63 7 E6
Lickey End B60 49 C6
Hillview Dr WR14 138 E4
Hillview Gdns WR8 169 E6
Hillview La GL20 183 F7
Hillview Rd
Birmingham B45 32 E8
Lickey End B60 49 C6
Hillville Gdns DY8 6 B3
Hillwood Rd
Birmingham B31 18 E7
Halesowen B62 8 C7
Hilston Ave B63 7 F4
Hilton Ave B28 21 F4
Hilton Cl DY8 6 A7
Hilton Rd WR14 153 C7
Himbleton CE Fst Sch WR9 105 D1
Himbleton Cl B98 70 F1
Himbleton Rd WR2 114 E4
Himley Gr B45 33 B6
Hinckley Ct 3 B68 9 B7
Hindhead Rd B14 21 C4
Hindlip CE Fst Sch WR3 103 A3
Hindlip Cl Halesowen B63 7 F2
Redditch B98 72 A3
Hindlip La WR3 103 C1
Hindon Wlk B32 9 C2
Hingley Ave WR4 116 B3
Hingley Rd DY9 7 A6
Hinton Ave B48 51 A6
Hinton Fields B61 48 E7
Hinton Rd WR12 176 D2
Hiplands Rd B62 8 F4
Hipton Hill WR11 147 C5
Hirdemonsway B90 36 F5
Hither Gn WR11 162 E4
Hither Gn La B98 70 F7
Hoarstone DY8 14 F5
Hoarstone Cl DY12 26 C5
Hoarstone La DY12 26 C6
Hob Gn Prim Sch DY9 6 E2
Hob Gn Rd DY9 6 E2
Hobacre Cl B45 33 A8
Hobbis House B38 34 C7
Hobhouse Gdns 6 WR4 116 C3
Hock Coppice 4 WR4 116 B4
Hockham's La WR6 80 D2
Hockley Brook La DY9 30 F3
Hoden La WR11 149 B7
Hodge Hill Ave DY9 6 F3
Hodge Hill Cotts DY10 28 C7
Hodges The 7 WR11 161 D5
Hodgetts Dr B63 16 C8
Hoggs La B31 18 E4
Holcroft Rd
Halesowen B63 7 C5
Stourbridge DY9 6 C4
Holdens The B28 21 E6
Holder Cl 10 B50 136 D5
Holdgate Rd B29 19 C7
Holdings La WR5 128 D1
Hole Farm Rd B31 19 C5
Hole Farm Way B38 34 F7
Hole La B31 19 C5
Hollams Rd GL20 196 F7
Holland Cl 4 B50 136 D4
Holland Gn WR4 116 C3
Hollaway Ct B63 7 D5
Hollie Lucas Rd B13 20 F7
Hollies Dr B62 8 E6
Hollies La Enville DY7 2 F7
Kidderminster Foreign DY11 11 F3
Hollies Mews The 4 WR14 139 B5
Hollies Rise B64 7 F8
Hollies The
Birmingham B45 33 A1
Charlton WR10 160 E8
2 Stourport-on-Severn DY13 43 E6
Hollins La WR6 99 A3
Hollister Dr B32 9 F3
Hollow Croft B31 19 B3
Holloway
Birmingham B31 18 E5
1 Pershore WR10 158 C8
Holloway Dr
Pershore WR10 144 B1
Redditch B98 71 B3
Holloway La B98 70 F3
Holloway Pk B98 71 A3
Holloway The
Alvechurch B48 51 D3
Bluntington DY10 29 E2
Chaddesley Corbett DY10 46 E8
Droitwich WR9 85 A2
Stourbridge DY8 5 F7
Hollowfields Rd B96 106 C6
Hollows The WR11 175 B2
Hollowtree La B60 50 A3
Holly Bush Gr B32 9 D7
Holly Bush La WR6 97 A7
Holly Cl
Bretforton WR11 163 B5
Droitwich WR9 104 A8
10 Evesham WR11 161 F2
Kinver DY7 3 F5
Holly Ct DY10 27 D8
Holly Dell B38 20 B2
Holly Dr B47 36 B7
Holly Gr
Birmingham, Bournville B30 19 F8
Bromsgrove B61 48 F3
Stourbridge DY8 5 F5
Holly Hill 4 B45 17 F1
Holly Hill Meth & CE Inf Sch B45 17 F2
Holly Hill Rd B45 18 A2
Holly La B48 52 F5
Holly Mount WR4 115 E4
Holly Mount Rd WR4 115 E4
Holly Rd
Birmingham, King's Norton B30 20 A4
Bromsgrove B61 48 F4
Oldbury B68 9 C8
Stourport-on-Severn DY13 44 B4
Tenbury Wells WR15 55 F6
Holly Tree La WR2 127 B8
Holly Well La DY14 40 E6
Hollybank Gr B63 7 D1
Hollybank Rd B13 21 A6
Hollyberry Cl B98 72 A4
Hollybrow B29 19 B7
Hollybush La DY8 5 F7
Hollyfield Dr B45 33 A1
Hollyhedge Cl B31 18 D6
Hollymoor Way
Birmingham B31 18 D1
Birmingham B31 18 B1
Hollymount B62 9 A7
Hollyoak Croft B31 34 B8
Hollywood By-Pass
Birmingham B47 20 F1
Hollywood B38, B47 35 E6
Hollywood Gdns B47 36 A8
Hollywood La B47 36 B7
Hollywood Prim Sch B14 21 A1
Holman St DY11 27 C5
Holmcroft Rd DY10 28 A5
Holme Rd 6 GL20 196 F3
Holmes Dr B45 32 F6
Holmes La Hanbury B60 87 A7
Stoke Prior B60 68 B1
Holmoak Cl 8 GL20 197 A4
Holmwood Ave DY11 27 A6
Holmwood Dr B97 70 C3
Holmwood Gdns 9 WR11 161 F2
Holmwood House B97 70 C3
Holt Fleet Rd WR9 82 E4
Holt Gdns B80 90 E2
Holt Hill B98 71 F8
Holt House B61 49 A3
Holt La B62 16 D4
Holt Rd B80 90 E2
Holy Cross Gn DY9 15 E2
Holy Cross La DY9 30 E8
Holy Oaks Cl B98 71 E2
Holy Redeemer RC Prim Sch The WR10 158 D8
Holy Well Rd
Great Malvern WR14 166 E8
Malvern Wells WR14 152 E1
Holyoakes Field Fst Sch B97 70 D4
Holyoakes La B97 69 C5
Holywell La B45 32 D6
Holywell Prim Sch B45 32 D7
Home Cl B28 21 F6
Home Mdw Ct B13 21 A5
Home Mdw La B98 71 E6
Home Piece WR9 84 D2
Homedene Rd B31 18 E7
Homefield Rd WR2 115 A1
Homemead Gr B45 32 F7
Homer Hill Rd B63 7 C7
Homestead Ave WR4 116 B7
Homestead Cl 6 GL20 184 F6
Homfray Rd DY10 12 F1
Honeybourne Airfield Ind Est WR11 164 B1
Honeybourne Cl 3 B63 8 A3
Honeybourne Fst Sch WR11 164 A4
Honeybourne Rd
Alveley WV15 1 C6
Bidford-on-Avon B50 136 E2
Halesowen B63 8 C3
Weston-sub-Edge WR11 164 B1
Honeybourne Sch B28 21 F8
Honeybourne Sta WR11 164 A6
Honeybrook Cl DY11 12 D2
Honeybrook La DY11 12 B1
Honeychurch Cl B98 70 F3
Honeycomb Way B31 18 E3
Honeysuckle Cl
Birmingham B32 9 B5
Evesham WR11 161 D1
Honeywood Rd WR2 114 E4
Honister Dr WR4 116 A6
Honiton Cl B31 18 E4
Honiton Cres B31 18 E4
Honnington Ct 2 B29 9 F1
Hoo Farm Ind Est DY10 27 F1
Hoo Rd DY10 27 E4
Hoobrook Ent Ctr DY10 27 E2
Hoobrook Ind Est DY10 27 E2
Hood Gr B30 19 D4
Hood St 6 WR1 115 B2
Hoopers Cl WR13 126 A2
Hoopers La B96 89 E1
Hoosen Cl B62 9 A6
Hop Gdns The WR11 162 C5
Hop Pole Gn WR13 125 F2
Hop Pole La DY12 25 E4
Hope La WR6 97 C6
Hope St B62 8 D8
Hopedale Rd B32 9 C5
Hopehouse La WR6 99 B3
Hopgardens Ave B60 49 B2
Hopkins Field CV37 151 C6
Hopton Dr DY10 27 E1
Hopton Gr B13 21 C5
Hopton La WR6 125 B6
Hopton St WR2 114 E2
Hopwood Cl B63 8 A2
Hopwood Gr B31 33 E6
Hopyard La B98 71 D4
Hopyard The GL20 184 D1
Hordern Cres DY5 6 D8
Horn La WR6 99 B7
Hornbeam Cl
15 Bewdley DY12 25 F3
Birmingham B29 19 B7
Hornby Gr B14 21 C4
Hornsby Ave WR4 116 C3
Hornyold Ave WR14 138 E3
Hornyold Rd WR14 138 E3
Horrell Rd B90 21 F2
Horse Bridge La DY7 4 C2
Horse Fair DY10 27 E7
Horsebridge Ave WR11 162 D4
Horsford Rd WR2 114 F5
Horton La WR9 65 A2
Horton Rd DY7 3 F5
Hoskyns Ave WR4 116 C3
Hospital Bank WR14 138 E3
Hospital La WR2 127 C2
Hospital Lea Castle DY10 13 C3
Hospital Rd WR14 138 D6
Hospital Tewkesbury GL20 196 F6
Hossil La
Belbroughton DY9 30 C8
Clent DY9 15 D1
Hough Rd B14 20 D6
Houghton Ct B28 21 D4
Houldey Rd B31 19 B1
Houndsfield Cl B47 36 C6
Houndsfield Farm B47 36 B5
Houndsfield Gr B47 36 A5
Houndsfield La B47 36 C6
Housman Cl B60 67 E8
Housman Ct B60 49 A3
Housman Pk B60 49 A2
Housman Wlk DY10 28 C6
Houx The DY8 5 E8
Hoveton Cl B98 71 B2
Howard Ave B61 48 E3
Howard Cl
Bidford-on-Avon B50 136 C4
Northway GL20 197 E8
Howard Rd
Birmingham, King's Heath B14 20 E7
Northway GL20 197 D8
Redditch B98 90 C8
Worcester WR2 114 C3
Howard Rd E B13 20 F7
Howcroft Gn 3 WR4 116 B6
Howells Rd GL20 196 E6
Howlett Pl WR4 116 C3
Howley Grange Prim Sch B62 8 F5
Howley Grange Rd B62 9 A4
Howsell Rd WR14 139 A4
Howsells The WR14 139 B6
Hoyland Way B30 19 E8
Huband Cl B98 71 A5
Huddington Ct* WR7 118 C6
Hudman's Cl GL20 184 A6
Hudson Cl
Honeybourne WR11 164 B5
Pershore WR10 144 C1
Worcester WR2 127 F7
Hudson's Dr B30 20 A4
Hudswell Dr DY5 6 D8
Hughes Cl
Harvington WR11 148 A7
Northway GL20 184 F1
Hughes La WR11 148 A7
Huins Cl B98 71 A4
Hullbrook Rd B13 21 C6
Hulls La WR9 104 A3
Humber Gdns B63 7 C5
Humber Rd WR5 115 E3
Hume St DY11 27 C5
Humphrey Ave B60 67 F7
Humphries Dr DY10 27 F2
Hungary Cl DY9 6 C5
Hungary Hill DY9 6 C5
Hungerford Rd DY8 5 E2
Hungerpit Wlk WR3 115 B6
Hunnington Cl B32 9 A1
Hunnington Cres B63 8 B2
Hunscote Cl B90 21 F1
Hunscote House B90 21 F1
Hunslet Cl B32 9 F4
Hunslet Rd B32 9 F4
Hunstanton Ave B17 9 F8
Hunstanton Cl
Brierley Hill DY5 6 C7
5 Worcester WR5 128 D6
Hunt Ave WR4 116 C4
Hunt End La B97 89 C5
Hunter Rise WR10 158 C8
Hunters Hill Sch B60 49 F6
Hunters Rise B63 7 D1
Hunters Way WR9 84 D4
Huntingdon Cl B98 71 F2
Huntingdon Gdns B63 7 C7
Huntingtree Prim Sch B63 7 E3
Huntingtree Rd B63 7 E3
Huntlands Rd B63 7 F2
Hunts Rd B30 20 B7
Hunts Rise DY12 26 C3
Huntsmans Cl 3 WR10 143 F6
Huntsmans Dr DY7 3 F5
Hurcott Ct DY10 28 A8
Hurcott La DY10 28 C8
Hurcott Rd DY10 28 B8
Hurst Ct DY9 6 F5
Hurst Gn Prim Sch B62 8 E8
Hurst Gn Rd B62 8 F8
Hurst La WR3 102 F2
Hurst Rd WR10 144 D2
Hurst The
Birmingham B13 21 D7
2 Cleobury Mortimer DY14 22 C4
Hollywood B47 36 A6
Husum Way DY10 28 C7
Huxleys Way 6 WR11 161 C4
Huxtable Rise WR4 116 B4
Hyacinth Cl 1 WR5 128 C4
Hyatt Sq DY5 6 C7
Hyde Cl Bromsgrove B60 49 B2
Kinver DY7 4 A5
Hyde La Kinver DY7 4 A6
Upton upon Severn WR8 168 E5
Hyde Pk Cnr GL19 192 A3
Hyde The DY9 6 D2
Hydefields WR8 169 A5
Hydrangea Cl WR5 128 D4
Hylton Rd
Evesham WR11 161 A4
Worcester WR2 114 F4
Hyperion Rd DY7 5 C7
Hytall Rd B90 21 C2

I

Ibberton Rd B14 21 B3
Ibis Cl DY10 28 B3
Ibstock Cl B98 71 E4
Ibstock Dr DY8 6 A4
Ibstock House B98 71 E4
Icknield Cl B50 136 E4
Icknield Fst Sch B98 71 D1
Icknield St
Alvechurch B38 35 B2
Beoley B98 52 C2
Bidford-on-Avon B50 136 E4
Redditch, Church Hill B98 71 C7
Redditch, Ipsley B98 71 D2
Rowney Green B48 52 B6
Icknield St Dr B98 90 D7
Ideal Bldgs 7 DY11 27 D6
Ideal Wks DY9 7 A6
Idleton 7 WR4 116 C3
Idmiston Croft B14 20 F2

Ikon Ind Est DY10 45 D6
Ilkley Cl WR4 116 A4
Illey Cl B31 18 C1
Illey La Birmingham B32 18 A7
Halesowen B62 17 E8
Illeybrook Sq B32 9 D2
Illshaw Cl B98 72 A4
Ilmington Cl B98 71 D1
Ilmington Rd B29 9 F1
Ilsham Gr B31 33 E6
Imber Rd DY10 28 A1
Imperial Ave DY10 27 F8
Imperial Gr DY10 27 F8
Imperial Rd WR14 153 A8
Impney Cl B98 71 E6
Inches La WR11 161 D5
Inett Way WR9 84 C3
Infirmary Wlk 5 WR1 115 B3
Ingestre Rd B28 21 F7
Ingeva Dr B45 33 A1
Ingham Pedl Cl 1 WR13 152 B2
Inglemere Gr B29 18 F7
Ingoldsby Rd B31 19 C3
Inkberrow Fst Sch WR7 120 F8
Inkberrow Rd B63 7 F2
Inn La DY11 45 A2
Innage Rd B31 19 B4
Innage The B47 36 A5
Innerstone La GL19 192 C1
Insetton Cl B98 71 D4
Institute Rd B14 20 F8
Instone Rd B63 8 A3
Insull Ave B14 21 B1
Intended St B63 7 C7
Inverlea Ct GL55 165 D4
Inverness Rd B31 18 F3
Io Ctr The B98 90 C8
Ipsley Alders Marsh Nature Reserve* B98 71 F4
Ipsley CE Mid Sch B98 71 E3
Ipsley Church La B98 71 C1
Ipsley La B98 71 D2
Ipsley St B98 70 E3
Iris Cl B29 19 B8
Iris Dr B14 20 D3
Iron Bridge Wlk DY9 15 B8
Ironside Ct 17 DY12 25 F3
Irwin Ave B45 33 C7
Isaac Wlk WR2 114 E1
Isaacs Way WR9 103 F7
Isbourne Cres WR11 161 D2
Island Dr DY10 27 E4
Islington B63 8 A4
Ismere Way DY10 12 F1
Ithon Gr B38 34 E8
Iverley Ct 6 WR15 55 F6
Iverley La DY10 14 C5
Iverley Rd B63 8 C4
Iverley Wlk DY9 6 C2
Ivor Rd B97 70 D2
Ivy La Bretforton WR11 163 B5
Fernhill Heath WR3 103 A2
Romsley B62 16 D5
Ivy Rd B30 20 A6
Ivy St WR3 115 A6
Ivyhouse Rd B38 34 C8
Izod St B97 70 D4

J

Jack Thomson Croft WR11 135 F3
Jackdaw La WR9 104 B7
Jackson Cres DY13 43 E1
Jackson St DY9 6 E6
Jackson Way B32 9 A5
Jacksons Mdw B50 136 C6
Jacksons Orch CV37 151 C6
Jacob Cl 4 WR3 115 E7
Jacobs Ladder WR3 102 D4
Jacomb Cl WR2 114 A7
Jacomb Dr WR2 114 A7
Jacomb Rd WR2 114 A7
Jakeman Cl B98 71 E4
Jamaica Cres WR14 139 A5
Jamaica Rd WR14 139 A5
James Cl WR1 115 C2
James Ct B38 19 F2
James Lloyd Trust Flats B30 19 C5
James Rd DY10 28 A8
James Scott Rd B63 7 A6
James St DY7 4 A4
Janice Gr B14 21 B4
Jarvis Dr WR10 171 E8
Jarvis St WR10 171 E7
Jasmin Croft B14 20 E3
Jasmine Cl 7 WR5 128 D5
Jasmine Gr B61 48 F4
Jasmine Rd WR14 152 F4
Jasmine Wlk 5 WR11 161 D1
Jason Rd DY9 6 F4
Jasper Rd 5 WR2 127 F7
Jay Pk Cres DY10 28 B2
Jays Cl B98 72 A3
Jays Cres B48 34 B1
Jeal Cl B47 35 E2
Jelleyman Cl DY11 27 C6
Jennett Tree La WR2 127 E1
Jennings Wood La DY13 43 A2
Jersey Cl B98 71 D7
Jerusalem Wlk DY10 27 E7
Jervoise Dr B31 19 B5
Jeynes Row GL20 196 F7
Jiggins La B32 9 D1
Jill La B96 90 B2
Jinnah Rd B98 70 E2
Jinney Ring Craft Ctr* B60 87 A5
Job's La GL20 185 D7
John Comyn Dr WR3 115 C8
John Moore Countryside Mus* GL20 196 E5
John Moore Prim Sch GL20 197 A3
John Rd B62 8 F3
Johns Cl B80 90 C4
Johnson Cl B98 71 A5
Johnsons Gr B68 9 D8
Joiners Cl 3 WR4 115 F6
Jordans Cl Redditch B97 89 D6
Willersey WR12 177 E3
Jorden's Wlk DY12 26 D4
Josiah Rd B31 18 D2
Joyberry Dr DY8 6 A3
Jubilee Ave B97 89 D7
Jubilee Cl B50 136 E5
Jubilee Dr
Bredon GL20 184 F6
Colwall WR14 152 D2
Jubilee Dr N DY11 27 B2
Jubilee Dr S DY11 27 B2
Jubilee Rd
Birmingham B45 17 E2
Worcester WR2 128 A8
Jubilee Terr B60 67 C1
Judge Rd DY5 6 F7
Juggins La B94 53 B7
Julian Cl B61 49 A8
Juliet Rd B62 8 F3
Junction Rd
Bromsgrove B61 48 E3
Stourbridge DY8 5 E8
Juniper Ct DY10 28 A4
Juniper Rise B63 7 C5
Juniper Way WR14 152 F4
Jury La WR6 99 A4
Jury Rd DY5 6 F7
Jutland Rd B13 21 B8

K

Karen Way DY5 6 D8
Katmandu Rd B60 49 C1
Katrine Rd DY13 43 E6
Keats Ave WR3 115 C6
Keats Cl DY8 6 A8
Keats House B97 89 C8
Keats Pl DY10 28 B6
Keble Cl WR4 115 E3
Kedleston Ct B28 21 F4
Kedleston Rd B28 21 F5
Keele Cl B98 71 E6
Keepers Cl WR10 143 F6
Keir Pl DY8 5 E8
Keith Winter Cl B61 48 F6
Kelby Cl B31 18 E4
Kelby Rd B31 18 F4
Kelling Cl DY5 6 C8
Kelverdale Gr B14 20 C4
Kelvin Cl DY11 27 A8
Kelvin Rd B31 19 B1
Kelwood Dr B63 8 A5
Kemelstowe Cres B63 16 C8
Kemerton House B97 70 B4
Kemerton Rd GL20 184 E6
Kempsey Cl
Halesowen B63 7 E4
Redditch B98 90 B7
Kempsey Covert B38 34 E7
Kempsey House B32 18 A8
Kempsey Prim Sch WR5 141 C7
Kempsford Cl B98 89 F6
Kempton Cl 4 WR11 161 C2
Kempton Ct B61 32 A1
Kempton Rd WR10 144 E4
Kempton Way DY8 5 E3
Kemshead Ave B31 33 E8
Kemsley Rd B14 20 F2
Kenchester Cl B98 71 F2
Kendal Ave B45 33 B7
Kendal Cl
Bromsgrove B60 49 B1
Redditch B98 72 A3
Kendal Ct 14 B29 19 C7
Kendal Dr B45 33 D1
Kendal End Rd B45 33 D1
Kendal Gn WR4 116 B6
Kendal Rise Rd B45 33 B7
Kendall St WR3 115 D4
Kendlewood Rd DY10 13 B1
Kenelm Cl WR6 97 E8
Kenelm Rd WR6 97 E8
Kenelm's Ct B62 17 A4
Kenilw Orth Cl WR1 115 C4
Kenilworth Cl B97 89 D6
Kenilworth Dr DY10 27 E2
Kenilworth House B13 21 A6
Kenilworth Rd B68 9 D7
Kenley Gr B30 20 B3
Kennedy Cl DY10 27 F3
Kennedy Ct DY8 5 F5
Kennedy Gr B30 20 B6
Kennel Bank WR10 160 B6
Kennels La WR3 102 F4
Kennet Gn WR5 115 D2
Kenswick Dr B63 8 A2
Kent Cl Evesham WR11 161 A3
Great Malvern WR14 139 C6
Kidderminster DY10 27 E3
Kent Rd Birmingham B45 17 F1
Halesowen B62 8 F5
Stourbridge DY8 5 D7
Kentmere Cl WR4 116 A5
Kentmere Rd B60 49 C1
Kenward Croft B17 9 F7
Kenway B47 36 A7
Kenwood Ave WR4 115 F4
Kenwood Cl WR4 115 F4
Kenyon Cl
Bromsgrove B60 49 A1
Stourbridge DY8 6 A7
Kepax Gdns WR3 115 A6
Keren Dr WR5 128 F3
Keresley Gr B29 9 F2
Kernthorpe Rd B14 20 D4
Kerry Cl B31 18 F6
Kerry Croft Cl B97 89 E5
Kerry Hill
3 Bromsgrove B60 67 E6
Worcester WR3 115 E8
Kerswell Cl 2 B97 70 B5
Kestrel Cl DY10 27 E3
Kestrel Dr 6 WR5 128 C5
Kestrel Gr B30 19 D8
Kestrel Rd B63 7 B7
Kestrel View B60 49 C7
Kestrel Way GL20 184 D1
Keswick Dr WR4 116 A6
Kettles Wood Dr B32 9 C2
Kewstoke Croft B31 18 E6
Key Ave WR4 116 C3
Keynell Covert B30 20 C2
Kidderminster Coll DY10 27 E4
Kidderminster General Hospl DY11 27 C5
Kidderminster Rd
Bewdley DY12 26 C4
Bromsgrove B61 48 C3
Chaddesley Corbett DY10 47 A6
Droitwich WR9 84 E4
Hagley DY9 15 B5
Iverley DY7, DY10 14 C7
Kidderminster Rd S DY9 14 F3
Kidderminster Sta DY10 27 F5
Kidderminster Town Sta* DY10 27 F5
Kielder Gdns DY9 6 B1
Kielder Rise WR2 127 F6
Kiftsgate Stone* GL55 178 E2
Kilbury Dr WR5 129 A8
Kilcote Rd B90 21 C2
Kilmore La GL20 183 F6
Kiln Cl B80 90 C4
Kiln La WR13 126 A2
Kilpeck Cl B98 71 F2
Kimberley Ave DY10 13 B4
Kimberley Cl B98 71 B7
Kimbolton Dr B60 50 A5
Kimpton Cl B14 20 E2
Kineton Cl B98 71 D1
Kineton Croft B32 18 D8
Kineton House B13 21 A6
Kineton Rd B45 32 E7
King Arthur's Cl WR2 114 F4
King Charles Ave WR2 127 C2
King Charles Cl DY11 27 C6
King Charles I High Sch DY10 28 A5
King Charles Rd B62 8 F4
King Charles Sq 4 DY10 27 E6
King Edmund Sq 1 WR1 115 B3
King Edward Ave B61 48 F5
King Edward Rd B61 48 F5
King Edward VI Camp Hill Schs B14 20 D7
King Edward VI Coll DY8 6 A6
King Edward VI Five Ways Sch B32 18 C8
King Edward's Rd WR14 152 E4
King George Ave
Bromsgrove B61 48 F4
Droitwich WR9 84 F1
King George Cl B61 48 F4
King George's Way
5 Pershore WR10 144 D1
Pershore WR10 158 E8
King Johns Ct GL20 196 E7
King St Brierley Hill DY5 7 A8
Halesowen B63 8 A4
Stourbridge DY8 5 E6
Stourbridge, Lye DY9 6 F5
Worcester WR1 115 C1
King St Pas DY5 7 A8
King Stephen's Mount WR2 114 F5
King William St DY8 5 F8
King's End Rd WR2 127 D4
King's Heath Boys Sch B13 21 A6
King's Hill WR5 141 C8
King's La
Bidford-on-Avon B50 136 B6
Norton & Lenchwick WR11 147 D3
King's Mdw DY9 15 E3
King's Norton Boys Sch B30 19 E4
King's Norton Girls Sch B30 19 F5
King's Norton Prim Sch B30 20 A2
King's Norton Sta B30 19 F4
King's Rd
Evesham WR11 161 F4
Kidderminster DY11 27 C6
King's Sch Playing Field WR2 115 B1
Kingcomb La GL55 178 F3
Kingfield Rd B90 21 C2
Kingfisher Cl WR5 128 D6
Kingfisher Ct B48 51 A7
Kingfisher Dr DY8 5 C4
Kingfisher Ent Pk B98 71 A3
Kingfisher Gr DY10 28 A3
Kingfisher Sh Ctr 2 B97 70 E3
Kingfisher Way B30 19 D8
Kingfisher Wlk B97 70 D4
Kingham Cl B98 72 A4
Kingham Covert B14 20 D2
Kings Arms La DY13 62 E8
Kings Cl B14 20 C6
Kings Coughton La B49 109 F2
Kings Ct DY8 5 E5
Kings Gate GL20 197 B6
Kings Gdn B30 19 E4
Kings Gn Ave B38 19 F2
Kings Hawford Sch WR3 102 A5
Kings Norton Bsns Ctr B30 20 A4
Kings Norton High Sch B38 34 F8
Kings Rd
Birmingham, Stirchley B14 20 C6
2 Great Malvern WR14 166 E7
Kings Sch WR5 115 C1
Kings Terr B14 20 D6
Kingsbridge Rd B32 9 D1
Kingsbury Ave WR2 127 F8
Kingscote Cl B98 71 D7
Kingsdale Ct WR12 190 E8
Kingsdown Rd B31 9 F1
Kingsfield Rd B14 20 E8
Kingsford La Kinver DY11 3 C1
Wolverley & Cookley DY11 12 C7
Kingshill Cl WR14 139 A1
Kingshill Dr B38 19 F2
Kingshurst Rd
Birmingham B31 19 A3
Solihull B90 21 F1
Kingsley Ave B98 71 A3
Kingsley Coll B98 90 C6
Kingsley Rd B30 19 D4
Kingsthorpe Rd B14 21 A3
Kingston Ave WR3 115 D6
Kingston Cl 1 WR9 104 A8
Kingston Ct 17 B29 19 C7
Kingston Rd GL20 197 E8
Kingsway Oldbury B68 9 B7
Stourbridge DY8 5 E8
Stourport-on-Severn DY13 43 F7
Kingsway Dr B38 19 F2
Kingswood Dr B30 20 C3
Kingswood House B14 20 E2
Kingswood Rd
Birmingham, Coft Common B31 33 F7
Hampton Lovett WR9 84 C7
Kinlet Cl B98 71 E3
Kinlet Gr B31 19 C2
Kinlet Rd DY12 24 A5
Kinloss Sch WR6 99 D4
Kinnersley Cl B98 71 E3
Kinnersley Rd WR14 138 E6
Kinnerton Cres B29 9 F2
Kinsey Gr B14 20 F4
Kinsham La GL20 185 C5
Kinthall La WR6 77 B6
Kintore Croft B32 18 B7
Kintyre Cl B45 17 E1
Kinver Ave DY11 27 A1
Kinver Dr DY9 15 C7
Kinver La DY11 13 B7
Kinver Rd
Birmingham B31 19 D2
Enville DY7 3 E8
Kinverdale DY11 12 B6
Kipling Cl
Great Malvern WR14 139 A2
Worcester WR3 115 C6
Kipling Rd B30 19 C4
Kipling Wlk 3 DY10 28 B6
Kirkstone Ct DY5 6 B8
Kirkstone Dr WR4 115 F4
Kirkstone Way DY5 6 B8
Kirkwall Rd B32 9 D1
Kitchener Rd CV37 151 E4
Kite La B97 70 A5
Kitebrook Cl B98 71 E4
Kitswell Gdns B32 18 A8
Kittiwake Dr
Brierley Hill DY5 6 D7
Kidderminster DY10 28 B3
Kitwell Jun & Inf Sch B32 18 A7
Kitwell La B32 18 A8
Knapp Pl WR5 128 E6
Knapp The WR11 162 D3
Knapp Way WR14 138 F4
Knaresdale Cl DY5 6 C8
Knight House B13 21 D7
Knight Rd DY11 12 C3
Knight St WR2 114 F2
Knighton Rd B31 19 C4
Knights Way GL20 197 A6
Knightsford Cl B97 69 F2
Knoll La WR14 153 B6
Knoll Sch The DY11 27 A7
Knoll The B32 9 C1
Knottesford Cl B80 90 C3
Knotts Ave WR4 116 C4
Knowesley Cl B60 49 B2
Knowle Cl
Birmingham B45 33 D7
Redditch B98 71 C6
Knutswood Cl B13 21 D7
Kohima Dr
Stourbridge DY8 5 E5
Worcester Norton WR5 128 F4
Kylemilne Way DY13 44 C3
Kyles Way B32 18 B7
Kyre Pk Gdns* WR15 75 F3
Kyreside WR15 55 F4

L

Labrador Rd 5 WR2 127 F6
Laburnum Cl
Hollywood B47 36 A5
Kinver DY7 3 F5
Redditch B98 70 E2
Stourbridge DY8 5 E7
Laburnum Dr WR11 161 F1
Laburnum Gr
Bromsgrove B61 48 F4
Kidderminster DY11 27 B8
Laburnum Rd
Birmingham B30 19 F8
Worcester WR4 115 E4
Laburnum St DY8 5 E7
Laburnum Trees B47 35 F7
Laburnum Way B31 19 A1
Laburnum Wlk WR8 169 C5
Lacon Childe Sch DY14 22 C5
Lacon Cl DY14 22 B4
Ladbrook Cl B98 89 E7
Lady Bank B32 18 B7
Lady Bracknell Mews B31 19 C4
Lady Grey's Wlk DY8 5 D5
Lady Harriet's La B98 70 F4
Ladygo La WR2 101 C2
Ladygrove Cl B98 90 A8
Ladypool Cl B62 8 C4
Ladysmith Rd B63 7 C6
Ladywood Rd
Besford WR8 157 B7
Martin Hussingtree WR3 103 A5
Lahn Dr WR9 103 D8
Lakedown Cl B14 20 E1
Lakefield B31 18 F4
Lakehouse Gr B38 19 D3
Laker Cl DY8 6 A7
Lakes Cl DY11 27 C7
Lakes Ct DY12 25 F3
Lakes Halt The B94 53 F8
Lakes Rd The DY12 25 F3
Lakeside B97 69 D7
Lakeside Ct DY5 6 B8
Lakeside Ind Est B98 71 B3
Lakewood Dr B45 18 B1
Lamb Bank WR14 138 D3
Lambert Rd WR2 114 F2
Lambourne Ave WR14 139 A5
Lambourne Cl 2 B50 136 D5
Lambourne Cres WR2 114 E6
Lambourne Dr 2 DY12 25 F4
Lambourne Orch WR6 82 B3
Lambourne Way DY5 6 B8
Lambscote Cl B90 21 C2
Lamont Ave B32 9 F3
Lampitt La GL20 172 A3
Lamport House 5 B14 21 A3
Lancaster Ave B45 33 A8
Lancaster Cl B30 20 A6
Lancaster Rd 3 DY12 25 F3
Lancelot House DY10 28 C8
Lanchester Rd B38 20 A1
Lancing Cl 3 WR5 128 E8
Land Oak Dr DY10 28 B7
Lander Cl B45 33 A6
Landor Rd B98 71 A1
Landsdowne St WR1 115 B4
Landsgate DY8 6 A1
Lane The
Buckland WR12 189 F5
Elmley Castle WR10 159 E1
Strensham WR8 171 A6
Lane's End WR5 141 B7
Lanescourt GL20 196 F6
Lanesfield Pk WR11 161 E6
Langdale Cl WR4 116 A6
Langdale Dr WR4 115 F5
Langdale Rd
3 Stourport-on-Severn DY13 43 D1
10 Worcester WR1 115 A5
Langdale Way DY9 6 D4
Langland Ave WR14 139 C2
Langland Rd DY14 22 C5
Langland Stadium (Malvern Town Football Club) WR14 139 C2
Langley Cl Redditch B98 71 D1
6 Worcester WR2 114 E5
Langley Rd 4 WR9 85 A1
Langstone Rd B14 21 B3
Lankets The WR11 162 E3

Lannacombe Rd B31 .....33 E6
Lansbury Gn B64 ....8 B8
Lansbury Rd B64 ....8 B8
Lansdown Gn DY11 ......27 C5
Lansdowne Cl 8 WR14 ..139 B1
Lansdowne Cres
Great Malvern WR14 .....139 A1
Studley B80 ....90 D3
Worcester WR3 ....115 C4
Lansdowne Ct DY9 ....6 C1
Lansdowne Rd
4 Great Malvern WR14 ...138 F4
Halesowen, Hasbury B63 ....7 D2
Studley B80 ....90 D3
9 Worcester WR1 ....115 B4
Lansdowne Rise 1
WR3 ....115 C4
Lansdowne Terr
WR14 ....139 A1
Lansdowne Wlk 1
WR3 ....115 D4
Lapal Cl WR2 ....114 F2
Lapal La B62 ....9 A2
Lapal La N B62 ....8 E3
Lapal La S B32, B62 ....8 F2
Lapal Prim Sch B62 ....8 F4
Lappath House B32 .....18 D8
Lapwing Cl
Kidderminster DY10 ....28 B1
Northway GL20 ....184 D1
Lapworth Cl B98 ....89 F7
Larch Cl DY7 ....4 C3
Larch House DY8 ....5 C6
Larch Rd
11 Evesham WR11 ....161 F2
Worcester WR4 ....115 D4
Larches Cottage Gdns
DY11 ....27 C3
Larches Rd DY11 ....27 D4
Larchfield Cl WR14 .....138 E4
Larchmere Dr
Birmingham B28 ....21 F8
Bromsgrove B61 ....48 E3
Larford Wlk DY13 ....43 F1
Lark Cl B14 ....21 A2
Lark Hill WR5 ....115 E1
Lark Hill Rd WR5 ....115 E1
Larkfield Rd B98 ....71 A1
Larkhill DY10 ....27 E7
Larkhill Rd DY8 ....5 C4
Larkhill Wlk B14 ....20 D1
Larks Rise DY14 ....22 B4
Larksfield Mews DY5 .....6 C7
Larkspur Ct B62 ....8 F7
Larkspur Dr WR11 ....161 C1
Larkspur Rd 8 WR5 .....128 D5
Lashbrooke House B45 ...32 F7
Laslett St WR3 ....115 D4
Lassington Cl B98 ....71 E4
Latchford Cl B98 ....71 E6
Latimer Rd B48 ....51 A5
Laugherne Rd WR2 ......114 F3
Laughton Cl B31 ....34 B7
Launceston Pl 11 WR4 ..116 C6
Launde The B28 ....21 E3
Laurel Ave
4 Evesham WR11 ....161 F2
9 Walton Cardiff GL20 ...197 A4
Laurel Bank Mews B60 ...49 F4
Laurel Cl
Drakes Broughton WR10 ..143 F6
Redditch B98 ....70 E2
Laurel Gr
Birmingham B30 ....19 E6
Bromsgrove B61 ....48 F4
Laurel La B63 ....8 B3
Laurel Rd
Birmingham, King's Norton
B30 ....20 A4
Worcester WR4 ....115 E5
Laurel Wood Cl 6 WR9 .104 A8
Laurel Wood Rd WR9 ...104 A8
Laurels Ave WR11 ......162 B8
Laurels Rd WR11 ....162 B8
Laurels The B68 ....9 B6
Laurence Ct B31 ....19 B5
Lavender House B38 .....34 F8
Lavender La DY8 ....5 D3
Lavender Rd WR3 ......115 A6
Lavender Wlk WR11 ....175 C8
Lavinia Rd B62 ....8 E3
Lawford Gr B90 ....21 D2
Lawley The B63 ....7 D1
Lawn Ave DY8 ....5 E4
Lawn St DY8 ....5 E4
Lawnsdown Rd DY5 ......6 F6
Lawnside 1 WR14 ......153 A8
Lawrence Ct 6 B68 ....9 B8
Lawrence St DY9 ....6 C6
Lax La DY12 ....26 B3
Laxton Ave WR2 ....114 E5
Laxton Cl WR7 ....117 F4
Laxton Dr 3 DY12 ....25 F4
Layamon Wlk DY13 ......43 F2
Laylocks La WR2 ....113 F4
Layton Ave WR14 ....139 B3
Lazy Hill B38 ....20 B2
Lazy La WR10 ....146 A1
Lea Bank Ave DY11 .....27 B5
Lea Castle Cl DY10 ......12 F1
Lea Castle Dr DY10 .....13 C2
Lea Cl WR3 ....102 B1
Lea Croft Rd B97 ....89 D5
Lea Cswy The DY11 .....27 A4
Lea End La B48 ....34 D3
Lea Gn La B47 ....36 C5
Lea Hill Cl WR14 ....138 F2
Lea House Rd B30 ......20 A7
Lea La DY10 ....12 F4
Lea Meml CE Fst Sch
DY14 ....24 C2
Lea Pk Rise B61 ....48 F5
Lea St DY10 ....27 F6
Lea St Fst Sch DY10 .....27 F6
Lea The Alveley WV15 ......1 C6
Kidderminster DY11 ....27 A5
Throckmorton WR10 .....145 E8
Lea Vale Rd DY8 ....5 F3
Lea View DY14 ....22 B4
Lea Wlk B45 ....32 F8
Lea Wood Gr DY11 ......27 A5
Lea Yield Cl B30 ....20 A7
Leabank Dr WR3 ....102 A1
Leach Gn La B45 ....33 B6
Leach Heath La B45 .....33 A7
Leadbetter Dr B61 ....48 D2
Leadon Rd WR14 ....153 D7
Leafield Gdns B62 ....8 D8
Leaholme Gdns DY9 ......6 B2
Leamington Rd WR12 ..177 D2
Leander Gdns B14 ....20 F5
Leander Rd DY9 ....6 F4
Leapgate Ctry Pk*
DY13 ....44 C2
Leapgate La DY13 ....44 E5
Lear Cl WR2 ....114 D3
Leasowe Cl 5 WR2 ......114 D1
Leasowe Rd B45 ....32 F8
Leasowes DY14 ....40 B7
Leasowes Com Coll B62 ..8 E6
Leasowes Ct B63 ....7 F3
Leasowes La B62 ....8 D4
Leasowes Rd WR11 .....162 B8
Lechlade Cl B98 ....71 B7
Lechmere Cres
6 Great Malvern WR14 ...138 F5
Worcester WR2 ....114 E5
Leckhampton Cl WR4 ...116 A7
Ledbury Cl B98 ....71 F2
Ledbury House B97 ......70 B4
Ledsam Gr B32 ....9 F6
Ledwych Cl WR9 ....84 D3
Ledwych Gdns WR9 .....84 E3
Ledwych Rd 1 WR9 ......84 E3
Lee Rd Blackheath B64 .....7 F8
Hollywood B47 ....36 A7
Northway GL20 ....197 E8
Leebank Rd B63 ....7 E2
Leeds Ave WR4 ....116 C6
Lees The WR14 ....152 F6
Legion Rd B45 ....32 E7
Leicester Gr WR11 .....161 D5
Leicester St 5 WR1 .....115 B4
Leigh & Bransford Prim Sch
WR13 ....126 B2
Leigh Gr WR9 ....84 E4
Leigh Sinton Rd
Leigh WR13 ....126 A1
Malvern WR13 ....125 F1
Leith Gr B38 ....34 E8
Lench Cl B97 ....70 A5
Lenchs Trust B32 ....9 E6
Lenwade Rd B68 ....9 D8
Leominster Ct B45 ....32 F8
Leominster Wlk B45 .....32 F8
Leonard Ave DY10 ....13 A1
Leonard Rd DY8 ....5 C5
Leopard Rise WR5 ......116 B3
Leslie Ave WR3 ....102 A1
Leswell Gr DY10 ....27 F6
Leswell La DY10 ....27 F6
Leswell St DY10 ....27 F6
Leven Dr WR5 ....128 E6
Lewes Gdns WR4 ....116 C6
Lewis Cl WR10 ....143 F6
Lewis Rd
Birmingham B30 ....20 C7
Oldbury B68 ....9 B7
Stourbridge DY9 ....6 D5
Lewkner Almshouses The
B48 ....51 A5
Lexington Cl 4 GL20 ...197 A4
Lexington Gn DY5 ....6 C7
Ley Hill Farm Rd B31 ...18 E5
Ley Hill Prim Sch B31 ...18 E5
Ley Orch WR12 ....177 F4
Leybrook Rd B45 ....33 B8
Leycester Cl B31 ....34 A7
Leycroft 4 WR9 ....85 B1
Leydon Croft B38 ....20 B2
Leylan Croft B13 ....21 D7
Leyman Cl B14 ....21 C4
Leys Cl
Hinton on the Green
WR11 ....175 A5
Stourbridge DY9 ....6 C2
Leys Rd WR11 ....134 D1
Leys The
Bidford-on-Avon B50 ....136 E5
Birmingham B31 ....19 B5
Evesham WR11 ....161 E4
Leys Wlk 4 WR11 ......161 E4
Leysfield WR11 ....147 F7
Leysters Cl B98 ....71 E3
Leyton Cl DY5 ....6 D8
Library Way B45 ....32 F7
Lichen Gdns B38 ....34 D7
Lichfield Ave
Evesham WR11 ....161 F4
Kidderminster DY11 ......26 F6
Worcester WR5 ....116 A2
Lichfield Ct B90 ....21 D2
Lichfield St DY13 ....44 A3
Lickey Coppice B45 .....33 C4
Lickey End Fst Sch B60 ..49 C6
Lickey Gr DY11 ....27 B2
Lickey Grange Dr B60 ...32 E1
Lickey Hills Ctry Pk*
B45 ....33 B3
Lickey Hills Prim Sch
B45 ....32 F3
Lickey Rd
Birmingham B45 ....33 C6
Stourbridge DY8 ....6 B6
Lickey Rock B60 ....32 D1
Lickey Sq B45 ....33 A2
Lickhill Lodge Fst Sch
DY13 ....43 D5
Lickhill Mid Sch DY13 ...43 F4
Lickhill Rd DY13 ....43 F4
Lickhill Rd N DY13 ......43 D6
Liddiard Ct DY8 ....5 E6
Lifford Cl B14 ....20 C4
Lifford Gdns WR12 .....190 C7
Lifford La B30 ....20 B4
Lightning Way B31 ......34 B7
Lightoak Cl B97 ....89 C6
Lightwood La WR2 .....113 D3
Lightwoods Hill B67 ......9 E8
Lightwoods Jun & Inf Sch
B68 ....9 D8
Lightwoods Rd DY9 ......6 C1
Lilac Ave WR4 ....115 E4
Lilac Cl Droitwich WR9 ...104 A8
Evesham WR11 ....161 B2
Redditch B98 ....70 E2
Lilac Gr 17 DY13 ....43 E4
Lilac Way B62 ....8 F8
Lilleshall Cl B98 ....71 E3
Lilley Gn Rd B48 ....52 D5
Lilley La B31 ....34 B8
Lily Gn La B97 ....70 A4
Lilycroft La B38 ....35 A7
Limbrick Cl B90 ....21 F2
Lime Ave WR4 ....115 E6
Lime Cl Alveley WV15 ......1 D6
Hollywood B47 ....36 A5
Lime Ct DY10 ....28 A4
Lime Gr Bromsgrove B61 ..48 F4
Kinver DY7 ....4 C3
Welland WR13 ....167 C5
Lime Kiln Cl B38 ....34 D7
Lime Rd 2 GL20 ....197 A3
Lime St
Eldersfield GL19 ....193 F3
Evesham WR11 ....161 E4
Lime Tree Ave
Broadway WR12 ....177 E1
Great Malvern WR14 ....152 E4
Lime Tree Cres B97 .....70 B4
Lime Tree Gr B31 ....19 C3
Lime Tree Wlk DY13 ....43 E5
Limekiln La B14 ....21 A4
Limes The WR5 ....141 D8
Lincoln Cl GL20 ....196 D4
Lincoln Cres DY11 ....26 F6
Lincoln Ct 9 B29 ....19 C7
Lincoln Gn 2 WR5 .....115 F1
Lincoln Gn La GL20 ....196 D4
Lincoln Rd B61 ....48 E4
Lincomb La DY13 ....63 D7
Lindale Cres DY5 ....6 B6
Linden Ave
Halesowen B62 ....8 E7
Kidderminster DY10 ......28 A7
5 Stourport-on-Severn
DY13 ....43 E1
Stourport-on-Severn
DY13 ....62 E8
Linden Cl 10 WR11 ....161 F2
Linden Dr DY8 ....6 A3
Linden Gdns DY10 ....28 A6
Linden Glade B63 ....8 A4
Linden Gr DY10 ....28 A7
Linden Rd
Birmingham B30 ....19 E7
6 Worcester WR4 ....115 F5
Lindens The B32 ....9 E7
Lindford Way B38 ....20 B2
Lindridge CE Prim Sch
WR15 ....58 D6
Lindridge Cl B98 ....72 A3
Lindridge Rd B90 ....21 F1
Lindsey Ave
Birmingham B31 ....19 C4
Evesham WR11 ....161 E3
Lindsworth App B30 .....20 C3
Lindsworth Ct 2 B30 ....20 C3
Lindsworth Rd B30 ......20 C3
Lindsworth Specl Sch
B30 ....20 C3
Lineholt Cl B98 ....90 A6
Lineholt La WR9 ....63 E1
Linehouse La
Catshill B60 ....49 D8
Marlbrook B60 ....32 D1
Lingen Cl B98 ....71 E3
Lingfield Rd
Bewdley DY12 ....26 D5
Evesham WR11 ....161 C2
Lingfield Wlk B61 ....32 B1
Link Rd Evesham WR11 ..161 E1
Tewkesbury GL20 ....196 F5
Link Terr WR14 ....138 F2
Link Way WR14 ....139 A4
Linkend Rd GL19 ......194 E3
Links Cres B68 ....9 B8
Links Dr Birmingham B45 ..33 A5
Stourbridge DY8 ....5 E2
Links Rd
Birmingham B14 ....21 A1
Oldbury B68 ....9 B8
Links The DY10 ....28 A4
Links View B62 ....8 D4
Linksview Cres WR5 ....116 A2
Linkwood Ind Est DY8 ....5 F6
Linley Cl WR3 ....102 A1
Linley Gr B14 ....20 C6
Linnet Cl
Birmingham B30 ....19 E8
Halesowen B62 ....8 B6
Linnet Rise DY10 ....27 F1
Linpole Wlk B14 ....20 D2
Linthurst Fst Sch B60 ...50 A6
Linthurst Newtown
B60 ....50 B5
Linthurst Rd B45, B60 ...50 A7
Linton Cl Halesowen B63 ...7 D5
Redditch B98 ....71 F2
Linton Mews B98 ....71 F2
Lion Ct WR1 ....115 C3
Lion Hill DY13 ....44 A3
Lion La DY14 ....22 D4
Lion Pas DY8 ....5 F5
Lion Sq DY10 ....27 E6
Lion St
Kidderminster DY10 ......27 E6
Stourbridge DY8 ....5 F5
Lionfields Cl DY10 ....13 A5
Lionfields Rd DY10 ......13 A4
Lisko Cl DY5 ....6 A8
Lisle Ave DY11 ....27 D3
Lismore Cl B45 ....17 E1
Lismore Gn 11 WR5 ....128 E6
Lister Ave WR4 ....116 C3
Lister Rd DY11 ....27 B4
Listowel Rd B14 ....20 D6
Little Acre B97 ....89 D6
Little Battenton WR9 ....63 D1
Little Boughton St 4
WR2 ....114 E1
Little Chestnut St
WR1 ....115 C4
Little Cornbow B63 ....8 B3
Little Forge Rd B98 ......90 C8
Little Gn GL19 ....192 A4
Little Grebe Rd DY10 ....28 B3
Little Hayes DY11 ....12 C3
Little Heath La B60 ......49 D6
Little Hill WR9 ....84 C2
Little Hill Gr B38 ....20 A1
Little Hill Way B32 ....9 D2
Little London 8 WR1 ....115 B4
Little Mdw Croft B31 ....18 F4
Little Penny Rope
WR10 ....158 C7
Little Piece 7 WR4 .....116 B5
Little Pk B32 ....9 B4
Little Pk St 15 WR5 ....115 C2
Little Priest La 5
WR10 ....158 D8
Little Rd WR11 ....163 E8
Little Southfield St 1
WR1 ....115 C3
Little Woods B97 ....89 E6
Littlecote Croft 1 B14 ...21 A3
Littlemead Ave B31 ......19 C1
Littlemead Rd B90 ....36 E8
Littleover Ave B28 ....21 F6
Littleshaw Croft B47 ....36 C4
Littleshaw La B47 ....36 C4
Littletons Sch The
WR11 ....148 F1
Littlewood Gn B80 ......90 D3
Littleworth La B96 ......88 B1
Littleworth St WR11 ....161 D4
Liverpool Rd WR5 ......115 F1
Livingstone Rd B14 ......20 E6
Livingstone St 7 WR5 ..128 E8
Llangorse Cl DY13 ......43 E7
Lloyd Cl WR11 ....147 E3
Lloyds Rd B62 ....8 C8
Load St DY12 ....26 B3
Lobelia Cl
Kidderminster DY11 ......12 C1
Worcester WR5 ....128 D5
Lock Cl B97 ....70 A4
Lock Keepers Reach
B48 ....50 F6
Lock St WR5 ....115 C2
Lockeridge La WR8 ....168 B3
Lockington Croft B62 .....8 F6
Lockside Dr DY7 ....4 B4
Lockton Rd B30 ....20 C8
Lockwood Rd B31 ....18 F4
Lodge Bank WR9 ....63 C3
Lodge Cl Bewdley DY12 ..26 D4
Halesowen B62 ....8 E3
Worcester WR2 ....114 E4
Lodge Cres DY9 ....15 B5
Lodge Croft B31 ....18 E6
Lodge Dr WR14 ....138 E2
Lodge Forge Trad Est
B64 ....7 C7
Lodge Hill WR10 ....157 D4
Lodge Pool Dr B98 ......70 F1
Lodge Rd Redditch B98 ..70 E3
5 Stourport-on-Severn
DY13 ....44 A3
Lodgefield Rd B62 ....8 B7
Lofthouse Cres B31 .....18 F3
Lofthouse Gr B31 ....18 F3
Loftus Cl B29 ....18 F8
Lomaine Dr B30 ....19 E4
Lomas Dr B31 ....18 E3
Lombard St DY13 ....44 A3
Lombardy Croft 3 B62 ....9 A6
London La
Bromsgrove B60 ....68 F7
Tardebigge B60 ....69 A6
2 Upton upon Severn
WR8 ....169 C6
London Rd WR5 ....115 D1
Long Acre DY10 ....27 F7
Long Bank DY12 ....25 C1
Long Cl DY9 ....15 A4
Long Compton Dr DY9 ...15 A6
Long Eights GL20 ......184 D1
Long Hedges WR10 ....158 B7
Long Hyde Rd WR11 ...148 E1
Long Innage B63 ....7 B6
Long La Halesowen B62 ....8 E8
Peopleton WR10 ....131 F1
Pinvin WR10 ....132 A1
Throckmorton WR10 ....145 B8
Long Leasow B29 ....19 B7
Long Marston Rd
Mickleton CV37 ....165 C7
Pebworth CV37 ....150 F3
Welford-on-Avon CV37 ..151 C8
Long Mdw Rd B60 ......49 C6
Long Mynd B63 ....7 D1
Long Mynd Rd B31 ......18 F6
Long Nuke Rd B31 ......18 E7
Long Saw Dr B31 ....18 D1
Long Sling WR9 ....84 D1
Long Wood B30 ....19 E5
Longboat La DY13 ......44 A4
Longborough Cl B97 ....89 B6
Longbow Rd B29 ....18 F7
Longbridge La B31 ......33 E8
Longbridge Sta B31 .....33 E8
Longcroft The B63 ....7 E4
Longdales Rd B38 ....34 E7
Longdon Cl B98 ....90 B7
Longdon Hill
Evesham WR11 ....162 B1
Wickhamford WR11 ....176 C8
Longfellow Cl B97 ....89 C7
Longfellow Gn DY10 ....28 C6
Longfellow Rd
Birmingham B30 ....19 D4
Worcester WR3 ....115 C6
Longfield WR8 ....169 C5
Longfield Cl B28 ....21 F6
Longfield Rd
Birmingham B31 ....18 E8
Stourbridge DY9 ....6 D5
Longford Cl
Bidford-on-Avon B50 ...136 F5
Birmingham B32 ....18 A7
Longham Croft B32 ....9 F4
Longheadland WR9 .....83 A5
Longhope Cl B98 ....72 B4
Longhurst Croft B31 .....34 B7
Longlands Cl B38 ....34 C8
Longlands Rd B62 ....8 E3
Longlands The B45 ......50 D7
Longmeadow Dr 5
WR15 ....55 F6
Longmeadow Gr B31 ....34 A6
Longmoor Cl B97 ....70 B5
Longmoor Rd B63 ....7 E3
Longmore Hill DY13 .....62 F6
Longmynd Way DY13 ....43 D1
Longridge Rd WR14 ....153 B5
Longtown Rd 7 GL20 ..197 A4
Longwill Prim Sch For Deaf
Children B31 ....19 A5
Longwood Rd B45 ....33 A7
Lord Austin Dr B60 ......32 E1
Lord's Heath 4 WR4 ....116 B5
Lords La B80 ....90 E2
Lordswood Cl B97 ....69 F2
Lorne Gr DY10 ....28 A6
Lorne St
Kidderminster DY10 ......28 A5
Stourport-on-Severn
DY13 ....44 A5
Lorrainer Ave DY5 ....6 A8
Loughmill Rd WR10 ....144 C1
Loughton Gr B63 ....7 F4
Louise Croft B14 ....20 E2
Lovage Rd B98 ....71 F6
Love La
Cleobury Mortimer DY14 ...22 C4
Hollywood B47 ....35 F7
Stourbridge, Lye DY9 ......6 F5
Stourbridge, Old Swinford
DY8 ....6 A3
Love Lyne
Feckenham B97 ....88 F6
Redditch B97 ....89 B5
Love's Gr WR1 ....115 B4
Lovell Cl B29 ....19 B6
Lovett Pl WR4 ....116 C4
Lovett Rd WR9 ....84 D7
Lovington La WR2 .....114 B7
Low Fold Cl WR2 ......114 D1
Low Rd WR11 ....134 B4
Low Thatch B38 ....34 E7
Lowans Hill View B97 ...70 C4
Lowbrook La B90 ....36 D4
Lowe La Alveley WV15 .....1 D2
Wolverley & Cookley
DY11 ....12 B2
Lowell St WR1 ....115 C4
Lower Barbourne Terr 8
WR1 ....115 A5
Lower Beeches Rd B31 ..18 C2
Lower Bentley La B60 ...68 F1
Lower Bull Entry 5
WR1 ....115 B2
Lower Chase Rd 6
WR14 ....153 B8
Lower Chestnut St
WR1 ....115 C4

Lower Cladswell La B49 108 F2
Lower Comm La B97 70 B2
Lower Croft WR10 160 B6
Lower Dr WR8 157 C7
Lower Ferry La WR2 140 F7
Lower Field Terr WR5 128 C8
Lower Gambolds La B60 68 B6
Lower Grinsty La B97 89 A8
Lower High St
Blackheath B64 7 C8
Stourbridge DY8 5 F6
Lower Higley Cl B32 9 E4
Lower Howsell Rd
Leigh WR13 126 A1
Malvern WR13 139 A8
Lower Inhedge 5 DY14 22 D5
Lower Leys WR11 161 E4
Lower Lickhill Rd DY13 43 E5
Lower Lode La GL20 196 C4
Lower Mill St DY11 27 D6
Lower Montpelier Rd WR14 138 C1
Lower Moor B30 19 E8
Lower Parklands DY11 27 C5
Lower Pk DY12 26 B3
Lower Priest La 6 WR10 158 D8
Lower Quest Hills Rd 3 WR14 138 F4
Lower Rd WR14 138 C2
Lower Shepley La B60 49 E6
Lower St DY14 22 D4
Lower White Rd B32 9 D5
Lower Wilton Rd 2 WR14 153 B8
Lower Wyche Rd WR14 152 E6
Lowesmoor WR1 115 C3
Lowesmoor Terr WR1 115 C3
Lowesmoor Trad Est WR1 115 C3
Loweswater House B38 20 B1
Loweswater Rd DY13 43 E7
Lowfield Cl B62 9 A3
Lowfield La B97 70 B5
Lowhill La B45 33 D6
Lowlands La B98 71 D3
Lowndes Rd DY8 5 E6
Loxley Ave
Birmingham B14 21 C3
Solihull B90 21 F1
Loxley Cl
Birmingham B31 18 E8
Redditch B98 71 D6
Loynells Rd B45 33 B7
Lucerne Ave WR14 153 A5
Lucerne Cl 1 WR3 115 A8
Lucy Baldwin Unit Hospl DY13 43 F5
Lucy Edwards Ct DY11 27 C5
Ludford Rd B32 9 A1
Ludgate Ave DY11 27 A4
Ludlow Ave WR4 116 B6
Ludlow House B13 21 A6
Ludlow Rd
Cleobury Mortimer DY14 22 A4
Kidderminster DY10 27 E3
Redditch B97 70 E3
Ludstone Rd B29 9 F1
Lugano Rd WR3 115 A8
Lulworth Cl B63 7 C6
Lundy Row WR5 128 E6
Lunnon La WR9 46 C2
Lunt Gr B32 9 D5
Lupton Ct B60 49 A1
Lusbridge Cl B63 7 B4
Lutley Ave B63 7 E4
Lutley Dr DY9 6 C3
Lutley Gr B32 9 B1
Lutley La B63 7 C2
Lutley Mill Rd B63 7 E4
Lutley Prim Sch B63 7 D1
Lutterworth Cl 3 WR4 115 F4
Lyall Gdns B45 17 E1
Lychgate Ave DY9 6 C1
Lydate Rd B62 8 F4
Lydbrook Covert 5 B38 34 E8
Lyddington Dr B62 8 B7
Lyde Gn B63 7 B7
Lydes Rd 5 WR14 153 B8
Lydford Terr Ave 13 WR4 116 C6
Lydham Cl B98 70 E5
Lydiate Ash Rd B60 32 C3
Lydiate Ave B31 18 D1
Lydney Cl B98 71 D7
Lydney Gr B31 18 F3
Lye Ave B32 9 A2
Lye Bsns Ctr DY9 6 F6
Lye By-Pass DY9 6 E6
Lye Cl La B32 9 A2
Lye Sta DY9 6 E6
Lye Valley Ind Est DY9 6 F6
Lyf's La WR5 141 B7
Lygon Bank WR14 138 F2
Lygon Cl B98 71 A5
Lygon Gr B32 9 E4
Lynbrook Cl B47 36 A7
Lynch La SY8 54 B4
Lyncourt Gr B32 9 B6
Lynden Cl B61 48 E3
Lyndenwood B97 70 A2
Lyndholm Rd DY10 28 A6
Lyndhurst Dr DY10 27 E8
Lyndon Cl B63 7 F4
Lyndon House B31 19 B3
Lyndon Rd B45 32 E7
Lyndworth Rd B30 20 C8
Lyneham Cl 5 WR4 115 F7
Lynfield Cl B38 34 F7
Lynn Cl WR13 125 F2
Lynval Rd DY5 6 F7
Lynwood Cl WR11 161 B4
Lynwood Dr DY10 14 C2
Lynworth La GL20 183 F6
Lyppard Grange Prim Sch WR4 116 C4
Lysander Rd B45 18 A2
Lyth La WR9 63 B2
Lytham Cl DY8 5 F2
Lythwood Dr DY5 6 C8
Lyttelton Pl DY9 15 C6
Lyttelton Rd
Bewdley DY12 26 A4
Droitwich WR9 84 F1
Stourbridge DY8 5 D5
Lyttelton St 4 WR1 115 A5
Lyttleton Ave
Bromsgrove B60 67 E7
Halesowen B62 8 E7
Lyttleton House B63 8 A2
Lyttleton Rd WR10 144 E4
Lytton La B32 9 F3

M

Maas Rd B31 19 A4
Mabey Ave B98 70 F5
Macarthur Rd B64 7 C8
Macaulay Rise WR14 139 A2
Madeley Rd
Belbroughton DY9 31 D6
Redditch B98 71 F5
Madge Hill WR8 155 E5
Madinatul Uloom Al-Islamiya Sch DY10 28 D1
Madley Cl B45 32 E8
Madresfield CE Prim Sch WR13 139 E3
Madresfield Dr B63 8 B2
Madresfield Rd WR14 139 A1
Mafeking Villas B62 8 B7
Magnolia Cl
Birmingham B29 19 A7
Drakes Broughton WR10 143 F6
9 Worcester WR5 128 D5
Magpie Cl WR5 128 D5
Magpie Way DY10 28 B2
Main Rd Kempsey WR5 141 C5
Wyre Piddle WR10 145 B3
Main St
Aldington WR11 162 C5
Beckford GL20 186 D4
Bishampton WR10 132 F3
Bretforton WR11 163 B5
Church Lench WR11 134 A3
Cleeve Prior WR11 149 B7
Cropthorne WR10 160 B6
Defford WR8 157 D3
Offenham WR11 148 A1
Pershore/Pinvin WR10 144 E6
Sedgeberrow WR11 175 A1
South Littleton WR11 148 F1
Willersey WR12 177 E4
Mainstone Cl B98 71 E3
Maisemore Cl B98 71 D6
Malcolm Ave B61 48 E3
Malcolm Gr B45 33 A7
Malfield Ave B97 69 F3
Malham Pl 1 WR5 128 E6
Malham Rd DY13 43 E7
Malinshill Rd WR11 161 B3
Mallaby Cl B90 36 F8
Mallard Ave DY10 28 B3
Mallard Cl
Brierley Hill DY5 6 C7
Redditch B98 70 F5
Worcester WR5 128 A6
Mallard Pl WR9 85 B3
Mallard Rd B80 90 F4
Mallards Cl WV15 1 D5
Mallory Dr DY11 12 D1
Mallow Cl WR14 153 D7
Mallow Dr B61 48 F6
Malmesy Cl GL20 196 F3
Malpas Dr B32 18 C8
Malpass Rd DY5 6 F7
Malt House La WR11 134 B3
Malt Mill La B62 8 D8
Malt Mill La Trad Est B62 8 D8
Malthouse Cres WR7 120 E7
Malthouse La B94 53 F7
Malthouse Pl 2 WR1 115 B2
Maltings The B80 90 D4
Malton Cl WR14 138 E6
Malton Gr B13 21 B7
Malus Cl WR14 139 C3
Malvern Ave DY9 6 C5
Malvern Cl
Broadheath WR2 114 A7
Stourport-on-Severn DY13 62 D8
Malvern Coll WR14 152 F7
Malvern Com Hospl WR14 139 A1
Malvern Dr DY10 27 E3
Malvern Girls' Coll WR14 153 A8
Malvern House
7 Halesowen B63 8 A3
Redditch B97 70 C1
Malvern Link CE Prim Sch WR14 139 A4
Malvern Link Sta WR14 139 A4
Malvern Mus* WR14 152 E8
Malvern Parish CE Prim Sch WR14 153 A8
Malvern Rd
Barnt Green B45 33 A2
Bromsgrove B61 67 D7
Newland WR2 126 F1
Oldbury B68 9 B8
Powick WR2 127 D3
Redditch B97 89 D8
Worcester WR2 114 F1
Malvern Theatre* WR14 152 F8
Malvern View
Bluntington DY10 29 E1
Kidderminster DY11 27 B1
Mamble DY14 40 E4
Malvern Wells Prim Sch WR14 166 E7
Mamble Craft Ctr* DY14 39 F4
Mamble Rd DY8 5 E5
Manby Rd 3 WR14 153 A8
Mandalay Dr WR5 128 F4
Mandarin Ave DY10 28 B3
Mandeville Way B61 48 F5
Manitoba Cl 3 WR2 127 E6
Manitoba Croft 2 B38 34 F8
Manning Rd WR9 84 E2
Manningford Ct B14 20 F3
Manningford Rd B14 20 E3
Manor Abbey Rd B62 8 E4
Manor Ave DY11 27 A7
Manor Ave S DY11 27 A6
Manor Cl Badsey WR11 162 D3
Droitwich WR9 85 A2
Honeybourne WR11 164 A4
Kidderminster DY11 27 A6
Stourport-on-Severn DY13 44 B5
Wickhamford WR11 176 D8
Manor Ct
Broughton Hackett WR7 117 E1
Cleeve Prior WR11 149 B7
5 Halesowen B62 9 A7
Manor Ct Rd B60 67 F8
Manor Dr B80 91 F7
Manor Farm WR7 143 A8
Manor Farm Craft Ctr* B94 36 F2
Manor Gdns
Aldington WR11 162 C5
Pershore WR10 158 E7
Manor House Cl B29 9 F1
Manor House La B96 89 E3
Manor La
Bretforton WR11 163 C4
Halesowen B62 8 E4
Hartlebury DY11 64 B8
Little Comberton WR10 159 B2
Lydiate Ash B61 32 C4
Stourbridge DY8 5 D3
Manor Mews B80 90 E4
Manor Pk
Harvington WR11 148 B6
Tewkesbury GL20 197 A8
Manor Pk Gr B31 18 C1
Manor Pk Specl Sch WR2 114 F4
Manor Pl 1 GL20 196 F3
Manor Rd
Clifton upon Teme WR6 97 E8
Eckington WR10 171 D7
Hill & Moor WR10 145 D3
South Littleton WR11 148 F2
Stourport-on-Severn DY13 44 A5
Studley B80 90 E4
Upper Bentley B97 69 B1
Wickhamford WR11 162 D1
Worcester WR2 127 F8
Wythall B47 36 A3
Manor Side WR11 162 D3
Manor Side Ind Est B98 71 E6
Manor Way B62, B63 8 D3
Manor Way Prim Sch B63 8 C3
Manorfield WR2 114 A7
Manse Gdns B80 90 E3
Mansell Cl B63 7 B7
Mansell Rd B97 89 D7
Mansfield Rd 1 WR14 139 C3
Mansion Ct B62 8 E7
Mansion Gdns WR11 161 D3
Mapit Pl WR4 116 C4
Maple Ave
5 Pershore WR10 144 D2
Worcester WR4 115 E4
Maple Cl
5 Evesham WR11 161 F2
Kidderminster DY11 27 B8
Kinver DY7 4 A5
Stourbridge DY8 5 D2
11 Stourport-on-Severn DY13 43 E4
Maple Cres WV15 1 C6
Maple Croft B13 20 F5
Maple Gr WR9 103 F8
Maple House B97 70 B2
Maple Rd
Birmingham, Eachway B45 32 F6
Birmingham, Selly Oak B30 19 E8
Halesowen B62 8 D8
Maple Tree La B63 7 C6
Maple Way B31 18 F1
Mappleborough Gn CE Prim Sch B98 72 B2
Mappleborough Rd B90 21 E1
Marans Croft B38 34 D7
Marble Alley B80 90 E4
Marbury Cl B38 19 D2
March Gr DY12 26 B4
March Hare Leisure Ctr WR7 117 F1
Marchwood Cl B97 70 A5
Marcliff Cres B90 21 C2
Marden Gr B31 34 A7
Margaret Ave B63 7 F4
Margaret Cl DY5 6 E8
Margaret Dr DY8 6 B4
Margaret Rd
Tewkesbury GL20 196 F4
Worcester WR2 128 A8
Margesson Dr B45 33 D1
Marhon Cl 5 WR9 85 B1
Marigold Cl 8 WR5 128 C5
Marion Cl WR3 115 B8
Marion Way B28 21 E7
Marjoram Cl B38 34 F8
Marjorie Ave B30 20 B3
Mark Cl
Great Malvern WR14 138 E6
Redditch B98 70 E2
Market Pl
Bromsgrove B61 48 F2
Redditch B98 70 E4
Market Sq B64 7 C8
Market St
Bromsgrove B61 48 F2
Kidderminster DY10 27 E5
Stourbridge DY8 6 A5
Tenbury Wells WR15 55 F5
Market Way DY9 15 C6
Market Wlk 4 B97 70 E4
Marl Bank WR3 115 D4
Marl Top B38 19 F2
Marlbank Rd WR13 167 B5
Marlborough Ave B60 68 A8
Marlborough Ct B60 68 B8
Marlborough Dr
Astley & Dunley DY13 62 F8
Stourbridge DY8 6 A3
Marlborough Gdns WR14 139 B6
Marlborough Rd WR10 171 D7
Marlborough St
2 Kidderminster DY10 27 E5
4 Worcester WR5 128 E8
Marlbrook Gdns B61 32 B1
Marlbrook La
Crowle WR9 105 A1
Marlbrook B60 32 D2
Marlcliff Gr B13 21 A6
Marldon Rd B14 20 E6
Marleigh Rd B50 136 E5
Marlfield Farm Fst Sch B98 71 C6
Marlfield La B98 71 B4
Marlow Rd WR2 114 D2
Marlowe Cl DY10 28 B6
Marlpit La B97 70 C1
Marlpool Cl 4 DY11 12 B1
Marlpool Ct DY11 27 C8
Marlpool Dr B97 70 C3
Marlpool Fst Sch DY11 27 C8
Marlpool La DY11 12 B1
Marlpool Pl DY11 27 C8
Marquis Dr B62 8 A7
Marsden Rd B98 70 E3
Marsh Ave WR4 116 A5
Marsh Cl WR14 139 B2
Marsh End B38 35 A8
Marsh Gr DY10 27 E8
Marsh Way B61 31 F1
Marsham Rd B14 20 F3
Marshfield Cl B98 71 B7
Marshwood Croft B62 9 A3
Marston Cl DY8 5 D4
Marston Rd B29 18 F8
Mart La DY13 44 A3
Marten Croft WR5 128 F5
Martin Ave WR11 161 A2
Martin Cl
Bromsgrove B61 48 E1
Great Malvern WR14 139 C1
Martin's Orch WR13 166 A8
Martindale Cl WR4 116 B6
Martindale Wlk DY5 6 B6
Martingale Cl 4 B60 67 E6
Martins Cnr CV37 151 A5
Martins Way DY13 43 F3
Martley CE Prim Sch WR6 99 B4
Martley Cl B98 90 B7
Martley Croft B32 9 E4
Martley Ct DY9 6 C4
Martley Dr DY9 6 C4
Martley Rd
Broadheath WR2 114 E5
Great Witley WR6 80 B7
Stourport-on-Severn DY13 62 D8
Mary Vale Rd B30 19 F6
Maryland Dr B31 19 B5
Maryland Rd DY5 6 F7
Marylebone Cl DY8 6 A7
Maryman's Rd WR11 161 B2
Maryvale WR15 55 D4
Marywell Cl B32 18 B7
Masefield Cl WR3 115 C6
Masefield Gdns 1 DY10 28 B6
Masefield Rise B62 8 D3
Masefield Sq B31 19 C4
Mashie Gdns B38 19 D1
Maslen Pl B63 8 B3
Mason Cl
Bidford-on-Avon B50 136 E5
Great Malvern WR14 139 B3
Redditch B97 89 D7
Mason La B94 36 F1
Mason Rd
Kidderminster DY11 27 C6
Redditch B97 89 D8
Masonleys Rd B31 18 D3
Masons Cl B63 7 C6
Masons Dr WR4 115 F6
Masons Ryde 11 WR10 158 D8
Masshouse La B38 19 F1
Masters Cl 2 WR11 161 E3
Masters La B62 8 E8
Matchborough Ctr B98 71 E1
Matchborough Way B98 71 E1
Math Mdw B32 9 F5
Mathon Rd
Great Malvern WR14 138 C1
Mathon WR13 152 A6
Matravers Rd WR14 139 B2
Matthew La (Road 3) DY10 27 F1
Matthias Cl WR14 139 A5
Maughan St DY5 7 A8
Maund Cl B60 67 E7
Maund St WR2 114 E4
Maurice Rd B14 20 E5
Mavis Gdns B68 9 B8
Mavis Rd B31 18 E1
Mawley Hall* DY14 22 F3
Max Rd B32 9 D5
Maxstoke Cl
Birmingham B32 18 A7
Redditch B98 71 D1
May Ave WR4 115 E4
May Farm Cl B47 36 A6
May La Birmingham B14 20 F5
Hollywood B47 36 A7
May Tree Hill WR9 104 A8
May Trees B47 35 F6
Mayalls The GL20 183 F6
Maybank WR14 139 C3
Mayberry Cl
Birmingham B14 21 B2
5 Stourport-on-Severn DY13 43 E4
Maycroft WR11 161 B2
Mayfair
1 Evesham WR11 161 D2
Stourbridge DY9 6 D2
Mayfield Ave WR3 115 C5
Mayfield Cl Catshill B61 31 F1
Kidderminster DY11 27 A8
Mayfield Ct DY11 27 C7
Mayfield Rd
Birmingham, Stirchley B30 20 A6
Great Malvern WR14 139 C2
Halesowen, Hasbury B63 7 E2
Pershore WR10 144 D2
Worcester WR3 115 D5
Mayfields The B98 70 E2
Mayflower Cl
4 Great Malvern WR14 153 B8
2 Stourport-on-Severn DY13 44 A2
Mayflower Rd WR9 85 B2
Mayford Gr B13 21 B6
Mayhurst Cl B47 36 C6
Mayhurst Rd B47 36 B6
Maynard Ave DY8 5 D3
Maypole Cl
Bewdley DY12 26 C3
Blackheath B64 7 B8
Maypole Dr DY8 5 E5
Maypole Fields B63 7 A7
Maypole Gr B14 21 B2
Maypole Hill B63 7 A7
Maypole La B14 21 A2
Mayswood Gr B32 9 D4
Maytree Rd WR10 145 D3
McConnell Cl B60 68 B7
McCormick Ave 2 WR4 116 C3
McIntyre Rd WR2 114 F2
McNaught Pl 12 WR1 115 B4
Meaburn Cl B29 19 A7
Mead The WR2 114 E4
Meadfoot Ave B14 20 F3
Meadow Brook Rd B31 18 F5
Meadow Cl
Kempsey WR5 141 C6
Kington WR7 119 E4
Tewkesbury GL20 197 A8
Meadow Croft
Hagley DY9 14 F4
Wythall B47 36 A3
Meadow Ct WR5 141 B7
Meadow Gn WR6 110 F6
Meadow Gn Prim Sch B47 36 A3
Meadow Hill Cl DY11 27 A5
Meadow Hill Rd B38 19 E2
Meadow La B48 51 B6

Meadow Mill WR15 ... 55 F3
Meadow Mills Ind Est DY10 ... 27 E5
Meadow Rd
Birmingham, Quinton B32 ... 9 A6
Catshill B61 ... 48 F8
Droitwich WR9 ... 84 E4
Great Malvern WR14 ... 139 A2
Halesowen B62 ... 8 C8
Honeybourne WR11 ... 163 D8
Worcester WR3 ... 102 B1
Wythall B47 ... 36 A3
Meadow Rise
Bewdley DY12 ... 26 D5
Birmingham B30 ... 19 E7
2 Tenbury Wells WR15 ... 55 F6
Meadow St B64 ... 7 F8
Meadow View
Birmingham B13 ... 21 C8
9 Stourport-on-Severn DY13 ... 62 E8
Meadow Way WR9 ... 84 D5
Meadow Wlk
Birmingham B14 ... 20 E1
Blackheath B64 ... 7 D8
4 Colwall Stone WR13 ... 152 B2
Meadowbank Dr WR2 ... 114 D1
Meadowbrook Cl WV15 ... 1 C5
Meadowbrook Rd B63 ... 7 E3
Meadowfield Rd B45 ... 33 A6
Meadowhill Cres B98 ... 70 F5
Meadowhill Rd B98 ... 70 F5
Meadowpark Rd DY8 ... 5 D8
Meadows End WR11 ... 161 B3
Meadows Fst Sch B61 ... 49 A3
Meadows Prim Sch The B31 ... 18 E1
Meadows The
Bidford-on-Avon B50 ... 136 C4
Stourbridge DY9 ... 15 B7
Meadowsweet Ave B38 ... 34 F8
Meadowsweet Pl DY10 ... 27 D8
Meadowvale Rd B60 ... 49 C6
Meadvale Rd B45 ... 33 B6
Meadway WR14 ... 138 F4
Meadway The B97 ... 70 C1
Mears Coppice DY5 ... 6 E6
Mearse La
Barnt Green B45 ... 33 A1
Belbroughton DY9 ... 31 B6
Cookhill WR7 ... 108 E2
Meaton Gr B32 ... 18 B8
Meaton La DY14 ... 23 E8
Meddins Cl 1 DY7 ... 4 A4
Meddins La DY7 ... 3 F4
Meddins Rise DY7 ... 3 F4
Medici Rd B60 ... 49 C2
Medway Gr B38 ... 34 E8
Medway Rd
Evesham WR11 ... 161 F3
Worcester WR5 ... 115 E2
Meer End B38 ... 34 D7
Meeting House La B31 ... 19 A4
Meir Rd B98 ... 90 C8
Melbourne Ave B61 ... 48 E4
Melbourne Cl B61 ... 48 E3
Melbourne Rd
Bromsgrove B61 ... 48 E3
Halesowen B63 ... 8 B5
Melbourne St 7 WR3 ... 115 B6
Melbury Gr B14 ... 20 E5
Melchett Rd B30 ... 20 A4
Melen St B97 ... 70 D4
Melfort Gr B14 ... 21 A3
Melrose Ave DY8 ... 6 A2
Melrose Cl
Birmingham B38 ... 19 F1
Worcester WR2 ... 114 F3
Melstock Rd B14 ... 20 D7
Melton Rd B14 ... 20 F8
Melzer House DY10 ... 27 E7
Mendip Cl
Bromsgrove B61 ... 49 A5
Great Malvern WR14 ... 139 B1
Mendip Cl Kenwood Ave WR4 ... 115 F4
Mendip House B98 ... 71 D6
Mendip Rd
Halesowen B63 ... 7 D1
Stourbridge DY8 ... 6 B6
Menin Cres B13 ... 21 B7
Menin Rd B13 ... 21 B8
Menston Cl WR4 ... 116 A4
Menteith Cl DY13 ... 43 E7
Meon Rd GL55 ... 165 E5
Meon Rise DY9 ... 6 C3
Mercia Cl B60 ... 67 F7
Mercot Cl B98 ... 90 A6
Mere Hall* WR9 ... 105 E8
Mere Rd DY8 ... 5 E3
Merebrook WR14 ... 166 F7
Meredith Gn DY11 ... 27 A1
Meres Rd B63 ... 7 C5
Merevale Cl B98 ... 90 D8
Merganser Way DY10 ... 28 B3
Merick Rd WR14 ... 139 C4
Meriden Ave DY8 ... 5 D6
Meriden Cl Redditch B98 ... 72 A3
Stourbridge DY8 ... 5 D6
Meridian Pl B60 ... 49 A1
Merino Ave B31 ... 34 A8
Merlin Dr DY10 ... 28 B3
Merrick Cl B63 ... 7 D2
Merricks Cl 1 DY12 ... 25 F3
Merricks La 7 DY12 ... 25 F3
Merriemont Dr B45 ... 33 A1
Merrill Gdns B60 ... 32 D2
Merriman's Ct 1 WR3 ... 115 C5
Merriman's Hill Rd WR3 ... 115 C5
Merriman's Wlk 5 WR3 ... 115 C5
Merrishaw Rd B31 ... 34 A8
Merritt's Brook La B31 ... 18 E5
Merritts Brook Cl B29 ... 19 A5
Merritts Hill B31 ... 18 E6
Merrivale Rd B62 ... 8 F8
Merry La WR11 ... 148 D1
Merrybrook WR11 ... 161 A4
Merryfield WR10 ... 160 E8
Merse Rd B98 ... 71 E6
Mersey Gr B38 ... 34 E8
Mersey Rd WR5 ... 115 E2
Merstow Gn 5 WR11 ... 161 C4
Merstow Pl 4 WR11 ... 161 C4
Merton Cl
4 Bewdley DY12 ... 25 F4
Kidderminster DY10 ... 28 B7
Worcester WR4 ... 115 E3
Merton Rd WR14 ... 139 A4
Michael Cres WR14 ... 138 F5
Michaelwood Cl B97 ... 69 F2
Michelle Cl B13 ... 21 A5
Mickleton Cl B98 ... 89 E7
Mickleton Prim Sch GL55 ... 165 D4
Mickleton Rd GL55 ... 164 D5
Middle Acre Rd B32 ... 9 E2
Middle Dr B45 ... 33 D4
Middle Field Rd B31 ... 19 D2
Middle Hollow Dr WR4 ... 116 A5
Middle House Dr B60 ... 32 D1
Middle La
Cropthorne WR10 ... 160 B6
Hadzor WR9 ... 104 C7
Wythall B38 ... 35 D5
Middle Leasowe B32 ... 9 D4
Middle Mdw Ave B32 ... 9 C5
Middle Piece Dr B97 ... 70 B1
Middle Pk Cl B29 ... 19 B8
Middle Pk Rd B29 ... 19 C8
Middle Rd
Stock & Bradley B96 ... 106 E3
Upper Bentley B60 ... 69 A2
Wildmoor B61 ... 31 F4
Worcester WR2 ... 114 F1
Middle St WR1 ... 115 C3
Middlefield Gdns B62 ... 8 F8
Middlefield House B14 ... 20 F3
Middlefield La DY9 ... 15 B6
Middlefield Rd B60 ... 68 B7
Middlehill Rise B32 ... 9 D3
Middlehouse La B97 ... 70 E6
Middlemore Cl B80 ... 90 D3
Middlemore Rd B31 ... 19 B3
Middles Ave WR4 ... 116 B4
Middleton Cl B98 ... 71 F2
Middleton Gdns
Birmingham B30 ... 19 D4
1 Worcester WR4 ... 116 B5
Middleton Grange B31 ... 19 C4
Middleton Hall B30 ... 19 E4
Middleton Hall Rd B30 ... 19 E4
Middleton Rd
Birmingham B14 ... 20 F7
Bromsgrove B61 ... 48 F4
Kidderminster DY11 ... 12 C1
Middletown B80 ... 90 D1
Middletown La B96, B80 ... 90 D1
Middletree Rd B63 ... 7 C7
Midhurst Cl 1 WR5 ... 128 E8
Midhurst Rd B30 ... 20 B3
Midland Rd
Birmingham B30 ... 19 F5
Worcester WR5 ... 115 D3
Midsummer Hill (fort)* HR8 ... 179 C8
Midsummer Mdw WR7 ... 120 F6
Midvale Dr B14 ... 20 D2
Mikado Rd B60 ... 49 D1
Milcote Cl B98 ... 90 A7
Milcote Rd B29 ... 19 A8
Mile Post La B96 ... 108 B5
Milebrook Gr B32 ... 18 B8
Milestone Dr DY9 ... 14 F4
Milestone Rd WR8 ... 168 F4
Milford Ave 4 DY13 ... 43 E6
Milford Cl B97 ... 89 C6
Milford Rd B14 ... 20 E8
Milhill Rd B98 ... 71 E1
Mill Ave WR12 ... 190 B7
Mill Bank
Evesham WR11 ... 161 E4
Fladbury WR10 ... 146 B1
Mill Cl
Bidford-on-Avon B50 ... 136 B7
Blakedown DY10 ... 14 B2
Bromsgrove B60 ... 67 F6
Hollywood B47 ... 36 A7
4 Stourport-on-Severn DY13 ... 44 B4
Mill Fields DY7 ... 4 B3
Mill Gdns B14 ... 21 D5
Mill La Aldington WR11 ... 162 C5
Badsey WR11 ... 162 D2
Bidford-on-Avon B50 ... 136 B7
Birmingham, Northfield B31 ... 19 A2
Birmingham, Woodgate Valley B32 ... 9 E2
Blakedown DY10 ... 14 B2
Bromsgrove B61 ... 48 F2
Cleeve Prior WR11 ... 149 A8
Colwall Stone WR13 ... 166 A8
Mill La *continued*
Dodderhill WR9 ... 66 E1
Drakes Broughton & Wadborough WR8 ... 143 C5
Earlswood B94 ... 53 B8
Eckington WR10 ... 171 D6
Elmley Castle WR10 ... 173 E7
Feckenham B96 ... 107 D8
Halesowen B63 ... 8 C4
Kidderminster, Blakebrook DY11 ... 27 D6
Kidderminster, Hoobrook DY10 ... 27 F2
Kinver DY7 ... 4 B3
Knighton on Teme WR15 ... 57 C7
Lindridge WR15 ... 59 A4
Malvern WR14 ... 153 D6
Mickleton GL55 ... 165 D4
Offenham WR11 ... 162 B7
Pershore WR10 ... 144 D2
Redmarley D'abitot GL19 ... 192 F4
Rous Lench WR7 ... 120 D3
Staunton GL19 ... 193 A2
Stourport-on-Severn DY13 ... 44 B4
Strensham WR8 ... 171 C3
Wildmoor B61 ... 31 F3
Wolverley & Cookley DY11 ... 12 D2
Wythall B47, B94 ... 36 B1
Mill La Cl WR10 ... 144 E3
Mill Lodge Prim Sch B90 ... 21 E2
Mill Mound* WR11 ... 164 A4
Mill Pleck B80 ... 90 E3
Mill Pool Cl DY9 ... 15 A4
Mill Pool Pl DY14 ... 22 D5
Mill Race La DY8 ... 6 A6
Mill Rd Blackheath B64 ... 7 E7
Evesham WR11 ... 161 B2
Stourport-on-Severn DY13 ... 44 B4
Mill St Evesham WR11 ... 161 D4
Halesowen B63 ... 7 C7
Kidderminster DY11 ... 27 D6
Redditch B97 ... 70 D4
Tewkesbury GL20 ... 196 D6
Worcester WR1 ... 115 C1
Mill Wlk The B31 ... 18 F1
Mill Wood Dr WR4 ... 116 B4
Millbank Cotts DY11 ... 27 D6
Millbrook Cl WR3 ... 115 A7
Millbrook Ct B62 ... 8 A7
Millbrook Dr B31 ... 33 E8
Millbrook Rd B14 ... 20 C6
Millbrook Way DY5 ... 6 B8
Millcroft Cl B32 ... 9 E2
Milldale Cl DY10 ... 27 E8
Millend WR10 ... 173 E7
Millennium Cl 2 GL20 ... 197 A4
Miller Cl B60 ... 67 E6
Miller St WR9 ... 84 F3
Miller's Ct Rd WR13 ... 180 D5
Millers Bank B50 ... 136 B7
Millers Cl 12 WR4 ... 115 F6
Millers Ct
1 Kidderminster DY11 ... 27 D6
Solihull B90 ... 21 F2
Millers Gn WR6 ... 60 F4
Millfield Birmingham B31 ... 19 A4
Elmley Castle WR10 ... 173 E7
Hinton on the Green WR11 ... 175 B2
Millfield Gdns 2 DY11 ... 27 D6
Millfield Rd B61 ... 48 E1
Millfield View B63 ... 7 E4
Millfields Fst Sch B61 ... 48 E1
Millhams Ave WR4 ... 116 B5
Millhaven Ave B30 ... 20 B6
Millmead Rd B32 ... 9 E1
Millpool Gdns B14 ... 20 F3
Millpool Hill B14 ... 20 F4
Millrace Rd B98 ... 70 E5
Millridge Way DY11 ... 64 A8
Mills Cl WR12 ... 190 D8
Millsborough Rd B98 ... 70 F3
Millside B28 ... 21 E3
Milne Pastures GL20 ... 197 C7
Milner Way B13 ... 21 D8
Milret Cl 2 WR3 ... 115 C5
Milston Cl B14 ... 20 E1
Milton Cl
Kidderminster DY11 ... 27 A6
Redditch B97 ... 89 C8
Worcester WR3 ... 115 C6
Milton Dr DY9 ... 15 D7
Milton House B63 ... 7 B5
Milton Rd B61 ... 49 A8
Milverton Cl B63 ... 8 A6
Milverton Ct 3 B62 ... 9 A7
Milward Sq 8 B97 ... 70 E3
Mimosa Cl B29 ... 19 B7
Minett Ave WR2 ... 127 B8
Minge La WR8 ... 169 C5
Minley Ave B17 ... 9 F7
Minster Rd 5 DY13 ... 44 A4
Minster Wlk B61 ... 48 F8
Minter Ave WR9 ... 84 F2
Minton Mews B60 ... 68 B8
Minton Rd B32 ... 9 F4
Minworth Cl B97 ... 70 B2
Miranda Cl B45 ... 18 A2
Mitcheldean Cl B98 ... 89 E7
Mitcheldean Covert B14 ... 20 D2
Mitre Ct B61 ... 49 A3
Mitre Rd DY9 ... 6 E5
Mitten Ave B45 ... 18 A1
Mitton Cl DY13 ... 44 A4
Mitton Gdns DY13 ... 44 A3
Mitton Manor Prim Sch GL20 ... 197 A8
Mitton St DY13 ... 44 A3
Mitton Way GL20 ... 197 A8
Moat Bank GL20 ... 181 F5
Moat Coppice B62 ... 9 A1
Moat Cres WR14 ... 139 D1
Moat Farm Dr B32 ... 9 A1
Moat Farm La WR10 ... 132 F3
Moat House Ct B80 ... 90 F8
Moat Mdws B32 ... 9 E4
Moatfield Mid Sch B98 ... 71 E1
Moatway WR14 ... 139 C1
Moatway The B38 ... 34 E7
Modbury Ave B32 ... 9 D1
Moffit Way 10 DY13 ... 43 E4
Mogul La B63 ... 7 A7
Moira Cres B14 ... 21 C4
Monarch Dr WR2 ... 114 E6
Monarch Pl 7 WR2 ... 114 E5
Monckton Rd B68 ... 9 A7
Money La B61 ... 32 A7
Mongcroft Rd WR10 ... 158 F1
Monkey Mdw 6 GL20 ... 184 E1
Monks Cl 4 WR10 ... 158 D8
Monks Dr B80 ... 90 D4
Monks La GL20 ... 197 E3
Monks Path B97 ... 69 F4
Monks Way WR10 ... 131 B2
Monksfield La WR2 ... 126 E1
Monkshood Retreat B38 ... 34 F8
Monksway B38 ... 20 B1
Monkswood Rd B31 ... 19 C2
Monkwood Nature Reserve* WR6 ... 100 E6
Monmouth Rd
Birmingham B32 ... 18 D8
Smethwick B67 ... 9 E8
Monnow Cl
Droitwich WR9 ... 103 E8
Great Malvern WR14 ... 153 D8
Monsell La WR8 ... 169 A4
Monsieurs Hall La B61 ... 48 B3
Monterey Rd 3 GL20 ... 197 A3
Montfort St WR11 ... 161 F4
Montfort Wlk B32 ... 9 A2
Montgomerie Cl WR2 ... 127 B2
Montgomery Cl B61 ... 32 A1
Montgomery Cres DY5 ... 6 F7
Montpelier Rd WR14 ... 138 C1
Montreal Cl WR2 ... 127 E6
Monument Ave DY9 ... 6 E4
Monument La
Barnt Green B45 ... 32 F4
Hagley DY9 ... 15 D7
Monyhull Hall Rd B30 ... 20 C3
Monyhull Hospl B14 ... 20 D3
Moons Moat Dr B98 ... 71 E5
Moons Moat Fst Sch B98 ... 71 D5
Moons Pk B98 ... 71 E6
Moor Hall Dr DY9 ... 16 A1
Moor Hill Dr 5 DY13 ... 43 F4
Moor House B14 ... 20 C2
Moor Leasow B31 ... 19 C2
Moor St WR1 ... 115 B3
Moorcroft Cl B97 ... 89 B6
Moorcroft Gdns B97 ... 89 B6
Moorend Rd GL19 ... 193 F1
Moorfield Dr
Bromsgrove B61 ... 48 F3
Halesowen B63 ... 8 A5
Moorfoot Ave B63 ... 7 C1
Moorgate Cl B98 ... 71 E6
Moorgate Rd B60 ... 68 A2
Moorhall La DY13 ... 43 E3
Moorlands Rd WR14 ... 138 F2
Moorlands The WR14 ... 152 F2
Moorpark Rd B31 ... 19 A1
Moors Ave DY11 ... 45 B2
Moors Croft B32 ... 9 B1
Moors La
Birmingham B31 ... 18 E7
Feckenham B96 ... 107 E7
Moors The WR1 ... 115 A4
Moorside Rd B14 ... 21 D3
Moorsom Way B60 ... 68 B7
Moray Cl B62 ... 8 E8
Mordiford Cl B98 ... 71 E4
Moreland Rd WR9 ... 84 E2
Morelands The B31 ... 19 B1
Morella Cl 13 DY12 ... 25 F3
Moreton Cl B32 ... 9 F5
Moreton La GL20 ... 184 F7
Moreton Pl 1 WR1 ... 115 B2
Morgan Cl B80 ... 90 F2
Morillon Ct DY10 ... 28 A1
Morlich Rise DY5 ... 6 B8
Morning Pines DY8 ... 5 E4
Morningside WR15 ... 55 E4
Morrin Cl WR3 ... 102 B1
Morris Ave WR3 ... 115 B8
Morris Field Croft B28 ... 21 E4
Morris Rd WR12 ... 190 D8
Morris Wlk B60 ... 67 E8
Morsefield La B98 ... 71 D1
Mortimer Gdns 5 DY14 ... 22 C4
Mortimer Gr DY12 ... 26 C4
Mortimers Cl B14 ... 21 B1
Mortimers Quay 2 WR11 ... 161 E4
Mortlake Ave WR5 ... 128 F8
Mortlake Dr WR6 ... 99 A4
Morton Ave WR3 ... 102 E2
Morton Hall La B96 ... 107 F3
Morton House B97 ... 70 A3
Morton La B97 ... 89 B7
Morton Rd
Brierley Hill DY5 ... 6 D7
Fernhill Heath WR3 ... 102 E2
Harvington DY10 ... 29 B2
Morvale Ct DY9 ... 6 E5
Morvale Gdns DY9 ... 6 E5
Morvale St DY9 ... 6 E5
Mosel Dr WR9 ... 103 D8
Moseley Rd WR2 ... 101 B3
Moss Gr B14 ... 20 D6
Moss La Beoley B98 ... 71 F8
Mappleborough Green B98 ... 72 A7
Moss La Cl B98 ... 71 F8
Mossfield Rd B14 ... 20 F7
Mostyn Rd DY13 ... 43 E6
Moulder Rd GL20 ... 197 A6
Moule Cl DY11 ... 27 C6
Mounds The B38 ... 34 E8
Moundsley Gr B14 ... 21 A3
Moundsley House B14 ... 20 F2
Mount Carmel RC Fst Sch B97 ... 70 A2
Mount La DY9 ... 15 E4
Mount Orch 4 WR15 ... 55 E4
Mount Pleasant
Pershore WR10 ... 144 D2
Redditch B97 ... 70 D2
3 Tenbury Wells WR15 ... 55 E4
Mount Pleasant Barns 1 WR10 ... 144 D2
Mount Pleasant La DY13 ... 63 F4
Mount Rd
Evesham WR11 ... 161 F3
Fairfield B61 ... 31 E2
Stourbridge, Stambermill DY8 ... 6 B5
Mount St Halesowen B63 ... 8 A3
Redditch B98 ... 70 E3
Stourbridge DY8 ... 6 B5
Mount Vernon Dr B61 ... 49 A5
Mountain Ash Dr DY9 ... 6 C2
Mountbatten Rd WR14 ... 139 C2
Mountfield Cl B14 ... 21 A2
Mountford Rd B90 ... 21 D1
Mountserrat Rd B60 ... 49 B1
Mouse La DY11 ... 27 B8
Mousehall Farm Rd DY5 ... 6 D7
Mousesweet Wlk B64 ... 7 B8
Mowbray Ave GL20 ... 196 F3
Mowbray Cl B45 ... 18 A2
Moyle Dr B63 ... 7 B7
Mucklow Hill B62 ... 8 D5
Mucklow Hill Trad Est B62 ... 8 C5
Muirfield Gdns B38 ... 19 D1
Mulberry Dr
Great Malvern WR14 ... 152 F4
Upton upon Severn WR8 ... 168 F5
Mulberry Rd B30 ... 19 C5
Mulberry Terr WR4 ... 115 E4
Mulberry Tree Hill WR9 ... 104 A8
Mull Cl B45 ... 17 E1
Mullion Croft B38 ... 19 E1
Munro Cl DY10 ... 28 C6
Munsley Cl B98 ... 71 F2
Munslow Gr B31 ... 33 F8
Murcot Rd WR12 ... 176 D4
Murcroft Rd DY9 ... 6 E1
Murren Ave WR14 ... 153 A5
Mus of Worcester Porcelain The* WR1 ... 115 B1
Museum of Local Life* WR1 ... 115 C2
Musket Cl 14 GL20 ... 197 A4
Musketts Ct B97 ... 70 B2
Muskoka DY12 ... 25 F3
Myatt Rd WR11 ... 148 A1
Myatt's Field WR11 ... 148 A7
Mynors Cres B47 ... 36 A6
Myrtle Ave
Birmingham, Highter's Heath B14 ... 20 F2
Redditch B98 ... 70 E2
Mythe Rd GL20 ... 196 E8
Myton Dr B90 ... 21 D1
Mytton Rd B30 ... 19 C5

N

Nafford Gr B14 ... 20 F2
Nafford Rd WR10 ... 171 F8
Nailers Cl Birmingham B32 ... 8 F2
Stoke Heath B60 ... 67 E6
Nailers Ct 3 B60 ... 48 F2
Nailsworth Cl 9 WR4 ... 115 F7
Nailsworth Rd B98 ... 70 F2
Nairn Cl Birmingham B28 ... 21 F5
Redditch B98 ... 71 E4
Nantmel Gr B32 ... 18 C8
Napleton La WR5 ... 141 D6
Napton Cl B98 ... 71 D1
Napton Gr B29 ... 9 F2
Narrow La B62 ... 8 E8
Narrow Wlk 11 WR2 ... 114 F1
Narrows The GL55 ... 178 E2
Naseby Cl B98 ... 71 D6
Naseby Dr B63 ... 7 D2
Naseby House 4 B14 ... 21 A3

Nash Cl Martley WR6 ...99 A4
Worcester WR3 ...102 A1
Nash Ct (School) SY8 ...37 A4
Nash Gn WR13 ...126 A2
Nash La DY9 ...30 D7
Nash Rd B98 ...71 B1
Nashe Cl DY10 ...28 C5
Naunton Cl B29 ...19 A7
Navenby Cl B90 ...21 C3
Navigation Rd WR5 ...128 B7
Naylor Cl DY11 ...27 B3
Near Lands Cl B32 ...9 B4
Near Oak House B32 ...18 D8
Nearhill Rd B38 ...34 C8
Neason Cl 8 WR4 ...116 B4
Needle Cl B80 ...90 E4
Needle Mill La B98 ...70 E6
Neigh La WR10 ...160 C7
Neighbrook Cl B97 ...69 F2
Nelson Rd
Stourport-on-Severn DY13 ...44 B1
Worcester WR2 ...114 F2
Nelson St 6 GL20 ...196 E6
Nene Cl DY8 ...6 A5
Nesfield Cl B38 ...19 C1
Nestor House B13 ...21 D7
Netheravon Cl B14 ...20 D1
Nethercote Gdns B90 ...21 E3
Netherdale Rd B14 ...21 A1
Netherend Cl B63 ...7 A7
Netherend La B63 ...7 B7
Netherend Sq B63 ...7 A7
Netherfield B98 ...90 A8
Netherley La
Berrow WR13 ...180 B1
Pendock GL19 ...193 B8
Netherton La
Bewdley DY12 ...26 C2
Netherton WR10 ...173 F7
8 Worcester WR1 ...115 B3
Netherton Rd
Astley & Dunley DY13 ...62 A8
Rock DY13 ...61 E7
Netherwood La
Crowle WR9 ...117 D8
Oddingley WR9 ...104 D1
Netley House B32 ...9 F5
Neville Ave DY11 ...27 D3
Neville Cl B98 ...71 A5
Neville Ct
Birmingham B13 ...20 F6
Kidderminster DY11 ...27 D3
Neville Rd Solihull B90 ...36 F8
Tewkesbury GL20 ...196 F5
New Bank St WR3 ...115 B6
New Bldgs B63 ...7 A7
New Chawson La WR9 ...84 C1
New England B62 ...8 E7
New Farm Rd DY9 ...6 C4
New Forest Cl DY14 ...24 C2
New Inn La
Salford Priors WR11 ...135 C2
Shrawley WR6 ...62 D1
New Inns La B45 ...17 E1
New John St B62 ...8 C8
New Mdw Cl B31 ...19 B2
New Mdw Rd B98 ...71 B3
New Pool Rd B64 ...7 B8
New Rd
Astwood Bank B96 ...89 E1
Bewdley DY12 ...26 D5
Birmingham B45 ...32 F7
Bromsgrove B60 ...49 A1
Bromsgrove, Sidemoor B61 ...48 E3
Castlemorton WR13 ...166 F1
Cleobury Mortimer DY14 ...22 D5
Doverdale WR9 ...64 F3
Eckington WR10 ...171 E8
Evesham WR11 ...161 B3
Fairfield B61 ...31 E2
Halesowen B63 ...8 B4
Hanley WR6 ...58 C1
Hollywood B47 ...36 A8
Kidderminster DY10 ...27 E5
Offenham WR11 ...162 B8
Pebworth CV37 ...150 E2
Pershore WR10 ...158 C8
Rock DY14 ...24 B2
Stourbridge DY8 ...6 A5
Studley B80 ...90 E3
Wolverley & Cookley DY11 ...13 B7
Worcester WR2 ...115 A2
New Rd Est WR6 ...124 A3
New St
Birmingham, Frankley B45 ...18 A1
Bretforton WR11 ...163 C5
Brierley Hill DY5 ...7 A8
Childswickham WR12 ...176 E2
Stourbridge DY8 ...5 F5
Stourport-on-Severn DY13 ...43 F3
Upton upon Severn WR8 ...169 C6
Worcester WR1 ...115 C2
New Wharf Cotts B60 ...69 B7
New Wlk 3 B97 ...70 E4
New Wood Cl DY7 ...5 C8
New Wood Dr B31 ...18 D1
New Wood La DY10 ...29 B8
Newall House B97 ...70 D2
Newark Gn WR4 ...116 D6
Newbold Ct B63 ...8 B3
Newborough Gr B28, B90 ...21 F3
Newborough Rd B28 ...21 F4
Newbourne Hill B48 ...51 E4
Newburn Croft B32 ...9 B5
Newbury Cl Catshill B61 ...32 B1
Halesowen B62 ...8 D3
Newbury Rd WR2 ...114 E3
Newcastle Cl 3 WR5 ...115 F1
Newent Cl B98 ...72 A3
Newent Rd B31 ...19 C4
Newey Cl B45 ...33 A6
Newey Rd B28 ...21 F6
Neweys Hill WR3 ...115 A7
Newfield Cres B63 ...8 A5
Newfield Gdns DY9 ...15 A4
Newfield La B63 ...8 B5
Newfield Pk Prim Sch B63 ...8 A5
Newfield Pl DY9 ...15 A4
Newfield Rd DY9 ...15 A4
Newhouse La B61 ...66 D8
Newick Gr B14 ...20 C4
Newland Cl B98 ...90 B7
Newland Comm Rd WR9 ...104 A5
Newland Cres WR2 ...127 D8
Newland Dr WR9 ...84 F1
Newland Gdns B64 ...7 E7
Newland Rd WR9 ...84 F1
Newlands WR10 ...158 C8
Newlands Cl DY11 ...27 C7
Newlands Dr B62 ...8 E7
Newlands Rd B30 ...20 C7
Newlands The B80 ...90 D3
Newlyn Rd
Birmingham B31 ...18 F3
Blackheath B64 ...7 D8
Newman Coll Cl B32 ...18 C8
Newman Coll of Higher Ed B32 ...18 C8
Newman Way B45 ...33 A6
Newport Cl B97 ...89 B6
Newport St 3 WR1 ...115 B2
Newton Cl
5 Bewdley DY12 ...25 F4
Crowle WR7 ...117 F4
Redditch B98 ...90 A6
Newton Rd B60 ...68 A7
Newton Works B60 ...68 A6
Newtown Hospl WR5 ...116 B2
Newtown La
Romsley B62 ...17 D2
Wildmoor B62 ...31 D8
Newtown Rd
Great Malvern WR14 ...138 E3
Worcester WR4 ...115 D3
Nibletts Hill B61 ...48 B7
Nibley Cl 11 WR4 ...115 F7
Nigel Ave B31 ...19 A5
Nightingale Ave WR4 ...116 C3
Nightingale Cl WR9 ...104 B7
Nightingale Cres DY5 ...6 D7
Nightingale Dr DY10 ...28 B2
Nightingale La WR11 ...149 A8
Nightingale Rd WR14 ...139 C2
Nimmings Cl B31 ...33 F6
Nimmings Rd B62 ...8 D8
Nina Cl DY13 ...44 B3
Nine Acres Gn 6 WR4 ...116 B4
Nine Days La B98 ...90 B6
Ninesquares 3 WR10 ...171 E7
Nixon Ct WR2 ...140 F8
No Man's Gn La DY7 ...2 F6
Noble View WR14 ...138 D3
Nodbury Hill WR7 ...120 F6
Node Hill B80 ...90 D3
Node Hill Cl B80 ...90 D3
Noel Ct B97 ...89 C8
Nogains WR10 ...158 D7
Nonsuch Prim Sch B32 ...9 D2
Noonan Cl B97 ...70 B2
Norbury Cl B98 ...71 B7
Norchard La WR10 ...131 B1
Norfolk Cl
Birmingham B30 ...20 B6
Worcester WR2 ...114 C3
Norfolk Ct 6 B29 ...19 C7
Norfolk House B30 ...20 A3
Norfolk Rd
Birmingham B45 ...17 F2
Oldbury B68 ...9 B7
Stourbridge DY8 ...5 D8
Norgrove La B97 ...88 D6
Norham Pl WR4 ...116 C6
Norlan Dr B14 ...20 F3
Norley Gr B13 ...21 C7
Norman Ave B32 ...9 E7
Norman Cl
Twyning GL20 ...183 F6
5 Worcester WR4 ...116 B6
Norman Rd B31 ...19 B3
Norrington Gr B31 ...18 C3
Norrington Rd B31 ...18 D3
North Bromsgrove High Sch B60 ...49 B3
North Croft WR2 ...127 E8
North E Worcestershire Coll (Bromsgrove Campus) B60 ...49 B3
North E Worcestershire Coll (Redditch Campus) B98 ...70 E4
North End La WR14 ...139 B2
North Hill Gdns WR14 ...138 E3
North Malvern Rd WR14 ...138 E2
North Rd
Bromsgrove B60 ...49 A2
Evesham WR11 ...161 F4
Stourport-on-Severn DY13 ...44 A5
North St WR9 ...84 F3
North Wlk
Birmingham B31 ...19 C1
Malvern WR14 ...138 E2
Northampton La WR9 ...82 F7
Northbrook Cl WR3 ...115 B6
Northcliffe Hts DY11 ...27 C7
Northcote St 12 WR3 ...115 B6
Northfield Children's Farm* B31 ...18 C4
Northfield Cl
Fernhill Heath WR3 ...102 F3
Redditch B98 ...71 D6
Northfield Manor Jun & Inf Sch B29 ...19 B7
Northfield Rd B30 ...19 E4
Northfield St WR1 ...115 C4
Northfield Sta B31 ...19 B2
Northgate B64 ...7 D8
Northgate Cl DY11 ...27 A4
Northleach Ave B14 ...20 D2
Northleach Cl
Redditch B98 ...71 B5
1 Worcester WR4 ...115 F7
Northleigh CE Prim Sch WR14 ...138 D4
Northside Cl B98 ...89 E7
Northumberland Ave DY11 ...27 D3
Northway La GL20 ...184 D1
Northwick Ave WR3 ...115 A6
Northwick Cl WR3 ...115 A7
Northwick Manor Jun & Inf Sch WR3 ...115 A7
Northwick Rd
Evesham WR11 ...161 E4
Worcester WR3 ...102 A1
Northwick Wlk WR3 ...115 A7
Northwood Halt Sta DY12 ...25 F7
Northwood La DY12 ...10 F1
Northwood Way DY5 ...6 B8
Norton Cl
Birmingham B31 ...19 A3
Redditch B98 ...71 F2
Worcester WR5 ...128 C6
Norton Gate B38 ...19 F1
Norton Juxta Kempsey CE Fst Sch WR5 ...129 C1
Norton La B47, B90, B94 ...36 E3
Norton Mews B61 ...49 A4
Norton Rd
Kempsey WR5 ...128 E4
Kidderminster DY10 ...28 B6
Stourbridge DY8 ...5 E2
Norton Terr B30 ...20 B6
Norton View
Birmingham B14 ...20 D7
Mickleton GL55 ...165 D3
Nortune Cl B38 ...19 D2
Norval Rd WR11 ...163 C8
Norwich Ave DY11 ...26 F6
Norwich Dr B17 ...9 F8
Norwich Rd WR5 ...115 F2
Norwood Ave B64 ...7 E7
Nuffield Cl WR2 ...114 E4
Nuffield Dr WR9 ...84 C3
Nunnery Ave WR9 ...84 E2
Nunnery La
5 Worcester WR5 ...115 F1
Worcester WR5 ...129 A8
Nunnery Way WR5 ...116 C1
Nunnery Wood High Sch WR5 ...116 A1
Nunnery Wood Nature Reserve* WR5 ...116 B2
Nunnery Wood Prim Sch WR5 ...115 F1
Nursery Cl
Birmingham B30 ...19 F5
Hagley DY9 ...15 A4
Kidderminster DY11 ...27 B8
Mickleton GL55 ...165 F5
2 Pershore WR10 ...144 D1
Nursery Dr B30 ...19 F5
Nursery Gdns B90 ...36 E8
Nursery Gr
5 Kidderminster DY11 ...12 B1
Kidderminster DY11 ...27 B8
Nursery Rd
Bewdley DY12 ...26 B4
Birmingham B30 ...19 E5
Great Malvern WR14 ...138 E3
Worcester WR2 ...127 E8
Nursery Wlk 15 WR2 ...114 F1
Nut Orch La GL20 ...183 F7
Nutbush Dr B31 ...18 D6
Nutfield Wlk B32 ...9 F5
Nutgrove Cl B14 ...20 F7
Nuthatch Dr DY5 ...6 C7
Nuthurst Gr B14 ...20 F2
Nuthurst Rd B31 ...33 F6

O

Oak Apple Cl DY13 ...62 E7
Oak Apple Rd B61 ...49 B8
Oak Ave
Madresfield WR13 ...139 F4
Worcester WR4 ...115 E5
Oak Barn Rd B62 ...8 E8
Oak Bridge Ct WR15 ...55 F3
Oak Cl Badsey WR11 ...162 E4
Kinver DY7 ...4 C3
Oak Cotts B14 ...21 C2
Oak Cres WR14 ...139 C1
Oak Ct Halesowen B63 ...7 F2
Stourbridge DY8 ...6 A4
Oak Dr
6 Colwall Stone WR13 ...152 B2
Hartlebury WR9 ...64 E8
Northway GL20 ...197 D8
Oak Farm Rd B30 ...19 E5
Oak Gdns GL20 ...184 F6
Oak Gr Birmingham B31 ...18 E1
Kidderminster DY10 ...28 A5
Oak Hill Fst Sch B98 ...71 A2
Oak La GL20 ...184 E6
Oak Leasow B32 ...9 B4
Oak Pk Ind Est DY10 ...45 E2
Oak Rd Catshill B61 ...49 B8
Oldbury B68 ...9 C7
Oak St WR8 ...169 C5
Oak Tree Ave B97 ...70 B4
Oak Tree Cl
6 Evesham WR11 ...161 F2
4 Tenbury Wells WR15 ...55 F6
Oak Tree Cres B62 ...8 F6
Oak Tree Dr WR9 ...65 B5
Oak Tree House B30 ...19 E7
Oak Tree La
Birmingham B29 ...19 E8
Cookhill B49 ...109 A2
Hollywood B47 ...36 B6
Sambourne B96 ...90 B2
Oak Tree Pk B98 ...71 F6
Oak Tree Rd WR11 ...147 F7
Oak Trees B47 ...36 A7
Oak Wlk The B31 ...19 A1
Oakalls Ave B60 ...49 B2
Oakcroft Rd B13 ...21 C7
Oakden Pl DY11 ...27 C7
Oakdene DY13 ...44 B3
Oakdene Dr B45 ...50 C8
Oakenshaw Rd B98 ...71 A1
Oakfield Cl WR5 ...141 D6
Oakfield Dr
Birmingham B45 ...33 D4
Kempsey WR5 ...141 C6
Oakfield Rd
Great Malvern WR14 ...139 A5
Kidderminster DY11 ...27 B5
Ombersley WR9 ...83 A5
Stourbridge, Wollescote DY9 ...6 F2
Oakham Cl B98 ...90 A5
Oakham Dr WR9 ...84 C2
Oakham House 7 B14 ...21 A3
Oakham Pl WR9 ...84 C2
Oakhampton Rd DY13 ...62 E8
Oakhill Ave DY10 ...27 E4
Oakhill Dr DY5 ...6 B7
Oakhill Infants Sch WR11 ...187 F5
Oakhurst Dr B60 ...49 A3
Oakland Ave WR9 ...84 E1
Oakland Cl WR8 ...168 F5
Oakland Gr B61 ...49 B4
Oaklands
Birmingham, Northfield B31 ...18 F4
Great Malvern WR14 ...152 E1
Halesowen B62 ...9 A4
Worcester WR5 ...116 B3
Oaklands The
1 Droitwich WR9 ...103 F8
Halesowen B62 ...8 F6
Kidderminster DY10 ...28 A7
Oaklands Way B31 ...18 C1
Oakleaf Cl B32 ...9 C2
Oakleaf Rise DY14 ...24 C2
Oakleigh B31 ...19 C2
Oakleigh Ave WR2 ...101 C2
Oakleigh Heath WR2 ...101 C2
Oakleigh Rd
2 Droitwich WR9 ...84 C1
Stourbridge DY8 ...6 B2
Oakley House B60 ...49 A1
Oakley Rd B30 ...20 B5
Oakly Rd B97 ...70 D3
Oakridge Cl
Redditch B98 ...71 C7
2 Worcester WR4 ...116 A7
Oaks The
Birmingham, Hawkesley B38 ...34 F7
1 Kempsey WR5 ...141 C6
Stoke Bliss WR15 ...75 F3
Oaktree Cl B48 ...51 A7
Oaktree Farm Mobile Homes Pk B94 ...53 B7
Oakwood Ct B63 ...8 A4
Oakwood Dr B14 ...20 D4
Oakwood Rd
9 Bewdley DY12 ...25 F3
2 Bewdley DY12 ...26 A3
Hollywood B47 ...36 A6
Oasis The DY9 ...14 F5
Oasthouse Cl B60 ...67 D6
Oat St WR11 ...161 D4
Oatlands Wlk 3 B14 ...20 C2
Oatsley La WR10 ...171 F7
Oberon Cl B45 ...18 A2
Ockam Croft B31 ...19 C2
Oddingley Rd B31 ...19 C2
Odnall La DY9 ...15 F3
Offenham CE Fst Sch WR11 ...148 A1
Offenham Cl B98 ...71 B6
Offenham Covert B38 ...34 E8
Offenham Rd 4 WR11 ...161 F4
Offerton La WR3 ...103 F1
Offley St WR3 ...115 B6
Offmoor Rd B32 ...18 B8
Offmore Ct DY10 ...28 C6
Offmore Farm Cl DY10 ...28 C6
Offmore Fst Sch DY10 ...28 B6
Offmore La DY10 ...28 A6
Offmore Rd DY10 ...27 F6
Offwell Rd B98 ...71 D1
Ogbury Cl B14 ...20 C2
Ogilvy Sq WR3 ...115 A8
O'key's La WR3 ...103 A2
Old Bakery Ct DY9 ...15 A5
Old Bank Top B31 ...19 B2
Old Barn Rd B30 ...19 D6
Old Birmingham Rd
Alvechurch B48 ...51 B8
Catshill B60 ...49 C8
Marlbrook B60, B45 ...32 E1
Old Bowling Gn Cl WR15 ...55 E6
Old Chawson La 4 WR9 ...84 C1
Old Chester Rd S DY10 ...27 E2
Old Church Rd WR13 ...152 A2
Old Coach Rd WR9 ...84 E2
Old Cres Ct 9 B68 ...9 B8
Old Crest Ave B98 ...70 E2
Old Crown Cl B32 ...9 B1
Old Dr The WR3 ...103 C2
Old Farm Gr B14 ...21 D5
Old Forge WR6 ...110 F6
Old Forge Bsns Ctr B98 ...90 C8
Old Forge Dr B98 ...90 C8
Old Forge Gdns 4 DY11 ...45 B2
Old Forge Trad Est DY9 ...6 E6
Old Glebe Pastures WR10 ...131 B1
Old Gr Gdns DY9 ...6 D3
Old Hall Cl
Aston Somerville WR12 ...175 E1
Stourbridge DY8 ...6 A8
Old Ham La DY9 ...6 D2
Old Hawne La B63 ...8 A5
Old Hill WR7 ...119 D2
Old Hill Sta B64 ...8 A8
Old Hollow WR14 ...138 C3
Old Hospl La GL20 ...196 F7
Old House La B62 ...17 B1
Old La B48 ...52 D4
Old Lime Gdns B38 ...34 E8
Old Malvern Rd WR2 ...127 C3
Old Manor Cl WR10 ...145 D3
Old Manor Gdns GL55 ...165 E4
Old Manor La GL20 ...197 A8
Old Mdw Rd B31 ...34 C7
Old Mill Cl B90 ...21 D2
Old Moat Dr B31 ...19 B3
Old Northwick La WR3 ...114 F8
Old Oak Rd B38 ...20 A2
Old Orch WR8 ...169 A5
Old Pk B29 ...19 A5
Old Portway B38 ...34 E7
Old Post Office La WR11 ...162 E3
Old Quarry Cl B45 ...32 F8
Old Rd
Clifton upon Teme WR6 ...97 F7
Powick WR2 ...127 F5
Old Rd N WR5 ...141 C7
Old Rd S WR5 ...141 B5
Old Rectory Cl WR2 ...127 E3
Old Rectory Gn WR10 ...146 B1
Old Rectory La B48 ...51 B7
Old Sch Cl WR11 ...148 A1
Old Sch La WR15 ...55 F6
Old St WR8 ...169 C5
Old Sta Rd B60 ...49 A1
Old Stone Cl B45 ...17 F1
Old Stratford Rd B60 ...49 C2
Old Swinford CE Prim Sch DY8 ...6 A3
Old Town Cl B38 ...19 F2
Old Turnpike Rd WR7 ...117 F6
Old Vicarage Cl 3 WR5 ...141 C6
Old Vicarage Gdns B80 ...90 E4
Old Wharf Rd DY8 ...5 F6
Old Woodyard The DY9 ...15 D6
Old Wyche Rd WR14 ...152 E5
Oldacre Rd B68 ...9 A7
Oldbury Cl B98 ...71 B6
Oldbury Pk Prim Sch WR2 ...114 F3
Oldbury Rd
Broadheath WR2 ...114 B4
Tewkesbury GL20 ...196 E6
Worcester WR2 ...114 E3
Oldfield GL20 ...196 F6
Oldfield Dr DY8 ...6 A3
Oldfield La WR9 ...83 C7
Oldfields Blackheath B64 ...7 D8
Hagley DY9 ...15 B6
Oldhouse Farm Cl B28 ...21 F6
Oldington La DY13 ...44 B8
Oldington Trad Est DY11 ...27 B1
Oldnall Cl DY9 ...6 F4
Oldnall Rd
Kidderminster DY10 ...28 A4
Stourbridge B63, DY9 ...7 A4
Oldswinford Hospl Sch DY8 ...6 A4
Oldwood Rd WR15 ...55 D1
Olive Dr B62 ...8 C8
Olive Gr DY13 ...43 F4

Olive Hill Prim Sch B62 8 D7
Olive Hill Rd B62 8 D8
Olive La B62 8 D8
Olive Pl B14 20 E7
Olliver Cl B62 9 A3
Olympus Gdns DY13 44 C3
Ombersley Cl B98 90 C7
Ombersley Endowed Fst Sch WR9 83 B4
Ombersley Pk* WR9 83 A3
Ombersley Rd
Droitwich WR9 84 E3
Halesowen B63 7 F2
Worcester WR3 102 A1
Ombersley St E 4 WR9 84 F3
Ombersley St W WR9 84 E3
Ombersley Way WR9 84 D2
Ongrils Cl WR10 144 C1
Ontario Cl
Birmingham B38 35 A8
Worcester WR2 127 E6
Open Field Cl B31 19 C2
Orangery The DY9 15 D7
Orchard Ave WR12 190 E8
Orchard Cl
Bidford-on-Avon B50 136 D5
Bredon GL20 185 A6
Bretforton WR11 163 C4
Earl's Croome WR8 155 F1
Hagley DY9 15 B4
Halesowen B63 7 C6
Hallow WR2 101 D1
Mickleton GL55 165 E5
3 Pershore WR10 158 C8
Rock DY14 41 F6
Ryall WR8 169 E6
Severn Stoke WR8 155 D6
3 Stourport-on-Severn DY13 44 B4
Worcester WR2 127 B8
Orchard Cres B60 67 C3
Orchard Croft B45 50 D8
Orchard Ct 5 GL20 196 F6
Orchard Dr
Birmingham B31 33 F7
Little Comberton WR10 159 A3
Twyning GL20 184 A6
Orchard End DY14 22 C5
Orchard Gdns WR6 77 E3
Orchard Gr
Cookhill B96 108 E7
Cookley DY11 13 A6
Kinver DY7 4 B4
Norton Juxta Kempsey WR5 129 D1
Orchard Holmes WV15 1 C6
Orchard Lea The 1 WR9 85 A1
Orchard Mead WR7 120 E7
Orchard Pl
Harvington WR11 147 F7
Redditch B80 90 F8
Orchard Rd
Bromsgrove B61 48 F4
4 Great Malvern WR14 152 F8
Pershore WR10 158 C8
Wolverley & Cookley DY10 13 C4
Orchard Ridge GL20 181 F5
Orchard Rise
Bewdley DY12 26 A3
Droitwich WR9 103 E8
Orchard St
Kidderminster DY10 27 E6
Redditch B98 70 E3
Worcester WR5 128 C7
Orchard The
Bewdley DY12 25 E3
Bowling Green WR2 127 C3
Bromsgrove B61 48 E4
Orchard Villas
Fairfield B61 31 D2
Wythall B47 35 F1
Orchard Way
Bransford WR6 126 C5
Callow End WR2 140 F7
Hollywood B47 36 A8
Studley B80 90 E2
Orchardlea WR10 132 A5
Orchards The
Astwood Bank B96 89 D1
Hollywood B47 36 A7
2 Kidderminster DY11 12 B1
Orcheston Wlk B14 20 D2
Orchid Cl WR5 128 C4
Orford Way WR14 139 C1
Oriel Cl WR4 115 E3
Oriole Gr DY10 28 B2
Orleans Cl 1 WR11 161 D1
Orleton Cl WR13 167 C4
Orleton La WR15 58 F4
Ormande Cl B63 7 B7
Orme Cl DY5 6 B8
Ormond Rd B45 17 F1
Ormscliffe Rd B45 33 B6
Orwell Cl DY8 5 D4
Orwell Dr B38 34 C8
Orwin Gn 1 WR4 116 B3
Osborne Cl
Brierley Hill DY5 6 F8
Kidderminster DY10 28 B6
Osborne Rd WR14 139 A3
Osier Cl WR5 128 C7
Osmaston Rd DY8 5 F2
Osmington Gr B63 7 D6
Osnor Ct B60 68 B7
Osprey Cl WR2 128 A6
Osprey House B80 90 D4
Osprey Pk Dr DY10 28 B3
Ostler Dr WR2 114 E3
Oswald St B98 70 E3
Oswestry Cl B97 89 C7
Other Rd B98 70 E4
Otherton La WR2 113 E1
Otley Cl WR4 116 A4
Ottawa Cl WR2 127 E7
Otter Cl B98 72 A3
Otter La WR5 128 F6
Ottilie Hild Sch B60 67 E5
Oulton Cl DY11 12 D1
Ounty John La DY8 6 A1
Our Lady & Kenelm RC Sch B63 8 A4
Our Lady of Fatima RC Prim Sch B17 9 F7
Our Lady of Lourdes RC Prim Sch B13 21 D5
Our Lady Queen of Peace RC Prim Sch WR2 114 F1
Out Wood Dr B31 18 D1
Outfields B13 20 E6
Outwood Cl B98 89 E7
Over Brunton Cl B31 19 B2
Overbrook WR11 161 E3
Overbury CE Fst Sch GL20 185 F7
Overbury Cl
Birmingham B31 19 C3
Halesowen B63 8 B2
Overbury Rd B31 19 C3
Overdale B96 89 E1
Overdale Rd B32 9 E5
Overend Rd B63, B64 7 D7
Overfield Rd B32 9 F1
Owens Croft B38 20 A1
Owlets End B50 136 F3
Owletts End WR11 161 E3
Owletts La
Pershore/Pinvin WR10 144 F7
Wick WR10 159 B7
Owlhill La WR9 63 E2
Ox Leasow B32 9 C2
Oxbow Way DY10 27 E8
Oxenton Croft B63 7 D2
Oxford Cl WR5 115 F2
Oxford Ct 8 B29 19 C7
Oxford Dr DY8 5 F4
Oxford St
Birmingham, Stirchley B30 20 A7
Kidderminster DY10 27 E5
Oxhill Cl B98 71 E1
Oxhill Rd B90 21 C2
Oxleasow Rd B98 71 E4
Oxley Gr B29 19 A8
Oxwood La B32 17 D4

P

Packers Hill WR8 169 A5
Packhorse Cl WR2 114 E3
Packhorse La B38, B47 35 E6
Packington Rd
Droitwich WR9 84 E2
3 Worcester WR2 114 E5
Packs Cl WR11 162 D4
Packwood Cl B97 69 F1
Packwood Cl 1 B29 9 F1
Padbury House B31 18 D5
Paddock Cl
Bidford-on-Avon B50 136 C5
Pershore WR10 144 C1
Paddock La B98 89 E7
Paddock The
Birmingham B31 19 C4
Stoke Heath B60 67 D6
Stourbridge DY9 15 C8
Paddock Way WR9 84 D5
Paddocks Rd B47 35 F6
Paddocks The
Cleobury Mortimer DY14 22 C5
Norton & Lenchwick WR11 147 C3
Padgets La B98 71 D4
Padgewell Hill 1 WR9 84 D1
Padmore St WR1 115 C3
Padua Rd B60 49 C1
Page's La GL20 183 D5
Paget Cl B61 48 E2
Pagnell Gr B13 21 C6
Painswick Cl
Redditch B98 89 E6
Worcester WR4 116 A7
Painswick Rd B28 21 F7
Pakefield Rd B30 20 C3
Palfrey Rd DY8 5 D5
Palm Croft DY5 6 C8
Palm Rd GL20 197 A4
Palmcourt Ave B28 21 E7
Palmers Gn
10 Worcester WR2 114 F1
2 Worcester WR2 114 E1
Palmers Rd B98 71 F5
Palmyra Rd B60 49 C2
Pamela Rd B31 19 A3
Paper Mill Cotts B97 69 E5
Paper Mill Dr B98 71 B5
Paper Mill La WR9 66 E2
Papworth Dr B61 48 F5
Par Gn B38 19 D1
Parade The B64 7 E8
Paradise Ct B28 21 D6
Paradise La B28 21 E6
Paradise Row B60 48 F2
Pargeter St DY8 5 F4
Parish Gdns DY9 6 C1
Parish Hill B61 31 D1
Park Ave
Birmingham, King's Norton B30 20 A5
Stourport-on-Severn DY13 43 F4
Studley B80 90 E3
Worcester WR3 115 A6
Park Butts Ringway DY11 27 D6
Park Cl Bewdley DY12 26 B3
Great Malvern WR14 139 B4
Northway GL20 184 D1
Park Cres DY13 43 F4
Park Croft B47 36 A5
Park Ct
Kidderminster DY11 27 D5
Redditch B98 71 A3
Park Dingle DY12 25 E2
Park End Dr B32 9 D1
Park Farm Ind Est B98 90 C7
Park Gate Rd DY10 13 B2
Park Hall Mews WR11 135 D4
Park La Bewdley DY12 25 F2
Halesowen B63 7 B6
Hallow WR2 114 D8
Harvington DY10 29 A2
Kidderminster DY11 27 D6
Rushock WR9 46 D2
Upper Sapey WR6 78 C5
West Malvern WR14 152 C6
Worcester WR3 115 A6
Park Rd Brierley Hill DY5 6 F8
Great Malvern WR14 152 C8
Hagley DY9 15 B6
Halesowen B63 7 B5
Stourbridge DY8 5 D5
Park Rd W DY8 5 D5
Park Ridge Dr B63 7 B6
Park Rise DY11 27 D5
Park St
Kidderminster DY11 27 D5
Stourbridge, Lye DY9 6 F5
Stourbridge, Stambermill DY8 6 A5
Stourbridge, Amblecote DY8 5 F8
Worcester WR5 115 C2
Park St Gdns DY11 27 D6
Park The
Northway GL20 184 D1
Redditch B97 69 C7
Park View B49 122 F6
Park View Rd
Birmingham B31 18 F3
Stourbridge DY9 6 F4
Park View Terr WR3 115 A6
Park Way
Birmingham B45 33 B8
Droitwich WR9 84 D4
Redditch B98 71 A5
Park Wlk Brierley Hill DY5 6 F8
4 Redditch B97 70 E3
Parkbrook Ind Est 5 DY9 6 F5
Parkdale Dr B31 34 A7
Parker House B14 20 F3
Parker Pl
Broadway WR12 190 D8
Kidderminster DY13 44 C7
Parkes Pas 2 DY13 44 A3
Parkes Quay 3 DY13 44 A3
Parkfield B32 9 A2
Parkfield Cl
Halesowen B62 9 A5
Hartlebury DY11 45 A2
Redditch B98 71 B6
Parkfield La WR2 114 D7
Parkfield Rd DY8 6 B5
Parkland Ave DY11 27 B5
Parklands Rd 2 WR3 102 A1
Parklands Cl B97 70 A5
Parklands The
3 Droitwich WR9 103 F8
Stourbridge DY9 6 D3
Parks The WR11 162 A6
Parkside Birmingham B32 9 C2
Colwall WR13 152 B1
Parkside Mid Sch B61 49 A3
Parkside Rd B63 7 D5
Parkside Way B31 18 C1
Parkstone Ave B61 67 D8
Parkview Trad Est B38 19 F3
Parkwood WR10 173 E7
Parkwood Rd B61 48 E3
Parlows End B38 34 D7
Parmington Cl B97 89 B6
Parry Rd DY11 27 B3
Parsonage Dr
Birmingham B45 33 D4
Halesowen B63 7 A7
Parsonage La WR9 82 F4
Parsonage Way WR4 116 D5
Parson's Hill B30 20 B2
Parsons La
Hartlebury DY11 44 F1
Redmarley D'abitot GL19 192 E3
Weston-sub-Edge GL55 178 D6
Parsons Rd B98 70 E2
Partons Rd B14 20 D6
Partridge Cl 3 WR5 128 D5
Partridge Gr DY10 28 A2
Partridge House B97 70 D2
Partridge La
Broadheath WR2 114 A6
Redditch B97 89 A7
Partridge Rd DY8 5 C4
Pass St WR10 171 E8
Pastures Wlk B38 34 D7
Pat Davis Ct DY10 27 E7
Patch La B98 89 F6
Paternoster Row 4 DY11 27 D6
Pathway The B14 20 C5
Patios The DY11 27 C7
Patricia Ave B14 21 C4
Patterdale Dr WR4 116 A5
Patterdale Way DY5 6 B8
Pavilion Gdns B61 48 F5
Paxford Cl B98 71 B6
Paxford Way B31 18 F6
Paxhill La GL20 183 F7
Paxton Cl B60 49 B1
Paxton Rd DY9 7 A4
Paynes La WR10 146 A1
Peabody Ave WR4 116 C4
Peach Cl 1 GL20 197 A3
Peach Ley Rd B29 18 F7
Peachfield Cl WR14 152 F5
Peachfield Rd WR14 152 F5
Peachley Cl 8 B63 8 B3
Peachley Gdns WR2 113 F7
Peachley La WR2 113 F8
Peacock Cl 8 WR5 128 E5
Peacock Mews DY10 27 E8
Peacock Rd B13 20 F6
Peak Rd DY8 6 B6
Peakman Cl B45 33 A6
Peakman St B98 70 E4
Pear Orch The 2 GL20 184 E1
Pear Tree Cl
Great Malvern WR14 152 E4
Kidderminster DY10 28 B7
Solihull B90 21 D2
Pear Tree Cres B90 21 C2
Pear Tree Dr
Leigh WR13 126 A2
Sedgeberrow WR11 175 A1
Pear Tree Gr B90 21 D2
Pear Tree Way
Crowle WR7 117 E4
2 Dodderhill WR9 66 E1
Pearl La DY13 43 D1
Pearmain Cl WR2 114 E6
Pearman Rd B45 17 D1
Pearmans Croft B47 36 A6
Pearson St DY9 6 F4
Peart Dr B80 90 C4
Peartree Dr DY8 6 A2
Peason La WR10 171 D8
Pebble Cl DY8 6 B5
Pebworth Cl B98 71 C7
Pebworth Fst Sch CV37 150 E2
Peckingham St 2 B63 8 B3
Pedmore CE Prim Sch DY9 6 C1
Pedmore Cl B98 90 B7
Pedmore Ct Rd DY8 6 B1
Pedmore Hall La DY9 15 C8
Pedmore La Hagley DY9 15 F8
Stourbridge DY9 6 E1
Pedmore Rd DY9 6 E5
Peel St DY11 27 D5
Peel Wlk B17 9 F7
Peewit Rd WR11 161 B2
Pegasus Ct B62 8 F5
Pegleg Wlk 2 B14 20 C2
Pelham Lodge DY10 28 A5
Pelham Rd WR9 103 E8
Pemberton Cres DY10 13 C3
Pembridge Cl
Birmingham B32 18 A7
Redditch B98 71 D2
Pembroke Ave WR15 55 F5
Pembroke Pl WR4 116 D5
Pembroke Way DY13 43 E6
Penbury St WR3 115 B7
Pendeen Rd B14 21 C4
Pendennis Cl B30 19 D5
Pendock CE Prim Sch GL19 193 B7
Pendragon Cl WR14 139 C3
Penelope Gdns WR11 176 D8
Penfields Rd DY8 6 B6
Penhill Cres WR2 114 D3
Peninsula Rd WR5 129 A4
Penlu Rd 7 WR15 55 F6
Penmanor B60 68 D8
Penmanor Cl WR2 114 E2
Penn Hall La WR6 59 E7
Penn La B94 53 C4
Pennard Gr B32 9 F4
Pennine Rd B61 49 A5
Pennine Way DY8 6 A6
Penny Cl WR13 154 A7
Penny La WR13 154 A7
Pennyacre Rd B14 20 D2
Pennyfold Cl B97 70 A5
Pennylands Bank WR12 177 A2
Penrice Rd WR9 84 E1
Penrith Cl
Brierley Hill DY5 6 B8
Worcester WR4 116 B6
Penrith Croft B32 18 D8
Pensax CE Prim Sch WR6 60 A6
Pensax Rd Pensax WR6 60 A5
Stockton on Teme WR6 59 F3
Pensby Cl B13 21 B8
Pensford Rd B31 19 C3
Pensham Hill WR10 158 E6
Penshurst Rd B60 49 C1
Penstock Ct DY10 28 C8
Penzer Dr B45 50 D8
Peplins Way B30 20 B3
Pepper Hill DY8 6 A4
Pepper St WR7 120 F6
Pepper Wood Dr B31 18 C1
Pepperpot* WR8 169 C6
Pepperwood Cl B61 31 C3
Perch Rd WR5 128 C5
Percheron Way
7 Droitwich WR9 85 B1
Droitwich WR9 104 B8
Perdiswell Leisure Ctr WR3 115 D7
Perdiswell Prim Sch WR3 115 C7
Perdiswell St WR3 115 B7
Peregrine Gr DY10 28 A2
Perivale Way DY8 6 A8
Perkins Cl WR11 135 D4
Perrett Wlk 8 DY11 27 D6
Perrie Dr WR11 164 B5
Perrin Ave DY11 27 B4
Perrins Cl WR14 138 E4
Perrins Field WR8 168 F5
Perrins La DY9 6 F4
Perrins Rise DY9 6 F4
Perry Ct B68 9 B7
Perry Hill Cres B68 9 B7
Perry Hill House B68 9 C8
Perry Hill La B68 9 B7
Perry Hill Rd B68 9 B7
Perry La Bromsgrove B61 48 F2
Hartlebury DY10 45 B5
Perry Mill Rd 2 WR10 131 B2
Perry Wood Cl WR5 115 E1
Perry Wood Wlk WR5 115 E1
Perrycroft Cl WR3 102 F3
Perryfields Cl B98 89 F6
Perryfields Cres B61 48 F5
Perryfields High Sch B68 9 A8
Perryfields Prim Sch B68 9 A7
Perryfields Rd B61 48 D4
Perrymill La B96 90 B1
Perscoran Way WR10 158 D7
Pershore & Hindlip Coll WR10 158 F6
Pershore Cottage Hospl WR10 158 D7
Pershore Ct DY11 27 D5
Pershore High Sch WR10 144 E3
Pershore La WR3 103 D2
Pershore Rd
Birmingham, Breedon Cross B30 20 A5
Birmingham, Ten Acres B30 20 B8
Eckington WR10 157 E1
Evesham WR11 161 C3
Halesowen B63 8 A2
Kidderminster DY11 27 A6
Upton Snodsbury WR7 131 C8
Pershore Rd S B30 19 F3
Pershore Sta WR10 144 E5
Pershore Trad Est WR10 144 E4
Perton Gr B29 19 A8
Perwell Cl GL20 184 E7
Pestilence La B48 51 C8
Peter's Finger B60 48 F1
Peter's Hill Prim Sch DY5 6 C7
Peter's Hill Rd DY5 6 C6
Peterborough Cl WR5 115 F2
Peterbrook Cl B98 89 F7
Peterbrook Prim Sch B90 21 D2
Peterbrook Rd B90 21 D1
Peterbrook Rise B90 21 D1
Peters Ave B31 18 F2
Petersbourne Ct B28 21 F8
Petersfield Ct B28 21 F8
Petersfield Rd B28 21 E7
Petland Trad Ctr B98 71 D4
Pettitt Cl B14 20 E2
Petton Cl B98 71 F3
Petunia Cl WR5 128 D5
Pevensey Cl 9 WR5 128 E8
Pevensey Rd B60 49 C1
Peverell Dr B28 21 F7
Pheasant Cl DY10 28 A2
Pheasant La B98 89 F7
Pheasant St WR1 115 C3
Philip Rd Halesowen B63 7 F3
Worcester WR3 102 B1
Philipscote 2 WR11 161 F4
Phillips La GL19 192 E3
Phillips Rd WR12 177 D1
Phillips Terr B98 70 F4
Pickenham Rd B14 21 A1
Pickering Croft B32 9 D1
Pickering Gn 7 WR4 116 C6
Pickersleigh Ave WR14 139 B4
Pickersleigh Cl
Great Malvern WR14 139 A4
6 Halesowen B63 8 A3
Pickersleigh Gr WR14 139 B2
Pickersleigh Rd WR14 139 B1
Picton Gdn The* WR13 152 B3
Picton Gr B13 21 B6
Pierpoint St 4 WR1 115 B3
Piers Cl WR14 153 A5
Pig Pen The* WR6 123 A7
Pigeon La GL20 186 A8

Pike Cnr 2 WR12 ....177 E4
Pike Hill B60 ....50 A7
Pikes Pool La B60 ....49 E2
Pikes The B45 ....32 F8
Pilgrim Rd WR9 ....85 B2
Pillow Mounds★
WR12 ....191 C6
Pinchers Cl DY9 ....30 E7
Pine Cl
Fernhill Heath WR3 ......103 A3
Kinver DY7 ....4 C3
Pine Ct DY9 ....6 B1
Pine Gr Barnt Green B45 ...32 F2
Birmingham B14 ....21 A5
Pine Tree Cl B97 ....69 F3
Pine Way WR4 ....115 E6
Pine Wlk
Birmingham B31 ....19 B3
Stourbridge DY9 ....6 D3
2 Stourport-on-Severn
DY13 ....43 E4
Pine Woods B32 ....9 A2
Pineapple Gr B30 ....20 C8
Pineapple Rd B30 ....20 C7
Pinedene DY13 ....44 C3
Pinehurst Dr B38 ....19 F3
Pineridge Dr DY11 ....27 B5
Pines The B45 ....18 A1
Pinetree Rd 1 DY12 ....25 F2
Pineview B31 ....18 F2
Pinewall Ave B38 ....20 A1
Pinewood Cl
Birmingham, Eachway
B45 ....32 D8
1 Kidderminster DY11 .....12 C1
Pinewood Dr B32 ....9 A1
Pinewoods
Birmingham B31 ....18 F8
Halesowen B62 ....9 A7
Pinewoods Ave DY9 .....14 F4
Pinewoods Cl DY9 ....14 F4
Pinewoods Ct DY9 ....14 F4
Pinfield Dr B45 ....33 B1
Pink Gn La B98 ....72 B8
Pinkett St WR3 ....115 A7
Pinkham DY14 ....22 D4
Pinkham La DY14 ....22 D5
Pinkus Cl 3 WR4 ....116 C3
Pinner Gr B32 ....9 E4
Pinta Dr DY13 ....44 B3
Pintail Gr DY10 ....28 B3
Pinvin CE Fst Sch
WR10 ....144 E6
Pinvin House B97 ....70 A3
Pioneer Cl B97 ....70 D4
Piper Pl DY8 ....5 F8
Pipers Cl B61 ....67 D7
Pipers Gn B28 ....21 F5
Pipers Rd B98 ....90 D7
Pipit Ct DY10 ....28 A2
Pippen Field WR4 ......116 C5
Pippin Ave B63 ....7 B7
Pippin Cl 6 B50 ....136 D5
Pippins Rd GL20 ....184 F6
Pippins The 2 WR10 ....171 E7
Pirie Ave WR4 ....116 C3
Pit Leasow Cl B30 ....20 B8
Pitcairn Cl B30 ....20 B6
Pitcairn Dr B62 ....8 B5
Pitchard Cl HR7 ....96 D7
Pitchcroft La WR1 ......115 A5
Pitcheroak Cotts B97 ....70 A3
Pitcheroak Specl Sch
B97 ....70 B4
Pitchers Hill WR11 .....176 D7
Pitclose Rd B31 ....19 B1
Pitfields Cl B68 ....9 A8
Pitfields Rd B68 ....9 A8
Pitman Rd B32 ....9 C5
Pitmaston Prim Sch
WR2 ....127 F8
Pitmaston Rd WR2 ......114 F1
Pitmeadow House B14 ..20 E2
Pitt Ave WR4 ....116 B3
Pitt St DY10 ....13 A1
Pitts La DY10 ....27 E6
Pixham Ferry La WR5 ..141 B5
Plane Tree Cl DY10 ......27 F7
Planetree Cl B60 ....49 B2
Plantation Cres 3 GL20 .184 F6
Plantation Dr WR4 .....116 C5
Plantation Sch WR6 ......82 B3
Platts Cres DY8 ....5 E8
Platts Dr DY8 ....5 F8
Platts Rd DY8 ....5 E8
Playdon Gr B14 ....21 A3
Players Ave WR14 ......139 A5
Pleasant Harbour DY12 ..26 B4
Pleasant St DY10 ....27 E7
Pleck House B14 ....20 C1
Pleck The
Bidford-on-Avon B50 .....136 D4
Inkberrow WR7 ....120 E8
Pleck Wlk B38 ....20 A1
Plimsoll Gr B32 ....9 C5
Plimsoll St DY11 ....27 D5
Plough Ave B32 ....9 C2
Plough Croft 12 WR4 ....116 B5
Plough La
Oddingley WR9 ....104 B2
Rock DY14 ....24 C1
Plough Rd WR9 ....117 A7
Ploughmans Cl 11 WR4 ..115 F6
Ploughmans Way 1
WR9 ....84 D5
Ploughmans Wlk B60 ....67 D6
Plover Gr DY10 ....28 B1
Plovers Rise 7 WR5 ....141 C6
Plymouth Cl
Birmingham B31 ....34 A7
Redditch B97 ....70 C1
Plymouth Ct B97 ....70 C1
Plymouth Dr B45 ....50 A8
Plymouth Rd
Barnt Green B45 ....50 A8
Birmingham B30 ....20 B7
Redditch B97 ....70 D2
Pochard Cl DY10 ....27 F1
Poden La
Aston Subedge GL55 .....178 E8
Honeybourne GL55 ......164 D4
Pointon Way WR9 ....84 C6
Polden Cl B63 ....7 C1
Pole Elm Cl 2 WR2 .....140 F8
Polesworth Cl B98 ....71 D1
Polly Brooks Yd DY9 ......6 E5
Polo Fields DY9 ....6 B1
Pomeroy Rd B32 ....9 C1
Pool Bank B98 ....70 E2
Pool Cl WR10 ....159 B4
Pool Field Ave B31 ....18 E7
Pool Furlong DY9 ....15 E1
Pool Rd Halesowen B63 ....8 B3
Studley B80 ....90 E4
Poolbrook Prim Sch
WR14 ....153 D7
Poolbrook Rd WR14 ....153 B5
Poole St DY8 ....5 E4
Pooles Ct DY10 ....27 E7
Poolhead La
Earlswood B94 ....53 C7
Tanworth-In-A B94 ....53 E5
Pooltail Wlk B31 ....18 D1
Pope Iron Rd WR1 ......115 A5
Popes La
Astwood Bank B96 ....89 E2
Birmingham B30, B31,
B38 ....19 D3
Poplar Ave
Birmingham, King's Heath
B14 ....20 F8
Worcester WR4 ....115 E5
Poplar Cl Catshill B61 .....48 F8
7 Evesham WR11 ....161 F2
Poplar Cres DY8 ....5 D3
Poplar Dr B45 ....50 D8
Poplar La B62 ....17 A4
Poplar Piece WR7 ......120 F6
Poplar Rd
Kidderminster DY11 ....27 C4
Redditch B97 ....70 A3
Stourbridge DY8 ....5 E3
Wichenford WR6 ....99 E5
Poplar Row DY11 ....27 C4
Poplar Trees B47 ....36 A6
Poplars La
Astwood Bank B96 ....89 A1
Feckenham B96 ....107 F8
Poplars The
Badsey WR11 ....162 D3
Bidford-on-Avon B50 .....136 D5
Poplars Trad Est B80 ....90 D6
Poplarwoods B32 ....9 B2
Popular Ave WR10 ......145 A4
Porlock Cres B31 ....18 D3
Porlock Rd DY8 ....6 A6
Port St WR11 ....161 E4
Portefields Rd WR4 .....115 F4
Porter Rd WR11 ....161 F3
Porters Mill La WR9 ....102 E6
Portersfield Ind Est B64 ....7 D8
Portersfield Rd B64 ....7 C8
Portland Cres DY9 ....6 B1
Portland Dr DY9 ....6 B1
Portland Rd
1 Droitwich WR9 ....85 B1
Great Malvern WR14 .....138 F1
Portland St WR5 ....115 B1
Portland Wlk WR2 ......115 B1
Portman Rd B13 ....20 F7
Portrush Ave B38 ....19 D1
Portsdown Rd B63 ....7 D2
Portsmouth Cl 3 WR5 ...115 F2
Portway Pl DY10 ....13 A5
Post Office La
Bransford WR6 ....126 D6
Fernhill Heath WR3 ......103 A3
Kempsey WR5 ....141 D7
8 Tewkesbury GL20 ......196 E6
Post Office Wlk B96 ......89 E1
Poston Croft B14 ....20 D3
Potters Cl WR4 ....115 F6
Pouk La WR6 ....77 F6
Pound Bank Rd WR14 ..139 C1
Pound Cl GL20 ....183 F6
Pound La
Birmingham B32 ....17 F3
Mickleton GL55 ....165 D3
Rock DY14 ....41 C7
Pound Rd B14 ....20 E2
Poverty B96 ....89 E2
Powderham Ave WR4 ...116 C6
Powell Ave B32 ....9 A6
Powell St 7 B63 ....8 B3
Powell's Row WR2 ......115 A1
Power Sta Rd DY13 ......44 B2
Powick Bridge★ WR2 ...127 E5
Powick CE Prim Sch
WR2 ....127 D3
Powlers Cl DY9 ....6 E2
Powyke Ct Cl WR2 .....127 D3
Pratts La
Mappleborough Green
B80 ....91 A8
Redditch B80 ....90 F7
Preece Cl WR14 ....138 F6
Premier Bsns Ctr 3 DY9 ....6 F5
Premier Ct B30 ....20 C3
Prescot Rd DY9 ....6 C3
Prescott Dr WR4 ....116 A8
Prestbury Cl
Redditch B98 ....72 A3
6 Worcester WR4 ....115 F7
Presthope Rd B29 ....19 B7
Preston Cl B98 ....71 B6
Prestwich Ave WR5 .....115 F1
Prestwood Dr Kinver DY7 ....4 F8
Stourbridge DY7 ....5 B7
Prestwood Rd
Birmingham B29 ....19 B8
Stourton DY7 ....4 E6
Price Rd DY9 ....7 A6
Price St WR3 ....115 B6
Price's La WR8 ....169 C5
Pridzor Rd WR9 ....85 A4
Priest La 6 WR10 ....144 D1
Priest Mdw Cl B96 ....89 D1
Priestfield Rd B97 ....89 E5
Priestley Cl B63 ....7 B6
Primrose Cl
Blackheath B64 ....7 B8
Great Malvern WR14 .....153 C7
Lickey End B60 ....49 C6
Primrose Cres WR5 .....128 D5
Primrose Croft B28 ......21 F5
Primrose Dr 10 WR5 .....128 D5
Primrose Gdns B38 ......34 F8
Primrose Hill B38 ....35 A8
Primrose Hill Prim Sch
B38 ....34 F8
Primrose La B28 ....21 F5
Primrose Twr B38 ....34 E8
Primrose Woods B32 ......9 B2
Primsland Dr 3 WR9 .....85 B1
Primsland Pl 3 WR9 ....104 A8
Primsland Way WR9 ....103 E8
Prince Andrew Cres
B45 ....17 E2
Prince Charles Cl B45 ...17 E2
Prince Edward Dr B45 ...17 E2
Prince Edward's Cl
WR11 ....161 E7
Prince Henry's High Sch
WR11 ....161 E6
Prince of Wales La B14 ..21 C3
Prince Philip Cl B45 .....17 E2
Prince Rd B30 ....20 A3
Prince Rupert Ave
WR2 ....127 B2
Prince Rupert Rd
3 Stourport-on-Severn
DY13 ....43 E2
16 Worcester WR5 ....115 C2
Prince St B64 ....7 D8
Princes Ave 2 WR9 .....103 F8
Princes Rd DY8 ....5 D3
Princess Anne Dr B45 ...17 E2
Princess Cres B63 ....7 E6
Princess Margaret Ave 6
WR14 ....139 B5
Princess of Wales Com Hospl
The B61 ....49 A4
Princess Rd WR11 ......161 E6
Princess Way DY13 ......43 E1
Prior Ave B60 ....67 C3
Prior Cl DY10 ....28 C5
Priors Grange WR11 ....135 E4
Priors Oak B97 ....70 B4
Priors Wlk WR11 ....161 E3
Priory Cl DY8 ....6 B3
Priory Ct Stourbridge DY8 ...6 B3
Studley B80 ....90 E5
Priory Gdns 1 WR9 ......84 F3
Priory House B63 ....7 F5
Priory La WR9 ....84 F3
Priory Rd
Birmingham, Stirchley
B14 ....20 C7
Birmingham, Warstock
B28 ....21 D3
Dodford B61 ....48 A6
Great Malvern WR14 .....152 F7
Halesowen B62 ....8 F4
Stourbridge DY8 ....6 B3
Worcester WR2 ....127 F8
Priory Sq B80 ....90 E5
Priory The 1 DY13 ....44 A5
Pritchard Ct DY12 ....26 C3
Pritchett Rd B31 ....34 B7
Private Way B45 ....33 C4
Proctors Barn La B98 ....71 B4
Prophets Cl B97 ....70 D3
Prospect Gdns DY8 ....6 A4
Prospect Hill
Kidderminster DY10 ....27 E6
Redditch B97 ....70 E4
Stourbridge DY8 ....6 A4
Prospect La DY10 ....27 E6
Prospect Pl 9 WR5 ......115 C1
Prospect Rd
Halesowen B62 ....8 C5
Stourport-on-Severn
DY13 ....44 B4
Prospect Rd N B98 ....71 A4
Prospect Rd S B98 ....71 A4
Prospect Row DY8 ....6 A3
Prospero Cl B45 ....18 A2
Proud Cross Ringway
DY11 ....27 C6
Providence Ct B64 ....7 C8
Providence Dr DY9 ....6 E6
Providence Ind Est DY9 ....6 E6
Providence Rd B61 ......48 F3
Providence St
Stourbridge DY9 ....6 F6
5 Worcester WR1 ....115 C2
Pry Cl The WR15 ....59 A8
Pry La WR12 ....190 A8
Puckrup La GL20 ....183 C6
Pudford La Martley WR6 ...98 F7
Shelsley Beauchamp WR6 ...79 E1
Pulley La WR9 ....103 E7
Pullman Cl 4 DY13 ....44 A4
Pump St
Great Malvern WR14 .....138 E3
Kidderminster DY10 ....27 E4
Worcester WR1 ....115 C2
Pumphouse La
Bentley Pauncefoot B97 ....88 B8
Blackwell B45, B60 ....49 F7
Hanbury B60 ....86 E3
Redditch B97 ....69 D1
Purbeck Cl B63 ....7 D1
Purbeck Croft B32 ....9 F4
Purefoy Rd B13 ....21 C5
Purleigh Ave WR4 ......116 C5
Purlieu The WR14 ....152 D5
Purshall Cl B97 ....70 C3
Purshull Gn La
Elmbridge WR9 ....47 A2
Upton Warren B61 ....66 B8
Purslow Gr B31 ....19 A1
Putney La B62 ....17 B1
Puxton Dr DY11 ....12 D1
Puxton La DY11 ....27 C7
Pyke Rd GL20 ....197 B7

Q

Quail Pk Dr DY10 ....28 A2
Quantock Cl
Birmingham B45 ....18 B2
Halesowen B63 ....7 D2
Quantock Dr DY10 ....28 A6
Quantock Rd DY8 ....6 B6
Quantry La DY9 ....31 F8
Quarrington Gr B14 ......21 A3
Quarry Bank DY11 ....45 A2
Quarry Hill B63 ....7 F2
Quarry House Cl B45 ....17 F1
Quarry La
Birmingham B31 ....19 A2
Bromsgrove B61 ....67 D8
Cleeve Prior WR11 ....149 B7
Halesowen B63 ....8 A2
Quarry Pk Rd DY8 ....15 A8
Quarry Rd B29 ....19 A8
Quarry The DY10 ....27 F8
Quarry Wlk B45 ....33 A7
Quay La
Earl's Croome WR8 ....155 F1
Great Comberton WR10 ...158 E2
Hanley Castle WR8 ....169 A8
Quay St
1 Tewkesbury GL20 ......196 E6
Worcester WR1 ....115 B2
Quebec Cl WR2 ....127 E6
Queen Elizabeth Dr
WR10 ....144 D1
Queen Elizabeth Rd
Birmingham B45 ....17 E2
Kidderminster DY10 ....28 B5
Queen Margaret Prim Sch
GL20 ....196 E4
Queen St
Astwood Bank B96 ....89 E1
Brierley Hill, Quarry Bank
DY5 ....7 A8
Droitwich WR9 ....85 A3
Halesowen B63 ....8 A4
Kidderminster DY10 ....27 E7
Redditch B98 ....70 E4
Stourbridge, Wollaston DY8 ...5 F6
Worcester WR1 ....115 C3
Queen St Pas DY5 ....7 A8
Queen's Cl WR14 ....138 E4
Queen's Cotts B97 ....70 B4
Queen's Cres DY8 ....6 A7
Queen's Dr WR14 ....138 E1
Queen's Pk Rd B32 ....9 F6
Queen's Rd
Evesham WR11 ....161 D5
Great Malvern WR14 .....138 E3
Stourbridge DY8 ....5 F6
Stourport-on-Severn DY13 ..43 F1
Queen's Way DY12 ....26 C4
Queens Ave B14 ....20 E8
Queens Dr B30 ....20 A4
Queens Dr The B62 ....8 C5
Queens Hill DY9 ....30 D7
Queens Mead WR8 ......169 C4
Queens Rd GL20 ....196 F4
Queensmead GL20 ......185 A6
Queensway
2 Bidford-on-Avon B50 ...136 C5
Halesowen B63 ....8 B3
Oldbury B68 ....9 B8
Stourbridge DY9 ....6 E2
Wichenford WR6 ....100 B6
Queenswood Dr 4
WR5 ....128 D5
Quest Hills Rd WR14 ....138 F4
Quibery Cl B98 ....71 F3
Quincy Rise DY5 ....6 C7
Quinneys Ct B50 ....136 E4
Quinneys La
Bidford-on-Avon B50 .....136 E4
Redditch B98 ....90 B6
Quinton Church Prim Sch
B32 ....9 A6
Quinton Cl B98 ....71 D1
Quinton Expressway B32 ..9 B4
Quinton La B32 ....9 D6
Quinton Rd W B32 ....9 D4
Quisters 13 WR4 ....116 B5

R

Race Field 3 WR4 ......116 B5
Racecourse La DY8 ....5 F1
Racecourse Rd WR10 ...144 E4
Racks La WR9 ....83 B5
Radbourne Dr B63 ....7 A7
Radcliffe Dr B62 ....8 E6
Raddens Rd B62 ....8 F3
Raddlebarn Farm Dr
B29 ....19 F8
Raddlebarn Rd B29 ......19 F8
Radford Ave DY10 ....27 E7
Radford Cl DY10 ....27 E7
Radford House 2 B97 ....70 A4
Radford Rd
Alvechurch B48 ....51 D7
Birmingham B29 ....19 A6
Flyford Flavell WR7 ......119 D2
Rous Lench WR11 ....120 D1
Radley Rd DY9 ....6 F4
Radnor Cl B45 ....18 B2
Radnor Croft 3 WR3 ....115 E7
Radnor House B31 ....18 D6
Radnor Rd B68 ....9 B7
Radway Cl B98 ....71 B6
Raglan Ct B60 ....49 A1
Raglan St WR3 ....115 B6
Ragley Cres B60 ....68 A8
Ragley Hall★ B49 ....122 E4
Ragley House 8 B97 ......70 A4
Ragley Rd WR11 ....148 A7
Raglis Cl B97 ....70 A1
Rail Gd 6 WR10 ....144 C1
Railway Cl B80 ....90 D4
Rainbow Hill WR3 ......115 D4
Rainford Way B38 ....34 C8
Rainthorpe Ave 3 WR5 ..128 E6
Raleigh Cl WR2 ....114 D2
Ralphs Mdw B32 ....9 D2
Ramble Cl WR7 ....120 F6
Ramillies Dr WR5 ....128 F4
Ramsden Cl B29 ....19 B7
Ramsey Cl B45 ....17 F1
Ramsons Cl WR14 ......139 C3
Randall Ave B48 ....51 A6
Randle Rd DY9 ....6 C4
Randwick Cl 14 WR4 .....115 F6
Randwick Dr WR4 ....115 F7
Ranelagh Rd WR14 .....139 C5
Rangeways Rd DY11 .....27 A8
Rangeworthy Cl B97 ......89 C7
Rannoch Ave 10 WR5 ....128 E6
Rannoch Cl
Brierley Hill DY5 ....6 B8
Stourport-on-Severn
DY13 ....43 E7
Ransom Ave WR5 ....128 D7
Ran-Tan The B97 ....89 E5
Rathmore Cl DY8 ....5 E2
Rathvilly Sch B31 ....19 B3
Raven Dr WR5 ....128 D5
Raven Hays Rd B31 .....18 C2
Raven Scroft Dr 1 WR9 ...85 B2
Raven St DY13 ....43 F3
Ravenhayes La B32 ......18 A6
Ravens Bank Dr B98 .....71 E7
Ravens Bank Fst Sch
B98 ....71 D6
Ravenscroft DY8 ....5 C6
Ravenshill Cl 2 WR5 ....128 E5
Ravenshill Rd B14 ....21 D4
Ravenshill Wood Nature
Reserve★ WR6 ....124 D8
Ravensmere Rd B98 ......71 B1
Raybon Croft B45 ....33 A6
Rea Ave B45 ....32 E8
Rea Cl B31 ....34 A7
Rea Fordway B45 ....17 F1
Rea Valley Dr B31 ....19 B2
Rea Way WR2 ....114 D2
Reabrook Rd B31 ....33 F8
Reades Piece WR11 .....164 A4
Rear Cotts B48 ....50 F6
Reaside Cres B14 ....20 B5
Reaside Dr B45 ....18 B1
Reaside Mid Sch B45 ....17 E1
Rebecca Pl WR8 ....156 F7
Rebekah Gdns WR9 ....103 F7
Recreation Rd B61 ......48 F3
Rectory Cl
Broadheath WR2 ....114 A7
Harvington WR11 ....148 A6
Stourbridge DY8 ....6 B3
Rectory Ct B97 ....70 D1
Rectory Gdns
Hartlebury DY11 ....45 A3
Stourbridge DY8 ....6 B3
Worcester WR2 ....115 A2
Rectory La
Guarlford WR13 ....154 A7
Hartlebury DY11 ....45 A3
Harvington WR11 ....148 A6
Madresfield WR14 ....139 D3
Malvern WR13 ....153 F6
Rock DY14 ....41 B5

Rectory La *continued*
Shrawley WR6 .... 81 D7
1 Stourport-on-Severn DY13 .... 43 E2
Upton Warren B61 .... 66 F3
Rectory Rd
Birmingham B31 .... 19 B3
Redditch B97 .... 70 D1
Stourbridge DY8 .... 6 B3
Upton upon Severn WR8 .... 169 C4
Red Brick Cl B64 .... 7 D7
Red Ditch La GL19 .... 192 A2
Red Earl La WR14 .... 153 D8
Red Hill Bewdley DY12 .... 26 B2
Redditch B98 .... 70 F2
Stourbridge DY8 .... 6 B4
Red Hill CE Prim Sch WR5 .... 128 E8
Red Hill Cl B80 .... 90 E6
Red Hill Gr B38 .... 34 F7
Red Hill La WR5 .... 128 F7
Red Hill Pl B62 .... 17 A7
Red House Rd DY13 .... 62 D8
Red La Evesham WR11 .... 161 B5
Tewkesbury GL20 .... 196 E6
Red Leasowes Rd B63 .... 8 A3
Red Lion St
Alvechurch B48 .... 51 B6
Redditch B98 .... 70 E4
Red Sands Rd DY10 .... 27 E8
Redbrook Covert 7 B38 .... 34 E8
Redburn Dr B14 .... 20 D2
Redcar Cl B61 .... 32 B1
Redcliffe St WR3 .... 115 A7
Reddings The B47 .... 36 A5
Redditch Rd
Alvechurch, Arrowfield Top B48 .... 51 B8
Alvechurch, Rowney Green B48 .... 51 C3
Birmingham B31, B38 .... 34 C8
Hopwood B48 .... 34 B1
Stoke Heath B60 .... 67 D5
Studley B80 .... 90 D5
Redditch Ringway B97 .... 70 D4
Redditch Sta B97 .... 70 D4
Redfern Ave WR5 .... 115 F1
Redgate Ave WR15 .... 55 E4
Redgate Cl B38 .... 19 D2
Redhall Rd B32 .... 9 E7
Redhill Cl DY8 .... 6 B4
Redhill Ct DY8 .... 6 B4
Redhill La B45, B61 .... 32 C5
Redhill Rd B38 .... 34 D7
Redhill Sch DY8 .... 6 B4
Redlake Dr DY9 .... 15 B8
Redlake Rd DY9 .... 6 B1
Redland Cl B60 .... 32 C1
Redland Dr WR13 .... 152 A3
Redland Rd WR14 .... 139 A4
Redlands 4 WR10 .... 144 D1
Redmarley CE Prim Sch GL19 .... 192 A3
Redmead Cl B30 .... 19 C4
Rednal Hill Jun & Inf Schs B45 .... 33 C7
Rednal Hill La B45 .... 33 A6
Rednal Mill Dr B45 .... 33 C7
Rednal Rd B38 .... 19 E1
Redstart Ave DY10 .... 28 B2
Redstone Cl B98 .... 71 C6
Redstone La 4 DY13 .... 62 F8
Redwing Cl WR14 .... 138 D6
Redwing Ct DY10 .... 28 A1
Redwood Cl
Birmingham B30 .... 19 E4
Worcester WR4 .... 115 E6
Redwood Croft B14 .... 20 E7
Redwood Ct 10 GL20 .... 184 E1
Redwood Rd
Birmingham B30 .... 19 E4
Kinver DY7 .... 4 C3
Reedham Cl WR3 .... 115 A7
Reedmace Cl B38 .... 34 F8
Reeve Ct DY10 .... 28 A1
Reeves Rd B14 .... 20 C6
Regan House B13 .... 21 D7
Regency Dr B38 .... 19 F2
Regency Gdns B14 .... 21 C3
Regency Rd 3 WR14 .... 139 B5
Regent Cl B63 .... 8 A4
Regent Ct 4 B62 .... 9 A7
Regent Mews B60 .... 67 E8
Regent St B30 .... 20 A7
Regents Pk Rd B60 .... 49 C2
Regiment Cl WR5 .... 128 E4
Regina Cl
Birmingham B45 .... 17 E2
Worcester WR2 .... 127 F6
Renfrew Gdns DY11 .... 27 C5
Rennie Gr B32 .... 9 D5
Renshaw Ind Est B80 .... 90 D4
Reservoir La 5 WR3 .... 115 D4
Reservoir Rd
Birmingham, Rednall B45 .... 33 C3
Kidderminster DY11 .... 27 C3
Resolution Way 3 DY13 .... 44 B2
Retreat St B96 .... 89 E1
Retreat The B64 .... 7 E7
Reyde Cl B97 .... 70 A2
Reynard Cl B97 .... 69 F3
Reynolds Cl WR13 .... 167 C5
Reynolds Ct 8 B68 .... 9 B8
Rhayader Rd B31 .... 18 E5
Rhuddlan Way DY10 .... 27 E1
Rhydd Cl WR14 .... 153 C7
Ribbesford Cl B63 .... 7 D6
Ribbesford Dr DY13 .... 43 E4
Ribbesford Rd DY13 .... 43 C2
Ribble Cl WR5 .... 115 E2
Ribblesdale Rd B30 .... 20 A8
Ribston Cl 2 WR2 .... 114 E5
Richard Pl 2 GL20 .... 196 F3
Richard's Cl WR14 .... 138 E5
Richards Cl B31 .... 33 F6
Richardson Cl WR9 .... 85 E8
Richardson Dr DY8 .... 5 E8
Richmond Ct
4 Birmingham B29 .... 19 C7
Halesowen B63 .... 7 E3
Stourbridge DY9 .... 6 B1
Richmond Gdns DY8 .... 5 F7
Richmond Gr DY8 .... 5 E8
Richmond Pl B14 .... 20 F8
Richmond Rd
Bewdley DY12 .... 25 F4
Birmingham, Eachway B45 .... 32 E7
Great Malvern WR14 .... 139 B4
Hollywood B47 .... 36 C7
5 Walton Cardiff GL20 .... 197 A3
Worcester WR5 .... 115 D2
Richmond St B63 .... 8 A4
Richmonds Pitch 1 WR14 .... 166 E7
Rickets Cl DY13 .... 44 B7
Rickett's La 12 WR9 .... 84 F3
Ricketts Pl DY12 .... 26 B3
Rickyard Cl B29 .... 19 A6
Rickyard La B98 .... 71 D5
Rickyard Piece B32 .... 9 E4
Riddings Cl DY12 .... 26 C5
Riddings The DY9 .... 6 D2
Ridgacre La B32 .... 9 C6
Ridgacre Rd B32 .... 9 C6
Ridgacre Rd W B32 .... 9 A6
Ridge Cl B13 .... 21 C6
Ridge Gr DY9 .... 6 C5
Ridge Prim Sch The DY8 .... 5 C5
Ridge St DY8 .... 5 C6
Ridgefield Rd B62 .... 8 C7
Ridgemount Dr B38 .... 34 D8
Ridgewater Cl B45 .... 33 B6
Ridgeway WR13 .... 166 B4
Ridgeway Ave B62 .... 9 A6
Ridgeway Cl B80 .... 90 E2
Ridgeway Mid Sch The B96 .... 108 E8
Ridgeway The
Cookhill B96 .... 109 A6
Droitwich WR9 .... 85 B3
Stourport-on-Severn DY13 .... 43 F5
Worcester WR5 .... 128 E7
Ridgeway Trad Est B96 .... 89 E1
Ridgewood Ave DY8 .... 5 C7
Ridgewood High Sch DY8 .... 5 C5
Ridgmont Croft B32 .... 9 E5
Ridings La B98 .... 71 B6
Ridleys Cross DY13 .... 62 E6
Ridsdale Cl WR11 .... 135 E4
Rifle Range Rd DY11 .... 27 B3
Rigby Hall B60 .... 68 C8
Rigby Hall Sch B60 .... 68 C8
Rigby La B60 .... 68 C8
Rightons Ct 5 WR11 .... 161 D5
Riley Rd B14 .... 21 D3
Rilstone Rd B32 .... 9 F5
Ringway The DY10 .... 27 F5
Ringwood Dr B45 .... 18 A1
Ripley Gdns WR4 .... 116 D6
Ripon Rd
Birmingham B14 .... 21 C4
Worcester WR5 .... 116 A3
Ripple Rd
Birmingham B30 .... 20 B7
Droitwich WR9 .... 84 E2
Rise Ave B45 .... 33 A7
Rise La WR15 .... 56 B6
Rise The B48 .... 34 B4
Rissington Ave B29 .... 20 A8
River Brook Dr B30 .... 20 B8
River Sch The WR3 .... 102 D2
Riversdale Rd B14 .... 21 D3
Riverside Studley B80 .... 90 F5
1 Tenbury Wells WR15 .... 55 E5
Riverside Cl
Lickey End B60 .... 49 C6
3 Upton upon Severn WR8 .... 169 C6
Riverside Cres B28 .... 21 D4
Riverside Ct B38 .... 19 D3
Riverside N DY12 .... 26 B4
Riverside Rd 3 WR9 .... 85 A3
Riverside Way WR9 .... 85 B3
Riversleigh Dr DY8 .... 5 E8
Riverview Cl WR2 .... 114 F6
Riverway Dr DY12 .... 26 B4
Rivington Cl DY8 .... 5 E4
Rnib New Coll WR5 .... 129 A7
Roach Cl 1 WR5 .... 128 C5
Road No 1 DY10 .... 27 E2
Road No 2 DY10 .... 27 E2
Road No 3 DY10 .... 27 E2
Roberts La
South Littleton WR11 .... 148 F1
Stourbridge DY9 .... 15 B8
Robeson Cl WR9 .... 85 B3
Robin Cl
Northway GL20 .... 184 D1
Worcester WR5 .... 128 D5
Robin Ct DY10 .... 28 A2
Robin Hood Cres B28 .... 21 E7
Robin Hood Croft B28 .... 21 F6
Robin Hood La
Birmingham B28 .... 21 F6
Birmingham B28 .... 21 E7
Robina Cl 2 WR11 .... 175 D8
Robin's Cl DY8 .... 6 A3
Robins Hill Dr B48 .... 51 A5
Robinsfield Dr B31 .... 34 A7
Rochester Cl B97 .... 89 C8
Rochester Rd B31 .... 19 A4
Rochester Wlk DY10 .... 28 C5
Rochford Cl
Birmingham B45 .... 32 E7
Halesowen B63 .... 7 F2
Rock Ave B45 .... 33 C7
Rock Cotts 6 DY11 .... 27 D6
Rock Hill
Bromsgrove B61 .... 67 D7
Inkberrow WR7 .... 120 F6
Rock La WR6 .... 78 C4
Rock St GL19 .... 195 D2
Rockford Cl B98 .... 89 F5
Rockhill La B96 .... 107 F8
Rockingham Hall Gdns DY9 .... 15 D7
Rockingham La WR4 .... 116 D6
Rockley Bank 3 DY14 .... 22 D5
Rockley Gr B45 .... 33 B7
Rockwell La B48 .... 51 E4
Rocky La B61 .... 48 E7
Rocky Wall DY7 .... 3 E4
Rodborough Cl WR4 .... 116 A7
Rodborough Dr WR4 .... 116 A7
Roden Ave DY10 .... 28 A7
Rodway Cl DY5 .... 6 D7
Rogers Hill WR3 .... 115 C4
Rolan Dr B90 .... 36 E8
Roman Ct B38 .... 35 B8
Roman Rd (Sandy La) DY8 .... 5 C3
Roman Way
Bromsgrove B61 .... 49 B4
Droitwich Spa WR9 .... 84 F4
Great Malvern WR14 .... 139 C5
Salwarpe WR9 .... 84 C1
Roman Way Bsns Pk WR9 .... 84 E5
Roman Way Fst Sch B98 .... 71 E3
Romany Rd B45 .... 17 D1
Romany Way DY8 .... 5 C3
Romilly Cl DY8 .... 5 E6
Romney Cl B28 .... 21 F7
Romsley Cl
Birmingham B45 .... 32 E8
Halesowen B63 .... 8 B2
Redditch B98 .... 71 F3
Romsley Hill Grange B62 .... 16 F1
Romsley La
Romsley WV15 .... 2 A2
Upper Arley DY12 .... 11 B8
Romsley Rd
Birmingham B32 .... 18 B8
Stourbridge DY9 .... 6 C5
Romsley View WV15 .... 1 C6
Rona Gdns WR5 .... 128 F6
Ronhill Cres DY14 .... 22 C5
Ronhill La DY14 .... 22 C5
Ronkswood Cres WR5 .... 115 E3
Ronkswood Hill WR4 .... 115 E3
Ronkswood Jun Sch WR5 .... 115 F3
Rookery Cl B97 .... 70 D1
Rookery Rd WR5 .... 141 C7
Rookery The B62 .... 9 A2
Rooks Mdw DY9 .... 15 B6
Rope Wlk GL20 .... 196 F6
Rosafield Ave B62 .... 8 F6
Rose Ave Alvechurch B48 .... 51 A5
Droitwich WR9 .... 85 A3
Oldbury B68 .... 9 C7
Worcester WR5 .... 115 D1
Rose Bank
1 Evesham WR11 .... 161 F4
Worcester WR5 .... 115 D1
Rose Cotts B30 .... 20 A6
Rose Dene 12 DY13 .... 43 E4
Rose Hill
Barnt Green B45 .... 33 B4
Worcester WR5 .... 115 D1
Rose Hill Sch WR4 .... 115 F6
Rose La B61 .... 48 A6
Rose Terr
Barnt Green B45 .... 50 D8
Worcester WR5 .... 115 D1
Rosebay Ave B38 .... 34 F8
Roseberry Gdns DY10 .... 13 C3
Rosebriars B90 .... 36 E7
Rosedale WR6 .... 60 E4
Rosedale Cl B97 .... 70 A4
Rosefield Cres GL20 .... 197 A6
Rosehall Cl B98 .... 89 E6
Roseleigh Rd B45 .... 33 B6
Rosemary Ave WR2 .... 114 D1
Rosemary Cl WR11 .... 161 B2
Rosemary Dr B60 .... 67 C1
Rosemary La DY8 .... 5 D3
Rosemary Rd
Halesowen B63 .... 7 E2
Kidderminster DY10 .... 28 B7
Rosemoor Dr DY5 .... 6 B7
Rosemoor Gdns 5 WR5 .... 128 E6
Rosemount B32 .... 9 E5
Rosenhurst Dr 6 DY12 .... 26 A3
Rosetti Cl DY10 .... 28 C6
Rosewood Cl WR3 .... 102 F2
Rosewood Dr B45 .... 50 C7
Roslin Cl B60 .... 49 B1
Rossees La WR6 .... 99 D7
Rossendale Cl
Fernhill Heath WR3 .... 102 F3
Halesowen B63 .... 7 D6
Rothesay Croft B32 .... 18 B7
Rothley Wlk B38 .... 34 C8
Rothwell Rd WR14 .... 152 F1
Rough Hill Dr B98 .... 89 F6
Rough Mdw 9 WR4 .... 116 B5
Rough The B97 .... 89 D8
Round Hill Ave DY9 .... 6 C1
Round Hill Wharf DY11 .... 27 D5
Round Saw Croft B45 .... 32 F8
Roundabout The B31 .... 18 D1
Roundhills Rd B62 .... 8 F8
Roundlea Rd B31 .... 18 E7
Rousay Cl B45 .... 17 F1
Rowan Ave WR4 .... 115 E4
Rowan Cl
Bromsgrove B61 .... 48 E2
Droitwich WR9 .... 103 F8
1 Evesham WR11 .... 161 F2
Hollywood B47 .... 36 B5
Rowan Cres B97 .... 70 A4
Rowan Ct B30 .... 20 A2
Rowan Rd B97 .... 70 A4
Rowan Way B31 .... 33 F8
Rowanberry Cl 4 DY13 .... 43 E4
Rowans The WR11 .... 148 A8
Rowantrees B45 .... 33 B5
Rowborough Cl B96 .... 89 E2
Rowbrook Cl B90 .... 36 E8
Rowcroft Covert B14 .... 20 C2
Rowheath House B30 .... 19 E5
Rowheath Rd B30 .... 19 F4
Rowland Ave B80 .... 90 E3
Rowland Hill Ave DY11 .... 27 B5
Rowland Hill Ctr 9 DY10 .... 27 E6
Rowland Way (Road 1a) DY11 .... 27 E1
Rowley Hill St WR2 .... 114 F2
Rowley Hill View B64 .... 7 F8
Rowney Croft B28 .... 21 E4
Rowney Gn La B48 .... 51 F5
Rowntree Gdns WR4 .... 116 C2
Roxall Cl DY10 .... 14 C2
Roxboro House B97 .... 70 D2
Royal Albert Cl 6 WR5 .... 115 C1
Royal Cl DY5 .... 6 C8
Royal Gram Sch WR1 .... 115 B4
Royal Oak Rd B62 .... 8 F5
Royal Orthopaedic Hospl The B31 .... 19 B5
Royal Sq 6 B97 .... 70 E3
Royal Worcester Cres B60 .... 49 C1
Rozel Ave DY10 .... 13 B1
Rubery Farm Gr B45 .... 32 F7
Rubery Field Cl B45 .... 18 B1
Rubery La B45 .... 18 A1
Rubery La S B45 .... 32 F8
Ruckley Rd B29 .... 19 B8
Rudge Rd 3 WR11 .... 161 D5
Rufford Prim Sch DY9 .... 6 C5
Rufford Rd DY9 .... 6 C4
Rufford St DY9 .... 6 D5
Rugby Rd DY8 .... 5 D7
Rumbow B63 .... 8 B4
Rumbow La B62 .... 16 D3
Rumbush La B90, B94 .... 36 F3
Runcorn Cl B98 .... 89 F8
Rush Gn B32 .... 9 E2
Rush La B98 .... 71 B6
Rushall Cl DY8 .... 5 E8
Rushbrook Gr B14 .... 20 C4
Rushbrook La B94 .... 53 D3
Rusher's Cl WR10 .... 144 C1
Rushleigh Rd B90 .... 36 E8
Rushmead Gr B45 .... 33 A7
Rushock Cl B98 .... 90 C7
Rushock Trad Est WR9 .... 46 A2
Rushwick Prim Sch WR2 .... 127 C8
Rushy Piece B32 .... 9 D3
Ruskin Ave DY10 .... 28 C6
Ruskin Ct 5 B68 .... 9 B8
Russel Croft B60 .... 68 A7
Russell Cl
Bowling Green WR2 .... 127 C2
Great Malvern WR14 .... 139 B3
Russell Dr
Eckington WR10 .... 171 E8
Great Malvern WR14 .... 139 B3
Russell Rd DY10 .... 27 F4
Russell St WR10 .... 158 F1
Russet Cl
4 Bredon GL20 .... 184 F6
1 Worcester WR2 .... 114 E5
Russet Way B31 .... 18 E6
Russett Way 1 DY12 .... 25 F4
Ruth Chamberlain Ct 3 DY11 .... 27 D6
Ruthall Cl B29 .... 19 C7
Rutherford Rd B60 .... 68 B7
Rutland Ct 2 B29 .... 19 C7
Rutland Dr B60 .... 68 A8
Rutland Pl
9 St. Peter the Great County WR5 .... 128 E6
Stourbridge DY8 .... 5 D8
Rutley Gr B32 .... 9 F4
Rutters Mdw B32 .... 9 B4
Ryall Gr WR8 .... 169 F6
Ryall La WR8 .... 169 E5
Ryall Mdw WR8 .... 169 E5
Rydal Cl
Stourport-on-Severn DY13 .... 43 F6
5 Worcester WR4 .... 115 F5
Rydal Way B28 .... 21 F7
Ryde Pk Rd B45 .... 33 C7
Ryden La WR10 .... 160 E8
Rye Cl WR9 .... 85 A2
Rye Croft Hollywood B47 .... 36 A5
Stourbridge DY9 .... 6 E2
Rye Hill La WR7 .... 117 E2
Ryebank Cl B30 .... 19 C5
Ryefield Cl DY9 .... 15 A4
Ryefields Rd B60 .... 67 C3
Ryegrass La B97 .... 89 C6
Ryeland Cl 5 WR3 .... 115 E7
Ryeland La
Elmley Lovett WR9 .... 45 F2
Hartlebury WR9 .... 64 F8
Ryelands WR10 .... 145 A4
Ryemarket DY8 .... 6 A5
Ryland Cl B63 .... 7 E2
Rynal Pl WR11 .... 161 E5
Rynal St WR11 .... 161 D5
Ryton Cl B98 .... 71 D1
Ryvere Cl 2 DY13 .... 43 F2

S

Sabrina Ave WR3 .... 115 A6
Sabrina Dr DY12 .... 26 A4
Sabrina Terr 13 WR1 .... 115 A5
Sabrina Wlk WR3 .... 115 A7
Saddlers Cl B63 .... 7 B5
Saffron House 3 B38 .... 34 E8
Saffron Rd 7 GL20 .... 196 E6
Sage Croft B31 .... 18 F5
Sagebury Dr B60 .... 67 C1
St Agatha's Cl
7 Pershore WR10 .... 144 D1
3 Pershore WR10 .... 158 D8
St Agathas Rd
8 Pershore WR10 .... 144 D1
2 Pershore WR10 .... 158 D8
St Agnes Cl B80 .... 90 C4
St Alban's Ave DY11 .... 27 A7
St Alban's RC Prim Sch B14 .... 20 F4
St Albans Cl WR5 .... 115 F3
St Albans House B32 .... 9 F5
St Ambrose Cl B62, B65 .... 8 C8
St Ambrose RC Prim Sch DY10 .... 27 F6
St Andrew Rd WR11 .... 161 A3
St Andrew's Cl 8 WR9 .... 84 F3
St Andrew's Dr WR9 .... 84 F2
St Andrew's Fst Sch B45 .... 50 D8
St Andrew's Rd
Great Malvern WR14 .... 153 A6
Pershore WR10 .... 158 C7
St Andrew's St WR9 .... 84 F3
St Andrews CE Fst Sch WR11 .... 161 B2
St Andrews Cl DY8 .... 5 F2
St Andrews Gn DY10 .... 27 E4
St Andrews Rd 9 WR9 .... 84 F3
St Andrews Way B61 .... 67 D8
St Ann's Rd WR14 .... 138 E1
St Anne's CE Mid Sch DY12 .... 25 F2
St Anne's Cl WR3 .... 102 B1
St Anne's Rd
Blackheath B64 .... 7 C8
Worcester WR3 .... 102 B1
St Anns Sch WR5 .... 129 F8
St Asaphs Ave B80 .... 90 D4
St Audrie's Rd WR5 .... 128 C8
St Augustine Dr WR9 .... 85 A4
St Augustine's Cl WR9 .... 85 A4
St Augustine's RC High Sch B97 .... 89 D5
St Barnabas CE Fst & Mid Sch WR10 .... 143 F6
St Barnabas CE Fst Sch DY11 .... 12 B1
St Barnabas CE Prim Sch WR3 .... 115 D5
St Bartholomew's Rd 5 DY13 .... 43 E2
St Bede's RC Mid Sch B98 .... 70 F3
St Bernard Dr WR14 .... 153 A5
St Brigid's RC Prim Sch B31 .... 18 F3
St Catherine's Hill WR5 .... 115 D1
St Catherine's Rd B60 .... 50 A5
St Catherine's Vale 2 WR5 .... 115 E1
St Catherines Cl B60 .... 50 A5
St Catherines Rd 2 WR11 .... 161 D1
St Cecilia Cl DY10 .... 27 E2
St Chad's Rd B45 .... 32 F7
St Chads Rd B80 .... 90 C4
St Clement's CE Prim Sch WR2 .... 114 F2
St Clement's Cl 3 WR2 .... 115 A2
St Clement's Ct 1 WR2 .... 115 A2
St Clement's Gdns WR2 .... 115 A2
St Columba's RC Prim Sch B45 .... 33 D7
St Columbas Dr B45 .... 33 D7
St David's Cl 1 DY13 .... 43 E6
St Davids Dr
Birmingham B32 .... 9 B5

St Davids Dr *continued*
Evesham WR11 ....161 D1
St Davids Rd GL20 ....197 F7
St Denis Rd B29 ....19 B7
St Dunstan's Cl WR5 ....128 C8
St Dunstan's Cres
13 Worcester WR5 ....115 C1
Worcester WR5 ....128 C8
St Dunstan's La WR15 ....57 A4
St Dunstan's RC Prim Sch
B14 ....20 F8
St Egwin's Cl WR11 ....147 D3
St Egwin's Rd 6 WR11 ....161 D5
St Egwine Cl WR3 ....115 C5
St Egwins CE Mid Sch
WR11 ....161 D6
St Francis CE Prim Sch
B30 ....19 D6
St Gabriel With St Mary CE Prim Sch WR8 ....154 A1
St George's CE Fst Sch
Kidderminster DY10 ....27 F7
Redditch B98 ....70 F3
St George's CE Prim Sch
WR1 ....115 B5
St George's Cres 4 WR9 .85 A3
St George's Ct B30 ....19 E7
St George's Gdns 3 B98 .70 F4
St George's La N WR1 ..115 B5
St George's La S WR1 ..115 B5
St George's Pl DY10 ....27 E7
St George's Rd DY8 ....5 D2
St George's Sq WR1 ....115 B5
St George's Terr DY10 ....27 F6
St George's Wlk WR1 ....115 B5
St Georges Cath Sch
WR1 ....115 A5
St Georges Cl 5 WR11 ..161 E1
St Georges Ct 10 DY10 ....27 E6
St Georges Rd B98 ....70 F4
St Giles Row DY8 ....6 A6
St Giles's Rd GL20 ....184 E6
St Godwald's Cres B60 ....68 B8
St Godwald's Rd B60 ....68 C7
St Heliers Rd B31 ....18 F4
St Hubert's RC Prim Sch
B68 ....9 C8
St James CE Prim Sch
DY8 ....5 D7
St James Cl
Badsey WR11 ....162 E3
Harvington WR11 ....148 B6
Norton Juxta Kempsey
WR5 ....129 C1
St James Ct B60 ....49 A3
St James Dr 3 WR11 ....161 D1
St James Prim Sch
WR14 ....138 C1
St James' RC Jun & Inf Sch
B45 ....33 A7
St James's & the Abbey
WR14 ....138 C1
St James's Dr WR14 ....138 F2
St John Fisher RC Fst Sch
B98 ....71 D6
St John Fisher RC Prim Sch
B31 ....34 B7
St John St B61 ....48 F2
St John's WR2 ....115 A1
St John's Ave DY11 ....27 B6
St John's CE Foundation Mid Sch B61 ....48 F1
St John's CE Fst Sch
Kidderminster DY11 ....27 B6
Stourport-on-Severn
DY13 ....44 A6
St John's CE Mid Sch
DY11 ....27 B6
St John's Cl
6 Kidderminster DY11 ....27 C6
Worcester WR3 ....102 B1
St John's La DY12 ....25 A2
St John's Rd
Halesowen B63 ....7 E4
Stourbridge DY8 ....6 A5
Stourport-on-Severn
DY13 ....44 A5
St John's St 5 DY11 ....27 C6
St Johns Cl 3 WR11 ....161 E1
St Johns Ct B31 ....19 B1
St Johns Wood B45 ....33 B5
St Joseph's Cl WR9 ....84 D2
St Joseph's RC Prim Sch
WR9 ....84 D2
St Josephs Ave B31 ....19 B5
St Josephs Prim Sch
WR14 ....138 E3
St Josephs RC Prim Sch
Birmingham B30 ....19 F5
Worcester WR4 ....116 B7
St Judes Ave B80 ....90 D4
St Judes Cl B14 ....20 F2
St Judes Ct B14 ....20 F7
St Judes RC Jun & Inf Sch
B14 ....20 F2
St Kenelm's CE Sch
B62 ....17 A4
St Kenelm's Rd B62 ....16 E5
St Kenelms Ave B63 ....7 E1
St Kitts Cl 5 WR14 ....138 F5
St Laurence CE Inf Sch
B31 ....19 B4
St Laurence CE Jun Sch
B31 ....19 B4
St Laurence Cl B48 ....51 B6
St Laurence Rd B31 ....19 B5
St Laurence Way 3
B50 ....136 D5
St Lawrence Cl 4 WR2 ..127 F7
St Lawrence Rd 3
WR11 ....161 C4
St Loye's Cl B62 ....8 D8
St Luke's CE Fst Sch
B97 ....70 D1
St Luke's Cotts B97 ....70 D1
St Lukes Bsns Ctr B64 ....7 E8
St Lukes Cl 7 WR11 ....161 D1
St Margarets Dr B63 ....7 F2
St Margarets Rd 4
WR11 ....161 D1
St Mark's Cl WR5 ....128 C7
St Mark's Rd DY9 ....6 D5
St Marks Cl 6 WR11 ....161 D1
St Martins Ave B80 ....90 D4
St Mary's CE Prim Sch
DY10 ....27 E8
St Mary's Cl
Kempsey WR5 ....141 B7
4 Tenbury Wells WR15 ....55 E5
St Mary's Convent Sch Mount Battenhall WR5 ....128 E8
St Mary's La
Stourbridge DY8 ....6 B3
9 Tewkesbury GL20 ....196 E6
St Mary's Pl 1 DY14 ....22 C4
St Mary's Prep Sch
WR15 ....56 D4
St Mary's RC Prim Sch
B80 ....90 E4
St Mary's Rd
Droitwich WR9 ....84 F2
Evesham WR11 ....161 D5
Tewkesbury GL20 ....196 D6
St Marys CE Prim Sch
GL20 ....181 F5
St Marys RC Prim Sch
Broadway WR12 ....190 D8
Evesham WR11 ....161 E5
St Marys Ringway DY10 ..27 E6
St Matthews Cl
2 Evesham WR11 ....161 E1
Salford Priors WR11 ....135 D4
St Michael's CE Jun & Inf Sch
B32 ....18 C8
St Michael's Cl
2 South Littleton WR11 ...148 F1
6 Stourport-on-Severn
DY13 ....44 A4
St Michael's Coll WR15 ..74 C8
St Michael's Rd WR3 ....115 B8
St Michaels Cl 3 WR11 .175 D8
St Milburgh Cl WR11 ....148 A1
St Moritz Cl WR3 ....114 F8
St Nicholas CE Mid Sch
WR10 ....144 E6
St Nicholas La WR4 ....116 D6
St Nicholas Rd WR10 ....131 B2
St Nicholas St
Droitwich WR9 ....84 E3
Worcester WR1 ....115 B3
St Nicolas Gdns B38 ....19 F2
St Oswald's Rd WR1 ....115 B4
St Oswalds CE Fst Sch
DY10 ....13 A1
St Oswalds Cl DY10 ....27 F8
St Patrick's Ct DY11 ....27 B1
St Patricks Cl
Birmingham B14 ....20 E5
9 Evesham WR11 ....161 D1
St Paul's Ave DY11 ....27 A6
St Paul's RC Prim Sch
B38 ....20 A1
St Paul's St WR1 ....115 C2
St Pauls Cl WR11 ....175 E8
St Peter's Church La
WR9 ....85 A2
St Peter's Cl
Evesham WR11 ....161 E3
Hinton on the Green
WR11 ....175 A5
Redditch B97 ....89 E5
St Peter's Cres WR9 ....85 A3
St Peter's Dr
Martley WR6 ....99 A4
St. Peter the Great County
WR5 ....128 E5
St Peter's La WR8 ....157 C6
St Peter's RC Fst Sch
B61 ....67 E8
St Peter's Rd
Droitwich WR9 ....84 F2
Great Malvern WR14 ....138 E3
Stourbridge DY9 ....6 C1
St Peter's Wlk WR9 ....85 A3
St Peters CE Fst Sch
WR9 ....85 A2
St Peters Cl
Birmingham B28 ....21 D6
Bromsgrove B61 ....48 E1
Malvern Wells WR14 ....166 F7
St Peters RC Prim Sch
B32 ....9 C1
St Peters St 5 WR5 ....115 C1
St Philips Dr
8 Evesham WR11 ....161 D1
Evesham WR11 ....175 D8
St Richard's Gdns 9
WR9 ....84 E3
St Richards Cl WR9 ....85 E8
St Richards Rd
Dodderhill WR9 ....85 E8
Evesham WR11 ....161 D1
St Saviour's Ct DY9 ....15 A6
St Stephen's House
B97 ....70 E4
St Stephen's CE Fst Sch
B98 ....70 F5
St Stephen's St 5 WR3 .115 B6
St Stephen's Terr 1
WR3 ....115 B6
St Stephens Gdns B98 ....70 F5
St Stephens Rd B29 ....20 B8
St Swithin's St 1 WR1 ..115 C2
St Swithuns Cl WR5 ....128 D8
St Thomas Aquinas RC Sch
B38 ....19 D3
St Thomas More RC Fst Sch
B98 ....90 B7
St Wulstan's Cres 1
WR5 ....115 D1
St Wulstans Cl 6 WR11 .161 E1
St Wulstans Dr WR14 ....167 A7
St Wulstans RC Prim Sch
DY13 ....43 D4
Salamanca Dr WR5 ....128 F4
Salcombe Dr DY5 ....6 C7
Salford Cl B98 ....90 B6
Salford Priors CE Sch
WR11 ....135 E4
Salisbury Cl WR5 ....115 F2
Salisbury Dr
6 Evesham WR11 ....161 C2
Kidderminster DY11 ....26 F6
Sallis Cl GL20 ....184 D2
Sally Cl WR11 ....176 D7
Salop Rd B97 ....70 D3
Salt Way Cookhill B96 ....108 D5
Feckenham B96 ....107 A8
Hadzor WR9 ....85 F2
Saltbox La WR15 ....55 F2
Saltbrook Rd B63 ....7 A7
Saltbrook Trad Est B63 ....7 A7
Salter's La B97 ....70 B5
Salters Cl WR4 ....115 F6
Salters La Besford WR8 ..143 E1
Defford WR8 ....157 D6
Fladbury WR10 ....145 E2
Saltway WR9 ....84 F3
Saltwood WR4 ....116 C6
Salwarpe Ct* WR9 ....84 B1
Salwarpe Gr B29 ....9 F2
Salwarpe Rd
Bromsgrove B60 ....67 F8
Droitwich WR9 ....84 E3
Sam Spencer Ct DY10 ....29 A2
Sambourne La
Astwood Bank B96 ....89 F1
Coughton B96 ....109 E6
Sambourne B96 ....90 A1
Sambourne Pk B96 ....109 A8
Sambourne Pk La B96 ....90 A1
Samuels Rd B32 ....9 A5
Sanctuary Cl WR2 ....114 E2
Sandalls Cl B31 ....18 D1
Sandals Rise B62 ....8 D3
Sandbourne Dr DY12 ....26 C3
Sanderling Ct DY10 ....28 A1
Sanders Cl B97 ....70 B4
Sanders Ind Est B61 ....48 E1
Sanders Rd
Bromsgrove B61 ....48 E1
Salford Priors WR11 ....135 F3
Sanderson Ct DY11 ....27 C5
Sandfield La WR11 ....174 E2
Sandfield The GL20 ....184 E1
Sandgate Rd B28 ....21 F4
Sandhills Gn B48 ....50 E7
Sandhills La B45 ....50 D7
Sandhills Rd B45 ....50 D8
Sandhurst Ave DY9 ....6 D2
Sandhurst Cl B98 ....71 C6
Sandhurst House B38 ....20 B1
Sandicliffe Cl DY11 ....27 C8
Sandles Cl WR9 ....103 F7
Sandles Rd WR9 ....103 F7
Sandmartin Way DY10 ....28 A2
Sandmere Gr B14 ....21 D3
Sandmere Rd B14 ....21 D3
Sandon Cl B98 ....71 A3
Sandon Rd DY9 ....6 F4
Sandown Ct 18 B29 ....19 C7
Sandown Dr B61 ....32 B1
Sandown Rd 5 WR11 ....161 C2
Sandown Twr 3 B31 ....19 A1
Sandpiper Cl
Kidderminster DY10 ....28 B2
Stourbridge DY9 ....6 F5
6 Worcester WR5 ....128 E6
Sandpiper Cres WR14 ....138 D6
Sandpiper Gdns B38 ....34 F7
Sandpits Cl WR6 ....99 A3
Sandpits The B30 ....19 E8
Sandringham Cl
Evesham WR11 ....161 D6
Great Malvern WR14 ....139 C6
Sandringham Rd B62 ....8 B7
Sandringham Way DY5 ....6 C8
Sands Cl 3 WR12 ....177 D1
Sands Croft Ave
WR12 ....177 E1
Sands La WR11 ....162 E2
Sands Rd B96 ....107 F1
Sands The
4 Broadway WR12 ....177 D1
Broadway WR12 ....190 D8
Sandstone Ave B45 ....33 A8
Sandstone Rd 5 DY12 ....26 C3
Sandway Gr B13 ....21 C7
Sandy Bank DY12 ....26 A3
Sandy Croft B13 ....21 C7
Sandy La
Blakedown DY10 ....29 C7
Kidderminster Foreign
DY11 ....12 A1
Kinver DY7 ....3 F1
Stourport-on-Severn
DY13 ....44 B1
Wildmoor B61, B62 ....31 E5
Sandy La Ind Est DY13 ....44 B1
Sandy Rd DY8 ....5 D1
Sandyacre Way DY8 ....6 B5
Sandy's Rd WR14 ....139 C3
Sandygate Cl B97 ....69 F2
Sandys Ave WR11 ....176 D7
Sandys Cl 2 WR10 ....146 A1
Sandys Rd WR9 ....83 A5
Sandys' Rd WR1 ....115 A5
Sansome Pl WR1 ....115 C3
Sansome Rd B90 ....21 F2
Sansome Rise B90 ....21 F2
Sansome Wlk WR1 ....115 B3
Sant Rd B31 ....34 B7
Santa Maria Way DY13 ....44 B3
Santridge Ct B61 ....49 A4
Santridge La B61 ....49 A4
Sapphire Cres WR2 ....114 E3
Sarah Seager Cl 5 DY13 .43 E6
Sarehole Mill Mus*
B13 ....21 D8
Sarehole Rd B28 ....21 E8
Sargent Turner Trad Est
DY9 ....6 F6
Saunders St WR3 ....115 A7
Saunderton House B31 ....18 E5
Savernake Cl B45 ....18 A2
Saville Cl B45 ....33 B7
Saxelby Cl B14 ....20 E2
Saxelby House B14 ....20 E2
Saxilby Pl 1 DY13 ....44 B4
Saxon Bsns Pk B60 ....67 E2
Saxon Cl
Clifton upon Teme WR6 ....97 F7
Studley B80 ....90 E5
Saxon Wood Cl 2 B31 ....19 A4
Saxonbury WR11 ....161 E2
Saxonfields 2 B50 ....136 D4
Saxons Way B14 ....21 A2
Sayers Ave WR14 ....138 E4
Scafell Cl WR4 ....116 A5
Scafell Rd DY8 ....6 B6
Scaife Rd B60 ....68 B7
Scarfield Hill B48 ....50 E5
School Ave WR11 ....135 E4
School Bank WR9 ....83 B4
School Dr
Bromsgrove B60 ....49 A3
Stourbridge DY8 ....5 F8
Wythall B47 ....36 A3
School La
Alvechurch B48 ....51 B5
Badsey WR11 ....162 E3
Bretforton WR11 ....163 C4
Crowle WR7 ....117 E5
Eckington WR10 ....171 E7
Hagley DY9 ....15 D6
Halesowen B63 ....7 F2
Lickey End B60 ....49 B6
North & Middle Littleton
WR11 ....149 A3
Overbury GL20 ....185 F7
South Littleton WR11 ....148 F2
Upton Snodsbury WR7 ....131 C8
Upton upon Severn WR8 ...169 C5
Upton Warren B61 ....66 F3
Wick WR10 ....159 A7
School Rd
Aston Somerville WR12 ....175 E1
Birmingham B28 ....21 F8
Birmingham, Eachway
B45 ....32 E6
Birmingham, Yardley Wood
B14 ....21 C4
Dodderhill WR9 ....85 E8
Elmley Lovett WR9 ....65 B6
Evesham WR11 ....161 B4
Hanbury B60 ....87 A5
Pebworth CV37 ....150 E2
Salford Priors WR11 ....135 E3
Worcester WR2 ....114 F1
School St
Honeybourne WR11 ....164 A4
Stourbridge DY8 ....5 F6
Schoolhouse Cl B38 ....20 B2
Scobell Cl 3 WR10 ....144 C1
Scotland La B32 ....18 C7
Scotland Pl 3 WR15 ....55 E5
Scots Cnr B14 ....20 E8
Scots La DY13 ....62 F5
Scott Rd B97 ....89 C8
Scott's Rd DY8 ....5 F6
Scribers La B28 ....21 E4
Sculthorpe Rd DY10 ....14 B2
Seabright Way WV15 ....1 C5
Seafield La Beoley B98 ....53 A2
Portway B48 ....52 E4
Seaford La
Naunton Beauchamp
WR10 ....132 A4
Peopleton WR10 ....131 F3
Seals Gn B38 ....34 D7
Sebright Ave
3 Worcester WR5 ....115 E1
Worcester WR5 ....128 D8
Sebright Cl WR10 ....144 C1
Sebright Gn DY11 ....12 C3
Sebright Rd DY11 ....12 C3
Securehold Bsns Ctr
B98 ....71 B2
Sedge Ave B38 ....19 F3
Sedge Cl WR2 ....114 D2
Sedge Dr B61 ....49 A6
Sedgeberrow CE Fst Sch
WR11 ....175 A1
Sedgeberrow Covert 4
B38 ....34 E8
Sedgeberrow Rd B63 ....8 A2
Sedgebourne Way B31 ....18 C1
Sedgefield Wlk B61 ....32 B1
Sedgeford Cl DY5 ....6 D8
Sedgley Cl B98 ....70 F4
Seedgreen Cl 3 DY13 ....62 E8
Seedgreen La DY13 ....63 A5
Seedhouse Ct B64 ....8 B8
Segbourne Rd B45 ....32 F8
Selba Dr DY11 ....26 F6
Selborne Gr B13 ....21 C5
Selborne Rd 7 WR1 ....115 A5
Selborne Rd W WR1 ....115 A5
Selby Gr B13 ....21 C6
Selcombe Way B38 ....34 F7
Selcroft Ave B32 ....9 F5
Selly Hall Croft B30 ....20 A6
Selly Manor Mus* B30 ....19 F7
Selly Oak Colls B29 ....19 D8
Selly Oak Rd B30 ....19 E5
Selly Oak Specl Sch
B29 ....19 E8
Sellywood Rd B29,
B30 ....19 E8
Selma Gr B14 ....21 D5
Selsdon Cl
Kidderminster DY11 ....27 B5
Wythall B47 ....36 C5
Selsey Cl WR4 ....116 A7
Senneleys Pk Rd B31 ....9 E1
Sensall Rd DY9 ....6 F3
Serin Cl DY10 ....28 A1
Serpentine The DY11 ....27 C4
Servite Ct B14 ....21 A2
Seven Acres WR4 ....116 A4
Seven Acres La B98 ....71 C5
Seven Acres Rd
Birmingham B31 ....19 C1
Halesowen B62 ....9 A5
Sevenhills Dr DY13 ....62 D8
Severn Cl B61 ....49 A8
Severn Ct 10 WR9 ....84 F3
Severn Dr
Ashchurch GL20 ....184 C1
Great Malvern WR14 ....153 D8
Upton upon Severn WR8 ...169 C6
Severn Gr DY11 ....27 B3
Severn House 4 B68 ....9 B8
Severn Hts WR6 ....82 B3
Severn Rd Halesowen B63 ..7 B5
Stourbridge DY8 ....5 F3
Severn Side DY13 ....44 A2
Severn Side N DY12 ....26 B4
Severn Side S DY12 ....26 B3
Severn St WR1 ....115 B1
Severn Terr WR1 ....115 B3
Severn Way
Bewdley DY12 ....25 F3
Wythall B47 ....35 E2
Severndale WR9 ....84 D1
Severnside Bsns Pk
DY13 ....44 A2
Seward Rd WR11 ....162 D3
Seymour Ave WR3 ....115 A8
Seymour Dr B98 ....71 A5
Seymour Pl GL20 ....196 E5
Seymour Rd
Kidderminster DY11 ....27 B8
Stourbridge DY9 ....7 A4
Shadymoor Dr DY5 ....6 C8
Shaftesbury Ave DY9 ....6 C2
Shaftesbury Cl B60 ....49 B2
Shaftesbury Gn 8 WR4 .116 C3
Shaftland Cross WR9 ....118 B7
Shaftsbury Ave B63 ....7 B7
Shakells Cl B97 ....89 E4
Shakespeare Ave B98 ....71 A2
Shakespeare Ct 4
GL20 ....196 E6
Shakespeare Dr DY10 ....28 B6
Shakespeare House
B31 ....34 A8
Shakespeare La WR11 ..148 B6
Shakespeare Rd
6 Worcester WR2 ....114 D2
1 Worcester WR2 ....114 D2
Shalnecote Gr B14 ....20 C5
Sham La WV15 ....1 F3
Shambles The WR1 ....115 C2
Shandon Cl B32 ....9 F3
Shannon Rd B38 ....34 E7
Shannon Way
Ashchurch GL20 ....197 C8
Evesham WR11 ....162 A3
Tewkesbury GL20 ....197 C8
Shap Dr WR4 ....116 B6
Shapinsay Dr B45 ....17 F1
Sharman Rd WR1 ....115 A5
Sharpe Rd WR2 ....128 A7
Sharps Cl B45 ....33 A7
Sharpway Gate B60 ....86 E8
Sharry La CV37 ....151 E2
Shatterford Wildlife Sanctuary* DY12 ....11 D6
Shaw Ave DY10 ....28 B6
Shaw Hedge Rd DY12 ....26 C4
Shaw La Dodderhill B60 ....86 B8
Stoke Prior B60 ....67 C3
Shaw La Ind Est B60 ....67 C2
Shaw St WR1 ....115 B3
Shawbank Rd B98 ....71 B3

Shawbrook Gr 10 B14 21 A3
Shawbury Cl B98 71 E3
Shawfield B47 36 A5
Shawhurst Croft B47 36 A7
Shawhurst Gdns B47 36 B7
Shawhurst La B47 36 A6
Shaws Cl B97 69 F2
Shearwater Cl
Birmingham B45 32 F6
Kidderminster DY10 28 B1
Sheenhill Rd
Honeybourne WR11 164 A7
South Littleton WR11 163 F8
Sheepcote Grange B61 48 F5
Sheepcroft Cl B97 69 F2
Sheepmoor Cl B17 9 F8
Sheepscombe Dr
WR4 116 A6
Sheepwalks La DY7 3 A6
Sheepwash La
Kinver DY7 3 C3
Wolverley & Cookley DY11 12 C8
Sheerwater Dr DY5 6 D7
Sheffield Cl 4 WR5 115 F1
Shelah Rd B63 8 A6
Sheldon Cl 1 WR10 144 C1
Sheldon Dr B31 18 D2
Sheldon Pk Rd WR3 102 A2
Sheldon Rd B98 90 A8
Shelduck Cl DY10 28 B3
Shelfield Rd B14 20 C3
Shell Cnr Trad Est B62 8 D8
Shelley Ave DY10 27 E7
Shelley Cl Catshill B61 49 A8
Redditch B97 89 C8
Stourbridge DY8 6 A8
Worcester WR3 115 C7
Shelley House B63 7 B5
Shelly Twr B31 19 C3
Shelsley Dr WR13 152 D3
Shelton La B63 7 E5
Sheltwood Cl B97 70 A2
Sheltwood La B60, B97 69 A3
Shenley Ct Sch B29 18 F7
Shenley Fields Dr B31 18 F8
Shenley Fields Rd B29 19 B8
Shenley Gdns B29 19 A7
Shenley Gn B29 18 F6
Shenley Hill B31 18 F6
Shenley La B29 18 F7
Shenstone Ave
Halesowen B62 8 E5
Stourbridge DY8 5 D3
Shenstone Cl B60 49 B3
Shenstone Ct
Bromsgrove B60 49 B3
Solihull B90 21 D2
Shenstone Flats B62 8 F5
Shenstone Rd B14 21 A1
Shenstone Trad Est B63 8 C4
Shenstone Valley Rd
B62 8 F6
Shephard Mead GL20 196 D5
Shepherds Brook Rd
DY9 6 D5
Shepherds Cl 5 WR9 84 D5
Shepherds Hill 4 WR9 84 D5
Shepherds Pool 1
WR11 161 D5
Shepherds Way WR9 84 D5
Shepherds Wlk B60 67 E7
Shepley Mdw B45 50 B8
Shepley Rd
Barnt Green B45 50 A7
Birmingham B45 33 B6
Sheraton Dr DY10 28 B6
Sheraton Grange DY8 5 F2
Sheraton Rd B60 49 C1
Sherbourne Cl B98 71 D2
Sherbourne Rd
Blackheath B64 8 B8
Stourbridge DY8 6 B4
Sheridan Row 1 WR4 116 C3
Sheringham Rd
Birmingham B30 20 B3
Worcester WR5 128 D6
Sherrard's Gn Rd
WR14 139 C1
Sherratts The WR9 65 B6
Sherridge Rd WR6 125 E5
Sherriff St WR4 115 D3
Sherston Covert 11 B30 20 C2
Sherwood Cl B28 21 F5
Sherwood House B64 7 F8
Sherwood La WR2 127 F7
Sherwood Mews B28 21 E6
Sherwood Rd
Birmingham B28 21 E7
Bromsgrove B60 68 A6
Stourbridge DY8 5 E7
Sherwood Wlk B45 18 B2
Shetland Cl 2 WR3 115 E7
Shifnal Wlk B31 33 F8
Shilton Gr B29 18 F8
Shinehill La WR11 149 B1
Ship Wrights Cl 6 WR4 115 F6
Shipbourne Cl B32 9 F5
Shipley Gr B29 19 A8
Shipston Cl WR4 115 F8
Shipston Rd B31 19 B1
Shire Bsns Pk WR4 116 B8
Shire Way WR9 85 B1
Shirehampton Cl B97 69 F2
Shireland La B97 70 A4
Shirley Cl 4 WR14 139 B1
Shirley Jones Cl WR9 84 C3
Shirley Rd
Birmingham, King's Norton B30 20 A5
Droitwich WR9 84 E1
Shirley Sta B90 21 F1
Shop La WR11 163 C5
Shor St 6 WR11 161 E4
Short St Halesowen B63 7 F5
Stourbridge DY8 5 F5
Shorters Ave B14 21 B4
Shortlands Cl B30 20 A2
Shortyard The DY11 12 E4
Shoulton La WR2 101 C2
Showell Cl WR9 103 E7
Showell Gn WR9 103 E7
Showell Gr WR9 103 E7
Showell Rd WR9 103 E7
Shrawley Ave DY11 27 B3
Shrawley Cl
Birmingham B45 32 F7
Halesowen B63 8 A2
Shrawley Rd
Birmingham B31 19 C2
Fernhill Heath WR3 102 E3
Shrewsbury Rd DY11 27 A6
Shrewton Ave B14 20 D2
Shrub Hill WR1 115 D3
Shrub Hill Rd WR1 115 D3
Shrubbery DY10 13 B5
Shrubbery Ave WR1 115 B5
Shrubbery Ct DY10 27 F7
Shrubbery Rd
Bromsgrove B61 48 E1
Drakes Broughton WR10 143 F6
Worcester WR1 115 B5
Shrubbery St DY10 27 F7
Shrublands Ave B68 9 B7
Shut Mill La B62 16 D2
Shuttlefast La WR13 153 A1
Sibdon Gr B31 34 A8
Sidbury WR5 115 C1
Sidemoor Fst Sch B61 48 E3
Sidings La WR10 160 D8
Sidings Rd WR8 142 E2
Sidings The DY9 15 A6
Sidlaw Cl B63 7 D2
Silk Printing Ctr The*
GL20 186 D5
Sillins Ave B98 71 A3
Sillins La B97 88 E6
Silver Birch Dr
Hollywood B47 36 B6
Kidderminster DY10 28 C5
Kinver DY7 3 F5
Silver Birches Bsns Pk 3
B60 67 F6
Silver Innage B63 7 C7
Silver St Birmingham B14 20 E8
9 Colwall Stone WR13 152 B2
Hollywood B47 35 E5
Kidderminster DY10 27 E7
Redditch B97, B98 70 E4
Worcester WR1 115 C3
Silverdale B61 48 F4
Silverdale Ave WR5 115 F1
Silverfield Cl B14 20 E8
Silvermead Ct B47 35 F5
Silverstone Ave DY11 12 D1
Silverthorne La B64 7 B8
Silvester Way DY5 6 B8
Silvington Cl B29 19 C7
Simcox Gdns B32 9 D2
Simeon's Wlk DY5 6 F7
Simmons Dr B32 9 D4
Simmons Leasow B32 9 E2
Simms La B47 36 A5
Simon De Montfort Dr 1
WR11 161 E7
Simon de Montfort Mid Sch
WR11 161 E2
Simon Evans Cl DY14 22 D4
Simon Rd B47 36 A7
Simon's Way 3 WR11 161 E3
Sinderberry Dr GL20 184 E1
Sinton La WR9 83 B3
Sinton Terr WR2 114 F1
Sion Ave DY10 13 A1
Sion Gdns 1 DY13 44 A3
Sion Hill DY10 12 F1
Sion Hill Mid Sch DY10 13 A2
Sir George's Mall 6
DY10 27 E6
Sir Hilton's Rd B31 34 C7
Sir Richards Dr B17 9 F7
Sir Theodore Pritchett Inf & Jun Sch B14 20 D2
Sir Walter's Mall 8 DY10 27 E6
Sisefield Rd B38 20 A1
Siskin Rd DY9 6 C3
Siskin Way DY10 28 B1
Site 7 Trading Est WR9 65 B8
Siviter St B63 8 B4
Six Acres B32 9 C4
Six Acres Croft 3 WR4 116 B4
Six Ashes DY14 22 E7
Sixteen Acres La B50 149 E8
Skenfrith Pl 9 WR4 116 C6
Skiddaw Cl WR4 116 B5
Skilts Ave B98 70 F1
Skilts Sch B98 72 C4
Skinner Rd WR2 114 F1
Skinner St WR2 114 F1
Skipton Cres 2 WR4 116 C7
Skomer Cl B45 17 E1
Skylark Way DY10 28 A2
Skyrrold Rd WR14 153 C8
Slad The DY13 44 D6
Sladd La DY11 12 A5
Slade Ave WR4 116 B5
Slade La Birmingham B28 21 E3
Shrawley WR6 62 D2
Slade Rd B63 7 C6
Sladen CE Mid Sch The
DY10 27 F7
Sladepool Farm Rd
B14 21 A2
Slideslow Ave B60 49 B2
Slideslow Dr B60 49 B3
Slimbridge Cl
Redditch B97 89 E5
5 Worcester WR5 128 E5
Slims Gate B63 8 A4
Sling La
Great Malvern WR14 139 A1
Hindlip WR3 103 B2
Sling The DY10 27 E6
Slingfield Mills DY10 27 D6
Slingfield Rd B31 19 C1
Slingpool Wlk WR2 115 A1
Slough The B97, B80 90 B4
Small La B94 53 E6
Smallbrook Rd WR12 177 D2
Smallshire Way DY8 5 E8
Smallwood Almshouses
B98 70 E3
Smallwood Arch 5 B98 70 E4
Smallwood St B98 70 E3
Smedley Crooke Pl
B48 34 C2
Smirrells Rd B28 21 E5
Smite La WR3 103 E2
Smith's La 2 GL20 196 E6
Smithfields 3 DY8 6 A5
Smiths Ave WR2 114 E1
Smiths Cl B32 9 B1
Smiths Ct 10 GL20 196 E6
Smiths Way WR10 158 C7
Smokey La WR10 160 B4
Snake La B48 51 A6
Snake Terr B48 51 A6
Snakes Lake La B61 48 D6
Sneechill WR7 130 B7
Snowberry Ave WR4 116 A4
Snowberry Cl 8 DY13 43 E4
Snowdon Cl DY11 12 C1
Snowdon Gr B63 7 D1
Snowdon Rd DY8 6 B6
Snowdonia Rd GL20 197 A4
Snowford Cl B90 21 F1
Snowshill Cl
Redditch B98 71 B6
2 Worcester WR4 116 B7
Snowshill Rd WR12 190 D6
Snuff Mill Wlk DY12 26 A2
Solcum La DY11 12 D6
Solent Pl WR11 161 F3
Solent Rd WR5 115 E3
Solitaire Ave WR2 114 D3
Somerdale Rd B31 19 C4
Somerford Rd B29 18 F8
Somerleyton Ave DY10 28 A5
Somerleyton Ct 3 DY10 28 A5
Somers Cl WR13 125 F2
Somers Pk Ave WR14 138 F4
Somers Pk Prim Sch
WR14 138 F4
Somers Rd
Great Malvern WR14 138 F3
Halesowen B62 8 C5
Somers' Rd WR1 115 A5
Somerset Dr
Birmingham B31 33 F7
Kidderminster DY11 12 C1
Stourbridge DY8 5 D7
Somerset Pl
Tewkesbury GL20 196 F3
Worcester WR1 115 B5
Somerville Rd WR4 115 E3
Sommerfield Rd B32 9 D3
Sonata Rd B60 49 C1
Sorrell Wlk DY5 6 B6
Soudan B97 70 D2
Souters House B32 18 D8
South Ave DY8 5 F4
South Bank Rd B64 7 E8
South Birmingham Coll (Hall Gn Campus) B28 21 E8
South Bromsgrove Com High Sch (Tech Coll) B60 67 F8
South Cres B60 49 A1
South Croft WR2 127 E8
South E Quadrant 8 B98 70 E4
South Gdns DY9 15 A4
South Lawn WR14 152 E5
South Moons Moat Ind Est
B98 71 D4
South Par WR1 115 B2
South Pk Dr WR9 84 D4
South Quay WR1 115 B2
South Rd
Birmingham, King's Heath B14 20 E8
Birmingham, Northfield B31 18 F2
Bromsgrove B60 68 B7
Hagley DY9 15 A4
Stourbridge DY8 5 E4
South St
3 Kidderminster DY10 27 F6
Redditch B98 70 E3
10 Worcester WR1 115 C2
South Wlk B31 19 C1
Southall Ave WR3 115 A8
Southall Dr DY11 45 A1
Southam Cl B28 21 E8
Southam Rd B28 21 E8
Southbank Rd B64 7 F8
Southcote Gr B38 19 D1
Southcott Ave DY5 6 D8
Southcrest Gdns B97 70 D1
Southcrest Rd B98 71 A2
Southdown Rd 6 WR3 115 E7
Southern House B13 21 A7
Southfield St WR1 115 C3
Southgate B64 7 D8
Southgate Cl DY11 27 A4
Southmead Cres B98 70 F3
Southmead Dr B60 49 B6
Southmead Gdns B80 90 E3
Southminster Dr B14 20 E6
Southview Ridge DY5 6 D7
Southville Bglws For Old People B14 21 B4
Southwick Rd B62 8 D8
Southwold Ave B30 20 C3
Southwold Cl 6 WR5 128 D6
Southwood Covert B14 20 C2
Sovereign Hts B31 18 C1
Sovereign Rd B30 20 A4
Spa Gdns GL20 197 B7
Spa Gr B30 20 C8
Spa Rd WR9 84 F2
Spadesbourne Rd B60 49 C6
Sparrey Dr B30 20 A8
Sparrowhall La WR2 127 B3
Sparrowhawk Cl
WR14 139 C4
Speedwell Gdns DY5 6 B6
Speedwell House B38 20 A1
Spencer Ave DY12 26 C4
Spencer Dr WR14 153 A7
Spencer St DY11 27 C4
Spennells Fst Sch
DY10 28 A2
Spennells Valley Rd
DY10 28 A3
Spenser Rd WR2 114 D3
Spenser Wlk B61 49 A8
Spernal Ash B80 90 F1
Spernal La B80 91 B1
Spetchley Cl B97 89 C6
Spetchley Pk & Gdns*
WR5 129 F8
Spetchley Rd WR5 116 B1
Spiceland Rd B31 18 F6
Spies Cl B62 8 F6
Spies La B62 8 F5
Spindle Cl DY11 12 D1
Spindle Rd 2 WR14 139 C3
Spinney Cl
Birmingham B31 19 B3
Kidderminster DY11 27 A7
Spinney Mews B97 70 C1
Spinney The
Worcester WR2 114 E5
Wythall B47 36 B4
Spion Kop WR10 144 E5
Spiral Cl B62 8 E8
Spiral Ct DY8 6 A4
Spire View B61 48 F3
Spirehouse La B60 49 E5
Splash Leisure Complex The
WR14 152 F8
Spoon Dr B38 19 D2
Spreadbury Cl B17 9 F8
Spring Bank
Defford WR8 157 D3
Worcester WR3 102 E1
Spring Cl
2 Colwall Stone WR13 152 B2
Hagley DY9 14 F4
Kinver DY7 3 F5
3 Tenbury Wells WR15 55 F6
Spring Cres B64 7 F7
Spring Gdns
Great Malvern WR14 139 B5
Tenbury Wells WR15 55 F5
Worcester WR1 115 C2
Spring Gr Cres DY11 27 B3
Spring Gr La WR15 55 E2
Spring Gr Rd DY11 27 B3
Spring Hill WR5 115 D2
Spring La
Great Malvern WR14 139 B4
Romsley B62 16 D4
Worcester WR5 115 D2
Spring La N WR14 139 C4
Spring La S WR14 139 C3
Spring Mdw
Halesowen B63 7 F2
1 Worcester WR4 116 B4
Spring St Halesowen B63 7 D6
Stourbridge DY9 6 E4
Spring Wlk B63 7 D1
Springbrook La B94 53 F7
Springfield GL20 197 B7
Springfield Ave
Bromsgrove B60 68 A8
Stourbridge DY9 6 E4
Springfield Cl 2 WR5 128 D6
Springfield Ct B28 21 F8
Springfield Dr
1 Evesham WR11 161 E1
Halesowen B62 8 D7
Springfield Glade 1
WR14 138 F5
Springfield House
DY10 27 F8
Springfield La
Broadway WR12 177 C1
Kidderminster DY10 27 F8
Springfield Rd
Birmingham, King's Heath B14 20 F8
Springfield Rd *continued*
Halesowen B62 8 D7
Worcester WR5 128 D6
Springhill Gdns B97 69 F2
Springhill Rise DY12 26 C4
Springs Ave B61 32 A1
Springside B98 90 C8
Springslade B32 9 F5
Springvale Rd B97 69 F2
Springwater Cl 8 GL20 184 E1
Spruces The DY9 14 F4
Square Cl B32 9 C3
Square The B48 51 B6
Squire's Cl WR5 141 C7
Squire's Wlk WR5 141 B6
Squires Ct DY5 6 C8
Squires The
Childswickham WR12 176 F2
Evesham WR11 161 C8
Norton & Lenchwick WR11 147 B1
Squirrel Dr WR5 128 F6
Squirrels Hollow B68 9 D7
Stable Way B60 67 E6
Stableford Cl
Birmingham B32 9 F3
Redditch B97 89 D7
Stacey Dr B13 21 A5
Stacey Grange Gdns
B45 33 A6
Stadium Cl DY10 27 F4
Stafford Ave WR4 116 D6
Stagborough Way DY13 43 E4
Stainburn Ave WR2 114 D1
Stainburn Cl WR2 114 D2
Staite Dr DY10 13 A5
Stakenbridge La DY10 14 D4
Stallard Rd WR2 114 E5
Stalls Farm Rd WR9 84 E3
Stambermill Cl DY9 6 D5
Stambermill House DY9 6 E5
Stamford Rd DY5 6 C6
Stamford St DY8 5 F7
Stanage Cl 10 WR4 116 B5
Stanbrook Abbey
WR2 140 E8
Stanbrook House Rd 4
WR2 140 F8
Stanbrook Rd WR15 55 F6
Stanbury Rd B14 21 B4
Standlake House B31 18 E5
Stanfield Rd B32 9 E6
Stanford Cl B97 89 B6
Stanford Gr B63 7 C1
Stanford Rd
Great Witley WR6 60 F1
Northway GL20 197 E8
Stanhoe Cl DY5 6 D8
Stanier Rd WR4 116 B7
Stanklyn La Stone DY10 28 C1
Summerfield DY10 45 A8
Stanks La WR8 168 F2
Stanley Ave B32 9 E7
Stanley Cl B98 71 A5
Stanley Rd
Birmingham, King's Heath B14 20 D7
Great Malvern WR14 139 B1
Oldbury B68 9 C7
Stourbridge DY8 5 F3
Worcester WR5 115 D2
Stanley Rd Prim Sch
WR5 115 D2
Stanley St WR5 128 C7
Stanmore Gr B62 9 A3
Stanmore Rd WR2 127 F7
Stanton Fields WR10 132 F3
Stanton Rd GL20 196 F7
Stanway Cl WR4 115 F7
Stanway Rd WR12 189 C1
Staple Flat B60 49 C8
Staple Hall Rd B31 19 B2
Staple Lodge Rd B31 19 C2
Stapleford Croft B14 20 C2
Staplehurst Rd B28 21 F8
Stapleton Cl
Redditch B98 71 D3
Studley B80 90 D3
Stapleton Rd B80 90 D4
Staplow Rd WR5 129 A8
Star La 7 WR2 114 F1
Star St DY9 6 F5
Starling Cl 2 WR5 128 C5
Station App
Barnt Green B45 50 D8
Kidderminster DY10 27 F5
Station Cl WR7 143 D8
Station Cotts B60 50 A4
Station Dr
Blakedown DY10 14 C2
Bredon GL20 184 F6
Earlswood B94 36 D1
Hagley DY9 15 A6
Station Gdns 5 WR10 171 E7
Station Hill 3 DY11 45 B2
Station La GL20 196 F7
Station Rd
Alvechurch B48 51 A5
Ashton under Hill WR11 187 C8
Beckford GL20 186 D4
3 Bewdley DY12 26 C3
Birmingham B13 20 D8
Birmingham, King's Norton B30 19 E4

Station Rd *continued*
Birmingham, Northfield B31 19 A2
Blackheath, Haden Cross B64 8 A8
Blackwell B60 50 A5
Bretforton WR11 163 B5
Broadway WR12 177 B1
Central Engineer Park CV37 151 E4
Cleobury Mortimer DY14 22 D5
Drakes Broughton & Wadborough WR8 142 E4
Eckington WR10 171 E7
Fernhill Heath WR3 103 A4
Fladbury WR10 146 A2
Hagley DY9 15 A6
Hartlebury DY11 45 B2
Harvington WR11 148 B7
Hinton on the Green WR11 174 F5
Honeybourne WR11 164 B5
Offenham WR11 162 C7
Pershore WR10 144 D2
Ripple GL20 183 A8
Rock DY12 24 A5
Salford Priors WR11 135 F3
South Littleton WR11 162 F8
Stourbridge DY9 6 E6
Studley B80 90 D4
Tewkesbury GL20 196 F6
Wythall B47 36 B3
Station St Blackheath B64 7 C8
Bromsgrove B60 48 F1
4 Droitwich WR9 84 E3
Tewkesbury GL20 196 F6
Station Way B97 70 D3
Staveley Rd B14 20 D6
Steamer Point WR14 139 B2
Steatite Way DY13 43 E5
Steel Rd B31 18 F2
Steelpark Rd B62 8 C7
Steene Gr B31 18 D3
Steeple Cl 3 DY14 22 C4
Steeples The DY8 6 B3
Steepwood Croft B30 19 D4
Stennels Ave B62 8 E4
Stennels Cres B62 8 E4
Stephenson Pl 2 DY12 26 C3
Stephenson Rd WR1 115 A4
Stephenson Terr WR1 115 A4
Stephenson Way WR11 164 A6
Steppes Piece B50 136 C5
Stepping Stones
Bidford-on-Avon B50 136 C5
Stourbridge DY8 6 B5
Sterrymere Gdns DY7 4 B4
Stevens Ave B32 9 D2
Stevens Rd DY9 6 D2
Stevenson Ave B98 70 F3
Steward Rd GL20 197 E8
Stewart Ct DY10 27 F5
Stewarts Rd B62 8 D7
Stewkins DY8 5 E8
Steynors Ave WR9 84 E2
Steynors Cl WR9 84 E2
Stilthouse Gr B45 33 A7
Stirchley Com Sch B30 20 A6
Stirchley Trad Est B30 20 B6
Stirling Ave WR4 116 C6
Stock Coppice Cl 1 WR4 116 B6
Stockhill Dr B45 32 F6
Stocking St DY9 6 F5
Stockmans Cl B38 34 E8
Stocks La Leigh WR13 126 B2
Newland WR13 139 C8
Stocks Rd WR6 124 E4
Stocks Wood B30 19 F8
Stockton Rd
Abberley WR6 60 B3
Stockton on Teme WR6 59 F3
Stockwell Ave DY5 6 D8
Stockwood La WR7 107 C1
Stoke Cross B60 68 E7
Stoke Gdns WR8 155 D4
Stoke La Dodderhill WR9 85 E7
Redditch B98 71 B7
Stoke Pound La
Stoke Pound B60 68 A4
Stoke Prior B60 67 F3
Stoke Prior Fst Sch B60 67 C3
Stoke Rd
Bromsgrove, Aston Fields B60 68 A7
Bromsgrove, Charford B60 67 F7
Stokes Rd GL20 183 A1
Stokesay Cl DY10 27 E2
Stokesay Gr B31 33 F8
Stokesay La 5 WR4 116 C6
Stone CE Fst Sch DY10 28 E2
Stone Cl Birmingham B38 19 F2
Colwall WR13 152 A2
Stone Cotts B31 19 A3
Stone Dr WR13 152 A2
Stone Hill DY10 28 E2
Stone La DY7 4 A4
Stone Yd B64 7 C8
Stonebow Rd
Drakes Broughton WR10 143 F6
Drakes Broughton & Wadborough WR10 144 A7
Stonebridge Cross Bsns Pk WR9 84 C6
Stonebrook Way B29 9 F2
Stonechat Cl DY10 28 B2
Stonecroft Ave B45 33 A7
Stonecrop Cl B38 34 F8
Stoneford La WR11 163 D2
Stonehenge Croft B14 20 D1
Stonehouse Cl B97 70 D1
Stonehouse Gr B32 9 D2
Stonehouse La
Birmingham B32 9 E2
Hopwood B48 34 E2
Stonehouse Rd B60 49 A1
Stoneleigh Cl
Redditch B98 89 F6
6 Worcester WR5 128 E5
Stoneleigh House B32 9 F5
Stonepit La WR7 120 F7
Stonepits La B97 89 D4
Stonerwood Ave B28 21 E8
Stoneton Gr B29 19 A8
Stoney Hill Cl B60 49 A1
Stoney La
Birmingham, Quinton B32 9 B6
Blackwell B60 50 C2
Churchill DY10 14 E3
Hartlebury DY13 64 A6
Himbleton WR9 105 E3
Kidderminster DY10 27 E8
Stoney La Ind Est DY10 27 E8
Stoneycroft Cl WR3 102 F2
Stoneyford Gr B14 21 B4
Stonnall Cl WR8 155 D5
Stony Furlong La WR10 171 F7
Storrage La B48 51 E3
Storrs Way The B32 18 B7
Stotfield Ave WR4 116 C4
Stotfold Rd B14 20 F2
Stour Cl B63 7 E6
Stour Hill DY5 7 A8
Stour House 2 B68 9 B8
Stour La 4 DY13 44 A3
Stour Vale Rd DY9 6 F6
Stour Valley Cl DY5 6 D7
Stourbridge Coll (Church St Ctr) DY8 6 A5
Stourbridge Coll (Westhill Ctr) DY8 6 B4
Stourbridge Coll
Stourbridge DY8 5 E5
Stourbridge, Old Swinford DY8 6 A4
Stourbridge Juntion Sta DY8 6 B3
Stourbridge Rd
Belbroughton DY9 31 B7
Blakedown DY9 14 F1
Catshill B61 48 F7
Churchill DY10 14 A6
Churchill & Blakedown DY10 13 D2
Fairfield B61 31 D2
Hagley DY9 15 C7
Halesowen B63 7 F5
Kidderminster DY10 27 F8
Lower Clent DY9 15 E3
Stourbridge DY9 6 D5
Stourbridge Town Sta DY8 6 A5
Stourbridge Trad Est DY8 6 A6
Stourdale Rd B64 7 C8
Stourdell Rd B63 7 E6
Stourminster Sch DY10 28 B4
Stourport Rd
Bewdley DY12 26 C3
Great Witley WR6 61 B1
Hartlebury DY13 63 D8
Kidderminster DY11 27 C2
Stourport-on-Severn Fst Sch DY13 44 A4
Stourport-on-Severn High Sch DY13 44 A5
Stourton Cres DY7 4 F7
Stourton Rd B32 9 B5
Stourvale Ind Est DY9 6 F6
Stourvale Trad Est B63 7 D6
Stouton Croft WR9 84 E4
Stow Dr DY5 6 B6
Stowe La WR13 166 A8
Strand La WR3 103 B4
Strand The
Bromsgrove B61 49 A3
Charlton WR10 160 D8
Stratford Rd
Bidford-on-Avon B50 137 A5
Birmingham B28 21 F7
Bromsgrove B60 49 A2
Harvington WR11 148 B6
Honeybourne WR11 164 B5
Mickleton CV37 165 D6
Strensham Bsns Pk WR8 171 A2
Strensham Gate WR8 171 A4
Stretton Dr B45 33 A2
Stretton House 7 B97 70 A4
Stretton Rd DY11 27 B4
Stroma Ave 13 WR5 128 E6
Stronsay Cl B45 17 F1
Stroud Rd B90 21 F2
Stuart Rd B62 8 F5
Stuart Rise WR5 128 F8
Stuarts Ct DY9 15 A5
Stuarts Gn DY9 15 B8
Stuarts Way B32 18 B7
Stud La WR6 60 C4
Studley Dr DY5 6 C8
Studley Gate DY8 5 D5
Studley High Sch B80 90 E3
Studley Inf Sch B80 90 E4
Studley Rd B98 71 A2
Studley St Mary's CE Jun Sch B80 90 E3
Suckley Prim Sch WR6 124 A4
Suckley Rd
Bransford WR6 126 B6
Leigh WR6 125 F5
Sudeley Ave 8 WR4 116 C6
Sudeley Cl WR14 138 F6
Sudgrove Cl 2 WR4 115 F7
Suffield Cl WR13 126 B4
Suffolk Dr
Brierley Hill DY5 6 C7
Worcester WR3 115 E7
Suffolk La WR6 60 F5
Suffolk Way 1 WR9 104 B8
Sugar Loaf La DY10 14 B7
Sugarbrook Ct 1 B60 67 F6
Sugarbrook La B60 68 A5
Sugarbrook Rd B60 68 A7
Summer Hill 6 B63 8 B3
Summer Hollow WR2 127 A8
Summer Pl DY11 27 C5
Summer Rd DY11 27 C3
Summer St Redditch B98 70 E3
Stourbridge, Lye DY9 6 E5
Stourbridge, Wollaston DY8 5 F5
2 Worcester WR3 115 B6
Summercroft 7 DY13 62 E8
Summerfield Dr 2 B29 19 A7
Summerfield Gdns WR11 161 B2
Summerfield La DY11 44 F7
Summerfield Rd
Clent DY9 15 E2
Great Malvern WR14 139 B5
2 Stourport-on-Severn DY13 44 B4
Summerfields Ave B62 8 F7
Summerhill Ave DY11 27 A5
Summerhouse Cl B97 89 A6
Summervale Cl DY9 15 A5
Summervale Rd DY9 15 A5
Summerway La DY11 44 F6
Summit Gdns B63 7 F3
Summit Rd DY14 40 E4
Summit The DY9 6 D4
Sun St GL20 196 E7
Sunbury Cotts B31 19 A4
Sunbury Rd
Birmingham B31 33 E7
Halesowen B63 7 F4
Suncroft B32 9 C5
Sundbury Rise B31 19 B5
Sunderland Dr DY8 6 A8
Sunderton Rd B14 20 E4
Sunningdale
Bromsgrove B60 49 A1
Halesowen B62 8 E4
Sunningdale Cl
Redditch B98 70 F4
Stourbridge DY8 5 F2
Sunningdale Holiday Est WR6 111 D6
Sunningdale Rd B61 67 D8
Sunny Bank Rd B68 9 C7
Sunnymead B60 49 A1
Sunnyside Gdns 1 DY11 12 B1
Sunnyside Rd WR1 115 B5
Sunnyside Sch WR1 115 A5
Sunrise 6 WR14 139 B1
Surfeit Hill Rd B64 7 D8
Surman St WR1 115 B4
Sussex Ct 7 B29 19 C7
Sutherland Rd B64 7 E8
Suthill Bridge WR6 59 B5
Sutton Cl B98 71 D2
Sutton Pk Fst Sch DY11 27 B4
Sutton Pk Gr DY11 27 C3
Sutton Pk Rd DY11 27 B3
Sutton Pk Rise DY11 27 B3
Sutton Rd DY11 27 C4
Swale Gr B38 19 F1
Swaledale Cl B60 67 E6
Swallow Cl 1 WR5 128 D5
Swallow Dr DY10 28 A2
Swallow Pl WR9 104 B7
Swallowfall Ave DY8 5 C4
Swallowfields WR4 116 C4
Swan Cl Blakedown DY10 14 B1
9 Tenbury Wells WR15 55 F6
Swan Ct 8 WR15 55 F6
Swan Ctr 7 DY10 27 E6
Swan Dr WR9 85 B3
Swan La
Evesham WR11 161 D5
Fairfield B61 31 E3
Tenbury Wells WR15 55 F6
Upton Warren B61 66 E5
Swan Orch WR6 125 A7
Swan St Alvechurch B48 51 B5
Stourbridge DY8 5 E5
Swan Theatre* WR1 115 A3
Swanley Cl B62 9 A3
Swanpool Wlk WR2 115 A1
Swans Length B48 51 A7
Swansbrook Gdns 4 B38 20 C2
Swansbrook La B96 88 E1
Swanshurst La B13 21 C8
Swanshurst Sch B13 21 B7
Swarthmore Rd B29 19 B7
Sweden La GL20 186 D2
Sweetpool La DY8 14 F5
Swift Cl B61 67 E8
Swift Pk Gr DY10 28 B2
Swilgate Rd GL20 196 E6
Swinburne Rd B97 89 C7
Swincross Rd DY8 6 B3
Swindell Rd DY9 6 C1
Swineshead Way WR5 116 C1
Swinford Old Hall DY8 6 B3
Swinford Rd DY8 6 A3
Swinton Cl
3 Worcester WR2 114 E1
Worcester WR2 127 E8
Swinton La
5 Worcester WR2 114 E1
Worcester WR2 127 E8
Swiss Hts 3 DY13 43 E1
Sycamore Ave
Evesham WR11 161 F2
Redditch B98 70 E2
Sycamore Cl
Great Malvern WR14 139 A5
Kidderminster DY10 27 F7
Stourbridge DY8 5 D2
Sycamore Ct B30 19 E4
Sycamore Dr B47 36 B6
Sycamore Rd
Birmingham, Bournville B30 19 F7
11 Northway GL20 184 E1
Northway GL20 197 E8
Worcester WR4 115 E5
Sycamore Terr B14 20 C7
Sycamores The DY9 14 F5
Sydnall Cl B97 69 F2
Sydney Rd Blackheath B64 7 C8
Bromsgrove B61 48 E3
Sydney St WR3 115 B6
Sylvan Ave B31 18 F3
Sylvan Gn B62 8 D5
Sylvia Ave B31 34 B8
Synehurst WR11 162 D4
Synehurst Ave WR11 162 D4
Synehurst Cres WR11 162 D4
Sytchampton Endowed Fst Sch WR9 64 B1

T

Tabberness Cl WR6 112 C3
Tabbs Gdns DY10 28 A6
Tagwell Cl WR9 104 B8
Tagwell Rd 2 WR9 85 A1
Tailor's La CV37 151 F1
Talavera Rd WR5 128 F3
Talbot Cl 1 DY11 45 A1
Talbot Pass 5 DY8 6 A5
Talbot Rd B60 67 E7
Talbot St Halesowen B63 7 C6
Kidderminster DY11 27 C4
Stourbridge, Lye DY9 6 F5
Talbotshill La DY10 13 C4
Talgarth Covert B38 34 E7
Tall Trees Cl B61 48 F8
Tall Trees Dr DY9 6 D2
Talladale B32 18 B7
Tallow Hill WR5 115 D3
Tamar Cl WR5 115 E3
Tamar Pl WR11 161 F3
Tamar Rise DY8 6 A8
Tamarisk Cl
Birmingham B29 19 B8
North Claines WR3 102 E3
Tame Rd B68 9 B8
Tame Rise B68 9 B8
Tamerton Rd B32 9 D1
Tamworth Ave 12 WR4 116 C6
Tan House La WR2 127 C7
Tan La 2 DY13 43 F4
Tandy Dr B14 20 F3
Tandy's La DY10 29 E4
Tanglewood Cl
Birmingham, Quinton B32 9 B4
Blackwell B60 50 A5
Tanhouse La
Great Malvern WR14 138 F6
Halesowen B63 7 C5
Redditch B98 71 C6
Tanners Cl 7 WR4 115 F6
Tanners Gn La B47, B94 36 B2
Tanners Hill DY12 25 E3
Tansy Cl WR5 128 D4
Tantallon Dr B32 9 D1
Tanwood Cl B97 89 A6
Tanwood Cross DY10 30 B2
Tanwood La DY10 30 A2
Tanworth La B98 72 C7
Tanyard Cl B48 51 B6
Tanyard La B48 51 B6
Tapenhall Rd WR3 102 E2
Tardebigge CE Fst Sch B60 69 B7
Tardebigge Ct B97 69 C6
Tardebigge House B60 49 B3
Tarragon Gdns B31 18 C2
Tarrant Gr B32 9 F5
Tarrington Covert 6 B38 34 E8
Tattersall 2 WR4 116 B3
Taunton Cl B31 18 C2
Tavern La WR15 57 C7
Tavern Orch WR4 116 B5
Tawny Cl GL20 184 D1
Tay Ave WR5 128 E6
Tay Gr Birmingham B38 34 F8
Halesowen B62 8 E8
Tay Rd B45 18 B1
Taylor Rd B13 20 F5
Taylor's La 3 WR1 115 B3
Taylors La WR5 128 D4
Taynton Covert 4 B30 20 C3
Taysfield Rd B31 18 E6
Tayson Way 2 WR14 138 F5
Teal Cres DY10 28 B3
Teal Rd B80 90 F4
Tearne St WR2 114 F4
Teasdale Way DY9 6 D4
Teasel Cl WR5 128 D4
Teasel Way WR3 102 D2
Teazel Ave B30 19 D6
Ted Preston Cl GL20 196 F4
Tedstone Rd B32 9 E5
Tees Gr B38 34 F8
Teesdale Cl 4 WR9 84 D1
Teeswater Cl
Bromsgrove B60 67 E6
1 Worcester WR3 115 E7
Telford Dr DY12 26 A3
Teme Ave
Great Malvern WR14 153 D8
Kidderminster DY11 27 B3
Teme Cres 7 WR9 84 D1
Teme La WR6 112 E1
Teme Rd Halesowen B63 7 B5
Stourbridge DY8 5 F3
Worcester WR4 115 F3
Teme St WR15 55 F5
Temeside Cl 10 WR15 55 F6
Temeside Way WR2 127 F5
Temperance St 7 WR1 115 C2
Temple Ave WR13 139 F4
Temple Cl B98 70 F4
Temple Mews 1 WR11 161 D4
Ten Acres End B30 20 B8
Ten Ashes La B45 33 C4
Tenacres Fst Sch B98 71 F3
Tenacres La B98 71 F3
Tenbury & District Hospl WR15 55 F6
Tenbury CE Prim Sch WR15 55 F4
Tenbury Cl B98 71 C6
Tenbury High Sch WR15 55 E3
Tenbury House 2 B63 8 A3
Tenbury Mead 6 DY14 22 C4
Tenbury Mus* WR15 55 F5
Tenbury Rd
Birmingham B14 20 E6
Cleobury Mortimer DY14 22 B3
Tenbury Swimming Pool WR15 55 F5
Tenbury Wells Bsns Pk WR15 56 A3
Tenbury Wells Pump Rms* WR15 55 F5
Tenby Twr 2 B31 19 A1
Tenby Way DY13 43 E5
Tenlands Rd B63 7 F3
Tennal Dr B32 9 F6
Tennal Gr B32 9 F6
Tennal La B32 9 F6
Tennal Rd B32 9 F6
Tennis Ct B30 19 D4
Tennis Wlk WR1 115 B4
Tennyson Cl WR3 115 C7
Tennyson Dr WR14 139 A2
Tennyson House B31 34 A8
Tennyson Rd B97 89 C8
Tennyson Way DY10 28 C6
Tenter Ct B63 8 B4
Tenter Dr B63 8 C4
Tenterfields B63 8 B4
Tenterfields Prim Sch B63 8 C4
Tern Gr B38 19 E1
Terrace Rd WR10 144 E4
Terrace The B64 7 E8
Terrill Ct 4 WR11 161 D5
Terrills La WR15 55 F1
Terrys Cl B98 70 F5
Tessall La B31 18 D2
Tetbury Dr WR4 116 A6
Tetbury Gr B31 18 D3
Teviot Gr B38 34 F8
Tewkesbury Borough Mus* GL20 196 E6
Tewkesbury CE Prim Sch GL20 196 F6
Tewkesbury Ind Est GL20 197 C8
Tewkesbury Rd
Bredon GL20 184 B2
Eckington WR10 171 F6
Thackeray Rd B30 19 D5
Thackholme 7 WR4 116 C5
Thame Ct B47 35 E2
Thames Cl WR5 115 E2
Thames Dr WR9 84 D1
Thane Cl B80 90 F4
Thatcham Rd 4 GL20 197 A3
Thatchers Ct WR9 84 D5
Thatchers The B62 8 E8
Thatchers Way WR9 84 D5
Thatchway Gdns B38 34 E7
Thelbridge Rd B31 33 E6
Theocs Cl GL20 196 E4
Thicknall Dr DY9 6 C2
Thicknall La DY9 15 B3
Thicknall Rise DY9 15 B4
Third Rd B61 31 F4
Thirlmere Cl 4 WR4 116 B6
Thirlmere Dr B13 21 D8
Thirlmere Rd DY13 43 F6

Thirlmere Wlk DY5 ....6 B7
Thirlstane Rd WR14 ....152 F6
Thirsk Way B61 ....32 B1
Thistle Cl 11 WR5 ....128 D5
Thistle Downs GL20 ....184 D1
Thistle Gn B38 ....34 E7
Thistle La B32 ....18 B7
Thistledown WR11 ....161 C1
Thomas Cl WR3 ....102 E2
Thomson Ave B38 ....19 D1
Thorn Ave WR4 ....115 E6
Thorn Lea WR11 ....162 A2
Thorn Rd B30 ....19 E7
Thornbury La B98 ....71 C7
Thorncliffe Cl B97 ....89 A6
Thorneloe Rd WR1 ....115 A5
Thorneloe Wlk WR1 ....115 A4
Thorngrove Rd 2
WR14 ....153 A8
Thornham Way B14 ....20 D1
Thornhill Rd
Brierley Hill DY5 ....6 E8
Halesowen B63 ....7 E3
Redditch B98 ....71 E6
Thornhurst Ave B32 ....9 E7
Thorns Com Coll DY5 ....6 E8
Thorns Prim Sch DY5 ....6 E7
Thorns Rd DY5 ....6 E7
Thornthwaite Cl B45 ....18 B2
Thornton House Sch
WR5 ....115 D1
Three Acres La B90 ....36 F6
Three Cnr Cl B90 ....36 E8
Three Cocks La WR11 ....148 B1
Three Counties
Showground* WR13 ....153 B2
Three Oaks Rd B47 ....36 B4
Three Springs Rd 7
WR10 ....144 C1
Three Springs Trading Est
WR5 ....115 D2
Threlfall Dr DY12 ....26 D4
Threshfield Dr WR4 ....116 A4
Throckmorton Rd
Hill & Moor WR10 ....145 E4
Redditch B98 ....90 A8
Thruxton Cl
Birmingham B14 ....20 F3
Redditch B98 ....71 E3
Thurleigh Cl DY9 ....6 C2
Thurlestone Rd B31 ....33 E7
Thurloe Cres B45 ....17 E1
Tibbats Cl B32 ....9 C3
Tibberton CE Fst Sch
WR9 ....117 A8
Tibberton Cl B63 ....8 C4
Tibberton Ct B60 ....67 E7
Tibberton Rd WR14 ....153 A8
Ticknall Cl B97 ....70 A4
Tidbury Cl B97 ....89 C6
Tidbury Gn Sch B90 ....36 E4
Tidworth Croft 2 B14 ....21 A3
Tigley Ave B32 ....9 D1
Tilehouse B97 ....70 D2
Tilehouse La B90 ....36 E6
Till St WR3 ....115 C5
Tillington Cl B98 ....71 E3
Tilshead Cl B14 ....20 E3
Timber Down WR10 ....158 F7
Timber La WR10 ....158 F7
Timberdine Ave WR5 ....128 C7
Timberdine Cl
Halesowen B63 ....7 D6
Worcester WR5 ....128 D7
Timberdyne Cl DY14 ....41 C3
Timberhonger La
Bromsgrove B61 ....48 B2
Dodford with Grafton B61 ....47 F1
Timbertree Cres B64 ....7 E7
Timbertree Prim Sch
B64 ....7 E7
Timbertree Rd B64 ....7 F7
Timmis Rd DY9 ....6 C6
Timms Gn 1 WR12 ....177 E4
Tinker's Cross WR3 ....102 D3
Tinkers' Cross WR6 ....113 B5
Tinkers Farm Gr B31 ....18 E3
Tinkers Farm Rd B31 ....18 E3
Tinmeadow Cres B45 ....33 C7
Tintern Ave WR3 ....115 D5
Tintern Cl
Bromsgrove B61 ....48 E1
Kidderminster DY11 ....26 F6
Tintern House B32 ....9 F5
Tipper Trad Est DY9 ....7 A5
Tipping's Hill B97 ....89 C5
Tiree Ave WR5 ....128 E6
Tirle Bank Way GL20 ....197 B6
Tirlebrook Cty Prim Sch
GL20 ....197 C6
Titania Cl B45 ....18 A3
Tithe Ct WR11 ....148 F3
Titheway WR11 ....148 F3
Titterstone Rd B31 ....34 A8
Tiverton Cl 5 WR4 ....116 B7
Tixall Rd B28 ....21 E5
Toftdale Gn WR4 ....116 B4
Toll House Cl WR2 ....127 B8
Toll House Rd B45 ....33 C7
Tolladine Rd WR4 ....115 E3
Tolley Rd DY11 ....27 B1
Tollgate Cl B31 ....33 F8
Tollhouse Dr WR2 ....114 F3
Tollhouse Rd B60 ....67 E6
Tolsey La 5 GL20 ....196 E6
Tomkinson Dr DY11 ....27 B4
Tomlan Rd B31 ....34 C7
Toms Town La B80 ....90 E3
Top Field Wlk B14 ....20 D2
Top Rd B61 ....32 A4
Top St WR10 ....160 E8
Topfield House B14 ....20 E1
Topham Ave WR4 ....116 B3
Topland Gr B31 ....18 C2
Topsham Croft B14 ....20 D5
Toronto Cl 5 WR2 ....127 E6
Toronto Gdns B32 ....9 E6
Torre Ave B31 ....18 E2
Torridon Cl DY13 ....43 E7
Torrs Cl B97 ....70 D2
Torton La DY10 ....45 B5
Toulouse Dr WR5 ....128 F4
Towbury Cl B98 ....89 F5
Towbury Hill (Fort)*
GL20 ....183 C6
Tower Croft 4 B50 ....136 E5
Tower Dr B61 ....49 A6
Tower Hill
Bidford-on-Avon B50 ....136 E4
6 Droitwich WR9 ....85 A3
Tower House Dr GL19 ....192 E3
Tower Rd WR1 ....115 A6
Towers Cl DY10 ....28 B5
Town Acres 11 WR4 ....116 A5
Towneley WR4 ....116 C3
Townsend Ave B61 ....49 B4
Townsend St 5 WR1 ....115 A5
Townsend Way WR14 ....139 D4
Toy City* WR15 ....75 F4
Toys La B63 ....7 C5
Traceys Mdw B45 ....33 A7
Trafalgar Ct 1 B50 ....136 D4
Trafford Pk The B98 ....70 F3
Tram St DY10 ....27 E5
Tranter Ave B48 ....51 A5
Treacle Nook 2 WR4 ....116 B5
Tredington Cl
1 Birmingham B29 ....19 A7
Redditch B98 ....90 B7
Tree Acre Gr B63 ....7 C4
Trefoil Cl
Birmingham B29 ....19 A7
Great Malvern WR14 ....153 D7
12 Worcester WR5 ....128 D5
Tregarron Rd B63 ....7 C5
Trehearn Rd WR9 ....85 B3
Trehernes Dr DY9 ....6 B1
Trejon Rd B64 ....7 E8
Trelawney Ct 10 WR2 ....114 F1
Trench La
Huddington WR9 ....118 B8
Oddingley WR9 ....104 D5
Trench Wood Nature
Reserve* WR9 ....104 F2
Trent Cl DY8 ....6 A4
Trent Cres B47 ....35 E2
Trent Rd WR5 ....115 F3
Tresco Cl B45 ....17 E1
Trescott Jun & Inf Sch
B31 ....18 D3
Trescott Rd
Birmingham B31 ....18 D4
Redditch B98 ....70 F3
Tretawn Gdns GL20 ....197 B6
Trevanie Ave B32 ....9 C6
Treville Cl B98 ....71 E3
Trevithick Cl
5 Stourport-on-Severn
DY13 ....44 A5
4 Worcester WR4 ....116 C4
Trianon Rd B60 ....49 C1
Trickses La B97 ....88 D4
Trimpley Dr DY11 ....27 A7
Trimpley La
Bewdley DY12 ....26 D5
Kidderminster Foreign
DY12 ....11 C5
Trimpley Rd B32 ....9 B1
Trinity Cl WR11 ....161 E2
Trinity Ct
Bromsgrove B60 ....68 B7
1 Kidderminster DY10 ....27 F6
Trinity Fields DY10 ....27 F6
Trinity Grange DY10 ....27 F7
Trinity High Sch & Sixth
Form Ctr B98 ....70 F4
Trinity Pas 4 WR1 ....115 C2
Trinity Rd
Great Malvern WR14 ....138 E2
Stourbridge DY8 ....6 A8
Trinity St
3 Tewkesbury GL20 ....196 E6
2 Worcester WR1 ....115 C2
Trinity The 3 WR1 ....115 C3
Trippleton Ave B32 ....18 B8
Tristram Ave B31 ....19 B1
Trittiford Rd B13 ....21 C6
Trotshill La E WR4 ....116 C5
Trotshill La W WR4 ....116 B5
Trotshill Way WR4 ....116 D4
Troughton Pl GL20 ....197 B6
Trout Beck Dr WR4 ....115 F5
Troutbeck Dr DY5 ....6 B8
Trow Way WR5 ....128 B7
Troy Gr B14 ....20 D4
Troy Ind Est B96 ....90 A3
Truemans Heath La
B47, B90 ....36 C7
Truro Dr DY11 ....27 A5
Tryst The B61 ....49 B5
Tudbury Rd B31 ....18 E4
Tudor Bsns Ctr B98 ....70 E3
Tudor Cl
Birmingham, Highter's Heath
B14 ....21 A1
Tudor Cl *continued*
Birmingham, King's Heath
B13 ....20 F6
Great Malvern WR14 ....153 C6
Tudor Gdns DY8 ....5 E5
Tudor House Mus*
WR8 ....169 B6
Tudor Pl GL20 ....196 F4
Tudor Rd DY12 ....25 F3
Tudor Way WR2 ....114 C3
Tuer The WR11 ....134 A3
Tuer Way WR7 ....120 E7
Tuffery Cl WR3 ....115 B6
Tug Wilson Cl GL20 ....184 E2
Tugford Rd B29 ....19 C7
Tugwood La DY13 ....64 B6
Tunnel Dr B98 ....70 E2
Tunnel Hill
Upton upon Severn WR8 ....169 B4
Worcester WR4 ....115 F5
Tunnel La B14 ....20 C4
Turbary Ave WR4 ....116 C5
Turgo Gdns WR5 ....116 A1
Turner Dr DY5 ....6 D7
Turners Cl WR4 ....115 F6
Turney Rd DY8 ....5 F6
Turnpike Cl WR2 ....114 F3
Turnpike La B97 ....70 A4
Turnstone Rd DY10 ....28 A1
Turrall St WR1 ....115 B6
Turton St DY10 ....28 A8
Turves Gn
Birmingham, Turves Green
B31 ....19 A1
Birmingham, West Heath
B31 ....33 F8
Turves Gn Boys' Sch
B31 ....34 A8
Turves Gn Girls Sch & Tech
Coll B31 ....19 A1
Turves Gn Prim Sch
B31 ....19 A1
Tutbury Row WR4 ....116 D6
Tutnall Cl B60 ....49 F1
Tutnall La Blackwell B60 ....50 A1
Finstall B60 ....49 F1
Twarnley Rise 3 WR4 ....116 B3
Twatling Rd B45 ....33 A2
Tweed Cl WR5 ....115 E2
Tweeds Well B32 ....18 B7
Twickenham Ct DY8 ....5 C7
Twiners Rd B98 ....70 F1
Twixtbears GL20 ....196 E7
Two Gates B63 ....7 C5
Two Gates La B63 ....7 C5
Twyning Cty Prim Sch
GL20 ....184 A6
Twyning Rd
Birmingham, Stirchley
B30 ....20 B7
Strensham WR8 ....171 A3
Tybridge St WR2 ....115 A2
Tye Gdns DY9 ....6 B1
Tylers Gn B38 ....20 B1
Tyndale WR4 ....116 C4
Tyndall Wlk B32 ....9 A2
Tyne Cl WR5 ....115 E2
Tyne Dr WR11 ....162 A3
Tynes The B60 ....67 E7
Tynings Cl DY11 ....12 B1
Tynsall Ave B97 ....69 F2
Tyrol Cl DY8 ....5 D6
Tysoe Cl B98 ....71 D2
Tythe Barn Cl B60 ....67 D6
Tythe Rd 1 WR12 ....177 D1
Tythebarn La B90 ....36 F6
Tything The WR1 ....115 B4

U

Uffculme Rd B30 ....20 D8
Uffmoor Est B63 ....7 E2
Uffmoor La B62 ....16 D7
Ullapool Cl B97 ....89 D5
Ullenhall La B95 ....72 E6
Ullswater Ave DY13 ....43 F6
Ullswater Cl
Birmingham B32 ....9 F2
Worcester WR4 ....116 A5
Ulverston Gn 1 WR4 ....115 F5
Ulwine Dr B31 ....19 A4
Umberslade Rd B29 ....20 A8
Underhill Cl B98 ....89 F6
Underwood Cl B97 ....89 A7
Unicorn Hill B97 ....70 D4
Union La WR9 ....84 E3
Union Pl WR3 ....115 A7
Union St
Kidderminster DY10 ....27 E7
Redditch B98 ....70 F3
Stourbridge, Lye DY9 ....6 E5
Stourbridge, Stambermill
DY8 ....6 A4
Worcester WR1 ....115 C2
Unwin Cres DY8 ....5 E5
Upland Gr B61 ....49 A4
Upland Rd B61 ....49 B4
Uplands B63 ....7 E2
Upleadon Cl B97 ....89 A6
Upper Arley CE Fst Sch
DY12 ....10 D5
Upper Chase Rd
WR14 ....153 B8
Upper Cl B32 ....9 D3
Upper Crossgate Rd
B98 ....90 C8
Upper End WR10 ....171 F8
Upper End Ct WR11 ....163 C4
Upper Ferry La WR2 ....140 E7
Upper Field Cl B98 ....71 C6
Upper Gambolds La
B60 ....68 C5
Upper Gd WR4 ....116 B5
Upper Hall Cl B98 ....71 D2
Upper Hook Rd WR8 ....168 E6
Upper House WR6 ....124 F6
Upper Howsell Cl 4
WR14 ....138 F5
Upper Howsell Rd
WR14 ....138 F5
Upper Mdw Rd B32 ....9 C5
Upper Norgrove House
B97 ....69 F1
Upper Pk St WR5 ....115 D1
Upper St WR8 ....157 E3
Upper Tything WR1 ....115 B4
Upper Welland Rd
WR14 ....166 F7
Upper Wick La WR2 ....127 C8
Upton Cl B98 ....71 F3
Upton Gdns WR8 ....169 D4
Upton Rd
Callow End WR2 ....140 E8
Kidderminster DY10 ....12 F1
Powick WR2 ....127 E2
Upton Snodsbury CE Fst Sch
WR7 ....131 C8
Upton Snodsbury Rd
WR10 ....144 E7
Upton upon Severn CE Prim
Sch WR8 ....169 C5
Usmere Rd
Kidderminster DY10 ....12 F1
Kidderminster DY10 ....27 F8
Uxbridge Ct DY11 ....27 D5

V

Valbourne Rd B14 ....20 C4
Vale Bsns Pk WR11 ....175 F8
Vale Cl B32 ....9 F3
Vale Ct B64 ....7 D7
Vale Ind Est DY11 ....27 C1
Vale of Evesham Sch
WR11 ....161 E2
Vale Rd DY13 ....44 A3
Vale St DY8 ....6 A8
Vale Wildlife Visitor Ctr*
WR11 ....147 E1
Valencia Rd B60 ....49 D1
Valentines Cl 3 WR9 ....104 B8
Valerian DY10 ....27 E2
Valley Cl
Kidderminster Foreign
DY11 ....26 E8
Redditch B97 ....89 A6
Valley Farm Rd B45 ....33 A6
Valley Rd Blackheath B64 ....7 E7
Bournheath B61 ....48 E7
Halesowen B62 ....8 F8
Stourbridge DY9 ....6 F6
Valley Stad (Redditch FC)
B97 ....70 C4
Valley View DY12 ....25 E2
Valley Way WR9 ....84 D2
Vancouver Cl 1 WR2 ....127 E6
Vandra Cl WR14 ....139 B5
Vardon Way B38 ....19 D1
Varlins Way B38 ....34 D6
Vaughan Rd DY14 ....22 B4
Vauxhall Rd DY8 ....6 A5
Vauxhall St WR3 ....115 D5
Vawdrey Cl
4 Stourport-on-Severn
DY13 ....43 E1
1 Stourport-on-Severn
DY13 ....62 E8
Vaynor Dr B97 ....89 D8
Vaynor Fst Sch The
B97 ....89 C7
Ventnor Cl B68 ....9 C7
Venus Bank 1 DY12 ....26 A3
Vera Roberts Way
DY11 ....27 B3
Verbena Cl B60 ....67 C1
Verbena Rd B31 ....18 F6
Vernon Cl Halesowen B62 ....8 D8
Martley WR6 ....99 A4
Redditch B98 ....71 A5
Vernon Ct 2 B68 ....9 B7
Vernon Gr WR9 ....84 D3
Vernon Pk Rd 16 WR2 ....114 F1
Vernon Rd
Halesowen B62 ....8 C8
Stourport-on-Severn
DY13 ....44 A4
Vernon Trad Est B62 ....8 C8
Veronica Cl B29 ....19 A6
Verstone Croft B31 ....19 A3
Vestry Ct DY8 ....5 E6
Vetch Field Ave WR4 ....116 B4
Vicar St
Kidderminster DY10 ....27 E6
Worcester WR3 ....115 D4
Vicarage Bank WV15 ....1 B5
Vicarage Cl
Birmingham, Stirchley
B30 ....20 C7
Brierley Hill DY5 ....6 C8
Bromsgrove B60 ....68 B8
Hallow WR2 ....101 D1
Vicarage Cres
Kidderminster DY10 ....27 F5
Redditch B97 ....70 C3
Vicarage Ct DY7 ....4 A3
Vicarage Dr DY7 ....4 A3
Vicarage Gdns 1 WR10 ....171 E7
Vicarage Hill B94 ....53 F3
Vicarage La
Childswickham WR12 ....176 E2
North Claines WR3 ....102 C3
Vicarage Rd
Birmingham, King's Heath
B14 ....20 D7
Brierley Hill DY5 ....6 C7
Stone DY10 ....28 E2
Stourbridge DY8 ....5 D7
Stourbridge, Lye DY9 ....6 F5
Vicarage Rd S DY9 ....6 E5
Vicarage View B97 ....70 D3
Vicars Wlk DY9 ....6 E2
Victor Bsns Ctr B98 ....71 B3
Victoria Ave
Droitwich WR9 ....84 F1
Evesham WR11 ....161 D6
Halesowen B62 ....8 F6
Worcester WR5 ....115 D1
Victoria Ct
6 Halesowen B62 ....9 A7
2 Kidderminster DY10 ....27 F6
Victoria La WR3 ....115 A6
Victoria Mews B45 ....50 D8
Victoria Pass 4 DY8 ....6 A5
Victoria Pk Rd WR14 ....139 B4
Victoria Pl
Kidderminster DY11 ....27 B2
5 Worcester WR5 ....115 D1
Victoria Rd
Bidford-on-Avon B50 ....136 C5
Birmingham, Stirchley
B30 ....20 A7
Bromsgrove B61 ....49 A3
Dodford B61 ....47 F6
2 Great Malvern WR14 ....152 F8
Halesowen B62 ....8 D8
Victoria Specl Sch B31 ....19 A5
Victoria Sq 5 WR9 ....84 F3
Victoria St
Halesowen B63 ....8 A4
7 Redditch B98 ....70 E4
Stourbridge DY8 ....6 A5
Worcester WR3 ....115 A6
Victory Cl 1 DY13 ....44 B2
Viewfields 6 WR5 ....116 B3
Vigornia Ave WR3 ....115 D5
Villa St DY8 ....6 A8
Village St
Aldington WR11 ....162 C5
Harvington WR11 ....148 B7
Village The WR6 ....97 E8
Villette Gr B14 ....21 C4
Villiers Rd B60 ....67 E7
Villiers St DY10 ....28 A5
Vimiera Cl WR5 ....128 F4
Vimy Rd B13 ....21 B8
Vincent Rd WR5 ....115 D2
Vine Ct B64 ....7 D8
Vine La Clent DY9 ....15 F3
Halesowen B63 ....8 B3
Kyre WR15 ....75 C5
Vine St Evesham WR11 ....161 D4
Kidderminster DY10 ....28 A8
Redditch B97 ....70 D4
Worcester WR3 ....115 A7
Vine Way GL20 ....196 E3
Vines La WR9 ....84 F4
Vineyard Rd B31 ....18 F5
Vinnall Gr B32 ....18 B8
Vintners Cl 5 WR4 ....115 F6
Violet La DY9 ....15 E4
Viols Wlk 4 DY14 ....22 C4
Virginia Rd GL20 ....197 E8
Vista Gn B38 ....20 B1
Vivian Ave WR2 ....127 C8
Vyrnwy Gr B38 ....34 E8

W

Wadborough Rd
Norton Juxta Kempsey
WR5 ....129 C1
Stoulton WR7 ....143 A7
Waggon La
Churchill DY10 ....14 A3
Churchill & Blakedown
DY10 ....13 F3
Waggon Pl 6 WR4 ....116 B5
Waggon Wlk B38 ....34 C8
Waggoners Cl 1 B60 ....67 E6
Wagtail Dr GL20 ....184 D1
Wain Gn WR4 ....116 B5
Wainwright Rd WR4 ....116 B8
Wake Gn Rd B13 ....21 D8
Wakefield Cl WR5 ....115 F2
Wakeford Rd B31 ....19 C1
Wakeman St 10 WR3 ....115 B6
Walcot La WR10 ....143 F5
Waldrons Moor B14 ....20 C5
Walford Gn B32 ....18 B7
Walford Wlk 7 B97 ....70 E3
Walker Ave
Brierley Hill DY5 ....6 D7
Stourbridge DY9 ....6 E3
Walker Dr DY10 ....13 A1
Walkers Heath Rd B38 ....20 B1
Walkers La WR5 ....129 A7
Walkers Rd B98 ....71 E6
Walkley Rd GL20 ....196 F7

Walkmill Dr WR9 85 D8
Walkwood CE Mid Sch B97 89 C8
Walkwood Cres B97 89 C6
Walkwood Rd B97 89 D6
Walkworth Ave 6 WR4 116 C6
Wall Well B63 7 F3
Wall Well La B63 7 F3
Wallace Rise B64 7 E7
Wall's Rd B60 67 C3
Wallcroft Cl WR2 114 E4
Wallhouse La
Feckenham B97 88 B5
Hanbury B60 87 F5
Walmead Croft B17 9 F7
Walmers Cres WR4 116 C7
Walmers Wlk The B31 18 D1
Walmesley Way B31 18 E3
Walmley Cl B63 7 B7
Walnut Ave WR4 115 F5
Walnut Cl
Broadway WR12 190 C8
Harvington WR11 148 B6
Stourbridge DY9 6 B1
Walnut Cres WR14 152 F4
Walnut La B60 68 D8
Walnut Way B31 33 F8
Walnuts The WR8 154 A2
Walter Nash Rd E DY11 27 B2
Walter Nash Rd W DY11 27 A1
Walters Cl B31 33 F6
Walters Rd B68 9 B6
Waltham Cl B61 48 E1
Waltham House B38 20 B1
Walton Ave B65 8 B8
Walton Cl Halesowen B63 7 F2
Kidderminster DY11 27 B2
Redditch B98 71 E3
2 Stourport-on-Severn DY13 43 D1
Tewkesbury GL20 197 B7
Walton Ct B63 7 F3
Walton Dr DY9 6 C5
Walton Gdns GL20 197 B6
Walton Gr B30 20 B2
Walton La
Elmley Lovett DY10 45 D2
Grimley WR2 101 C5
Walton Pool La DY9 15 F2
Walton Rd
Bromsgrove B61 49 B4
Elmley Lovett DY10 45 D2
Stourbridge DY8 6 A6
Walton Rise DY9 16 A3
Walwyn Rd
Colwall Stone WR13 152 A1
Great Malvern WR13 152 C3
Wannerton Rd DY10 14 B1
Wansbeck Gr B38 34 E8
Wapping La B98 72 B7
Warbage La
Belbroughton DY9 30 F1
Dodford B61 48 A7
Warbank Cl B48 51 A6
Warbler Pl DY10 28 A2
Ward Rd 2 DY13 44 B1
Wardle Way DY11 12 B3
Wardoor Place' 1 WR4 116 C5
Wards Cl WR11 162 A3
Wareham House B28 21 E3
Wareham Rd B45 18 B2
Waresley Ct Rd DY11 45 A1
Waresley Pk DY11 64 A8
Waresley Rd DY11 45 A1
Warley Croft B68 9 E8
Warmington Rd B47 36 A6
Warmstry Ct 4 WR1 115 B2
Warndon Bsns Pk WR4 116 A8
Warndon Gn WR4 116 A5
Warndon Infants Sch WR4 116 B6
Warndon Jun Sch WR4 116 B6
Warndon La WR4 116 D6
Warndon Way WR4 116 D7
Warple Rd B32 9 C5
Warren La B45 33 B3
Warren Rd
Birmingham, Stirchley B30 20 A6
Northway GL20 197 D8
Warrens End 1 B38 19 F1
Warstock La B14 21 A4
Warstock Rd B14 21 A3
Warston Ave B32 9 D3
Warstone Cl DY12 26 D4
Warwards La B29 20 A8
Warwick Ave B60 68 A8
Warwick Cl B80 90 D3
Warwick Ct 1 B29 19 C7
Warwick Hall Gdns B60 68 A8
Warwick Highway B98 71 C2
Warwick Pl GL20 196 F5
Warwick Rd B68 9 D7
Warwick St DY13 44 A5
Wasdale Rd B31 18 F4
Waseley Cl 3 WR5 128 E5
Waseley Hills Ctry Pk* B45 32 C8
Waseley Hills High Sch B45 32 D7
Waseley Rd B45 32 E8
Washbrook Cl 3 WR4 116 B7
Washford Dr B98 90 D7
Washford Ind Est B98 90 E8
Washford La B98 90 D8
Washington Rd WR11 176 D8
Washington St
Kidderminster DY11 27 C5
3 Worcester WR1 115 C4
Washpole La WR9 104 B4
Wassage Way WR9 84 D7
Wassage Way N WR9 84 C7
Wassage Way S WR9 84 C7
Wassell Ct B63 7 E2
Wassell Dr DY12 26 C4
Wassell Gr Rd
Hagley DY9 15 F8
Halesowen B63 7 A2
Wassell Rd
Halesowen B63 7 E2
Stourbridge DY9 6 E2
Wassell Wood Nature Reserve* DY12 26 D7
Wast Hill Gr B38 34 F7
Wasthill La B38, B48 34 D5
Watchetts Gn 1 WR4 116 C4
Watchman Ave DY5 6 F7
Watchtower Rd DY13 44 D6
Water Croft 5 WR4 116 B5
Waterfall Rd DY5 6 D7
Waterford Cl WR3 115 A7
Watergrip La GL20 186 A7
Waterhaynes Cl B45 33 A6
Waterlade Cl 2 DY11 45 B2
Waterlaide Rd DY11 45 A2
Waterloo Cres B50 136 E5
Waterloo Ind Est B50 136 E6
Waterloo Pk B50 136 E6
Waterloo Rd
Bewdley DY12 25 F2
Bidford-on-Avon B50 136 E6
Birmingham, King's Heath B14 20 E8
Waterloo St DY10 27 E6
Waterloo Way GL20 185 A6
Waterside
Droitwich WR9 85 A3
Evesham WR11 161 D3
Upton upon Severn WR8 169 C6
Waterside Cl 2 WR9 85 A3
Waterside Grange DY10 27 E8
Waterside Orch B48 34 B2
Waterside View DY5 6 B8
Waterworks Dr B31 18 D4
Waterworks Rd WR1 115 A5
Watery La
Alvechurch B48 35 C1
Belbroughton DY9 29 F7
Birmingham B62 9 A3
Hopwood B48 34 F2
Portway B48 52 D7
Redditch B98 71 B2
Welland WR14 166 F5
Worcester WR2 114 E1
Watford Rd B30 19 F5
Watkins Gdns B31 19 C4
Watkins' Way WR14 153 C7
Watledge Cl 2 GL20 196 F6
Watleys Cl 5 B50 136 D5
Watt Ct 3 DY13 44 A4
Watts Rd B80 90 E2
Watwood Rd B28, B90 21 F3
Waugh Dr B63 16 D8
Wavell Rd DY5 6 F7
Waveney Rd 5 WR9 84 D1
Waverley Cl DY10 28 A8
Waverley Cres B62 16 F4
Waverley St WR5 128 C7
Waxland Rd B63 8 B2
Way Croft DY11 44 A8
Waystone La DY9 30 D4
Weather La DY13 62 F4
Weatheroak Cl B97 70 A1
Weatheroak Hill B48 35 B1
Weatheroaks B62 9 A7
Weaver Cl WR9 85 A3
Weavers Cl B97 89 D4
Weavers Hill B97 89 D4
Webb La B28 21 E6
Webheath Fst Sch B97 70 A2
Wedderburn Rd WR14 153 C8
Wedgberrow Cl WR9 84 F2
Wedgewood Rd B32 9 D5
Wedley Pl WR4 116 C3
Weethley House 6 B97 70 A4
Weights Farm B97 70 C7
Weights La B97 70 C7
Weir La WR2 128 A7
Weirbrook Cl B29 19 C7
Welbeck Cl B62 8 E6
Welbeck Dr DY11 27 B5
Welch Gate DY12 26 A3
Welches Cl B31 19 B5
Welcome Dr B61 32 A1
Welford Cl B98 89 F5
Welford Rd
Bidford-on-Avon B50 137 A3
Long Marston CV37 151 C6
Well Cl Northway GL20 184 E1
Redditch B97 89 E5
Well La Little Witley WR6 81 B4
Rushock WR9 46 B2
Well Mdw B45 33 A6
Welland Cl WR9 84 D1
Welland Dr DY8 6 A8
Welland Gdns WR13 167 C4
Welland Prim Sch WR13 167 C5
Welland Rd
Halesowen B63 8 A2
Upton upon Severn WR8 168 D4
Wellesbourne Cl B98 70 E4
Wellfield GL20 197 B7
Wellington Cl 4 WR1 115 C2
Wellington Ct
Birmingham, Beech Lanes B32 9 F5
Kidderminster DY11 27 C5
Wellington House B32 9 F4
Wellington Lodge Cl GL20 185 A6
Wellington Rd
Bromsgrove B60 68 A8
Ombersley WR9 83 A5
Wellington St 6 B98 70 E4
Wellington Twr 4 B31 19 A1
Wellmead Wlk B45 32 F8
Wells Cl
4 Great Malvern WR14 166 E7
Kidderminster DY11 27 A6
Wells Gdns WR12 190 E8
Wells Rd
Great Malvern WR14 166 E8
Malvern Wells WR14 152 E5
Worcester WR5 116 A2
Welsh House Farm Com Sch B32 9 F4
Welsh House Farm Rd B32 9 F4
Wendron Cl B60 49 B2
Wendron Gr B14 20 D4
Wenlock Cl B63 7 D2
Wenlock Dr B61 49 A5
Wenlock Rd
Stourbridge DY8 6 B6
Tewkesbury GL20 196 F5
Wenlock Way 1 DY13 43 E1
Wensleydale 2 WR9 84 D1
Wensleydale Dr WR3 115 E7
Wentworth Dr B60 50 A5
Wentworth Rd DY8 5 E7
Wentworth Rise B62 8 D3
Wentworth Way B32 9 F3
Weoley Castle Rd B29 9 F1
Weoley Hill B29 19 C8
Werstan Cl WR14 153 C7
Werth La GL19 195 D2
Wesley Ave
Halesowen B63 7 B8
Stourport-on-Severn DY13 43 E1
Wesley Ct B64 7 F8
Wesley Wlk B60 67 E7
Wesson Gdns B63 8 A3
Wessons Rd B50 136 E5
West Ave B98 70 E3
West Bvd B32 9 F4
West Ct B60 67 F6
West End WR11 149 A8
West End La WR12 190 C7
West End Villas B38 19 F2
West Heath Hospl B38 34 C8
West Heath Jun & Inf Sch B38 34 C8
West Heath Rd B31 19 B1
West Hill Ct B14 20 C4
West Malvern Rd
Great Malvern WR14 138 C1
West Malvern WR14 152 D6
West Mead Dr B14 20 E6
West Midland Safari Pk* DY12 26 E3
West Midlands (Private) Hospl B63 7 D5
West Mill Croft B38 34 E7
West Pk Ave B31 18 E2
West Rd Bromsgrove B60 49 A2
Halesowen B63 7 B6
West Rd S B63 7 B6
West Side WR11 149 A4
West St Brierley Hill DY5 6 F8
Droitwich WR9 84 E3
Evesham WR11 161 C4
Redditch B98 70 E3
Stourbridge DY8 5 F5
West Way B31 34 B7
Westacre Dr DY5 6 F8
Westacre Mid Sch WR9 84 D3
Westbourne WR11 164 B5
Westbourne Cl B61 48 E1
Westbourne Rd B62 8 E7
Westbourne St 1 DY12 26 C3
Westbourne Terr B61 48 E1
Westbury Ave WR9 84 C1
Westbury House B97 70 B2
Westbury St WR1 115 C3
Westcliff Pl B31 18 F4
Westcombe Gr B32 9 A1
Westcote Ave B31 18 C2
Westcroft Gr B38 19 D3
Westcroft St 5 WR9 84 E3
Westcroft Way B14 21 B1
Westdean Cl B62 8 C4
Western Ave B62 8 E4
Western Bsns Pk B62 8 B7
Western Hill Cl B96 89 E1
Western Hill Rd GL20 186 D2
Western Rd
Blackheath B64 7 E8
Hagley DY9 15 B4
Stourbridge DY8 5 F4
Western Way DY11 27 A5
Westfield Ave
Birmingham B14 21 B1
Northway GL20 197 D8
Westfield Cl WR3 102 F3
Westfield La WR8 156 B7
Westfield Rd
Birmingham B13 20 D8
Brierley Hill DY5 6 F8
Fernhill Heath WR3 102 E3
Westfields B61 48 F8
Westford Gr B28 21 E3
Westhaven Dr B31 18 E7
Westhaven Pl 8 WR2 114 E5
Westhead Rd DY10 13 A4
Westhead Rd N DY10 13 A4
Westhill Coll (Univ Birmingham) B29 19 D8
Westhill Rd B38 19 F3
Westholme Croft B30 19 E8
Westholme Rd B50 136 D5
Westhouse Gr B14 20 D4
Westland Gdns DY8 5 F7
Westlands Fst Sch WR9 84 D5
Westlea Cl WR2 114 C1
Westlyn Cl WR14 139 B3
Westmead Ave B80 90 E4
Westmere WR8 154 A2
Westminster Bank
Great Malvern WR14 138 C1
West Malvern WR14 152 C8
Westminster Cl B61 48 D1
Westminster Ct 2 B60 49 A2
Westminster Dr B14 20 E6
Westminster Rd
Birmingham, Stirchley B29 20 A8
Great Malvern WR14 152 E4
Kidderminster DY11 27 A6
Worcester WR5 115 F2
Westmount Cl 2 WR2 127 F6
Weston Hill WR6 112 D4
Weston Orch WR10 146 A1
Weston Pk* GL55 178 E3
Weston Rd
Bretforton WR11 163 D3
Honeybourne WR11 164 B3
Westonbirt Cl 1 WR5 128 E5
Westonhall Rd B60 67 D1
Westray Cl B45 17 F1
Westridge Rd B13 21 C6
Westside Dr B32 9 D1
Westview Cl WR2 114 D2
Westville Ave DY11 27 A5
Westward Rd WR14 138 E6
Westwood Ave
Droitwich WR9 84 F1
Stourbridge DY8 5 D3
Westwood Cl WR9 84 C2
Westwood Dr B45 18 B1
Westwood La HR6 94 A3
Westwood Pk* WR9 84 B4
Westwood Rd WR9 84 D4
Westwood Way WR9 84 C3
Wey Cl WR9 84 D2
Weyburn Cl WR2 127 E6
Wharf La B60 50 B1
Wharf Rd B30 20 A2
Wharfedale Cres 7 WR9 84 C1
Wharfedale Dr WR4 116 A5
Wharrington Cl B98 90 A8
Wharrington Hill B98 90 A8
Wheatcroft Ave DY12 26 C4
Wheatcroft Cl B62 8 F8
Wheatfield Ave WR5 128 C5
Wheatfield Ct GL55 165 D4
Wheatfield View B31 18 D6
Wheatley Cl B68 9 C8
Wheatley La WR8 168 F3
Wheatley Rd B68 9 D8
Wheatmill Cl DY10 14 B2
Wheatridge Rd B60 67 E6
Wheatstone Cl 5 GL20 184 E1
Wheeler Cl WR2 114 F2
Wheeler Orch WR15 55 E3
Wheeler St DY8 5 F5
Wheeler's La B13 21 A7
Wheelers La B13 20 F7
Wheelers La Inf Sch B13 20 F7
Wheelers La Jun Sch (Annexe) B13 21 A6
Wheelers La Jun Sch B13 20 F7
Wheelers La Sch B13 20 F7
Wheeley Rd B48 50 D5
Wheelwright Cl
Bromsgrove B60 67 E6
Worcester WR4 115 E6
Whetty La B45 32 F7
Whettybridge Rd B45 32 E6
Whimbrel Gr DY10 28 A1
Whinchat Gr DY10 28 A2
Whinfield Rd
Dodford B61 48 B6
Worcester WR3 102 B1
Whiston Gr B29 19 B8
Whitborn Cl WR14 153 C7
Whitborn End WR14 153 C8
Whitbourne VC Prim Sch WR6 110 F6
Whitburn Cl DY11 27 B5
Whitchurch Cl B98 89 F6
Whitcomb's Orch DY14 22 C3
Whitcot Gr B31 33 F8
Whitcroft Rd WR10 144 D1
White Castle WR4 116 D6
White Cl DY9 6 C2
White Cottage Gdn* WR9 106 C1
White Heart Cl 18 DY12 25 F3
White Hill
Birmingham B31 19 B6
Kinver DY7 3 E5
Worcester WR4 116 A4
White House Ct WR6 124 A6
White House Dr B45 33 A2
White Ladies Cl WR1 115 B4
White Ladies Wlk 6 WR1 115 B4
White Rd B32 9 D6
Whitebeam Croft 3 B38 19 E1
Whitefriars Dr B63 8 A4
Whitegate Dr DY11 27 A3
Whitehall Cl WR2 127 C8
Whitehall Dr B63 8 B4
Whitehall Rd
Blackheath B64 7 C8
Halesowen B63 8 B4
Stourbridge DY8 6 B2
Whitehill La B29, B31 19 A5
Whitehill Rd DY11 27 A4
Whitehorse Cl 4 WR2 127 E6
Whitehouse La B98 71 E4
Whitehouse Pl B45 32 F6
Whitehouse Rd DY10 27 D4
Whitemoor La B96 109 B7
Whitepits La B48 52 F4
Whites Rd 2 WR2 127 F7
Whitesmith Croft B14 20 E8
Whitestone Rd B63 8 A6
Whitethorn Gr 3 WR14 139 C3
Whitewood Cl WR5 129 A8
Whitewood Way WR5 129 A8
Whitford Bridge Rd B60 68 A2
Whitford Cl
Bretforton WR11 163 C4
Bromsgrove B61 67 D8
Whitford Gdns B61 48 D2
Whitford Hall Dodderhill Sch WR9 85 A4
Whitford Rd B61 48 D2
Whitland Cl B45 33 B6
Whitland Dr B14 20 F3
Whitlenge La DY10 45 C3
Whitley Ct Rd B32 9 C6
Whitlock Gr B14 21 A3
Whitlocks End Halt B90 36 E7
Whitmore Rd
Stourbridge DY8 5 D5
Worcester WR2 114 D1
Whitney Ave DY8 5 D6
Whittakers Cl 1 WR10 144 D1
Whittal Cl WV15 1 C5
Whittall Dr E DY11 27 B1
Whittall Dr W DY11 27 A1
Whittingham Rd B63 8 A5
Whittington CE Prim Sch WR5 129 B6
Whittington Cl B14 20 E5
Whittington Hall La
Kinver DY7 4 F2
Stourbridge DY7 5 B3
Whittington Rd
Stourbridge DY8 5 E3
Worcester WR5 129 A8
Whitville Cl DY11 27 C7
Whyle La HR6 92 D5
Whynot Cl B60 67 C2
Whynot St B63 7 B5
Wichenford Dovecote (NT)* WR6 100 B4
Wick House Cl WR10 158 F7
Wick Rd WR10 159 B2
Wickham Cl WR11 176 D8
Wickham Rd B80 90 F4
Wicklow Cl B63 7 D1
Wide Acres B45 17 F1
Widney House B97 70 C4
Wigeon La GL20 197 A5
Wigland Way B38 20 A1
Wigley Bank Rd DY7 3 D6
Wigorn House B67 9 F8
Wigorn La DY9 15 B8
Wike La B96 109 C8
Wilberforce Pl 9 WR4 116 C3
Wild Goose La B98 90 D8
Wildacres DY8 5 C6
Wilde Cl B14 20 D4
Wilden Cl B31 18 C3
Wilden Ind Est DY13 44 C6
Wilden La
Kidderminster DY10 27 E1
Stourport-on-Severn DY13 44 C6
Wilden Top Rd DY13 44 D5
Wildmoor La B61 32 A3
Wilfred Cl 3 WR3 115 C5
Wilkes Way 9 B50 136 D5
Willersey Bsns Pk WR12 177 E5
Willersey Prim Sch WR12 177 F4
Willersey Rd
Badsey WR11 162 F1
Birmingham B13 21 D8
Willes Ct 2 B62 9 A7
Willets Rd WR9 103 F8
Willetts Dr B63 7 B4
Willetts Rd B31 19 A1
William Bullock Cl DY13 43 F3
William Coley Pl 3 DY13 43 F1
William Shakespeare Pl 7 WR9 103 F8
William St B97 70 E4

William Tennant Way WR8 169 D4
Willis St DY11 27 C5
Willis Wlk GL20 184 D1
Willmore Gr 4 B38 34 F8
Willow Bank Cl WR10 145 A8
Willow Brook Rd B48 51 A7
Willow Cl
  Ashton under Hill WR11 187 B7
  Bromsgrove B61 48 E2
  Fernhill Heath WR3 103 A3
  Hagley DY9 14 F5
  4 Pershore WR10 144 C1
  Ripple WR8 169 F6
Willow Coppice B32 9 C1
Willow Ct B61 48 E3
Willow Dr WR9 103 F8
Willow End DY9 6 D3
Willow Gdns B61 48 E3
Willow Gr WR14 139 A3
Willow Hts B64 8 A8
Willow Pk Dr DY8 6 B2
Willow Rd
  Birmingham, Bournville B29, B30 19 F8
  Bromsgrove B61 48 E3
  Evesham WR11 161 F2
  Kinver DY7 4 C3
  Martley WR6 112 C8
  Wichenford WR6 99 D1
  Willersey WR12 177 E3
Willow St WR5 115 C1
Willow Tree Dr B45 50 D8
Willow Way
  Redditch B97 70 B4
  Studley B80 90 E2
Willowdene DY13 44 C3
Willowfield Dr DY11 12 C1
Willows The
  Hollywood B47 36 A6
  Stourport-on-Severn DY13 44 C3
Willowsbrook Rd B62 8 F8
Willowslea Rd WR3 102 A1
Willsbridge Covert 8 B14 20 C2
Willson Croft B28 21 D3
Wilmcote Ct B61 67 D8
Wilmcote House B97 70 B4
Wilmington Rd B32 9 B6
Wilmore La B47 35 F4
Wilmot Rd WR14 138 F5
Wilsford Cl B14 20 D1
Wilson Rd DY11 45 A1
Wilson St 3 WR3 115 D4
Wilton Ave DY11 27 B8
Wilton Rd WR14 153 B8
Wiltshire Ct 10 B29 19 C7
Wiltshire Dr B63 7 B7
Wimbledon Dr DY8 6 B2
Winbrook DY12 26 A3
Winchcombe Dr WR4 115 F7
Winchcombe Rd WR11 175 B2
Winchester Ave
  Kidderminster DY11 27 A6
  Worcester WR2 127 F8
Winchester Cl DY9 15 A6
Winchester Dr DY8 6 A3
Winchester Gdns B31 19 A3
Winchfield Dr B17 9 F7
Windermere Dr WR4 115 F7
Windermere House DY10 27 E7
Windermere Way 1 DY13 43 F5
Winding Mill N DY5 6 E7
Winding Mill S DY5 6 E7
Windles Row 8 WR4 116 B5
Windmeres 4 WR11 161 F3
Windmill Ave B45 32 E8
Windmill CE Mid Sch DY13 43 E1
Windmill Cl
  Birmingham B31 19 C5
  4 Stourport-on-Severn DY13 43 F1
  1 Stourport-on-Severn DY13 62 F8
  3 Worcester WR1 115 B4
Windmill Dr B97 89 C6
Windmill Gdns B97 89 B6
Windmill Hill
  Birmingham B31 19 B5
  Halesowen B63 7 D5
  Temple Grafton B49 137 C8
Windmill La
  Inkberrow WR7 120 E7
  Kempsey WR5 141 C8
  Stoulton WR7 143 D8
Windmill Rd B90 21 E2
Windrush Cl
  Redditch B97 89 D6
  Worcester WR5 115 E2
Windrush Cres WR14 153 D8
Windrush Gr B29 20 A8
Windrush House B31 18 E5
Windrush Rd B47 36 B7
Winds Point DY9 15 A6
Windsor Ave WR2 114 E2
Windsor Cl
  Birmingham, Coft Common B31 34 A6
  Birmingham, Frankley B45 18 A2
  Halesowen B63 7 F3
  Newland WR14 139 C6
Windsor Cres DY7 3 F4
Windsor Ct B38 19 F1
Windsor Dr
  Astley & Dunley DY13 62 F8
  Kidderminster DY10 27 E7
Windsor Gdns B60 49 A2
Windsor High Sch B63 7 F4
Windsor Holloway DY7 4 C1
Windsor Rd
  Birmingham, Stirchley B30 20 B5
  Droitwich WR9 103 F8
  Evesham WR11 161 E6
  Halesowen B63 7 F4
  Redditch B97 70 D5
  Stourbridge DY8 5 E3
Windsor St B60 49 A2
Windsor View B32 18 D7
Winforton Cl B98 71 E3
Wing La GL20 185 D8
Wingate Cl B30 19 F4
Wingfield Ave WR4 116 C7
Winnall La DY13 63 B4
Winnington Cl WR6 97 E8
Winnington Gdns WR8 154 A2
Winnipeg Cl WR2 127 E6
Winnipeg Rd B38 35 A8
Winsford Cl B63 8 A6
Winslow Ave WR9 85 B3
Winslow Cl B98 71 F3
Winsmore WR2 127 E3
Winston Dr B62 17 A4
Winston Rd DY11 13 A6
Winstone Cl B98 71 A4
Winterbourne Croft B14 20 C1
Winterburn Rd WR2 114 E6
Winterfold Cl DY10 28 B6
Winterfold House Sch DY10 46 A8
Wintour Wlk B60 67 E7
Winward Rd B98 71 F1
Winwood Ct DY8 5 F4
Winwood Heath Rd B62 16 E2
Winwoods Gr B32 18 A8
Winyate Hill B98 71 A2
Winyates Crafts Ctr* B98 71 E3
Winyates Ctr B98 71 E3
Winyates Way B98 71 E4
Wirehill Dr B98 70 F1
Wirlpiece Ave WR4 116 C5
Wirral Rd B31 18 F6
Wiseacre Croft B90 21 E2
Wiselack Pl 7 WR4 116 B4
Wishaw Cl Redditch B98 90 A8
  Solihull B90 21 E2
Wisley Way B32 9 F5
Wistaria Cl B31 19 A6
Witherford Cl B29 19 C8
Witherford Way B29 19 C8
Withers Rd WR2 115 A1
Withincroft 5 WR4 116 B4
Withington Covert B14 20 D2
Withy Trees Rd WR11 163 C8
Withybed Cl B48 51 A6
Withybed La
  Alvechurch B48 51 A6
  Inkberrow WR7 120 D8
Withymoor Rd DY8 6 A7
Witley Ave B63 7 E4
Witley Cl DY11 27 B2
Witley Ct* WR6 80 D6
Witley Rd
  1 Birmingham B31 19 D2
  Holt WR6 81 E3
Witley Way DY13 62 D8
Witton Ave WR9 84 D1
Witton Bank B62 8 F7
Witton Mid Sch WR9 84 E1
Witton St DY8 5 F4
Wivelden Ave DY13 44 D6
Wixford Rd B50 137 A8
Woburn Cl B61 48 D1
Woburn Dr
  Brierley Hill DY5 6 B8
  Halesowen B62 8 B7
Wold Wlk B13 21 C6
Wolferlow Medieval Village of* HR7 96 B8
Wollaston Ct DY8 5 C6
Wollaston Rd
  Stourbridge DY7 5 C7
  Stourbridge, Amblecote DY8 5 F8
Wollescote Bsns Pk 6 DY9 6 F5
Wollescote Prim Sch DY9 6 F4
Wollescote Rd DY9 6 D3
Wolsey Cl WR4 115 E3
Wolverhampton Rd
  Kidderminster DY10 13 A1
  Oldbury B68 9 D8
  Stourton DY7 4 E7
Wolverhampton Rd S B32 9 E7
Wolverley Ave DY8 5 C6
Wolverley High Sch DY11 12 D4
Wolverley Rd
  Birmingham B32 18 B8
  Halesowen B63 7 F2
  Kidderminster DY11 12 B1
Wolverley Sebright Prim Sch DY11 12 D3
Wolverly Rd DY10 13 A2
Wolverton Cl B98 71 E2
Wolverton Rd B45 33 C6
Wood Croft B47 36 B6
Wood Ct B97 70 C1
Wood End Dr B45 50 A8
Wood End La B94 53 F5
Wood End Sta B94 53 F4
Wood Farm Rd WR14 152 E2
Wood Hill Cl WR4 116 B4
Wood La
  Ashton under Hill WR11 174 B2
  Birmingham, Woodgate B32 9 A1
  Cookhill B96 108 F3
  Earlswood B94 36 E1
  Edwyn Ralph HR7 95 B2
  Fairfield B61 31 C3
Wood Leason Ave WR4 116 B5
Wood Leasow B32 9 D2
Wood Leigh Cl B63 8 A6
Wood Piece Cl 4 WR4 116 B7
Wood Piece La B98 71 D7
Wood St Bushley GL20 182 E1
  Kidderminster DY11 27 D5
  Stourbridge DY8 5 D6
  Stourbridge, Lye DY9 6 F5
Wood Terr
  Sambourne B96 90 B1
  Worcester WR1 115 B4
Woodbank Dr B61 48 F8
Woodberrow La B97 89 D6
Woodbine Rd 6 WR1 115 A5
Woodbridge Cl WR5 128 D6
Woodbrooke Rd B30 19 E7
Woodbury Cl
  Great Witley WR6 61 B1
  Halesowen B62 8 F8
  Hartlebury DY11 45 A1
  Redditch B97 89 A6
Woodbury La WR5 129 C3
Woodbury Pk Holt WR6 82 B3
  Norton Juxta Kempsey WR5 129 D3
Woodbury Rd
  Halesowen B62 9 A8
  Kidderminster DY11 27 B2
  Stourport-on-Severn DY13 43 F5
Woodbury Rd N DY13 43 A5
Woodbury Rise WR14 138 E3
Woodchester DY9 15 B4
Woodcock Cl
  Birmingham B31 18 C1
  Tanworth-In-A B94 53 E3
Woodcock Hill Jun & Inf Sch B31 18 E7
Woodcock La B31 18 E8
Woodcombe Cl DY5 6 B7
Woodcote Cl B98 71 E3
Woodcote La
  Belbroughton DY9 30 E1
  Dodford with Grafton B61 47 D5
Woodcroft Cl
  Blackheath B64 7 F8
  Blackwell B60 49 F5
Woodend Cl B97 70 B2
Woodfall Ave B30 19 F5
Woodfarm Rd WR14 152 F2
Woodfield DY9 30 E7
Woodfield Ave
  Blackheath B64 7 D8
  Stourbridge DY9 6 F2
Woodfield Cl B98 71 A5
Woodfield Cres DY11 27 D5
Woodfield La
  Ombersley WR9 83 A8
  Romsley B62 31 D8
Woodfield Mid Sch B98 71 A2
Woodfield Rd
  Birmingham, King's Heath B13 20 F8
  1 Droitwich WR9 85 A3
Woodfield St 4 DY11 27 C6
Woodfields WR9 85 A4
Woodgate Bsns Pk B32 9 B2
Woodgate Dr B32 9 A1
Woodgate Gdns B32 9 A2
Woodgate House B97 70 B4
Woodgate Jun & Inf Sch B32 9 B1
Woodgate La B32 9 A2
Woodgate Rd
  Bentley Pauncefoot B60 87 D8
  Stoke Prior B60 68 B1
Woodgate Valley Ctry Pk* B32 9 D3
Woodgate Way DY9 30 E7
Woodglade Croft B38 19 E2
Woodgreen Cl B97 89 B7
Woodgreen Croft B68 9 C7
Woodgreen Dr WR4 116 B7
Woodgreen Rd B68 9 C7
Woodhall Cl WR9 83 A5
Woodhall La WR9 83 A5
Woodham Cl B45 17 E1
Woodhampton Cl 6 DY13 62 F8
Woodhouse Orch DY9 30 E7
Woodhouse Prim Sch B32 9 E6
Woodhouse Rd B32 9 E5
Woodland Ave
  Hagley DY8 14 F5
  Kidderminster DY11 27 C7
Woodland Cl
  Aston Somerville WR12 175 F1
Woodland Cl continued
  2 Drakes Broughton WR10 143 F6
  Stourbridge DY9 6 D2
  Worcester WR3 115 D6
Woodland Dr B45 33 A2
Woodland Gr DY10 13 C3
Woodland Rd
  Birmingham, Northfield B31 19 B3
  Dodford B61 47 F6
  Halesowen B62 8 D8
  Redditch B97 70 B3
  Suckley WR6 124 A3
  Worcester WR3 115 D6
Woodland Rise
  Blackheath B64 7 F8
  2 Cleobury Mortimer DY14 22 D5
Woodlands WR11 161 E1
Woodlands Cl
  3 Great Malvern WR14 166 E7
  1 Hartlebury DY11 45 B2
Woodlands Pk Rd B30 19 C5
Woodlands Rd
  Birmingham, Rubery B45 32 D7
  Cookley DY10 13 A4
Woodlands The
  Blackheath B64 8 A7
  Ryall WR8 169 E6
  Stourbridge DY8 6 A2
Woodleaves B47 35 F8
Woodleigh WR10 143 F6
Woodleigh Ct B38 19 F1
Woodleys The B14 21 B4
Woodman Cl B63 8 C3
Woodman La DY9 15 E4
Woodman Rd
  Birmingham B14 21 A1
  Halesowen B63 8 C3
Woodmancote 10 WR4 115 F7
Woodmans Way WR9 84 D5
Woodmeadow Rd B30 20 B3
Woodpecker Gr DY10 28 B2
Woodridge Ave B32 9 B4
Woodridge Rd B63 8 A5
Woodrow Cl B61 31 F1
Woodrow Ctr B98 90 B8
Woodrow Dr B98 90 B6
Woodrow Fst Sch B98 90 B7
Woodrow La
  Bluntington DY10 29 E3
  Catshill B61 32 B2
Woodrow N B98 90 A7
Woodrow S B98 90 B7
Woodrow Wlk B98 90 A7
Woodrush Dr B47 36 A5
Woodrush High Sch The B47 36 A6
Woodrush Rd 16 GL20 197 A4
Woods La Blackheath B64 7 C8
  Brierley Hill DY5 6 D7
Woodshears Dr WR14 153 A7
Woodshears Rd WR14 153 A7
Woodshill Ave B45 33 A2
Woodside Ave B97 70 B2
Woodside Dr B45 50 B8
Woodside Rd 1 WR5 115 E1
Woodside Way B32 18 A8
Woodstock House B13 21 A7
Woodstock Rd WR2 114 E3
Woodthorpe Dr
  Bewdley DY12 26 A4
  Stourbridge DY9 6 D3
Woodthorpe Gdns B14 20 E5
Woodthorpe Prim Sch B14 20 E5
Woodthorpe Rd B14 20 E5
Woodvale Dr B28 21 E4
Woodvale Rd
  Birmingham, Woodgate B32 9 A1
  Birmingham, Yardley Wood B28 21 E4
Woodville Rd
  Birmingham, King's Heath B14 20 F8
  5 Tewkesbury GL20 196 F3
Woodward Cl WR10 158 C7
Woodward Parks 5 WR10 146 A1
Woodward Pl DY9 6 C4
Woodward Rd
  Kidderminster DY11 27 C4
  Pershore WR10 158 C7
Woolaston Rd B98 90 C8
Woolhope Cl B98 71 F3
Woolhope Rd WR5 115 C1
Woollas Hall* WR10 172 D6
Woolmead Row WR4 116 D5
Wooton Cl B97 70 A4
Wootton Rd B31 34 A6
Worboys Rd WR2 127 F8
Worcester 6th Form Coll WR5 129 A8
Worcester City Art Gall & Mus* WR1 115 B3
Worcester Cl DY9 15 A5
Worcester Coll of Tech WR1 115 B2
Worcester Cross 3 DY10 27 E5
Worcester House 4 B63 8 A3
Worcester La DY9 15 B7
Worcester Porcelain Works* WR5 115 C1
Worcester Racecourse* WR1 115 A3
Worcester Rd
  Bromsgrove B61 48 F1
  Dodderhill WR9 66 E1
  Evesham WR11 161 C7
  Great Witley WR6 61 A1
  Hagley DY9 14 F3
  Harvington DY9, DY10 29 C4
  Kidderminster DY10 27 E2
  Mustow Green DY10 28 F1
  Newland WR2 126 F1
  Oldbury B68 9 A8
  Ombersley WR3 102 A7
  Pershore WR10 144 C1
  Pirton WR8 142 B4
  St. Peter the Great County WR5 128 C4
  Stoke Heath B61 67 B4
  Stone DY10 45 D7
  Stourport-on-Severn DY13 44 B3
  Wyre Piddle WR10 145 A4
Worcester Shrub Hill Sta WR4 115 D3
Worcester Sixth Form Coll WR5 116 A1
Worcester Sq 1 B97 70 E4
Worcester St
  Kidderminster DY10 27 E5
  Stourbridge DY8 6 A4
  Stourport-on-Severn DY13 44 A4
Worcester Swimming Pool & Fitness Ctr WR1 115 B4
Worcester Univ Coll WR2 114 F4
Worcester Woods Ctry Pk* WR5 116 B1
Worcestershire Royal Hospl WR5 116 B2
Worcestershire Sch of Ag WR6 99 A3
Word Hill B17 9 F7
Wordsley Cl B98 71 B7
Wordsworth Ave
  Redditch B97 89 C8
  Worcester WR3 115 C6
Wordsworth Cres DY10 28 B6
Wordsworth Gn WR14 139 A2
Wordsworth House
  Birmingham B31 34 A8
  Halesowen B63 7 B5
Workman Rd WR11 161 B3
World's End Ave B32 9 D6
World's End Jun Sch B32 9 D5
World's End La B32 9 D5
Worth Cres DY13 43 D5
Worthen Gr B31 34 A8
Worthings The B30 20 B6
Worton Rd DY9 6 F2
Wrekin Cl Halesowen B63 7 C1
  Kidderminster DY11 27 B2
Wrekin Dr
  Bromsgrove B61 49 A5
  Stourbridge DY9 6 D4
Wrekin Wlk 5 DY13 43 D1
Wren Ave WR14 139 C2
Wren Cl WR3 102 E3
Wribbenhall Fst Sch DY12 26 C5
Wribbenhall Mid Sch DY12 26 C3
Wright St B63 8 B4
Wroxall Cl DY5 6 C8
Wroxall Gr B13 21 A6
Wryflatt 3 WR4 116 C5
Wych Rd WR9 84 E2
Wychall La B38 19 E2
Wychall Pk Gr B38 19 D2
Wychall Prim Sch B31 19 C2
Wychall Rd B31 19 C3
Wychbold Cl B97 89 A6
Wychbold Ct DY9 15 C8
Wychbold Fst Sch WR9 85 E8
Wychbury Ct B63 8 A3
Wychbury Dr DY9 15 C7
Wychbury Grange DY9 6 C1
Wychbury Rd
  Birmingham B32 18 B7
  Brierley Hill DY5 6 E8
  Stourbridge DY9 6 E2
Wyche Ave B14 20 D4
Wyche CE Prim Sch WR14 152 E4
Wyche Cotts B60 67 C1
Wyche Rd WR14 152 E5
Wychelm Cl 2 WR5 128 E8
Wychelm Farm Rd B14 21 A1
Wychwood Dr B97 89 D6
Wye Ave WR14 153 D8
Wye Cl Droitwich WR9 103 E8
  Worcester WR5 115 E2
Wykewane WR14 153 D7
Wyld's La WR5 115 C2
Wynall La S DY9 6 F3
Wyndbrook La GL19 192 F7
Wyndham Gdns B30 19 D4
Wynds Covert B14 20 D2
Wynds Point B31 19 B5
Wynfield Gdns B14 20 F5
Wynn Cl DY12 26 D5
Wynniattes Way WR6 60 F3
Wynstead Covert 6 B14 20 C2
Wynyards Cl 1 GL20 196 F6
Wyre Cl B45 18 B1

Wyre Forest Nature Reserve* DY12 ....25 B5
Wyre Hill Bewdley DY12 ...25 F2
Pinvin WR10 ....144 F4
Wyre La CV37 ....151 D6
Wyre Rd
Pershore WR10 ....144 E3
Stourbridge DY8 ....5 E7
Wyrebrook Gdns WR15 ..57 A7
Wythall Gn Way B47 .....35 E3
Wythall Rd B63 ....8 A2
Wythall Sta B47 ....36 C4
Wythwood Cl DY9 ....6 D1
Wythwood Gr B47 ....36 C6
Wythwood Rd B47 ....36 C6

Y

Yard The WR11 ....175 B2
Yardley Cl B98 ....71 E3
Yardley St DY9 ....6 C6
Yardley Wood Com Prim Sch B14 ....21 D4
Yardley Wood Rd B13, B14 ....21 B5
Yardley Wood Sta B28 ...21 D5
Yardley Works DY9 ....6 C5
Yarn Cl B47 ....36 A5
Yarnborough Hill DY8 .....6 A2
Yarnbury Cl B14 ....20 E1
Yarningale Cl B98 ....89 F6
Yarningale Rd B14 ....20 D5
Yarnold La
Bournheath B61 ....48 C8
Fairfield B61 ....31 C1
Yarranton Cl 2 DY13 .....62 E8
Yarrow Cl WR5 ....128 D4
Yarrow Dr B38 ....34 F8
Yates Hay Rd WR14 .....138 F5
Yeadon Cl B97 ....70 A1
Yellowhammer Ct DY10 ....28 A1
Yeoman Cl DY10 ....27 E3
Yeomans Wlk B60 ....67 E8
Yessell La WR11 ....160 E6
Yew Tree Ave DY9 ....30 E8
Yew Tree Cl
4 Bewdley DY12 ....25 F3
Redditch B97 ....70 A4
Worcester WR5 ....128 F8
Yew Tree La
Bewdley DY12 ....25 F3
Birmingham, Frankley B32 ....17 E3
Fairfield B61 ....31 D2
Fernhill Heath WR3 ......103 A3
Malvern Wells WR14 ......166 F7
Yew Tree Pl B62 ....17 A5
Yew Tree Rd
Halesowen B63 ....7 F3
Kidderminster DY10 ....27 F5
Yew Tree Wlk 10 DY13 ....43 E4
Yewleigh La WR8 ....168 F4
Yewtree Cl WR11 ....161 F2
Yewtree Dr B60 ....49 B2
Yewtree Hill WR9 ......103 F8
York Ave
Bromsgrove B61 ....48 E4
Droitwich WR9 ....84 F1
York Cl Birmingham B30 ...20 A6
Bromsgrove B61 ....48 E4
Malvern WR14 ....139 B5
Studley B80 ....90 C4
York Cres DY8 ....5 D7
York Ct DY10 ....27 E7
York La WR10 ....144 F1
York Pl WR1 ....115 A4
York Pl La WR1 ....115 A4
York Rd Bewdley DY12 ....25 F4
Birmingham, King's Heath B14 ....20 E8
Bromsgrove B61 ....48 F4
Tewkesbury GL20 ....196 F4
York St
Kidderminster DY10 ....27 E7
Stourport-on-Severn DY13 ....44 A3
Yvonne Rd B97 ....89 D7

Z

Zermatt Cl 2 WR3 ......115 A8
Zetland Rd WR14 ....138 F2
Zortech Ave DY13 ....44 A8
Zouche Cl DY8 ....5 E8

Using the Ordnance Survey National Grid

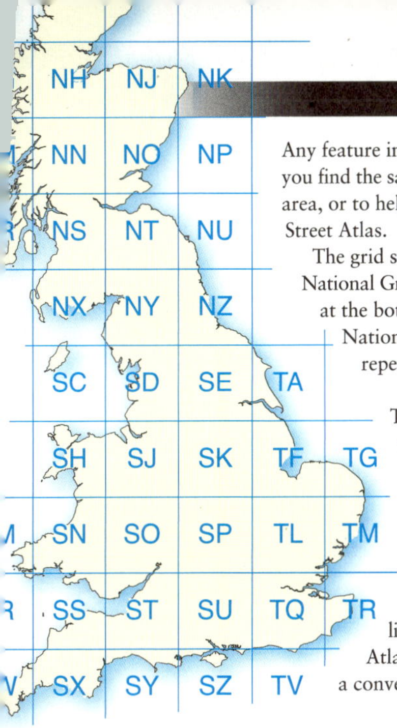

Any feature in this atlas can be given a unique reference to help you find the same feature on other Ordnance Survey maps of the area, or to help someone else locate you if they do not have a Street Atlas.

The grid squares in this atlas match the Ordnance Survey National Grid and are at 500 metre intervals. The small figures at the bottom and sides of every other grid line are the National Grid kilometre values (**00** to **99** km) and are repeated across the country every 100 km (see left).

To give a unique National Grid reference you need to locate where in the country you are. The country is divided into 100 km squares with each square given a unique two-letter reference. Use the administrative map to determine in which 100 km square a particular page of this atlas falls.

The bold letters and numbers between each grid line (**A** to **F**, **1** to **8**) are for use within a specific Street Atlas only, and when used with the page number, are a convenient way of referencing these grid squares.

Example The railway bridge over DARLEY GREEN RD in grid square B1

Step 1: Identify the two-letter reference, in this example the page is in **SP**

Step 2: Identify the 1 km square in which the railway bridge falls. Use the figures in the southwest corner of this square: Eastings **17**, Northings **74**. This gives a unique reference: **SP 17 74**, accurate to 1 km.

Step 3: To give a more precise reference accurate to 100 m you need to estimate how many tenths along and how many tenths up this 1 km square the feature is (to help with this the 1 km square is divided into four 500 m squares). This makes the bridge about **8** tenths along and about **1** tenth up from the southwest corner.

This gives a unique reference: **SP 178 741**, accurate to 100 m.

Eastings (read from left to right along the bottom) come before Northings (read from bottom to top). If you have trouble remembering say to yourself "Along the hall, THEN up the stairs"!

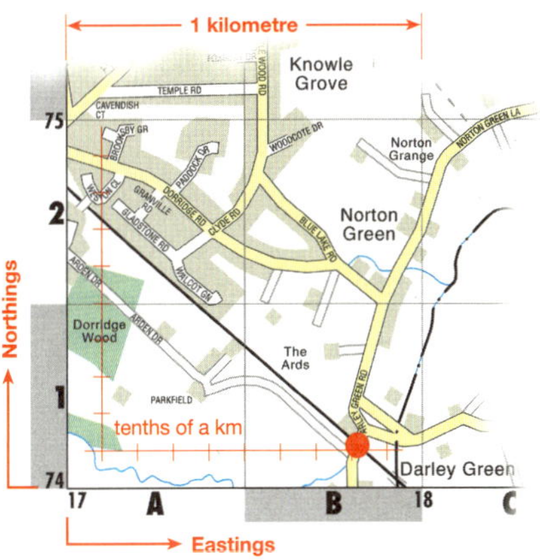

Notes

me and Address	Telephone	Page	Grid reference

PHILIP'S MAPS

the Gold Standard for serious driving

- Philip's street atlases cover every county in England and Wales, plus much of Scotland
- All our atlases use the same style of mapping, with the same colours and symbols, so you can move with confidence from one atlas to the next
- Widely used by the emergency services, transport companies and local authorities
- Created from the most up-to-date and detailed information available from Ordnance Survey
- Based on the National Grid

BEST BUY • BEST BUY • Auto EXPRESS • BEST BUY • BEST BUY

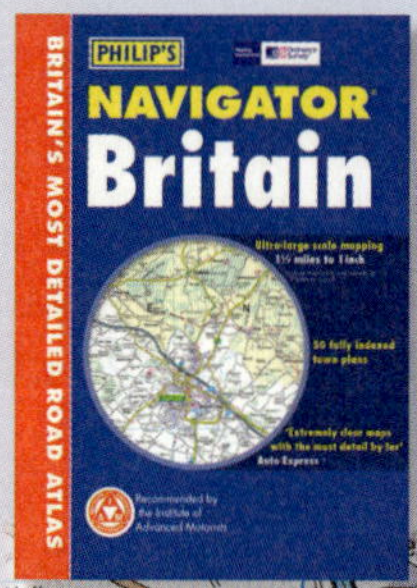

For national mapping, choose **Philip's Navigator Britain** – the most detailed road atlas available of England, Wales and Scotland. Hailed by Auto Express as 'the ultimate road atlas', this is the only one-volume atlas to show every road and lane in Britain.

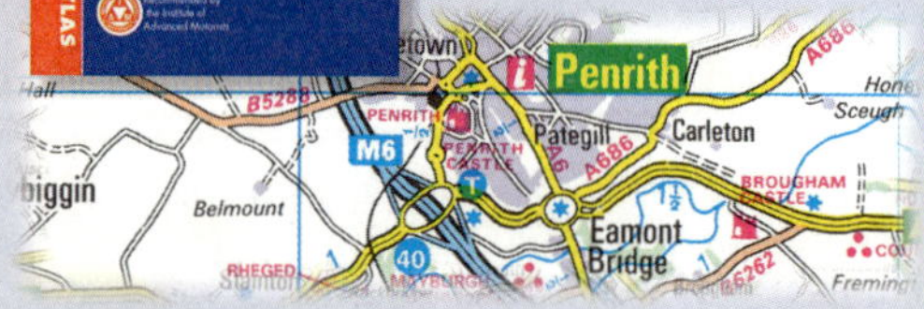

Street atlases currently available

All England and Wales coverage

England

Bedfordshire
Berkshire
Birmingham and West Midlands
Bristol and Bath
Buckinghamshire
Cambridgeshire
Cheshire
Cornwall
Cumbria
Derbyshire
Devon
Dorset
County Durham and Teesside
Essex
North Essex
South Essex
Gloucestershire
North Hampshire
South Hampshire
Herefordshire Monmouthshire
Hertfordshire
Isle of Wight
Kent
East Kent
West Kent
Lancashire
Leicestershire and Rutland
Lincolnshire
London
Greater Manchester
Merseyside
Norfolk
Northamptonshire
Northumberland
Nottinghamshire
Oxfordshire
Shropshire
Somerset
Staffordshire
Suffolk
Surrey
East Sussex
West Sussex
Tyne and Wear
Warwickshire
Birmingham and West Midlands
Wiltshire and Swindon
Worcestershire
East Yorkshire Northern Lincolnshire
North Yorkshire
South Yorkshire
West Yorkshire

Wales

Anglesey, Conwy and Gwynedd
Cardiff, Swansea and The Valleys
Carmarthenshire, Pembrokeshire and Swansea
Ceredigion and South Gwynedd
Denbighshire, Flintshire, Wrexham
Herefordshire Monmouthshire
Powys

Scotland

Aberdeenshire
Ayrshire
Edinburgh and East Central Scotland
Fife and Tayside
Glasgow and West Central Scotland
Inverness and Moray
Lanarkshire

How to order

Philip's maps and atlases are available from bookshops, motorway services and petrol stations. You can order direct from the publisher by phoning **01903 828503** or online at **www.philips-maps.co.uk**
For bulk orders only, phone 020 7644 6940